4C

as 1s

MALINGERING, LIES, AND JUNK SCIENCE IN THE COURTROOM

MALINGERING, LIES, AND JUNK SCIENCE IN THE COURTROOM

Edited by Jack Kitaeff

CAMBRIA
PRESS

YOUNGSTOWN, NEW YORK

Copyright 2007 Jack Kitaeff

Library of Congress Cataloging-in-Publication Data

Malingering, lies, and junk science in the courtroom / Edited by Jack Kitaeff.
      p. cm.
Includes bibliographical references and index.
ISBN 978-1-934043-58-5 (alk. paper)
1. Insanity—Jurisprudence—United States. 2. Liability (Law)—United States. 3. Capacity and disability—United States. 4. Forensic psychology—United States. 5. Malingering—Diagnosis. I. Kitaeff, Jack. II. Title.

KF9242.M35 2007
345.73'04—dc22

2007009278

CONTENTS

FOREWORD

In a 1967 Clint Eastwood Western film, *The Good, the Bad, and the Ugly*, Eastwood faced four gunslingers intent on killing him. He then shot all four men dead and survived without a scratch. A cowboy who witnessed the shootout asked him, "How'd ya know which one would draw first?" He answered, "The guy on the right had nervous eyes, so I figured he was too scared. The two in the middle were slightly behind the other two; they wouldn't have had clear shots. The guy on the left kept twichin' his fingers. I knew he'd be the first to draw" (Leone, 1967; see also Slovenko, 2002).

Such was the silver screen's version of the "expert." It would not have been surprising to find Eastwood's character called into a 19th-century Western court to offer expert testimony on "behavioral signs of anxiety," "gunslinger's neurosis," or "traumatic decision-making in a shootout"—no need to be concerned with niceties such as his educational background, empirical peer-reviewed research, or acceptance in the scientific community. He would have been accepted in the 1870s as an expert nonetheless, and everyone would thereafter base their shooting strategy on his personal and unsupported recommendations.

One hundred years in the future, the psychoanalyst Bruno Bettelheim decreed that autistic children were produced by "refrigerator moms," mothers who, according to Bettelheim, were not competent to bond emotionally with their children, eventually resulting in a complete incapacity for emotional attachment in the children. Aside from some clinical or anecdotal experiences, Bettelheim presented no supporting evidence whatsoever. But his pronouncement had a significant impact on society and on how mothers regarded themselves. One could only imagine an "expert" testifying in court for the defense of such an "adult child of a refrigerator mom" who had been charged with a violent crime. The defendant might be suffering from "refrigerated child syndrome" without the ability to feel for another person, and therefore could not be held responsible for committing neglectful, harmful, or even violent acts. If found innocent, however, social workers and others should be concerned that the defendant herself might one day become a refrigerator mother.

Not many people realize that Sigmund Freud (the "father of psychoanalysis") was interested in the idea of expert testimony in court and that he pushed for further psychological involvement in the courtroom setting. In 1906 he delivered a lecture to a law class at the University of Vienna entitled "Psychoanalysis and the Ascertaining of Truth in Courts of Law," in which he said:

> There is a growing recognition of the untrustworthiness of statements made by witnesses, at present the basis of so many judgments in Courts of Law; and this has quickened in all of you, who are to become judges and advocates, an interest in a new method of investigation, the purpose of which is to lead the accused person to establish his own guilt or innocence objectively. This method is of a psychological and experimental character and is based upon psychological research; it is closely connected with certain views which have only recently been propounded in medical psychology. (Banay, 1966, p. 433)

In 1908 Hugo Münsterberg (the "father of forensic psychology") and a professor of psychology at Harvard, continued the push for psychology's increased involvement in the courts and legal system. Münsterberg recommended that prospective witnesses be tested for reliability in experimental situations before their testimony is accepted. He also criticized the legal profession for its failure to apply psychological principles to the evaluation of testimony (Münsterberg, 1923).

Dean John Wigmore (you guessed it, the "father of evidence law"), in a scathing article responding to Münsterberg's suggestions, challenged the psychology professor to produce these psychological principles. Wigmore (2002) asked: "[W]here are the exact and precise experimental and psychological methods of ascertaining and measuring the testimonial certitude of witnesses and the guilty consciousness of accused persons?" The concern implicit in Wigmore's challenge was that psychological testimony be based on scientific principles and research, and not just on "clinical experience," anecdotal accounts, or gut feelings. Perhaps he foresaw the outrageous and unsubstantiated claims that would be made in the future by well-meaning, but naïve, unscientific and uncritical psychologists, psychiatrists, or social workers.

For example, Carol Tavris reported in *Science and Pseudoscience in Clinical Psychology* (Church, 2006; Frenkel, 2006), that "In [a] courtroom, I heard a social worker explain why she had decided to remove a child from her mother's custody: The mother had been abused as a child, and 'we all know' that this is a major risk factor for the mother's abuse of her own child one day." In fact, in the mid-1980s, the panics relating to recovered-memory therapy, day-care sex-abuse scandals, multiple personality disorder (dissociative identity disorder), and others were all based on erroneous and scientifically invalidated claims by psychotherapists, using subjective and unreliable methods (Jenkins, 1998; Showalter, 1997).

Psychologist Margaret Hagen (1997) wrote a telling book, *Whores of the Court: The Fraud of Psychiatric Testimony and the Rape of American Justice.* In it she talks about the wasted resources caused by the business of expert testimony, and the ludicrous verdicts due to the testimony of these "experts" injecting fanciful psychological theories into life-and-death settings. Hagen describes modern psychiatry as "junk science," overly influenced by faddists who have invented numerous syndromes and dysfunctions and placed them into the American legal system. These include the battered wife syndrome, recovered-memory syndrome, intermittent-explosive disorder, urban psychosis, and posttraumatic stress syndrome (Salerno, 2005).

Consider the case of the McMartin preschool. The school was founded by Virginia McMartin, who lived in the small oceanfront community of Manhattan Beach, California, just south of Los Angeles. She had opened the school and hired members of her family and church to help build and run it. Her daughter, Peggy Buckey, was the administrator. The school was considered so exemplary that the town of Manhattan Beach had given Virginia an award. But the fanciful beliefs of one vindictive parent would change all that when she made allegations that her son was sexually abused by staff members at the school.

> The school was termed a "sexual house of horrors" and the prosecutor claimed that the defendants in the case were a danger to the community. One of the allegations against the school was that its true purpose was to procure young children for adult pleasures. An assistant DA insisted that there were *millions* of pornographic photographs. But no one ever produced them, and the FBI never found them. What is particularly disturbing about this case is that the charges of physical and sexual horrors and abuse were based on no real evidence other than stories "retrieved" from children. The situation was so outrageous that almost anything was construed as a sign of child abuse even if concrete evidence refuted it. (Earl, 1995)

The prosecution's cases rested on the results of interviews at Children's Institute International (CII) at UCLA. One doctor, William E. Gordon, testified that the photographs did show evidence of abuse. He was reported to be an "expert" who had previously testified in some 300 trials on the same issue. But he admitted he was not a certified pediatrician, but a professor, and had no formal education in diagnosis.

In the end, 360 children were diagnosed at CII as having been abused at the McMartin preschool. It was the longest and most expensive legal proceeding in American history. After 7 years from the first accusations and endless heartache to the defendants, no one was convicted. It had cost the community almost $16 million and had cost many parents their peace of mind (Showalter, 1997).

These are not isolated events. A study by Poole, Lindsay, Memon, and Bull (1995) found that large numbers of certified psychotherapists were using subjective, highly influential techniques such as hypnosis, dream analysis, and guided imagery in order to "uncover" repressed memories of childhood sexual abuse. In a 1995 study by Michael Yapko, more than 1,000 members of the American Association of Marriage and Family Therapists reported believing that "hypnosis can be used to recover memories from as far back as birth." One third agreed that "the mind is like a computer, accurately recording events that actually occurred." And one fourth of them agreed that "someone's feeling certain about a memory means the memory is likely to be correct" (Lilienfeld, Lynn, & Lohr, 2003; Poole et al., 1995). What is particularly concerning is that none of these statements are likely to be true.

All this is not surprising considering flaws in our higher educational system. Professors in colleges, graduate schools and professional schools have complained about the lack of critical thinking on the part of students. One study on the training of psychiatrists suggested that residents learn how to make diagnoses, prescribe appropriate medication, and perform therapy, but rarely do they learn to be skeptical, ask questions, analyze research, or consider alternative explanations or treatments (Luhrmann, T. M., *Of two minds: The growing disorder in American psychiatry*, as cited in Tavris, 2003).

The reliance on expert testimony—whether psychological or otherwise—has resulted in litigants, claimants, and (of course) lawyers, benefiting from significant monetary settlements.

Witnesses are relied upon in modern tort cases to help "prove" injury. In their book *Phantom Risk*, Foster, Bernstein, and Huber (1999) examine the havoc that proving environmentally induced syndromes, for example, create in the courtroom. This would include things such as:

> ...miscarriages resulting from work at video display terminals, birth defects in children caused by the mother's use of the drug Bendectin, cancer from low-intensity magnetic fields, lung cancer produced by very slight levels of airborne

asbestos in buildings with intact asbestos insulation, or cancer resulting from a slip and fall in a grocery store.... . (Foster et al., 1999, p. 1)

"Phantom risks" are alleged cause-and-effect relationships whose very existence is unproven and perhaps even unprovable. Yet such effects are presented into evidence in civil suits all the time by "experts" in their fields using a type of deduction referred to by the authors as *post hoc, ergo prompter hoc* or "after which, therefore because of which." The authors point out:

> The outcome of such cases is likely to depend on testimony of expert witnesses with radically different views of the supposed hazards involved. Even for [things like] ionizing radiation, whose hazards are surely well studied, one can pick and choose among the epidemiologic studies and find support for the claim that exposure to low-level radiation is far more hazardous than the consensus of scientific opinion would admit. The adversarial process naturally amplifies these differences, and often obscures the differences between well-established scientific fact, consensus scientific opinion, and idiosyncratic views of some scientists. (Foster et al., 1999, p. 33)

Experts file *amicus* briefs in major cases in an attempt to shape the law and social policy. Sometimes these result in complete changes in psychological and psychiatric diagnostic and classificatory nomenclature. One of the outcomes, for example, of such trends is that alcoholism is now a "disease." What are the implications of this? In his book *SHAM*, Steve Salerno (2005) outlines some of these:

> This forces companies or their insurers to assume billions of dollars in treatment costs and to look the other way when marginal employees relapse time and time again. Firing workers for [having the alcoholism disease], without taking every possible step to help rehabilitate them and reintegrate them unto the corporate culture, can open a company to seven-figure civil lawsuits as well as other governmental sanctions.

Exxon learned this firsthand when it hired "recovered alcoholic" Joseph Hazelwood to captain the *Exxon Valdez*. One night in March 1989, after having a few, Hazelwood left the oil tanker in a subordinate's hands. It ran aground. The result was one of the worst ecological disasters on record, which involved Exxon in a $2 billion cleanup and opened the company to a $900 million settlement of federal and state claims, as well as a $4.5 billion fine. (p. 229)

Many in politics have been concerned with this march of experts. During the 1992 presidential campaign, Vice President Dan Quayle called for extensive practice reform of using expert witnesses in the federal courts for Slovenko (2002). He got his wish but not in the direction he hoped for. For Quayle and others, the Ninth Circuit's decision 2 years later in *Daubert v. Merrell Dow Pharmaceuticals* (1995) was not a happy one. Under *Daubert*, the "general acceptance" test in the relevant scientific community established in *Frye v. United States* in 1923, became just one of the considerations in determining reliability or validity of expert testimony. *Daubert* incorporated the general acceptance test as one of the various factors to be considered when evaluating whether to admit scientific evidence. Much more was now left to the trier of fact, and many feared that the gates were now thrown open for all manner of junk science to be admitted into evidence.

But all this is not necessarily new. In the 1983 Supreme Court's decision in *Barefoot v. Estelle* (1983), the prosecution's psychiatric expert "predicted" that the defendant was likely to engage in future dangerous behavior. In response to the defense's argument that the weight of empirical studies did not support a claim of predicting future dangerousness by psychiatrists, the Court assumed that "all of these professional doubts about the usefulness of psychiatric predictions can be called to the attention of the jury." It further concluded that the jury could understand and assess the evidence and thus it merely applied a general standard of relevance (*Barefoot*, Federal Rules of Evidence, Rules 401–401).

The best way for the legal system to deal with the question of experts is certainly not to dismiss them completely for they often make valuable contributions. The authors of *Phantom Risk* suggest:

> Probably the best that legal reformers can do is to suggest ways to help improve the quality of the scientific evidence that is presented in court. The goal is not to raise standards of proof to levels so high that no plaintiff could hope to win but rather to ensure that the scientific testimony that is presented to juries is as reliable as possible. Expert testimony needs to be *verifiable*, and, where possible, *consistent with a consensus of scientific opinion*. (Foster et al., 1999, p. 34)

The format of this book is straightforward. The contributors, all experts in their respective fields, were asked to write about what I call "phantom psychological phenomena" (pseudoscience, dubious psychological and psychiatric syndromes, and psychological myths and false beliefs), malingering, junk science in the courtroom, problems with expert testimony, or the intersection of any of these areas within the mental health and the legal system. The result is a scholarly and fascinating compendium.

Jack Kitaeff, PhD, JD

REFERENCES

Banay, R. (1966). The psychiatrist in court. In R. Slovenko (Ed.), *Crime, law and corrections* (p. 433–456). Springfield, IL: Thomas.

Barefoot v. Estelle, 463 U.S. 880 (1983).

Betts, H. B. (Ed.). (1999). Disabled. In *The world book encyclopedia* (Vol. 5, p. 220). World Book Company.

Church, E. (2006, August 8). *News photography and photoshop.* Retrieved October 21, 2006, from http://blogs.reuters.com/2006/08/08/news-photography-and-photoshop

Daubert v. Merrell Dow Pharmaceuticals, 20. 43 F.3d 1311 (9th Cir. 1995).

Earl, J. (1995). The dark truth about the dark tunnels of the McMartin. *Issues in Child Abuse Accusations, 7*(2).

Foster, K. R., Bernstein, D. E., & Huber, P. W. (1999). *Phantom risk.* Cambridge, MA: The MIT Press.

Frenkel, S. (2006, August 7). *Reuters admits doctoring Beirut photo.* Retrieved October 21, 2006, from http://www.jpost.com/servlet/Satellite?apage=1&cid=1154525816599&pagename=JPost%2FJPArticle%2FShowFull

Frye v. United States, 293 Fed. 1013 (D.C. Cir. 1923).

Hagen, M. (1997). *Whores of the court: The fraud of psychiatric testimony and the rape of American justice.* New York: Regan Books.

Jenkins, P. (1998). *Moral panic: Changing concepts of the child molester in modern America.* New Haven, CT: Yale University Press.

Leone, S. (Director). (1967). *The good, the bad, and the ugly* [motion picture]. United States: United Artists.

Lilienfeld, S. O., Lynn, S. J., & Lohr, J. M. (2003). *Science and pseudoscience in clinical psychology.* New York: The Guilford Press.

Münsterberg, H. (1923). *On the witness stand.* New York: Clark Boardman.

Poole, D. A., Lindsay, D. S., Memon, A., & Bull, R. (1995). Psychotherapy and the recovery of memories of childhood sexual abuse: U.S. and British practitioners' opinions, practices, and experiences. *Journal of Consulting and Clinical Psychology, 63*, 426–437.

Ramsland, K. (2003), *The McMartin nightmare and the hysteria puppeteers.* Retrieved June 18, 2007, from http://www.crimelibrary.com/criminal_mind/psychology/mcmartin_daycare/2.html

Salerno, S. (2005). *SHAM.* New York: Crown.

Showalter, E. (1997). *Hystories: Hysterical epidemics and modern media.* New York: Columbia University Press.

Slovenko, R. (2002). *Psychiatry in law/law in psychiatry. New* York: Brunner-Routledge.

Tavris, C. (2003). The widening scientist-practitioner gap: A view from the bridge [Foreword]. In S. O. Lilienfeld, S. J. Lynn, & J. M. Lohr (Eds.), *Science and pseudoscience in clinical psychology* (p. ix). New York: The Guilford Press.

Wigmore, J. (2002). Professor Münsterberg and the psychology of testimony. In R. Slovenko (Ed.), *Psychiatry and law/law and psychiatry* (pp. 103–124). New York: Brunner-Routledge.

MALINGERING, LIES, AND JUNK SCIENCE IN THE COURTROOM

CHAPTER ONE

THE NEED FOR CRITICAL THINKING IN FORENSIC PSYCHOLOGY

Harvey Schlossberg, PhD
Antoinette Collarini Schlossberg, PhD

The study of psychology always appeals to college students. Today, more than ever before, media productions and attention to real and fictional stories on television or in the movies have resulted in popular portrayals of the work of psychologists. Profilers delineate characteristics of criminals from crime scene evidence, the type of crime itself, and the behavior of the victim. Situations dramatized from real life, displaying the work of hostage negotiators in resolving life and death crisis situations, and the tracking and prediction of serial sexual predators and murderers, have excited many young people to enter the field of forensic psychology. When we asked high school students what they want as a career, many stated they wanted to become psychologists, particularly with the aim of working within the criminal justice system as forensic psychologists. The lure of the field is linked to the fact that we are curious about ourselves and want to know as much as possible about how and why we respond to stimuli and analyze our world. Students are often excited when they read about these exploits and want to understand behavior and motivation. They discover that they often do things that are difficult for them to explain and are surprised by their own motives. They are so excited by the discoveries that they read about and hear in class that they are often overwhelmed and anxious to accept explanations even when these explanations are questionable. We often do things that are difficult for us to explain, and so the thought of finding the answers to our many internally asked questions makes psychology a desirable field of study. Often, the inability to distinguish between explanations, facts, biases, and research validity confirms the student's own natural fears of inadequacy and guilt. It is at this point that it is necessary to teach and to help students to understand that critical thinking is often the backbone of creating a core of knowledge in forensic psychology (Kuhn, 2005).

"Critical thinking" is the process of questioning research, statements, findings, and assertions to determine truth and validity. By examining all elements and possibilities in an unbiased, objective, and impersonal way while remaining open and cautious, we are able to accept or reject proposed solutions or offer alternative ones. Critical thinking can be described as a combination of stages. The first step is identifying a problem or issue, for example, the need for psychologically well-adjusted people for police work. For the second step it is necessary to gather information in an unbiased quest to examine various aspects of this problem. For our example, this is done by examining research studies and the literature, as well as prior approaches that deal with special job applicant selection. This may include psychological personality testing, getting samples of behaviors typical of successful police officers, and a general survey of police departments for what they consider to be necessary abilities for job success. The third step of critical thinking would include examination of the materials obtained in

Step 2 in an attempt to eliminate or question which elements are valid and reliable. This selection by critical evaluation would use techniques that are based on logic in giving weight to those factors that prevent wrong or erroneous conclusions (Shafersman, 1991). This, of course, does not eliminate all errors but permits a broader range of decision making that is likely to be more accurate. In our example of police officer candidate selection, we would observe that this selection process often consists of a background investigation of prior experiences and behaviors, psychological testing of both subjective and objective techniques, or a psychiatric interview. The fourth step would incorporate examination and selection by critical evaluation of what appear to be the best of those techniques that are used or proposed. This means that we would select those techniques that would be likely to give us candidates who will perform successfully. The material should be evaluated and the best approaches could be compared and tested to determine which one would be able to provide the solution to our problem. The testing of assertions and suggestions that explain facets of the problem are weighed, and the credibility and veracity of the explanations that are offered are explored for consistency and validity. Supporting evidence is then evaluated and all findings would be synthesized into a reasonable judgment that is based on a wide variety of information sources such as cross-cultural comparisons of experiences by additional police agencies using the same techniques, an ongoing collection of data to measure success of prediction, and the elimination of erroneous materials. In psychology in particular, it is necessary to learn how to ask the right questions and to deal with ambiguities that tend to be used in explaining behaviors found in the personal beliefs and prejudices of a particular evaluator. Therefore, in the study of psychology it is necessary not only to understand but also to appreciate the similarities and differences among people. Particularly in the clinical field, we are encouraged, both as students and as practitioners, to be accepting of individual differences and to be nonjudgmental about the way people express their feelings and behaviors. Psychologists are very encouraging and open to theories and hypotheses about varieties of behavior. We are taught early that it is easy to be a critic; it is difficult to be a creator. The fact that we would reject or discourage a theory suggests we are narrow-minded and judgmental. With these concepts in mind it becomes easy to see why the entire field of science, and particularly psychology, is replete with fringe theories and approaches to issues that run the gamut of a variety of quack conclusions (Digdon, 1999).

Forensic psychology in particular must guard itself against the pitfalls of unquestioning acceptance and openness to any theory that is offered but is recognized as not meeting the guidelines of scientific research and reason. In psychology there are a wide variety of hypotheses based on observation, clinical experience, and anecdotal record to choose from, but they do not necessarily meet the rigors of scientific methods of investigation. The forensic psychologist must arm himself or herself with unwavering commitment to questioning the techniques by which individuals reach their conclusions.

Forensic psychology is loosely defined as the use of psychological concepts and techniques as they apply to the legal system. The reason we say loosely defined is that the expertise of psychologists is often sought in areas that may not be of a criminal nature but involve incidents of questionable antisocial behavior, and the methods of arriving at theories of behavior are often attributable to clinical experience and observations, with the scientific component frequently dependent on loose multivariate research of sociological factors that show inconclusive cause and effect. Quantifying psychosocial research with a degree of statistical significance often remains elusive. Further, studies in psychology often defy attempts at replication for a variety of unidentifiable reasons. These methods are applied in the legal system, which tends to be rigid and structured, particularly with awareness that theories that are accepted in the legal system must withstand the rigors of scientific method to be credible. Psychosocial research often cannot withstand this test, although within the practices of psychological testing, evaluation, and clinical practice this research has face validity and operational usefulness. When we take this from the psychological practice to the courtroom, or when it is evaluated under the same conditions as the physical sciences, it is clear that the results of psychological research are not as precise and defendable in this courtroom setting. The burden of defense falls upon the shoulders of the forensic psychologist to justify which of the many theories he or she is going to use in evaluating a case (B. E. Bell & Loftus, 1989).

Situations such as a disgruntled and nonproductive employee who may sabotage or delay projects, while perhaps not criminal, become costly to society. Individuals injured in automobile or other accidents often exaggerate or invent symptoms for profit. Similarly, faking or presenting a psychological syndrome in order to avoid work or deception for gain or for special consideration is often evaluated by forensic psychologists. On many occasions, in the absence of physical symptomatology, individuals select psychological symptoms because they are more difficult to diagnose and quantify: If I feel an emotion, it is difficult to determine if I am acting or actually feeling it. Malingering and faking psychological symptoms have serious social and criminal aspects through which a forensic psychologist must wade. Our definition also embraces an understanding of the elements of the legal system as they impact and interact between police, criminals, victims, witnesses, courts, and correctional systems.

Forensic psychology weighs all aspects of these elements and at the same time tries to balance between the needs of society and those of the individual. Forensic psychologists are called upon to deal with issues such as sanity, mental competence, rehabilitation, benefits of incarceration, issues of adoption, occupational issues such as malingering, and psychological pain and trauma from a variety of incidents. These expectations, especially within the adversarial U.S. legal system, often place psychologists in positions of conflict with opposing positions, sometimes from ill informed, poorly trained but well-meaning practitioners. In those cases that ultimately go before courts and juries, it is often the work of attorneys to discredit or question the competence of a witness. Therefore, in these types of cases a psychologist must be comfortable and armed with knowledge so that he or she may reject the conclusion of another practitioner by questioning how and why the other psychologist arrived at his or her position. Psychologists must recognize that their challenge of motives and possible misinterpretations and deriving a different opinion from examination of all the factors are not because of arbitrary stubbornness or pomposity.

Psychologists by nature and by their training indoctrination become uncomfortable and self-doubting for not embracing a position or theory that is offered, and they often refuse to pick up the challenge to question the issues for fear that it will be seen as a personal attack rather than questioning the reason and sources for the conclusions. The psychologist's role is to encourage thinking and the expression of feelings without hurting or degrading the source. Therefore, the psychologist will search hard to find a redeeming concept that will enable the acceptance of a theory. To function in the legal system and to apply reasonable judgments based on carefully carried out research, forensic psychologists must learn that not all positions are equal. The psychologist may not want to hurt the credibility of another theorist, or he or she may not be able to offer an alternate explanation, but the person who can do so is not necessarily correct. Sometimes it is difficult to engage in critical thinking because questioning an issue is not politically, or socially, correct or popular. It is also necessary to recognize that just because a concept is subjected to rigorous thinking it may not result in validation or rejection. The concept may, in fact, still be worthless or in spite of the findings be quite valuable. For example, one of our students recently wrote a paper that evaluated the following question: Are serial killers religious or spiritual? She was dismayed and troubled by the fact that a serial killer could be religious but not spiritual, or spiritual but not religious. The student had a difficult time accepting that both explanations could be true. The important issue is to subject the concept to as much question as possible. For example, although many tests have validity and reliability, their application remains an inexact art. Their usefulness is often criticized not on the basis of conclusions but rather on the basis that they may discriminate against a particular group or derive a conclusion that may not be popular. Therefore, rather than encouraging the use of tests and improvement of their utility as a tool, many groups use political or social arguments to reject the concept of screening, although the tests may be necessary especially for some safety-sensitive occupations.

There is no doubt that critical thinking in the field of medicine, for example, has been responsible for careful checks on development of new drugs and medical procedures by questioning hypotheses developed on the basis of research and possible flaws in that research. We know that the public generally accepts most research on face value when it is reported in the media and readily embraces these pronouncements. Part of the reason is lack of training in critically evaluating research— for example, in a research report, what population does the sample represent, who was included and who was eliminated, who sponsored and funded the research, were there proper control groups, would the results be applied to another population, has the study been replicated numerous times before advancing a causative relationship, and can the study be replicated and under what circumstance will we get the same results? Forensic psychology, on the other hand, deals with individual cases on a case-by-case basis, and these become a repertoire of case studies for future evaluation and analyses. However, we know that the range of individual differences prevents application to each case as if they are all the same.

Recently, in addition to the classic forensic psychological work, some psychologists have been called upon to evaluate the social and political pressures on shaping the personalities of terrorists and in particular defining the characteristics influencing responses to the impact of terrorist activity responsible for carnage and indifferent killing. However, psychologists in their evaluations are influenced by the same stimuli that influence the public.

Predicting future behaviors is subject to the available information that is provided, and this is frequently based on the same information provided to the public. People's perceptions and subsequent attitudes and conclusions can be manipulated quite easily. A good example is the recent coverage by major news networks and media of the Israeli/Lebanese conflict in which doctored photographs were used to influence public perception about which side was the aggressor and responsible for the carnage and indifferent killing (Church, 2006; Frenkel, 2006). The viewers' conclusions were understandable when we knew the version of the conflict they had seen. This manipulation of public opinion by doctoring supposedly live, authentic photos and film from the warfront was done in Iraq and Afghanistan as well. A figure of a British soldier superimposed over a crowd in a photograph made it appear as if he were pointing a gun at an Iraqi woman and child. The addition of extra smoke to pictures of bombings and the use of models with mislabeling of situations shaped public opinion quite dramatically. It is interesting to note that an Al Qaeda chief called for volunteers to join the militant group with special emphasis on the need for media experts. Without critical thinking, this variety of misinformation shapes the political and social world we live in.

For forensic psychologists it becomes necessary to be very cautious in analyzing motivations and behaviors in order to understand the reasons why an individual will embrace a particular approach to a political or social situation and how this may lend itself to predicting behaviors or reactions that may otherwise seem irrational or disturbed.

In medical research there is generally a controlled setting in a laboratory that lets the researcher question all the variables that affect the outcome; on the other hand, the laboratory is not present in the study of many social and behavioral settings and so the many existing variables are difficult to isolate, making it impossible to question and challenge their effects on the situation. For this reason the theories that are developed in forensic psychology are constantly evolving and changing, as well as increasing the need to think critically and to question every aspect of conclusions that are drawn, whether they are in a courtroom or a classroom. There should be a strong recognition that nothing should be accepted without asking the appropriate questions such as: who said it, what was his or her motivation, does he or she have a prejudice or bias, and how were the facts obtained? It is even more difficult when the result of an evaluation causes the need to change a preconceived notion or theoretical bias that contradicts already established theories.

A review of the types of situations that a forensic psychologist may find himself or herself in clearly supports the need for critical thinking. The first and most important involves the forensic psychologist who testifies in court. In some cases, this testimony can result in loss of large amounts of money and break up of families or commitment to an institution. The law is generally blind to individual differences. To dispense justice so that it is meaningful, it must be done with an even hand regardless of the individual's economic or social position. Since human behavior tends to be individual and unique to a particular person and situation, there tends to be a great deal of latitude in the evaluation of that behavior. Since the nature of the courts is an adversarial structure, it is not uncommon to have two or more experts viewing the behavior and interpreting it in very different ways. For example, a child custody case frequently involves testimony by a court-appointed psychologist, who may render a decision that is not consistent with the belief of the parent on the opposing side, who deems the conclusion as unacceptable. He then can bring in another expert for an evaluation to challenge the court-appointed or first psychologist's evaluation. The goal of the psychologist is to find the truth and to act in the role of a friend of the court by rendering an impartial evaluation as to which parent is capable of better raising the child. It is interesting that both psychologists are attempting to do the same job in an impartial way and to offer what is best for the child, but both can have totally different opinions. This should not be surprising since any evaluation is limited in time and the subjects are seen in limited situations. For the opposing psychologist who is testifying, it is necessary to be able to analyze what the other psychologist is saying and to evaluate critically his or her statements so that he or she may offer a reasonable explanation that brings out the weaknesses or errors in the contrary explanation. The statement "I know what I am saying and he doesn't" is not adequate. To point out critical error in his or her judgment based on the factors or elements he or she used to form the opinion becomes a powerful tool. Unfortunately, this child custody issue is often the most difficult type of testimony that a forensic psychologist will encounter; however, in terms of the child's welfare, his or her willingness to have an open mind to double question all the facts will have the most impact on the child and will affect the child's life permanently. While explanations may differ sometimes, the psychologist's testimony, while not really accepted on a factual basis, has an impact on the judge, jury, litigants, and lawyers to help them understand variations, and while explanations may be different, this difference does not imply a positive or negative value but rather that there are often many explanations for the same behaviors. This same concept in the same way helps the police, witnesses, and the public in looking for suspected criminals. Suggestion of possible causes of behavior, while not necessarily right or wrong, helps bring a focus on possible suspects by presenting a broad profile. In reality, this profile fits many people but enables the focus on specific variables; while not scientifically based, they have observational characteristics that people can recognize and forces them to focus on a particular suspect. Profiling of personality variables of serial killers or other predators then becomes a valuable tool for stimulating attention on possible types of suspected personalities. A criminal's personality profile may be based on behavioral aspects during the crime or the use of a factorial or statistical analysis of social demographics. We may find that these social demographic variables used to describe the perpetrator include alternate theories such as early school behavior, interactions with or the number of siblings in a family, and parental supervision. These may better describe personality than the statistical criteria.

Another important type of forensic psychological testimony centers on the insanity plea. From evaluation after the occurrence of the criminal incident, a forensic psychologist must attempt to evaluate the state of the mind of an individual at the time he or she committed a crime. Evaluation of the person at the moment the crime was committed is based upon historical information as reported by the record or by the suspect and those elements that can be obtained from others, such as school records, prior criminal record, statements by neighbors, friends, and family, and information about what happened at the time of the crime. Once again this calls on critical evaluation— who is making the statements, the motivation as to why they are making them, issues of personal gain, and the circumstances under which this information is obtained. The psychologist must keep in mind that the aim of this evaluation is to determine if this person knew the difference between right and wrong at the time of the incident and knew whether or not his or her actions were wrong. As with most forensic situations, differing expert opinions will surface; it is only through critical evaluation of all the circumstances that the psychologist will feel comfortable in defending his or her position. For example, a suspect may benefit by trying to manipulate the court to accept "guilty by virtue of insanity" in order to avoid a long commitment to a penal institution as opposed to a term in a psychiatric facility. The secondary gains of psychiatric treatment could result in a rapid cure and subsequent early release from incarceration.

Another example for the need to question alternate explanations is the issue of mental competency as this relates to inheritance or other life situations up to and including the right to commit suicide. Different psychologists can argue very different points of view. Forensic psychologists have been called upon to evaluate the use of force in requiring mentally disturbed people to take medication or in an extreme case to evaluate the effectiveness of psychotherapy and the type that would be most beneficial for a particular type of illness or person. All these illustrations point to the need for careful observation and thinking on the part of the psychologist.

In summary, educators are responsible for equipping future forensic psychologist practitioners with tools and methods of rigorous critical thinking. This is especially important for psychology, where frequently the scientific method cannot be applied completely. Concepts such as unconscious motivation for behaviors, subliminal stimulus, defense mechanisms, parental influence, and the symbolic nature of dreams (to mention just a few areas) are not concrete, visible, or measurable easily. We can interpret these constructs and understand them in a variety of ways; we cannot dismiss and replace them with equally vague concepts without being able to understand and explain the alternate view. To be a social scientist does not imply that one must blindly accept all manner of nonsense (Gambrill, 2006). For psychology students to learn methods of critical thinking is as important as learning how to think about issues. Logical thinking does not guarantee the truth but does prepare the person for decision making. Methods of designing and questioning alternate statements to explain a variety of behaviors prepares an individual to defend or change his or her position in the face of alternate proposals. Asking the right questions and collecting the proper information in an unbiased manner helps organize thoughts and decision making and provides confidence in one's conclusions.

REFERENCES

Bell, B. E., & Loftus, E. F. (1989). Trivial persuasion in the courtroom: The power of (a few) minor details. *Journal of Personality and Social Psychology*, 56(5), 669–679.

Bell, J. (1997). *Outcomes assessment with a focus on critical thinking in psychology: Sources and ideas*. Columbia, MD: Howard Community College. Retrieved September 5, 2006, from http://academic.pg.ccmd.us/wpeirce/MCCCTR/bell2.html

Church, A. (2006, August 8). *Dodge and burn*. Retrieved October 21, 2006, from http://www. ABCnews.com.archived.article.com

Digdon, N. (1999, April). *Critical thinking in psychology*. Grant MacEwan Community College. Retrieved from http://www.artscigmcc.ab.ca/courses/psych104/think.htm

Frenkel, S. (2006, August 7). *Reuters admits doctoring Beirut photo*. Retrieved October 21, 2006, from http://www.jpost.com/servlet/Satel lite?apage=1&cid=1154525816599&pagename=JPost%2FJPArticle%2FShowFull

Gambrill, E. (2006). *Critical thinking in clinical practice*. New York: Wiley.

Kuhn, D. (2005). *Education for thinking*. Cambridge, MA: Harvard University Press.

Shafersman, S. D. (1991). *An introduction to critical thinking*. Retrieved September 6, 2006, from http:/www.freeinquiry.com/critical-thinking.html

CHAPTER TWO

HOW SCIENCE BY MEDIA CREATES FALSE CERTAINTIES AND RESISTANCE TO CONCEPTUAL CHANGE

Diane F. Halpern, PhD
Ariana Brooks, MA
Clayton Stephenson

Being the social animals that humans are, we tend to engage in conversation with people in situations where we are confined in a small place. For example, consider the confinement of an airplane. Eventually, the question of what you do for work will come up. Psychologists fret answering this question because of the response we typically get. "So, you've been analyzing me, haven't you?" Occasionally, a psychologist may get the response, "So, I had this dream the other night..." Sometimes psychologists get the response of silence from people who are usually loquacious because they are afraid you can read their mind. They implicitly reason that because you know so much about the human mind, you must be able to read them.

These classic responses result from misconceptions that people have about psychologists, and these misconceptions get played out and reinforced in the courtroom whenever psychologists provide expert testimony. These ideas about psychologists are fostered in media depictions in which psychologists are seen as providing "deep" interpretations of the everyday problems of troubled people who are seen lying on a couch. Misconceptions fostered by the media create confidence about knowledge gained through the media and the flawed lens of everyday experiences. More specifically, the general public's understanding of science is often misconstrued somewhere along the communication line between scientific writings and the way science is explained in the popular outlets where the general public reads about science. In this chapter, we will focus on the way in which misconceptions about scientific findings are created and maintained by the media and how our everyday experiences with the media can create false certainties among the public. We will also discuss how to avoid and dispel such misconceptions through the use of critical thinking skills.

THE TWINKIE DEFENSE

One of the most outrageous psychological misconceptions created by the media involved the case of Dan White, who killed two elected officials in San Francisco's City Hall (Ewing & McCann, 2006). White was charged with first- and second-degree murder but was convicted only of two counts of voluntary manslaughter and was given a mere 8-year prison sentence for taking two innocent lives. The general public could not understand how a cold-blooded hate crime could end with such a short prison term. They needed to understand how a jury could have come up with this seemingly light sentence for such a heinous crime. The oddity in this case was the testimony provided by a psychiatrist who explained how White's eating habits had changed as a result of his manic-depressive syndrome. The psychiatrist stated that the changes in White's eating habits were cyclical, alternating with manic and depressive phases of the syndrome such that White would eat junk food to deal with his problems, which in turn made him feel worse, and so forth. The psychiatrist did not claim that White's bad eating habits caused him to commit the crime; rather, they were described as being caused by his mental disorder.

The trial for double murder concluded without reference to White's poor eating habits. It was not until after the jury's verdict and the judge's sentencing were made public that the issue of sugar consumption as an influence on White's criminal behavior was raised. The idea that high sugar consumption contributed to his murderous actions became the inflamed public discourse known as the "Twinkie Defense." The public was outraged by the short jail term White received and concluded that the jurors must have been swayed by the idea that the consumption of Twinkies could change someone's behavior without their control. In fact, the jury had decided that White did not premeditate the shootings with malicious intent and reiterated that the statement about the consumption of Twinkies and other junk food influencing the defendant's behavior had nothing to do with their decision. But a disbelieving public needed a better explanation of the seemingly light sentence. It was a short, logical leap to infer that the jurors were duped by Twinkies—the ultimate high-sugar, high-fat food that came to represent all that is wrong with America.

Although it is popularly believed that eating large quantities of sweet food causes children to be hyperactive, a review of the scientific literature reveals that sugar does not influence behavior. Wolraich, Wilson, and White (1995) performed a meta-analysis on 16 studies that tested the relationship between sugar consumption and the behavior of children. In a meta-analysis, effect sizes are used to calculate the extent to which two variables covary when averaged over multiple studies. The effect size found for the relationship between sugar and aggression was a Cohen's d of -0.10, which is not only a small effect size but also with a negative value. The negative value indicates that the direction of the relationship was actually opposite of what was expected! The effect sizes for the relationship between sugar and teacher and parent ratings, of children's behaviors and mood ranged from −0.02 to 0.03. In other words, the relationship is essentially 0. In contrast, relationships were found between sugar consumption and motor skills (0.20) and sugar consumption and academic scores (0.30).

Expectancies Influence What We See and Know

If there is no (or only a minimal) relationship between sugar and behavior in children, then how can we expect an adult male's behavior to be directly affected by the intake of Twinkies and other junk food? Wolraich et al. (1995) concluded that parents' beliefs of children's behavior changing as a result of ingesting sugar can be explained as a bias for confirming expectancies. That is, parents expect the child's behavior to become more rowdy after eating sugary foods because of past experiences where eating foods high in sugar is a critical part of the activities. For example, birthday parties usually include sugary cakes and other sweets. These are occasions when groups of children get overexcited and overactive. Parents come to believe that sugar is the cause of overactive behavior; they rarely stop to think that the relationship between the two variables may only be correlational. Other causes of a change in the child's behavior could be the large number of other children at the birthday party, or the excitement of special stimuli such as balloons, music, games, or new toys in the form of mysterious presents.

The belief that sugar consumption causes hyperactivity creates an expectancy, which can be strong and overrule the critical thinking process when it comes to formulating conclusions about experienced events, such as the relationship between sugar consumption and behavior. One possible source for the creation and support for misconceptions like this one is the simplistic way that complex scientific relationships are described in the media. When media reports are congruent with a person's expectancies, the result is an even stronger belief in the hypothesized relationship.

Consider this example: After the White case, *The Washington Post* printed an article titled "Diet and Crime" with the beginning line stating, "Diet deficiencies in general and the 'junk food syndrome' in particular may be in part to blame for a variety of antisocial behavior ranging from youthful hyperactivity to adult crime, a diet researcher says" (Crenshaw, 1981, p. D8). If this sentence is read carefully, it is clear that there is no direct statement asserting that sugar is the *cause* of antisocial behavior. The words "may be in part" are used to indicate sugar might contribute to a very large spectrum of behaviors. The same article claims that antisocial behavior is related to exposure to industrial metals and specific vitamins that can lead to or inhibit some behaviors, which only supports the general notion that diet affects behavior but does not support the specific causal link between sugar consumption and hyperactive behavior. Nothing about causation was claimed, but for the reader who already believes in the effect of sugar on hyperactive behavior, it is easy to see how these sentences appear to confirm this relationship.

Even when newspapers publish information about studies that disconfirm the links between sugar and hyperactivity, they use hedge terms that act as a double negative, and thus have the reverse effect. For example, approximately a year and a half after the article in *The Washington Post* (Crenshaw, 1981) was published, *The New York Times* (Brody, 1982) published an article stating that there *was very little evidence* that sugar made children hyperactive. That same newspaper published another article in 1984 that quoted the clinical psychologist Dr. Prinz stating, "...sugar consumption in particular and nutritional intake in general cannot *be labeled the primary cause* of childhood hyperactivity. A child's social environment coupled with his or her biological characteristics still is seen as the *major explanation*, while dietary variables must be viewed as minor influences [italics added]" (p. C1). Furthermore, Schoenthaler (1991) stated that malnutrition in general is *more likely to* influence antisocial behavior than sugar. Finally, in 1987 there was a clear refutation. The *Toronto Star* published an article in which a public health nutritionist was quoted, "Myths take a long time to die. There is no evidence that sugar cause these things [hyperactivity]" (Horgan, 1987, p. E7). Even after the disconfirming statements made in the media, the misconception that sugar causes antisocial behavior persists. Why is this? What are the key factors in creating and maintaining a misconception that could carry on as a bias in understanding courtroom proceedings?

In the case of the Twinkie defense, there are two major possibilities as to why it became a prototype for the way misconceptions are formed and retained. First, the Twinkie defense was blown out of proportion by the media as a result of the verdict. The jury was not swayed by the Twinkie defense, despite the common belief that it was. The second possibility is that the jury really was influenced by the Twinkie defense in a very subtle way, perhaps without their conscious awareness. How else could the public understand the jury's decision? The jury may have been persuaded by the statement made by the psychiatrist during the trial because the explanation was congruent with their schemas and intuitions. Either way, the media and the psychiatrist share the common characteristic of being perceived as credible authorities who can substantiate the Twinkie defense.

THE POWER OF AUTHORITIES

Another possible source of misconceptions is the tendency to listen to people in positions of authority (e.g., media, parents, teachers, and doctors) without questioning the information they are providing (Petty & Caciappo, 1981). According to the research literature on persuasion, the source of a message is a strong determinant of the effectiveness of a persuasive communication. The credibility of the source is an influential characteristic of persuasive messages. Hovland, Janis, and Kelley (1953) conducted classic studies on source credibility. They hypothesized that credibility involved two types of variables, those related to the source's expertise and those related to the source's trustworthiness. Expertise is not objectively established; it is a subjective trait estimated by the person receiving the information. Expertise is also specific. For example, a psychologist is a credible expert on human behavior but not art history. Trustworthiness, on the other hand, involves an assessment of the source's motives. A source that is in a position to gain from acceptance of the message is perceived as less trustworthy, and thus less persuasive than one that has little to gain (Petty & Cacioppo, 1981). The statement made about sugar and junk food consumption and its relationship to White's behavior was made by a psychiatrist, who would have been seen be seen by a jury as an authority on behavior. The psychiatrist is also a trustworthy source. Many of the failures to think critically about scientific issues in court cases occur when jurors automatically accept the testimony of experts. When an expert's testimony corroborates the beliefs of jurors, they are not motivated to seek disconfirming evidence.

Research on expert testimony has shown that they often have an impact on jury decision making. Research has also shown that concrete testimony, which is a tight linking of research to the facts of the case, is more effective than standard expert testimony that does not provide case-specific links (Brekke & Borgida, 1988). One explanation for this finding is that by creating links between research and the facts of the current case, jurors elaborate more on the testimony, thus making it memorable and more influential in their decision-making process. Petty and Cacioppo's (1981) elaboration likelihood model for persuasion provides an explanation. According to the model, the more we think about the content of the message the more influential it will be.

Another court-related example of the way in which expert testimony can mislead jurors is in judgments of dangerousness. Psychiatrists and psychologists are often asked to provide an opinion or prediction about how dangerous a defendant will be in the future. These estimates often affect capital punishment cases (Krauss & Sales, 2001). The American Psychiatric Association provided a brief (1983) in which they presented research showing that experts are correct in their predictions of dangerousness only about two out of three times. In at least one case, when the Supreme Court learned that predictions about dangerousness of a defendant are frequently wrong, they decided not to overturn a death penalty decision (cited in Krauss & Sales, 2001). Some court experts have argued that psychologists and psychiatrists should not testify about the dangerousness of a client because there is no ethical, scientific way to predict which defendant poses a future danger and which does not. There is no valid, reliable research to inform these judgments (Faust & Ziskin, 1988; Lavin & Sales, 1998). Krauss and Sales further investigated the effect of opinion-based expert testimony. They found that mock jurors rated expert testimony based on "clinical opinion" as more influential and persuasive than testimony that was based on research findings. Additionally, they found that jurors rated the expert opinion based on their judgment as being as credible as expert testimony backed by research.

We may never know the truth as to whether the jury in the White trial was swayed by the information they received about junk food and the cyclical variations with White's manic-depressive episodes. It is easy to understand how members of a jury could be consciously or unconsciously swayed by the statement that junk foods, especially sweets, can change a person's behavior and how the media and general public will look for reasons for light sentence he received.

WHY DO BELIEFS PERSIST?

Schemas are cognitive representations used to organize and understand the social and physical world. These internal representations are developed though personal experience and observations. We use schemas as knowledge structures to help us understand new information and organize it in ways that are congruent with existing information. Schemas are very general structures that include knowledge about ourselves, other people, social roles, and events. They are a very influential force on how we perceive the world because they create expectations that guide attention, perception, and memory (Bartlett, 1932; Markus, 1977; Taylor & Crocker, 1981). When people receive new information that fits one of their basic schemas, it is more likely that they will not seek alternative explanations compared with when new information is inconsistent with their world view.

Schemas make information processing automatic, which increases cognitive efficiency. They reduce ambiguity by providing a template to filter new information. However, when the information is incomplete, we use schemas to fill in the blanks. Once we complete missing information, information processing halts, and the result can be faulty interpretations and judgments about new information.

We often look at ourselves and our environments when developing schemas about the social world; these schemas in turn help us develop attitudes and beliefs about people and objects in that world. Chaiken, Wood, and Eagly (1996) pointed out that our attitudes may be affected, or maybe even created, by our own behavior. There is considerable evidence that in some circumstances we use our own actions to infer our beliefs. In this view, our attitudes do not cause our behavior; rather, our behaviors cause our attitudes. Some of social psychology's most controversial theorists have made this claim (Bem, 1967; Festinger, 1957). Thus, many of our misconceptions may have been formed by simply reflecting on our own and others' actions. Noticing that we have more energy or that children are hyperactive after consumption of sugar can easily lead to the misconception that a causal relationship exists. Moreover, to many people, these observations serve as legitimate evidence for this relationship.

MISCONCEPTIONS

Research shows that misconceptions are often difficult to correct (Otero, 1998; Vosnaidou, 2001). One explanation for the difficulty in changing misconceptions is the effort it takes to change our basic schemas (Dole & Sinatra, 1998). Schemas are very hard to change even in the face of discrediting information. Research has shown that our beliefs often persist after they have been discredited, referred to as *perseverance effect*. For example, Ross, Lepper, and Hubbard (1975) studied this phenomenon by asking participants to judge the validity of various suicide notes. After participants judged whether or not the various notes were real or fake, they were given feedback on their accuracy in detecting "real suicide notes." Eventually, participants developed the schema (organizing belief) that they were either good or bad at this task. Later, the experimenters told the participants that the feedback they got was given at random, and thus it was bogus and unrelated to their performance on this task. Despite this information, participants who got more positive feedback still believed that they were good at this task.

Once incorrect information enters a person's knowledge base, new information that is inconsistent with what is known is often distorted or ignored—an unconscious process that strengthens or aids in the retention of the misconception. The tendency to ignore or discount inconsistent information while focusing on information that is consistent with one's beliefs is referred to as *confirmation bias*. This bias is displayed when people seek information consistent with their beliefs about the world. Most people want to be correct in their world views, and thus they often pay attention to or recognize information that is consistent with their existing beliefs. Unfortunately, this means that most people tend to ignore information that is contrary to their beliefs. Thus, once someone decides that she thinks hyperactivity is indeed caused by sugar consumption, she will pay much more attention to instances when this relationship is supported and ignore or discredit observations or evidence when the relationship is not supported. As hard as it may be to accept, even if we learn that credible studies have been conducted that show that hyperactivity is not caused by sugar consumption, we are more inclined to find ways to dismiss these studies or be skeptical of them when we believe in the truth of the relationship.

The ways in which misconceptions are formed may also contribute to their resistance to change. That is, information sources (e.g., parents, media) may provide intermittently repeated messages that strengthen the belief with a learning schedule that make the original learning highly resistant to change. For example, parents may continually warn children that if they eat too much candy they will not be able to fall asleep. Children typically receive this message intermittently, perhaps only when a parent is concerned about the child's behavior. Intermittent reinforcement to avoid overeating is a good way to enhance the retention of information.

Changing beliefs, whether they are correct or incorrect, can be a difficult task. People often walk out of a classroom, study, or persuasive situation still holding the beliefs and misconceptions they came in with even when they received contrary information (Halpern, 2003). Those who are less able to understand new information (Guzzetti, 2000) and students with poor metacognitive abilities may be less able to decipher inconsistencies between the new information and information they believe to be true (Dole & Sinatra, 1998; Maki, 1998; Otero, 1998). Dole (2000) also found that the more strongly held a belief, the more difficult it is to comprehend new information that conflicts with the belief. Thus, research suggests that cognitive skills that help people deal effectively with information that does not confirm their existing beliefs are important tools aiding conceptual change.

How to Dispel False Beliefs

One possible way to counter misconceptions about scientific findings is by tapping an individual's critical thinking skills. Critical thinking is defined as

> the use of those cognitive skills or strategies that increase the probability of a desirable outcome. It is used to describe thinking that is purposeful, reasoned, and goal directed—the kind of thing involved in solving problems, formulating inferences, calculating likelihoods, and making decisions, when the thinker is using skills that are thoughtful and effective for the particular context and type of thinking task. (Halpern, 2003, p. 6)

There is a wide range of evidence showing that people can learn to improve how they think, but often, they possess the necessary thinking skills but fail to use them when they are needed. In an exemplary study, Kowalski and Taylor (2004) found that critical thinking skills predicted changes in students' posttest misconception scores regarding psychology. Their results suggest that students who think critically are likely to leave an introductory course with a more accurate understanding of psychology than are students who do not think critically. Other studies published in the conceptual change literature also suggest that teaching students the skills of critical thinking can be especially helpful to low performing students.

Metacognition
Metacognition refers to each person's knowledge, understanding, and control of his or her own cognitive processes. Psychologists study metacognition by examining three types of learning phenomena: (1) estimating how easy new material will be to learn, (2) rating subjective feelings of knowing, and (3) judging how well new information is learned (Jost, Kruglanski, & Nelson, 1998). To make these estimates, learners have to reflect on their own state of knowing and recognize that confidence in what one knows can vary, depending on circumstances that are often known only to the learner.

When people make judgments about their state of knowing, they are engaging in controlled information processing (Hastie & Dawes, 2001). Controlled processing is effortful. It is usually contrasted with automatic information processing, in which the thinker and the learner respond easily and without the sort of conscious effort involved in assessing the thinking process. People also tend to use more controlled thinking to carefully monitor their abilities when accomplishing something new. For example, learning how to drive is a very taxing task, and new drivers cannot attend to other information such as adjusting the radio or even listening to it. Once the task is practiced, the new driver is able to free up the cognitive resources that were used to learn the task and the driving process becomes more automatic.

When the information fits a current belief or conceptual framework to process it more automatically, the usual response is that there is no need to monitor that information. But when the information does not fit with existing beliefs, it requires much more conscious control. Anyone who engages in controlled processing may have to go through the process of unlearning, relearning, and formulating a new conceptual framework and possibly going through the very painful process of changing one's world views. No wonder most people prefer to take in information without the conscious effort of thinking critically.

Cognitive Dissonance

There is agreement both in critical thinking and persuasion literature that an effective way to change a person's beliefs is to make inconsistencies salient, causing disequilibrium between his or her thinking and the evidence that the thinking is flawed. Cognitive dissonance involves the recognition of inconsistency between beliefs, behavior, and knowledge, which creates discomfort. Cognitive dissonance was first thought to be caused by any conflicting cognitions; however, dissonance is most often experienced when our behaviors do not match our beliefs or attitudes (Festinger, 1957). Research has also shown that dissonance is most threatening when behaviors threaten one's self-image (Brehm & Cohen, 1962; Festinger, 1957; Festinger & Aronson, 1960). For example, you may think you are a kind person, but if you treated someone from another racial group badly based on a stereotypical belief you have of that group, either your self-image as a kind person will need revision or you will have to decide that your actions were justified. It is easier to justify one's actions than it is to change a self-concept.

Moreover, it is suggested in both persuasion and critical thinking literature that repeated exposure to new information, especially dissonance-creating information, increases the likelihood of changing the original belief. For most people, it will take more than one study, or one review of a study to change their existing beliefs. By repeatedly showing that the relationship does not exist, which creates repeated episodes of dissonance, the motivation to reduce the dissonance will increase enough to bring about change. However, to increase the likelihood that misconceptions will change, we need to teach people how to effectively evaluate scientific evidence and arguments.

CRITICAL THINKING STRATEGIES

Critical thinking strategies are embedded in the scientific method, which requires comprehension of hypothesis testing, theory building, bias, and determining causation.

Causation Versus Correlation

One consistently misunderstood scientific principle is the difference between causation and correlation. Correlation is not causation, although it can provide support for causal claims if the research design supports it. When discussing research, certain words and phrases (e.g., effect) insinuate a causal relationship. Correlation is not a "bad" concept. When researchers find relationships, they can gain great insight into how the world works. Causal statements can be made from correlated data only when subjects are randomly assigned to different conditions—so causality lies in the experimental design—a fact that is not well understood. If we can get people to think about control groups and how people vary in many ways, we would have come a long way toward getting important notions about causality into common thinking.

Disconfirming Evidence

As stated earlier, there is a general tendency to ignore evidence or information that contradicts our beliefs about the world. However, we can consciously learn to seek out, or at least be open to, information that is not in line with our beliefs. One skill commonly used to resist persuasion is the deliberate consideration of counterarguments or possible alternative explanations. Willingness to consider or practice in developing counterarguments can reduce susceptibility to persuasive techniques that are faulty or unjust.

Fallacies are common persuasive tools based on unsound reasoning. One commonly used fallacy is the use of weak or invalid analogies. Although the use of analogies is a basic thinking skill, analogies can also mislead thinking. An analogy can be used to compare two events or objects when they share certain properties. However, an analogy is weak or inappropriate when the objects being compared have important dissimilarities. Analogies are commonly used by politicians to persuade the public to support an action. For example, the current administration is fond of saying that Iran in 2006 is like Germany in 1938. The implications of this analogy are clear: Unless we act quickly we will have consequences similar to those we experienced when we did not respond to Germany's early aggressive acts. In fact, modern Iran is like 1938 Germany in some important ways and not like it in other important ways. Critical thinkers need to consider the similarities and differences to determine which are more critical and whether other events in the world today render that direct comparison meaningful. The conscious effort needed to think through the parallel relationships between Iran and Germany is effortful. The more automatic and unthinking acceptance of this analogy requires much less mental work. How can we develop the disposition to think critically, especially when we identify a topic that is important enough to invest mental energy into thinking about it? We need to develop the attitudes of critical thinking. In other words, there needs to be a predisposition to engage in the effortful thinking needed for critical analysis.

Another commonly used fallacy is the bandwagon technique. This technique creates the impression that there is a widespread support for a position or an argument. It is frequently used in television commercials, where we are told that some car is the best selling or a designer is the most coveted by everyone "in the know." Learners can all be taught to recognize the use of fallacies, which is a first step toward defending against them. Card stacking or suppressing information is a potent persuasive technique that operates by omitting information that supports the opposite position. The entire system of legal advocacy is based on the idea that each side in a legal case presents its best case, which means that important information that might weaken their case will be omitted or made to appear weak. Again, people can learn to ask for missing information and to independently weigh information. It is important to consider what information is not being presented in the face of a persuasion attempt.

CONCLUSION

As psychologists, we have a good understanding of the cognitive processes that can lead jurors and others astray as they think through complex issues. We have a large body of evidence showing that people can learn to think more critically with appropriate instruction and the opportunity to practice critical thinking in multiple settings (Moseley et al., 2005). Based on a large number of research findings, we suggest that instruction in the skills of critical thinking be mandatory in high schools and colleges and that all attorneys lead jurors and others through the process of thinking more critically about evidence and testimony. In a court case, each side could lead the jurors in thinking about causal claims, weak analogies, or any of the other common fallacies that are used during a trial. They can point out key information that may be accepted too readily because it conforms to a preexisting schema or rejected too quickly because it does not fit with preexisting schemas and explain why critical information of both sorts needs the extra effort of a critical thinker. We can improve how information is processed in the courtroom and other places, but it will take conscious effort and knowledge of how we think and understand the world. It is not easy, but it may be the most important discourse in a courtroom or anywhere else.

REFERENCES

American Psychiatric Association as ami-cus curiae in support of petitioner [Brief], Barefoot v. Estelle, 463 U.S. 880 (1983).

Bartlett, F. C. (1932). *Remembering: A study in experimental and social psychology.* Cambridge, UK: Cambridge University Press.

Bem, D. J. (1967). Self-perception: An alternative explanation of cognitive dissonance phenomena. *Psychological Review, 74*, 183–200.

Brekke, N., & Borgida, E. (1988). Expert psychological testimony in rape trials: A social-cognitive analysis. *Journal of Personality and Social Psychology, 55*, 372–386.

Brehm, J. W., & Cohen, A. R. (1962). *Explorations in cognitive dissonance.* Oxford, UK: Wiley.

Brody, J. E. (1982, November 17). How diet can affect mood and behavior. *The New York Times,* p. C1. Retrieved on September 6, 2006 from http://web.lexis-nexis.com/universe/document?_m=16840ffa8b96ce7 cb9b41cc861da7191&_docnum=14&wchp=dGLbVlz-zSkVb&_md5 =60c2fd093fec69f096ee929fce5beb82

Chaiken, S., Wood, W., & Eagly, A. H. (1996). Principles of persuasion. In E. T. Higgins & A. W. Kruglanski (Eds.), *Social psychology: Handbook of basic principles* (pp. 702–742). New York: Guilford Press.

Crenshaw, A. B. (1981, April 12). Diet and crime. *The Washington Post,* p. D8. Retrieved on September 6, 2006 from http://web.lexis-nexis. com/universe/document?_m=16840ffa8b96ce7cb9b41cc861da7191& _docnum=16&wchp=dGLbVlz-zSkVb&_md5=0ea29879d4115e0b5 11791c14dba16ab

Dole, J. A. (2000). Readers, texts and conceptual change learning. *Reading and Writing Quarterly, 16*, 99–118.

Dole, J. A., & Sinatra, G. M. (1998). Reconceptualizing change in the cognitive construction of knowledge. *Educational Psychologist, 33*, 109–128.

Ewing, C. P., & McCann J. T. (2006). *Minds on trial: Great cases in law and psychology.* New York: Oxford University Press.

Faust, D., & Ziskin, J. (1988). The expert witness in psychology and psychiatry. *Science, 241*, 31–35.

Festinger, L. (1957). *A theory of cognitive dissonance.* Oxford, UK: Row, Peterson & Co.

Festinger, L., & Aronson, E. (1960). Arousal and reduction of dissonance in social contexts. In D. Cartwright & A. Zander (Eds.), *Group dynamics: Research and theory* (pp. 125–136). Oxford, UK: Row, Peterson & Co.

Guzzetti, B. (2000). Learning counter-intuitive science concepts: What have we learned from over a decade of research? *Reading and Writing Quarterly, 16*, 89–98.

Halpern, D. F. (2003). *Thought and knowledge: An introduction to critical thinking* (4th ed.). Mahwah, NJ: Lawrence Erlbaum Associates.

Hastie, R., & Dawes, R. M. (2001). *Rational choice in an uncertain world: The psychology of judgment and decision making.* Thousand Oaks, CA: Sage.

Horgan, M. A. (1987, September 22). Hyperactivity and sugar not linked, report finds. *The Toronto Star*, p. E7. Retrieved on September 5, 2006 from http://web.lexis-nexis.com/universe/document?_m=16840ffa8b 96ce7cb9b41cc861da7191&_docnum=5wchp=dGLbVlz-zSkVb&_m d5=7641c96257c134220a4834295568261f

Hovland, C. I., Janis, I. L., & Kelley, H. H. (1953). *Communication and persuasion: Psychological studies of opinion change.* New Haven, CT: Yale University Press.

Jost, J. T., Kruglanski, A. W., & Nelson, T. O. (1998). Social metacognition: An expansionist review. *Personality and Social Psychology Review, 2*, 137–154.

Kowalski, P. & Taylor, A. K. (2004). Ability and critical thinking as predictors of change in students' psychological misconceptions. *Journal of Instructional Psychology, 31*, 297.

Krauss, D. A., & Sales, B. D. (2001). The effects of clinical and scientific expert testimony on juror decision making capital sentencing. *Psychology, Public Policy, and Law, 7*, 267–310.

Lavin, M., & Sales, B. (1998). Moral justification for limits of expert testimony. In S. J. Ceci & H. Hembrooke (Eds.), *Expert witnesses in child abuse cases: What can and should be said in court* (pp. 59–81). Washington, DC: American Psychological Association.

Maki, R. H. (1998). Test predictions over text materials. In D. J. Hacker, J. Dunlosky, & A. C. Graesser (Eds.), *Metacognition in educational theory and practice* (pp. 117–144). Mahwah, NJ: Lawrence Erlbaum Associates.

Markus, H. (1977). Self-schemata and processing information about the self. *Journal of Personality and Social Psychology, 35*, 63–78.

Moseley, D., Baumfield, V., Elliot, J., Gregson, M., Higgins, S., Miller, J., et al. (2005). *Frameworks for thinking: A handbook for teaching and learning.* New York: Cambridge University Press.

Otero, J. (1998). Influence of knowledge activation and context on comprehension monitoring of science texts. In D. J. Hacker, J. Dunlosky, &
A. C. Graesser (Eds.), *Metacognition in educational theory and practice* (pp. 145–164). Mahwah, NJ: Lawrence Erlbaum Associates.

Petty, R. E., & Cacioppo, J. T. (1981). *Attitudes and persuasion: Classic
and contemporary approaches*. Dubuque, IA: Wm C. Brown.

Ross, L., Lepper, M. R., & Hubbard, M. (1975). Perseverance in self-
perception and social perception: Biased attributional processes in the
debriefing paradigm. *Journal of Personality and Social Psychology,
32*, 880–892.

Taylor, S. E., and Crocker, J. (1981). Schematic bases of social information
processing. In E. T. Higgins, P. M. Herman, & M. P. Zanna (Eds.).
Social cognition: The Ontario symposium. Hillsdale, NJ: Lawrence
Erlbaum Associates.

Vosniadou, S. (2001). What can persuasion research tell us about conceptual
change that we did not already know? *International Journal of Educational Research, 35*, 731–737.

Wolraich, M. L., Wilson, D. B., & White, J. W. (1995). The effects of sugar
on behavior or cognition in children: A meta-analysis. *Journal of the
American Medical Association, 274*, 1617–1621.

CHAPTER THREE

MEDICAL MALINGERING AND DISABILITY: HISTORIC, ECONOMIC, AND MODERN PERSPECTIVES WITH MANAGEMENT CONSIDERATIONS

M. Nicholas Coppola, PhD, MHA, MSA, FACHE
Lee Bewley, PhD, MHA
Jeffrey P. Harrison, PhD, MBA, MHA, FACHE
Meghan Shapiro, MHA, CHE

INTRODUCTION

Health care executives and their associated colleagues find it difficult to understand the impact of medical malingering on organizations and society due to the inability to manage direct and incremental costs associated with waste, fraud, and abuse. Various third-party payers, industry prepaid premiums, and fee-for-service schedules superficially appear to cover direct expenditures toward malingering individuals; however, they often do not cover the full cost of care. Most health care organizations fail to recognize the significant cost associated with the delivery of care to certain fraudulent medical cases and the lost opportunity costs associated with recapturing and reprogramming those scarce health care resources. Patients attempting to abuse the health care system for personal or secondary gain have a direct impact on the health care industry. For example, these patients often fail to show up for appointments, fail to properly follow physicians' directives, neglect to return phone calls, and may deliberately destroy medical records. Furthermore, these patients may disrupt normal cycle flow, adversely affect human resource relationships within the health care system, and cause ancillary hospital personnel to spend a disproportionate amount of time and attention on one case.

In addition, physicians are often challenged with a continued patient trend known as "somatization." With burgeoning managed care penetration and gatekeeper access in America, somatization, the reporting of somatic symptoms with no pathophysiological explanation, has become more problematic in health care as patients exaggerate symptoms to ensure care or future compensation. Somatization may increase malingering duration and cost by causing physicians to refer patients for special or additional screening during the beneficiary process due to the lack of clinical evidence of pathology, often at unreimbursed expense.

Self-directed patient and employer activities associated with health care fraud produce agency costs every health maintenance organization (HMO) is struggling to identify and solve in today's competitive and rapidly penetrating managed care market. Illegal workers' compensation claims cost insurance companies and managed care organizations millions of dollars each year. According to the National Health Care Anti-Fraud Association (NHCAA), health care fraud is defined as the intentional deception or misrepresentation that an individual or entity makes when the misrepresentation could result in some unauthorized benefit to the individual, entity, or some third party.

In 2004 America spent over one trillion dollars financing health care. It is estimated that approximately 16% of these health care dollars may be attributable to health care fraud, generally gained through workers' compensation programs. Of this amount, approximately one-third is directly attributed to claimant fraud activities, while the remaining two thirds can be traced to actions of provider fraud. How did the health care profession end up in such a state? When did the early economic incentives for perpetrating health care and insurance fraud for personal or secondary gain from the claimant standpoint begin? Historical analysis of some of the earliest cases of fraud reveals where the trend may have begun, and focused considerations for management practitioners can be developed for current problems.

HISTORIC PERSPECTIVE

The Emergence of Malingering

The history of workers' compensation, fraud, disability, and economic incentives as they relate to malingering and false claims is difficult to trace and more difficult to accurately represent from both a medical and legal perspective. There are always two sides to every story, and the truth is difficult to discern. However, several authors have attempted to compartmentalize this phenomenon from both qualitative and descriptive methodologies (Coppola, 1998; Kent, 2001; Kudlick, 2003; Lockhart, n.d.; McWhinnie, 1982; Rhodes, 1998).

Workers' compensation programs are one of the many benefits sought out by employees. The world's earliest documented case of workers' compensation is probably in Great Britain. Britain's parliament enacted a program of compensation in 1593 to recognize disabled naval officers (Library of Congress Study, 1984). The program served as an *incentive* to retain regular naval officers on active duty in case family finances or misfortunes removed the presence of economic security for the officer.

The earliest case on record of an established system of benefits provided by an employer to an employee in the United States is also documented in the military (Coppola, 1997a). One of the earliest enactments by the fledgling U.S. Congress in 1790 was the Act of April 30, 1790, which provided "the list of invalids of the United States." The provision provided for the payment of $5.00 each month to enlisted personnel and one-half pay to officers for life, although the payments were distributed with great difficulty, at best, generally with restrictions to those injured during war (not from illness or age), and may not have reached all those deserving the benefit. However, for military personnel, this loose system of compensation was all that was available through 1861 when the Congress passed the first recognized series of workers' compensation benefits in America called "An Act for the Better Organization of the Military Establishment." This law provided for the separation/retirement of officers with 40-plus years of service and for the medical separation of soldiers who had incurred injuries while in the line of duty (Coppola, 1997b; Department of Defense, 1996).

According to one author, the earliest case of claimant misbehavior in America may be documented within the U.S. Navy. In 1855 the navy established the lead in what would inevitably become a successive series of mandates shaping the modern military physical disability system. That same year, the House of Military Affairs established "An Act to Promote Efficiency in the Navy." This mandate required that officers no longer capable of performing their duties under field/sea conditions be expeditiously retired. The intent of the mandate was, of course, to "promote efficiency in the Navy." Until this mandate, officers appointed on active duty remained in service until they were cashiered, resigned, or died. It was only in cases of extreme and unmistakable debilitating conditions that a soldier would be involuntarily separated from service. The impetus prior to 1855 was on *hiding* debilitating conditions and keeping the medical record clean to avoid involuntary separation from military service. There simply existed no economic incentive for the soldier-patient to fabricate injuries prior to 1855. On the contrary, it was in the patient's best economic interest to always give the appearance of being healthy. Failing to give the perception of fitness might result in the loss of job, pay, and medical benefits simultaneously. Rumors of medical board coercion and manipulation of medical records during the 1855 mandate was so prevalent that the legislation was repealed in 1857 (Coppola, 1998).

In 1861 the economic incentive for a physically impaired soldier to imitate fitness changed when Congress passed "An Act for the Better Organization of the Military Establishment." This law provided for the separation/retirement of officers with 40-plus years of service and for the medical separation of soldiers who had incurred injuries while in the line of duty. This congressional mandate was one of the first of its kind in America to offer a recognized series of workman's compensation benefits to an employee by an employer.

In the early 1900s, a burgeoning national trend for providing workers' compensation began to emerge throughout America, too. However, early 20th-century management theory at the time advocated what was known as Wood's Law (Evens, 1992). Wood's Law stated that without a specific contract, employees could be fired without cause and were provided with no compensation benefits if injured in the workplace. In fact, many employees were required to sign a form stating that they would not enter into legal action with an employer or request compensation if injured while working. Working itself was considered a privilege, not a right.

As the century developed, the industrial and steel age revealed more unskilled laborers working than at any other time in American history. Henry Ford's introduction of the assembly line in 1913 revolutionized industry but increased worker boredom, attracted unskilled laborers at lower wages than skilled workers, and resulted in an increase in industry-related accidents. Around that same time, with the introduction of integrated transportation networks across America, employees were able to unite and press for change nationwide. Contemporary management responded to burgeoning union and worker demands by replacing low wages (in lieu of salary increases) with limited health and injury benefits. In 1914 New York State passed the first workers' compensation law as nonoccupational disability benefits gained acceptance after a fire killed or injured over 100 employees in the garment district. The industrial workforce soon pursued this trend. In the 1920s, civilian industry began to offer benefit packages designed to replace declining wages, and in 1942 nonoccupational disability benefits gained acceptance with the introduction of congressionally mandated disability worker plans (Coppola, 1998). In 1935 Congress had passed the National Labor Relations Act, which included foundations for the remaining states that had no workers' compensation legislation to provide it. By 1950, every state in America had passed some type of workers' compensation plan. As of 1994, more than 80% of all U.S. employers offered some kind of disability benefit (Fossum, 1995; Williams & Torrns, 1993).

As of 2005, 92% of all employers offered some kind of disability benefit. However, with the change in economical incentive came a change in patient behavior patterns. Rather than a debilitated worker attempting to imitate a fully capable employee, which had been the case in the latter half of the 19th century, it may now be in a perfectly healthy claimant's best economic interest to imitate symptoms of a debilitated person.

Malingering Emerges
Through the early part of the 20th century, people worked until the day they died or could seek refuge with working family members. In limited circumstances, homeless and indigent workers found refuge in charitable institutions in larger communities. Factory conditions for workers in the northern United States were so bad in the late 19th century that the U.S. Supreme Court cited them in a legal ruling in the 1857 court case of *Dred Scott v. Sanford.* Dred Scott (a slave) attempted to sue his plantation owner for his freedom. The U.S. Supreme Court ruled against Scott stating that slaves were better off than northern factory workers because slaves enjoyed such fringe benefits as "care in illness" and old age security (Fraze & Finney, 1988). As preposterous as this decision may sound today, it emulated the thoughts of many 19th-century Americans. Slaves *might* be guaranteed food, shelter,

and health care by the homeowner; the same could not be said for the typical unskilled laborer injured and without work in a northern factory. In the later part of the 1900s, all that began to change. For hundreds of years employees worked because they had to earn money to survive. The economic incentive prior to most of 1950 throughout America was to perpetuate health and fitness for fear of being dismissed or replaced in the work environment. From about that time, and with the recently passed legislation regarding payments to disabled workers, a paradigm shift occurred, which for the first time created an opportunity for the healthy worker to commit health fraud and imitate illness or injury for personal financial gain.

It is difficult to determine exactly when these disreputable individuals manifested themselves in complex fraud projects for personal gain. The slow evolution of indemnity and service plans in the mid-1930s and 1940s transferred risk from the patient to the insurer. Additionally, through the 1950s and 1960s, several new avenues for collecting benefits existed for the patients to exploit as the result of new legislation in state worker compensation plans. Although most workers (85%) do not respond to an injury this way, the 15% who do account for a disproportionate share of disability cost. It was not until 1968 that the health and insurance industry responded. Health care antifraud programs began to emerge as a deterrent to claimant fraud. However, 70% of all programs in health care antifraud that currently exist have only been around since 1985 due to the increased emphasis of managed care (Health Insurance Association of America, 1994). According to a survey by Ernst & Young, over 70% of large hospital organizations have *some* sort of system in place to track and monitor workers' compensation issues.

ECONOMIC PERSPECTIVES

Consider a world where citizens have free, uninhibited access to a common, desirable resource that was subject to limited replenishment. In this world, we can expect that citizens will seek to obtain quantities of this resource in order to enhance their own well-being.

Furthermore, we can expect that each rational citizen will seek to maximize his or her own well-being or utility. Consequently, we can assume that citizens will pose the following question to themselves prior to obtaining an additional quantity of the resource, "Am I better off with more of this resource?" Holding all other considerations constant, rational citizens will answer this question with an unequivocal "yes" and proceed to obtain additional quantities of the resource. In time, this resource will diminish and then disappear from availability. This scenario is consistent with "The Tragedy of the Commons" posited by the theorist Garrett Hardin, who outlines societal consequences associated with the unbounded utilization of resources driven by the rational pursuit of utility maximization by individuals (Adnett & Dawson, 1998).

Malingering is associated with a universally accessible resource with limited replenishment capabilities: an individual's working capacity (Carroll, 2003). With obvious exceptions, including incarceration, forced servitude, and incapacity, each individual has broad access to his or her own ability to work on any given day. The choices that an individual makes with regard to the utilization of his or her capacity to work are essentially segmented into a binary choice of to work or not to work. Individuals weigh tradeoffs between benefits and opportunity costs in making decisions to work or not to work in the rational pursuit of maximizing utility. Malingering exists as a variable inherent in the calculus of an individual's working capacity utilization that potentially enables an individual to enjoy the benefits of working while choosing not to work (Ruser, 1998). In the aggregate, the societal effects of malingering are consistent with the theme of inefficient resource utilization outlined by Hardin's Tragedy of the Commons. Although the resource of working capacity will not be lost to society in the future, society does irrevocably lose the working capacity of the individual during the period of malingering. The effects on society and root causes of malingering can at least be partially explained by basic economic principles (Wang & Kleiner, 2005).

Economics concerns the study and application of principles focused on the efficient utilization of resources in markets. Classical economic tenets, based largely on the works of Adam Smith, hold that the market, consisting of consumers and producers, through an "invisible hand," will efficiently find prevailing prices to allocate scarce resources and effectively ration goods and services within the market (Rice, 2003).

Classical economics is based on a key assumption of behavioral rationality where consumers are expected to pursue utility maximization and producers are expected to pursue profit maximization (Smith, 2003). The inherent drive of individuals to better their lives is an essential element of economics. The belief that individuals will enter markets in search of goods and services that will bring them enjoyment and satisfaction is predicated on this behavioral rationality. Similarly, the expectation of earning at least a normal profit serves as the prime incentive for rational producers of goods and services to enter the market, start a business, and attempt to meet the demands generated by individuals in the market.

Markets are environments where consumers and producers engage in exchange processes while simultaneously seeking to improve their own well-being (Santerre & Neun, 2004). Economic principles provide for basic conditions that facilitate efficient exchanges between consumers and producers that result in the efficient distribution of resources within the market. Characteristics of efficient markets include (Santerre & Neun):

- Many buyers and sellers
- Producers offer identical products
- Low transaction costs
- No barriers to entry or exit
- Perfect information

Finally, efficient allocation of resources requires an equitable balance of benefits in market transactions. Economists call the equitable balance of benefits Pareto optimality, where allocations of resources to one individual that result in an increase in benefits to that individual do not make another individual worse off as a consequence of the transaction (Rice, 2003). For instance, if an individual purchases a premium bottle of bourbon from a store owner in exchange for $100, Pareto optimality holds that the individual and the store owner each perceives that the utility that he or she received in the transaction was equivalent to the consideration that he or she transferred. Pareto optimality would not be achieved in this example if the individual discovered that the premium bottle of bourbon was, in fact, a cheap bottle of whisky covered with a counterfeit premium bourbon label.

From an economic perspective, malingering is considered an inefficient allocation of resources (Adnett & Dawson, 1998). The root cause of this market inefficiency is based on the assumption of rationality of individual behavior as individuals are expected to take actions that will enhance their own utility. Individuals who feign illness, disease, or disability perceive that they will receive levels of utility beyond the opportunity costs of foregoing work as a consequence of their claim that will be greater than if they chose to work in a manner that is consistent with their true capacity to work.

Individuals who rationally follow their own self-interests and employ malingering often rely on deviations from characteristics of efficient markets. Variations in work environments in regards to the quantity and quality of market participants may enable or constrain malingering. A market rich with available workers could moderate the incidence of malingering as employers have ready, viable substitutes for workers. On the other hand, a labor market consisting largely of low-quality workers may serve to support malingering efforts of relatively higher-quality workers in the market. Similarly, barriers to exit or entry from a labor market can effect malingering. A market with low or no barriers to entry or exit will moderate malingering activities as workers may be hired or fired readily, whereas a market with barriers such as a collective bargaining unit or craftsmen's guild could enable malingering efforts due to the inhibited ability of managers to seek substitute labor. Finally, since malingering is predominantly based on the internal assessment and report of health and ability to work by an individual, defects from perfect market information are increasingly likely as only the individual concerned clearly knows the true extent of his or her own capacity to work (Adnett & Dawson, 1998; Rice, 2003).

Economic Concepts Associated With Malingering
The rational pursuit of self-interests coupled with taking advantage of deviations from efficient market conditions to achieve individual utility maximization provides a broad economic synopsis for malingering in markets. These two variables, drive and opportunity, may account for much of the basic economic foundation underlying malingering in markets; however, more refined explanatory and predictive concepts with the field of economics exist to supplement the basic primers. The following economic concepts, utility maximization, asymmetrical information, morale hazard, and compensating differentials, further illuminate the theoretical foundation for malingering in a market or society.

Utility Maximization
A primary assumption of economic analysis is that individuals will seek to fulfill their own self-interests and thus will make choices oriented toward utility maximization. Utility maximization choices involve weighing the aggregate value of benefits, costs, and opportunity costs to determine a choice that will yield the highest net utility. Aggregating these variables for each of the various choices will yield corresponding individual assessments of net benefits or utility. Rational individuals will pursue the choice with the greatest net benefit (Santerre & Neun, 2004).

In the context of work capacity utilization and malingering, benefits for working may include pay, job satisfaction, job security, camaraderie, or perquisites. Conversely, benefits for not working range from leisure to avoidance of occupational health risk. Benefits accrued from not working as a consequence of malingering can include access to workers compensation insurance, sympathy from third parties, or offers of workplace accommodation (Rice, 2003).

Costs associated with work capacity utilization and malingering result in decrements to individual utility. An individual's choice to work may yield costs to the individual, including physical exertion, mental stress, or exposure to occupational health hazards. Costs borne by individuals choosing not to work include loss of income, loss of accrued sick/vacation time, and reduction in vocational ability. Meaningful costs potentially assumed by individuals who choose not to work in conjunction with malingering are increases in the likelihood for employment termination and diminished work ethic reputation among peers and colleagues.

Utility maximization of working capacity is achieved when individuals judge the aggregate benefits of work utilization choices, including malingering, against costs incurred by those choices and the opportunity costs of foregoing other choices. Utility maximization is achieved with the choice that results in the greatest positive difference between benefits and costs. In some market instances, individuals may judge that the net benefits of not working in conjunction with malingering justify this choice and they will expect to be better off as a consequence of that choice.

Asymmetrical Information
Conditions for efficient markets include the characteristic of perfect information. To establish an equitable basis for individuals in a market in order to properly evaluate the potential benefits and costs of various transactions involving goods and services, perfect information is required to thoroughly and exhaustively impart decision variables such as attributes, characteristics, tendencies, limitations, or requirements. Perfect information exists as a standard for an efficient market to facilitate cogent decision making by parties in a transaction that results in Pareto optimality. Unfortunately, perfect information is a gold standard that is rarely achieved in markets, particularly with regard to conveying health status. When market participants such as an employer and employee have unequal levels of knowledge regarding health status, this circumstance is known as asymmetrical information (Fuchs, 1998).

The sources of asymmetrical information related to health status and malingering include lack of medical training, individual perception, and opportunity. As most individuals have limited or nonexistent medical training, accurate assessments of health status are difficult to obtain from self-reports by individuals, or the true extent of an injury or malady may be misstated as a consequence of simple medical ignorance. Individuals' perceptions of their own health status is subject to variance, which may result in inaccurate conveyance of information between individuals. Finally, as individuals have a nearly unique perspective of their own state of disease or injury, they also have the opportunity to report information to individuals that may not be completely synchronous with their true medical condition.

Malingering can be facilitated by asymmetrical information. Individuals who seek to further their own interests may leverage ignorance, perception, or opportunity in order to project a health status that is contrary to reality. Projecting a health status other than reality results in the malingering individual creating a level of information that exceeds the information level of other individuals in market or social interactions. The effect of asymmetrical information is that employers, health care providers, or colleagues engage in transactions with individuals that will likely result in inefficient allocation of resources consistent with imperfect market characteristics (Wang & Kleiner, 2005).

Moral Hazard

The circumstance where individuals alter their consumption or behavioral choices as a consequence of having insurance is known as moral hazard. A classic example of moral hazard involves the change in likelihood of utilization of health services that occurs when individuals have health insurance. Since rational self-interested individuals with health insurance do not normally bear the full costs of health services, they tend to consume more health services than they would in the absence of health insurance. The concept of moral hazard encapsulates an idea that this type of behavior is subjectively immoral and results in some type of societal danger (Rice, 2003).

Moral hazard is associated with malingering, specifically in the areas of health insurance and workers' compensation insurance. Malingering enables individuals with the potential to enjoy benefits entitled to legitimate claimants of insurance coverage. By effectively feigning an illness or injury, individuals may receive benefits, including medical care, pharmaceuticals, compensated time off from work, or vocational retraining that would otherwise be unavailable to them. The net result of moral hazard enabled by malingering is another example of a deviation from Pareto optimality where an individual enhances his total utility without a corresponding transfer in consideration utility to another party (Adnett & Dawson, 1998).

Compensating Differentials

The concept of compensating differentials in economics concerns the application of Pareto optimality in the compensation process between an employer and an employee. In simple terms, to engage in an employment contract, an employee must agree to a compensation package provided by an employer in exchange for the performance of work. The compensation package may consist of several components, including wages, salary, working conditions, health insurance, or other perquisites. Similarly, the performance of the work assumes a constant expectation of productivity, working environment, and occupational hazards. The concept of compensating differentials holds that an individual assigns a set utility level to the compensation package necessary to engage in the performance of work in a constant environment (Morrisey, 2001). Changes to the equation of compensation package and work expectations in the course of employment require a rebalancing of the compensation package or work expectations in order to maintain Pareto optimality. For instance, if an employer decides to drop employer-sponsored health insurance for all employees while simultaneously maintaining a status quo for job performance expectations, employees will have effectively received a decrease in compensation unless the employer increases other elements of compensation such as wages or perquisites (Miller, 2004).

Malingering is relevant to compensating differentials in employment areas considered employee fraud and misconduct. Employees may perceive that the equitable balance of compensation and work expectations that existed at the onset and during subsequent periods of their employment contract has changed. If employees perceive that the utility that they receive from their compensation package has become deficient relative to the expectations of job performance, they may seek to achieve compensating differentials through deviant means such as malingering in the absence of equitable redress from their employers. Malingering to achieve compensating differentials may be manifested in employee efforts to slow the pace of work in the face of increased productivity demands and unchanged compensation levels. For instance, garbage collectors who are required to double the number of residences served in their weekly routes with no change in compensation may suddenly develop back, shoulder, and leg ailments that appear to convey an inability to expand garbage collection capacity. In this manner, the garbage collectors may be malingering to maintain what they consider Pareto optimality through compensating differentials (Morrisey, 2001).

Summary of Economic Perspective

The economic basis for malingering is simply that it is a mechanism for enhancing an individual's perception of his or her own well-being by seeking to maximize utility. Rationality serves as the foundation for this mechanism as individuals are expected to act in their own self-interest and to judge and then select economic and societal choices that enable them to achieve higher levels of utility. Lapses in the characteristics of efficient markets such as few buyers and sellers of labor, significant variance in labor quality, barriers to entry and exit within a labor market, and the absence of perfect information enhance the opportunity and likelihood of malingering in a market. Finally, a more thorough explanation of the economic aspects of malingering must include the concepts of utility maximization, asymmetric information, moral hazard, and compensating differentials.

MODERN PERSPECTIVE

Modern Health Care Fraud

Fraud is defined as the "intentional perversion of truth in order to induce another to part with something of value or to surrender a legal right" (Betts, 1999). Estimates of annual losses due to health care fraud range from 3% to 16% of all health care expenditures. Health care fraud increases the cost of health care for everyone and in general reduces the quality of care provided due to the cost of fraud detection and the types of fraud themselves. For health care insurers and providers to combat health care fraud, more money is being spent on organizations and the formation of compliance committees in organizations, resulting in an increase in the cost of providing health care (Betts, 1999; Swedlow & Johnson, 2001; Ziel, 1998).

False diagnosis is a prime example of modern health care fraud. This form of fraud is associated with malingering to a minor extent by requests of the patient in order to ensure insurance coverage. It is a widely accepted form of health care fraud. Greater restrictions in health care and insurance will amplify this problem as physicians will be determined to ensure their patients get the treatment they need by making certain that they are able to be covered under insurance (National Health Care Anti-Fraud Association [NHCAA], 1995; Zimmerman, 1984).

Determinants of Malingering
There are four sources of information for making the determination of malingering. Interviews that discuss past history of achievement and past work as well as past mental health issues are critical. Also important are the examiners' observations and the results of testing. This along with the reports of collateral informants such as past treatment providers and family members can help shed light on the functioning of the individual; however, such reports cannot be taken at face value as some family members may not be truthful in an attempt to help the defendant's cause. Treatment providers as well may be convinced of the authenticity of the defendant's allegations and may not be objective, and jail personnel may be prejudiced against the defendant and also fail to be objective. Sometimes, the best evidence of malingering is found by observing the change in demeanor when an individual leaves the examining area (American College of Occupational and Environmental Medicine [ACOEM], 2003; Cloeren, 2002; Cheadle et al., 1999; DON, 2002; GAO Report, 2004).

Sometimes malingerers overplay their part: They are often unfriendly or uncooperative. They may give short, uninformative answers. They may refuse to sign authorizations to release medical records or maintain that they do not know the phone numbers of family members. Prior to the establishment of standardized testing, examiners would ask questions that even severely impaired people should know, such as the color of grass. Malingerers will often allege hallucinations that are significantly more frequent than for actual psychiatric patients (Rubenzer, 2004).

Many defendants in criminal cases may limit their presentation to very specific symptoms such as amnesia about the events of the crime. Faked amnesia can be detected by a forced choice memory test, an example of which is a test of about 20 questions that are salient to the crime. Each question has two plausible answers.

Someone with no prior knowledge of the crime should be able to score 50% because blind guesses should lead to about half of the answers being right. A malingerer will overexaggerate the responses and score at a statistically significant level, which implies concealed knowledge of the crime (Glassmire et al., 2003).

A malingering scale, the Atypical Presentation Scale (APS) has recently been developed as a competency screening for the purpose of standing for a trial. The APS is a companion test to the Evaluation for Competency to Stand Trail—Revised, which is a standardized competency interview. It asks the defendant questions about the alleged symptoms and how they interfere with the ability to function in a court setting. This was originally designed as a screening measure for faked incompetence. A recent study found that the APS is very effective for sorting suspected malingerers from defendants with legitimate mental problems (Rubenzer, 2004).

When conducting a forensic examination, nothing can be taken for granted or at face value. It is no longer an acceptable clinical practice for a forensic examiner to accept a defendant's presentation without looking at all the evidence. When an examination does not address the possibility of malingering, it is almost worthless. Examiners who work this way are asking to be manipulated by criminal defendants. It must also be noted that even when someone fakes his or her responses on a test, he or she may still be significantly impaired due to fear, anxiety, or other personality disorders.

Positron emission tomography (PET) scans are another option recently found to be a possible aid in determination of malingering. PET scans are a minimally invasive nuclear medicine imaging system that uses radiopharmaceuticals that are short lived to detect perfusion and metabolic activity in the various organ systems and can provide information about function and metabolism that is comparable with anatomical information obtained from radiographic studies. Clinical applications of PET are seen in oncology, cardiology, and neuropsychiatric disorders. The creation of 18F-fluordeoxyglucose (18F-FDG), a primary radiopharmaceutical tracer that measures the metabolic rates of glucose, and $^{15}OH_2O$, which measures regional cerebral blood flow, allowed the PET scan to reveal brain metabolism and function. These tracers are thought to facilitate the study of a variety of neurologic disorders such as dementia and other mental illnesses and have also been used to study the effects of different stimuli to the central nervous system (GAO Report, 2004; Martin, 2003).

Models of Malingering

There are four models of malingering: the pathogenic model, the criminological model, the puritanical model, and the adaptational model.

1. *Pathogenic model:* The pathogenic model refers to individuals who are motivated by an underlying pathology. This includes the voluntary production of faked symptoms that will later be replaced by an actual disorder. Research indicates that this model may have a small role in explaining the behavior of nonforensic malingerers, but it is limited in explaining the behavior of forensic malingerers.
2. *Criminological model:* The criminological model states that there is an antisocial and oppositional motivation for malingering.

This model deals with people who have personality disorders and who will not be deterred by social norms or criminal law. Such people may fake other mental disorders to obtain undeserved rewards. This is the model that is described by the American Psychiatric Association, *Diagnostic and Statistical Manual of Mental Disorders (DSM)*. The *DSM-III, DSM-III-R*, and *DSM-IV* descriptions of malingering are an extreme departure from the pathogenic model and a shift toward a moralistic view of malingering.

3.   *Puritanical model:* The puritanical model is a combination of personal characteristics, contextual variables combined with a general tendency to be uncooperative. There is only one theme in this model, and it is a bad person, in a bad situation, who is also a bad participant.

4.   *Adaptational model:* The adaptational model describes malingering as a constructive attempt to survive in extremely adversarial circumstances. It is a kind of risk benefit analysis where malingering is chosen over other alternatives. There are three basic assumptions of this model: The person perceives the evaluation as adversarial; the person believes there is something to lose by being honest; and the person is not aware of a more effective method of achieving his or her goal. This model can be further divided into two dimensions: cost-benefit analysis and adversarial setting.

Studies have shown that the cost-benefit analysis of the adaptational model seems to be the most representative aspect of forensic cases, followed by adversarial circumstances in the criminological model. Nonforensic cases were most accurately characterized by the adversarial circumstances, which were followed by the cost-benefit analysis and the criminological model. In forensic settings, medical symptoms are more frequently faked than are cognitive impairments. Half of nonforensic malingerers who were female focused on medical symptoms. The hardest malingering to detect, however, is that done by people who also have a genuine disorder.

Differentiating Between Physical Malingering and Other Nonorganic Pathology

There are physical exam techniques that are used to make a determination of the functional (organic) or nonorganic basis of subjective complaints of limitation. Both nonorganic pathology and malingering indicate that there is not a physiological basis for the allegations of the patient. Included here would be mental disorders as well, which may look very much like malingering (Department of Health and Human Services, n.d.; Feinberg, Kirz, & Mackey; 2003; GAO Report, 2004).

The most notable test used is known as Waddell's behavioral signs. This was developed by Dr. Gordon Waddell et al. in 1980, and they organized eight signs into five types. The types are tenderness, simulation, distraction, regional disturbances, and overreaction. When three or more of these signs are present, it is considered a positive finding. This is associated with other clinical measures of behavior and suggests that the patient does not have a straightforward medical issue (Waddell, 1993).

1. *Tenderness:* Tenderness is skin discomfort that is nonanatomical in nature secondary to light palpation. Tenderness that is due to physical disease is localized. Physical back pain does not make the skin tender to light touch.

2. *Simulation:* Simulation is represented by axial loading or putting pressure on the top of the head of a patient who is standing—this should not cause low back pain. When the shoulders and hips are rotated at the same time, the back structures are not stressed. If the patient reports back pain when this is done, the test is considered to be positive for a nonorganic basis of the allegations.

3. *Distraction:* An example of distraction is the straight leg raise test. This can be done any time the hip is flexed with the knee straight. The foot can be examined with the patient seated with one knee extended. Another example of a distraction test is when the patient uses the injured limb when he or she has been distracted.

4. *Regional disturbances:* Regional disturbances are sensory changes or weaknesses. A widely distributed numbness that involves the whole extremity or side of the body and is not consistent with expected neurological patterns is suspicious. A sudden or uneven weakness such as cog wheeling, give away weakness, or break away weakness is a sign of nonorganic pathology.

5. *Overreaction:* Overreaction is when there is an inconsistency in patient reaction, with a reaction to a light touch at one moment and then no reaction when he or she is distracted. This is a positive sign of overreaction and is notable for disproportionate facial grimacing, exaggerated verbalizations, sweating, or collapse. Other behavioral signs of overreacting are questionable use of assistive devices for ambulation, inappropriate sighing, and rubbing.

The original purpose of the Waddell signs was to make clinical assessment more streamlined by separating out the nonorganic and the organic elements of the alleged symptoms, to allocate appropriate resources toward the treatment of physical pathology, to help identify illness behavior, and to reduce the waste of resources by eliminating unneeded procedures and diagnostic studies and treatments. Sometimes, behavioral signs can be present in the context of organic pathology. Behavioral signs only represent a red flag and are not meant to be a substitute for a psychological assessment. By themselves, these tests are not tests of credibility or validity (Feinberg et al., 2003).

Another test is called Mankopf's Test. This is based on the theory that heart rate increases with pain. Greer et al. discuss a study of this test that used 20 patients with chronic back pain, which is felt to be nonorganic, and 20 patients who were pain free. A mechanical pain stimulus applied to the patient's fingers was used. There was no clinically significant difference to the effect of pain on the heart rate of either group. There is no mention of blinding in the test; nor were there any individuals with organic-based pain in the study (Greer, Chambliss, & Mackler, 2005).

Hoover's Test is used to detect the nonorganic basis of paralysis. In this test, the patient is asked to press down with the paralyzed leg and lift up with the unaffected leg to resistance while the examiner holds the heel of the unaffected leg. There was a small diagnostic case-control study that used a computer-assisted strain gauge to measure movement effort during Hoover's Test. The subjects were 7 women with true paresis, 9 with nonorganic paresis, and 10 controls. Nonorganic paresis was diagnosed based on history, neurological examination, and the lack of positive neurodiagnostic findings. A calculation was made that rendered a maximum involuntary to voluntary ratio for each patient's extremities. The calculation was able to discriminate between all the nonorganic patients, the normal controls, and true paresis. A similar test is called the Abductor Sign and is based on the theory that thigh abductors work together with each other. The investigator reported 100% accuracy in determining organic paresis from nonorganic using this sign.

The Midline Split Test is used to try and detect nonorganic causes of sensory loss. This is based on the cutaneous nerves that cross the midline, and the idea is that a sharp midline split denotes nonorganic sensory loss. The study consisted of 100 people who presented to a neurology department due to complaints of decreased sensation to the side of their face. Of the 100, 80 were determined to have organic deficits such as multiple sclerosis or stroke (cerebrovascular accident [CVA]). There was no information about how these were diagnosed. Most likely brain computed tomography (CT) or magnetic resonance imaging (MRI) scans were utilized. Of the patients with organic disease, 7.5% demonstrated midline splitting of memory loss, which falsely suggested a nonorganic issue. Twenty percent of the nonorganic patients demonstrated sensory loss due to the midline split. There was no blinding or independent confirmation of the findings.

The AMA published a guide to the evaluation of permanent impairments. This states that it is very difficult to confirm malingering and it usually depends on accidental or purposeful surveillance (Gale, 2006).

Differentiating Between Malingering and Factitious Disorder
The primary feature of malingering is the purposeful production of either false or grossly exaggerated psychological or physical symptoms. The motivation for malingering is external, such as avoiding employment, obtaining money, evading criminal prosecution, avoiding work, or obtaining drugs. Malingering, however, can easily be mistaken for a real disease as it is similar to many other mental health disorders.

Factitious disorder is described as feigning, exaggerating, or inducing illness to assume the role as a patient. Unlike malingerers, patients with factitious disorder have no secondary financial gain leading to their factitious disease; they only wish to fulfill the patient role or to live the patient role through others, known as Munchausen's syndrome, where the person with the disorder deliberately makes someone else sick, most often their children, in order to live the patient role through someone else (ACOEM, 2003; DON, 2002; Feldman, 1996).

One of the first people to ever describe factitious disorders was Galen, the Roman physician, first writing about them in the second century. In 1843 Gavin wrote, "On Feigned and Factitious Diseases" dealing with the issue of soldiers and seamen who faked illness to get attention. Little interest was given to this issue until Asher wrote an article on Munchausen's syndrome in 1951. The first person to describe the psychiatric presentation was Gellenberg in 1977. Prior to this, no distinction was made between malingering, conversion disorder, or factitious symptoms. There is little known information about the cause of this disorder, largely due to the reluctance of the patients to take psychological testing.

There have been many theories proposed for the cause of factitious disorder. It has been remarked by some researchers that these people frequently have a history of abuse and deprivation and numerous past hospitalizations. As adults, they often lack support from friends or family, and it is considered a coping mechanism that is learned and reinforced in childhood (Szoke & Boillet, 1999).

This disorder is characterized by unstable interpersonal relationships, recurrent suicidal or self-harming behaviors, and unstable identity features. In this regard, patients with factitious disorder are similar in presentation to individuals who have a borderline personality disorder. Characteristics of deceitfulness, lack of concern for personal safety and remorse, lack of work behavior, and unwillingness to conform to social norms are also consistent with people who have an antisocial personality disorder.

Diagnostic criteria suppose that the individual fakes the symptoms to assume the patient role. It is usually combined with marked personality and relationship disorders. The diagnostic criteria rely on information from the patient and are difficult to use when the presentation is psychological. As with malingerers, the production of symptoms is conscious. Unlike malingering, the motivation is unconscious. This is distinguished from a conversion disorder, in which the symptom production and the motivation are unconscious. Little is known about the clinical course and prognostic features of this disorder because most of the patients are lost to follow up (Feldman, 1996).

From reports in the literature, the course of factitious disorder is characterized by numerous hospitalizations, which start in adolescence or young adult periods and extend into the late 40s. Cases where the person is older than 45 are rare. Possible explanations for this are patients improving at faking illnesses and are therefore harder to detect and diagnose; as they age, the illness becomes milder; or as patients age, they develop real illnesses and they no longer have to fake an illness. An important goal of management and treatment of this disorder is to recognize and treat concurrent disorders that may have an impact on the course of the illness (Elwin & Iqbal, 2002).

GOVERNMENTAL BODIES RESPONSIBLE FOR FRAUD DETECTION

Several federal enforcement agencies have responsibility for health care fraud investigation. These include the Department of Justice, the Internal Revenue Service, the Federal Bureau of Investigation, the U.S. Postal Service, and various Offices of Inspector General (OIG) within the Department of Health and Human Services (HHS). Fraud detection efforts on the part of HHS OIG include looking for the illegal screening of Medicare beneficiary health status prior to enrollment, detecting fraud schemes involving plans that disenroll the sick, charge unauthorized premiums, misrepresent benefits to enrollees, inflate the reported number of treated patients and raise treatment costs to increase patient fixed fees, use unapproved treatment or equipment, and employ medical providers who have been excluded from participating in federal health insurance programs.

In addition to the effort on the part of the federal government, states have created insurance fraud bureaus of their own. These fraud bureaus, as well as the NCHCAA, which was established by several private health insurers and public agencies, aid the federal agencies in addressing health care fraud. Several important acts, including the Health Insurance Portability and Accountability Act (HIPAA) of 1996 and the Balanced Budget Act of 1997, contain substantial antifraud provisions and new programs to detect fraud, abuse, and intentional deception.

Federal and state agencies, however, will not find a solution to this growing problem without the support of health care industry members. Important steps for any health care organization to deter and reduce health care fraud include recognizing what the different types of health care fraud are, understanding the government's laws regarding health care fraud, and creating a corporate compliance program for your organization (Wojcik, 2003; Ziel, 1998).

Health insurance fraud continues to reach epidemic proportions. This problem is exacerbated in an environment in which 1 in 10 people think it is acceptable to falsify insurance claims and more than 70% of doctors admit to lying for their patients to obtain coverage; also adding to the problem are prompt payments of insurance claims through electronic claims filing and the confidentiality of patient records required by the HIPAA, which makes health care fraud a federal criminal offense. The insurance industry estimates that between 5% and 10% of all health claims submitted nationwide are incorrectly paid due to fraudulent or abusive billing practices. Equally disturbing are the results of a government audit that found that 6.3% of the Medicare program's fee-for-service claim payments in 2001 should not have been paid due to erroneous billing, inadequate provider documentation to support the claims, and/or outright fraud (Feinberg et al., 2003; Kalb, 1999).

Fraud and Abuse Laws and Statutes

The federal government has increasingly focused on health care fraud due to the increasing costs of health care and as a result of the industry consolidation during recent years. This has been demonstrated in legislative initiatives such as the Stark laws and the HIPAA of 1996 as well as through increasing federal enforcement efforts within departments such as the DOJ (Department of Justice) and HHS (Kalb, 1999; Shepherd, 1997; Werner, 1998).

The False Claims Act (FCA) prohibits the submission of false claims, statements, or certifications to the government either knowingly or for items that it is deemed the provider should have known were false or illegal, such as providing services that were not medically necessary. Any provider who does submit such claims risks criminal charges and civil penalties (NHCAA, 1994).

The FCA was enacted during the Civil War. It was amended in 1986 to protect and reward whistleblowers under the *qui tam* provision, allowing them to act in the name of the United States in order to file suits. Whistleblowers, as private citizens, are eligible under this statute to receive a reward, typically 15% to 30% of any amounts collected. The state also permits individuals who participated in the illegal actions to file a suit against others involved (Haron, 1998; Poston, 1999; Shepherd, 1997).

The Anti-Kickback Statute states that it is forbidden to receive payment, either in cash or in kind, of kickbacks, bribes, and other incentives, including rebates, with the specific intent of influencing the referral of patients or the purchase or sale of health care-related goods or services. Receiving any such payment or remuneration is a felony. Most states have enacted more restrictive versions of this statute. While managed care arrangements are also covered in this statute, the regulations provided by the law and HCFA do provide for exceptions and define "safe harbors" in remuneration (Kalb, 1999).

Stark I and Stark II, also known as the Ethics in Patient Referral Act, forbid physician referral of patients for a designated service to certain types of facilities or entities with which they, or any immediate family member, "has a financial relationship...(including) ownership or investment interest or a compensation arrangement between the physician and the entity" (Ethics in Patient Referrals Act, as cited in Hirschtick & Chenen, 1989, p. 9). The entity may not bill the government for services rendered to a patient referred to them in the manner described. Exemptions are made when there is a group practice-type of relationship that involved investment by the physician, so long as the investment is at fair market value (Werner, 1998). These laws, however, only carry civil penalties and are only applicable to the physician, although intent by the physician is not required (Kalb, 1999; Levin, 1998).

Individuals or entities that are found to have violated one of the health care fraud statutes may be subjected not only to the specific statutory penalties but also to a variety of "collateral" consequences. This includes exclusion from participation in the federal health care programs, civil monetary penalties, loss of licensure, and loss of staff privileges. These collateral consequences can be more severe and costly than the direct penalties. These penalties usually result from a criminal conviction or a finding of civil liberty, but they can be imposed even without a conviction or finding (Polston, 1999).

Effects of Litigation on Malingering
Increasingly, illnesses that are not easily diagnosed or have few definite symptoms have begun to become more and more involved in personal injury litigation as they are easily simulated. These allegations include brain damage, toxic encephalopathy, neurobehavioral deficits, and issues of sick building syndrome or environmental sickness. Symptoms include memory problems, concentration and language problems, fatigue, depression, and anxiety (Rubenzer, 2004).

It appears as though elements of litigation are having an impact on neuropsychological evaluations. Individuals with known severe brain injury do better on testing than people who make allegations of mild brain damage due to mold exposure. The issue of litigation introduces biases that have a contaminating effect on the test data. There is a growing body of evidence that suggests lawyers and other advocates who are associated with litigation claims have a misleading influence on test data that results in misleading conclusions. This, along with the degree of effort put forth by the patient during psychometric testing, has a greater impact on the results than the actual degree of injury. This is true even when severe brain-injured individuals are tested.

Another prominent illness that malingerers take advantage of is mental health diseases, often spending time in psychiatric hospitals at the cost of the tax payers so as not to be caught malingering. When defendants are successful in faking a mental impairment, they take advantage of our society's sense of compassion for people who are mentally ill and help to create a skeptical attitude toward those individuals who are truly incompetent. Their actions contribute additional costs to the court system in the way of increased transportation costs and psychiatric care. When one spends time in a mental hospital, the chances of successfully winning a court case due to mental malingering increases.

Since the Supreme Court has decided that the execution of mentally retarded persons is illegal, there is increased incentive for criminals to fake mental problems. Mental health providers who work in forensic settings have reported that malingering happens in about 16% to 18% of people who present as being significantly impaired. This is seen as an underestimation because those individuals who are successful cannot be counted. There is very little evidence that clinicians can detect malingers without specialized testing. Rubenzer states that a recent study found that psychiatrists who worked in a state forensic facility and relied on interviews and medical records were unable to detect 50% of malingerers who were detected through testing. It is estimated that the incidence of incorrect identification in nonforensic settings is much higher (Rubenzer, 2004).

MANAGEMENT CONSIDERATIONS

Malingering, Workers' Compensation, and Managed Care

Many hospital administrators have yet to grasp the reality that the impact of workers' compensation on their facility continues to increase every year, although administrator attitudes toward the program have remained largely unchanged since 1950. The NHCAA estimates that approximately 2% of the over one trillion dollars spent on health care each year are attributed to activities involving health care fraud (NHCAA, 1994). This amount has grown steadily every year since 1985. Of the aforementioned 2%, the Health Insurance Association of America (HIAA) estimates that approximately 35% of fraudulent behavior is attributed to claimant activities. However, the National Insurance Crime Bureau (NICB) is quick to point out that the percentage is probably much higher because claimant misbehavior is so difficult to detect if executed subtly.

From a reductionism point of view, activities with claimants attempting to commit health care fraud and receive financial gain through workers' compensation mechanisms have grown through the following five avenues over the years (Coppola, 1998).

1. *Increased financial rewards available for the degree of injury or illness:* The OIG estimates the average lump sum payment a claimant can expect to receive through a successfully litigated (or settled) workers' compensation case is $25,000. The paydays can get even higher in many cases, too. For example, one sales representative sued his company for nearly one million dollars when he was fired for refusing to work 8-hour days after being diagnosed with AIDS. Another individual sued her company for nearly two million dollars for mental distress after other employees made frequent complaints about her perverse body odor, which, she claimed, was due to a medical condition.

2. *Lax oversight for distribution of monetary benefits:* According to the National Council on Compensation Insurance (NCCI) and the NICB, claimants who receive monetary

benefits may have successfully defrauded over half a dozen medical organizations and insurance companies prior to getting caught. This is most successfully achieved through perpetrating the same injury or illness across state lines or through claiming benefits through different HMOs. A woman in Florida was successful in receiving monetary benefits through her maiden name, her husband's last name, and her own again while using an alias in another HMO for the same injury.

3. *Poor reporting systems for initiating and archiving data reference questionable patient compensation cases:* Hospital policies concerning categorizing a patient's situation based on the potential of secondary gain in a workers' compensation case may often come into conflict with the health of the patient and the patient's right to privacy. Due to dilemmas such as these, many health care organizations are beginning to question some patients' rights and issues of confidentiality. Many large corporations are actually campaigning for the designation of established employee responsibilities when pursuing workers' compensation cases (Evens, 1992).

4. *Gross lack of coordination of effort along the continuum of care for both providers and administrators:* Physicians and administrators may often act as *enablers* for disgruntled employees attempting to fraud their employer for a medically related injury. For example, a patient undergoing workers' compensation review in the Washington metro area for a minor shoulder injury told her attending physician that she was not going to leave his office until he wrote down in her medical file that she was unable to go back to work and that he (the physician) was going to be responsible if she did and was further injured. The physician's diagnosis for the patient was positive and without concern; however, he felt uncomfortable arguing with her. He ultimately provided her with a referral to a specialist rather than go on record as stating that nothing was wrong with her. The same physician later discussed the

case with the facilities director of admitting; however, no other coordination was made. The same patient eventually met with a specialist and confided in the physician that she was involved in an ongoing compensatory review process and needed (at least) to be referred for physical therapy. The specialist reluctantly agreed rather than argue with the patient and later confided with the hospital's same director of admitting about the event. Again, no additional action was ever taken. The patient eventually did receive severance pay from her employer and spent over 90 days in and out of the hospital facility despite the absence of any clinical pathology.

5. *Ignorance of the financial scope of the impact:* The auditor general of the United States estimated that delays in processing worker compensation cases through one very large managed care organization cost upward of $450,000 per day in lost productivity, medical expenses, and other resources. In addition to the drain on scarce personnel and health care resources, most hospital administrators fail to realize the financial impact of workers' compensation cases on their facility. Capturing the direct costs of such expenses is arduous. However, one small hospital belonging to a larger HMO in Kansas calculated the expense that approximately 35 claimants had on the organization over a 12-month period by tracking the financial and hourly workload (full time equivalent) information on claimants. The marginal (in this instance, unreimbursed) expense of treating workers' compensation cases was estimated to be $317,470 (Goforth, 1996). Additionally, the facility lost the opportunity cost associated with reprogramming and redelivering the financial resource in another manner, which may have generated revenue.

Malingering and Workers' Compensation
Is Not Solely an Insurance Company Problem

In managing worker compensation cases, the pragmatic administrator must be cognizant of the concept of *Res ipsa loquitur*, or "the thing speaks for itself." In legal terms, the philosophy refers to the rebuttal presumption that the defendant was negligent, which arises from proof that the instrumentality causing injury was in the defendant's exclusive control and that the accident was one that ordinarily does not happen in the absence of the negligence. However, for the purpose of this discussion, it is necessary for the administrator to see himself or herself as the *negligent enabler*, allowing mismanagement of workers' compensation to continue within the facility at cost to others.

As previously discussed, workers' compensation cases create unreimbursed human and financial expenses to the hospital. While the ultimate payer for financial resources to the claimant may be delivered from a third-party insurer, hospital administrators must be aware that their facilities act as enablers. Prior to any delivery of monetary or other benefits to the claimant, the claimant must first get the hospital facility to buy into his or her illness/injury claim. While many cases may be clear cut and easily diagnosable, many others are not. Claimants who are pursuing workers' compensation cases may cause administrative and human resource problems beyond the financial impact, including lost productivity and frustration (Swedlow, 2001).

Furthermore, the development of managed care systems discourages facilities along the continuum of care to shift the financial burden and other unreimbursed expenses with workers' compensation cases to other payers. A hospital administrator who shifts or delays his or her responsibility for cost-effective care for a disability claim will later repay the effort through increased insurance/reinsurance premiums, additional administrative fees, and other ancillary services in the long term. Lastly, the hospital administrator who places himself or herself in the passive or adaptive mode is continually in a reactive rather than a proactive decision-making process. Externalities such as the claimant or the insurance company control the direction of the case rather than the hospital maintaining control. Accordingly, some decisions concerning workers' compensation management are made incrementally rather than unilaterally. In this respect, long-term goals of decreasing average length of stay (ALOS) and cost may be compromised for the short-term satisfaction of resolving immediate issues with case or risk management.

What Every Medical Administrator Should Know
There are essentially three types of data that a prudent hospital administrator should review when reference tracking the management/mismanagement of worker compensation cases in his or her facility. They are physician/administrator efficiency, claimant behavior, and population characteristics.

Physician/Administrator Efficiency
A 1994 study of several hundred worker compensation files being processed in various stages of delivery revealed a large disparity in ALOS for the physicians completing the physical review. Analysis of physician efficiency and productivity found that some physicians were taking an inordinate amount of time to complete a workers' compensation review, some taking upward of 3 months to complete despite all the medical and administrative actions having already been completed. The physician just had not gotten around to completing his or her case report. Factors influencing this ranged from lack of physician management to apathy in the system. Such reasons included the following (Coppola, 1996).

1. Physician sabbatical, time-off, or teaching/research constraints
2. Failure of the facility to track the progress of patient appointments
3. Lost medical or patient case files
4. Inadequate human resource paradigms for managing disability cases
5. Outdated patient processing protocols, internal controls, and management initiatives
6. Lack of communication with other echelons along the continuum of care

Claimant Behavior
As far as patient misbehavior and management are concerned, the potential for secondary gain to an individual if pursuing

monetary benefits from a job-related accident can be extremely tempting even to the most honest individuals. Research has found that many patients deliberately delay the processing of their cases for periods of days to months. Such behaviors may include the following:

1. Scheduling an appointment as far out as possible and then canceling it the day before: In many cases it may take weeks to months to get a new appointment for various specialties.
2. Removing documentation from the medical record for deception purposes
3. Withholding pertinent medical information from the attending physician
4. Failing to appear for a medical appointment
5. Refusing to follow physician directives
6. Imitating or exaggerating behavior characteristics of an ill patient
7. Intentionally making oneself sick
8. Educating oneself on workers' compensation benefits and procedures to identify avenues to prolong disability evaluation

It was found that this behavior in the workers' compensation system may not be uncommon when examining a 1997 survey of 1,324 employees by the American Society of Chartered Life Underwriters & Chartered Financial Consultants. The study found that 48% of all U.S. workers admitted to taking unethical or illegal actions at least once in the last 12 months, with the motivation behind the unethical actions related to job insecurity, personal debt, company politics, and long hours, among others.

Population Characteristics

Dozens of agencies such as the NCCI, the NICB, and the American Re-Insurance Company have compiled and identified leading indicators and predictors for workers' compensation duration for persons perpetuating medical review for personal or secondary gain. These indicators were developed through retrospective review of worker compensation case studies. While no single independent variable or set of variables can indicate definitively whether persons are manipulating the medical system for personal or secondary gain, certain behavior patterns can act as flags for further inspection. Some of these predictors include the following:

1. Employee experiencing labor problems
2. Rumors in the workplace that the claimant is malingering
3. Altered patient or personnel documents
4. History of adverse disciplinary or personnel actions
5. Worker having history of poor attendance record
6. Worker resisting physician's suggestions to do light work
7. Employee being resistant to outside review of medical history/second opinion
8. Substantial treatment with no diagnosis
9. Degree of disability not consistent with lost work time
10. Frequency of doctor visits abnormally high
11. Injured worker experiencing financial difficulty/financial future uncertain
12. Injured worker disgruntled, soon-to-retire, or facing imminent firing or layoff

Additional population characteristics point toward patients who are under 38, who may not be receiving social security benefits, and who may be out on disability leave longer than the standard means and averages of patients with similar medical conditions. The last leading indicator is unemployment. There is an increased trend with patient disabilities when plant shutdowns or massive unemployment layoffs are imminent (Thomas, Guire, & Horvat, 1997).

Finally, although it would not be prudent for a physician and administrator to make a determination of patient misbehavior individually, one key to deterring this type of behavior is to be aware and educated on the potential of the activity. Who is normally in charge of tracking patient misbehavior or on keeping metrics on patients who may be abusing the medical system for personal gain? Often no one is, although it is within the resource availability of the hospital administrator to detect and decrease this behavior.

Procedural Deficiencies in Established Hospital Procedures Concerning Workers' Compensation Management

Hospital administrators often have two major problems with managing workers' compensation cases in their organization. The first is that many administrators use duration of treatment (primarily through exhaustion of all ancillary occupational services in the facility) as a metric for determining quality of care. The second flaw is failing to designate an individual as the facility's disability case manager (DCM).

Despite success stories in many HMOs concerning reducing ALOS in the workers' compensation system, many hospitals and their associated administrators may still perceive *duration of medical treatment as a metric for determining quality of care*. Retrospective examination of hospitals finds that administrators still gauge workers' compensation outcomes on two criteria:

1. The claimant's length of reimbursement potential (Arndt, 1995)
2. Exhausting the full range of occupational services offered in the facility along the continuum of care

As a result of following these behavior patterns, physicians and administrators become weary of aggressive discharge planning processes that can shorten days in the workers' compensation system for patients and save the hospital critical resources (Carol, 1994; Thomas et al., 1997). Furthermore, a hospital supporting a *duration = quality* posture may actually contribute to the deteriorating health of the claimant in the long term and ultimately cause the hospital to expend additional resources to achieve the same healthy end state.

Some claimants undergoing workers' compensation processing in the hospital are still maintained as inpatients in the facility, adversely affecting the hospital in its optimal allocation and use of resources. Furthermore, it has been demonstrated that people undergoing disability evaluation use two to three times as much health care utility as persons without disabilities entering the health care system. Additionally, this increase in health care utility continues to multiply, the longer the individual is allowed to remain in a treatment state; however, the patient receives no greater advantage in health benefit through the increased use and access to medical care.

Legal and Ethical Issues
in Managing Workers' Compensation Cases

Ethical issues regarding patient care generally revolve around four commonly accepted and established health care practices. They are as follows (Coppola, 1998):

1. *Autonomy:* The patient's right to self governance.
2. *Beneficence:* The requirement of the facility to do good.
3. *Nonmaleficence:* The requirement for the facility to do no harm.
4. *Justice:* The obligation to give each patient his or her due.

However, in workers' compensation cases, the tenets of patient autonomy and justice may often come into conflict with the hospital's obligations for beneficence and nonmaleficence, especially if the patient is deliberately seeking financial reward or some other secondary benefit.

The ethical considerations of the health care administrator and CFO are often tied into those of the physician, but not always. While the physician's ethical duty is tied into Section Five of the Code of Ethics of The American Medical Association, which states that in an emergency physicians should do their best to render service to the patient, despite prejudice of any kind, the health care administrator and CFO's ethical duties are not. Health care administrators may often find themselves torn between owing allegiance to the financial stability of the organization and the charitable nature of the health care profession. Many hospitals attempt to overcome this dilemma by achieving a balance between the business aspect of operating a health care facility and the social aspect of caring for the indigent through the establishment of ethics committees within their facility.

Another debate in workers' compensation cases is the dilemma of specialty care and gatekeeper approval. The 1986 case of *Elsesser v. Hospital of the Philadelphia College of Osteopathic Medicine* found that HMOs can be liable for the alleged negligence for primary care physicians who fail to refer patients for specialty care when practice guidelines gauge it possible. As a result, and as discussed, physicians may often refer a patient for the additional care rather than risk the tort associated with the potential liability. The key to these dilemmas is education, communication, documentation, and quality first time care.

What Physicians Need to Know About Workers' Compensation and Disability Case Management

Since the late 1980s, the concept of somatization has received increased recognition in the medical community. Somatization is the self-directed patient reporting of somatic symptoms in response to psychological distress. Patients then seek clinical treatment for this distress; however, there is no pathophysiological explanation for the disorder. Many physicians specializing in workers' compensation are beginning to recognize that there is a difference between the behavior (somatic) and medical (clinically diagnosed) model of managing workers' compensation cases (Escobar et al., 1987). With a continued trend toward managed care penetration and gatekeeper approval in America, patient's feel that they have little choice but to exaggerate symptoms to ensure care or potential compensation (Barsky & Borus, 1995). As a result, incidences of somatization increase disability duration by causing physicians to refer patients for special or additional screening during the beneficiary process even in the absence of clinical evidence of pathology (Liowiski, 1988). This further ties up the personnel in the human and hospital resource pool.

The Journal of the American Medical Association has published several articles on this issue with the underlying recommendation being to educate physicians on the ultimate source of suffering and its impact on hospital expenditures and disability management. They continue the discussion by stating, "Technological and procedural medical management can provide the transient somatizer with an identity as a sick patient and allow him or her to become ill" (Barsky & Borus, 1995). Hospital administrators who *allow* physicians to inflate workers' compensation medical costs through these activities also act as enablers and contribute to this negative cycle. The key for hospital administrators is to partner with their physicians and remind them that not every symptom denotes disease. Physicians must understand that the motivation behind a patient seeking care may not always be to exclusively receive treatment for illness.

A research project conducted in the Washington metro area of several physicians examined perceptions relating to patient behavior patterns. The physicians were requested to write down the three leading assumptions they make when evaluating a patient. The three major assumptions were as follows (Coppola, 1997a).

1. The patient is injured or ill.
2. The patient wants to get healthy.
3. When the patient is healthy, he or she will return to work or his or her former status.

As fundamental as this study's outcome may seem, it reaffirms the educational philosophy physicians have learned for hundreds of years in medical institutions. However, the premise that the patient is honest is no longer a valid and reliable assumption. Issues of secondary financial gain, time off from work, and other factors have an impact on a patient's decision to seek care in the hospital facility.

As a result, hospital administrators and physicians have a responsibility to develop a reliable mechanism for physical and medical parameters through establishing practice guidelines for disability management. Such guidelines may (for instance) require certain worker compensation cases to be evaluated on three different occasions (over time) and agree with one another within a 5% level of deviation. In some cases, an opinion of a member of the American Academy of Disability Evaluating Physicians (AADEP) must be obtained to discern which finding accurately describes the patient's medical condition.

For example, the AADEP was formed in 1987 by a group of medical doctors who realized the need to develop a new organization that specialized in educating physicians and other professionals in the medical science of disability evaluation. The AADEP is the only organization in America that is dedicated to teaching health care professionals in the evaluation of the injured worker. In 1996 over 1,100 professionals were educated in AADEP evaluation and training methodologies.

Additionally, the AADEP provides educational courses for medical professionals and legal counselors. AADEP courses deal with such issues as impairment ratings based on the American Medical Association *Guides to the Evaluation of Permanent Impairment*, return to work evaluations, which place the injured person in a category based on the *Dictionary of Occupational Titles* (*DOT*), and determination of maximum medical improvement (MMI). Many state workers' compensation systems use AADEP as the teaching organization for their health care providers. AADEP is capable of providing teaching courses in Federal Social Security evaluations and in such areas as the American with Disabilities Act (ADA) (American Academy of Disability Evaluation Physicians, 1996).

Finally, physicians must be made aware that back injuries are the easiest impairment to imitate when disgruntled employees are seeking compensation benefits for personal gain. Additionally, few established and uniform mechanisms are in place in most hospitals to evaluate the semantic differences in back injuries despite the established validity and reliability of the Waddell Test (Waddell, 1987; Wiesel, Weinstein, Herkowitz, Dvorak, & Bell, 1996). The Waddell Test is commonly used by insurance companies and providers to identify patients who may be imitating injuries for personal or secondary gain. Waddell scores are generated that identify variances in patient behavioral models of impairment and physiological models from reliable samples (Waddell, 1993). The Waddell Test distinguishes between nonorganic physiological signs (tenderness, simulation, distraction, regionalization, and overreaction) that are independent of those commonly used to detect organic disease, but correlate with treatment failure, with long standing symptoms, with elevated hypochondriasis and hysteria scores on the Minnesota Multiphasic Personality Inventory, and with various other psychological factors. Waddell scores may be used to normalize responses between patients (Waddell, 1987; Wiesel et al., 1996).

Identifying Malingerers for Workers' Compensation Claims
In some cases, an employer and the insurance company may feel as though an injured employee is exaggerating his or her injury. There are a variety of methods used to try and differentiate between feigned illness and genuine illness. Three tools utilized frequently in determining malingering in workers' compensation cases are independent medical examination, surveillance, and functional capacity evaluations (FCEs).

1. *Independent medical examination:* An independent medical examination is a complete examination by a nontreating physician. Private disability contracts often specify that recipients of disability payments submit to any examination that may be requested by the insurance company. If someone refuses to submit to such an examination, that is grounds for denying benefits.

2. *Surveillance:* Surveillance is also very helpful in determining if allegations are consistent with the way someone behaves when he or she thinks that he or she is unobserved. Insurance companies often have their own fraud departments and farm out surveillance to independent investigators, including professional investigators and off-duty state bureau-of-investigation officers.

3. *Functional capacity evaluations:* The use of FCEs is common in private disability claims. This is an examination where the capacity of the patient to perform repetitive actions, lift, bend, stoop, and walk is tested.

There is a statement as to the perceived level of cooperation from the patient in the report. Some agencies do not rely on FCEs due to the subjective nature of the outcome. Patients have been known to overwork themselves the day before an FCE so that they perform poorly while giving the impression of full cooperation. They will come in genuinely limping and in pain due to an extreme workout the day before.

Why Employees May Fake an Illness or Disability
There are several reasons why employees may fake an illness or disability. The first is, of course, to get a check without having to come to work. Retaliation against the employer is also a basis for malingering. Another reason is avoidance of work due to psychological effects of being out on extended leave. In other words, people begin to believe that they cannot work, and this undermines their recovery. The attitude injured workers have toward their job, coworkers, and managers is a more accurate predictor of disability than the actual medical factors. This can have more of an impact toward chronic disability than the actual injury.

**Actions to Prevent Protracted Malingering
or Length of Stay in the Compensation System**
The major findings of studies concerning outcomes for workers' compensation cases show that hospital administrator management of workers' compensation cases does not produce the same outcome for claimants with similar conditions each time. The primary factor in protracted processing is lack of coordinated management within the facility and abandonment of established case management practices. For some reason, hospital administrators often manage workers'

compensation cases differently than standard primary care cases. Therefore, hospital administrators are encouraged to hire/appoint a case manager for workers' compensation cases and develop a systems-oriented (team) approach to disability management applying total quality management (TQM) principles. These actions may be implemented within a year by the hospital administrator in their facility and do not require dramatic reengineering or cost increases.

Each hospital that processes workers' compensation cases on a regular basis or has identified a high percentage of malingering episodes should establish a locally implemented patient management team (PMT) for the purpose of achieving integrated disability management within the facility. Personnel on the PMT should include representatives from the nursing staff and clinical, administrative, financial, patient administration, legal, and patient representative offices. The PMT should meet on a weekly basis and concentrate efforts on those personnel who have exceeded the average workers' compensation duration for that particular facility. Additional discussion items should incorporate the tenets of concurrent review, case management, and retrospective review. Furthermore, critical pathways and standard protocols should be developed locally in each facility. Presentation of locally developed protocols should be made to the governing board of directors. Furthermore, DCMs should be assigned to patients whose appointment history and medical progress is less than predictable as compared with patients occupying similar points in space in the same facility. The suggested charter for the hospital administrator to implement and present to the governing board is provided in Figure 3.1. Establishment of a DCM and PMTs proved effective in managing the high disability volume at many army medical centers during the global war on terror. Although the DCM and PAT were not vested with the mission to identify or detect malingering, the establishment of the DCM did assist in lowering protracted processing for disability evaluations associated with the normal administrative burdens of such processing.

Figure 3.1. Suggested charter for establishment of a disability case manager in the hospital.

Coppola's DCM Hospital Charter

1. The hospital administrator will designate a disability case manager (DCM) whose responsibility it is to expedite processing of workers' compensation cases within the facility. The DCM will act as the sole point of contact for workers' compensation proceedings in the hospital facility. The DCM should be a senior nurse practitioner or physician assistant with managed care and case management experience, or a similarly qualified individual. The DCM will report directly to the hospital administrator.
2. The hospital administrator will ensure that declaration of workers' compensation proceedings are forwarded to the DCM. The DCM will track all outpatient and inpatient data on these patients and report on the progression of all disability claimants. It will be the responsibility of the DCM to establish, collect, review, and report on all benchmarks and outcomes reference workers' compensation within the facility.
3. The DCM will ensure that claimants undergoing physical evaluation receive priority of care within the facility, if necessary. It is the responsibility of the DCM to identify critical pathways and to break down barriers that result in protracted physical evaluation processing. Additionally, the goal of the comprehensive DCM should be to minimize administrative expenses by creating centralized management of the entire range of health care services provided to claimants. The DCM will share, with discretion and the approval of the governing board and legal counsel, all material leading to the identification of claimant fraudulent activities. This information should be provided to appropriate internal and external organizations.
4. The DCM, under the authority of the hospital administrator, will organize a patient management team (PMT). Representatives on the PMT should include individuals from the nursing staff and clinical, administrative, financial, patient administration, legal, and patient representative departments. The PMT should meet on a weekly basis and concentrate efforts on those personnel who have exceeded the ALOS for that particular facility. Items to be discussed should incorporate the tenets of concurrent review, case management, cost containment, practice guidelines and retrospective review. Presentation of locally developed protocols by the PMT should be made to the governing board of each hospital facility.

Source. Coppola (1998)

Conclusion

No one knows exactly what the costs to business of malingering are, but the evidence suggests that malingering is pervasive. Almost 80% of high-cost permanent disability claims involve an attorney. This is the step that workers' compensation laws were designed to prevent. The involvement of attorneys indicates that employees are resistant to returning to work. In California, the average cost of litigation in contested workers' compensation claims is $30,000. It has been found that employees who rarely enjoy their job are 2.5 times more likely to report a back injury than those who do enjoy their jobs. Fifteen percent of all workers' compensation claims are due to mental problems from the inability to balance work and family demands. These claims have an average disability period of 39 weeks compared with 24 weeks for traumatic injury claims. Stress claims also cost about 50% more than physical injury claims.

The National Insurance Crime Board estimates that workers compensation fraud is the fastest growing insurance scam in the country. The estimated cost is about $5 billion per year. Ten cents out of each dollar spent on insurance premiums is wasted on fraud.

The behavioral aspect of disability is just now being addressed. According to Burke, if a company has 1,000 employees, about 40 of them will file for short-term disability in 1 year. Of those 40, 6 will have a mental disability such as depression, and many of the remaining will have secondary mental issues. Even a single episode of malingering is very expensive. An employer will usually pay $3 to $4 in adjusted premiums for every dollar spent on claims.

The linkage of medical malingering and disability exists as a tremendous challenge for practitioners of management and medicine in the marketplace. This modern human behavioral challenge has a well-developed, evolutionary history and considerable economic bases for its existence. By studying the historical, economic, and modern perspectives of medical malingering, managers may be better prepared to develop solutions and processes to identify, minimize, and potentially eliminate the sources and incidence of malingering in our society.

REFERENCES

Adnett, N., & Dawson, A. (1998). The economic analysis of industrial accidents: A re-assessment. *International Review of Applied Economics, 12*(2), 241–256.

American Academy of Disability Evaluating Physicians (AADEP). (1996). Retrieved January 29, 2006, from the AADEP home page: http://www.aadep.org/

American College of Occupational and Environmental Medicine (ACOEM). (2003). *Occupational medicine practice guidelines: Evaluation and management of common health problems and functional recovery in workers* (2nd ed.). Beverly, MA: OEM Press.

Arndt, M. (1995, summer). Admission severity of illness and resource utilization comparing Medicaid and privately insured patients. *Hospitals and Health Service Administration, 40*, 210–226.

Barsky, A. J., & Borus, F. J. (1995, December). Somatization and medicalization in the era of managed care. *Journal of the American Medical Association, 274*(24), 1931–1934.

Betts, H. B. (Ed.). (1999). Disabled. In *The world book encyclopedia* (Vol. 5, pp. 218–223). Chicago: World Book.

Carol, J. G. (1994). *Monitoring with indicators: Evaluating the quality of patient care.* Gaithersburg, MD: Aspen.

Carroll, M. (2003). Malingering in the military. *Psychiatric Annals, 33*(11), 732–736.

Cheadle, A., Wickizer, T. M., Franklin, G., Cain, K., Joesch, J., Kyes, K., et al. (1999). Evaluation of the Washington state workers' compensation managed care pilot project II: Medical and disability costs. *Medical Care, 37*, 982–993.

Cloeren, M. (2002). *Workers' compensation part 2: Introduction to case management.* Retrieved January 28, 2004, from http://chppmwww.apgea.army.mil/doem/OMP-fi les/BasicsofOWCP2.ppt

Coppola, M. N. (1996, April 16). *The United States army physical disability evaluation system: Quality management and reengineering initiatives* (A preceptor project, Office of the Surgeon General).

Coppola, M. N. (1997a, March–April). Identifying and reducing health care fraud in managed care. *Group Practice Journal, 46*(2), 46–54.

Coppola, M. N. (1997b). *Statistical measurement and analysis of claimant and demographic variables affecting processing and adjudication duration.* Washington, DC: Library of Congress.

Coppola, M. N. (1998). The hidden value of managing worker's compensation costs in the hospital setting. In J. Burns & M. Sipkoff (Eds.), *1999 Hospital strategies in managed care* (pp. 227–255, chap. 15). New York: Faulkner & Gray.

Department of Defense. (1996). *Compensation elements and related manpower cost items: Their purpose and legislative backgrounds* (5th ed.). Washington, DC: Government Printing Office.

Department of Health and Human Services. (n.d.). *New freedom initiative.* Retrieved January 16, 2004, from http://www.hhs.gov/newfreedom/init.html

DON. (2002). *Disability evaluation manual.* (SECNAVINST 1850.4E). Retrieved March 10, 2004, from http://neds.nebt.daps.mil/1850_4e.htm

Elwin, T., & Iqbal, A. (2002). *Factitious disorder.* Retrieved January 6, 2006, from http://www.psychiatrymatters.md/International/Authfiles/ErrorPage.asp?C=54548387239390740741

Escobar, J., Golding, J. M., Hough, R., Karno, M., Burnam, A., & Wells, K. B. (1987, July). Somatization in the community: Relationship to disability and use of services. *American Journal of Public Health, 77*(7), 837–840.

Evens, B. (1992, November). Will employers and unions cooperate? *HR-Magazine, 37,* 59–63.

Feinberg, S., Kirz, J., & Mackey, S. (2003). *Symptom magnification & Waddell behavioural signs.* Retrieved January 29, 2006, from http://www.cwce.com/feinbergarticles/symtommagnifi cation.htm

Feldman, M. (1996). *Disease or deception? The mystery of factitious disorders.* Retrieved January 6, 2006, from http://www.selfhelpmagazine.com/articles/chronic/factit.html

Fossum, J. (1995). *Labor relations.* Chicago: Irwin.

Fraze, J., & Finney, M. (1988, March). Employee rights between our shores. *Personnel Administrator,* 50–53, 79–80.

Fuchs, V. (1998). *Who shall live? Health, economics, and social choice.* River Edge, NJ: World Scientific.

Gale, T. (2006). *Behavioural health Fe-Mu.* Retrieved January 29, 2006, from http://www.humanillnesses.com/Behavioral-Health-Fe-Mu/index.html

GAO Report. (2004). *Health care fraud: Information-sharing proposals to improve enforcement efforts.* Washington, DC: General Accounting Office.

Glassmire, D. M., Bierley, R. A., Wisniewski, A. M., Greene, R. L., Kennedy, J. E., Date, E. (2003). Using the WMS-III faces subtest to detect malingered memory impairment. *Journal of Clinical and Experimental Neuropsychology, 25*(4), 465–481.

Goforth, W. (1996). Baylor University Hospital Research Study, Texas.

Greer, S., Chambliss, L., & Mackler, L. (2005). What physical exam techniques are useful to detect malingering? *Journal of Family Practice, 54*(6), 547–548. Retrieved January 29, 2006, from http://www.jfponline.com/toc.asp?FID=216&issue=June%202005&folder_description=June%202005%20(Vol.%2054,%20No.%206)

Haron, D. (1998). Waste and neglect: Fraud and abuse in the health care industry. *The Health Care Supervisor, 16*(4), 61–68. Retrieved January 23, 2004, from the ProQuest database.

Health Insurance Association of America. (1994). *Health insurers anti-fraud programs.* Managed care and insurance products report. Washington, DC: Author.

Hirschtick, S. R., & Chenen, A. R. (1989, summer). The Ethics in Patient Referrals Act of 1989: What will it mean to physicians? *The Medical Staff Counselor, 3*(3), 9.

Kalb, P. (1999). Health care fraud and abuse. *The Journal of the American Medical Association, 282*(12), 1163–1168. Retrieved January 22, 2004, from the Ovid database.

Kent, D. (2001, December). Review of the new disability history: American perspectives and a history of disability. *Journal of Visual Impairment & Blindness*, 765–767.

Kudlick, C. (2003). Disability history: Why we need another "other." *American Historical Review, 108*(3), 763–793.

Levin, A. (1998). Compliance programs stop health care fraud. *National Underwriter, 102*(49), 7–9. Retrieved January 24, 2004, from the ProQuest database.

Library of Congress Study. (1984). *Staff disability retirement pay of US military personnel: History and analysis of pertinent legislation, 1861–1949.* Washington, DC: Congressional Research Service.

Lipowiski, Z. J. (1988, November). Somatization: The concept and its clinical application. *American Journal of Psychiatry, 145*(11), 1358–1368.

Lippman, H. (1995, August). New ways to fight fraud. *Business Health*, 44–46.

Lockhart, P. (n.d.). *Understanding the disability evaluation system.* Retrieved March 10, 2004, from http://www.lifelines2000.org/services/articles/20020926/151413.asp?RootID=534

Martin, C. W., WCB of BC Evidence Based Practice Group. (2003, September). *Detecting malingerers. Hidden truths?* Retrieved January 8,

2006, from http://www.worksafebc.com/health_care_providers/Assets/PDF/detecting_malingerers.pdf

McWhinnie, J. R. (1982). Measuring disability (section). *The OECD social indicator development programme*, no 5. Paris: OECD Publications Office.

Miller, R. (2004). Estimating the compensating differential for employer provided health insurance. *International Journal of Health Care Finance and Economics, 4*(1), 27–41.

Morrisey, M. (2001). Why do employers do what they do? Compensating differentials. *International Journal of Health Care Finance and Economics, 1*(1), 195–201.

Myers, M. T. (2000). Lying for patients may be a violation of federal law. *Archives of Internal Medicine, 160*(14), 2223–2224. Retrieved January 22, 2004, from the Ovid database.

National Health Care Anti-Fraud Association (NHCAA). (1994, December). *Fraud in managed health care delivery and payment* (Report to the NHCAA Board of Governors). Washington, D.C.

National Health Care Anti-Fraud Association (NHCAA). (1995). *Guidelines to health care fraud, fact sheet T278.* Washington, DC: Author.

Polston, M. D. (1999). Whistleblowing: Does the law protect you? *American Journal of Nursing, 99*(1), 26–31. Retrieved January 22, 2004, from the Ovid database.

Rhodes, R. S. (February 26, 1998). Statement of Robert S. Rhodes, MD, President, American College of Occupational and Environmental Medicine before the House Ways and Means Subcommittee. Retrieved January 29, 2004, from http://www.acoem.org/news/news/default.asp?NEWS_ID=79

Rice, T. (2003). *The economics of health reconsidered* (2nd ed.). Chicago: Health Administration Press.

Rubenzer, S. (2004). Malingering of psychiatric disorders and cognitive impairment in criminal court settings. *The Prosecutor, 38*, 5.

Ruser, J. (1998). Does workers' compensation encourage hard to diagnose injuries? *Journal of Risk and Insurance, 65*(1), 101–124.

Santerre, R., & Neun, S. (2004). *Health economics: Theories, insights, and industry studies* (3rd ed.). Cincinnati, OH: South-Western.

Shepherd, S. R. (1997). Role of "whistleblowers" is curbing health care fraud and abuse. *Employee Benefit Plan Review, 52*(1), 54–56. Retrieved January 24, 2004, from the ProQuest database.

Smith, A. (2003). *The wealth of nations* (Bantam Classics ed.). New York: Bantam.

Swedlow, A. L., & Johnson, G. L. (2001). Workers' compensation managed care: The search for integration. In P. R. Kongstvedt (Ed.), *The managed health care handbook* (4th ed., pp. 1154–1161). Gaithersburg, MD: Aspen.

Szoke, A., & Boillet, D. (1999). Factitious disorder with psychological signs and symptoms: Case reports and proposals for improving diagnosis. *Psychiatry On-Line.* Retrieved January 6, 2006, from http://www.priory.com/psych/factitious.htm

Thomas, W. J, Guire, K. E., & Horvat, G. (1997, winter). Is patient length of stay related to quality of care? *Hospitals and Health Service Administration, 42*, 489–507.

Waddell, G. (1987, spring). A new clinical model for the treatment of low back pain. *Spine, 12*, 632–644.

Waddell, G. (1993, spring). A fear avoidance beliefs questionnaire (FABQ) and the role of fear avoidance in chronic low back pain and disability. *Pain, 52*, 157–168.

Wang, Y., & Kleiner, B. (2005). Defining employee dishonesty. *Management Research News, 28*(2/3), 11–22.

Werner, M. J. (1998). Understanding the fraud and abuse laws: Guidance for internists. *Annals of Internal Medicine, 128*(8), 678–684. Retrieved January 23, 2004, from the Ovid database.

Wiesel, S. W., Weinstein, J. N., Herkowitz, H., Dvorak, J., & Bell, G. (1996). *The lumbar spine* (Vol. 2, 2nd ed.). Philadelphia: W. B. Saunders.

Williams, S., & Torrens, P. (1993). *Health services.* New York: Delmar.

Wojcik, J. (2003). Fraud a costly component of health care expenses. *Business Insurance, 37*(10), 1–3. Retrieved January 24, 2004, from the ProQuest database.

Ziel, S. E. (1998). The "essentials" of an effective corporate compliance program. *The Association of Perioperative Registered Nurses, 67*(5), 1032–1034. Retrieved January 22, 2004, from the Ovid database.

Zimmerman, R. R. (1984). *Disability evaluation in biomedicine: Subjective analysis and research guide with bibliography.* Washington, DC: Abbe.

CHAPTER FOUR

PSYCHIATRIC SYNDROMES OF THE CONDEMNED

Alan A. Abrams, MD, JD, FCLM
Maheen Patel, MD
Nesibe Soysal, MD
Alan Newman, MD

In the history of murder, the onset of insanity while awaiting execution of a death sentence is not a rare phenomenon.
—Frankfurter (1950)

There are prisoners who have received the death penalty with long prior histories of severe and persistent mental illness but whose insanity defense was rejected at trial (*Arizona v. Clarke*, 2006). Other condemned prisoners' mental illness was not even raised at trial but was well documented prior to the offense that led to their sentencing to suffer death. This chapter will focus on those condemned prisoners with little or no past history of severe mental illness who become, or raise claims that they have become, severely mentally impaired while on death row, and whose sentence should therefore be commuted or stayed. This chapter will also briefly touch on the issue of death row syndrome and death penalty volunteers.

In *Ford v. Wainwright* (1986), the Supreme Court narrowly decided that a state cannot constitutionally execute an insane person because that would be a fundamental violation of the Eighth Amendment's protection against cruel or unusual punishment. As articulated in *Ford*, by Justice Powell, the substantive standard for staying the execution of a mentally ill inmate is "a person is legally insane for the purpose of execution when by reason of mental disease or mental defect he is unaware of the fact of the impending execution, and the reason for it" (*Ford*, 1986). The petitioner has the burden of proving legal insanity by a preponderance of the evidence. Justice Rehnquist in dissent raised the specter of a condemned prisoner "malingering" mental illness to stay alive.

The defendant has already had a full trial on the issue of guilt and a trial on the issue of penalty; the requirement of still a third adjudication offers an invitation to those who have nothing to lose by accepting it to advance entirely spurious claims of insanity. A claim of insanity may be made at any time before sentence and, once rejected, may be raised again; a prisoner found sane 2 days before execution might claim to have lost his sanity the next day, thus necessitating another judicial determination of his sanity and presumably another stay of his execution. The passage of the Antiterrorism and Effective Death Penalty Act (AEDPA) restricting successive habeas appeals has also increased the gains from developing a debilitating mental disorder to toll time limitations and avoid denials based on successive appeals, that could have been raised earlier (AEDPA, 1996).

Ford v. Wainwright is the most significant case in the evolution of constitutional limits on executing the mentally ill, juveniles, and the retarded. The actual story of the petitioner, Alvin Bernard Ford, is typical for the spectrum of condemned prisoners we are discussing here. Alvin Ford was convicted of first-degree murder in the slaying of a police officer in a failed robbery attempt in Florida in 1974. Ford was committing an armed robbery of a Red Lobster restaurant in Ft. Lauderdale with several accomplices. He shot an officer twice in the abdomen and once in the back of the head while retrieving the officer's car keys. After being apprehended at his mother's home in Gainesville, Florida, Ford spent his first 6 years in prison under normal health conditions. In late 1981, at the end of the appeals process and within hours of his execution, Ford's mental condition deteriorated dramatically. His mental disturbance initially began as an occasional peculiar idea or confused perception but became more serious over time. Apparently, after reading in the newspaper that the Ku Klux Klan had held a rally in nearby Jacksonville, Ford developed an obsession focused on the Klan. He began to refer to himself as "Pope John Paul, III." He reported that he would not be executed because he owned the prisons and could control the Governor through mind waves. Over time, Ford regressed further into nearly complete incomprehensibility, speaking only in a code characterized by intermittent use of the word "one" and making statements such as "Hands one, face one. Mafia one. God one, father one, Pope one. Pope one. Leader one." Ford died of natural causes while on death row.

A similar story is presented in *Rohan, ex rel Gates v. Woodford* (*Rohan*, 2003). The appellant, Oscar Gates, was convicted of murder and robbery, with prior convictions for kidnapping, robbery, and rape. Mr. Gates' crime was not irrational—he killed a crime partner in a forgery ring because he wanted a bigger "cut." At trial no mental health defense was raised, and Gates was described by a psychologist as well-adjusted. Gates was sentenced to death. Mr. Gates was found incompetent by the federal district court after he began filing long and incoherent court papers, claiming that he was an heir to Howard Hughes' trust and that Howard Hughes told him how to cure AIDS with yellow chilli peppers.

Though specifics vary to some degree, a review of state Supreme Court opinions on death sentence appeals, Federal habeas appeals, death penalty abolition Web sites, and the Amnesty International Web site reveal a number of condemned inmates with a similar history—a troubled childhood without evidence of significant mental illness, no meaningful mental health defense at trial, the onset of a severe "psychotic" illness characterized by grandiosity, claims of not really being on death row, claims of actually being someone else with the power to halt the execution, claims of not dying after execution or of reincarnation, refusal of treatment with medication, and communication with incoherent gibberish. Smearing, eating, or storing feces is also often found. The mental health experts hired by the state report this is a malingered psychosis; the petitioner's experts report marked loss of reality testing, severe schizophrenia, and hence incompetence.

We suggest that the "conscious" versus "beyond willful control" dialectic prevents an accurate mental health understanding of the occurrence of these unusual presentations, and interferes with a meaningful Ford or Gates analysis. We further suggest that these presentations associated with impending execution have much more in common with what we are calling chronic Ganser syndrome, which could equally as well be labeled hysterical psychosis, hysterical pseudodementia, or stress-induced psychosis. Mayer-Gross postulated that there is a continuum between acute Ganser's syndrome and chronic prison psychoses (Anderson, Trethowan, & Kenna, 1959). The *Diagnostic and Statistical Manual of Mental Disorders (4th ed.) Text Revision (DSM-IV-TR)* (American Psychiatric Association [APA], 2000) places the Ganser syndrome into dissociative disorder not otherwise specified (NOS), which minimizes the hysterical phenomena, the cognitive distortions, and the unique "psychotic" communication style. The *DSM* classification does underscore the relationship to environmental stress, prior trauma, and limited coping skills. The hysterical element is clearest in that it is the mental image of madness that is portrayed rather than schizophrenia or affective psychosis, just as hysterical anesthesia portrays the mental image of sensory innervation rather than anatomical nerve distribution. Ganser syndrome has predominantly been defined as an acute twilight state, primarily in prisoners, that resolves rapidly. This has perhaps hindered recognition of these death row "psychoses" as having many similarities to acute Ganser's syndrome. A recognition of the relatedness deepens the recognition that this presentation contains a complex mixture of avoidance, evasion, denial, and "cognitive paralysis," that is, a complex mixture of willful malingering, dissociation of the self, and hysterical terror.

In 1897 Dr. Sigbert J. M. Ganser wrote a paper in which he described four cases that had many traits in common—fluctuating consciousness, hallucinations, hysterical stigmata, and defects of memory or knowledge. The most outstanding phenomenon was that the patients:

> were unable to answer the most simple questions put to them, although they acknowledged by the way they answered that they had grasped the sense of the question. They also revealed in their answers an amazing lack of general knowledge and a perplexing loss of knowledge they must have once acquired or that they still possessed. (Schlesinger, 1996)

This has come to be known in English as approximate answers or talking past the point. This has been referred to as the Ganser symptom in the absence of the full syndrome.

Ganser titled his paper "A Peculiar Hysterical State" (Schorer, 1965). Ganser wondered if this was just "crude malingering" or whether it could be malingering coexisting with a true form of mental illness. He characterized the mental illness as a hysterical twilight state, adding presciently, "I am far from assuming that these disturbances are solved by recognizing their hysterical nature" (Ganser, 1898).

Following Ganser's presentation, other forensic psychiatrists reported similar combinations of symptoms in incarcerated patients. Presently, Ganser syndrome refers to a phenomenon often associated with prisoners, in which the patient gives:

> ...an utterly incorrect and often ridiculous reply, although it is quite clear that he [has] understood the sense of the question. Furthermore, although these patients often appear to be disoriented in time and place, their general behavior gives the distinct impression that they are alert. They are not confused in the usual sense; they are capable of comprehending

> the meaning of questions. ...the patient in a Ganser state talks
> past the point by design, even though the design is not neces-
> sarily conscious. ...This condition has never been observed in
> persons of superior intelligence. (Schlesinger, 1996)

Ganser symptoms have been described as "corresponding to the
layman's imperfect notion of madness" (Goldin & MacDonald, 1959).
The *DSM-IV-TR* categorizes Ganser's syndrome as a dissociative
disorder, not otherwise specified (NOS) characterized by "the giving
of approximate answers to questions when not associated with Dissociative Amnesia or Dissociative Fugue" (APA, 2006). The incorrect
answers are clearly not the result of misinformation or forgetting.

The Ganser syndrome has received much consideration, especially
in the European literature. In the United States, Weiner and Braiman
(1955) wrote that although encountered in prisoners, it is also occasionally found in the general population by people who have to
face unpleasant conditions. Jolly reported that one third of his cases
were noncriminal civilians. Of the six cases reported by Weiner and
Braiman, only one was a prisoner.

In almost all cases reported, the patient is disoriented as to time and
space and gives absurd answers to questions. Often, he claims he does
not know who he is, where he comes from, or where he is. When he
is asked to do simple calculations he makes obvious mistakes—for
instance, giving 5 as the sum of 2 plus 2. When he is asked to identify
objects, he gives the name of a related object. On being shown a pair
of scissors, the patient may say that they are knives; a picture of a
dog may be identified as a cat, a yellow object may be called red, and
so on. If he is asked what a hammer is used for, he may reply "to cut
wood." If he is shown a dime he may state that it is a half dollar. If he
is asked how many legs a horse has, he may reply "six" and so on.

Weiner and Braiman (1955, p. 770) report other symptoms in Ganser patients such as mild degrees of mental defect (dull borderline);
hysterical symptoms of various kinds, such as amnesia, analgesia,
incontinence, confusion, and so forth; and epileptic-like convulsions
and tremors. It is pointed out by Weiner and Braiman that Ganser's
syndrome may be confused with voluntary malingering in prisoners

who want to escape indictment, but that the malingerer will at times lose the air of bewilderment and confusion when he is not watched, whereas the Ganserian patient remains in that state all the time. The answers to questions of the Ganserian patient are reminiscent of those given by schizophrenics but seem even sillier, however, almost as if a voluntary effort had been made to say something ridiculously inappropriate.

A third misdiagnosis easily made is one of mental deficiency or organic conditions. But a mental deficiency of a degree that would explain such absurd answers would have been known prior to the onset of the disorder. Similarly, an organic condition that might lead to these symptoms would have to be at a very advanced stage; again, there would be no difficulty in making the diagnosis. Is the Ganser syndrome a psychosis? Ganser himself (as well as Kraepelin) felt that it is a psychoneurosis, similar to what Wernicke called hysterical pseudodementia, and should be included in the group of hysterias (Schlesinger, 1996).

The psychodynamic mechanism involved in the Ganser syndrome seems surprisingly simple: It is obvious that the patient wants to avoid the unpleasant situation and the burden of responsibility. Perhaps, as Weiner and Braiman have stated, he wants to do more than that. By unconsciously selecting symptoms that make him lose his rationality and often forget his personal identity and his past, he wants to reject his whole self, his whole life history—a denial of his total self. We encounter difficulties when we try to explain the symptoms from a formal point of view. The answers of the patient are related to the questions, although inappropriately, and are reminiscent of the metonymic distortions of the schizophrenic and, in particular, of the negativistic answers of some catatonics. The similarity is, however, only apparent. The Ganserian seems almost to make an effort to give a silly answer. A catatonic would not say that a horse has six legs.

A recent review of the Ganser syndrome by Dwyer and Reid presents the history and acknowledges the uncertainty regarding the mixture of conscious and unconscious elements in the disorder. The authors report:

[Ganser] noted a syndrome in three prisoners, the features of which included approximate answers to simple questions, perceptual abnormalities such as visual and auditory hallucinations, clouding of consciousness, and symptoms of somatic conversion (also known as functional or hysterical symptoms). Approximate answers refer to responses that are incorrect, but indicate that the question has been understood. For example, when asked, "How many legs does a cow have?" The patient might reply "five." Although clearly incorrect, this answer demonstrates an understanding of the question and required answer. The unusual nature of this symptom combined with the fluctuating level of consciousness has prompted extensive debate as to whether Ganser's Syndrome represents organic brain impairment, an hysterical conversion disorder, or malingering. As such, the syndrome has frequently undergone reclassification, a fact reflected by its alternative titles— balderdash syndrome, prison psychosis, nonsense syndrome. ...Ganser, however, with characteristic clarity, preferred the term "vorbeigehen" (to pass by, meaning that the patient passes by the correct answer to choose another) and stated that "The most obvious sign which they present consists of their inability to answer correctly the simplest of questions which are asked of them, even though by many of their answers they indicate that they have grasped, in a large part, the sense of the question, and in their answers they betray at once a baffling ignorance and a surprising lack of knowledge which they most assuredly once possessed, or still possess. ...The cause of Ganser's Syndrome remains uncertain. Current psychiatric classification categorizes it as a dissociative disorder, the symptoms of which are judged as psychogenic in origin. This view has been greeted with skepticism by those who suspect deliberate simulation and malingering, most notably Wertham who stated that "a Ganser reaction is a hysterical pseudo stupidity which occurs almost exclusively in jails and old fashioned German textbooks." ...An association with head injury has been noted ...The diagnosis of Ganser's Syndrome is often problematic, especially in view of the frequency with which the symptom of approximate answers arises in other psychiatric disorders. The identification of malingering, in order to gain an obvious benefit such as accommodation, is important although not nearly as straightforward as it might seem. The two are not mutually exclusive, a point emphasized by Ganser himself. (Dwyer & Reid, 2004)

The authors distinguish between the Ganser symptom of only approximate answers versus the full Ganser syndrome, which includes approximate answers, somatic conversion symptoms, clouding of consciousness, and perceptual disturbances.

The role of neurological injury in Ganser symptoms also appears significant. The neurologist Critchley remarked that there is a striking similarity between "vorbeireden" and regressive metonymy (one of the first symptoms of a sensory or jargon aphasia). However, differentiating malingering from a neurological or psychiatric condition is problematic. In a study by Anderson, Trethowan, and Kenna (1959), it was found that the fatigue, which develops as the examination of simulators is conducted longer, causes their answers to be more and more normal, while in pseudodementia, fatigue causes an increase in uncooperativeness. Another study examined 15 new cases of Ganser syndrome in Israel in which a high percentage belonged to an ethnic minority and were suspected of having symptoms of premorbid neurological pathology. Of the 15, 6 had suffered head injury in the past with loss of consciousness and ensuing chronic headaches and other symptoms of chronic postconcussion syndrome. Three of the 15 patients were diagnosed as suffering from schizotypal personality disorder; 14 were diagnosed as antisocial. The authors noted an association between Cluster A personality disorder and severity of Ganser syndrome: "Eighty percent ($n = 4$) of those patients suffering from the severest form of Ganser syndrome ($n = 5$) were in the schizophrenic end of the personality disorder spectrum" (Sigal, Altmark, Alfici, & Gelkopf, 1992). The authors noted the difficulty of distinguishing malingering from Ganser's syndrome and put forward the conceptualization that Ganser's syndrome is:

> ...a polymorphic entity on a continuum between dissociative and psychotic disorders. Our findings point out that the lower

the level of personality organization and ego resources, the higher the risk of developing Ganser Syndrome. ...Members of minority [populations] may harbor feelings of discrimination and such feelings may bring about the development of Ganser Syndrome or other dissociative defenses when they are confronted with serious charges by the legal system, which they may feel they lack the adequate means of support to deal with. If our data are representative of the Ganser Syndrome population, we can tentatively understand Ganser Syndrome as a maladaptive way of dealing with a "no way-out" situation by "going crazy" in organically and/or functionally disturbed individuals. (Tsoi, 1973)

The nature and course of Ganser syndrome is quite variable, from transient to chronic. One study described a 54-year-old male who presented over a period of 7 years with a state akin to dementia that included approximate answers, the patient's symptoms improving during hospitalization and then reappearing prior to discharge (Hampel, Berger, & Muller, 1996).

This kind of "hysterical pseudodementia" is not limited to people involved in the criminal justice system.

The essential features common to all these cases is a syndrome of dependency and behavioral problems resembling dementia-related conduct disorders, but with stable cognitive performance over a period of years, investigations that do not support a neurodegenerative condition and a prolonged survival that is not in keeping with the common organic dementias... . Hospitalization or institutionalization can lead to feelings of abandonment, depression and rage and a further retreat into pseudodementia and dependency...conversion pseudodementia in older people can be seen as a severe regression in the face of overwhelming anxiety and cumulative losses in individuals with borderline, narcissistic and dissociative personality traits stemming from earlier abuse, trauma, abandonment or emotional repression. The syndrome is worsened rather than helped by approaches to care appropriate to the organic dementias. (Hepple, 2004)

If the social justification for capital punishment is that it is the ultimate punishment, mental terror is an integral part, as opposed to physical pain, which is not. Chronic Ganser presentations among the condemned restate the paradox initially posed by Justice Traynor, that is: Is it more cruel to execute someone oblivious of his fate or crueler to execute the person aware of it? If this is a peculiar hysterical state, perhaps more responsive to antianxiety medications, should there be limits to "synthetic calm?" Does a condemned prisoner have a right to effective treatment, if the effective treatment is the commutation of the death sentence, more than any medication?

More recently, there has been litigation around what has been called "Death Row syndrome." This has been used to refer to the psychological changes that some condemned prisoners experience from living on death row after many years of appeals, that is, the dehumanizing effects of living for a prolonged period on death row. Back in 1890 the Supreme Court noted "when a prisoner sentenced by a court to death is confined in the penitentiary awaiting the execution of the sentence, one of the most horrible feelings to which he can be subjected during that time is the uncertainty during the whole of it" (In re Medley, 1890). This psychological concern was taken up again in Justice Stevens's dissent from the denial of certiorari in *Lackey v. Texas* (Stevens, 1995). Justice Stevens begins to address this significant issue: "Petitioner raises the question whether executing a prisoner who has already spent some 17 years on death row violates the Eighth Amendment's prohibition against cruel and unusual punishment." He speculated that the lengthy delays prior to execution might constitute "psychological torture" (*People v. Anderson*, 1972; see also Breyer, 1998, 1999). The few studies or reports on the actual effects of solitary confinement or living conditions on death row are very preliminary, with many methodological problems (Grassian, 1983).

The Death Row syndrome has also been related to death penalty volunteers, that is, prisoners who refuse to appeal their sentence, with claims that Death Row syndrome makes them incompetent to waive their appellate rights. In *Rees v. Peyton*, the Supreme Court decided that the standard for testing competency to waive a death penalty appeal is whether a defendant has the "capacity to appreciate his position and make a rational choice with respect to continuing or abandoning further litigation or on the other hand whether he is suffering from a mental disease, disorder, or defect which may substantially affect his capacity" (*Rees v. Peyton*, 1966). The special counsel for condemned prisoner Michael Ross in Connecticut recently raised this argument, ultimately unsuccessfully (see Schwartz, 2005). Not all death penalty volunteers have experienced long years as condemned prisoners. Gary Gilmore was the first individual to be executed after the Supreme Court reinstated the death penalty, and Timothy McVeigh, the Oklahoma City bomber, spent few years on death row. Prisoners waive appeals for many reasons, not all psychiatric or related to extreme demoralization, despair, isolation, hopelessness, anxiety, anger, depression, and posttraumatic stress. Nonetheless, it is likely that these relentless living conditions are so stressful that condemned prisoners drop their appeals rather than stay the course. J. C. Oleson, in a thoughtful article, suggests that death row is so inherently coercive that competence to waive appeals cannot exist (Oleson, 2006).

Death row is not the only place where people suffer a sentence of death. Prison gangs and street gangs have a long tradition of executing associates who fail or snitch or break gang rules in other ways. The author Jorge Luis Borges has a short story on the topic called "The Waiting," which captures the hysterical dissociative state of mind awaiting execution. In the story, a gangster has been targeted for assassination by a rival gangster and goes into hiding. He is preoccupied with the moment when the assassins will arrive, constantly anticipating and dreading that possibility. When the assassins finally arrive in his room to kill him, he:

> gestured at them to wait, and he turned over and faced the wall, as though going back to sleep. Did he do that to awaken the pity of the men that killed him, or because it's easier to endure a terrifying event than to imagine it, wait for it endlessly—or (and this is perhaps the most likely possibility) so that his murderers would become a dream, as they had already been so many times, in that same place, at that same hour? ... He was in this act of magic when the blast obliterated him. (*The Jorge Luis Borges Collection*, n.d.)

References

American Psychiatric Association (APA). (2000). *Diagnostic and statistical manual of mental disorders* (*DSM-IV-TR*). Washington, DC: Author.

American Psychiatric Association (APA). (2006). *Diagnostic and statistical manual of mental disorders* (*DSM-IV-TR*). Washington, DC: Author.

Anderson, E. W., Trethowan, W. H., & Kenna, J. C. (1959). An experimental investigation of simulation and pseudodementia. *Acta Psychiatrica et Neurologica Scandinavica, 34*(Suppl. 132), 1–42.

Antiterrorism and Effective Death Penalty Act (AEDPA), *8 U.S.C. § 1182* (1996).

Arizona v. Clarke, 548 U.S. (2006).

Breyer, J. (dissenting) in Elledge v. Florida, 525 U.S. 944, 944 (1998).

Breyer, J. (dissenting) in Knight v. Florida, 528 U.S. 990, 993 (1999).

Dalfen, A. & Feinstein, A. (2000). Head injury, dissociation and the Ganser syndrome. *Brain Injury, 14*(12), 1101–1105.

Dwyer, J., & Reid, S. (2004). Ganser's Syndrome. *Lancet, 364,* 471–473.

Ford v. Wainwright, 477 U.S. 399 (1986), 106 S. Ct. 2595, 91 L.Ed. 2d 335.

Frankfurter, J. (dissenting) in Solesbee v. Balkcom, 339 U.S. 9, 14, 94 L. Ed. 604, 70 S. Ct. 457 (1950).

Ganser, S. J. M. (1898).Üer einen eigenartigen hysterischen Dämmerzustand. *Archiv für Psychiatrie und Nervenkrankheiten (Berlin), 30,* 633–640. [English translation by Schorer C. E. (1965). A peculiar hysterical state. *British Journal of Criminology, 5,* 120–126].

Goldin, S., & MacDonald, J. E. (1959). The Ganser state. *Journal of Mental Science, 101,* 267.

Grassian, S. (1983). Psychopathological effects of solitary confinement. *American Journal of Psychiatry, 140,* 1450.

Hampel, H., Berger, C., & Muller, N. (1996). A case of Ganser's state presenting as a dementia syndrome. *Psychopathology, 29*(4), 236–241.

Hepple, J. (2004). Conversion pseudodementia in older people: A descriptive case series. *International Journal of Geriatric Psychiatry, 19,* 961–967.

In re Medley, 134 U.S. 160, 172, 33 L. Ed. 835, 10 S. Ct. 384 (1890).

Jorge Luis Borges Collection, The. (n.d.). Retrieved, November 10, 2006, from http://www.lib.virginia.edu/small/collections/borges.html

Oleson, J. C. (2006, winter). Swilling Hemlock: The legal ethics of defending a client who wishes to volunteer for execution. *Wash & Lee Law Reviews, 63*, 147.

People v. Anderson, 6 Cal. 3d 628, (1972).

Rees v. Peyton, 384 U.S. 312 (1966).

Rohan, ex rel Gates v. Woodford, (2003) 334 F.3d 803.

Schlesinger, L. B. (1996). *Explorations in criminal psychopathology: Clinical syndromes with forensic implications.* Springfield, IL: Charles Thomas.

Schorer, C. E. (1965). The Ganser syndrome. *British Journal of Criminology, 5*, 120–126.

Schwartz, H. I. (2005). Death Row syndrome and demoralization: Psychiatric means to social policy ends. *Journal of American Academy of Psychiatry Law, 33*, 153–155.

Sigal, M., Altmark, D., Alfici, S., & Gelkopf, M. (1992). Ganser syndrome: A review of 15 cases. *Comprehensive Psychiatry, 33*(2), 134–138.

Stevens, J. (dissenting), 514 U.S. 1045, 1045 (1995) (mem.).

Tsoi, W. F. (1973). The Ganser syndrome in Singapore: A report of ten cases. *British Journal of Psychiatry, 123*, 567-572.

Weiner, H., & Braiman, A. (1955). The Ganser syndrome: A review and addition of some unusual cases. *American Journal of Psychiatry, 111*, 767–773.

CHAPTER FIVE

THE MYTH OF THE SUCCESSFUL INSANITY DEFENSE

Robert W. Bigelow, JD

A gruesome, heinous crime or series of crimes occur. The crimes appear to be the work of a mad person. When the suspect is apprehended, he or she is found to be a person with a history of mental illness. The media and public express a fear that this "monster" will get away with it by acting crazy and raising an insanity defense. Contrary to popular misconception, this last step is virtually guaranteed not to occur. From the 15-year-old Kip Kinkel who shot 27 people in a school massacre after killing his parents, to "Son of Sam" killer David Berkowitz, to Ted Bundy, Sirhan Sirhan, John Wayne Gacy, and Jeffrey Dahmer, the insanity defense has been raised, withdrawn, or rejected to resounding failure.

There are a variety of reasons why the insanity defense is not successful. This chapter will trace the history of this defense and the varied legal definitions that have been applied over time. We will see that the term *insane* in the context of this defense is a legal definition rather than a medical diagnosis and the law itself is changed by lawmakers when the defense is seen as "successful" as in the case of John Hinckley Jr., whose "success" has not set him free in the 23 years since he was found not guilty by reason of insanity. The public's misunderstanding of the insanity defense is more firmly rooted in fear than in fact.

MEDICAL VERSUS LEGAL INSANITY

Colaizzi (1989) traces the history of how the medical field has diagnosed and defined the dangerously insane through recent history. Significant is the debate between the psychiatric and legal professions as to defining and punishing the varying degrees of insanity. Although a doctor may find a patient medically insane, this does not mean that the person is insane by the legal definition. Most mentally ill persons—including those diagnosed with psychosis or schizophrenia—are, in fact, unlikely to prevail using an insanity defense. Rolf (2006) points out that by the year 2000 there were estimated to be over 250,000 people in jails or prisons who meet the medical definition of being mentally ill.

INSANITY DEFENSE VERSUS COMPETENCY TO STAND TRIAL

The insanity defense must be differentiated from competency to stand trial. The distinction is largely one of timing. The insanity defense pertains to the defendant's mental state at the time of the alleged criminal acts, whereas competency to stand trial pertains to the mental state of an individual at the time of trial.

DEFINING LEGAL INSANITY

The legal definition of insanity in the Unites States is traced to the M'Naghten case in England (1843). M'Naghten was a delusional woodworker who believed he was the target of a conspiracy of the Tories. M'Naghten shot and killed Edward Drummond, the personal secretary of Tory Prime Minister Sir Robert Peel, mistaking him for the prime minister. There was substantial testimony regarding M'Naghten's mental condition. The jury acquitted M'Naghten, who as a result of this "success" was confined to a mental institution for the rest of his life.

The queen and the public were outraged by this perceived miscarriage of justice and lack of a prison term. After the public outcry, the House of Lords crafted the M'Naghten test, which required that a defendant should be acquitted if the proof establishes a "disease of the mind" caused a "defect of reason" such that the defendant did "not know the nature and quality of the act or did not know it was wrong" (*M'Naghten's Rule*, 1843). M'Naghten's rule replaced the long-standing "wild beast" insanity defense and became the standard in American jurisprudence for many years.

Most significant is that M'Naghten presented a purely cognitive standard. It was not a defense to assert that a defendant could not control his or her actions because of mental illness. The case of *Parsons v. State* (1877) presented an alternate or more expansive view by acknowledging that a person can suffer from a mental illness that makes him or her "unable to control his actions or conform his conduct to the law." Although often criticized, this test is known as the "irresistible impulse test." This standard is not widely accepted, but some jurisdictions (CO, NM, TX, VA) follow M'Naghten and the irresistible impulse test. Most notable was the introduction of a volitional perspective as opposed to the purely cognitive paradigm, which certainly expanded the availability of the insanity defense to more mentally ill defendants.

In 1954 the D.C. Circuit in *Durham v. U.S.* (1954) held that a defendant is not responsible if the proof establishes that his or her crime was the "product of mental disease or defect" (p. 875). With this test, the crime must not only be a product of the mental disease but would not have been committed "but for" the disease. This court was reacting to an increased awareness for and validation of modern psychiatry. This decision was roundly criticized for allowing psychiatrists to venture into the legal and factual realm of jurists and juries. This criterion is known as the *Durham* test.

In 1972 D.C. would join numerous other jurisdictions in adopting the standard put forth by the American Law Institute in the Model Penal Code, which was created in 1962. The case adopting this standard was *United States v. Brawner* (1972). Using this standard, the accused is entitled to acquittal if at the time of such conduct "as a result of mental disease or defect he lacks substantial capacity to appreciate the criminality [wrongfulness] of his conduct or confirm his conduct to the requirements of the law" (ALI Model Penal Code, 1985). This test appears to be a hybrid of the M'Naghten test and the irresistible impulse test by considering both cognitive and volitional aspects. Rolf (2006) refers to this standard as "a softer version of the M'Naghten right or wrong test" (p. 7).

Everything changed in 1981, when John Hinckley Jr. attempted to assassinate President Ronald Reagan. Hinckley pled not guilty by reason of insanity. Unlike countless unsuccessful defendants before him, Hinckley was acquitted. At this time, all federal courts followed the standard of the Model Penal Code and, like M'Naghten over 100 years before, the public, politicians, and media called for reform of the standard.

Perlin (1997) states that the public's outrage reflects "society's basic dissatisfaction with perceived incompatibility of the due process and crime control models of criminal law, and with the notion that psychiatric excuses can allow a guilty defendant to 'beat a rap and escape punishment'" (p. 1381). It is notable that this success has not resulted in Hinckley being free in the 23 years since the verdict.

Congress reacted swiftly to the public outcry with legislation intended to abolish or modify the insanity defense. Perlin (1997) points out that the Reagan administration called for the abolition of the defense altogether. When confronted with actual data and facts about the defense, Congress appeared to compromise and enacted the Insanity Defense Reform Act (IDRA) (1988), which provides for a M'Naghten exclusively cognitive type of standard. The volitional approach was completely eliminated in the federal courts.

At the state level (nonfederal cases) the legislators reacted as well. Utah, Idaho, and Montana eliminated the defense altogether, and other states raised the standard of proof for the defense from a preponderance of evidence to clear and convincing evidence of insanity. Some states in a far from semantic change enacted "guilty but mentally ill" (GBMI) or "guilty but insane" (GBI) standards rather than, or in addition to, not guilty by reason of insanity (NGRI). The first two allow for the acknowledgment of mental illness without excusing the conduct and call for the balance of the prison sentence to be served following the treatment (usually at the discretion of the court), which ordinarily takes place at the correctional facility.

MENS REA: DIMINISHED CAPACITY DEFENSE

Although the insanity defense exists in some form in all but three states, these states and others allow evidence of mental illness to rebut mens rea or the requisite mental state to have the intent to commit the crime charged. Federal courts and many other states allow "diminished capacity" evidence. Although this evidence is often intertwined with the insanity defense, this defense should not be confused with the insanity defense. If successful using the insanity defense, the defendant will be confined to a mental institution, whereas a successful attack on mens rea can result in an outright acquittal or a conviction on a lesser charge requiring a state of mind less than intent such as reckless or negligent.

OBSTACLES FOR THE INSANITY DEFENSE

The insanity defense presents numerous problems for the criminal defense attorney and is often accurately referred to as a tactic of last resort. First and foremost, the defense attorney must admit to the horrible acts for which the client is accused. This means that the attorney must overcome the anger, horror, and fear that can be evoked in a jury. The jury may also have a predisposition to be afraid of the mentally ill.

Another obstacle in the insanity defense is that the jury is not allowed to consider sentencing. Rightly or wrongly, it is the realm of the judge not the jury to mete out punishment. As a result, the jury will not be aware, and the defense attorney will not be allowed, to explain that a defendant found not guilty by reason of insanity is not released back onto the streets and into our society. In fact, the defendant acquitted in this manner is committed to an institution often for a longer period of time than if the crime had resulted in a conviction. This is a factor to consider in raising the defense, and why it is often more worthy of consideration only in serious cases when the defendant is facing a substantial period of incarceration as opposed to a case where the defendant is facing little if any jail time.

An additional issue for the defense is that a severely mentally disturbed defendant may appear totally sane at the time of trial as he or she may now (since arrest) be heavily medicated and under psychiatric care. Reid (2006) cites the "controversial strategy" that is occasionally raised by defense attorneys arguing for allowing the client to remain psychotic in order to allow the jury to get a more accurate picture of the defendant's mental state. Reid (2006) accurately points out several flaws in this plan. First, it might deprive the defendant of his or her right to be competent during trial. There is simply no trial if the defendant is not competent. Second, there is also no guarantee as to how an unmedicated psychotic might present at the time of trial. Third, there are significant ethical issues for a physician denying treatment to one in psychiatric need. Finally, the jury may actually be afraid of seeing the defendant in this state, thus having a negative effect on defense strategy.

A further problem with raising the insanity defense is that psychiatry is not an exact science. Many of the most famous insanity cases involved a battle of experts who disagree as to the mental state of the defendant. Although the burden of proof lies with the prosecutor to prove a defendant guilty beyond a reasonable doubt as to each and every element of the crimes charged, by raising the insanity defense, which is an "affirmative defense," the defense assumes a burden of producing evidence to overcome a presumption of sanity. Depending on the jurisdiction, the defense must show evidence ranging from a scintilla to evidence sufficient to raise a reasonable doubt to even allow the defense to be raised. Most jurisdictions in the post-Hinckley era require the defense to prove insanity by a preponderance of the evidence, and federal courts require the defense to prove insanity by clear and convincing evidence to achieve acquittal. A small number of states still place the burden on the prosecution to prove sanity beyond a reasonable doubt once the issue has been raised.

The defense must also overcome the public perception reinforced in popular media that faking insanity is an easy way to avoid punishment. Perlin (1997) states that this "fear is unfounded" and "there is virtually no evidence that feigned insanity has ever been remotely significant problem in criminal procedure" (p. 1410).

The jails and prisons of the county are filled with the mentally ill. Prejean (2006) cites fear of malingering, a hostility toward the mentally ill, and the notion that the mentally ill are merely of weak character, which can lead many to the conclusion that mentally ill people should be held accountable "regardless of their real or perceived problems" (p. 1498).

STRATEGIC MANEUVERS

Criminal law always raises issues of strategy within the framework of the law and ethics. The insanity defense has been invoked for strategic purposes. It has been suggested that the attorneys for Lee Boyd Malvo (the young "Beltway Sniper") raised the insanity defense in order to be able to introduce evidence about Malvo's relationship with John Allen Muhammad (the older Beltway Sniper) and difficult childhood, which would not have been admissible with another defense, in order to invoke the sympathy of the jury in a strategic move to avoid the death penalty. Lee Boyd Malvo was found guilty but not sentenced to death. However, legal maneuvering exists on both sides of a criminal case. For instance,

Steele (2006) relates that Professor Bard of the University of Texas asserts that the prosecutors in the first trial of Andrea Yates sought the death penalty to get jurors who would be more conservative and less likely to accept an insanity defense.

AN INFAMOUS INSANITY SAMPLER

Gado (2005) suggests that journalists and politicians manipulate the insanity defense for their purposes as well. Politicians utilize the defense as a way of capturing attention and journalists because they know it is of great public interest. Often, lost in the notoriety of an insanity defense case is the fact that its use did not accomplish the desired result.

Jeffrey Dahmer

The trial of Jeffrey Dahmer was one of the most high-profile insanity defense cases of recent times. Forty-five witnesses took the stand for the defense to speak about Dahmer's bizarre behavior, including severed heads found in his refrigerator, an altar of candles, skulls in a closet, and his practices of necrophilia and cannibalism as he ate the biceps of one of his victims.

Despite the fact that Dahmer suffered from severe mental disorders, his lawyers were unsuccessful using the insanity defense. Dahmer was found guilty and sentenced to 15 consecutive life sentences in prison. He was later murdered in prison by a schizophrenic named Christopher Scarver.

The Son of Sam

David Berkowitz terrorized New York in the mid-1970s with a string of killings. Labeled the "Son of Sam" because he believed he was the son of a 6,000-year-old man inhabiting the body of his neighbor Sam Carr, Berkowitz believed that demons were ordering him to kill using the Carrs' dog as the medium to instruct him.

Originally found incompetent to stand trial, a second hearing found him competent. The defense team was to make use of the insanity defense but ultimately Berkowitz pled guilty and received sentences of 25 years to life for each of six murders and additional time for attempted murder and assault. He is serving his life sentence at the Sullivan Correctional Facility in New York State.

Ted Bundy

Ted Bundy was the infamous serial killer who killed at least 30 women. Bundy represented himself in his first trial for a murderous attack on women at the Chi Omega House on the campus of Florida State University. After being found guilty and receiving two death sentences, he allowed lawyers to represent him in a second trial for the murder of Kimberly Leach. Bundy pled not guilty by reason of insanity.

Again, Ted Bundy was found guilty by a jury in seven hours and sentenced to death. He was executed on January 24, 1989.

John Wayne Gacy

John Wayne Gacy raped, tortured, and murdered at least 30 young men and buried many of them in the floorboards of his home. The insanity defense was raised in his case.

Despite testimony of schizophrenia and multiple personality disorder and medical experts finding him insane, Gacy was found guilty and executed on May 10, 1994, in Joliet, Illinois.

Kip Kinkel

Fifteen-year-old Kip Kinkel murdered his parents and then went on a murderous rampage at Thurston High School in Springfield, Oregon. His attorneys were preparing an insanity defense, but he ultimately pled guilty to murder and attempted murder and is serving just over 111 years in prison.

Sirhan Sirhan and Ted Kaczynski

Not all who could raise the defense want it raised. Sirhan Sirhan, the killer of Robert Kennedy, tried to withdraw his plea and plead guilty rather than have defense medical experts continue to discuss his mental state. He had been diagnosed psychotic before trial, and there was testimony during trial as to his diminished capacity. Ted Kaczynski, the "Unabomber," pled guilty in part to avoid having the insanity defense raised. A court-appointed psychiatrist diagnosed him as a paranoid schizophrenic. There is very little argument that both men suffered from forms of mental illness. Sirhan Sirhan was found guilty after trial of first-degree murder and was sentenced to death. The death penalty was abolished in California in 1972, so he will likely spend the rest of his life in prison. Kaczynski was sentenced to life in prison without the possibility of parole.

LACK OF SUCCESS

Despite a plethora of high-profile cases covered on television or print media, as well as television series and movies that show a clever and evil criminal escaping culpability and punishment by acting crazy, the reality is far different. Perlin (1994) states that virtually all studies show that the insanity defense is rarely raised. It is estimated that the insanity defense is raised in only 1% of cases and success is only realized in a fourth of those cases (p. 108). That figure can be misleading as to the success of the defense. Cirincione (1996) and Rogers, Bloom, and Manson (1984) point out that many of these successes are arrived at through plea agreement with the cooperation of the prosecutor. A number of contested successful insanity defenses are via bench trial with the judge as the finder of fact rather than a jury. The benefit of having a judge in many instances is that a judge is often aware of the myths associated with the insanity defense and may prove a more fair and less-afraid trier of fact.

AFTER THE "SUCCESS"

History has proven that "success" is a relative term when it comes to the insanity defense. M'Naghten died in a mental institution. Hinckley is still not free 23 years after his controversial success. Defendants found guilty but mentally ill (GBMI) or guilty but insane (GBI) will receive varying degrees of psychiatric treatment before serving the balance of their sentence as any other inmate. A person found not guilty by reason of insanity (NGRI) will be institutionalized. This may involve a civil commitment proceeding. There will also be periodic reviews. In most jurisdictions, the decision of release is made by the court.

ANDREA YATES AND THE FUTURE

Andrea Yates, who had a significant history of mental illness, drowned her five children in a bathtub. In an odd mix of notoriety and media, her first trial, which resulted in conviction, was overturned because a prosecution witness had testified falsely that Yates had been a fan of the show *Law and Order* and had seen an episode where a mother drowned her children and successfully pled insanity. The show had not aired by the date of the killings. This witness was the only witness to testify that Yates knew right from wrong. It might be suggested that this false testimony elicited in the jury the misconceptions, mythology, and fear that many have toward the insanity defense. In her second trial Ms. Yates was found not guilty by reason of insanity.

If the history of the evolution of the legal definition of insanity has shown anything, it is that a success like that of Andrea Yates is likely to prove controversial despite the fact that she will likely spend the rest of her life in an institution. This result may lead to further scrutiny of an already tenuous proposition for success in raising the insanity defense.

REFERENCES

American Law Institute. (1985). *Model penal code: Official draft and explanatory notes*. Philadelphia: Author. [ALI Model Penal Code § 4.01(1) (1985).]

Cirincione, C. (1996). Revisiting the insanity defense: Contested or consensus. *Bulletin of the American Academy of Psychiatry and the Law, 24*(2), 165–176.

Colaizzi, J. (1989). *Homicidal insanity, 1800–1985*. Tuscaloosa: University of Alabama Press.

Durham v. U.S., 214 F. 2d 864 (D.C. Cir. 1954).

Gado, M. (2005). The insanity goes on. *Court TV's crime library: Criminal minds and methods*. Retrieved November 12, 2005, from http://www.crimelibrary.com/criminal_mind/psychology/insanity/ll.html

Insanity Defense Reform Act, 18 U.S.C. § 17 (1988).

M'Naghten's Rule, 8 Eng. Rep. 718 (1843).

Parsons v. State, 81 Ala. 577, 2 So. 854 (Ala. 1877).

Perlin, M. (1994). *The jurisprudence of the insanity defense*. Durham, NC: Academic Press.

Perlin, M. (1997). "The borderline which separated you from me": The insanity defense, the authoritarian spirit, the fear of faking, and the culture of punishment. *Iowa Law Review, 82*, 1375–1426.

Prejean, M. (2006). Texas law made this mad woman sane. *Houston Law Review, 42*, 1487–1522.

Reid, W. (2006, May). The insanity defense: Bad, or mad or both. *Journal of Psychiatric Practice,* 169–200.

Rogers, J. L., Bloom, J. D., & Manson, S. M. (1984). Insanity defenses: Contested or conceded? *American Journal of Psychiatry, 141*, 885–888.

Rolf, C. (2006, spring). From M'Naghten to Yates—Transformation of the insanity defense in the United States—Is it still viable? *Rivier College Online Academic Journal,* (2), 1–18. Retrieved from http://www.rivier.edu/journal/ ROAJ-2006-Spring/J41-ROLF.pdf

Steele, B. (2006, October 24). Misconceptions muddle insanity defense debate, law lecturer says. *University Times Faculty and Staff,* p. 35. (Citing lecture at University of Pittsburgh Law School on October 17, 2002 by University of Texas Professor Jennifer S. Bard). Retrieved from http://mac10.umc.pitt.edu/u/FMPro?-db=ustory&-lay=a&-format=d.html&storyid=2711&-Find

United States v. Brawner, 471 F.2d 969 (D.C. Cir. 1972).

CHAPTER SIX

PSYCHOLOGICAL AND NEUROPSYCHOLOGICAL TESTING IN WORKERS' COMPENSATION: PARADOXICAL OBJECTIVE PSYCHOMETRIC FINDINGS VERSUS SUBJECTIVE COGNITIVE, PSYCHOLOGICAL, AND PAIN COMPLAINTS

Richard G. Salamone, PhD, ABPP

INTRODUCTION

The better part of a century ago, Symonds (1937), referring to a patient's clinical presentation following head injury, noted, "it is not only the kind of injury that matters, but the kind of head" (p. 1092). With regard to chronic pain, the Cartesian view involving anything close to a one-to-one correspondence between tissue damage and subjective pain complaints, impairment, and disability has been discredited at least since Melzack and Wall's (1965) classic paper arguing for more comprehensive *gate control theory* of pain and more recently evolving into a *neuromatrix theory* of pain (Melzack, 1999). The research literature has failed to consistently demonstrate strong and consistent relationships between pain, disability, and tissue damage (Turk & Melzack, 1992). Indeed, low back pain patients often lack objective findings commensurate with their complaints of pain, and asymptomatic individuals are sometimes demonstrated to have objective abnormalities on, for example, imaging studies (Waddell & Turk, 1992). Furthermore, the prevalence of psychiatric disorder (e.g., various forms of adjustment, depression, anxiety, and personality disorders) among the general population is not at all uncommon as revealed in the American Psychiatric Association (APA), *Diagnostic and Statistical Manual of Mental Disorders*, fourth edition, text revision (*DSM-IV-TR*) (APA, 2000) and tends to be elevated in chronic pain populations (Gatchel, 1996). Using examples of head injury and pain and expanding them to other injuries, a crucial corollary to Symonds' (1937) caution would be Sir William Osler's often quoted sage advice that "it's more important to know what kind of patient has the disease than what kind of disease the patient has."

Within the workers' compensation arena, debate regarding the type and degree of sequelae from injury, impairment, and disability frequently rages not simply between plaintiff and defense attorneys but even within the various specialties that evaluate and treat injured workers. While some injuries and their physical, psychological, and/or cognitive sequelae are quite clear based upon the nature of the accident (e.g., coal miner with a traumatic below-the-knee amputation in a rock fall who also evinced very brief loss of consciousness associated with a head strike [without radiologic abnormality and being fully alert and oriented on initial emergency room evaluation] who has difficulty with ambulation and can no longer ambulate effectively in low coal). Some are reasonably clear (e.g., miners' claims of emotional distress secondary to the loss of a leg and/or posttraumatic stress disorder [PTSD]). Some are not so clear (e.g., that head injury resulting in miners' claims of concentration and memory difficulties 1 year post accident). And some can be preposterous (e.g., a miner claiming that he cannot recall his siblings' names or how to operate a shuttle car 1 year post accident). However, even what is "clear" can sometimes be deceptive; for example, schizophrenic patients who will, by virtue of their psychiatric disease, evince symptoms and signs of psychosis can also make false or exaggerated claims of psychotic symptoms. Furthermore, a particular patient symptom (e.g., memory complaint) or sign (e.g., stuttering) can be associated with factors other than the injury to which it may be attributed (e.g., brain injury).

The field of medicine uses various procedures (e.g., physical exam) and tests (e.g., radiologic and laboratory studies) to objectify and quantify the assessment of various injury and disease states and their sequelae. Of course, some methods may be "more objective" than others (e.g., quantifying levels of pain based upon patient physical exam behavior and response vs. determining the probability of a compressive lesion to a spinal nerve root with radiologic procedures and electrodiagnostic studies). As indicated above, pain is a complex, if not elusive, phenomenon to assess and manage, and it is common for neurosurgeons and orthopedic surgeons to use objective measures in an attempt to correlate findings from those measures with a patient's subjective complaints as part of the diagnostic workup.

Within the psychological and psychiatric arenas, however, diagnosis is largely symptom- versus sign-based, easily discerned when diagnostic criteria such as the *DSM-IV-TR* (APA, 2000) are evaluated and tallied; probably this is even more so when it comes down to the reality of day-to-day evaluative decisions by the psychologist and/or psychiatrist clinician. Diagnosis is by far largely based upon a patient's subjective reports; we hope for an accurate reporting of symptoms that many times, if not most of the time, depending upon the setting and patient population, we obtain. However, there are times when we may not receive an accurate reporting but, instead, minimization or exaggeration of symptoms. Simply accepting this, without some objective method of verification, a patient's symptom complaints, particularly when there may be complex and multiple incentives to report nonexistent symptoms or exaggerate existent symptoms, such as in the workers' compensation arena (or to minimize symptoms or problems such as in a child custody evaluation case to briefly acknowledge the opposite end of the continuum), is done at no small diagnostic peril. Indeed, work by Green and associates with regard to cognitive claims in head injured, depressed, and pain patients has resulted in remarkably compelling evidence of response bias not only in substantial percentages of patients with obvious incentives to exaggerate such claims but also in patient samples with no apparent incentives of this kind (Gervais, Rohling, Green, & Ford, 2004; Gervais, Russell, Green, Ferrari, & Pieschl, 2001; Green, 2001, 2003a; Rohling, Green, Allen, & Iverson, 2002).

This chapter discusses the basis and utility of the use of psychometric studies when confronted with an injured worker for evaluation and treatment or in the context of an independent medical (i.e., psychological or neuropsychological) examination. This method is demonstrated to add objectivity to the evaluation of patient claims of psychiatric disorder, cognitive disorder, and pain complaints. Experience within the workers' compensation arena suggests acknowledgment of pain, psychiatric, and/or cognitive sequelae to various occupational injuries by treating doctors but frequent skepticism and resistance for evaluation and treatment by carriers for fear of adding the nebulous black hole of a "mental health claim card" to physical complaints (e.g., low back pain, mild head injury), which itself may defy substantiation from objective diagnostic medical testing. Given the complexities of various psychosocial factors operating within the workers' compensation arena, both from patient and carrier perspectives that affect a case, whether or not acknowledged, a method is needed to objectively evaluate the veracity and consistency of patient clinical complaints and presentation. What is required is an objective method that results in data to assist in detection and assessment of clinical disorders and syndromes (e.g., involving pain, mood, and/or cognitive complaints) as well as *response bias*, most typically in the workers' compensation arena, involving the range of mild exaggeration (e.g., so-called symptom magnification or functional augmentation) associated with somatization-type factors (e.g., anxiety) to that which is more malignant, involving malingering (ignoring for the moment that multiple factors and motivations can coexist for response bias). The method must be a sword that cuts both ways and allows data supportive of a patient's clinical claims, as well as being demonstrative of response bias, should either (or both) exist. That method will be argued to involve appropriate psychological and neuropsychological testing.

PHYSICAL COMPLAINTS FREQUENTLY HAVE PSYCHOLOGICAL OR PSYCHOSOCIAL COMPLICATIONS

Primary care physicians will tell you that people vary markedly in how frequently they complain about physical symptoms, their propensity to visit physicians when experiencing identical physical symptoms, and even their response to the same treatment. On what basis can we explain such variance? A 20-year study of Kaiser Permanente revealed that about 60% of medical visits were by patients without a diagnosable medical disorder (Cummings & Follette, 1968). Indeed, while sometimes from clinical evaluation it is clear, for example, that anxiety or depression accounts for physical symptoms, not infrequently "medically unexplained symptoms" have no such clear association and are likely explained by more complex psychological or psychosocial mechanisms (Brown, 2004). For common physical symptoms (e.g., chest pain, fatigue, dizziness) in an internal medicine clinic, with more than two thirds of patients undergoing objective diagnostic medical testing, only 16% were determined to have an organic cause to their complaint(s) (Kroenke & Mangelsdorff,

1989). Eisenburg (1992) noted that "the frequency of diagnosable psychiatric disorder found in studies of general practice varies from as low as 11 percent to as high as 36 percent" (p. 1080). Spitzer et al. (1994) found that the diagnosis of common psychiatric disorders was missed 50% to 75% of the time by primary care physicians. And finally, chronically ill patients are at higher risk for depressive symptoms and disorders than is the general population (Clark, Cook, & Snow, 1998).

With regard to chronic low back pain, traditional (e.g., radiologic) methods such as advanced imaging identify the cause of pain in only a minority of cases (Bogduk & McGuirk, 2002). This is improved with additional methods such as discography. However, a compelling physical etiology for chronic pain remains elusive in many patients. While symptomatic individuals tend to have elevated rates of spinal disk protrusions and herniations, the incidence of such, particularly with regard to protrusions (vs. herniation with clear nerve root compromise), in asymptomatic individuals makes a purely structural model of back pain problematic (Boos et al., 1995). On one hand, it could be hypothesized that technology is as yet insufficiently developed to detect the physiologic cause; on the other hand, there is a substantial body of research that compellingly indicates no small role of nonphysiologic factors in pain complaints and disability claims. "There is a significant, and seemingly predominant, psychosocial component that produces the prolonged disability... . These results show that there is not a close relationship between physically related variables and self-reported pain and disability" (Gatchel, Polatin, & Mayer, 1995, pp. 2706, 2707). Indeed, injury severity and physical job demands were poorly correlated with return to work after 1 year. Boos et al. (1995) found that "work perception and psychosocial factors were helpful in discriminating between symptomatic and asymptomatic disc herniations" (p. 2613). Burton, Tillotson, Main, and Hollis (1995) observed that "multiple regression analysis showed the level of persisting disability to depend principally on measures in the psychosocial domain" (p. 722). In a very large sample prospective study at the Boeing aircraft company, Bigos et al. (1991) found that, in addition to a history of recurrent back pain, work perceptions and a psychological test scale were most predictive for the new onset of back pain complaints in uninjured workers.

Important to note is that the issue of psychological and psychosocial factors operating to affect a patient's physical complaints and presentation is a rather ubiquitous one, whether it involves cause, effect, or a synergistic relationship. This is not to say that psychological and psychosocial factors carry the lion's share of the variance in all cases; a brain tumor interfering with the visual pathways causing blindness is hardly "psychological" (discounting any depressive disturbance secondary to the loss of sight for now). However, many common physical symptoms, including pain, have been shown to be rather closely associated with psychological and psychosocial factors. The research to date suggests that the more likely error is to underdiagnose rather than to overdiagnose such factors in medical patients.

As noted in the previous discussion, this phenomenon is not unique to workers' compensation; nor is this arena immune to its presence. Neither is it suggested that such a lack of correspondence of patient complaints to objective physical (or psychological) pathology is necessarily monetarily driven; in the primary care studies that would not generally appear to be the case. Notably, however, there are obvious potential financial incentives that operate within the workers' compensation system (Hadler, 1995; Hadler, Carey, Garrett, & the North Carolina Back Pain Project, 1995) and tort compensation system (Cassidy et al., 2000), and this has been demonstrated to be a factor with at least some patients.

Despite the more typical lack of attention and perhaps ambivalence toward assessment and treatment of such nonmedical or nonsurgical factors, the ambiguity (manifested by medical and surgical factors frequently leaving much of the variance in symptoms unaccounted for) itself merits critical appraisal of patient complaints in any context, but particularly so when potential psychosocial factors and motivations can reasonably be determined to have entered into the fray and, therefore, need to be ruled out to assure appropriate assessment, treatment, and management and avoiding unnecessary and/or inappropriate medical and/or surgical treatments.

Taking the issue of pain as an example, a common focus in the workers' compensation arena, Turk and Nash (1996) note that the evidence of one-to-one correspondence of physiologic factors and pain is tenuous and challenge the heuristic robustness of the traditional "sensory-physiologic model" of pain. They note that:

> [a] Patients with objectively determined, equivalent degrees and types of tissue pathology vary widely in their reports of pain severity. [b] Asymptomatic individuals often reveal objective radiographic evidence of structural abnormalities. [c] Patients with minimal objective physical pathology often complain of intense pain. [d] Surgical procedures designed to inhibit symptoms by severing neurologic pathways believed to be subserving the reported pain may fail to alleviate pain. [e] Patients with objectively equivalent degrees of tissue pathology and treated with identical interventions often respond in widely disparate ways. [f] Physical impairment, physical functioning, pain report, disability, and response to rehabilitation appear to be only modestly correlated. (p. 324)

Similarly, the head injury literature, particularly regarding the mild end of the continuum, is notable for (a) vastly different subjective complaint rates following injury and abating of such complaints over recovery in different subject and context samples (e.g., compensation or litigating samples [Rohling, Allen, & Green, 2002] vs. athletic samples [Bleiberg et al., 2004; Iverson, 2005]); (b) less than robust correspondence of the objective severity of the injury with the number, severity, and persistence of expected and unexpected complaints (Larrabee, 1990); (c) positive radiologic findings in asymptomatic individuals (Katzman, Dagher, & Patronas, 1999); and (d) poor correspondence of the severity of the injury with neuropsychological testing unless invalid profiles are eliminated with response bias testing (Green, Rohling, & Lees-Haley, 2001).

The scientific literature indicates that for no small number of patients with chronic medical disease or frequently recurring illness, factors other than (solely) the physiologic can and do operate to synergistically worsen (or improve) a patient's clinical presentation. Of course, there can be many factors such as premorbid psychiatric disorder (e.g., depression) lowering the threshold for pain and symptom complaints, family stress, a history of psychological trauma, and certain personality styles where more active coping is impeded. With a work injury, those factors remain, and in addition there are issues of fault, felt employer support or lack thereof, fear of navigating the future injured or disabled, problematic relationships with different doctors sometimes, and so forth.

For injured workers, there is also the issue of monetary compensation. Most would probably agree that societal support is both necessary and fair for those who truly cannot work owing to injury. The issue, of course, is validly determining who is truly impaired past the threshold of precluding work activity. While it would most certainly be unfair to a priori conclude that monetary compensation is a factor substantially impacting all claimants, studies indicate that it is a factor for some patients (Cassidy et al., 2000; Hadler, 1995; Hadler et al., 1995; Rohling, Binder, & Langhinrichsen-Rohling, 1995), and this effect across patient samples appears, indeed, to be rather substantial. Although it is no simple task to be able to tease apart patients whose manifestation of illness or injury is more directly and less directly related to that illness or injury, it is crucial to do so, particularly in the context of workers' compensation, where treatment and disposition are limited to that which is specific and directly related to the work injury. Again, given that symptoms do not necessarily reliably correlate with objective physiologic markers of injury and that objective physiologic markers of injury do not necessarily reliably correlate with impairment and associated disability, a method is needed to assist in determining the presence of response bias in patient verbal complaints and overt clinical presentation if such exists. Whereas negative findings with such a method would not "prove" a patient's claim, it potentially can eliminate likely invalid claims and raise the level of confidence in a patient's claim when there is a lack of evidence of response bias.

The Problem With Symptoms

As indicated, physical complaints not infrequently have psychological or psychosocial complications. Physical complaints (e.g., pain) and symptoms do not necessarily reflect the entirety of physiologic aberration or functional limitation from such. For that matter, psychological complaints cannot be presumed necessarily directly associated with physical complaints or even reported stressful circumstances (such as in the context of a "traumatic" accident). For psychological complaints, the typical diagnostic endeavor is largely associated with eliciting symptoms as there are few objective signs or reliable biologic markers of psychological or psychiatric dysfunction. However, many of those symptoms are rather ubiquitously experienced, well known, or easily coached. Although there are clinical interviewing methods that, for example, look for objective evidence such as whether or not claimed symptoms match observed behavior, whether symptom constellations are consistent with known psychiatric groups, and whether patients endorse atypical or preposterous symptoms (Hall & Pritchard, 1996; Rogers, Bagby, & Dickens, 1992; Rogers & Resnick, 1988), the literature (Ziskin, 1981) generally indicates rather poor ability by clinicians to reliably determine who may be exaggerating or even faking, particularly when relying solely on interview methods. This is not simply limited to the psychological/psychiatric interview. Studies (Ekman, 1996; Ekman & O'Sullivan, 1991) indicate that other professions are similarly handicapped and, while some might be somewhat better than others, there is no profession that has been demonstrated to consistently detect and distinguish honesty from deception. Although symptoms are not unimportant, they are not sufficient as they can mislead as well as lead.

I will focus on the issue of mild head injury and postconcussive type complaints, not an atypical clinical presentation in workers' compensation, as an exemplar.

Of 538 consecutively admitted emergency room patients with mild head injury (e.g., with loss of consciousness of 0 to 20 minutes and a Glasgow Coma Scale rating of 13–15), Rimel, Giordani, Barth, Boll, and Jane (1981) were able to examine 424 at 3 months postinjury and found that 78% complained of headache, 59% complained of memory problems, 15% complained of a change in transportation, and 14% complained of difficulty with household chores. Thirty-four percent of those employed at the time of their injury were not working. Only 16% had no complaints. Despite normal neurologic exams, most of 69 patients undergoing neuropsychological testing evinced results suggestive of impairment in various neuropsychological domains. At first glance, these would be worrisome if not ominous findings. However, there was no control group with which to compare complaints types and frequencies and no response bias testing of the neuropsychologically tested patients.

Using a symptom checklist to evaluate for complaints, Lees-Haley and Brown (1993) evaluated 170 claimants filing claims for emotional distress or industrial stress. Claimants with head injuries, toxic exposure, and other factors that could potentially directly impact brain function were excluded. They ultimately used 50 primary care patients as medical controls. (They were unable to find a similar number of mild head injury patients in a clinic in their area who were not litigating.) They found generally higher levels of symptom complaints among the claimants and argued that such a level of symptom complaints merited "methods for differentiating styles of complaint...for distinguishing symptoms of a specific injury from base rates" (p. 208). In other words, the remarkably elevated rate of symptoms frequently attributed to brain injury reported by claimants excluded for brain injury raises no small question regarding their cause. An important and alternative conclusion to their results is that the base rate of endorsement by the medical control group would make clinically distinguishing these groups by their subjective complaints (e.g., anxiety or nervousness 93% vs. 54%, sleep disturbance 92% vs. 52%, headache 88% vs. 62%, concentration problems 78% vs. 26%, memory problems 53% vs. 20%, word finding problems 34% vs. 20%) problematic at the individual level. And this is not even considering the issue of the veracity of the symptom complaints and concomitant behavioral deficits demonstrated.

Continuing research on this issue, Fox, Lees-Haley, Earnest, and Dolezal-Wood (1995) evaluated 1,116 subjects (1,107 when nine invalid protocols were eliminated) from a California HMO. Four hundred patients were seeking outpatient psychotherapy (OP), 104 were neurological patients (NP), 124 were family practice patients (FP), 192 were internal medicine patients (IM), and 296 were patients undergoing initial routine evaluation to join an HMO (RE). The method of the study involved a symptom checklist with instruction to endorse symptoms that have been present in the past 2 years. Notably, of the NP group, only one endorsed any history of loss of consciousness. Also relevant for this discussion is that the RE group could most logically be presumed to be motivated to be relatively conservative in symptom endorsement, given the context of their examination.

Symptom reports, at least for the presence or absence of a symptom or group of symptoms commonly associated with mild head injury and postconcussive syndrome, are shown to be rather ubiquitous and poorly distinguishing between groups. For example, for the OP, NP, FP, IM, and RE groups, respectively, headache was reported quite commonly (52% vs. 49% vs. 50% vs. 38% vs. 43%) as were memory problems (31% vs. 36% vs. 33% vs. 23% vs. 18%) and dizziness (30% vs. 30% vs. 27% vs. 24% vs. 24%). Regrouping the patients into categories of a history of being knocked unconscious (25), bumped on the head (82), involved in a lawsuit (75), or none of these conditions (940) revealed, respectively, complaints of, for example, headache (52% vs. 72% vs. 53% vs. 44%), memory problems (68% vs. 46% vs. 43% vs. 23%), and dizziness (60% vs. 46% vs. 23% vs. 25%), at levels that occur frequently and are certainly not particularly discriminating at a clinical level.

Indeed, Iverson and McCracken (1997) evaluated 170 chronic pain patients without mild head injury or involvement in workers' compensation or litigation. Sleep problems (83%), fatigue (76.5%), and irritability (73%) were noted to be symptoms with the highest rates of endorsement. However, cognitive complaints involving memory problems (29%), difficulty maintaining attention (18%), and concentration problems (16.5%) were also notable. More to the point, 42% of the pain patients had one or more cognitive symptoms, and 80.6% reported three or more noncognitive symptoms traditionally associated with mild head injury and postconcussive syndrome. Of the 42% of pain patients with one or more cognitive symptoms, 94.4% reported three or more noncognitive symptoms involving *DSM-IV* (APA, 1994) criteria for postconcussional disorder. Therefore, 39% of the chronic pain sample met criteria (barring an actual head injury) for postconcussional disorder.

In a follow up study, Iverson, King, Scott, and Adams (2001) evaluated workers' compensation chronic pain patients (WCCP), nonworkers' compensation patients who were candidates for spinal cord stimulators (NWCSCS), litigating head injury patients (LHI), and nonlitigating head injury patients (NLHI) with 20 subjects in each group. They found the WCCP group to evince four times the number of cognitive symptoms as the NWCSCS patients, despite the latter probably being more severe patients by virtue of the nature of their referral for such an invasive procedure. Additionally, the WCCP, LHI, and NLHI groups were commensurate with regard to cognitive complaints. The caveat to clinicians is that "one should not assume that self-reported cognitive problems are indicative of, or specific to, acquired brain injury" (p. 28).

Mittenberg, DiGiulio, Perrin, and Bass (1992) evaluated, an average of 1.7 years post injury, 100 consecutively clinic referred mild head injury patients (with a mean loss of consciousness of 23 minutes; 27 subjects with no loss of consciousness) for postconcussive complaints and 223 nonmedical control subjects. They used a 30-item symptom checklist of common postconcussion complaints. The patient group was instructed to endorse symptoms experienced after the injury and then, in retrospect, before the injury. The control group was instructed to endorse current symptoms and then symptoms imagined if they were to evince a mild head injury. Twenty-two of 30 symptoms did not differ between the control group's imagined profile of symptoms and the mild head injury group's reported profile of symptoms. That is not particularly exiting news; the control group may just have been accurate in their knowledge and prediction of mild head injury symptoms. What was revealing and quite interesting, however, was that the mild head injury group, when reporting preinjury symptoms, endorsed 21 of 30 symptoms at a lower rate compared with the control group who were reporting their current (noninjury related) symptoms. Analysis revealed no observed relationship between reported symptom frequencies and demographics for patients versus controls. Nor was there any observed relationship between patients' number of postconcussive symptoms and length of loss of consciousness, time since injury, type of injury, age, gender, or occupational status. Mittenberg et al. (1992) suggested that anticipation of symptoms plays a role in postconcussive syndrome. It was hypothesized that patients may tend to reattribute benign emotional, physiologic, and memory symptoms to mild head injury, which itself may activate typical symptom expectancies when such an injury occurs. Mild head injury is stressful and believed to induce autonomic and emotional arousal. The patient's symptom expectancies bias selective attention to their internal state. Attentional bias and arousal, in turn, augment symptom perception, which then elicits additional autonomic and emotional responding, in vicious circle fashion, reinforcing misattributed expectations. Mittenberg et al. note that the diminished rate of persistent postconcussion syndrome in children and athletes supports this notion. They contend that the so-called medical student disease phenomena prevalence rate of approximately 70% is also supportive of the notion of expectancies playing a role.

This is not to say that evaluation of symptoms is irrelevant; hardly so. Evaluating for the typicality and atypicality of symptoms during the interview is necessary; it is simply not sufficient in many cases. Symptom complaints, especially associated with workers' compensation patients or litigants, are frequently poorly discriminatory relative to other various patient and nonpatient groups.

Psychosocial Issues and Workers' Compensation:
Summary and Conclusions
Just as with many individuals with chronic illness outside of the workers' compensation arena, injured workers with chronic conditions frequently have at least some degree of psychological distress. Contending with recovery from actual serious injury and/or surgery, pain that is not infrequently chronic, actual or threatened (e.g., based upon physical capacity or restrictions) job loss, diminished finances, system issues involving sometimes supportive and sometimes adversarial interactions with case managers, carriers, and doctors, and so forth impinge upon workers' compensation patients more times than not. As noted previously, psychosocial factors frequently complicate the outcome of chronic medical patients and, given the additional stress-related factors associated with being within the workers' compensation system, injured workers are at particular risk. There is a tendency, in my experience, with many carriers to avoid "going there," that is, acknowledging, evaluating, and treating such psychosocial factors even when overt psychological symptom complaints or signs are present. Psychology and psychiatry tend to be viewed as a black hole for the patient frequently owing to skepticism regarding the objectivity of evaluation and the efficacy of treatment particularly if there is suspicion that the patient is attempting to "pad" his or her physical complaints by "playing the psychiatric card." While this has, in part, been brought on by psychology and psychiatry themselves owing to a social-political role of being a "helper," which is an issue unto itself that will not be discussed further here, it is crucial to understand that psychosocial factors operate to impact a case, whether or not they are acknowledged by the carrier, case managers, doctors, or even the patient. Experience in the workers' compensation arena reveals that some chronic pain patients with little objective evidence of spine pathology tend to shift complaints over to the psychological arena. Although not all patients evidence response bias, exaggeration of physical, emotional, and cognitive complaints is no small problem in the workers' compensation arena. Although not all injured workers wish to "get on the dole," not all wish to return

to work. If psychosocial issues are not evaluated and managed, they will, ultimately, manage the case. Having a method that improves the ability to detect such both supports legitimate patient treatment needs and assists in the disposition of those who amplify symptoms for whatever reason.

PSYCHOLOGICAL AND NEUROPSYCHOLOGICAL EVALUATION PRELIMINARIES

In medicine and surgery, objective tests (e.g., imaging, electrodiagnostic studies) are used to assist in ruling out medical/surgical pathology and in evaluation of symptom magnification. Psychiatric evaluation and diagnosis, however, is largely based upon a patient's subjective complaints, the veracity of which is very much in question in workers' compensation cases. Objective data such as unobtrusive surveillance to determine whether or not a patient's subjective report is commensurate with his or her actual functioning can assist tremendously; however, it is most frequently unavailable. By the time it is, there is already a high index of suspicion of exaggeration or malingering that triggers the relatively expensive and time-intensive process that frequently is lacking in providing an adequate and representative true sample of patient behavior and so tends, in practice, to be used more to refute a patient's claim than to support it.

For psychologists, appropriate psychological and/or neuropsychological testing adds objectivity to the otherwise perilously subjective process of evaluation of psychological/psychiatric, pain, and cognitive claims. A patient's actual clinical status may be exactly as stated in his or her self-report; or it may not. Although clinical acumen and experience is not unimportant (Garb, 1989), and clinical judgment is frequently inevitable and necessary (Kleinmuntz, 1990), there are weaknesses to clinical judgment (Garb & Schramke, 1996). There is a long history in psychology since Meehl (1954, 1957) argued for the fallibility of the "head" (i.e., clinical prediction) relative to the more robust "formula" (i.e., statistical prediction) approach. Whereas some (Dawes, Faust, & Meehl, 1989) make this argument rather vehemently, others (Garb, 1989; Garb & Schramke, 1996; Kleinmuntz, 1990) acknowledge the issue, counter that judgment is not always quite so suspect, note that the realities of clinical practice necessitate both, and counter that there are methods to decrease the susceptibility of cognitive and judgment errors.

Psychological tests are correlated with prognosis and eventual return to work (or not) in pain patients (Gatchel & Epker, 1999). Also important is the fact that psychological and neuropsychological tests are very useful for evaluating response bias of various symptom complaints including psychological distress (Greiffenstein, Baker, Axelrod, Peck, & Gervais, 2004; Rogers, Sewell, & Salekin, 1994), cognitive dysfunction (Gervais et al., 2004; Lees-Haley, Iverson, Lange, Fox, & Allen, 2002), and pain-related impairment (Bianchini, Greve, & Glynn, 2005; Larrabee, 2003a; Meyers, Millis, & Volkert, 2002). Although some may argue that the use of tests to evaluate for response bias actually reveals bias on the part of the examiner, or even a predatorial approach to the patient, it can also be argued that the neglect of such procedures reveals examiner bias in the opposite direction. Additionally, the literature is quite clear that patients sometimes over-report symptoms (Green, 2001; Sumanti, Boone, Savodnik, & Gorsuch, 2006) and under-report them for that matter (Baer & Miller, 2002), and if this is not formally assessed the veracity of their complaints (or their minimization or absence) remains in question. In my experience, there is a relatively small but notable group of injured workers who are reluctant to report psychological symptoms such as those involving depression or anxiety for fear of presenting as weak or crazy or drawing attention away from their physical complaints. The use of tests that can assess for response bias is eminently fair; it can prompt confidence or cast doubt in a patient's symptom complaints. Not infrequently, the workers' compensation system itself tends to be rather skeptical of patient complaints, both physical and psychological, and psychometric evidence of cooperation and openness on self-report psychological inventories and intact effort on *effort tests* (i.e., cognitive response bias tests) bolsters the credence of the patient's symptom complaints. The sword cuts both ways.

Psychological and Neuropsychological Tests

What is a psychological test (of which a neuropsychological test is a subset)? Anastasi (1982) defines this as "essentially an *objective* and *standardized measure* of a *sample* of *behavior* [italics added]" (p. 22). It is objective insofar as it remains independent of observer bias. Whether I believe all patients are entirely accurate and honest in their presentation or that all patients are malingerers has no impact on the test results as long as standardized procedures are followed. By being standardized, the procedures of administration and scoring are uniform; explicit instructions guide all examiners to follow exactly the same procedures. For example, oral instructions and orally administered items are all given to the patient verbatim. Tests measure insofar as they quantify some behavior or related phenomena. That could involve recalling a brief story recited to the patient, hand speed and dexterity, or endorsing symptoms on a self-report inventory with the latter measuring the patient's endorsement or nonendorsement of an item, not whether the patient actually has a particular symptom, which is a subjective experience and not directly observable (vs. the report of a symptom, which is). Tests by necessity are geared toward sampling a representative and relevant set or subset of behavioral problems for efficiency's sake that allow the drawing of conclusions to a broader arena. For example, a memory test may involve verbal and nonverbal items to be recalled and recognized for some conclusions to be drawn about an individual's ability to function in a work environment that requires recalling verbal orders for parts as well as parts' locations that may change frequently.

Key Psychometric Concepts

If a psychological test, assessing for a specific cognitive ability, is given and, say, the patient obtains 20 items correct out of 40 or endorses 20 symptoms out of 40 on a self-report symptom complaint inventory, that is really all we know, which is not much or typically particularly helpful. Is identifying 20 of 40 items correct on a memory test normal or not? Are 20 symptoms endorsed on a self-report depression inventory indicative of depression or not? Are 20 items correct on a response bias test indicative of poor effort or intact effort? A *raw score* is largely meaningless in the absence of interpretive data. What is required is a clearly defined and uniform frame of reference with which to compare a patient's scores. Enter *normative data*, which represent the test performance of the *standardization sample* (or samples) and provide a benchmark against which to compare and interpret a patient's test performance (or score). Was the patient's memory score closer to the Alzheimer's patient group or to a group of independently living and well-functioning elderly individuals?

But there is a potential glitch here. Normative data need to be *representative*. Such data need to be collected from a group of individuals that includes those similar to the patient who is to be tested. Conversely, psychological tests must be given to individuals who are represented in the normative group. It would not be fair to compare a fifth grader's math score on the Graduate Record Examination with a college senior's score; neither would it likely be productive to compare a college senior's score on a fifth grade normed math test with other fifth graders. Indeed, it would make little sense to administer a college normed test to a fifth grader or a fifth grade normed test to a college senior. But once we have established that our normative group is representative of our patient, the patient's raw score can be referred to the normative data. This may be a nonpatient group (e.g., adult community subjects without any history of head trauma or psychiatric disturbance) or a patient group (e.g., adult head injured patients or psychiatric patients).

Actually, raw scores are typically converted to some relative measure, a *standard score*, to define the patient's position in reference to the standardization sample in uniform terms and to permit comparison against other tests (standard scores), although the latter is done imperfectly if tests involve different normative samples, even if drawn from the same population (e.g., two separate tests with two separate normative bases involving 500 healthy adults from ages 18 to 65 with education from eighth grade to graduate school). A standard score expresses the subject's distance from the mean in standard deviation units, which is a uniform method of describing performance. Each standard deviation unit (or part of one) defines exactly where that patient scored relative to the normative sample(s). So a raw score may represent two standard deviation units above the normative group's mean (e.g., robust performance) or two standard deviation units below the mean (e.g., poor performance). As can be imagined, it is crucial that the patient being tested is represented by the test's normative group for appropriate comparison of their score against the normative base of scores.

The *validity* of a test concerns what the test measures and how well it does so. For example, a memory test needs to be demonstrated to actually assess memory function. It is insufficient to include items on the test, no matter how obvious appearing, and presume that it measures memory. There needs to be an external criterion (e.g., another established memory test) and evidence that it distinguishes patients with different levels of memory ability. Sometimes it is very desirable to construct a test that is very obvious with regard to what it is testing (e.g., a memory test with a subtest instructing a patient to "Listen carefully to this story and repeat it back to me as exactly as possible when I am finished"). Sometimes, for example with self-report personality inventories, it is desirable to make the test or test items more obtuse so that the patient cannot easily determine what the test measures or at least which item groups assess for which behaviors or traits to decrease the chance of manipulation of the test (e.g., a parent in a child custody case wishing to "put his or her best foot forward" on the test or a patient malingering PTSD who is trying to appear maximally distressed). For example, a test to assess for response bias on memory tests, given that memory tests require good effort on the patient's part for confidence in the results as actually representative of his or her ability, should probably not have "Detection of Faked Memory Disorders Test" listed on the materials to which the patient is exposed and probably ought to be constructed to appear to be a memory test apparently representative of other memory tests to which the patient will be exposed. In psychological and neuropsychological testing, validity is the crucial concept. Of course, a valid test can be used for invalid purposes. A test of pull-ups may be a very valid test of upper body muscular endurance but a poor test to determine memory ability. What a test is valid for must be determined empirically. Empirical support is what is ultimately required to determine if a test measures what it purports to measure.

The *reliability* of a test concerns the consistency and stability of scores. This is necessary but not sufficient for validity. An intelligence test ought to result in a similar score if given to the same person twice, a week apart. If a particular intelligence test validly measures intelligence, such retest scores at brief intervals ought to be quite similar (barring error variance, practice effects, etc.). If the test is valid, it ought to be reliable; while reliability determines the upper limit of validity, validity is what is ultimately crucial. The converse, however, is not necessarily true. A broken scale may quite reliably read out 78 lbs. for all who stand on it. However, it is not validly measuring weight.

No test is perfect, psychological, neuropsychological, or otherwise. This is not an issue limited to psychology or neuropsychology but involves any field that uses tests to measure some phenomena. All tests are not equal, and some tests are better than others. If a test is being utilized for a particular purpose, it is crucial that one can have confidence in its results. For many years, the issues of *sensitivity* and *specificity* have been used to describe the utility of a test, particularly in psychology and neuropsychology. Using impaired brain damaged subjects as an example, the sensitivity of "Salamone's Test of Brain Damage" involves the number of actually impaired subjects with an abnormal score divided by the number of impaired subjects (i.e., valid acceptances of a positive test result [or true positives]) in the context of already knowing the outcome. The test's specificity involves the number of nonimpaired subjects with normal score divided by the number of nonimpaired subjects (i.e., valid rejection of a negative test result [or true negatives]) in the context of already knowing the outcome. In research settings, it is frequently known which subjects are, for example, brain damaged and which are not as subjects are placed in brain damaged and normal (or other medical) groups based upon other (than the test at issue) external criteria. However, already knowing the outcome (i.e., patient condition) is not the typical situation in clinical assessment. You are typically using the test results to predict whether or not, continuing with our example, a patient with an as yet undetermined clinical status, has cognitive impairment from brain damage. Enter *positive predictive power*. This involves the probability of a positive test result correctly identifying a patient, for example, with brain damage when we do not initially know to which group (non-brain-damaged or brain damaged) the patient belongs. Conversely, *negative predictive power* involves the probability of a negative test result correctly identifying a non-brain-damaged patient when we do not initially know to which group the patient belongs. The rub with this in practical terms is that both positive and negative predictive power are influenced by the *base rate*, that is, the current population prevalence of the phenomena of interest. And this becomes a particular issue and problem as the base rate moves increasingly away from 50%, either lower or higher but of particular relevance with regard to the clinical endeavor, which not infrequently involves the issue of diagnosis or detection of conditions with ostensibly low base rates (Gouvier, 1999). Although there are calculations beyond the scope of this chapter, a simple example will help at least make the concept clear with a fictitious example involving the "Honest Politician Detector Test." Let's presume the Honest Politician Detector Test has a sensitivity of 99% and a specificity of 99%. Not perfect but not bad. Let us further presume that the base rate of honest politicians is low, 1 in 1000. While it is tempting to think that our test would reliably identify honest politicians, with the base rate of honest politicians being so low, the positive predictive power is actually quite poor owing to the interaction of the test's sensitivity/specificity and the low base rate (of honest politicians). While the one politician for every thousand tested may be identified as honest, there would be so many more dishonest politicians misidentified as honest, such that determining who is who becomes futile based on the test results alone. In reality, for better or worse, judgment enters in here; this is no small dilemma. What is crucial to understand is that the error rate increases as the base rate diverges from 50%. A low base rate translates into decreasing positive predictive power and increases negative predictive power and increased rate of false positive errors. A high base rate translates into increasing positive predictive power and decreases negative predictive power and increased false negative errors. In other words, the base rate affects the utility of a test—even a valid test. These statistical realities affect all tests, not simply psychological and neuropsychological tests.

Actually, while some clinical disorders are of very low prevalence in the general population, it is not necessarily the case with the patient who comes to the examiner's door. For example, for the patient in his early to mid-50s who comes in for neuropsychological evaluation for dementia, a diagnosis of Alzheimer's disease might appear rather perilous (with regard to increased false positive error risk) when the prevalence is very low (41.2 per 100,000) before age 61 (Campion et al., 1999). However, this patient is not a random pick out of many community-dwelling individuals, rather, one who is observed to have trouble in his business, forgetfulness at home, difficulty organizing his activity, and so forth, which precipitated the evaluation in the first place. This is a real patient, autopsy confirmed some 20 years later. Despite the low base rate in the general population, valid diagnosis at the time of exam was possible.

The base rate issue, or problem, presumes random sampling and prevalence of a disorder or phenomenon can vary markedly with regard to the setting of the exam (S. R. Millis, personal communication, October 30, 2006). Some method skeptic types (e.g., Faust, Ziskin, & Heirs, 1991; Ziskin, 1981) seem to ignore this. And with regard to the issue of response bias, base rates of such in the medicolegal arena have been demonstrated to range from the teens (Sweet, 1999) to over 30% (Greiffenstein, Baker, & Gola, 1994; Larrabee, 2000) to over 40% (Gervais, Green, Allen, & Iverson, 2001; Richman et al., 2006). Therefore, the base rates of response bias, specifically referring to the medicolegal arena (including workers' compensation), are favorable for assessment, presuming tests of sufficient sensitivity and specificity. Fortunately, many clinical disorders and syndromes, for example, depressive disorders in chronic pain patients and memory dysfunction in moderately brain injured patients, do not occur at such low base rates as to cause serious problems for assessment. Given that the base rate of response bias is substantial in the medicolegal arena, this, in practical terms, buffers the issue of increased false negative errors of disorders with very high base rates in the general population.

The method skeptic might argue then that if actuarial prediction with tests has been demonstrated to be superior to clinical judgment in the research setting, it is not possible to validly diagnose low or high base rate disorders or syndromes, if such were the case within the context of the medicolegal arena, when the superior method itself may have a very worrisome error rate. After interviewing a medical inpatient, a psychological test (with medical patients as part of its normative base) administered suggested panic attacks and/or agoraphobia despite my interview failing to suggest an anxiety disorder. This patient's history of gastrointestinal distress and associated diarrhea inclined him to respond to the test items in a manner similar to panic disordered and agoraphobic patients, which I discovered in reinterviewing him based upon the results of psychological testing. Yes, judgment is fallible; that does not excuse us from using it. Real-world assessment will never eliminate clinical judgment totally, nor would that be desirable. At that point tests, not doctors, would be all that are required. When a patient has a disorder or syndrome, even if it occurs at a low base rate, he or she has the disorder or syndrome regardless of what any test suggests. The issue is the test and statistics interface. At that juncture human judgment comes into play even if imperfect. Of course, judgment is no more fallible in the clinical endeavor than in the administrative (law) endeavor.

It is more common for recently published tests to include data on the positive and negative predictive power of a test under various base rate conditions. Newer studies (e.g., Millis & Volinsky, 2001) also describe the diagnostic utility of tests in terms of effect sizes (i.e., standard deviation units separating groups), receiver operating characteristic curves (i.e., a graphic plot of true positive and false positives with the proportional area under the curve being assigned a numerical value defining the test's discriminability), and likelihood ratios (i.e., the incremental likelihood of a patient, with a positive test result, having a disorder relative to a patient with a negative test result), the latter of which are commonly utilized in medical research.

Why Use a Psychological or Neuropsychological Test?
The use of a psychological or neuropsychological test, in addition to an interview and record review, allows improved evaluation based upon the addition of objective test data regarding the patient's psychological or neuropsychological clinical status that improves precision of assessment. As noted, the use of psychometrics, with standardized and normed tests, allows the use of statistical and actuarial data to aid in decision making. The use of such procedures can assist in identifying and ruling out clinical problems such as mood or anxiety disorders or impairment from brain injury. Additionally, there are tests that assist in assessing the veracity of a patient's subjective psychological, cognitive, and pain complaints. Being able to determine whether a patient tends to magnify or minimize psychological distress or pain complaints or is performing with intact effort or not on cognitive testing is crucial for assessment, treatment, and administrative disposition of a case. Notably, psychological and neuropsychological tests, used for their intended purposes and with appropriate groups, compare very favorably with various medical tests (Meyer et al., 2001, 2002).

Context Matters: The Scaffolding and Compass for the Exam
At the beginning of the chapter, I suggested the importance of objective psychological and neuropsychological testing in evaluation of psychological, cognitive, and pain claims in the workers' compensation area. I noted research setting studies indicating the general superiority of such objective methods to guide actuarial style decision making. I also noted studies indicating that clinical judgment has its place and is, ultimately, an unavoidable part of the clinical assessment process. Tests do not assess or diagnose; clinicians do. The purpose of tests is to provide objective data to guide assessment and diagnosis. Additionally, even over and above the issue of base rates, context matters in the clinical evaluation of a workers' compensation patient.

Context questions to be asked include the following: (a) Was there an actual injury or traumatic event? (b) How severe was it according to objective criteria? (c) Did it cause the physical (e.g., associated with alleged pain) or psychological injury? (d) Are the claimed symptoms and problems consistent with the documented injury? (e) Has the history of symptoms and problems been consistent since the injury? (f) Is the patient postinjury history consistent with the scientific literature on recovery? (g) Are there intervening physical or psychological events impacting the patient's clinical status and symptoms? (h) Is there a premorbid or concurrent history of relevant injury, stress, or psychopathology? (i) What was the premorbid level of relevant abilities if loss of functioning (e.g., cognitive) is alleged? (j) Is there adequate supportive collateral information for the patient's claims of clinical disorder or syndrome and any diminution of function alleged associated with such? Context-related questions and issues, although outside of the realm of testing, remain imperative to address in the assessment process (Millis & Volinsky, 2001).

An objective history, for example, involving pre- and postaccident medical records, accident reports, and police reports and subjective history (i.e., patient interview, collateral interviews) are necessary data points despite the possibility of being misled by any or all of them. The notion that the use of such may run the risk of errors in judgment (Faust et al., 1991; Ziskin, 1981) merits caution (Borum, Otto, & Golding, 1993; Garb, 1998), not diagnostic or evaluative nihilism. A patient or claimant comes to the examiner in a particular context. Proper and rational interpretation of psychological and neuropsychological tests needs to account for that context (else irritable bowel patients may be misdiagnosed with panic disorder and/or agoraphobia owing to answering test items in a manner consistent with avoiding leaving the home and distancing themselves from a bathroom). This is no different than with medical diagnostic tests. For example, a neurosurgeon will likely be more concerned (e.g., in terms of considering surgical intervention) about an apparent disk herniation and spinal nerve root impingement on a radiologic scan when it is associated with symptom complaints (e.g., pain or paresthesias in a characteristic distribution) and signs (e.g., abnormal reflexes) consistent with the character and location of the particular disrupted disk.

Take Home Points

As noted, psychosocial factors can impact the expression of ostensibly physical or medical disease or distress. This is not limited to the workers' compensation arena. However, the base rate of different forms of response bias seems to vary at least with regard to some contexts. For example, in child custody evaluation and preemployment contexts there tend to be higher rates of defensiveness, that is, minimizing or denying symptoms or even typical faults and frailties (Rogers & Resnick, 1988). Conversely, misattribution, exaggeration, and fabrication of symptoms and clinical presentation, that is, the symptom magnification base rates, are quite elevated in workers' compensation cases (Sumanti et al., 2006). Adding of psychometric studies increases the objectivity and accuracy of the assessment of relevant and crucial issues involving, for example, psychiatric, pain, and cognitive complaints and response bias, which occurs in no insignificant percentage of workers' compensation patients. Without an objective and valid method to evaluate response bias to assist in determining which patients have legitimate psychological or cognitive dysfunction and to what level and with what likely impact on functioning, all cases are suspect, at least from the carrier's perspective, which only perpetuates his or her reluctance to approve care for all such ostensibly nebulous claims. Such a method serves legitimate patients well by assisting in substantiating their clinical claims and supporting their need for associated treatment and restrictions.

That being said, and this is a crucial point, while response bias is not uncommon, its detection only reveals symptom magnification (for this example, but it could also be minimization) and not necessarily, in and of itself, the particular motivation (e.g., sick role vs. monetary or other such external incentives) for such, that is, if the patient has a somatoform disorder, has a factitious disorder, or is malingering. Response bias, particularly in reference to symptom magnification or exaggeration, is not synonymous with malingering, which involves specific motivations (e.g., for certain external incentives such as financial compensation or avoiding legal prosecution (per *DSM-IV-TR*, APA, 2000). A response bias measure can reveal many levels of exaggeration or even fabrication, possibly volition in some circumstances (e.g., below chance performance on symptom validity testing), but not, in and of itself, the specific motivation to do so. Pankratz & Erickson (1990) argue that below chance performance indicates intent and malingering, and Slick, Sherman, and Iverson (1999) suggest that such "is closest to an evidentiary 'gold standard' for malingering" (p. 551). However, the *intent* to which below chance performance on symptom validity testing refers is the direction and perhaps vigor of effort, not the specific motivation(s) driving it. (This is particularly true in distinguishing a factitious disorder from malingering, where there is intent to produce false symptoms for both, but the former's motivation is pathological and the latter's is not.) Such requires information in addition to the response bias testing results, as well as clinical judgment as to a patient's motivation, which is ultimately decided by the administrative law judge. Motivation(s) associated with clinical disorders is most certainly within the purview of a psychologist, being mindful that malingering is not actually a clinical disorder but a set of behaviors with particular motivations that is not necessarily associated with psychopathology. As Gorman (1993) aptly notes, "malingering is an act, and is not a physical or mental disease or disorder. Not being a disorder, it is not diagnosed, but instead is detected" (p. 139). He goes on to argue that "being the simulation or exaggeration of disease, malingering is often best detected by a physician" (p. 139). Therefore, although the practicality of clinical practice in the workers' compensation arena thrusts this issue upon doctors, it is ultimately an administrative determination (albeit with input from the doctor), not a clinical one.

CATEGORIES OF FUNCTIONAL DISORDERS

There are three main categories of *functional* disorders, that is, disorders with psychosocial concomitants significantly impacting the expression of the disorder. I am including malingering in this discussion for parsimony's sake as it is most commonly included as a diagnosis despite the caveat noted in the previous discussion. Of course, *DSM-IV-TR* (APA, 2000) lists malingering under the section "Other Conditions That May Be a Focus of Clinical Attention" rather than under any of the "Disorders" sections.

DSM-IV-TR (APA, 2000) notes that somatoform disorders involve physical symptoms that are not fully attributable to a medical condition and that are not intentionally produced. Factitious disorders involve physical or psychological symptoms that are volitionally produced or exaggerated with the motivation being to assume a sick role. Malingering involves the intentional production of false or grossly exaggerated physical or psychological symptoms motivated by external incentives typically involving seeking something reinforcing (e.g., financial compensation) or avoiding something punishing (e.g., prison). A factitious disorder typically involves actual illness or injury, which is intentionally (but surreptitiously) self-inflicted, and the motivation is social, that is, to assume a sick role. So although there is volition in both a factitious disorder and malingering, and both are "faking" or constructing medical or psychological circumstances for a specific intent or aim, the former is considered psychopathologic and involves a psychiatric disorder; the latter does not and is simply viewed as fraud.

A Critical and Realistic Appraisal of the "M" Word
That being said, while *DSM-IV-TR* (APA, 2000) is commonly cited as the definition of malingering by virtue of being in the official diagnostic nomenclature for psychiatric disorders, it is actually rather lacking, and more robust and precise definitions exist (Slick et al., 1999).

Additionally, experience over the years in the workers' compensation arena has convincingly demonstrated to me that these circumstances yield multiple and complex motivations and pressures, that may and often do change over time, to which the patient responds. While there is a tendency to think of all such patients as dirty rotten scoundrels (and some may be), many patients are simply attempting to survive in a difficult, challenging, and not infrequently adversarial system. A coal miner, with no other work experience, in a small coal town with few other jobs has his back against the wall if he has a back injury where he believes, despite what his neurosurgeon tells him, he will not be able to return to his job or may be terminated (perhaps for some "other" reason) upon return. Claiming he cannot work may be malingering at this point. Add to that a family history of disability, feeling discouraged that they can no longer support their family, perhaps a history of childhood abuse or prior psychological trauma resulting in a resurgence of long dormant feelings of helplessness, family stress associated with the reduced finances, and so forth, and motivations become more complex and murky.

Deception is ubiquitous in human interactions for both the benefit and detriment of relationships. Sometimes deception involves making ourselves look better than we, in fact, are; sometimes it involves making ourselves look worse than we, in fact, are. There can be a single or multiple reasons for both. As noted, malingering is detected (albeit imperfectly), not diagnosed; it is not a mental disorder. It can occur in the context of a mental disorder (e.g., a schizophrenic patient faking a psychotic episode at the time of being caught for a murder in attempt to obtain commitment to a treatment facility rather than prison) or not (e.g., an individual claiming PTSD who does not actually have such symptoms, for purposes of civil litigation against a bank, following the witnessing of a bank robbery there, or a patient who was involved in a low-speed motor vehicle accident who is falsely claiming neck pain and associated physical dysfunction and limitation). Although *DSM-IV-TR* (APA, 2000) suggests that antisocial personality disorder may increase the index of suspicion of malingering, there is no evidence in the literature of which I am aware that indicates that most exaggeration, response bias, malingering, and so forth is done by individuals with antisocial personality disorder. Indeed, my experience suggests quite the opposite.

Malingering is not a disorder or trait. It is not a type of person. It is a behavior or a set of behaviors with specific intentions and goals. It is fairly common insofar as many excuses people make to avoid doing something are tainted with some degree of malingering (e.g., claiming to have a stomachache to avoid going to the store for your spouse because of the ball game on television) or the like (e.g., claiming other circumstances besides physical or mental symptoms such as "I was having car trouble" to avoid a task). In some instances, malingering is not considered to be malignant but can be adaptive (Rogers, 1997). For example, a nuclear scientist captured by terrorists and forced to design a nuclear bomb may overplay his or her heart condition to slow progress down on their forced labor for admirable reasons, perhaps even at the risk of being discovered and killed.

So malingering is not something intrinsic to an individual (i.e., "a malingerer") but rather represents an interaction (sometimes simple and sometimes complex) between the individual and the individual's circumstances. The difference between an individual who malingers and one who does not seems to me to frequently be a specific circumstance with motivation to do so—not necessarily any particular moral character (at least within the context of the workers' compensation). Just as with the classic ethical dilemma of whether or not it would be justified to steal medicine that you cannot afford for your critically ill child, we all have our limits. In the right circumstances, if push came to shove, we would all likely malinger or at least exaggerate "some." Circumstances in the workers' compensation system can put much pressure on patients to incline them to exaggerate the effects of their injury. That does not make it right, but it does make such behaviors understandable. Obviously, such behaviors need to be assessed.

Just as there are different types of individuals with different levels of education, experience, or savvy in such deception, there are differences in the expression of malingering in terms of the number, grouping, and severity of symptoms claimed. As with any behavior, there are those who are more adept and those who are less adept. Indeed, the effort and egregiousness of malingering is not necessarily tied to the number and/or severity of the symptom complaints or presentation. An unsophisticated individual malingering brain damage after a mild head injury may bungle his or her way through an exam that is poorly studied or prepared for credible complaints and performances and that is ridiculously out of proportion to or inconsistent with the alleged injury. A more sophisticated individual who chooses to malinger in similar circumstances may studiously explore the Internet for information assisting in the presentation of a brain injury and may rehearse such complaints and performances at length, avoiding patently ridiculous complaints, ultimately leading to a more subdued and credible interview and exam presentation. The level of deficit reported or presented is not necessarily synonymous with the effort to malinger if that is the patient's intent. Given that most tests of response bias are actually objectively easy so that getting most of the items correct requires little effort, getting most of them wrong requires little effort as well. The difference is motivation to respond in a particular direction, not the output of effort per se.

A PHILOSOPHICAL APPROACH TO THE EXAM

Psychologists tend to have rather hotly debated discussions with regard to the issue of response bias testing on professional Internet discussion lists. Actually, it seems to me that the more fundamental disagreement among list-members is not response bias testing, per se, but rather one's philosophical stance to the evaluative process, particularly in the workers' compensation and medicolegal arenas. One camp tends to suggest that the other are patient or plaintiff attorney advocates and the other camp suggests their accusers are company or defense attorney advocates. Each side accuses the other of bias and conspiracy. A rational and constructive view of response bias testing, however, is not about bias, per se (e.g., "to catch a malingerer"), but rather about ruling in and out what the patient has and what he or she does not have, clinically and psychosocially, that may affect his or her claims and presentation within the workers' compensation system. Assessment of possible response bias is one component of the exam just as the interview, collateral interview(s), review of medical records, psychological testing, cognitive testing, and so forth are. Bias occurs when anything is systematically ignored or overemphasized.

Colluding with patients is no more admirable than colluding with an insurance company. Within the workers' compensation system, it is not simply an issue of an isolated and insulated doctor-patient relationship. In the workers' compensation system, the relationship is considerably more complex. Ultimately, psychologists need to approach the exam not as helpers but rather umpires (who, unlike their baseball counterparts, of course, do not have the final say) who ought to favor no team. And like umpires, we need to be able to discern and make the call, regardless of what the crowd thinks, who gets on base (i.e., discerning impairment) and who does not (i.e., discerning no impairment). How can an umpire discern a strike if there is no criterion for a ball? Conversely, how can an umpire assess for a ball if there is no criterion for a strike? If we cannot, or choose not, to properly evaluate response bias, we cannot properly evaluate impairment. If some patients are nails and some are screws, we need both hammers and screwdrivers to work with them properly. You would not simply pound a screw with a hammer when a screwdriver is what is required.

It strikes me as ludicrous that response bias testing is maligned by some as nefarious. It can support the call of intact effort, as well as poor effort. It can support the call of open and cooperative reporting of symptoms or exaggeration (or defensiveness/minimization). It is a double-edged sword that can cast doubt or lend credence to patients' claims. That seems to me to be eminently fair to all.

My experience with the workers' compensation system in Virginia, at least, is such that the carriers and defense attorneys can generally accept an exam that supports patients' claims of impairment when they have some reasonable degree of confidence that our methods weed out those who are not legitimate in their presentation. This can make it result in quicker resolution of the case (for the company) and settlement (for the patient). If as psychologists we expect to keep our collective seat at the workers' compensation table, we need to be better perceived as fair and objective. I recall very early in my career, sitting down and talking with an administrative law judge to best understand how to interact with the workers' compensation system, and among other pearls and candid bits of advice he gave me was one regarding a local neurosurgeon who he trusted because [paraphrase] "he says what he thinks and doesn't give a damn about what anybody else thinks [about his opinion]." This has been good, sustaining advice for me in a rather contentious and tumultuous system with many pressures. Objective data regarding both clinical issues and response bias issues are one crucial way of helping to inoculate psychologists from these pressures and possible bias.

What Symptoms Tend to Involve Response Bias?

Patients need to be evaluated for response bias for the very disorders and symptoms they may claim. Commonly this involves various depressive and anxiety-related disorders. Cognitive complaints such as memory and concentration problems are also common, frequently associated with head trauma, pain, or emotional distress. In addition to having a psychological or neuropsychological disorder, the impact of such on a patient's functioning (i.e., impairment) from such requires evaluation for its presence, severity, and possible response bias. As noted previously, the rate of symptom magnification in patients claiming psychiatric, pain, and cognitive symptoms is over 40% in some samples. Recall that research by Green and associates indicates complaints of memory dysfunction are frequently exaggerated in depressed and pain patients.

How Do We Assess Response Bias?

In addition to evaluating the context issues previously noted and a clinical interview, the unique contribution of psychology, in addition to psychometric procedures to evaluate a patient's psychological status, typicality of pain complaints and associated psychological complications, and cognitive function, there are a number of psychometric procedures to evaluate response bias in these areas. Some tests are constructed for the purpose of the detection of simulated psychopathology (e.g., Structured Interview of Reported Symptoms [SIRS], Rogers et al., 1992). Some tests are constructed for the evaluation of psychopathology and somatic complaints but include validity scales to detect over- and under-reporting of symptoms (e.g., Minnesota Multiphasic Personality Inventory-2 [MMPI-2], Butcher et al., 2001;

Battery for Health Improvement-2 [BHI-2], Bruns & Disorbio, 2003). Similarly, in the cognitive area, there are cognitive tests constructed specifically to detect exaggerated cognitive deficits. Some are domain specific and involve assessing for response bias in the memory arena (e.g., Green's Word Memory Test [GWMT], Green, 2003b; Computerized Assessment of Response Bias [CARB], Allen, Green, Cox, & Conder, 2004; Test of Memory Malingering [TOMM], Tombaugh, 1996), problem-solving arena (e.g., Validity Indicator Profile [VIP], Frederick, 2003), and processing speed and accuracy (e.g., b Test, Boone, Lu, & Herzberg, 2002). Finally, there are neuropsychological tests that measure various cognitive abilities that either have normative data gathered at the time of test development or data obtained through subsequent research (e.g., Rey Complex Figure Test [RCFT], Meyers & Meyers, 1995; California Verbal Learning Test-2 [CVLT-2], Delis, Kramer, Kaplan, & Ober, 2000; Reliable Digit Span [RDS] of the Wechsler Adult Intelligence Scale-III, Babikian, Boone, Lu, & Arnold, 2006). Indeed, stand-alone and imbedded response bias measures and research associated with these in neuropsychology have burgeoned over the last decade and a half and include many of the more commonly used neuropsychological tests.

PSYCHOLOGICAL AND NEUROPSYCHOLOGICAL DISORDERS AND OCCUPATIONAL IMPAIRMENT

Injured workers tend to allege impairment in occupational function owing to three main issues: physical injury frequently associated with complaints of pain, psychological disorder, and/or cognitive dysfunction.

With regard to pain and physical capacity, appropriate medical and surgical evaluation along with functional capacity evaluation and, sometimes, videotaped surveillance are the most appropriate methods of assisting with the assessment of physical impairment claims. Psychometrics, however, can supplement these methods. For example, the BHI-2 has normative data for injured patients who have been instructed to present themselves as worse than they are (Bruns

& Disorbio, 2003). The MMPI-2 has been involved in a number of successful studies involving detecting symptom magnification by chronic pain patients (Arbisi & Butcher, 2004a; Bianchini et al., 2005; Meyers et al., 2002).

With regard to mood disorders, some degree of depressed mood and anxiety is commonly associated with prolonged illness, injury, or pain as noted previously. PTSD, however, is relatively rare and requires an objectively severe stressor, an appropriate constellation of symptoms, and impairment in functioning. Notably, a severe stressor is necessary but not sufficient to result in PTSD. There is a relatively wide range of prevalence of PTSD in the face of similar stressors and a far from perfect dose-response relationship between the objective level of the stressor and claimed symptoms (Greiffenstein et al., 2004; Perry, Difede, Musngi, Frances, & Jacobsberg, 1992; Yehuda & McFarlane, 1995). With a severe stressor, a patient may or may not evince PTSD. Psychological distress in the context of a severe stressor is not ipso facto PTSD and "backwards reasoning" is not an uncommon error in such circumstances. Indeed, psychosocial factors seem to be no small factor in a number of cases (Perry et al., 1992; Yehuda & McFarlane, 1995), some of which involves exaggeration or worse (Greiffenstein et al., 2004). Of import is that depressive and anxiety disorders are quite prevalent outside of the workers' compensation arena. Many, actually by far most, individuals with psychological disorders, barring those with severe chronic mental illness such as schizophrenia, remain productive and functional in the work environment. Psychological distress and psychopathology are not tantamount to impaired occupational functioning. The question is, ultimately, how much legitimate mood or anxiety disturbance is present and how this potentially interacts with the specific demands of the job task. Most typically, a patient too impaired to function at work is too impaired to function fully in most other social roles such as with family and friends. For the most part, psychological disorders are more or less pervasive in affecting a person's functioning. A coal miner involved in a roof collapse wherein he witnessed a coworker crushed to death and was trapped himself, fearing his own death before eventually being extricated, could be reasonably expected to be at high risk to develop PTSD. PTSD is not infrequently also associated with a depressive disorder (*DSM-IV-TR*, APA, 2000), and the combination can potentially be rather debilitating and impairing across a patient's range of functioning at least over the short term. On the other hand, PTSD is quite treatable and can improve with psychopharmacologic (Davidson & van der Kolk, 1996) and cognitive-behavioral treatment (Rothbaum & Foa, 1996). Most psychological disorders, with treatment and a patient motivated to get well and return to fully active life, remit or improve substantially over time. Depressive or anxiety disorders are not typically akin to an amputation where the loss of function remains permanent and is forever (functionally) compensated. And with regard to the issue of occupational impairment, a psychological disorder may preclude some types of work activity (e.g., fast paced, highly stressful, dangerous) but not others.

For example, the miner discussed previously is a real case; he not only saw his coworker die but observed this fellow's viscera spilled out of a wound to his abdomen, gruesome to say the least. All of this was confirmed by third party. This miner was reluctant to discuss his accident. He was reluctant to discuss his symptoms and presented as generally rather subdued, if not shut down. Contrast this with another miner more peripherally involved in the incident by virtue of rescue work (who witnessed the roof collapse but neither of the miners). Most of his rescue work was away from the accident site. He presented as the proverbial "bundle of nerves," quite animated in his complaints and quite adamant from the start that he had PTSD, complete with many of the buzzwords, and stating he would not be able to return to work, mining or otherwise. The first miner eventually received permanent restrictions from me for underground mining work; I felt that he had PTSD and that this precluded him from effectively and safely working in the mines. He was released to aboveground work and was able to perform that successfully. The second miner never returned to work but settled his workers' compensation claim and pursued Social Security disability benefits.

Additionally, my experience is that for a subset of patients with physical injuries who fail to meet a threshold to preclude their returning to work based upon objective medical/surgical and functional capacity testing, psychological claims tend to evolve and rise to prominence. Indeed, I have had numerous patients inform me outright they were informed by counsel that their Social Security claim would likely be quite dependent upon psychological impairment in addition to their mild to moderate low back pain to "get them over the top," to paraphrase these patients. Of course, all legitimate injury-related impairment, both physical and psychological, merits consideration for work restrictions within the workers' compensation system as does the addition of any other legitimate physical or psychological impairment with regard to Social Security claims, with one main difference. Within the workers' compensation system, psychosocial stressors and pressures not directly related to the injury, including stress from being within a sometimes rather adversarial system, are not typically considered "work related" and are not factored into any permanent impairment rating or restrictions associated with the work injury. It is crucial for the examiner to tease apart those psychological complaints that are related to the accident and injury and those that are not.

Cognitive complaints, particularly those within the memory and concentration arenas, are fairly common with pain, mood and anxiety, and mild head-injured patients as previously noted. While such complaints need to be taken seriously, particularly with regard to, for example, pain patients on numerous sedating medications and acutely mild head-injured patients, studies, particularly over the last 10 years, have demonstrated, in a sobering manner, a high rate of response bias when these were claims examined psychometrically (Green, 2001; Green et al., 2001). Indeed, a whole line of earlier research suggesting diminution of memory function (Burt, Zembar, & Niederehe, 1995) has been attacked owing to a failure of researchers to assess for response bias in mood-disordered patients (Rohling et al., 2002). It is generally felt presently that such complaints by patients are subjective and have little, if any, objective import. Similarly, the base rate for response bias in nonacute mild head injury has been shown to be remarkably elevated (Schmand et al., 1998).

The better part of 50 years ago, Miller (1961), in a seminal article focusing on psychosocial factors operating in patients evaluated in a medicolegal context, articulated observations that have only more recently become the focus of study. He noted that of 200 consecutive head injury cases, in his medicolegal practice, "47 had gross and unequivocally psychoneurotic complaints. In 22 other cases, a postconcussional or postcontusional syndrome was complicated by psychoneurotic features" (p. 919). He further noted "an inverse relationship of accident neurosis to the severity of the injury" (p. 920). He reported "in response to direct questions few of these patients are prepared to admit to anything other than robust physical and mental health until the very day of the accident...[despite that] evidence of some significant predisposing factor or factors was found in 20 of these 47 cases," which he felt to be an underestimate owing to "the tendency of these patients to conceal positive evidence in their pre-accident histories" (p. 920). Miller noted, in discussing patients claiming anxiety, that "objective signs of anxiety such as tachycardia, tremor, and axillary hyperhidrosis are, however, relatively uncommon, and have been found in less than 15% of personal cases" (p. 922). He noted "the most consistent clinical feature is the subject's unshakable conviction of unfitness for work, a conviction quite unrelated to overt disability even if his symptomatology is accepted at its face value" (p. 922). "Another cardinal feature is an absolute refusal to admit any degree of symptomatic improvement" (p. 922). Noting a tendency to add psychological distress claims to physical claims, Miller reported:

> Equally characteristic is the patient's attitude to medical attention and treatment. In industrial cases periodic attendance on the general practitioner is necessary in order to obtain successive certificates of unfitness for work, but in other instances it is remarkable that the patient will complain bitterly of disabling nervous symptoms lasting for many months—for which she has never once sought medical treatment. (p. 922)

Adding to his observation of psychosocial factors impacting general (i.e., not limited to the aforementioned head injury sample) "accident neurosis" cases, Miller noted:

> Amongst a number of patients personally seen in this or some other connexion [*sic*] who had previously suffered from and been compensated for a similar condition, not one has ever admitted to any psychiatric disability remaining from the first accident... .[,] patients with this disorder in whom the legal issue has been resolved are conspicuously rare amongst the thousands who seek treatment for functional nervous disorders...[, and] it is significant that of the many ex-service men who were drawing pensions for the rather similar condition of war neurosis at the end of the Second World War, in the vast majority of cases symptoms cleared up within a few years of demobilization. (p. 923)

In a follow up, after settlement, of 50 patients with accident neurosis, only two "were still disabled by their psychiatric symptoms on re-examination two years after settlement. Both instances were characterized by diagnostic confusion, substantial lump-sum payments, and continuing National Insurance pensions for the results of the accident" (p. 925).

THE DOSE-RESPONSE RELATIONSHIP IN EVALUATING PATIENT SYMPTOMS AND COMPLAINTS

Although I have argued for caution about uncritically accepting symptoms and complaints, and the need for methods to improve objectivity in psychological and neuropsychological evaluation of the injured worker, symptoms and complaints are not unimportant. Just as highly unusual or even patently absurd symptoms can cast doubt on the veracity of a patient's clinical presentation, common and consistent symptoms lend credence (barring successful attorney coaching) to such complaints. But not infrequently in the workers' compensation arena, it is not simply a matter of whether or not the patient has a physical, psychological, or neuropsychological injury but rather severity of the injury and the magnitude of any associated impairment. This is a crucial component in evaluation, particularly in psychological (and frequently neuropsychological) cases, where there is, more frequently than not, a lack of incontrovertible or nearly incontrovertible diagnostic test evidence, for example, an X-ray to unequivocally assess for fracture. One important benchmark in evaluating the veracity of an injured patient's symptoms and complaints is for the clinician to consider carefully *severity indexing* or the dose-response relationship (Larrabee, 1990).

For example, generally, one would expect a higher incidence of fractured feet from an elephant standing on your foot than a small child standing on your foot. Hitting your thumb with a well-swung hammer ought to result in more pain than a hangnail on that thumb. Likewise, a severe blow to the head ought to cause a more severe head (and brain) injury than a mild blow to the head and, related, a more severe head injury ought to result in greater (cognitive) impairment than a mild head injury. An unfractured leg ought to be able to kick a ball further than a fractured leg. A brain without a severe cerebral hemorrhage and/or contusions ought to be able to remember better than one with a severe cerebral hemorrhage and/or contusions.

**Related Expectations and Does Our Expectation
of the Dose-Response Relationship Fit the Data?**
Taking the brain injury analogy further as the model, there ought to be a positive correlation for severity of head injury (e.g., CT/MR scan), over its range, and cognitive impairment; the worse the structural damage, the worse ought to be the subsequent cognitive impairment. Strokes, brain tumors, and various dementias with verified and uncontestable brain damage ought to evince greater cognitive impairment than mild head-injured patients without such verified and uncontestable brain damage. Patients with verified and uncontestable severe brain damage ought to evince more cognitive impairment than patients with psychiatric (e.g., depression) and chronic pain disorders (i.e., without verified and uncontestable evidence of brain damage).

This is not what Paul Green, PhD, and associates have found with the GWMT in over 10 years of research with many thousands of patients. With regard to subjective patient (i.e., symptom) complaints, workers' compensation and disability patients without abnormal brain scans tend to have greater levels of memory complaints (on the Memory Complaints Inventory [MCI]) than such patients with abnormal brain scans (Green & Allen, 1996) and/or objective neurologic findings (Rohling et al., 2002) and perform more poorly on objective neuropsychological tests and response bias measures such as the GWMT (Rohling et al., 2002). Patients with brain injuries, depression, or chronic pain who fail either the GWMT or CARB evince greater subjective memory complaints on the MCI (CogniSyst, 1999). Interestingly, chronic (e.g., back) pain, fibromyalgia, and depressed patients tend to have a greater level of memory complaints than do neurologic patients (Gervais, Russell, et al., 2001). If individuals without leg fractures reported greater problems kicking a ball some distance than individuals with leg fractures, what would we think? How can we make sense of these paradoxical memory complaint findings?

Perhaps the culprit is lack of insight for severely head-injured patients. However, this does not explain such extremely elevated complaints in non-neurologically impaired (e.g., depression, chronic pain) patients when they fail response bias tests that severely head-injured patients tend to pass (P. Green, personal communication, November 9, 2006).

Perhaps the culprit is depression. However, this does not explain why mild head-injured patients report more depression as well as other psychological and physical problems and, again, tend to fail response bias tests that severely head-injured patients tend to pass (P. Green, personal communication, November 9, 2006).

Perhaps the culprit is pain. However, on what basis ought mild head-injured patients to report more pain than severely head-injured patients when the latter have evinced an objectively more severe physical trauma and, again, tend to fail response bias tests that severely head-injured patients tend to pass (P. Green, personal communication, November 9, 2006).

The question with which we are inevitably confronted is, "Is it better to have a mild or severe head injury?" Would you rather have an elephant stand on your foot or a child stand on your foot?

A Solution

The resolution of these—and other similar—paradoxical findings in the clinical setting is to evaluate the validity of a patient's symptom complaints. This involves, in addition to the context assessment described previously, response bias testing that objectively assists in evaluating the under- or over-reporting of symptoms (with regard to patient verbal reports) and symptom magnification (with regard to patient behavior) in the context of ability testing or psychological testing. "Effort testing" of learning/memory will be described in some detail as the prototype although there are a number of other cognitive domains where response bias may manifest itself and test procedures to evaluate for such. Valid neuropsychological test results (e.g., regarding a patient's memory function) are dependent upon full patient effort in engaging with those tests for accurate interpretation of their various neuropsychological abilities. Psychological test results (e.g., regarding patient psychological symptoms and distress) are dependent upon patient cooperation, openness/candor, and honesty. If not for objective assessment of response bias, on what basis can we have confidence in our testing results and, ultimately, our conclusions regarding a patient's clinical status particularly in evaluative contexts where there are psychosocial pressures for response bias and base rates of such demonstrated in the scientific literature confirming these concerns (Green, 2001, 2003a)?

WHY OBJECTIVELY EVALUATE THE VERACITY OF A PATIENT'S SYMPTOMS?

First, there is the problem about the ubiquity of many (e.g., postconcussive type) symptoms that may be attributed to a specific cause (e.g., head injury). The ubiquity of such symptoms merits critical evaluation as does their relationship to that to which they are alleged to be related. For example, as previously noted, postconcussive symptoms are notoriously common and not specific to mild head injury. Before one evaluates and comes to some conclusion regarding the relationship of a symptom to any alleged cause, the validity of the symptom (and any associated behavior) must first be established. Then and only then is it possible to draw inferences regarding the issue of causation (e.g., to the injury or alternative or contributing causes).

Second, the workers' compensation arena inherently involves pressures and incentives to exaggerate and exaggeration of symptoms has been shown, as indicated, to involve substantial percentages of patients. Indeed, as mentioned, compensation issues are more frequently than not shown to be related to increased complaints and increased response bias in studies that examine such. Binder and Rohling (1996) studied the impact of financial compensation on symptom severity and found an interaction between the two such that mild head-injured patients with financial incentives performed worse on neuropsychological testing than more severely head-injured patients without such financial incentives. Bianchini, Curtis, and Greve (2006), assessing for three levels of financial compensation incentive with head-injured patients, found a positive correlation between the level of financial incentive and failure on response bias testing assessing cognitive, physical, and psychiatric domains. Furthermore, whereas mild and moderate-severe head-injured patients with financial incentives demonstrated increased failure on response bias testing, the mild group tended to perform worse. The overall finding of a positive dose-response relationship for the level of financial compensation with failure on response bias testing, while needing to be replicated, suggests "that potential monetary compensation rather than nonspecific psychosocial factors associated with workers compensation claims is a major motive for exaggeration of problems attributed to work-related brain injuries" (p. 843). Third, people, including trained clinicians, mental health or otherwise, are notoriously poor at judging deception on their own (Ekman, 1996; Ekman & O'Sullivan, 1991; Heaton, Smith, Lehman, & Vogt, 1978). This is not to say that the most egregious instances will not be detected by interview or even unusual psychological or neuropsychological test results, only that overall accuracy rates in decision-making are less than desirable and objective psychometric procedures can improve detection (Green, 2001; Mittenberg, Rotholc, Russell, & Heilbronner, 1996).

The psychometric approach lends increased objectivity and precision to assessing a patient's psychological, neuropsychological, and pain disorder as well as response bias. Although not supplanting interview and observational information (and objective medical history via medical records, video surveillance, etc.), it provides crucial objective data, apart from the potential shortcomings of the interview and examiner bias or susceptibility to deception, with which to compare and contrast other exam findings.

WHAT RESPONSE BIAS TESTING DOES AND DOES NOT TELL US

Test results indicating response bias inform us that response bias exists. With regard to neuropsychological (i.e., ability) testing, that means that the patient has very likely evinced less than full effort to perform as best as possible. With regard to psychological testing, that means the patient very likely evinced either symptom magnification (from exaggeration of present symptoms and/or psychological distress to faking nonexistent symptoms and/or psychological distress) or defensiveness (whereby the patient minimized symptoms). Positive response bias test results, in and of themselves, will typically leave the question open as to what, if any, ability impairment or psychological distress exists, requiring information over and above the response bias testing results on which to construct an opinion. Furthermore, as noted previously, response bias testing does not reveal, in and of itself, the specific motivation (or motivations) for the aberrant cognitive effort or psychological symptom claims, that is the intent or aim of the response, even, for example, in the case of below chance level cognitive testing results which only indicate volition or will to do poorly, not the particular reason (or reasons) for doing so. In other words, response bias testing is not "malingering testing," despite some tests names and research papers implying that it is or can be synonymous with such. Response bias testing results, in and of themselves, do not distinguish response bias associated with a somatoform disorder, factitious disorder, or malingering. Assessment at this next level requires the addition of other information such as the medical record, accident reports, collateral information, clinical observation, and videotaped surveillance.

The conclusion of response bias is just of that; it does not necessarily impugn any malicious intent by the patient and does not necessarily warrant ceasing of treatment or benefits. Nor does it necessarily mean that all the patients' complaints involve response bias. These are areas of ambiguity for response bias testing results themselves that are essential to be squarely recognized. A finding of response bias on exam does merit further investigation of the nature and reason for such that may impact treatment or disposition. For example, a patient may evince indication of symptom magnification on a psychological test such as the MMPI-2 that could be due to malingering but also could be due to a tendency to be very anxious about some ominous physical pathology that the patient incorrectly believes he or she has in conjunction with feeling that his or her surgeon is not taking complaints seriously so that the patient's responding to test items on psychological testing is associated with a greatly lowered threshold for symptom endorsement compared with most patients to make the point and "to be heard."

Psychometric Approaches to Assess Response Bias

Psychometric approaches, depending upon the particular test, capitalize on a number of strategies to assess for response bias for both neuropsychological and psychological complaints enumerated below by Rogers, Harrell, and Liff (1993) and Bender and Rogers (2004). Most fundamentally, these involve evaluation of various types of inconsistencies in a patient's presentation and/or test performance(s) involving either excessive impairment or atypical patterns of impairment or claimed symptoms.

The *floor effect* strategy relies on the notion that individuals who evince response bias are frequently unaware of testing tasks or items that are so simple or unrelated to the type of impairment that ought to be manifested that even markedly impaired individuals would likely pass them easily and consistently. On what basis would a patient with an objective history of mild head injury fail items or a test that a patient with a severe brain injury can pass?

The *magnitude of error* strategy capitalizes on the idea that patients who are evincing response bias typically are unsure of the degree of error, from approximate to gross, to evince on test items. Rogers et al. (1993) noted "Powell (1991) found that simulators feigning schizo-phrenia tended to have higher proportions of both approximate and absurd errors on cognitive items of the Mini-Mental State" (p. 261).

The *performance curve* strategy assesses for effort and consistency of effort by examining a patient's pattern of performance over the course of items of known and graded difficulty from very easy to very difficult. At the easy end of the spectrum, items are constructed so that all but mentally retarded subjects ought to consistently choose the correct answer. At the very difficult end of the spectrum, items are constructed so all but the most intelligent of individuals will likely fail. The test items are typically administered in a random order (vs. graded order of difficulty) so as to make it more difficult for the patient to keep track of which items (i.e., beyond a particular level of difficulty) to fail, if that is their intent. Patients and nonpatients ought to evince a performance curve (when the items are reordered by graded difficulty after scoring) characterized by getting the easy items consistently correct, then evincing an gradually increased proportion of incorrect answers beginning with items of a difficulty that match and then exceed the limits of their ability to where the proportion of correct and incorrect answers eventually descends to chance levels.

The *symptom validity testing* strategy capitalizes on the notion that if a patient's rate of failure on test items drops below chance, they must know the correct answer to get the wrong answer so frequently. Patients who are putting forth good effort and are simply challenged by items beyond their ability will evince performance at chance lev-els on tasks. For example, if an individual flipped a coin 100 times, you would expect roughly 50 head and 50 tail landings. If the coin landed on heads 96 times, you would probably be rather suspicious of the coin being unbalanced. If a patient takes a multiple choice test with two response options and gets 95% of the items correct, we would conclude that he or she has the ability to answer most of the items correctly. If the patient said he or she did not know these items and only got 5% of the items correct, we might be inclined to conclude that he or she does not have the ability to answer most of the items correctly. Or would we? Actually, it takes the same level of ability to obtain 95% or 5% correct on this multiple choice test, with the difference being whether you are trying to answer the items correct or incorrect. A patient truly not being able to identify the correct items would evince a score somewhere around 50% because his or her best effort would only result in a random level of performance success. On one hand, below chance performance is very compelling evidence of volition to answer incorrectly (although, again, it does not identify the motivation for such); on the other hand, experience demonstrates that this occurs relatively infrequently with individuals who evince response bias and so is, consequently, not particularly sensitive to detect response bias. For patients who are not simply producing strong effort to do poorly but, rather, poor effort to do well, including normative data that compare patients with known good effort and response bias will increase the utility of such measures such as with the GWMT (Green, 2003b).

The *atypical presentation* strategy capitalizes on the notion that most patients are unaware of the details of performance profiles (e.g., within and between various domains of neuropsychological testing tasks) or symptom constellations typical or atypical of the disorder for which they are being examined. Of course, attorney coaching, which does occur (Bury & Bagby, 2002; Wetter & Corrigan, 1995), can diminish the utility of this strategy (Rose, Hall, & Szalda-Petree, 1998).

The *psychological sequelae* strategy capitalizes on the finding that patients simulating physical injury and/or complaints (e.g., brain injury) frequently evince elevated levels of psychological complaints relative to individuals with actual injury.

Referring to neuropsychological examinations in particular, Boone et al. (2002) summarize a number of strategies for detecting response bias including (a) "noncredible performance on effort tests," (b) "noncredible performance on measures of cognitive ability that have been found to be sensitive to feigned symptoms," (c) "marked inconsistency between test scores and behavior, within a testing session," (d) "inconsistency between cognitive test performance and daily functioning," (e) "exhibition of behaviors that are never witnessed in patients with actual brain injuries," (f) "unexpected patterns of cognitive test performance across separate testing sessions," (g) "pattern of neuropsychological performance that is not consistent with medical or psychiatric condition," (h) "severity of neuropsychological impairment that is not consistent with medical or psychiatric condition," (i) "noncredible findings on neurologic or other medial exam," (j) "implausible self-reported symptoms," and (k) "contradictions in symptoms and behaviors between the examination setting and daily life" (pp. 37–38).

Rogers et al. (1992, pp. 19–21) describe a number of response bias detection strategies, incorporated into the SIRS, which are geared mostly toward psychiatric symptomatology and complaints. (a) *Evaluation of rare symptoms* "includes bona fide symptoms that occur infrequently in psychiatric patients." (b) *Evaluation of symptom combinations* involves "items that ask about the existence of bona fide psychiatric symptoms which rarely occur simultaneously. (c) *Evaluation of improbable or absurd symptoms* involves identification of endorsed symptoms that "have a fantastic or preposterous quality …[that] makes it unlikely, by definition, that such symptoms could possibly be true." (d) *Evaluation of blatant symptoms* capitalizes on the finding that "malingerers over-endorse symptoms which are obvious signs of mental disorder." (e) *Evaluation of subtle symptoms* "is based on symptoms which untrained individuals would see as everyday problems and not indicative of mental illness." (f) *Evaluation of the severity of symptoms* "is based on the observation that malingerers often endorse an unlikely number of symptoms with extreme or unbearable severity." (g) *Evaluation of the selectivity of symptoms* involves the finding that "some feigning individuals are nonselective or indiscriminant in their endorsements of psychiatric problems." (h) *Evaluation of reported vs. observed symptoms* involves evaluating the consistency of a patient's claimed symptoms to observable behavior. (i) *Evaluation of direct appraisal of honesty* involves items that query the patient regarding "the honesty and completeness of their self-reports" across a variety of circumstances and scenarios. (j) *Evaluation of defensive symptoms* involves "symptoms [that] represent a variety of everyday problems, worries, and situations which most individual experience to some degree." (k) *Evaluation of symptom onset* involves assessing for the typicality or atypicality of the onset of the claimed symptoms or mental disorder. (l) *Evaluation of overly specified symptoms* focuses on the typicality or atypicality of the "degree of precision" of symptom endorsement. Finally, (m) *evaluation of inconsistency of symptoms* capitalizes on the notion that "malingerers often have difficulty remembering which symptoms they have endorsed and are, therefore, inconsistent in their responses."

A take home point that ought to be clear from the above is that evaluating for response bias requires a multifaceted approach in terms of factors and domains to be assessed (Millis & Volinsky, 2001). For example, as noted, patients with chronic pain and/or depression tend to have elevated complaint levels for memory problems and evince significant rates of failure on memory response bias testing. Patients goals and motivations, preparation, sophistication, and so forth may vary with regard to these various factors and necessitate multiple strategies to evaluate for response bias. One major advantage of the use of psychometrics (vs. solely an interview) for assessment of response bias is being able to utilize normative data comparing patients evincing and not evincing response bias to allow rational and objective decision making regarding identifying such. For the patients passing such an examination, confidence can increase commensurately with regard to the validity of their interview complaints and test performances.

CARB and GWMT as Models
for Cognitive Response Bias Testing

The CARB (Allen et al., 2004) is a response bias test within the symptom validity paradigm (that is also normed on "good" and "poor" effort patients) requiring recognition "memory" that patients with histories of objectively severe brain injury or neurologic disease generally easily pass (Iverson, Green, & Gervais, 1999). Green's Word Memory Test (Green, 2003) is a verbal memory test that simultaneously evaluates effort and ability (Iverson et al., 1999). It is a particularly powerful method as it (1) involves multiple primary and secondary effort measures, (2) allows a comparison of effort and ability measures, and (3) has a large and well-defined normative database for comparison of results that includes multiple clinical groups, many of which involve workers' compensation and/or disability seeking patients. Indeed, the normative data include some 50 comparison groups and over 2,800 cases.

Research on these, and other, subjects indicates that the severity of brain injury is positively correlated with performance on the effort measures (Green, 2001)—hence the name effort test, which is some-what of a misnomer as noted above insofar as a patient can potentially produce much effort to perform poorly and another patient could perform poorly simply by not trying hard, one way or the other. Nonetheless, this remains a common shorthand term that easily contrasts itself from ability and is not quite as obscure sounding and cumbersome as the more formal (and precise) term of response bias. In other words, if in large groups of patients, there is a tendency for the patients with objectively lesser head or brain injuries to perform worse on effort measures than patients with objectively more severe head or brain injuries, something else besides neurologic dysfunction must be associated with this poorer performance (and pulling the group mean of the effort testing results down) of the former group. If two groups of people had their feet stepped on by elephants and children, respectively, and the latter group complained of more foot pain, that would make little biologic sense. These results do not imply that more severe injuries are not associated with greater impairment; actual brain injury severity is positively correlated with impairment and vocational outcome (Millis & Putnam, 1996). They do indicate that significant portions of individuals claiming impairment from head injury, particularly at the milder end of the continuum, are not putting forth effort to perform maximally on neuropsychological and response bias testing.

Low response bias scores translate into invalid neuropsychological exam (i.e., cognitive testing) results and cast a doubt on the patient's symptom (e.g., memory dysfunction) claims. Without objective verification of effort, particularly in exam contexts with elevated base rates of symptom magnification, an examiner can have little confidence that neuropsychological testing results possibly suggestive of impairment are not, actually, a product of poor effort to do well or even effort to do poorly. Passing response bias testing in the framework of appropriate contextual relationships described above increases the confidence that diminished neuropsychological testing results are associated with, for example, the alleged head and brain injury.

With regard to patient CARB and GWMT effort measures, groups of mild head-injured patients tend to perform more poorly than severely brain-injured patients (Green, Iverson, & Allen, 1999). Mild head-injured patients with normal CT brain scans performed worse than severely head injured patients with abnormal CT brain scans (Green, 2003b; Green et al., 1999). Patients with shorter posttraumatic amnesia performed worse than patients with longer posttraumatic amnesia (Green et al., 2001). Non-neurologic patients perform worse than neurologic patients (Green et al., 2001). Chronic pain (e.g., low back pain), fibromyalgia, and depressed patients also evince very high rates of failure on response bias testing (Gervais, Green, et al., 2001; Gervais, Russell, et al., 2001; Rohling et al., 2002).

These findings revealed that memory complaints correlate most with other symptoms, particularly psychiatric symptoms, but not with memory impairment on objective testing.

Indeed, effort, in a workers' compensation patient sample, was associated with the lion's share of the variance on neuropsychological test results, over and above injury severity (Green et al., 2001).

Not infrequently, workers' compensation patients complain of memory dysfunction attributed to depressive disorder. Indeed, a review of research over the years has yielded findings indicative of diminished memory testing scores in depressed patients (Rohling, et al., 2002). Unfortunately, no small amount of neuropsychological research, particularly in less recent years when effort testing was not routinely administered, has erroneously resulted in conclusions of chronic neuropsychological impairment in various clinical groups (e.g., with depression, PTSD, chronic pain, mild head injury) commonly found within the workers' compensation or medico-legal arena. The results and conclusions of these older studies failing to utilize response bias testing are increasing demonstrated to be suspect.

In many subject groups, particularly in the medicolegal arena such as workers' compensation, effort is being demonstrated to contain a greater degree of statistical variance than with cerebral pathology across groups studied (Green et al., 2001). That is not to say that a brain injury or toxic exposure, and so forth, cannot result in cognitive deficits from that injury; these conditions can, most definitely, cause significant and even quite serious cognitive (as well as emotional and behavioral) problems. However, the results of response bias testing over more recent years underscore the need, when evaluating individual patients, to be able to distinguish those who are performing with intact effort and those who are not.

Along these same lines, many chronic pain patients complain of memory deficits, and the question arises if these complaints are objective or not. Gervais, Green, et al. (2001) evaluated disability applicants associated with work injuries and automobile. Disconcertingly, 41% failed CARB and 42% failed GWMT. Notably, these tests are essentially psychometrically equivalent in terms of difficulty (Allen et al., 2004). Then, half of the patients were informed that CARB (but not GWMT) is an effort test. The patients were then tested again. At that juncture, the coached group evinced a 6% failure rate on CARB and a 34% failure rate on GWMT, whereas the uncoached group evinced failure rates of 38% and 41%, respectively, not unlike initial testing. These pain patients evinced greater levels of memory complaints and performed worse on effort testing than did a group of neurologic patients. A neurologic or biologic argument as to the causation of such results is obviously strained; psychosocial factors associated with response bias is by far the most defensible explanation. Gervais, Russell, et al. (2001) compared working versus nonworking (i.e., disability seeking) fibromyalgia patients and found that claim status, not diagnosis, predicted effort testing failure.

**The Necessity of Evaluation of Response Bias
in Workers' Compensation Patients With Cognitive Complaints**
In patients with a history of mild head injury (as well as depression and chronic pain), memory complaints are remarkably common. Sometimes, patients may complain of memory (and other cognitive) problems from their medication. Not infrequently, claims of such enter into issues of occupational readiness or impairment. Research previously noted has clearly demonstrated that such complaints are not only remarkably ubiquitous but also prone to exaggeration, particularly in the medicolegal arena, such as workers' compensation. Notably, memory complaints correlate very poorly with actual impairment in (groups of) these patients. The veracity of such cognitive complaints is very much at issue owing to the typical lack of objective medical evidence of brain damage for head-injured (or toxic exposed, etc.) patients and/or a neurologic or biologic explanation to account for such with depressed or chronic pain patients. Neuropsychological testing is sensitive to brain injury, medication effects on the brain, and so forth, but also to patient effort. And effort has been shown to be associated with greater variance in neuropsychological test results than is injury severity in head-injured patients. Other high-risk groups include patients with chronic pain and depression. Therefore, evaluation of effort in patients claiming cognitive dysfunction from head injury (or pain or depression) is a critical component of objective evaluation of their complaints and claims. To use an electronics analogy, effort testing assists in the detection and evaluation of extraneous (psychosocial) "noise" over and above the "signal" complaint or performance (e.g., memory).

Neuropsychological testing, including effort testing, is a sound, fair, and objective method for evaluating cognitive complaints. Testing can assist in both detecting response bias and delineating and lending credibility to legitimate complaints in patients who are not exaggerating deficits associated with head injury (or toxic exposure, medication effects, etc.). Without such an objective method, patients with actual deficits may not be supported and treated appropriately, and patients without such deficits obtain needless or inappropriate treatment, with no small impact on ultimate dispositional issues such as occupational readiness or impairment.

Other Testing Approaches for Cognitive Response Bias

The GWMT is described as the model for response bias testing, in part owing to its utility, that is, having greater ability to discriminate low-effort patients (Green, 2001). This seems to be associated with the notion that patients who complain of memory problems, at least those who tend to evince response bias, tend to focus on the verbal memory domain. However, response bias can occur in other neuropsychological domains, and there are presently many stand-alone tests that assess for response bias in areas of verbal and nonverbal problem solving (Frederick, 2003), visual memory (Tombaugh, 1996; also Green's Nonverbal Medical Symptom Validity Test currently in development), and cognitive speed and accuracy (Boone & Herzberg, 2002), to name a few. Some tests have begun to include response bias measures in their original construction and norming (Delis et al., 2000; Meyers & Meyers, 1995). Furthermore, many of the most commonly utilized neuropsychological tests have been studied extensively over the last 15 years to now include data on response bias. Evaluation of response bias in neuropsychology has evolved tremendously over the last decade and a half, and knowledgeable neuropsychologists have multiple data points to objectively and validly draw conclusions regarding a patient's effort and whether the results are more consistent with legitimate impairment from a real injury or whether the results are more likely to be generated by something else.

The MMPI-2 and BHI-2 as Models
for Psychiatric and Somatic Response Bias Testing

The MMPI, and now its revision, the MMPI-2 (Butcher et al., 2001), "are currently the most widely used and researched objective personality inventories" (Greene, 2000). This test has a number of response bias measures to assess what is frequently called a "fake good" or "fake bad" response style, notwithstanding previous discussion that response bias measures assess response bias and not the specific motivation for such. With regard to the workers' compensation arena, the issue is more frequently in the domain of "fake bad" than "fake good." The MMPI-2 has been demonstrated to be robust in detecting "malingering" and "feigning" in the context of psychiatric complaints (Rogers et al., 1994). While perhaps not more important but perhaps more interesting is that the MMPI-2 has, in more recent years, been demonstrated to detect exaggeration and malingering in patients with somatic complaints such as those involving brain injury (Scott, Emick, & Adams, 1999; Youngjohn, Davis, & Wolf, 1997), pain (Arbisi & Butcher, 2004a), and seizures (Derry & McLachlan, 1996).

Over recent years, there has been increasing interest and research on the FBS scale developed by Lees-Haley (Lees-Haley, English, & Glenn, 1991), which was developed on personal injury litigants and has been subsequently studied with head injury (Larrabee, 2003b), pain (Meyers et al., 2002), and psychiatric claims (Greiffenstein et al., 2004). There has been some criticism of the scale (Arbisi & Butcher, 2004b; Butcher, Arbisi, Altis, & McNulty, 2003) although this itself has been criticized on methodological grounds (Greve & Bianchini, 2004; Lees-Haley & Fox, 2004) and studies with the FBS scale compared directly with the more traditional MMPI-2 "fake bad" indicators such as F, FB, FP, and F-K, with medicolegal patients (and independent criteria for response bias) have generally demonstrated their superiority (Greiffenstein et al., 2004; Larrabee, 2003a, 2003b; Nelson, Sweet, & Demakis, 2006; Ross, Millis, Krukowski, Putnam, & Adams, 2004).

The BHI-2 (Bruns & Disorbio, 2003) is a test normed on physical rehabilitation and chronic pain patients as well as a community (i.e., noninjured) sample. It assesses various physical, psychological, and psychosocial factors relevant to the treatment and recovery of rehabilitation and pain patients. Response bias assessment involves scales to assist in detecting defensiveness and exaggeration. Indeed, the norms associated with the latter involve the sample of patients who took the test a second time with instructions to exaggerate. The test also uses statistical algorithms to give probabilities that a patient's alleged pain problem (e.g., back injury) tends or tends not to match the patient normative sample with that problem.

Summary and Conclusions

Knowledgeable and qualified psychologists can provide assessment and consultative services useful for referring physicians, surgeons, case managers, carriers, and attorneys as they evaluate and contend with the merit of cases involving claims of cognitive dysfunction, pain, and psychological impairment in the workers' compensation arena associated with occupational injuries.

Mild head injury and associated alleged brain injury or persistent postconcussion syndrome (as well as associated claims of psychological problems or psychiatric disorders such as PTSD) from accidents or injuries in the medicolegal environment are typically problematic for physicians, surgeons, case managers, carriers, and attorneys to evaluate and contend with. Opinions in the medical record are frequently based largely upon the subjective report of the patient, the veracity of which is at issue and subject to no small uncertainty, given the potential for monetary or other gain. It is well established that negative imaging studies and/or a negative neurologic exam do not rule out mild brain injury. Opinion is, therefore, usually centered on the patient's subjective reports or uncritical acceptance of demonstrated performances on mental status exam or more detailed tests of cognitive ability.

The scientific arm of neuropsychology, particularly over the last 10 to 15 years, has been involved in much research regarding the issue of mild head injury and associated persistent postconcussion syndrome. A good portion of this research has involved the issue of distinguishing those who likely have legitimate complaints from those who are exaggerating their claims or providing incomplete (or decidedly poor) effort on tests of various cognitive abilities allegedly impacted negatively by their head—and ostensibly by extension—brain injury. There are currently a number of well-validated psychometric procedures and other clinical methods useful for determining whether a patient is likely exaggerating or fabricating his or her alleged cognitive impairments. The scientific literature demonstrates that neuropsychology, relative to other associated fields, has probably made the greatest strides with these types of cases in providing objective and valid methods for evaluating the veracity of such claims of cognitive impairment and, by extension, brain injury. Given that a convergence of recent studies suggesting that, in the context of workers' compensation and similar medicolegal circumstances, rates of response bias involving exaggeration and/or malingering are remarkably elevated, this is no inconsequential issue. Prudence in evaluating such claims merits objective and validated methods for discriminating those who are making legitimate claims of cognitive dysfunction secondary to a head injury from those who are not.

In many instances, claims of persistent postconcussion syndrome are largely or solely associated with psychological or psychiatric problems, not brain injury. A head injury is not tantamount to a brain injury. Even in instances with incontestable mild brain injury (e.g., contusion on brain scan) at the time of injury, it is not a foregone conclusion that there is forever impairment attributable to brain damage or that objective residual impairment is of a level precluding a successful return to work. Neuropsychological evaluation, with appropriate response bias testing, can be helpful in the discrimination of these patients.

Some patients without head injuries, for example, chronic pain patients and patients claiming depression, also allege impairing cognitive dysfunction (e.g., diminished memory and concentration ability). Similarly, appropriate neuropsychological testing can assist in determining which patients are exaggerating in these circumstances as well. Rates of exaggeration and malingering in these groups have been demonstrated to be high, with chronic pain patients evincing higher rates than even mild head injury patients.

Traditional psychological testing, that is, validated psychometric procedures focusing on the discrimination of various types of psychological and psychiatric disturbance and somatic complaints including pain, is also an important tool for determining which patients are likely exaggerating or malingering claims of psychological distress or psychiatric disturbance. Again, most typically, the medical record is replete with interview reports of subjective patient complaints. Accepting such as valid, under medicolegal circumstances, however, is done at no small peril. The scientific literature over the past 50 years has robustly demonstrated that the addition of formal psychometric procedures improves the accuracy of the diagnostic endeavor, as do objective tests in general medicine. A number of psychometric tests focusing on the assessment of general psychopathology and personality have various scales to assist in determining a patient's response style, for example, exaggerating or malingering. There are also psychometric tests that have been specifically developed to assist in the issue of detecting exaggerated or malingered psychopathology and psychological distress.

Therefore, current neuropsychological and psychological tests are indispensable for the objective evaluation of cognitive, psychological, and somatic and pain disturbance and impairment in the workers' compensation and associated medicolegal environment. These procedures allow improved discrimination of those patients who are legitimate from those who are not with regard to their complaints and presentation. These procedures add objectivity to an otherwise perilously subjective endeavor of the interview. The scientific literature is quite clear that psychologists and physicians (and virtually all other groups of professionals who are required to evaluate deception) are notoriously poor at formulating such opinions regarding the veracity of an examinee's reports based upon interview and observational data alone, particularly with regard to more sophisticated or coached subjects. These objective psychometric procedures also represent an approach that is fair and even-handed insofar as they also facilitate identifying those patients in whom we can have increased confidence that their problems are as claimed. Notwithstanding the general reluctance for involving psychology and neuropsychology, my experience is that case managers, carriers, and defense attorneys generally find this information palatable and helpful as well, so that a more rapid disposition can proceed with confidence that a patient (without such merit) is not simply poaching the system.

Injured workers frequently have at least some degree of psychological distress. Psychosocial factors frequently complicate the outcome with injured workers. Psychosocial factors operate to affect a case, whether or not they are acknowledged. Some patients with little objective spine pathology shift complaints over to the psychological arena. Exaggeration of physical, emotional, and cognitive symptoms is no small problem in workers' compensation (although not all patients exaggerate). Not all injured patients wish to return to work (although not all want to "get on the dole"). If psychosocial issues are present and impinging upon the patient's clinical presentation, if they are not appropriately evaluated and managed, they will manage the case.

Not atypically, a treating physician or surgeon will have some interest in psychological or neuropsychological evaluation although the case manager or carrier may be resistant. A patient who is complaining, genuinely or not, of psychological or cognitive problems is eventually going to be evaluated and/or treated by somebody; and this will filter down into the workers' compensation record. Who does the evaluation and follow up in terms of becoming the treating doctor is under the control of the referring physician and/or the carrier as long as that control is not abdicated by an unwillingness to acknowledge and deal with the psychological and psychosocial issues. Ultimately, a choice needs to be made between ignoring psychological and/or neuropsychological claims and psychosocial issues and hoping they go away or preemptively evaluating, managing, and treating (as warranted) and maintaining some modicum of control of the case, particularly in instances of symptom magnification of back pain, cognitive complaints, and psychological complaints.

REFERENCES

Allen, L. M., III, Green, P., Cox, D. R., & Conder, R. L., Jr. (2004). *Computerized assessment of response bias* [manual, updated 2004]. Durham, NC: CogniSyst.

American Psychiatric Association. (1994). *Diagnostic and statistical manual of mental disorders* (4th ed.). Washington, DC: Author.

American Psychiatric Association. (2000). *Diagnostic and statistical manual of mental disorders* (4th ed. text revision). Washington, DC: Author.

Anastasi, A. (1982). *Psychological testing* (5th ed.). New York: MacMillan

Arbisi, P. A., & Butcher, J. N. (2004a). Psychometric perspectives on detection of malingering of pain: Use of the Minnesota Multiphasic Personality Inventory-2. *Clinical Journal of Pain, 20,* 383–391.

Arbisi, P. A., & Butcher, J. N. (2004b). Failure of the FBS to predict malingering of somatic symptoms: Response to the critiques by Greve and Bianchini and Lees Haley and Fox. *Archives of Clinical Neuropsychology, 19,* 341–345.

Babikian, T., Boone, K. B., Lu, P., & Arnold, G. (2006). Sensitivity and specificity of various digit span scores in the detection of suspect effort. *The Clinical Neuropsychologist, 20,* 145–159.

Baer, R. A., & Miller, J. (2002). Underreporting of psychopathology on the MMPI-2: A meta-analytic review. *Psychological Assessment, 14,* 16–26.

Bender, S. D., & Rogers, R. (2004). Detection of neurocognitive feigning: Development of a multi-strategy assessment. *Archives of Clinical Neuropsychology, 19,* 49–60.

Bianchini, K. J., Curtis, K. L., & Greve, K. W. (2006). Compensation and malingering in traumatic brain injury: A dose-response relationship? *The Clinical Neuropsychologist, 20,* 831–847.

Bianchini, K. J., Greve, K. W., & Glynn, G. (2005). On the diagnosis of malingered pain-related disability: Lessons from cognitive malingering research. *The Spine Journal, 5,* 404–417.

Bigos, S. J., Battie, M. C., Spengler, D. M., Fisher, L. D., Fordyce, W. E., Hansson, T. H., et al. (1991). A prospective study of work perceptions and psychosocial factors affecting the report of back injury. *Spine, 16,* 1–6.

Binder, L. M., & Rohling, M. L. (1996). Money matters: Meta-analytic review of the effects of financial incentives on recovery after closed-head injury. *American Journal of Psychiatry, 153,* 7–10.

Bleiberg, J., Cernich, A. N., Cameron, K., Wenyu, S., Peck, K., Ecklund, J., et al. (2004). Duration of cognitive impairment after sports concussion. *Neurosurgery, 54*, 1073–1078.

Bogduk, N., & McGuirk, B. (2002). *Medical management of acute and chronic low back pain: An evidence-based approach.* Amsterdam: Elsevier.

Boone, K., Lu, P., & Herzberg, D. S. (2002). *The b Test* [manual]. Los Angeles: Western Psychological Services.

Boos, N., Rieder, R., Schade, V., Spratt, K. F., Semmer, N., & Aebi, M. (1995). The diagnostic accuracy of magnetic resonance imaging, work perception, and psychosocial factors in identifying symptomatic disc herniations. *Spine, 20*, 2613–2625.

Borum, R., Otto, R., & Golding, S. (1993). Improving clinical judgment and decision making in forensic evaluation. *Journal of Psychiatry and Law, 21*, 35–76.

Brown, R. J. (2004). Psychological mechanisms of medically unexplained symptoms: An integrative conceptual model. *Psychological Bulletin, 130*, 793–812.

Bruns, D., & Disorbio, J. M. (2003). *Battery for health improvement 2* [manual]. Minneapolis, MN: NCS Pearson.

Burt, D., Zembar, M., & Niederehe, G. (1995). Depression and memory impairment: A meta-analysis of the association, its pattern, and specificity. *Psychological Bulletin, 117*, 285–305.

Burton, A. K., Tillotson, K. M., Main, C. J., & Hollis, S. (1995). Psychosocial predictors of outcome in acute and subchronic low back trouble. *Spine, 20*, 722–728.

Bury, A. S. & Bagby, R. M. (2002). The detection of feigned uncoached and coached posttraumatic stress disorder with the MMPI-2 in a sample of workplace accident victims. *Psychological Assessment, 14*, 472–484.

Butcher, J. N., Arbisi, P. A., Atlis, M. M., & McNulty, J. L. (2003). The construct validity of the Lees-Haley fake bad scale: Does this scale measure somatic malingering and feigned emotional distress? *Archives of Clinical Neuropsychology, 18*, 473–485.

Butcher, J. N., Graham, J. R., Ben-Poarth, Y. S., Tellegen, A., Dahlstrom, W. G., & Kaemmer, B. (2001). *Minnesota multiphasic personality inventory-2* (rev. ed.) [manual]. Minneapolis, MN: NCS Pearson.

Campion, D., Dumanchin, C., Hannequin, D., Dubois, B., Belliard, S., Puel, M., Thomas-Anterion, C., et al. (1999). Early-onset autosomal dominant Alzheimer disease: Prevalence, genetic heterogeneity, and mutation spectrum. *American Journal of Human Genetics, 65*, 664–670.

Cassidy, J. D., Carroll, L. J., Cote, P., Lemstra, M., Berglund, A., & Nygren, A. (2000). Effect of eliminating compensation for pain and suffering on the outcome of insurance claims for whiplash injury. *The New England Journal of Medicine, 342,* 1179–1186.

Clark, D. A., Cook, A., & Snow, D. (1998). Depressive symptoms differences in hospitalized, medically ill, depressed psychiatric inpatients and nonmedical controls. *Journal of Abnormal Psychology, 107,* 38–48.

CogniSyst. (1999). *1999 Supplement for the computerized assessment of response bias, word memory test and memory complaints inventory* [manual]. Durham, NC: Author.

Cummings, N., & Follette, W. (1968). Psychiatric services and medical utilization in a prepaid health plan setting: Part 2. *Journal of Medical Care, 6,* 31–41.

Davidson, J. R. T., & van der Kolk, B. A. (1996). The psychopharmacologic treatment of posttraumatic stress disorder. In B. A. van der Kolk, A. C. McFarlane, & L. Weisaeth, L. (Eds.), *Traumatic stress: The effects of overwhelming experience on mind, body, and society* (pp. 491–509). New York: Guilford Press.

Dawes, R. M., Faust, D., & Meehl, P. E. (1989). Clinical versus actuarial judgment. *Science, 243,* 1668–1674.

Delis, D. C., Kramer, J. H., Kaplan, E., & Ober, B. A. (2000). *California verbal learning test—Second edition* [manual]. San Antonio, TX: The Psychological Corporation.

Derry, P. A., & McLachlan, R. S. (1996). The MMPI-2 as an adjunct to the diagnosis of pseudoseizures. *Seizure, 5,* 35–40.

Eisenberg, L. (1992). Treating depression and anxiety in primary care. *New England Journal of Medicine, 326,* 1080–1083.

Ekman, P. (1996). Why don't we catch liars? *Social Research, 63,* 801–817.

Ekman, P., & O'Sullivan, M. (1991). Who can catch a liar. *American Psychologist, 46,* 913–920.

Faust, D., Ziskin, J., & Hiers, Jr., J. B. (1991). *Brain damage claims: Coping with neuropsychological evidence* (Vols. I, II). Los Angeles: Law and Psychology Press.

Fox, D. D., Lees-Haley, P. R., Earnest, K., & Dolezal-Wood, S. (1995). Base rates of postconcussive symptoms in health maintenance organization patients and controls. *Neuropsychology, 9,* 606–611.

Frederick, R. I. (2003). *Validity indicator profile* (2nd ed.) [manual]. Minneapolis, MN: NCS Pearson.

Garb, H. N. (1989). Clinical judgment, clinical training, and professional experience. *Psychological Bulletin, 105,* 387–396.

Garb, H. N. (1998). *Studying the clinician: Judgment research and psychological assessment*. Washington, DC: American Psychological Association.

Garb, H. N., & Schramke, C. J. (1996). Judgment research and neuropsychological assessment: A narrative review and meta-analysis. *Psychological Bulletin, 120*, 140–153.

Gatchel, R. J.(1996). Psychological disorders and chronic pain: Cause- and effect relationships. In R. J. Gatchel & D. C. Turk (Eds.), *Psychological approaches to pain management* (pp. 33–52). New York: Guilford Press.

Gatchel, R. J., & Epker, J. (1999). Psychosocial predictors of chronic pain and response to treatment. In R. J. Gatchel & D. C. Turk (Eds.), *Psychosocial factors in pain: Critical perspectives* (pp. 412–434). New York: Guilford Press.

Gatchel, R. J., Polatin, P. B., & Mayer, T. G. (1995). The dominant role of psychosocial risk factors in the development of chronic low back pain disability. *Spine, 20*, 2702–2709.

Gervais, R. O., Green, P., Allen, L. M., & Iverson, G. L. (2001). Effects of coaching on symptoms validity testing in chronic pain patients presenting for disability assessments. *Journal of Forensic Neuropsychology, 2*, 1–19.

Gervais, R. O., Rohling, M. L., Green, P., & Ford, W. (2004). A comparison of WMT, CARB, and TOMM failure rates in non-head injury disability claimants. *Archives of Clinical Neuropsychology, 19*, 475–487.

Gervais, R. O., Russell, A. S., Green, P., Ferrari, R., & Pieschl, S. D. (2001). Effort testing in patients with fibromyalgia and disability incentives. *Journal of Rheumatology, 28*, 1892–1899.

Gorman, W. F. (1993). *Legal neurology and malingering: Cases and techniques*. St. Louis, MO: Warren H. Green, Inc.

Gouvier, W. D. (1999). Baserates and clinical decision making in neuropsychology. In J. J. Sweet (Ed.), *Forensic neuropsychology* (pp. 27–37). Lisse, The Netherlands: Swets & Zeitlinger.

Green, P. (2001). Why clinicians often disagree about the validity of test results. *NeuroRehabilitation, 16*, 231–236.

Green, P. (2003a). Welcoming a paradigm shift in neuropsychology. *Archives of Clinical Neuropsychology, 18*, 625–627.

Green, P. (2003b). *Green's word memory test (manual)*. Edmonton, Canada: Green's Publishing.

Green, P., & Allen, L. M. (1996). *Memory complaints inventory: A computerized test of memory complaints*. Durham, NC: CogniSyst.

Green, P., Iverson, G. L., & Allen, L. (1999). Detecting malingering in head injury litigation with the word memory test. *Brain Injury, 13*, 813–819.

Green, P., Rohling, M. L., Lees-Haley, P. R., & Allen, L. M., III. (2001). Effort has a greater effect on test scores than severe brain injury in compensation claimants. *Brain Injury, 15*, 1045–1060.

Greene, R. L. (2000). *The MMPI-2: An interpretive manual* (2nd ed.). Boston: Allyn and Bacon.

Greiffenstein, M. F., Baker, W. J., Axelrod, B., Peck, E. A., & Gervais, R. (2004). The fake bad scale and the MMPI-2 F-family in detection of implausible psychological trauma claims. *The Clinical Neuropsychologist, 18*, 573–590.

Greiffenstein, M. F., Baker, W. J., & Gola, T. (1994). Validation of malingered amnesia measures with a large clinical sample. *Psychological Assessment, 6*, 218–224.

Greve, K. W., & Bianchini, K. J. (2004). Response to Butcher et al., The construct validity of the Lees-Haley fake-bad scale. *Archives of Clinical Neuropsychology, 19*, 337–339.

Hadler, N. M. (1995). The disabling backache. *Spine, 20*, 640–649.

Hadler, N. M., Carey, T. S., Garrett, J., & the North Carolina Back Pain Project. (1995). The influence of indemnification by workers' compensation insurance on recovery from acute backache. *Spine, 20*, 2710–2715.

Hall, H. V., & Pritchard, D. A. (1996). *Detecting malingering and deception: Forensic distortion analysis (FDA)*. Delray Beach, FL: St. Lucie Press.

Heaton, R. K., Smith, H. H., Lehman, R. A. W., & Vogt, A. T. (1978). Prospects for faking believable deficits on neuropsychological testing. *Journal of Consulting and Clinical Psychology, 46*, 892–900.

Iverson, G. L. (2005). Outcome from mild traumatic brain injury. *Current Opinion in Psychiatry, 18*, 301–317.

Iverson, G. L., Green, P., & Gervais, R. (1999). Using the word memory test to detect biased responding in head injury litigation. *Journal of Cognitive Rehabilitation, 17*, 4–8.

Iverson, G. L., King, R. J., Scott, J. G., & Adams, R. L. (2001). Cognitive complaints in litigating patients with head injuries or chronic pain. *Journal of Forensic Neuropsychology, 2*, 19–30.

Iverson, G. L., & McCracken, L. M. (1997). "Postconcussive" symptoms in persons with chronic pain. *Brain Injury, 11*, 783–790.

Katzman, G. L., Dagher, A. P., & Patronas, N. J. (1999). Incidental findings on brain magnetic resonance imaging form 1000 asymptomatic volunteers. *Journal of the American Medical Association, 282*, 36–39.

Kleinmuntz, B. (1990). Why we still use our heads instead of formulas: Towards an integrative approach. *Psychological Bulletin, 107*, 296–310.

Kroenke, K., & Mangelsdorff, A. D. (1989). Common symptoms in ambulatory care: Incidence, evaluation, therapy, and outcome. *American Journal of Medicine, 86*, 262–266.

Larrabee, G. J. (1990). Cautions in the use of neuropsychological evaluation in legal setting. *Neuropsychology, 4*, 239–247.

Larrabee, G. J. (2000). Neuropsychology in personal injury litigation. *Journal of Clinical and Experimental Neuropsychology, 22*, 702–707.

Larrabee, G. J. (2003a). Exaggerated pain report in litigants with malingered neurocognitive dysfunction. *The Clinical Neuropsychologist, 17*, 395–401.

Larrabee, G. J. (2003b). Detection of symptom exaggeration with the MMPI-2 in litigants with malingered neurocognitive dysfunction. *The Clinical Neuropsychologist, 17*, 54–68.

Lees-Haley, P. R., & Brown, R. S. (1993). Neuropsychological complaint base rates of 170 personal injury claimants. *Archives of Clinical Neuropsychology, 8*, 203–209.

Lees-Haley, P. R., English, L. T., & Glenn, W. J. (1991). A fake bad scale on the MMPI-2 for personal injury claimants. *Psychological Reports, 68*, 203–210.

Lees-Haley, P. R., & Fox, D. D. (2004). Commentary on Butcher, Arbisi, and McNulty (2003) on the fake bad scale. *Archives of Clinical Neuropsychology, 19*, 333–336.

Lees-Haley, P. R., Iverson, G. L., Lange, R. T., Fox, D. D., & Allen, L. M., III. (2002). Malingering in forensic neuropsychology: Daubert and the MMPI-2. *Journal of Forensic Neuropsychology, 3*, 167–203.

Meehl, P. E. (1954). *Clinical versus statistical prediction: A theoretical analysis and a review of the evidence*. Minneapolis: University of Minnesota Press.

Meehl, P. E. (1957). When shall we use our heads instead of the formula? *Journal of Counseling Psychology, 4*, 268–273.

Melzack, R.(1999). Pain and stress: A new perspective. In R. J. Gatchel & D. C. Turk (Eds.), *Psychosocial factors in pain* (pp. 89–106). New York: Guilford Press.

Melzack, R., & Wall, P. (1965). Pain mechanisms: A new theory. *Science, 50*, 971–979.

Meyer, G. J., Finn, S. E., Eyde, L. D., Kay, G. G., Dies, R. R., Eisman, E. J., et al. (2002). Amplifying issues related to psychological testing and assessment. *The American Psychologist, 57*, 140–141.

Meyer, G. J., Finn, S. E., Eyde, L. D., Kay, G. G., Moreland, K. L., Dies, R. R., et al. (2001). Psychological testing and psychological assessment: A review of the evidence and issues. *The American Psychologist, 56,* 128–165.

Meyers, J. E., & Meyers, K. R. (1995). *Rey complex figure test and recognition trial* [manual]. Odessa, FL: Psychological Assessment Resources.

Meyers, J. E., Millis, S. R., & Volkert, K. (2002). A validity index for the MMPI-2. *Archives of Clinical Neuropsychology, 17,* 157–169.

Miller, H. (1961). Accident neurosis. *British Medical Journal, 1,* 919–925.

Millis, S. R., & Putnam, S. H. (1996). Detection of malingering in postconcussive syndrome. In M. Rizzo & D. D. Tranel (Eds.), *Head injury and postconcussive syndrome* (pp. 481-498). New York: Churchill Livingstone.

Millis, S. R., & Volinsky, C. T. (2001). Assessment of response bias in mild head injury: Beyond malingering tests. *Journal of Clinical and Experimental Neuropsychology, 23,* 809–828.

Mittenberg, W., DiGiulio, D. V., Perrin, S., & Bass, A. E. (1992). Symptoms following mild head injury: Expectation as etiology. *Journal of Neurology, Neurosurgery, and Psychiatry, 55,* 200–204.

Mittenberg, W., Rotholc, A., Russell, E., & Heilbronner, R. (1996). Identification of malingered head injury on the Halstead-Reitan Battery. *Archives of Clinical Neuropsychology, 11,* 271–281.

Nelson, N. W., Sweet, J. J., & Demakis, G. J. (2006). Meta-analysis of the MMPI-2 fake bad scale: Utility in forensic practice. *The Clinical Neuropsychologist, 20,* 39–58.

Pankratz, L., & Erickson, R. C. (1990). Two views of malingering. *The Clinical Neuropsychologist, 4,* 379–389.

Perry, S., Difede, J., Musngi, G., Frances, A. J., & Jacobsberg, L. (1992). Predictors of posttraumatic stress disorder after burn injury. *American Journal of Psychiatry, 149,* 931–935.

Richman, J., Green, P., Gervais, R., Flaro, L., Merten, T., Brockhaus, R., et al. (2006). Objective test of symptom exaggeration in independent medical examinations. *Journal of Occupational and Environmental Medicine, 48,* 303–311.

Rimel, R. W., Giordani, B., Barth, J. T., Boll, T. J., & Jane, J. A. (1981). Disability caused by minor head injury. *Neurosurgery, 9,* 221–228.

Rogers, R. (1997). Introduction. In R. Rogers (Ed.), *Clinical assessment of deception and malingering* (2nd ed., pp. 1-19). New York: Guilford Press.

Rogers, R., Bagby, R. M., & Dickens, S. E. (1992). *Structured interview of reported symptoms* [manual]. Odessa, FL: Psychological Assessment Resources.

Rogers, R., Harrell, E. H., & Liff, C. D. (1993). Feigning neuropsychological impairment: A critical review of methodological and clinical considerations. *Clinical Psychology Review, 13,* 255–274.

Rogers, R., & Resnick, P. J. (1988). *Malingering and deception: The clinical interview* [practitioner's manual]. New York: Guilford Publications.

Rogers, R., Sewell, K. W., & Salekin, R. T. (1994). A meta-analysis of malingering on the MMPI-2. *Assessment, 1,* 227–237.

Rogers, R., Sewell, K. W., & Ustad, K. L. (1995). Feigning among chronic outpatients on the MMPI-2: A systematic examination of fake-bad indicators. *Assessment, 2,* 81–89.

Rohling, M. L., Allen, L. M., & Green, P. (2002). Who is exaggerating cognitive impairment and who is not? *CNS Spectrum, 7,* 387–395.

Rohling, M. L., Binder, L. M., & Langhinrichsen-Rohling, J. (1995). Money matters: A meta-analytic review of the association between financial compensation and the experience and treatment of chronic pain. *Health Psychology, 14,* 537–547.

Rohling, M. L., Green, P., Allen, L. M., III, & Iverson, G. L. (2002). Depressive symptoms and neurocognitive test scores in patients passing symptom validity tests. *Archives of Clinical Neuropsychology, 17,* 205–222.

Rose, F. E., Hall, S., & Szalda-Petree, A. D. (1998). A comparison of four tests of malingering and the effects of coaching. *Archives of Clinical Neuropsychology, 13,* 349–363.

Ross, S. R., Millis, S. R., Krukowski, R. A., Putnam, S. H., & Adams, K. M. (2004). Detecting incomplete effort on the MMPI-2: An examination of the fake-bad scale in mild head injury. *Journal of Clinical and Experimental Neuropsychology, 26,* 115–124.

Rothbaum, B. O., & Foa, E. B (1996). Cognitive-behavioral therapy for posttraumatic stress disorder. In B. A. van der Kolk, A. C. McFarlane, & L. Weisaeth (Eds.), *Traumatic stress: The effects of overwhelming experience on mind, body, and society* (pp. 491–509). New York: Guilford Press.

Schmand, B., Lindeboom, J., Schagen, S., Heijt, R., Koene, T., & Hambeerger, H. L. (1998). Cognitive complaints in patients after whiplash injury: The impact of malingering. *Journal of Neurology, Neurosurgery, and Psychiatry, 64,* 339–343.

Scott, J. G., Emick, M. A., & Adams, R. L. (1999). The MMPI-2 and closed-head injury: Effects of litigation and head injury severity. *Journal of Forensic Neuropsychology, 1,* 3–13.

Slick, D. J., Sherman, E. M. S., & Iverson, G. L. (1999). Diagnostic criteria for malingered neurocognitive dysfunction: Proposed standards for clinical practice and research. *The Clinical Neuropsychologist, 13*, 545–561.

Spitzer, R. L, Williams, J. B., Kroenke, K., Linzer, M., Verloin Degruy, F., III, Hahn, S. R., et al. (1994). Utility of new procedure for diagnosing mental disorders in primary care: The PRIME-MD 1000 Study. *Journal of the American Medical Association, 272*, 1749–1756.

Sumanti, M., Boone, K. B., Savodnik, I., & Gorsuch, R. (2006). Noncredible psychiatric and cognitive symptoms in a workers' compensation "stress" claim sample. *The Clinical Neuropsychologist, 20*, 754–765.

Sweet, J. J. (1999). Malingering differential diagnosis. In J. J. Sweet (Ed.), *Forensic neuropsychology* (pp. 255–285). Lisse, The Netherlands: Swets & Zeitlinger.

Symonds, C. P. (1937). Mental disorder following head injury. *Proceedings of the Royal Society of Medicine, 30*, 1081–1092.

Tombaugh, T. N. (1996). *Test of memory malingering* [manual]. North Tonawanda, NY: Multi-Health Systems.

Turk, D. C., & Melzack, R. (1992). The measurement of pain and the assessment of people experience pain. In D. C. Turk & R. Melzack (Eds.), *Handbook of pain assessment* (pp. 3–12). New York: Guilford Press.

Turk, D. C., & Nash, J. M.(1996). Psychological issues in chronic pain. In R. K. Portenoy & Kanner, R. M. (Eds.), *Pain management: Theory and practice* (pp. 323–335). Philadelphia: F.A. Davis Company.

Waddell, G., & Turk, D. C. (1992). Clinical assessment of low back pain. In D. C. Turk & R. Melzack (Eds.), *Handbook of pain assessment* (pp. 15–136). New York: Guilford Press.

Wetter, M. W., & Corrigan, S. K. (1995). Providing information to clients about psychological tests: A survey of attorneys' and law students' attitudes. *Professional Psychology: Research and Practice, 26*, 474–477.

Yehuda, R., & McFarlane, A. C. (1995). Conflict between current knowledge about posttraumatic stress disorder and its original conceptual basis. *American Journal of Psychiatry, 152*, 1705–1713.

Youngjohn, J. R., Davis, D., & Wolf, I. (1997). Head injury and the MMPI-2: Paradoxical severity effects and the influence of litigation. *Psychological Assessment, 9*, 177–184.

Ziskin, J. (1981). *Coping with psychiatric and psychological testimony* (3rd ed.). Venice, CA: Law and Psychology Press.

CHAPTER SEVEN

GUARDING THE GATES: EXPERT WITNESS TESTIMONY AFTER *DAUBERT*[1]

Karin Horwatt Cather, JD

Modern science can reasonably be said to have come into being during the time of Queen Elizabeth I of England and William Shakespeare. Almost immediately, it came into conflict with the law.[2]

SCOPE

Expert testimony is testimony by a witness who has more knowledge, skill, experience, training or education about a given subject than a lay person does. Such testimony can take the form of an opinion and need not—as is usually required with lay witnesses—be based only on observations. The potential subject matter of the expertise is unlimited—from the standard of care in a medical malpractice case to the cause of a tire failure to whether an individual's drug possession is consistent or inconsistent with personal use. In state cases, the admissibility of DNA tests (both PCR and RFLP) and the statistical methods involved in their interpretation, of horizontal gaze nystagmus tests as circumstantial evidence of driving under the influence of alcohol, and of causation testimony in cases alleging injury from pharmaceuticals are heavily reported. So are cases involving the admissibility of polygraph evidence (which is, despite the multitude of standards for admissibility of scientific evidence, almost uniformly inadmissible), and syndrome evidence.

Expert testimony is essential in many cases. For example, in medical malpractice cases, expert testimony establishes the standard of care in the community; in murder cases, a medical examiner or coroner testifies as to the cause of death. In products liability cases, an expert must testify as to the source of malfunction. Of course, in most such cases, it is not uncommon to have experts from both sides satisfy admissibility requirements and testify to opposite conclusions.

Meanwhile, expert testimony is frequently viewed with distrust and cynicism—even by the experts, themselves.[3] Courts are concerned with the capacity of lay jurors to competently evaluate expert testimony from conflicting sources. For example, Judge Eastaugh, rendering an opinion on a leading case for the Alaska Supreme Court, observed that "(1) lay jurors can be overly-impressed by science; (2) lay jurors lack the capacity to evaluate scientific evidence critically; and (3) lay jurors are likely to give 'junk science' more weight than it deserves."[4] He went on to say that:

> Even when they apply the same methodology, experts for opposing parties may reach different results. Likewise, well-qualified experts may make rational conflicting choices in deciding which reliable methodology to apply. Juries, relatively ill-trained to resolve such conflicts on subtle or complex scientific grounds, may resort to credibility assessments which are unduly simplistic. Opinions of a practiced forensic expert may prevail over those of a true academic who makes a less impressive appearance on the witness stand. Assuming proper

execution of the judicial gatekeeping function, we think the risk to fair trials posed by junk science is lower than the risk posed by jurors' difficulty in critically assessing scientific evidence that is based on reliable methodologies.[5]

To complicate matters, during *voir dire*, lawyers for one side or the other frequently seek to ensure that jurors with the same expertise as their witnesses do not serve on the jury. Generally, the disqualifying question is some version of "if our expert testified to conclusions that, based on your professional experience, you believed were flawed would you be able to set your professional background aside and decide the case solely on the evidence before you, even if you felt that our expert was wrong?" This practice all but guarantees that no one on the jury will be able to assess the credibility of the relevant expert from the "inside."

But the admissibility of such evidence is far from automatic. As one dissenting Alabama Supreme Court justice aptly stated,

> [C]ourts must carefully scrutinize the opinions of so-called experts to ensure that a jury does not hear what has in recent years come to be known as "junk science." It is that very presumption—that "experts" know better than the average person—that makes "junk science" so dangerous. Peter W. Huber's book Galileo's Revenge: Junk Science in the Courtroom (1991), at pp. 2–3, gives an apt description of the junk science phenomenon:
>
>> Junk science cuts across chemistry and pharmacology, medicine and engineering. It is a hodgepodge of biased data, spurious inference, and logical legerdemain, patched together by researchers whose enthusiasm for discovery and diagnosis far outstrips their skill. It is a catalog of every conceivable kind of error: data dredging, wishful thinking, truculent dogmatism, and, now and again, outright fraud.[6]

Junk science pervades our experience, so it should not be surprising to find it in the courtroom. Syndrome evidence,[7] for example, has been introduced to explain all kinds of conduct.

When a relatively large number of persons, having the same symptoms, exhibit a combination or variation of functional psychiatric disorders that leads to purely emotional stress that causes intense mental anguish or emotional trauma, i.e., trauma having no direct physical effect upon the body, psychiatrists put those persons under one or more labels. Today, we have the following labels: "The Battered Wife Syndrome;" "The Battered Woman Syndrome;" "The Battered Child Syndrome;" "The Battered Husband Syndrome;" "The Battered Parent Syndrome;" "The Familial Child Sexual Abuse Syndrome;" "The Rape Trauma Syndrome;" "The Battle Fatigue Syndrome;" "The Viet Nam Post-Traumatic Stress Syndrome;" "The Policeman's Syndrome;" "The Post-Concussive Syndrome;" "The Whiplash Syndrome;" "The Low-Back Syndrome;" "The Lover's Syndrome;" "The Love Fear Syndrome;" "The Organic Delusional Syndrome;" "The Chronic Brain Syndrome;" and "The Holocaust Syndrome." Tomorrow, there will probably be additions to the list, such as "The Appellate Court Judge Syndrome."[8]

Ironically, the above-referenced list was written by the dissent, which supported the admissibility of the contested evidence, in a case in which a road-rage shooter proffered the "Holocaust syndrome" to bootstrap a nonexistent self-defense claim, and which the trial court properly refused to enable:

The evidence excluded only tended to show that possibly appellant was not an ordinary and prudent man with respect to self-defense. This did not entitle appellant to an enlargement of the statutory defense on account of his psychological peculiarities. A similar point was recently made in *Gonzales v. State*, 689 S.W.2d 900, 903 (Tex.Cr.App.1985), with regard to V.T.C.A., Penal Code, § 19.04(c) (Voluntary manslaughter), which also utilizes the "reasonable man."

Appellant seems to contend that because he is an Hispanic farm worker who was living with a Caucasian woman on a low income he should be granted more latitude in the degree of insult, etc., sufficient to enrage him. Yet appellant fails to recognize that the standard of the reasonable man, the person of ordinary temper, is employed precisely to avoid different applications of the law of manslaughter to defendants of different races, creed, color, sex, or social status.

Similarly, in a murder case in which there was no dispute that the victim was stalked before she was murdered, an expert witness attempted to testify to an impulse-control disorder in which the criteria were so broad that anyone could qualify and which would not have precluded the defendant from planning the attack; the defendant proffered this expert testimony—which the court fortunately prevented from reaching the jury—even though the defendant's defense was that he was totally uninvolved in the events that gave rise to the death of the victim. The following amazing colloquy results:

> [DEFENSE COUNSEL]: Is it a fair statement that not all individuals are equally capable of forming and possessing the same types and degrees of intent to commit a violent act?
>
> [DR. FIESTER]: You know, that is correct, yes. In addition, the ability to have that intent and the ability to control one's behavior can vary from moment-to-moment, day-to-day, month-to-month, or year-to-year in any given individual, even with a baseline set of personality or psychiatric symptoms.
>
> [DEFENSE COUNSEL]: So, if I understand your testimony, in determining the nature of, say, for example Mr. Bryant's intent, it is very relevant to consider whether he has this impulse control—
>
> [PROSECUTOR]: I object. That's leading. I mean, who is testifying here?
>
> THE COURT: Sustained.
>
> [DEFENSE COUNSEL]: Is it relevant to consider impulse control disorder in determining Mr. Bryant's intent to commit a particular violent act?
>
> [DR. FIESTER]: Yes.
>
> [DEFENSE COUNSEL]: If you could, again, just explain that for the Court.

[DR. FIESTER]: Again, it is a failure to contain what can be overwhelming, immediate aggressive impulses...

[DEFENSE COUNSEL]: Is there a connection or a nexus between an impulse control disorder of the type that you have determined that Mr. Bryant suffers from and the allegations that you have reviewed in the statement of events or summary of events?

[DR. FIESTER]: Yes.

[DEFENSE COUNSEL]: What is that?

[DR. FIESTER]: That my understanding is that Mr. Bryant has been charged with murder, essentially, and that the nexus between the two is that an impulse control disorder can lead an individual in certain circumstances to experience overwhelming aggressive urges that could result in them acting out those urges, and could result in an assaultive act.

[DEFENSE COUNSEL]: Again, when you're saying "impulsive," when I think of impulsive, that means sudden, spontaneous, without planning, and deliberation. Is that an accurate way to define impulse?

[DR. FIESTER]: Yes.

* * *

[DEFENSE COUNSEL]: Dr. Fiester, the question is, if the Defendant is in a Court proceeding and there is a voice speaking, and the Defendant appears agitated by that voice, and then interrupts that voice, and then has a verbal outburst and makes threats, is that evidence of an impulse control disorder?

* * *

[DR. FIESTER]: ...I can say yes, that information is consistent with an impulse control disorder. In fact, if you look at the associated features of the disorder as described in the DSM-IVTR, it says that signs of general impulsivity or aggression may be present between explosive episodes.

Let us not forget the impulse-control disorder means physically assaultive acts. So, it says that individuals with this disorder may report problems with chronic anger and frequent sub-threshold episodes. In other words, they don't lose it and attack someone, but they experience aggressive impulses, but either manage to resist acting on them or engage in less destructive aggressive behavior, such as screaming, punching a wall without damaging it, etc.

So, a verbal tirade instead of actually acting out the aggressive impulse by beating someone up or harming them seriously is completely consistent with the features of this intermittent explosive disorder.

During cross-examination, the following occurred:

[PROSECUTOR]: My question is you testified earlier that intermittent explosive disorder from month-to-month or from day-to-day in fact can be different, isn't that true, in terms of its impact on an individual? Just because you diagnose someone with impulse disorder or intermittent impulse disorder, the effect of that disorder can be different from day-to-day or month-to-month, to use your words. Isn't that correct?

[DR. FIESTER]: No. I believe that's not quite accurate. I said that each state of the individual and their degree to which they can resist an impulse, aggressive impulse can vary from time-to-time, but the key core characteristic of the disorder is having episodes where you are unable to resist that aggressive episode.

[PROSECUTOR]: So, the effect of the disorder does vary from day-to-day. The effect of the disorder varies from day-to-day and month-to-month by degree. Is that what you're saying?

[DR. FIESTER]: I'm not exactly sure I would say it is the effect of the disorder... The disorder is present all the time, but the ability of the individual to resist those impulses can vary.

Following the State's cross-examination of Dr. Fiester, the trial court inquired:

THE COURT: You are not saying, are you, that every person or even this person who has impulse control disorder isn't capable of controlling his actions, are you?

THE WITNESS: At all points in time, no. That's correct.

THE COURT: *So, anyone with this disorder is capable of planning a future action. Is that correct?*

THE WITNESS: *Yes. Just the presence of the disorder itself, without further information, would [lead] me to say that it's possible an individual that carries this diagnosis could plan a crime.*[9]

Sometimes, the science may be legitimate, but the methodology of the expert may be flawed, as in *Schafersman v. Agland Coop.*, where a party proffered an expert to testify about causation in a products liability case involving adulterated oats fed to cattle.

Wass admitted that he did not perform a clinical examination of any of the cows and did not treat the cows. Wass did not perform any tests on the cows to rule out other causes of the jaundice that had been observed in the cows by the Schafersmans' veterinarian, nor did he test for copper toxicity, which Wass opined was a contributing factor to the illness afflicting the cows. Wass performed no tests to rule out other potential causes for the alleged drop in milk production. Wass acknowledged that he should have tested for copper toxicity and performed other tests on the cows. Wass further testified that while he tested a sample of the mixture delivered to the Schafersmans by Agland, he did not test the composition of the total ration actually fed to the cows after it was combined by the Schafersmans with corn and other nutrients...

With respect to the theory of multiple mineral toxicity, Wass testified that he had neither studied multiple mineral toxicity nor authored any publications concerning multiple mineral toxicity. Wass testified that he was aware of no controlled studies that related to multiple mineral toxicity, although he claimed that people in the field have observed it. Wass conceded that the theory he proposed set forth no standard for determining what levels of any given minerals could result in a toxic effect. In his deposition, which was admitted at the hearing on Agland's motion in limine, Wass stated that he had seen a similar prior case, but he did not testify regarding the mineral levels present in that instance, nor did he discuss any testing that might have been performed in that instance. Wass conceded, in his deposition, that he had not conducted any tests that were intended to bear out his theory of multiple mineral toxicity.

In addition, Agland's expert witness, Dr. David Reed, a veterinarian who specializes in dairy cows and nutritional consulting for dairy producers, reviewed Wass' deposition testimony and the attached exhibits. Reed testified that the scientific literature did not contain a theory of multiple mineral toxicity and that in his opinion, that theory did not apply to the instant case.[10]

And, of course, there is the raft of litigation by parents who claim that autism is caused by Thimerosal, even though courts acknowledge there is no scientific evidence to support the claim.[11]

More ambiguously, there is silicon breast-implant litigation, which finds little scientific support. Indeed, the debate seems to be between law and science, and not between different scientific factions.

The best way to test the silicone poisoning theory was to conduct large population studies of women with and without implants. The Mayo Clinic was the first brand-name medical facility to undertake such an analysis. Its finding was published by the *New England Journal of Medicine* in June 1994. Mayo Clinic researchers found what study after study since their work has found, that women with silicone breast implants are no more likely to develop connective tissue diseases than women without them.

In the five years since the clinic's research, science has failed—with monotonous regularity—to demonstrate the link so many assumed existed. In 1995, the *New England Journal of Medicine* published another analysis which found no connection between silicone and connective tissue diseases. By 1996, the research was so conclusive that *Scientific American* reporter Sasha Nemecek wrote of the "scientific consensus" which had emerged on the subject: "Indeed, studies have not found evidence for a link between silicone implants and autoimmune disorders such as lupus, scleroderma and rheumatoid arthritis."[12]

A search on Entrez PubMed revealed, among other things, a meta-analysis study in a 2000 edition of *The New England Journal of Medicine* that supported the author's evidence,[13] as well as a meta-analysis in *Autoimmunity*.[14] The purpose of these citations is not to argue that silicone breast implants do or do not cause auto-immune disorder—such would be well beyond the scope of this chapter and my knowledge base—but to point out that the division between scientific research and court decisions.

Expert testimony is essential in certain kinds of cases and can be of immeasurable assistance to the trier of fact. A 1998 study by the Federal Judicial Center[15] established that experts testified most frequently in tort cases. This survey found that medical and mental health experts were the most common general category of testifying experts and that economists were the most frequent specific type of expert (because the amount of recovery to which a plaintiff is entitled must be offered in many such cases).[16]

Judges reported that the most frequent issues addressed were:

> the existence, nature, or extent of injury or damage (68% of the trials) and the cause of injury or damage (64%). Testimony as to the amount of recovery to which plaintiff was entitled was offered by experts in 44% of trials. Other issues addressed by expert testimony were the reasonableness of a party's actions (in 34% of trials), industry standards/'state of the art' (30%), standard of care owed by a professional (25%), design or testing of a product (25%), and knowledge or intent of a party (16%).[17]

However, experts may be needed to shed light on a surprising array of topics.[18] Indeed, a Google search of expert witness directories revealed hundreds of areas of witness expertise.[19] The Advisory Committee observed, in the Notes to FRE 702, that the:

> fields of knowledge which may be drawn upon are not limited merely to the "scientific" and "technical" but extend to all "specialized" knowledge. Similarly, the expert is viewed, not in a narrow sense, but as a person qualified by "knowledge, skill, experience, training or education." Thus within the scope of the rule are not only experts in the strictest sense of the word, e.g., physicians, physicists, and architects, but also the large group sometimes called "skilled" witnesses, such as bankers or landowners testifying to land values.[20]

Expert testimony is introduced to prove or explain facts introduced into evidence. Sometimes, expert testimony is required to explain why evidence is not introduced. This is called "negative evidence."[21] Jurors have come to expect expert testimony—even when such evidence is technologically impossible to obtain because the relevant test does not exist, has degraded due to exposure to the elements or the passage of time, is prohibitively expensive, or is irrelevant. But thanks to fictional criminal forensics television shows, prosecutors in criminal cases must now introduce "negative evidence" to establish to jurors the basis for the absence of such evidence.[22] For example, a prosecutor might have a medical examiner explain to the jury why it would be impossible to obtain DNA evidence of a rape from skeletal remains, or a fingerprint expert might testify that it is not possible to recover fingerprints off every surface or why, in a murder case where one spouse is charged with killing the other in the marital home, DNA or fingerprint evidence taken from the home would not prove the identity of the killer.[23] Such negative evidence must conform to the same requirements with regard to admissibility as other expert testimony.

The purpose of this chapter is to describe the legal standards for the admissibility—or not—of expert testimony.[24] This chapter contains an exploration of federal statutory and common law and a brief exploration of state laws, and an outline of ethical issues for the practitioner and of issues that affect the weight or admissibility of expert testimony.

LAWS GOVERNING EXPERT TESTIMONY

Statutory and common laws have evolved to attempt to ensure the relevance, accuracy, and reliability of expert testimony. Federal courts attempt to ensure that "[e]xperts must show that their conclusions were reached by methods that are consistent with how their colleagues in the relevant field or discipline would proceed to establish a proposition were they presented with the same facts and issues."[25]

Reduced to their fundamentals, laws governing the admissibility of expert testimony require that such evidence be relevant[26] and reliable. Moreover, the probative value of the evidence must not outweigh the prejudicial effect, and it must not be cumulative.[27] There may or may not be restrictions as to the extent to which it may speak to the ultimate issue—and vouching for a witness through expert testimony is generally prohibited.[28]

The Federal Rules of Evidence[29]

In the federal courts, the admissibility of expert testimony is governed by the Federal Rules of Evidence (FRE).[30] Notably, this section of the FRE begins by setting out restrictions on the extent to which lay witnesses may offer testimony in the form of opinions or inferences. With specifically delimited exceptions, lay witnesses must confine their testimony to what they can perceive from their senses.

The relevant FRE are as follows:

Rule 701. Opinion Testimony by Lay Witnesses

> If the witness is not testifying as an expert, the witness' testimony in the form of opinions or inferences is limited to those opinions or inferences which are (a) rationally based on the perception of the witness, and (b) helpful to a clear understanding of the witness' testimony or the determination of a fact in issue, and (c) not based on scientific, technical, or other specialized knowledge within the scope of Rule 702.

In the Notes to the FRE, the Advisory Committee indicates that the purpose of the amendments to FRE 701 was to "eliminate the risk that the reliability requirements set forth in Rule 702 will be evaded through the simple expedient of proffering an expert in lay witness clothing."[31]

Rule 702. Testimony by Experts

> If scientific, technical, or other specialized knowledge will assist the trier of fact to understand the evidence or to determine a fact in issue, a witness qualified as an expert by knowledge, skill, experience, training, or education may testify thereto in the form of an opinion or otherwise, if (1) the testimony is based upon sufficient facts or data, (2) the testimony

is the product of reliable principles and methods, and (3) the witness has applied the principles and methods reliably to the facts of the case.

Rule 703. Bases of Opinion Testimony by Experts

> The facts or data in the particular case upon which an expert bases an opinion or inference may be those perceived by or made known to the expert at or before the hearing. If of a type reasonably relied upon by experts in the particular field in forming opinions or inferences upon the subject, the facts or data need not be admissible in evidence in order for the opinion or inference to be admitted. Facts or data that are otherwise inadmissible shall not be disclosed to the jury by the proponent of the opinion or inference unless the court determines that their probative value in assisting the jury to evaluate the expert's opinion substantially outweighs their prejudicial effect.

Rule 703 was amended to ensure that, when an expert reasonably relies on inadmissible information to form an opinion or inference, the underlying information is not rendered admissible simply because the opinion or inference is admitted. This prohibition ensures that a forensic psychologist does not become a vehicle through which otherwise-inadmissible evidence is transported to the fact-finder.

A court must also weigh the issue of whether the probative value of the underlying, inadmissible information outweighs the prejudicial effect, even with a cautionary instruction to the jury. An example might be hearsay evidence provided to the expert to assist him in making a determination of sanity at the time of the offense.

Rule 704. Opinion on Ultimate Issue

(a) Except as provided in subdivision (b), testimony in the form of an opinion or inference otherwise admissible is not objectionable because it embraces an ultimate issue to be decided by the trier of fact.

(b) No expert witness testifying with respect to the mental state or condition of a defendant in a criminal case may state an opinion or inference as to whether the defendant did or did not have the mental state or condition constituting an element of the crime charged or of a defense thereto. Such ultimate issues are matters for the trier of fact alone.

Rule 705. Disclosure of Facts or Data Underlying Expert Opinion

The expert may testify in terms of opinion or inference and give reasons therefore without first testifying to the underlying facts or data, unless the court requires otherwise. The expert may in any event be required to disclose the underlying facts or data on cross-examination.

Rule 706. Court Appointed Experts

(a) *Appointment:* The court may on its own motion or on the motion of any party enter an order to show cause why expert witnesses should not be appointed, and may request the parties to submit nominations. The court may appoint any expert witnesses agreed upon by the parties, and may appoint expert witnesses of its own selection. An expert witness shall not be appointed by the court unless the witness consents to act. A witness so appointed shall be informed of the witness' duties by the court in writing, a copy of which shall be filed with the clerk, or at a conference in which the parties shall have opportunity to participate. A witness so appointed shall advise the parties of the witness' findings, if any; the witness' deposition may be taken by any party; and the witness may be called to testify by the court or any party. The witness shall be subject to cross-examination by each party, including a party calling the witness.

(b) *Compensation:* Expert witnesses so appointed are entitled to reasonable compensation in whatever sum the court may allow. The compensation thus fixed is payable from funds which may be provided by law in criminal cases and civil actions and proceedings involving just compensation under the fifth amendment. In other civil actions and proceedings the compensation shall be paid by the parties in such proportion and at such time as the court directs, and thereafter charged in like manner as other costs.

(c) *Disclosure of appointment:* In the exercise of its discretion, the court may authorize disclosure to the jury of the fact that the court appointed the expert witness.

(d) *Parties' experts of own selection:* Nothing in this rule limits the parties in calling expert witnesses of their own selection.

Each federal jurisdiction interprets these rules differently.

U.S. Supreme Court Rulings

FRE 702 was amended before the Supreme Court's opinion in *Daubert v. Merrell Dow Pharmaceuticals, Inc.*, 509 U.S. 579, 113 S.Ct. 2786, 125 L.Ed.2d 469 (1993). Before *Daubert*, most jurisdictions relied upon the "general acceptance standard," of *Frye v. United States*, which states the following:[32]

> Just when a scientific principle or discovery crosses the line between the experimental and demonstrable stages is difficult to define. Somewhere in this twilight zone the evidential force of the principle must be recognized, and while courts will go a long way in admitting expert testimony deduced from a well-recognized scientific principle or discovery, the thing from which the deduction is made must be sufficiently established to have gained general acceptance in the particular field in which it belongs.

As will be seen in the following text, the *Frye* test is still in use in many state courts.

But in 1993, the *Daubert* Court held that the FRE, not *Frye*, provided the standard in federal courts by which expert testimony should be evaluated for admissibility. Although some judges and commentators feared that *Daubert* would open the floodgates to junk science,[33] there seems to be a consensus that *Daubert* has resulted in a more stringent review of expert testimony by federal trial courts.[34] The majority opinion held that even though the:

> *Frye* test was displaced by the Rules of Evidence does not mean, however, that the Rules themselves place no limits on

> the admissibility of purportedly scientific evidence... . Nor is
> the trial judge disabled from screening such evidence. To the
> contrary, under the Rules the trial judge must ensure that any
> and all scientific testimony or evidence admitted is not only
> relevant, but reliable.[35]

The *Daubert* majority found that the trial court had a gatekeeping obligation; the trial court must evaluate scientific testimony to prevent irrelevant, unreliable, insufficiently probative, unfairly prejudicial evidence from being admitted. *Daubert* located this obligation squarely within the language of FRE 702, indicating that the Rule itself presupposed "some degree of regulation of the subjects and theories about which an expert may testify."[36]

The proffered testimony must be relevant; that is, it must "assist the trier of fact to understand the evidence or to determine a fact in issue."

> The consideration has been aptly described by Judge Becker as
> one of "fit." "Fit" is not always obvious, and scientific validity
> for one purpose is not necessarily scientific validity for other,
> unrelated purposes... . The study of the phases of the moon,
> for example, may provide valid scientific "knowledge" about
> whether a certain night was dark, and if darkness is a fact in
> issue, the knowledge will assist the trier of fact. However
> (absent creditable grounds supporting such a link), evidence
> that the moon was full on a certain night will not assist the trier
> of fact in determining whether an individual was unusually
> likely to have behaved irrationally on that night. Rule 702's
> "helpfulness" standard requires a valid scientific connection
> to the pertinent inquiry as a precondition to admissibility.[37]

The *Daubert* Court presumes that, faced with a proffer of scientific testimony, the trial court will conduct a hearing pursuant to FRE 104(a) to determine whether the proffered evidence will consist of (1) "scientific knowledge" which (2) will assist the trier of fact to understand or to determine a fact at issue. FRE 104(a) provides:

> Preliminary questions concerning the qualification of a person
> to be a witness, the existence of a privilege, or the admissibility

of evidence shall be determined by the court, subject to the provisions of subdivision (b) [pertaining to conditional admissions]. In making its determination it is not bound by the rules of evidence except those with respect to privileges.[38]

The Court held that the standard is that "[t]hese matters should be established by a preponderance of proof." The Court went on to state some general observations, not "a definitive checklist or test:"

1. Whether the theory can, and has been tested
2. Whether the theory has been subjected to peer review and publication—although the Court cautioned that this factor was relevant, but not dispositive
3. The known and potential rate of error, and the existence and maintenance of standards controlling the technique's operation
4. General acceptance—the explicit identification of a relevant scientific community and an express determination of a particular degree of acceptance within that community

The *Daubert* Court cautioned that "[t]he inquiry envisioned by Rule 702 is...a flexible one.[12] Its overarching subject is the scientific validity—and thus the evidentiary relevance and reliability—of the principles that underlie a proposed submission. The focus, of course, must be solely on principles and methodology, not on the conclusions that they generate" and urged trial judges to be especially mindful of FRE 403.[39]

In 1997 the Supreme Court determined in *General Electric Co. v. Joiner* that the standard of review for such decisions was "abuse of discretion."[40]

In *United States v. Scheffer*, the Court held that because "the exclusion of unreliable evidence is a principal objective of many evidentiary rules" and because "the jury is the lie detector," Rule 707, prohibiting polygraph evidence in military trials, was constitutional. Although the *Scheffer* Court cited the *Daubert* standard, its approach to polygraph evidence was more consistent with an analysis using the *Frye* test: "The contentions of respondent and the dissent notwithstanding, there is simply no consensus that polygraph evidence is reliable. To this day, the scientific community remains extremely polarized about the reliability of polygraph techniques."[41]

Two years later, the Supreme Court decided, in *Kumho Tire v. Carmichael*, that *Daubert's* holding applies not only to testimony based on "scientific" knowledge, but also to testimony based on "technical" and "other specialized" knowledge. The Court also concluded that a trial court was not obligated to consider every factor mentioned in *Daubert* in order to ascertain the reliability of expert witness testimony; rather, "the test of reliability is 'flexible,' and *Daubert's* list of specific factors neither necessarily nor exclusively applies to all experts or in every case. Rather, the law grants a district court the same broad latitude when it decides how to determine reliability as it enjoys in respect to its ultimate reliability determination."[42]

Finally, in *Weisgram v. Marley Co.*, the Supreme Court held that a party could secure a directed verdict[43] based on the state of the evidence after appellate determination that expert testimony was improperly admitted.

> Since *Daubert*...parties relying on expert evidence have had notice of the exacting standards of reliability such evidence must meet.... . It is implausible to suggest, post-*Daubert*, that parties will initially present less than their best expert evidence in the expectation of a second chance should their first trial fail.[44]

In the 2nd Circuit (the Southern District of New York), criminal defendants can be obligated to present their experts for a *Daubert* hearing, or the Court will bar those experts from testifying.[45]

The circuits have not decided uniformly whether a party gets a *Daubert* hearing as of right.[46]

Interestingly, at least one circuit has held that, although an expert witness's conviction for felony embezzlement (a crime of moral turpitude involving fraud) had a bearing on his credibility before the jury, it had no place in a *Daubert* analysis.[47]

State Laws

This section is not meant to constitute a complete review of the rules of evidence[48] pertaining to expert testimony in all states. For one thing, by the time this chapter goes to press, the law in any given state may have changed. Nevertheless, this review of state law is useful to show the multitude of issues that arise in cases involving expert testimony. These issues—such as whether certain kinds of expert testimony must be subject to judicial scrutiny at all—are not limited by geography. By 1999, 27 states had held that the *Daubert* standards were either helpful or controlling in their determinations regarding the admissibility of expert opinion evidence.[49]

An unofficial tally of the decisions in this chapter reveals that 21 states exclusively follow *Daubert*, 13 states follow their own standards, and 12 states follow *Frye*. Some states might follow *Daubert* for one kind of case and *Frye* for another, or might have deemed *Daubert* to be helpful, but not controlling, or are for some other reason not easily categorized.

The speed at which things can change is reflected in the fact that, although the Nebraska *Phillips* Court explicitly rejected *Daubert*, its *Schafersman* Court would endorse it 2 years later.[50]

Alabama

In *Barber v. State,* the Alabama Court of Criminal Appeals observed that in Alabama, by statute, courts apply the *Daubert* standard to the admissibility of DNA evidence; all other evidence is evaluated under *Frye*. With regard to nonscientific expert testimony, Rule 702, Ala. R. Evid., governs.[51]

But in Alabama, general physical comparisons do not fall under the ambit of *Frye*.[52] The general rule is that a lay witness may testify to the correspondence between shoeprints or bare footprints; however, that witness cannot testify as to the ultimate issue (that is, that the shoeprints were the defendant's).[53]

There is an excellent overview of the flaws inherent in expert testimony on the unreliability of eyewitness testimony, and the methodological flaws in research attacking the reliability of eyewitness testimony in Alabama state courts—Preussel (2006).[54]

Alaska

Alaska's rules of evidence mirror the Federal rules. In *State v. Coon*, the Alaska Supreme Court adopted the *Daubert* standard.[55] But Alaska courts hold that testimony based on personal experience, rather than scientific knowledge, does not need to meet what Alaska calls the *Coon-Daubert* test.[56] Furthermore, Alaska rejected *Kumho Tire*.[57]

Arizona

Arizona has explicitly rejected *Daubert*. The Arizona Supreme Court observed in *Logerquist v. McVey* that "*Daubert's* 'shift in perspective is subtle yet profound. Whereas *Frye* requires judges to survey the validity of the proffered scientific evidence, *Daubert* calls upon judges to assess the merits of the scientific research supporting an expert opinion.'"[58] The *Logerquist* Court took the position that:

> [o]ne of the arguments for adopting *Daubert* is to allow trial judges to put a halt to improper verdicts from jurors misled by junk science and experts ready at the drop of a hat (or a dollar) to say anything for any party. This, of course, is a two-edged sword—plaintiffs' lawyers do not have a monopoly on venal or inaccurate experts. But we do not believe *Daubert/Kumho* will prove to be a perfect or even a good antidote. Implicit in *Joiner* and *Kumho* is the assumption that trial judges as a group will be more able than jurors to tell good science from junk, true scientists from charlatans, truthful experts from liars, and venal from objective experts. But most judges, like most jurors, have little or no technical training "and are not known for expertise in science," let alone in the precise discipline involved in a particular case.[59]

In Arizona, a party is not entitled to a *Frye* hearing as of right, because the *Frye* test is inapplicable to scientific principles that are long recognized.[60] Furthermore, Arizona courts hold that the *Frye* test only applies to "opinion testimony based on novel scientific principles advanced by others" and has no application "when a qualified witness offers relevant testimony or conclusions based on experience and observation about human behavior for the purpose of explaining that behavior."[61]

To obtain a *Frye* hearing "on previously accepted scientific evidence, the party opposing its admissibility must preliminarily demonstrate that the method 'is no longer accorded general scientific acceptance.'"[62]

State v. Superior Court is a seminal case on the admissibility of horizontal gaze nystagmus testing.[63]

In *State ex rel Romley v. Fields*,[64] the Arizona Supreme Court gave a grocery list of categories of cases that did or did not fall within the ambit of *Frye*:

> In Arizona, *Frye* has usually been applied in cases involving the results of physical scientific tests. *See, e.g., Valdez*, 91 Ariz. at 277–79, 371 P.2d at 896–98 (polygraph evidence); *Scales v. City Court*, 122 Ariz. 231, 234–35, 594 P.2d 97, 100–01 (1979) (breathalyzer); *State v. Gortarez*, 141 Ariz. 254, 262–66, 686 P.2d 1224, 1232–36 (1984) ("voiceprint"evidence); *State v. Superior Court* (Blake), 149 Ariz. 269, 277–80, 718 P.2d 171, 179–82 (1986) (horizontal gaze nystagmus testing); *State v. Beaty*, 158 Ariz. 232, 241–42, 762 P.2d 519, 528–29 (1988) (phosphoglucomutase (PGM) blood grouping); *State v. Velasco*, 165 Ariz. 480, 486–87, 799 P.2d 821, 827–28 (1990) (silica gel blood alcohol test); *State v. Bible*, 175 Ariz. 549, 576–82, 858 P.2d 1152, 1179–85 (1993) (DNA evidence). However, *Frye* has also been applied to determine the basic reliability of techniques not necessarily involving "hard"science. *State v. Mena*, 128 Ariz. 226, 231–32, 624 P.2d 1274, 1279–80 (1981) (hypnotically refreshed testimony).
>
> In a variety of other situations, however, *Frye* has been found inapplicable. *See, e.g., State v. Roscoe*, 145 Ariz. 212, 219, 700 P.2d 1312, 1319 (1984) (dog tracking); *Baroldy v. Ortho Pharm. Corp.*, 157 Ariz. 574, 581–83, 760 P.2d 574, 581–83 (App. 1988) (scientific hypothesis of causation); *State v. Richards*, 166 Ariz. 576, 577–79, 804 P.2d 109, 110–12 (App. 1990) (bite mark comparison); *State v. Varela*, 178 Ariz.

319, 325–26, 873 P.2d 657, 663–64 (App. 1993) (general characteristics of child sexual abuse victims).

In *State ex rel Romley*, the issue was the admissibility of actuarial risk assessment of sex offenders, and that court held that *Frye* was inapplicable.

The standard for admissibility under *Frye* is set out in an Arizona Supreme Court opinion affirming the trial court's decision to take judicial notice of the reliability of DNA evidence. Three conditions must be satisfied for the receipt of such evidence.

1. The proponent must first demonstrate that the principles being applied are "generally accepted in the relevant scientific community."
2. The court must also decide the general acceptance of the technique(s) being used in the application of such principles.
3. Finally, there needs to be a foundational showing that correct procedures were followed in a given case. This foundation is distinct from the *Frye* finding itself and, in the judge's discretion, may initially be provided at trial in front of the jury rather than at a separate hearing.[65]

Arizona appellate courts review trial courts' *Frye* analyses *de novo*.[66]

In *Clark v. Arizona*, the U.S. Supreme Court affirmed the right of an Arizona court to exclude expert testimony from a psychologist about the defendant's mental illness, stating that expert testimony about mental state was irrelevant unless it was proffered in the context of an insanity defense.[67]

Arkansas

Arkansas embraced the *Daubert* standard in 2000, with its decision in *Farm Bureau Mutual Insurance v. Foote*. In that case, the Court affirmed the exclusion by the trial court of expert testimony that proffered that dogs trained to detect accelerants are better at it than the equipment used to conduct chemical tests; the basis for the exclusion was that the Farm Bureau Mutual Insurance failed to establish a foundation for the admissibility of the evidence pursuant to *Daubert*:

> [The witness] did not produce the study [in contention], so there was no way of ascertaining the techniques used or the potential rate of error. There was no evidence that this scientific theory had ever been tested or subjected to peer review, or that it had been otherwise embraced by the particular scientific community. In short, Farm Bureau, as the proponent of the novel scientific evidence, failed to carry its burden of proof on the issue of reliability.[68]

In *Coca-Cola Bottling Company of Memphis, Tennessee v. Gill*, the Arkansas Supreme Court adopted *Kumho Tire*. The *Gill* Court ruled that an electrician with an expired license who had not worked since 1970 could testify as an expert because he had sufficient basis for his opinion and because the issues with regard to the alleged "staleness" of his experience went to weight, not admissibility.[69]

The Arkansas Supreme Court, like other states, distinguishes expert testimony based on experience from that based on scientific knowledge. Gang testimony based on experience, interviews and conversations, familiarity with tattoos and graffiti, and gang locations and rivalries is deemed admissible:

> Accordingly, we agree with *Kumho Tire* that whether a trial court relies on the specific factors outlined in *Daubert* is within the circuit court's discretion and depends on the facts of the case. In the case before us, the circuit court did not employ the *Daubert* criteria, but Officer Hurd testified that he had been working in the gang intelligence unit of the Little Rock Police Department since 1995 and had personally interviewed over 300 gang members. ...He had also been qualified as a gang expert in other courts of law. Because Officer Hurd's testimony was premised upon his personal experiences in dealing with gangs over a number of years, it differs from expert testimony which rests purely on a scientific foundation. We conclude that the circuit court did not abuse its discretion in failing to conduct a *Daubert* analysis to determine the reliability of Officer Hurd's testimony. Moreover, the circuit court did not abuse its

discretion by ruling that the testimony was reliable based on Officer Hurd's knowledge and experiences.[70]

Interestingly, the party that bears the burden of proof in a controversy over the admissibility of expert testimony is the party contesting its admissibility.[71] Moreover, a party is not entitled to a *Daubert* hearing as of right.

The testimony of an emergency room physician based on experience and observations rather than methodology, expressing an opinion not buttressed by scientific or technical testing or analysis, did not warrant a *Daubert* inquiry.[72]

In *Turbyfill v. State*,[73] the Court found that *Daubert* did not apply to causation evidence when two emergency room physicians testified that the cause of an 8-month-old infant's severe vaginal lacerations had to have been caused by blunt force penetration to the vagina and that even though their evidence was not based on scientific testing, it was admissible:

> She was accompanied by her mother and her mother's fiance, Mark Turbyfill. One of S.R.'s attending emergency-room physicians, Dr. Valerie Borum Smith, testified that the infant had a life-threatening injury—she had a high heart rate and a low blood pressure. The child was pale and in shock due to the fact she had lost twenty-five percent of her blood supply. The infant had blood in her diaper, dried blood all over her genital area, and a large tear with a clot in her vaginal area. The tear was a third-degree tear, extending through the muscle all the way down to the rectal sphincter; a tear equivalent to the kind a woman would have from child birth. Dr. Smith testified that in order to have a vaginal tear of that degree, there would have to be penetration of the labia majora of the vagina. Dr. Smith further testified that S.R.'s was the worst tear she had ever seen—the child's vaginal opening had been torn to twice its normal size, and she was in danger of bleeding to death without surgical intervention. Dr. Smith also testified that the child's condition was so grave that they were unable to perform a rape kit on her for fear it would dislodge the clot and restart the bleeding.

Smith concluded by stating within a reasonable degree of medical certainty that the child's vaginal tear was consistent with an intentional injury, stating, "It's consistent with penetration by an object of some sort that caused this tear." She based this opinion on the fact that accidental tears (straddle injuries) are much more likely to be interior tears and they usually tear upward toward the clitoris—here the victim's tear went down, suggesting a significant amount of force penetrating her labia. Further, Dr. Smith also noted that the child was not yet walking, thus there was a low possibility for an accidental, recreation injury.[74]

The other emergency-room (ER) physician testified that this injury was the "worst he'd ever seen" and that the only time he had seen a similar tear was in the case of a woman after childbirth without an episiotomy. He testified that "blunt force caused the injury." The Court ruled that the evidence did not fall under the ambit of *Daubert* because it was not novel and because it was based on experience and observation rather than methodology and so was admissible under their Rule 702.[75] Furthermore,

...here, the doctors merely testified that [the victim's] injury was consistent with intentional penetration causing injury to the child as well as sexual abuse. Existing Arkansas law allows such testimony, because although it embraces the ultimate issue, it does not mandate a legal conclusion.[76]

Arkansas does not admit so-called expert testimony that attacks the reliability of eyewitness testimony.[77]

California
California expressly rejected *Daubert* in *People v. Leahy*, retaining the *Kelly/Frye*[78] test as the applicable California standard.[79] Leahy also clarified that "general acceptance" under *Kelly* "means a consensus drawn from a typical cross-section of the relevant, qualified scientific community."[80]

Under the *Kelly* test, evidence obtained through a new scientific technique may be admitted only after its reliability has been established under a three-pronged test.

1.   Proof that the technique is generally accepted as reliable in the relevant scientific community.
2.   Proof that the witness testifying about the technique and its application is a properly qualified expert on the subject.
3.   Proof that the person performing the test in the particular case used correct scientific procedures.[81]

But *Kelly* is only applicable to novel techniques, not to established ones.

> *Kelly* is applicable only to "new scientific techniques." It "only applies to that limited class of expert testimony which is based, in whole or part, on a technique, process, or theory which is *new* to science and, even more so, the law."... [*Kelly's*] narrow "common sense" purpose [is] to protect the jury from techniques which...convey a "misleading aura of certainty."[82]

Kelly also does not apply to medical causation testimony.[83]

Moreover, California outlawed the admission of polygraph evidence by California Evidence Code § 351.1. In the California Supreme Court case of *People v. Wilkinson*, the Court cited the *Scheffer* case when it held that that code section was not unconstitutional.[84] In *Wilkinson*, the Court observed that the studies proffered by Wilkinson in support of her motion to admit the polygraph testimony were the identical studies submitted by Scheffer—"materials which the United States Supreme Court expressly considered and cited in *Scheffer* in concluding there existed no scientific consensus on the reliability of polygraph evidence in general."

California accepts expert testimony about actuarial risk assessment of sex offenders but holds that *Kelly* is inapplicable.[85]

Colorado

Colorado follows its rule of evidence 702, rejects *Frye*, and indicates that *Daubert* may or may not apply:

> We now hold that CRE 702, rather than *Frye*, governs a trial court's determination as to whether scientific or other expert testimony should be admitted. Such an inquiry should focus on the reliability and relevance of the proffered evidence and requires a determination as to (1) the reliability of the scientific principles, (2) the qualifications of the witness, and (3) the usefulness of the testimony to the jury. We also hold that when a trial court applies CRE 702 to determine the reliability of scientific evidence, its inquiry should be broad in nature and consider the totality of the circumstances of each specific case. In doing so, a trial court may consider a wide range of factors pertinent to the case at bar. The factors mentioned *Daubert v. Merrell Dow Pharmaceuticals, Inc.*, 509 U.S. 579, 593-94 (1993), and by other courts may or may not be pertinent, and thus are not necessary to every CRE 702 inquiry. In light of this liberal inquiry, a trial court should also apply its discretionary authority under CRE 403 to ensure that the probative value of the evidence is not substantially outweighed by unfair prejudice. Finally, we hold that under CRE 702, *a trial court must issue specific findings as it applies the CRE 702 and 403 analyses.*

State v. Shreck, 22 P.3d 68 (Colo., 2001).[86] The "standard of admissibility for CRE 702 is reliability and relevance, not certainty."[87] Not only must the underlying subject matter be subject to a *Shreck* analysis, but so must the conclusions and methods of interpretation, including statistical/numerical conclusions.[88]

In Colorado, the *Shreck* analysis applies to experience-based testimony.[89] Colorado allowed expert testimony from a profiler to explain a defendant's actions as that of a serial killer, holding that "[e]vidence of a defendant's actions, demeanor, or appearance at the time he allegedly committed a crime generally is relevant to the defendant's state of mind."[90] Furthermore, a psychologist was permitted to testify that the victim's behavior was *consistent with* that of an individual who had been burned intentionally instead of accidentally.[91]

It should be noted that at least one Court of Appeals decision cited *Daubert* and *Kumho Tire* in the course of its *Shreck* analysis.[92]

Connecticut

Connecticut adopted the *Daubert* standard in 1997 with *State v. Porter.*[93] In *Porter*, Connecticut also renewed its *per se* exclusion of polygraph evidence.

In Connecticut, a party is not entitled to a *Porter* hearing as of right. In *Maher v. Quest Diagnostics, Inc.*, the court held that if the relevant expert testimony involves scientific principles whose reliability has been sufficiently established, then a *Porter* inquiry is unnecessary.[94]

Furthermore, cases involving physical comparisons rather than scientific analysis are also not subject to scrutiny under *Porter*.[95] And once the trial court "has served its gatekeeping function in accordance with *Porter* and determined that the expert testimony will be admitted, any challenges to the methodology used in the process generally go to the weight of the testimony and not its admissibility."[96]

The Connecticut Supreme Court also concluded that the same scrutiny is due to evidence in a bench trial as in a jury trial.[97]

Furthermore, testimony is inadmissible if it invades the province of the jury.

> In *State v. McClendon*, the Supreme Court excluded expert testimony from a psychologist impeaching the reliability of eyewitness testimony, ruling that "such testimony has been excluded on the grounds that the reliability of eyewitness identification is within the knowledge of jurors and...because...it invades the province of the jury to determine what weight...it wishes to give eyewitness testimony."[98]

The Connecticut Supreme Court also ruled in a child pornography case that although:

> ...at least in some cases, it may be difficult for a lay observer to distinguish between real and virtual images...the vast majority

of courts have rejected the claim that, in light of technological advances, the prosecution, in every case, must present expert testimony to establish that a particular image depicts a real child.[99]

Delaware

In 1980 Delaware's codified rules of evidence (Delaware Rules of Evidence, or DRE) became effective. In 1993 the Delaware Supreme Court in *Nelson v. State* ruled that the reliability requirements for expert testimony codified in the DRE were identical to the FRE and to *Daubert* in ruling DNA evidence admissible in a case involving the abduction of a woman from an ATM and her subsequent rape and robbery:[100]

1. The expert witness is qualified [D.R.E. 702];
2. the evidence is otherwise admissible, relevant, and reliable [D.R.E. 401 and 402];
3. the bases for the opinion are those reasonably relied upon by experts in the field [D.R.E. 703];
4. the specialized knowledge being offered will assist the trier of fact to understand the evidence or determine a fact in issue (D.R.E. 702); and
5. the evidence does not create unfair prejudice, confuse the issues, or mislead the jury [D.R.E. 403].[101]

The Delaware Supreme Court also immediately adopted *Kumho Tire*, observing that "[s]ince Delaware Rule of Evidence 702 is identical to its federal counterpart, we rely upon the United States Supreme Court's most recent authoritative interpretation of Federal Rule of Evidence 702."[102]

In *Minner v. American Mortg. & Guar. Co.*,[103] Judge Quillen, a Delaware Superior Court judge, chronicles the history of expert testimony from the time of Blackstone to the year 2000.[104] In *Minner*, a syndrome evidence case, Judge Quillen ruled that, while a *Daubert* hearing is not required in every case, the trial court must make some sort of pretrial ruling with regard to the admissibility of expert testimony,[105] observing that:

> The case currently before the Court is a prime example of how *Daubert* hearings could overwhelm. There are over 500 docket entries, and there are literally boxes of reports, depositions, and affidavits submitted in support of the parties' respective Motions to exclude experts. Recently, Plaintiffs' counsel has requested that the trial date be stayed so that the parties can have *Daubert* hearings in the time that is reserved for the trial (for a period of three weeks).[106]

Judge Quillen held that there was no basis under *Daubert* for the admission of expert testimony about multiple chemical sensitivity syndrome or sick building syndrome; furthermore, although he held that there was no disagreement as to the existence of the diagnoses of chronic fatigue syndrome and fibromylagia, the expert's conclusions were unreliable with respect to causation (that is, that working in the relevant building caused those disorders in the plaintiff). However, the Court ruled that the plaintiff could introduce expert testimony about reactive airway dysfunction syndrome and toxic encephalopathy and how exposure to toxins in the building may have caused those illnesses and remanded the matter back for trial.[107]

Judge Quillen's cogent and powerful analysis of large volumes of medical and epidemiological data in light of Delaware's treatment of expert testimony after *Daubert* should be required reading for any practitioner, regardless of whether he or she practices in Delaware.

Florida

Florida rejected *Daubert* in a footnote in *Flanagan v. State*[108] and still applies the *Frye* test—but not as of right now only "when the science at issue is new or novel."[109] In *Ramirez v. State*, Florida's Court outlined the test for admissibility:

1. First, the trial judge must determine whether such expert testimony will assist the jury in understanding the evidence or in determining a fact in issue... .

2. Second, the trial judge must decide whether the expert's testimony is based on a scientific principle or discovery that is "sufficiently established to have gained general acceptance in

the particular field in which it belongs." *Frye v. United States*, 293 F. 1013, 1014 (D.C. Cir. 1923)...

3. The third step in the process is for the trial judge to determine whether a particular witness is qualified as an expert to present opinion testimony on the subject in issue... .

4. Fourth, the judge may then allow the expert to render an opinion on the subject of his or her expertise, and it is then up to the jury to determine the credibility of the expert's opinion, which it may either accept or reject.[110]

Under the *Ramirez* test, the trial court makes the first three determinations alone and the party proffering the testimony bears the burden of proof. The fourth issue is for the jury.[111]

Expert testimony as to the causation of a medical condition is not subject to a *Frye* analysis.[112] However, evidence characterized by the Florida Supreme Court as "syndrome evidence" (in this case, child abuse accommodation syndrome) is subject to the *Frye* test, and was found to be inadmissible.[113]

The proponent of the questioned evidence bears the burden of proof in a *Frye* hearing by a preponderance of the evidence.[114]

> Florida courts have applied the *Frye* test to medical causation testimony which is predicated on a new or novel scientific theory or methodology. *See, e.g., Castillo*, 854 So.2d at 1264 (expert testimony involving cause of birth defects found properly admissible under *Frye*); *United States Sugar Corp. v. Henson*, 823 So.2d 104 (Fla.2002) (*Frye*-testing expert testimony that long-term exposure to pesticides caused the plaintiff's phrenic nerve mononeuropathy); *Poulin v. Fleming*, 782 So.2d 452, 455 (Fla. 5th DCA 2001) (excluding under *Frye* expert testimony that infant's schizencephaly was caused by prenatal exposure to radiation); *Cerna v. South Florida Bio-availability Clinic, Inc.*, 815 So.2d 652 (Fla. 3d DCA 2002) (*Frye*-testing expert testimony linking drug ingestion to blindness); *Kaelbel Wholesale, Inc. v. Soderstrom*, 785 So.2d 539 (Fla. 4th DCA 2001) (expert testimony linking ciguatera poisoning from fish to Guillian-Barre syndrome excluded under *Frye*); *Berry v. CSX Transp., Inc.*, 709 So.2d 552, 556 (Fla. 1st DCA 1998) (admitting under *Frye* expert testimony

linking long-term exposure to excessive levels of organic
solvents to toxic encephalopathy); see also *David v. National
R.R. Passenger Corp.*, 801 So.2d 223 (Fla. 2d DCA 2001)
(case remanded for *Frye* hearing regarding expert testimony
linking repetitive motion to carpal tunnel syndrome). To date,
however, the Supreme court has seemingly limited *Frye* to
cases in which the underlying basis of an expert's opinion
as to causation has been based on scientific studies or tests.
See, e.g., Castillo, 854 So.2d at 1264 (expert permitted to testify that he believed that fetal exposure to benomyl would
cause the birth defects in question in humans based on rat
gavage studies, lab experiments on human and rat cells, and
the results of dermal testing done by the manufacturer's own
scientist); *United States Sugar Corp. v. Henson*, 787 So.2d 3,
5 (Fla. 1st DCA 2000) (medical causation testimony based
on scientific textbooks and/or case studies describing well-
known effects of organophosphates), *approved,* 823 So.2d
104 (Fla. 2002).[115]

Florida appellate courts employ a *de novo* standard of review of trial
courts' application of the *Frye* test.[116]

General causation testimony is covered by *Frye*, even if it
comes in the form of a medical opinion, because "[t]he underlying scientific principle (sometimes referred to as the issue
of 'general causation') would appear to be subject to the tests
established in *Frye* and/or *Daubert*. This type of opinion testimony also implies the infallibility of the basis of the opinion."[117]
Evidence linking trauma to fibromyalgia was excluded because
it failed the *Frye* test.

Georgia

In February 2005 the Georgia legislature overruled its common law
with regard to expert testimony by statute, passing Senate Bill No. 3,
Georgia's Tort Reform Act.[118] Section 7 of the Bill pertains to expert
testimony:

Title 24 of the Official Code of Georgia Annotated, relating
to evidence, is amended by striking Code Section 24-9-67,

relating to expert opinion evidence, and inserting in its place new Code Sections 24-9-67 and 24-9-67.1 to read as follows:

"24-9-67.

In criminal cases, the opinions of experts on any question of science, skill, trade, or like questions shall always be admissible; and such opinions may be given on the facts as proved by other witnesses.

24-9-67.1

(a) The provisions of this Code section shall apply in all civil actions. The opinion of a witness qualified as an expert under this Code section may be given on the facts as proved by other witnesses. The facts or data in the particular case upon which an expert bases an opinion or inference may be those perceived by or made known to the expert at or before the hearing or trial. If of a type reasonably relied upon by experts in the particular field in forming opinions or inferences upon the subject, the facts or data need not be admissible in evidence in order for the opinion or inference to be admitted. *Facts or data that are otherwise inadmissible shall not be disclosed to the jury by the proponent of the opinion or inference unless* the court determines that their *probative value* in assisting the jury to evaluate the expert's opinion *substantially outweighs their prejudicial effect.*

(b) If *scientific, technical, or other specialized knowledge will assist the trier of fact* in any cause of action to understand the evidence or to determine a fact in issue, a witness qualified as an expert by knowledge, skill, experience, training, or education may testify thereto in the form of an opinion or otherwise, if:

(1) The testimony is based upon *sufficient facts or data which are or will be admitted into evidence at the hearing or trial;*
(2) The testimony is the product of *reliable principles and methods;* and
(3) *The witness has applied the principles and methods reliably to the facts of the case.*

(c) Notwithstanding the provisions of subsection (b) of this Code section and any other provision of law which might be construed to the contrary, in professional malpractice actions, *the opinions of an expert,* who is otherwise qualified as to the acceptable standard of conduct of the professional whose conduct is at issue, *shall be admissible only if, at the time the act or omission is alleged to have occurred,* such expert:

(1) *Was licensed* by an appropriate regulatory agency to practice his or her profession in the state in which such expert was practicing or teaching in the profession at such time; and

(2) In the case of a medical malpractice action, *had actual professional knowledge and experience* in the area of practice or specialty in which the opinion is to be given as the result of having been regularly engaged in:

(A) *The active practice of such area of specialty of his or her profession for at least three of the last five years,* with sufficient frequency to establish an appropriate level of knowledge, as determined by the judge, in performing the procedure, diagnosing the condition, or rendering the treatment which is alleged to have been performed or rendered negligently by the defendant whose conduct is at issue; *or*

(B) *The teaching of his or her profession for at least three of the last five years as an employed member of the faculty of an educational institution accredited in the teaching of such profession,* with sufficient frequency to establish an appropriate level of knowledge, as determined by the judge, in teaching others how to perform the procedure, diagnose the condition, or render the treatment which is alleged to have been performed or rendered negligently by the defendant whose conduct is at issue; and

(C) Except as provided in subparagraph (D) of this paragraph:

(i) Is a member of the same profession;

(ii) Is a medical doctor testifying as to the standard of care of a defendant who is a doctor of osteopathy; or

(iii) Is a doctor of osteopathy testifying as to the standard of care of a defendant who is a medical doctor; and

(D) Notwithstanding any other provision of this Code section, an expert who is a physician and, as a result of having, during at least three of the last five years immediately preceding the time the act or omission is alleged to have occurred, supervised, taught, or instructed nurses, nurse practitioners, certified registered nurse anesthetists, nurse midwives, physician's assistants, physical therapists, occupational therapists, or medical support staff, has knowledge of the standard of care of that health care provider under the circumstances at issue shall be competent to testify as to the standard of that health care provider. However, a nurse, nurse practitioner, certified registered nurse anesthetist, nurse midwife, physician's assistant, physical therapist, occupational therapist, or medical support staff shall not be competent to testify as to the standard of care of a physician.

(d) Upon motion of a party, the court *may* hold a pretrial hearing to determine whether the witness qualifies as an expert and whether the expert's testimony satisfies the requirements of subsections (a) and (b) of this Code section. Such hearing and ruling shall be completed no later than the final pretrial conference contemplated under Code Section 9-11-16.

(e) An affiant must meet the requirements of this Code section in order to be deemed qualified to testify as an expert by means of the affidavit required under Code Section 9-11-9.1.

(f) *It is the intent of the legislature that, in all civil cases, the courts of the State of Georgia not be viewed as open to expert evidence that would not be admissible in other states.* Therefore, in interpreting and applying this Code section, the courts of this state may draw from the opinions of the United States Supreme Court *in Daubert v. Merrell Dow Pharmaceuticals, Inc.,* 509 U.S. 579 (1993); *General Electric Co. v. Joiner,* 522 U.S. 136 (1997); *Kumho Tire Co. Ltd. v. Carmichael,* 526 U.S. 137 (1999); and other cases in federal courts applying the standards announced by the United States Supreme Court in these cases."[119]

The purpose of Senate Bill No. 3 was primarily, but not entirely, to "promote predictability and improvement in the provision of quality health care services and the resolution of health care liability claims and will thereby assist in promoting the provision of health care liability insurance by insurance providers."[120]

Interestingly, Section 24-9-67.1 appears to recognize the problem of "professional witnesses"who are retained "on account of their ability to express a favorable opinion, which...is in many instances the result alone of employment and the bias growing out of it"[121] since subsections 2(A) and 2(B) require that the expert actually practice or teach in the relevant field for three out of the preceding 5 years. That bill also provided statutory definitions for *competent evidence, cumulative evidence, direct evidence, indirect* or *circumstantial evidence, preponderance of the evidence, presumptive evidence* and *sufficient evidence.*[122]

The *Harper* Court abandoned the *Frye* test in 1982, observing that "[a]fter much consideration, we conclude that the *Frye* rule of 'counting heads' in the scientific community is not an appropriate way to determine the admissibility of a scientific procedure."[123] In *Harper*, the Court held that:

> It is proper for the trial judge to decide whether the proce-
> dure or technique in question has reached a scientific stage of
> verifiable certainty, or...whether the procedure "rests upon the
> laws of nature." The trial court may make this determination
> from evidence presented to it at trial by the parties; in this
> regard expert testimony may be of value. Or the trial court
> may base its determination on exhibits, treatises or the ratio-
> nale of cases in other jurisdictions... . The significant point
> is that the trial court makes this determination based on the
> evidence available to him rather than by simply calculating
> the consensus in the scientific community. Once a procedure
> has been recognized in a substantial number of courts, a trial
> judge may judicially notice, without receiving evidence, that
> the procedure has been established with verifiable certainty, or
> that it rests upon the laws of nature.[124]

In its holding that a probation revocation hearing was not a civil matter, the Court of Appeals held that:

> [i]n light of long-standing history of *Harper* and its prog-
> eny, which existed when the legislature enacted OCGA §
> 24-9-67.1 as a part of Georgia's Tort Reform Act, we do not
> conclude that the legislature intended to abandon the *Harper*
> evidentiary test in criminal cases. Indeed, the almost verbatim
> re-enactment of old Code section 24-9-67 as new Code section
> 24-9-67 would seem to affirm Georgia's traditional reliance
> upon *Harper* in criminal matters... .[125]

In *Barlow v. State*, the Georgia Supreme Court held that expert testimony in a sexual abuse case with regard to the propriety of interview techniques of child sex abuse victims is admissible as long as the expert does not attempt to impeach the credibility of the child witness.[126]

Hawaii
Hawaii has its own evidentiary standard, which was set forth in *State v. Montalbo*. It drew in part on a two-pronged analysis of expert testimony set forth in *State v. Kim*:[127]

> The critical inquiry with respect to expert testimony...is whether such testimony "will assist the trier of fact to understand the evidence or determine a fact in issue... ." Rule 702, Haw.R.Evid. Generally, in order to so assist the jury an expert must base his [or her] testimony upon a sound factual foundation; any inferences or opinions must be the product of an explicable and reliable system of analysis; and such opinions must add to the common understanding of the jury... . Haw.R.Evid.
>
> A court must consider whether the evidence presented at trial...would usurp the jury's function as a finder of fact, or would be likely to confuse and prejudice the jury. These determinations may only be made on examination of the scientific procedure...itself.
>
> We therefore "adopt" the *Frye* test of general acceptance in the relevant scientific community under the reliability prong of the *Kim* analysis. We hold that a court should weigh general acceptance along with the other factors listed below in order to determine, under Hawaii Rules of Evidence (HRE) Rules 702 and 703, whether scientific evidence should be admitted at trial. These factors include whether:
>
> (1) the evidence will assist the trier of fact to understand the evidence or to determine a fact in issue;
>
> (2) the evidence will add to the common understanding of the jury;

(3) the underlying theory is generally accepted as valid;

(4) the procedures used are generally accepted as reliable if performed properly;

(5) the procedures were applied and conducted properly in the present instance.

The court should then consider whether admitting such evidence will be more probative than prejudicial.[128]

Although the Hawaii Supreme Court "has not adopted the *Daubert* test in construing HRE Rule 702, it has found the *Daubert* factors instructive."[129] The Hawaii Intermediate Court of Appeals in *State v. Escobedo-Ortiz* undertook a *Daubert* analysis before holding that expert testimony about fingerprint comparisons was admissible under HRE 702, which tracks the Federal Rule.[130]

But in 2006, the Hawaii Intermediate Court of Appeals analyzed the admissibility of testimony concerning the alerting of narcotics detection dogs to currency purported to have been exposed to narcotics—relying both on the HRE and a case that relies in part on a *Daubert* analysis. The Court explores whether the evidence is inadmissible:

under HRE Rules 702 and 703[131] because the State failed to lay a proper foundation that the procedures employed in obtaining the evidence were sufficiently reliable; 2) under HRE Rule 402 because the evidence was irrelevant due to the widespread contamination of the money supply with drugs; 3) under HRE Rule 403 because the probative value of the evidence was substantially outweighed by the danger of unfair prejudice; and 4) under HRE Rule 404(b) because [the dog's] alert could have been based on the odor of drugs, such as cocaine and heroin, that were not seized in this case.[132]

State v. Vliet, in 2001, held that:

The prosecution is correct in contending that this court has not adopted the *Daubert* test, and we expressly refrain from doing so. However, because the HRE are patterned on the Federal

Rules of Evidence (FRE), construction of the federal counterparts of the HRE by the federal courts is instructive, but obviously not binding on our courts. HRE Rule 702, modeled on FRE Rule 702, pertains to admission of expert evidence.[133]

In Footnote 24 of the *Vliet* opinion, the Hawaii Supreme Court indicates that it applies a right/wrong standard to the ultimate conclusion reached by an expert, and rejects the SCOTUS's practice of ignoring the expert's conclusions.

It appears that applying the HRE using the *Montalbo* test, and keeping the *Daubert* test in mind, is useful in understanding Hawaii law on expert testimony.

Idaho

Idaho adopted the *Daubert* standard in *State v. Parkinson*, plus the additional factors set out as follows:[134]

> Other courts and commentators have used [*Daubert*] factors in analyzing proposed scientific evidence and have suggested additional factors, including: (1) the presence of safeguards in the technique; (2) analogy to other scientific techniques whose results are admissible; (3) the nature and breadth of inferences drawn; (4) the extent to which the basic data are verifiable by the court and jury; (5) availability of other experts to test and evaluate the technique; (6) the probative significance of the evidence in the circumstances of the case... . In light of these concerns we examine the testimony at issue in this appeal.

The admissibility of expert testimony in medical malpractice cases is governed by statute:

> The admissibility of the expert testimony is an issue that is separate and distinct from whether that testimony is sufficient to raise genuine issues of material fact sufficient to preclude summary judgment... . The liberal construction and reasonable inferences standard does not apply, however, when deciding whether or not testimony offered in connection with a motion for summary judgment is admissible. The trial court must look at the witness' affidavit or deposition testimony and determine

whether it alleges facts which, if taken as true, would render the testimony of that witness admissible. This Court reviews challenges to the trial court's evidentiary rulings under the abuse of discretion standard.

To avoid summary judgment for the defense in a medical malpractice case, the plaintiff must offer expert testimony indicating that the defendant health care provider negligently failed to meet the applicable standard of health care practice. In order for such expert testimony to be admissible, the plaintiff must lay the foundation required by Idaho Code § 6-1013. To do so, the plaintiff must offer evidence showing: (a) that such opinion is actually held by the expert witness; (b) that the expert witness can testify to the opinion with a reasonable degree of medical certainty; (c) that the expert witness possesses professional knowledge and expertise; and (d) that the expert witness has actual knowledge of the applicable community standard of care to which his expert opinion testimony is addressed.

The applicable community standard of care is defined in Idaho Code § 6-1012. It is: (a) the standard of care for the class of health care provider to which the defendant belonged and was functioning, taking into account the defendant's training, experience, and fields of medical specialization, if any; (b) as such standard existed at the time of the defendant's alleged negligence; and (c) as such standard existed at the place of the defendant's alleged negligence.[135]

A witness need not have formal education, but may base his testimony on experience:

Here, the officer did not render an opinion that [the defendant] was under the influence of drugs but, rather, that he displayed certain symptoms that *are consistent with* those shown by persons who are under the influence of methamphetamine or similar substances. While this distinction may be subtle, it is nevertheless real and significant.[136]

Often, parties solicit expert testimony with regard to whether a complainant was or was not sexually abused. Idaho elucidated the standard for the admissibility of such testimony in *State v. Konechny*:

We recognize that there is overlap between the realms of psychological diagnosis and treatment. However, the two roles are not identical and do not inherently call for the same skills. Indeed, a number of courts and scholarly publications have suggested that the roles of therapist and forensic diagnostician should not be served by the same person.... . [O]ne common concern about utilizing a therapist as an expert diagnostic witness stems from a mental health professional's training "to rely heavily on the reported feelings of the child and to base therapy on an assumption that abuse has occurred."

Mental health professionals who enter the forensic arena... are asked to shift from their more familiar role as the child's helping agent and instead seek to uncover truth, whatever its implications for the child's treatment. The mental health professional thus becomes a potential adversary to the child, and his or her engrained tendency to support or empathize may cloud objectivity.[137]

Illinois

Illinois still uses the *Frye* test.[138] In 2002 the Illinois Supreme Court explicitly clarified that it does not use what several Illinois appellate courts were calling "*Frye*-plus-reliability:"

Illinois law is unequivocal: the exclusive test for the admission of expert testimony is governed by the standard first expressed *Frye v. United States*, 293 F. 1013 (D.C. Cir. 1923).... . The *Frye* standard, commonly called the "general acceptance" test, dictates that scientific evidence is only admissible at trial if the methodology or scientific principle upon which the opinion is based is "sufficiently established to have gained general acceptance in the particular field in which it belongs."

First, "general acceptance" does not concern the ultimate conclusion. Rather, the proper focus of the general acceptance test is on the underlying methodology used to generate the conclusion. If the underlying method used to generate an expert's opinion are [*sic*] reasonably relied upon by the experts in the field, the fact finder may consider the opinion—despite the novelty of the conclusion rendered by the expert.

Second, general acceptance of methodologies does not mean "universal" acceptance of methodologies. The medical community may entertain diverse opinions regarding causal relationships, but this diversity of opinion does not preclude the admission of testimony that a causal relationship exists if the expert used generally accepted methodology to develop the conclusion. "In determining whether a novel scientific procedure is 'generally accepted' in the scientific community, the issue is consensus versus controversy over a particular technique. ""Moreover, the mere existence of a dispute does not preclude a finding that the procedure is generally accepted." .... Simply stated, general acceptance does not require that the methodology be accepted by unanimity, consensus, or even a majority of experts. A technique, however, is not "generally accepted" if it is experimental or of dubious validity. Thus, the *Frye* rule is meant to exclude methods new to science that undeservedly create a perception of certainty when the basis for the evidence or opinion is actually invalid.

Further, despite CIPS's contention, *Frye* does not make the trial judge a "gatekeeper" of all expert opinion testimony. The trial judge's role is more limited. The trial judge applies the *Frye* test only if the scientific principle, technique or test offered by the expert to support his or her conclusion is "new" or "novel"...Only novelty requires that the trial court conduct a *Frye* evidentiary hearing to consider general acceptance. We recognize that a "new" or "novel" scientific technique is not always easy to identify, especially in light of constant scientific advances in our modern era. Generally, however, a scientific technique is "new" or "novel" if it is "original or striking" or does "not resembl[e] something formerly known or used."

Once a principle, technique, or test has gained general acceptance in the particular scientific community, its general acceptance is presumed in subsequent litigation; the principle, technique, or test is established as a matter of law. For example, DNA analysis does not require a *Frye* hearing because the principle has been found to be generally accepted... . ("[w]here the question of the general acceptance" is raised the court often "establish[es] the law of the jurisdiction for future cases").[139]

The *Donaldson* Court stressed that reliability was implicit in the general-acceptance standard:

> Today, we clarify that ["*Frye*-plus-reliability"] is not the standard in Illinois. The trial court is not required to conduct a two-part inquiry into the both the reliability of the methodology and its general acceptance. The determination of the reliability of an expert's methodology is naturally subsumed by the inquiry into its general acceptance in the scientific community. Simply put, a principle or technique is not generally accepted in the scientific community if it is by nature unreliable. Additionally, the *Frye*-plus-reliability test impermissibly examines the data from which the opinion flows, while the technique remains generally accepted. Questions concerning underlying data, and an expert's application of generally accepted techniques, go to the weight of the evidence, rather than its admissibility.[140]

Expert witnesses may testify from sources that are themselves not admissible in formulating their opinions.

> (1) [E]xperts are permitted to testify based on inadmissible literature and [the defendant] was not precluded from cross-examining these experts; and (2) the record reveals that [the plaintiff's] experts relied on bases other than anecdotal case reports to support their causation theory.

> Addressing the first point, an expert witness may base an opinion on facts not in evidence if they are of a type reasonably relied upon by experts in the particular field in forming opinions. However, such facts and data can be obtained during cross-examination. Applying this rule, it was proper for [the plaintiff's] medical experts to base their testimony on literature without identifying it on direct exam. [The defendant] could have cross-examined these experts as to their opinions in light of the professional literature from which they formed their opinions as well as other relevant medical literature.[141]

Illinois has a statute governing the commitment of sexually violent predators. For *In re Commitment of Simons*, the Illinois Supreme Court held that "actuarial risk assessment" is "generally accepted by professionals who assess sexually violent offenders; therefore, it is perfectly admissible in a court of law," and that Illinois trial courts' *Frye* analysis is subject to *de novo* review. "In conducting such *de novo* review, the reviewing court may consider not only the trial court record but also, where appropriate, sources outside the record, including legal and scientific articles, as well as court opinions from other jurisdictions."[142]

Indiana

Indiana relied in part on the *Daubert* test in limiting the admissibility of evidence about child sexual abuse accommodation syndrome (CSAAS).[143] Indiana law finds *Daubert* to be a nonbinding but helpful standard.[144] The *Steward* Court evaluated CSAAS in light of Indiana Rules of Evidence 401 (relevancy), 403 (balancing probative value against unfair prejudice), 704(b) (prohibition against opinions concerning witness truthfulness), and Indiana Rule of Evidence 702:[145]

> Federal Rule of Evidence 702 was adopted as subsection (a) of the Indiana rule. Subsection (b) of the Indiana rule is unique in its express requirement that expert testimony must be based upon reliable scientific principles.
>
> (a) If scientific, technical, or other specialized knowledge will assist the trier of fact to understand the evidence or to determine a fact in issue, a witness qualified as an expert by knowledge, skill, experience, training, or education, may testify thereto in the form of an opinion or otherwise.
>
> (b) Expert scientific testimony is admissible only if the court is satisfied that the scientific principles upon which the expert testimony rests are reliable.
>
> Evid.R. 702.
>
> The United States Supreme Court's *Daubert* decision, coincidentally handed down just weeks after Indiana's Rule 702(b) was adopted, interpreted Federal Rule of Evidence 702 as requiring that expert testimony "be supported by appropriate validation—i.e., 'good grounds,' based on what is known," and as "establish[ing] a standard of evidentiary reliability." *Daubert*, 509 U.S. at ----, 113 S.Ct. at 2795, 125 L.Ed.2d at

481... [A]lthough not binding upon the determination of state evidentiary law issues, the federal evidence law of *Daubert* and its progeny is helpful to the bench and bar in applying Indiana Rule of Evidence 702(b). Of particular relevance to our inquiry here are *Daubert*'s statements that "scientific validity for one purpose is not necessarily scientific validity for other, unrelated purposes," and that Federal Rule of Evidence 702 "requires a valid scientific connection to the pertinent inquiry as a precondition to admissibility." *Id*. at ----, 113 S.Ct. at 2796, 125 L.Ed.2d at 482.

Child sexual abuse syndrome evidence must satisfy the reliability requirement of Rule 702(b) as well as the Rule 403 balancing test.

Although relevant, evidence may be excluded if its probative value is substantially outweighed by the danger of unfair prejudice, confusion of the issues, misleading the jury, or by considerations of undue delay or needless presentation of cumulative evidence.[146]

Courts can take judicial notice of reliability of scientific testimony.[147]

The *Steward* Court held that evidence with regard to CSAAS was dangerous under the Rule 403 analysis but held that it might be admissible under Indiana's test for the limited purpose of rehabilitating a child witness in the event that the defendant were to open the door to it by suggesting that certain behaviors of the victim were inconsistent with the claim of abuse:

Because research generally accepted as scientifically reliable recognizes that child victims of sexual abuse may exhibit unexpected behavior patterns seemingly inconsistent with the claim of abuse, such evidence may be permissible under Indiana Evidence Rule 702(a)'s authorization of "specialized knowledge [which] will assist the trier of fact to understand the evidence." Therefore, if the defense discusses or presents evidence of such unexpected behavior by the child, or if during trial testimony the child recants a prior allegation of abuse, a trial court may consider permitting expert testimony, if based upon reliable scientific principles, regarding the prevalence of the specific unexpected behavior within the general class of reported child abuse victims. To be admissible, such scientific evidence must assist the finder of fact in understanding a child's responses to abuse and satisfy the requirements of both Rule 702(b) and the Rule 403 balancing test.[148]

Thus, it appears that the *Steward* Court approaches the analysis in a like fashion to the *Daubert* Court. Evidence unreliable for one purpose (because of the possibility that a sympathetic evaluator will view the child's claims uncritically and because a jury will substitute the compelling authority of the expert for its collective judgment) may be reliable for another (the rehabilitation of a witness in the event that the defendant opens the door to the inquiry).

Nevertheless, the Indiana Supreme Court has ruled that:

[i]n determining reliability, while various factors have been identified, there is no specific "test" or set of "prongs" which must be considered in order to satisfy Indiana Evidence Rule 702(b). The decision of the trial court as to reliability under Indiana Evidence Rule 702(b) will be reviewed for abuse of discretion.[149]

In *Malinsky v. State*, the Indiana Court of Appeals held that a forensic pathologist who had performed multiple autopsies could explain to a jury that, based on photographs taken of a handcuffed woman who disappeared and was never found, the woman in the photographs was an unwilling participant in the sexual bondage activities engaged in by the defendant and that in some of the photographs she was incapacitated or unconscious and had lost bladder control—demonstrating that she was unconscious or unwilling; furthermore, such expert testimony did not require any analysis under *Daubert* or any other standard because it is more a "'matter of the observations of persons with specialized knowledge' than 'a matter of "scientific principles" governed by Indiana Evidence Rule 702(b).'"[150]

Iowa
Despite Iowa's "reference to *Daubert* in previous cases, [Iowa has] neither adopted nor rejected it as a standard test for all expert-testimony

cases."[151] Rather, as the Iowa Supreme Court said in *Leaf v. Goodyear Tire & Rubber Co.*:

> Rule 702 and our cases applying it have served us well, and we see no need to replace them in favor of a mandatory application of the *Daubert* test, whether the evidence is scientific or technical in nature. Nevertheless, we believe the "observations" in *Daubert* will be helpful to a court in assessing reliability of evidence in complex cases.[152]

On the other hand, that Court noted that "[s]uch evidence might be so novel or complex that the court, in its discretion, will require proof of acceptance of the theory or technique in the scientific community, one of the 'considerations' suggested by *Daubert*"[153]—and, of course, the essence of *Frye*.

The *Leaf* Court held that it was committed to a liberal view on the admissibility of expert testimony and that it has been "quite deferential to the district court in the exercise of its discretion in that area."[154] In *Leaf*, the Court held that objections to the admissibility of expert testimony should take place before trial.[155] Iowa applies an "abuse of discretion" standard of review to such cases.

In *Schlader v. Interstate Power Co.*, the Iowa Supreme Court held that expert testimony was not essential in a stray-voltage case brought by dairy farmers because it was not a professional negligence case. Expert testimony is required in actions based upon the negligence of a professional.

> It is the complexity of professional negligence cases that requires expert testimony. [The defendant] argues that stray-voltage cases are technical in nature and thus require such testimony. Although testimony of witnesses having specialized education and training, or special experience and knowledge, is often admitted into evidence on the ground of necessity, it is not necessarily required merely because a case involves matters of science, special skill, special learning, knowledge, or experience which may be difficult for jurors to comprehend.
>
> Causes of action which predicate recovery upon expert testimony are rare. Salem stands for the rule that expert testimony is generally unnecessary and may be properly excluded:

if all the primary facts can be accurately and intelligibly described to the jury, and if they, as men of common understanding, are as capable of comprehending the primary facts and of drawing correct conclusions from them as are witnesses possessed of special or peculiar training, experience, or observation in respect of the subject under investigation.[156]

This issue was further explored by the Iowa Court of Appeals in *Davis v. Montgomery County Memorial Hospital.*[157]

Kansas
Kansas is a *Frye* state.

Kansas *Frye* test cases have addressed a variety of scientific techniques. *State v. Shively*, 268 Kan. 573, 584–87, 999 P.2d 952 (2000) (polygraph evidence); *State v. Valdez*, 266 Kan. 774, 787–88, 977 P.2d 242 (1999) (statistical evidence accompanying a type of DNA testing known as polymerase chain reaction [PCR] testing); *State v. Heath*, 264 Kan. 557, 577–78, 957 P.2d 449 (1998) (battered child syndrome); *State v. Chastain*, 265 Kan. 16, 22–23, 960 P.2d 756 (1998) (the horizontal gaze nystagmus sobriety test); *State v. Canaan*, 265 Kan. 835, 852, 964 P.2d 681 (1998) (the luminol test for the presence of blood); *State v. Isley*, 262 Kan. 281, 290, 936 P.2d 275 (1997) (statistical evidence accompanying PCR testing); *State v. Haddock*, 257 Kan. 964, 985, 897 P.2d 152 (1995) (PCR testing); *State v. Hill*, 257 Kan. 774, 785, 895 P.2d 1238 (1995) (PCR testing); *State v. Colbert*, 257 Kan. 896, 910, 896 P.2d 1089 (1995) (DNA print testing and the process of restriction fragment link polymorphism [RFLP] analysis); *State v. Witte*, 251 Kan. 313, 329, 836 P.2d 1110 (1992) (the horizontal gaze nystagmus sobriety test); *Smith v. Deppish*, 248 Kan. 217, 238–39, 807 P.2d 144 (1991) (DNA print testing and the process of RFLP analysis); *State v. Butterworth*, 246 Kan. 541, 550, 556, 792 P.2d 1049 (1990) (hypnosis); *State v. Hodges*, 241 Kan 183, 187, 734 P.2d 1161 (1987) (theory and methodology underlying the battered woman syndrome); *State v. Miller*, 240 Kan 733, 735–38, 732 P.2d 756 (1987) (the Dequenois-Levine test for determining whether a substance is marijuana); *State v. Haislip*, 237 Kan. 461, 481–82, 701 P.2d 909 (1985) (use of hypnosis to induce witness testimony); *Neises v. Solomon State Bank*, 236 Kan. 767, 774, 696 P.2d 372 (1985) (a voice lie detector test called the PSE); *State ex rel. Hausner v. Blackman*, 233 Kan. 223, 228, 662 P.2d 1183 (1983) (human leukocyte antigen [HLA] test); *State v. Marks*, 231 Kan. 645, 654, 647 P.2d 1292 (1982) (psychiatric diagnosis on rape trauma syndrome admissible); *State v. Washington*, 229 Kan. 47, 53–54, 622 P.2d 986 (1981) (the Multi-System method of blood analysis of polymorphic enzymes; also lists examples of the application of the Frye test from other jurisdictions); *State v. Lowry*, 163 Kan. 622, 628-29, 185 P.2d 147 (1947) (the admissibility of a lie-detector test); *State v. Fuller*, 15 Kan. App. 2d 34,36, 802 P.2d 599 (1990) (a technique for identifying marijuana); *Tice v. Richardson*, 7 Kan. App. 2d 509, 510, 644 P.2d 490 (1982) (the admissibility of HLA test in a paternity suit). *See also* cases in which *Frye* did not apply, *State v. Warden*, 257 Kan. 94, 106, 891 P.2d 1074 (1995) (facilitated communication); *State v. Tran*, 252 Kan. 494, 502, 847 P.2d 680 (1993) (testimony of a "gang expert"); *State v. Barker*, 252 Kan. 949, 958, 850 P.2d 885 (1993) (the use of narcotics dog).[158]

Kansas employed the *Frye* test to decide the admissibility of testimony of an FBI behavioral scientist about whether a crime scene was staged and whether the murder was a "personal cause" homicide or a burglary gone bad. In *Patton*, the Court opined that:

> [t]he admissibility of expert testimony is subject to K.S.A. 60-456(b), but the *Frye* test acts as a qualification to the K.S.A. 60-456(b) statutory standard. *Frye* is applied in circumstances where a new or experimental scientific technique is employed by an expert witness. *Frye* requires that before expert scientific opinion may be received into evidence, the basis of the opinion must be shown to be generally accepted as reliable within the expert's particular scientific field.
>
> The *Frye* test does not apply to pure opinion testimony, which is an expert opinion developed from inductive reasoning based on the expert's own experiences, observations, or research. The validity of pure opinion is tested by cross-examination of the witness. The distinction between pure opinion testimony

and testimony based on a scientific method or procedure is rooted in a concept that seeks to limit application of the *Frye* test to situations where there is the greatest potential for juror confusion.[159]

The Court went on to rule that the expert testimony of the FBI agent was opinion testimony, and was therefore not subject to a *Frye* test, but was best handled through cross-examination.

It is clear from the evidence presented regarding the crime scene analysis that this testimony was based on specialized knowledge that would not be familiar to a lay person, as it was knowledge which the agent had gained through extensive specialized training through the FBI... . Once the trial court makes this determination, the validity of pure opinion testimony is challenged by cross-examination. The trial court did not abuse its discretion by admitting this testimony.[160]

In *State v. Heath*, the Kansas Supreme Court ruled that testimony from a forensic pathologist about battered child syndrome was admissible to prove that the victim's injuries resulted from an intentional act.

We have held that in order to be qualified as an expert, a witness must be skilled or experienced in the profession to which the subject relates and qualified to impart to the jury knowledge within the scope of his or her special skill and experience that is otherwise unavailable to the jury from other sources. It is within the trial court's discretion to determine the qualifications of an expert witness, and a trial court's determination will not be reversed on appeal absent a showing of an abuse of discretion. Judicial discretion is abused only when no reasonable person would take the view adopted by the trial court.[161]

After determining that the expert's testimony about battered child syndrome did not constitute an impermissible comment on the credibility of a witness, the court ruled that testimony about battered child syndrome did not require a *Frye* hearing because it was already widely accepted.[162]

The Supreme Court held that:

> [a] criminal defendant against whom a confession will be
> admitted may be permitted to introduce expert psychologi-
> cal or psychiatric testimony bearing on his or her ability to
> respond reliably to interrogation. It is essential, however, that
> the testimony actually tell jurors something they would not
> otherwise know from their usual human experience and that
> it remain hypothetical or theoretical. It must stop short of
> expressing the expert's judgment on the defendant's reliabil-
> ity in the specific instance of the confession submitted for the
> jury's consideration.[163]

But that court also ruled that the trial judge did not err in refusing to
admit expert testimony that the defendant lied in his confession to
murder because he has PTSD and "dependent personality" disorder
because "[a] judge who permits one witness to opine on the credibility of another witness errs as a matter of law; credibility judgments
are within the exclusive province of the jury."[164]

Kentucky

Kentucky is a *Daubert* state.[165] It adopted *Daubert* in *Mitchell v. Commonwealth*[166] and *Kumho Tire* in *Goodyear Tire & Rubber Co. v. Thompson.* However, a party is not entitled to a *Daubert* hearing as of right.

> ...[T]rial courts in the Commonwealth may take judicial notice
> of methods and techniques which already have been recog-
> nized by existing case law as reaching the status of scientific
> reliability, e.g., analysis of fibers, ballistics, and fingerprints.
> However, we noted that "judicial notice does not preclude
> proof to the contrary." Judicially noticed reliability shifts
> the burden to the opponent of the method or technique to
> prove to the trial judge's satisfaction that the method or tech-
> nique no longer meets KRE 702's standard of reliability. The
> proponent may rely entirely on the judicially noticed method
> or technique or may "introduce extrinsic evidence as addi-
> tional support or in rebuttal." Thus, while *Daubert* and *Mitchell*
> apply to all expert testimony pursuant to KRE 702, the appli-
> cation is markedly different depending on whether the method
> or technique, upon which the testimony is based, has been

recognized as reliable by existing case law. This difference is exemplified in the evolution of the reliability of certain methods of DNA analysis.

...Under *Fugate,* the PCR and RFLP methods of DNA analysis are no longer subject to a pre-trial *Daubert* hearing. In other words, a trial court may take judicial notice of the reliability of these methods of analysis. However, *Johnson, supra,* makes clear that these two methods of DNA analysis are not forevermore beyond the reach of the application of *Daubert* and *Mitchell.* Rather, a party still may challenge the reliability of the PCR and/or RFLP methods of DNA analysis, though he or she bears the burden of proving that the methods of analysis are not, or are no longer, reliable under KRE 702. This would result in a reverse *Daubert* hearing where the party moving to exclude the evidence tries to prove that the challenged expert testimony is based on "scientific, technical, or other specialized knowledge" that is not reliable.[167]

But the Court of Appeals suggested that it was not convinced that *Daubert* applied to witnesses in legal malpractice cases because "the performance of trial counsel is not something easily quantifiable."[168]

Louisiana

Louisiana adopted the *Daubert* standard in *Louisiana v. Foret*[169] and then held that expert testimony concerning child sexual abuse accommodation syndrome serves a "rehabilitative" function for a witness, but assessment of credibility is for the trier of fact and not for psychotherapists.[170]

Louisiana does not admit expert testimony with regard to polygraph examinations—or their results—in either civil or criminal cases[171] but does in some administrative hearings.[172]

In *Corkern v. Valve,* the intermediate appellate court remanded a worker's compensation case back to the trial court for a *Daubert* hearing on whether a psychological autopsy was admissible.[173]

The Lousiana Court of Appeals decided that *Daubert*:

comes into play only when the methodology used by the expert is being questioned. This court found it improper to use

Daubert analysis when questioning the conclusions reached by applying the methodology to the facts. Therefore, the [defendant's] argument that the trial court did not conduct a *Daubert* analysis on the application of [plaintiff's expert witness's] methodology to the facts of this case is misplaced.[174]

In a Court of Appeals case, a judge in a concurring opinion went to the extraordinary length of suggesting that, on remand, the case be assigned to another trial judge, because the original trial judge would already be "tainted" by the erroneously admitted polygraph evidence.[175]

Louisiana courts have ruled explicitly that:

> much of the Louisiana Code of Evidence is patterned after the Federal Rules of Evidence in an attempt to facilitate a "movement towards a uniform national law of evidence", it seems appropriate for Louisiana Courts to, "especially where the language of the Louisiana Code is identical or virtually identical with that used...in the federal rules" utilize this "body of persuasive authority which may be instructive in interpreting the Louisiana Code."[176]

Furthermore, in summary judgment motions:

> (1) the trial judge cannot make credibility determinations on a motion for summary judgment; (2) the court must not attempt to evaluate the persuasiveness of competing scientific studies, and in performing its gatekeeping analysis, must "focus solely on the principles and methodology, not on the conclusions they generate;"(3) the court "must draw those inferences from the undisputed facts which are most favorable to the party opposing the motion;" and, (4) because summary judgments deprive the litigants of their opportunity to present their evidence to a jury, they should be granted only when the evidence, including admissible expert opinion evidence, establishes that there is no genuine issue of material fact in dispute.[177]

Maine

Maine adopted the *Daubert* standard in 1996 in *Green v. Cessna Aircraft Co.*[178] But in 2005, in the case of *Searles v. Fleetwood Homes of Pennsylvania*, it appeared to have retreated from *Daubert* in favor of *State v. Williams*:

> The proponent of expert testimony must satisfy two require-
> ments: first, the testimony must be relevant pursuant to M.R.
> Evid. 401, and second, the testimony must assist the jury in
> understanding the evidence or determining the existence of a
> fact in issue.

> To meet the two-part standard for the admission of expert tes-
> timony, the testimony must also meet a threshold level of reli-
> ability. Although "general scientific acceptance" is not required
> to reach that threshold, it is often the case that "the easiest way
> this burden can be met is to show the acceptance of the theory,
> method, etc. by the expert community to which it relates."[179]

In 2005 the Supreme Judicial Court of Maine explicitly declined to utilize the *Daubert* standard[180] and held that the:

> Maine Rules of Evidence provide, "If scientific, technical,
> or other specialized knowledge will assist the trier of fact
> to understand the evidence or to determine a fact in issue, a
> witness qualified as an expert by knowledge, skill, experi-
> ence, training, or education, may testify thereto in the form
> of an opinion or otherwise." M.R. Evid. 702. A proponent
> of expert testimony must establish that (1) the testimony is
> relevant pursuant to M.R. Evid. 401, and (2) it will assist the
> trier of fact in understanding the evidence or determining a
> fact in issue.

> "To meet the two-part standard for the admission of expert
> testimony, the testimony must also meet a threshold level of
> reliability." In cases where expert testimony "rests on newly
> ascertained, or applied, scientific principles," a trial court
> may consider whether "the scientific matters involved in the
> proffered testimony have been generally accepted or conform
> to a generally accepted explanatory theory" in determining
> whether the threshold level of reliability has been met. Gen-
> eral acceptance is not a prerequisite for admission, however.
> A court has latitude to admit "proffered evidence involving
> newly ascertained, or applied, scientific principles [that] have

not yet achieved general acceptance...if a showing has been made [that] satisfies the [court] that the proffered evidence is sufficiently reliable to be held relevant."

Indicia of scientific reliability may include the following: whether any studies tendered in support of the testimony are based on facts similar to those at issue; whether the hypothesis of the testimony has been subject to peer review; whether an expert's conclusion has been tailored to the facts of the case; whether any other experts attest to the reliability of the testimony; the nature of the expert's qualifications and, if a causal relationship is asserted, whether there is a scientific basis for determining that such a relationship exists.

We review a court's foundational finding that expert testimony is sufficiently reliable for clear error. Assuming that a court finds that there is a proper foundation, its decision whether to admit the testimony is a matter of discretion. The question in the present case—whether Dr. Upham's testimony should have been excluded because it was not sufficiently supported by the medical literature—speaks to whether her testimony was sufficiently reliable. Therefore, we review the court's finding that it was for clear error.[181]

Moreover, a 2003 Maine Supreme Court case cited *Williams* and Maine Rules of Evidence when it ruled upon the admissibility of accident reconstruction experts as to the speed of an automobile in an involuntary manslaughter case:

The admissibility of expert evidence is set forth in M.R. Evid. 702: "If scientific, technical, or other specialized knowledge will assist the trier of fact to understand the evidence or to determine a fact in issue, a witness qualified as an expert by knowledge, skill, experience, training, or education, may testify thereto in the form of an opinion or otherwise." In *State v. Williams*, 388 A.2d 500, 504 (Me.1978), we stated:

The controlling criteria regarding the admissibility of expert testimony, so long as the proffered expert is qualified and probative value is not substantially outweighed by the factors mentioned in Rule 403, are whether in the sound judgment of the presiding Justice the testimony to be given is relevant and will assist the trier of fact to understand the evidence or to determine a fact in issue.[182]

That court also explicitly declined to adopt *Daubert*—although both the State and the defendant seemed to think it had.[183]

Maryland

Maryland is a *Frye* state, and it applies a *de novo* standard of review of *Frye* rulings, as it noted in *Clemons v. State*.[184]

> [In] *Reed v. State*, 283 Md. 374, 391 A.2d 364 (1978), this Court adopted the standard set forth in *Frye v. United States*, 293 F. 1013 (D.C.1923), to determine the admissibility of scientific evidence and expert testimony... . Writing for this Court in *Reed*, Judge Eldridge observed that prior to the admission of expert testimony based on the application of novel scientific techniques, the party seeking to use the expert testimony must establish that the particular methodology is valid and reliable. As we noted in *Wilson*, through our discussion of the reasoning in *Reed*,
>
> (1) Where the validity and reliability is so broadly and generally accepted within the scientific community, as is the case of ballistic tests, blood tests, and the like, a trial court may take judicial notice of its reliability.
>
> (2) Likewise, a court may take judicial notice that certain procedures, widely recognized as bogus or experimental, are unreliable.
>
> (3) When the reliability of a particular technique is not subject to judicial notice, however, "it is necessary that the reliability be demonstrated before testimony based on the technique can be introduced into evidence. Although this demonstration will normally include testimony by witnesses, a court can and should take notice of law journal articles, articles from reliable sources that appear in scientific journals, and other publications which bear on the degree of acceptance by recognized experts that a particular process has achieved." The Court concluded that the proper

> test for establishing the reliability of scientific opinion is whether the basis of that opinion is generally accepted as reliable within the expert's particular scientific field.

> If the trial court determines that the test is admissible, on appellate review, this Court must independently apply the *Frye-Reed* test to the scientific techniques at issue.[185]

The *Clemons* Court explicitly rejected the *Daubert* standard.[186]

> In Maryland, novel scientific evidence may become admissible in one of several ways. First, the evidence may be admitted by statute, if a relevant statute exists. Second, the proponent can prove that the evidence meets the Reed standard of "general acceptance" in the relevant scientific community. This can be accomplished through expert testimony, judicial notice, or a combination of the two. In the present case, the first method applies because the Legislature, by enacting § 10-915, declared DNA profiling evidence reliable and admissible.[187]

The Court held that a *Frye-Reed* hearing was required in order to evaluate the reliability of testimony by narcotics officers with regard to drug activity.[188] On the other hand, in *Fullbright vs. State*, the Maryland Court of Appeals distinguished *Ragland* in a case in which a fingerprint expert testified that "it's hard to get good prints off blood" on the grounds that the proffered testimony in *Fullbright* served the purpose of explaining the police officer's decision not to attempt to retrieve latent prints from a specific piece of evidence and not to establish any of the essential elements of the offense, and it also served as "anticipatory rehabilitation" in advance of any attempt by the opposing party to undermine the witness's credibility or the sufficiency of the investigation due to the witness's failure to attempt to get latent prints off such a surface.[189]

In the FELA case, the Court ruled that the *Frye-Reed* test was inapplicable to expert testimony from a physician with regard to the cause of plaintiff's arthritis because the principles underlying the testimony were not new:

The receipt of testimony from an expert is governed in Maryland by Rule of Procedure 5-702.

Expert testimony may be admitted, in the form of an opinion or otherwise, *if the court determines that the testimony will assist the trier of fact* to understand the evidence or *to determine a fact in issue*. In making that determination, *the court shall determine (1) whether the witness is qualified as an expert by knowledge, skill, experience, training, or education,* (2) the appropriateness of the expert testimony on the particular subject, and (3) whether a sufficient factual basis exists to support the expert testimony.

It is the third factor mentioned in Rule 5-702, the "sufficient factual basis...to support expert testimony,"at which CSX directs its fire. It seeks, moreover, to attack that threshold factor along three separate fronts. One of those attacks is that the testimony of the three experts failed the so-called *Frye-Reed* test of *Frye v. United States*, 293 F. 1013 (D.C. Cir. 1923), and *Reed v. State*, 283 Md. 374, 391 A.2d 364 (1978), in that the deductive techniques used by the three experts were not shown to have met with "general acceptance within the scientific community."

...The *Frye-Reed* test has absolutely nothing to do with the conclusions of Miller's doctors that the etiology of his osteoarthritis was his years of walking on mainline ballast or with the conclusion of Dr. Andres that, as a general ergonomic phenomenon, years of walking on mainline ballast can be injurious to the lower extremities of human beings. As Judge Eldridge made very clear for the Court of Appeals, *Reed v. State*, 283 Md. at 380, the *Frye-Reed* test does not apply to expert opinions generally.[190]

In *Bryant v. State*, the Court ruled that a defendant who asserted that he did not kill his ex-wife could not introduce expert testimony indicating that he suffered from an impulse control disorder and therefore, if he did stab his wife, it was not premeditated. The Court's reasoning was threefold. First, the expert testified that someone with an impulse-control disorder could sometimes control his impulses, and second, there was no evidence that the crime could possibly have been an impulsive act, under the circumstances of the case, and third, the defendant could not assert that he did not kill his wife because someone else did it, and simultaneously assert that he did kill his wife, but he was, due to a disease of the mind, incapable of forming the requisite *mens rea*. Therefore, the testimony could not assist the jury, would only confuse them, and was unreliable:

> Drawing on the cases and treatise cited above, it appears to us that there was no factual predicate for the expert testimony; there was no nexus between [the witness's] proffered testimony and the particular facts of this case. Among other things, appellant never acknowledged that he murdered [the victim]. Therefore, it is not clear how testimony about an alleged impulse disorder would have been relevant to explain conduct that appellant denied. Put another way, appellant did not intend to present any evidence that would make the testimony that he suffered from the impulse control disorder relevant to his ability to form the requisite *mens rea*.
>
> Moreover, the objective evidence clearly showed that the murderer acted with premeditation. We note, for example, that an individual was seen pacing near [the victim's] residence for hours before the murder, and the same person questioned a boy to learn where [she] lived. Inside [her] residence, the cord to one telephone was cut and the other was missing. Two knives were found, as was a stick used to sharpen knives. This conduct is the antithesis of an impulsive act. Therefore, [the witness's] testimony would not have made it more likely that the murderer acted without premeditation.
>
> In addition, although appellant sought to admit expert testimony that he suffered from an impulse disorder, [the witness] indicated that, even with the disorder, appellant was still sometimes able to control his impulses and he would be capable of planning a crime. Accordingly, the effect of the disorder on appellant's ability to form the requisite *mens rea*, and in explaining his earlier threats against [the victim], was speculative.[191]

Maryland does not always require expert testimony as to causation in a medical context. In *Giant Food, Inc. v. Booker*, the Maryland Court of Appeals noted that:

[to] the extent to which we can distill any general wisdom out of the case law, it seems to be this. A genuine jury issue as to the causal relationship between an earlier injury and a subsequent trauma may sometimes be generated, even in the absence of expert legal testimony, when some combination of the following circumstances is present: 1) a very close temporal relationship between the initial injury and the onset of the trauma; 2) the manifestation of the trauma in precisely the same part of the body that received the impact of the initial injury; 3) as in *Schweitzer v. Showell*, [19 Md. App. 537 (1974)] some medical testimony, albeit falling short of a certain diagnosis; and 4) an obvious cause-and-effect relationship that is within the common knowledge of laymen.

Conversely, the causal relationship will almost always be deemed a complicated medical question and expert medical testimony will almost always be required when one or more of the following circumstances is present: 1) some significant passage of time between the initial injury and the onset of the trauma; 2) the impact of the initial injury on one part of the body and the manifestation of the trauma in some remote part; 3) the absence of any medical testimony; and 4) a more arcane cause-and-effect relationship that is not part of common lay experience (the ileitis, the pancreatitis, etc.)

When all is said and done, we are perhaps reduced to a truism: the stronger the case for the causal connection, even absent expert medical testimony, the lesser the need for such testimony; the weaker the non-medical case for the causal connection, the greater the need for such testimony. There is more involved, of course, than a simply inverse proportion between the strength of the non-medical-expert case of causation and the need for expert medical testimony. Some questions of causation might involve medical knowledge so recondite that expert testimony would always be required. Other questions of causation would not. There can be no hard and fast rule controlling all cases.[192]

In *Todd v. State*, the Special Court of Appeals held that expert testimony was not required to establish that an injury was "life-threatening" for purposes of the Maryland Code when the victim suffered an open head injury and a subdural hematoma:

The State presented evidence that Sarah suffered a deep gash across her forehead that bled profusely and caused her to lose consciousness. Portions of her face were "completely crushed" in the accident. She was rushed to Peninsula Regional Medical Center, where physicians diagnosed bleeding on the brain. Hospital records that were admitted into evidence reflect that the emergency room physician determined that Sarah had suffered "severe cranial injury" and was in need of emergency surgery to repair it. Physicians at Peninsula attempted to stabilize Sarah's condition so that emergency surgery could be performed on her skull. The physicians were unable to stabilize her, however, and could perform no more surgery than that which was necessary to control the bleeding. The next day, when Sarah's condition was more stable, she was flown to Johns Hopkins Hospital, where a surgical team was waiting to perform more surgery to repair Sarah's head wound and to stop the bleeding on her brain. Sarah was later required to undergo several more surgeries as well.

We are convinced that, on this evidence, a rational trier of fact could have concluded beyond a reasonable doubt that Sarah's injury was of such a nature that, but for the intervening medical attention, she would have died. No expert medical testimony was necessary to establish that Sarah suffered a life-threatening injury.[193]

Massachusetts

Massachusetts evaluates its evidence under what it calls the *Daubert-Lanigan* standard. The Massachusetts Supreme Court adopted *Daubert*—but not wholesale—in *Commonwealth v. Lanigan*, in which the admissibility of DNA evidence was at issue:

> We accept the basic reasoning of the *Daubert* opinion because it is consistent with our test of demonstrated reliability. We suspect that general acceptance in the relevant scientific community will continue to be the significant, and often the only, issue. We accept the idea, however, that a proponent of scientific opinion evidence may demonstrate the reliability or validity of the underlying scientific theory or process by some other means, that is, without establishing general acceptance.[194]

A Massachusetts appellate court ratified the admissibility of expert testimony with regard to actuarial assessment of sex offenders and held also that a *Lanigan* hearing was not required in every instance:

> In the absence of specific, concrete evidence suggesting unre-
> liability, *Lanigan* should not be used to revisit areas where we
> have validated expert testimony based on properly conducted
> personal observations and clinical testing applying generally
> accepted scientific techniques. Testimony of the sort given
> in [Sexually Dangerous Predator] proceedings is not based
> on concepts that have only recently emerged in the scientific
> literature. The Supreme Judicial Court has previously con-
> sidered and rejected arguments that the concept of a sexually
> dangerous person is so inexact or vague that psychiatrists and
> psychologists are unable to opine about who may or may not
> meet the statutory criteria.[195]

The Massachusetts Court of Appeals applied the *Lanigan* test to an expert who testified in an employment discrimination case that the defendant's failure to accommodate the plaintiff was a proxi-mate cause of her disability; the appellate court agreed with the trial court that:

> [The expert's] testimony revealed her to have little grasp of
> the specifics of Smith's life. Although she knew that there
> were long periods when Smith was on medical leave and did
> no work at all, she did not know the dates or extent of her
> absences. She was not familiar with Smith's daily activities
> during the periods when she was out of work; nor was she
> aware of the number of hours that Smith spent working. She
> did not have a specific understanding of Smith's work activi-
> ties, the details and extent of Smith's surgeries and recover-
> ies, or whether and in what ways the company had provided
> accommodation.
>
> We agree with the judge that these gaps in Dr. Silver's
> knowledge about Smith called into question the reliability
> of her conclusion that it was more probable than not that
> Smith's worsening [post-polio syndrome] was due to the
> company's failure to accommodate, as opposed to other

potential causes. Whether these deficiencies are viewed as a failure of methodology (the flawed use of the differential diagnosis technique) or as a lack of factual foundation, the judge was entitled to exercise her discretion to exclude Dr. Silver's opinion.[196]

Massachusetts requires that "where an expert is basing his opinion on facts or data not admitted in evidence, those facts, or data, must be 'independently admissible,' and they must be 'of the sort that experts in that specialty reasonably rely on in forming their opinions.'"[197] Furthermore, applying the reasoning in *Kumho Tire*, Massachusetts holds that *Lanigan* applies to expert opinions based on personal observations and clinical experience, and to medical expert testimony concerning diagnosis and causation.[198] On the other hand,

> ...[e]xpert testimony concerning the standard of care generally need not be subject to a *Daubert-Lanigan* analysis. Such testimony is based on the expert's knowledge of the care provided by other qualified physicians, not on scientific theory or research: "How physicians practice medicine is a fact, not an opinion derived from data or other scientific inquiry by employing a recognized methodology." However, when the proponent of expert testimony incorporates scientific fact into a statement concerning the standard of care, that science may be the subject of a *Daubert-Lanigan* inquiry. Because expert opinion about increased risk, like diagnosis and causation, involves the application of science to patient care, *Daubert-Lanigan* would be applied to that portion of an expert's testimony, requiring the proponent of such evidence, if challenged, to demonstrate its relevance and reliability.[199]

The Court's explanation for this is that "[b]ecause the standard of care is determined by the care that the average qualified physician would provide, it is 'generally accepted' almost by definition. ...The focus, then,...is on whether the expert's qualifications create a foundation adequate to support the expert's statement of the standard of care."[200]

In *Canavan's Case*, the Court ruled that the "relevant scientific community must be defined broadly enough to include a sufficiently broad sample of scientists so that the possibility of disagreement exists;" thus, trial judges must be cautioned not to "define the 'relevant scientific community' so narrowly that the expert's opinion will inevitably be considered generally accepted."[201]

In *Commonwealth v. Patterson*, the Massachusetts Supreme Court ruled concerning fingerprint identification testimony that:

> Evidence of fingerprint individualization determined by application of the ACE-V method to single latent fingerprint impressions meets the *Lanigan-Daubert* reliability standard. The general acceptance of this application of ACE-V by the fingerprint examiner community leads us to this conclusion. However, the application of ACE-V to simultaneous impressions cannot rely on the more usual application of ACE-V for its admissibility, but must be independently tested against the *Lanigan-Daubert* standard. On the record before the motion judge, the Commonwealth has not yet established that the application of the ACE-V method to simultaneous impressions is generally accepted by the fingerprint examiner community or that a review of the other *Daubert* factors favors admission of evidence based on such an application.[202]

Michigan

In Michigan, MRE 702 governs the admissibility of expert testimony:

> If the court determines that recognized scientific, technical, or other specialized knowledge will assist the trier of fact to understand the evidence or to determine a fact in issue, a witness qualified as an expert by knowledge, skill, experience, training, or education, may testify thereto in the form of an opinion or otherwise.

In *People v. Beckley*, the Michigan Supreme Court ruled that admissibility under Michigan Rule of Evidence (MRE) 702 requires that the evidence comply with a three-part test.

1. First, the expert himself must be qualified.
2. Second, the evidence must serve to give the trier of fact a better understanding of the evidence or assist in determining a fact in issue.
3. Finally, the evidence must be from a recognized discipline. The determination of whether a witness is qualified to render an expert opinion rests within the discretion of the trial court. Such a determination will not be reversed absent an abuse of discretion.[203]

With regard to medical malpractice cases, the admissibility is governed by statute:

> In a medical malpractice action such as this one, the court's assessment of an expert's "qualifications" are now guided by MCL 600.2169(2):
>
> In determining the qualifications of an expert witness in an action alleging medical malpractice, the court shall, at a minimum, evaluate all of the following:
>
> (a) The educational and professional training of the expert witness.
> (b) The area of specialization of the expert witness.
> (c) The length of time the expert witness has been engaged in the active clinical practice or instruction of the health profession or the specialty.
> (d) The relevancy of the expert witness's testimony.[204]

Aiding in the *Beckley* analysis is *People v. Davis.* The relevant issue in *Davis* was the admissibility of polygraph evidence. The Court held that such testimony, which defendant wished to use to prove he was not lying when he said that he did not intentionally run over his wife with his automobile, was inadmissible because, due to its unreliability, subjectivity of interpretation, lack of consistent response among test-taking subjects, and error rate, "the technique is not an 'accepted' one among the scientists whose approval is a prerequisite to judicial recognition."[205]

Pursuant to MRE 702, the *Davis-Frye* rule limits the admissibility of novel scientific evidence by requiring the party offering such evidence to demonstrate that it has gained general acceptance in the scientific community. In conducting a *Davis-Frye* inquiry, a trial court is not concerned with the ultimate conclusion of an expert, but rather with the method, process, or basis for the expert's conclusion and whether it is generally accepted or recognized. General scientific recognition may not be established without the testimony of impartial experts whose livelihoods are not intimately connected with the evidence at issue. The party offering the evidence has the burden of demonstrating its acceptance in the scientific community.[206]

In *Clerc v. Chippewa War Memorial Hospital*, the Court of Appeals ruled that the by denying the plaintiff a *Davis-Frye* hearing on causation in a medical malpractice action before ruling the testimony inadmissible "the trial court failed to properly exercise its function as a gatekeeper of expert opinion testimony in striking plaintiff's experts' testimony without conducting a more searching inquiry:"

Under MRE 702, the trial court had an independent obligation to review *all* expert opinion testimony in order to ensure that the opinion testimony...was rendered by a "qualified expert," that the testimony would "assist the trier of fact," and...that the opinion testimony was rooted in "recognized" scientific or technical principles. These obligations applied irrespective of the type of expert opinion testimony offered by the parties. While a party may waive any claim of error by failing to call this gatekeeping obligation to the court's attention, the court *must* evaluate expert testimony under MRE 702 once that issue is raised.[207]

The *Davis-Frye* test applies only to new scientific principles or techniques. A party need not show the general acceptance of an already established test. Moreover, even if the *Davis-Frye* test did apply where a unique or novel purpose was the goal of applying generally accepted techniques, the evidence is still admissible. "Independent validation is not necessary where no significant dispute exists over the testing protocol."[208]

Minnesota

The admissibility of expert testimony in Minnesota is governed by Minn. R. Evid. 702, which is identical to its federal counterpart. The leading case for Minnesota's test for the admissibility of expert testimony is *State v. Mack*, in which the court held inadmissible testimony from a previously hypnotized witness in a criminal proceeding concerning the subject matter adduced at a pretrial hypnotic interview.[209] The Court, invoking the *Frye* test, held that:

> [u]nder the *Frye* rule, the results of mechanical or scientific testing are not admissible unless the testing has developed or improved to the point where experts in the field widely share the view that the results are scientifically reliable as accurate. Although hypnotically-adduced "memory" is not strictly analogous to the results of mechanical testing, we are persuaded that the *Frye* rule is equally applicable in this context, where the best expert testimony indicates that no expert can determine whether memory retrieved by hypnosis, or any part of that memory, is truth, falsehood, or confabulation—a filling of gaps with fantasy. Such results are not scientifically reliable as accurate.

The Court held that the testimony was inherently unreliable because:

> [e]xpert testimony further indicated that a hypnotized subject is highly susceptible to suggestion, even that which is subtle and unintended. Such suggestion may be transmitted either during the hypnotic session or before it... . The hypnotized subject is influenced by a need to "fill gaps." *When asked a question under hypnosis, rarely will he or she respond, "I don't know."*[210]

The Court relied on the consensus in the scientific community to conclude that:

> [t]he fact that a witness' memory results from hypnosis bears on the question of whether her testimony is sufficiently competent, relevant, and more probative than prejudicial, to merit admission at all. The crux of the problem is that hypnosis can create a memory of perceptions which neither were nor could have been made, and, therefore, can bring forth a "memory"

from someone who cannot establish that she perceived the events she asserts to remember. Neither the person hypnotized nor the expert observer can distinguish between confabulation and accurate recall in any particular instance.[211]

Nearly 50 years later, in *Goeb v. Tharaldson, Dow Chem. & Silberman*, the Minnesota Supreme Court expressly declined to reject the *Frye-Mack* standard and adopt the *Daubert* standard, observing that "*Frye* 'was perfectly suited to the court's competence,'" while Daubert requires 'a judge, a notable generalist, to second guess a scientist.'"[212] In contrast, "the *Frye* general acceptance standard ensures that the persons most qualified to assess scientific validity of a technique have the determinative voice."[213]

> In addition to these criticisms of the *Frye-Mack* standard, it is also argued that the Supreme Court's reasoning in *Daubert* should be persuasive because Rule 702 of the Minnesota Rules of Evidence is identical to its federal counterpart, and as such it does not contain any reference to the general acceptance standard. However, the Minnesota Rules of Evidence were promulgated in 1977.[214]

The Court's rationale for rejecting *Daubert* included a plea for uniformity in evidentiary rulings.

> Finally, the potential for non-uniformity in the law under *Daubert* gives us considerable cause for concern. Cases built on similar facts and offering similar scientific techniques could have widely disparate results. For example, the Fifth and Ninth Circuit Courts of Appeals have held that *Daubert* overruled the *per se* rule excluding polygraph evidence. As a result, each federal district court will need to consider the admissibility of polygraph evidence anew each time it is raised. While some argue that this would ensure that the courts have the flexibility to change as science evolves, this practice will also lead to greater variation in decisions at the district court level that may not be correctable at the appellate level under an abuse of discretion standard of review. In contrast, under the *Frye* prong of the *Frye-Mack* standard, the trial judge defers to the scientific community's

assessment of a given technique, and the appellate court reviews *de novo* the legal determination of whether the scientific methodology has obtained general acceptance in the scientific community. Thus, *Frye-Mack* is more apt to ensure "objective and uniform rulings" as to particular scientific methods or techniques-our primary concern in previously refusing to abandon *Frye-Mack*...[215]

Minnesota appellate courts employ two different standards of review, depending on what prong of the *Frye-Mack* test they are evaluating. For the general acceptance prong, courts view the matter as a question of law and employ a *de novo* standard of review. With regard to foundational reliability and determinations of witness qualifications and helpfulness, Minnesota uses an abuse of discretion standard.[216]

In *State v. MacLennan*,[217] the Minnesota Supreme Court addressed the battered child syndrome,[218] and the admissibility of syndrome evidence in general, and held that the *Frye-Mack* test did not apply to such evidence; rather, the admissibility of syndrome evidence is guided by Minnesota Rule 702. According to *MacLennan*, the:

> basic requirement of Rule 702 is the helpfulness requirement. If the subject of the testimony is within the knowledge and experience of a lay jury and the testimony of the expert will not add precision or depth to the jury's ability to reach conclusions about that subject which is within their experience, then the testimony does not meet the helpfulness test.[219]

As to battered child syndrome, the Supreme Court held that:

> As we did in *Hennum*, we limit expert testimony on battered child syndrome to a description of the general syndrome and the characteristics which are present in an individual suffering from the syndrome. *See Hennum*, 441 N.W.2d at 799. Each party may call witnesses to testify about characteristics possessed by the defendant that are consistent with those found in someone suffering from battered child syndrome. *See id*. But experts may not testify to the ultimate fact that the particular defendant suffers from battered child syndrome.[220]

Mississippi

The admissibility of expert testimony in Mississippi is guided by the Mississippi Rule of Evidence 702, which is identical to FRE 702. With regard to the interpretation of this Rule, Mississippi adopted *Daubert* and *Kumho Tire* in 2003 in the eminent domain case of *Miss. Transp. Commission v. McLemore.*[221]

> Under Rule 702, expert testimony should be admitted only if it withstands a two-pronged inquiry. First, the witness must be qualified by virtue of his or her knowledge, skill, experience or education. Second, the witness's scientific, technical or other specialized knowledge must assist the trier of fact in understanding or deciding a fact in issue. In addition, Rule 702 "does not relax the traditional standards for determining that the witness is indeed qualified to speak an opinion on a matter within a purported field of knowledge."[222]

That court held, in adopting the *Daubert* standard, that:

> ¶ 27. First, the Mississippi Rules of Evidence define relevant evidence as that which has "any tendency to make the existence of any fact that is of consequence to the determination of the action more probable or less probable than it would be without the evidence." M.R.E. 401. If the proffered evidence has any probative value at all, Rule 401 favors its admission. That is, "the threshold for admissibility of relevant evidence is not great. Evidence is relevant if it has any tendency to prove a consequential fact." Walker's testimony regarding damages and the methods he used in determining damages was clearly relevant in this eminent domain action. Therefore, Walker's testimony satisfies the first prong of the modified *Daubert* standard.

> ¶ 28. Second, in our following reliability analysis we do not intend to set forth a generic checklist of factors that our state courts shall use in every instance where parties present expert witness testimony. Rather, we choose to follow the lead of the federal courts, using the illustrative *Daubert* factors for guidance and leaving the determination of which reliability factors are applicable in particular cases to the sound discretion of our learned trial judges.[223]

In 2005 Mississippi applied *McLemore* to a case in which a serologist testified that she tested a portion of defendant's T-shirt and that portion contained human blood, and then a crime scene analyst testified that the blood stain pattern was indicative of a cast-off event in the course of a blunt force trauma or stabbing incident. The defendant's contention was that because the serologist had not tested the entire T-shirt, the state could not assert that the red substance she tested and found to be blood was the same red substance that covered the rest of the shirt from chest to navel, and so, therefore, the testimony of the crime scene analyst was unreliable, because he predicated his testimony on the substance being blood. The Court observed dryly:

> The trial court denied defense counsel's motion in limine to exclude the blood spatter testimony on the grounds that Graham's testimony was based on the assumption that the stains on the shirt were in fact human blood. In applying *Daubert* to the facts and circumstances peculiar to the case *sub judice*, the trial court quite appropriately denied Jones's motion to exclude Graham's testimony, which was relevant and reliable as to his bloodstain analysis of the stains on Jones's tee shirt, which had by that time been identified by Christie Smith before the jury as human blood. In our adversary system of justice, Jones, through counsel, was able to extensively cross-examine both Smith and Graham as to their testimony, including their opinions and conclusions. Graham readily admitted on cross-examination that if the serologist determined that certain stains he tested turned out not to be human blood, then so be it, because he had done his job. In other words, in today's case, it was Smith's "job" to determine if the stains were "human blood" and it was Graham's "job" to analyze the stain patterns on the shirt and come to conclusions as to how they got there.... . [N]o case is tried in a vacuum.[224]

That court also ruled that the coroner's report as to the time of death was excluded because it was based on hearsay information and because a deputy coroner testified that the coroner who prepared the report did not have a medical degree (and was dead, although not at the time he prepared the report), and that a coroner was not able to arrive at an exact time of death. Thus, that portion of the report was unreliable.[225]

Missouri

In Missouri, the admissibility of expert testimony in civil cases appears to be governed by statute.[226] In 2003 the Missouri Court of Appeals observed that:

> [s]ince the enactment of the statute in 1989, the Missouri Supreme Court has declined to directly decide whether section 490.065 supercedes application of the *Frye* rule in the same manner that *Daubert* changed the admissibility requirements for expert testimony in federal courts. Lasky v. Union Elec., 936 S.W.2d797, 801 (Mo.banc 1997), the Court gave remand instructions that the trial court was to "be guided by section 490.065...in evaluating the admission of expert testimony." Notably, the Court did not discuss either *Frye* or *Daubert* in directing application of the statute.[227]

Section 490.065 provides:

> 490.065 1. In any civil action, if scientific, technical or other specialized knowledge will assist the trier of fact to understand the evidence or to determine a fact in issue, a witness qualified as an expert by knowledge, skill, experience, training, or education may testify thereto in the form of an opinion or otherwise.
>
> 2. Testimony by such an expert witness in the form of an opinion or inference otherwise admissible is not objectionable because it embraces an ultimate issue to be decided by the trier of fact.
>
> 3. The facts or data in a particular case upon which an expert bases an opinion or inference may be those perceived by or made known to him at or before the hearing and *must be of a type reasonably relied upon by experts in the field in forming opinions or inferences upon the subject and must be otherwise reasonably reliable.*
>
> 4. If a reasonable foundation is laid, an expert may testify in terms of opinion or inference and give the reasons therefor

without the use of hypothetical questions, unless the court believes the use of a hypothetical question will make the expert's opinion more understandable or of greater assistance to the jury due to the particular facts of the case.[228]

Few cases have interpreted section 490.065, and the *McDonaugh* Court observed that:

> [t]hese decisions illustrate that no consistent standard has been applied to determine the admissibility of scientific evidence in civil cases.[229] Given the multiple approaches outlined by our courts, it is not surprising in this case that the Commission deemed it necessary to analyze the expert testimony in support of EDTA chelation therapy under both the Frye rule and section 490.065 using the *Daubert* factors. The Commission determined the testimony of the medical experts was admissible under both standards.[230]

McDonaugh rejected the *Frye* rule in the interpretation of Section 490.065.[231]

In a Court of Appeals case involving actuarial risk assessment of sex offenders, the Court held that *Daubert* applies to the interpretation of 490.061.1 because it is identical (except for the words "in a civil action") to FRE 702, and because *McDonaugh* implied that *Daubert* was the correct standard for the interpretation of that section.[232]

Goddard indicated that the purpose of section 490.065.3 "was to bring the legal practice in line with the standard practice exercised by experts in their respective fields."[233] The rationale for this is that professionals in life and death situations rely on information that would be otherwise inadmissible in court, but they could not then come to court and testify as to the bases of their actions, or their conclusions, because the underlying information would not be admissible without bringing the witnesses in to testify and then inviting the expert to testify in the form of a hypothetical.

> The legislature recognized that it was inconsistent to allow experts to rely on hearsay while practicing their profession,

but not let them rely on hearsay when rendering their opinion in court, unless substantial time and money were expended to bring those facts forth and put in evidence. It remedied this inconsistency by enacting section 490.065.3.

Under this subsection, "[t]he questions are...whether the hearsay [or lack of firsthand knowledge] as tested by professional acceptance standards in the field is reasonably reliable, and whether it is otherwise reasonably reliable as a matter of general evidentiary principle." The first mandate under subsection (3) requires a court to determine whether the facts and data are reasonably relied upon by experts in the particular field.[234]

The trial judge's next responsibility under this section is to "ensure that the facts and data are otherwise reasonably reliable. 'It is only in those cases where the source upon which the expert relies for opinion is so slight as to be fundamentally unsupported, that the finder of fact may not receive the opinion.'"[235]

Missouri defines "abuse of discretion" as follows: "An abuse of discretion occurs when the trial court's ruling is so arbitrary and unreasonable that it shocks this court's sense of justice and it is clearly against the logic of the surrounding circumstances."[236]

On the other hand,

Missouri courts, in criminal cases, still follow the test articulated in *Frye v. United States*, 293 F. 1013 (D.C.Cir.1923), for the admission of scientific evidence. To admit the testimony of an expert witness or the results of scientific procedures in a criminal case, "the testimony must be based on scientific principles that are generally accepted in the relevant scientific community." Whether a procedure has gained acceptance in the relevant field and is admissible scientific evidence is established in a *Frye* hearing—that is a hearing held outside of the presence of the jury.[237]

A party is not entitled to a *Frye* hearing as of right: "The failure to hold a *Frye* hearing does not require reversal unless the evidence was improperly admitted because there was insufficient evidence to prove that the scientific evidence had gained general acceptance in the scientific community."[238]

Montana
Montana rejected *Frye* in 1983:

> Rule 702, M.R.Evid., which is identical to its federal counterpart, governs the admissibility of expert testimony. Rule 702 provides that if scientific, technical, or other specialized knowledge will assist the trier of fact to understand the evidence or to determine a fact in issue, a witness qualified as an expert by knowledge, skill, experience, training, or education may testify in the form of an opinion or otherwise.
>
> "[I]t is better to admit relevant scientific evidence in the same manner as other expert testimony and allow its weight to be attacked by cross-examination and refutation."[239]

In 1995 Montana adopted the *Daubert* standard for the admission of expert testimony.[240] In Montana, a party is not entitled to a *Daubert* hearing, because *Daubert* applies only to novel scientific evidence.[241]

A party objecting to the admissibility of expert testimony must file a motion *in limine* in order to timely litigate the matter. The failure to object to expert testimony by filing a motion *in limine* barring its admission waives the objection.[242]

In *State v. Clifford*, the Montana Supreme Court ruled that an expert could testify that, based on his analysis of handwriting exemplars, the defendant was the author of certain letters.

> The *Daubert* test does not require a district court to determine whether the expert reliably applied expert methods to the facts. Rather, if the witness is a qualified expert in the field, he may testify. Under a *Daubert* analysis, the reliability of Blanco's application of his expert field to the facts is immaterial in determining the reliability of that expert field. Rule 702, M.R.Evid., did not require the District Court to hold a *Daubert* hearing...

...Rule 704, M.R.Evid., provides that "[t]estimony in the form of an opinion or inference otherwise admissible is not objectionable because it embraces an ultimate issue to be decided by the trier of fact." This rule allows Blanco to testify to the ultimate conclusion of who wrote the letters.[243]

The *Clifford* Court admonishes that "[e]xperts should explain their reasoning, so the opposing party can prepare for trial. With that information, the opposing party can attack the expert's reasoning as defective instead of merely attacking his conclusions as defective."[244] Furthermore, that court did not find error in the trial court's refusal to admit testimony from an evidence professor about the unreliability of handwriting analysis because he was not an expert in the relevant discipline, but an evidence professor who had criticized handwriting analysis evidence.[245]

In *Hulse v. State, Dept. of Justice, Motor Vehicle Div.*, the Montana Supreme Court held that before a law enforcement officer may testify regarding a correlation between alcohol consumption and HGN, the State must present foundation evidence establishing that the officer has special training or education qualifying him as an expert on the scientific basis for the HGN test, although *Daubert* isn't implicated because HGN testimony is not novel.[246]

Nebraska

The standard for admissibility of expert testimony in Nebraska can be found in *Schafersman v. Agland Coop.*[247] In that case, Nebraska rejected *Frye* and adopted *Daubert* and *Kumho Tire*.[248] In *Schafersman*, the plaintiffs asserted that their dairy cows died because the oats they purchased from Agland were contaminated with pig feed. Their expert testified that the pig feed caused "multiple mineral toxicity" in plaintiff's cows even though he did not examine the cows, did not determine the proportion of the offending feed to the oats to ascertain the "dosage" of contaminated feed, and admitted that there was nothing present in the contaminated feed that could give rise to the relevant conditions, and that:

With respect to the theory of multiple mineral toxicity, Wass testified that he had neither studied multiple mineral toxicity nor authored any publications concerning multiple mineral toxicity. Wass testified that he was aware of no controlled studies that related to multiple mineral toxicity, although he claimed that people in the field have observed it. Wass conceded that the theory he proposed set forth no standard for determining what levels of any given minerals could result in a toxic effect. In his deposition, which was admitted at the hearing on Agland's motion in limine, Wass stated that he had seen a similar prior case, but he did not testify regarding the mineral levels present in that instance, nor did he discuss any testing that might have been performed in that instance. Wass conceded, in his deposition, that he had not conducted any tests that were intended to bear out his theory of multiple mineral toxicity.[249]

The Court, in adopting *Daubert*, observed that:

[e]ssentially, the only basis for Wass' opinion, other than his theory of multiple mineral toxicity, was that since the cows consumed the feed and then became ill, the feed must have caused the illness. First, the assumption that correlation proves causation presents fallacious *post hoc propter hoc* reasoning that cannot be said to be helpful to the trier of fact under Neb. Evid. R. 702, even absent the application of a more stringent *Frye* or *Daubert* analysis. Second, this reasoning can be deduced equally by the trier of fact; Wass' opinion on the matter is superfluous and again fails to assist the trier in determining a factual issue.[250]

Its rationale for accepting *Daubert* is that:

[g]iven the number of jurisdictions that have adopted the *Daubert* standards and the extensive development of the *Daubert* standards in the state and federal courts, it can no longer be said that the nature and implications of *Daubert* are unknown. In fact, to the extent that this consideration is still relevant, it militates in favor of adopting the *Daubert* standards, as Nebraska courts risk losing the benefit of helpful and persuasive authority from other jurisdictions on newly presented evidentiary issues by their continued reliance on a test

that is being increasingly removed from the jurisprudential mainstream.[251]

Furthermore,

> [t]he concern about "junk science" expressed in *Carter, supra*, now also weighs in favor of adopting the *Daubert/Kumho Tire* standards. The "gatekeeper" function exercised by trial courts under the *Daubert/Kumho Tire* analysis is, in fact, a more effective means of excluding unreliable expert testimony than is the *Frye* test. The experience in jurisdictions which have adopted the *Daubert* standards suggests that the admission of so-called "junk science" evidence is a minimal risk.[252]

In *State v. Davlin*, the Court ruled that an expert was not required to rigidly follow a guide in order for their conclusions to be reliable.

> The court noted that although neither Scurto nor Nehe rigidly followed the guidelines of NFPA 921, such guidelines were intended as a model, and that Scurto's and Nehe's deviations did not affect the reliability of their opinions. The district court found that a reasonable basis existed for Scurto's and Nehe's opinions as to the origin of the fire and as to whether the fire was intentionally set.[253]

A court, in exercising its gatekeeping function, must adequately demonstrate that it has performed its gatekeeping duty by putting on the record (1) the court's conclusion whether the expert's opinion is admissible and (2) the reasoning the court used to reach that conclusion, specifically noting the factors bearing on reliability that the court relied on in reaching its determination:

> The type of ballistics and firearms testimony that Bohaty presented in this case was not novel and is fairly routine in cases involving the use of firearms. Therefore, the *Daubert* analysis did not need to be as extensive as it might have been if the testimony involved more complicated, less routine methods of testing. [In] *State v. Leibhart*,...with respect to a *Daubert* challenge to expert testimony regarding shaken baby syndrome, we stated:

We note that the evidence presented at the *Daubert* hearing in this case was not extensive and consisted mainly of [the expert's] testimony and his reference to the relevant literature. However, the level of inquiry in a *Daubert* hearing may vary depending on the nature of the expert testimony challenged, and the inquiry in the present case was appropriate and sufficient. As we stated in *Schafersman*,...*Daubert* "does not require that courts reinvent the wheel each time that evidence is adduced."[254]

Nevada

Nevada employs its own standard for the admissibility of expert testimony.

> NRS 50.275 provides, "If scientific, technical or other specialized knowledge will assist the trier of fact to understand the evidence or to determine a fact in issue, a witness qualified as an expert by special knowledge, skill, experience, training or education may testify to matters within the scope of such knowledge." Accordingly, the district court may generally admit expert testimony on matters outside the average person's common understanding. Such testimony must also be relevant and its probative value must not be substantially outweighed by the danger of unfair prejudice. Because the admission of expert testimony is in the sound discretion of the district court, we will not reverse the district court's decision absent an abuse of discretion.[255]

In *Banks*, the Nevada Supreme Court ruled that expert testimony from a forensic economist was admissible on the issue of "hedonic damages":

> The term "hedonic" is derived from the Greek language and refers to the pleasures of life. Hedonic damages are therefore monetary remedies awarded to compensate injured persons for their noneconomic loss of life's pleasures or the loss of enjoyment of life. The Supreme Court of South Carolina has succinctly explained hedonic loss, as distinguished from pain and suffering:
>
> > An award for pain and suffering compensates the injured person for the physical discomfort and the emotional response

to the sensation of pain caused by the injury itself. Separate damages are given for mental anguish where the evidence shows, for example, that the injured person suffered shock, fright, emotional upset, and/or humiliation as the result of the defendant's negligence.

On the other hand, damages for "loss of enjoyment of life" compensate for the limitations, resulting from the defendant's negligence, on the injured person's ability to participate in and derive pleasure from the normal activities of daily life, or for the individual's inability to pursue his talents, recreational interests, hobbies, or avocations.

Awarding damages for hedonic losses appears to be a recent concept.[256]

Soon afterward, the Supreme Court clarified *Banks* and held that "medical expert testimony on the issue of causation must be stated to a reasonable degree of medical probability."[257] During trial, the medical expert testified regarding possible ways anesthesia equipment could fail and admitted that, because he could not examine the actual machine used, he could not determine whether the equipment contributed to the victim's injury. The expert opinion testimony was based on less than a reasonable degree of medical probability:

[M]edical expert testimony regarding standard of care and causation must be stated to a reasonable degree of medical probability. In this case, [the witness] testified concerning an ultimate issue in the case, causation. He was not certain what caused [plaintiff's] injuries; however, he stated that he could offer a theory that was just as plausible as the theory that lindane caused the injury. He further testified that he ranked an autoimmune response as the most likely cause of the injury and recognized that this was inconsistent with Nevada's evidentiary standard. Only after the court explained that Dr. Schneck's testimony would be stricken unless he testified in accordance with Nevada law, did he state that more likely than not an autoimmune response was the most likely cause of the injuries. Dr. Schneck never stated his medical opinion to a reasonable degree of medical probability, however.

Dr. Schneck's testimony was highly speculative and failed to meet the admissibility standard.[258]

It is unclear from the opinion the extent to which the witness's failure to immediately say "more likely than not" instead of "most likely" contributed to the Court's opinion as to the witness's reliability.

In a case in which plaintiff sued defendant for manufacturing a silicon-based breast implant that ruptured and allegedly caused her debilitating injury, the Court observed that:

> [w]e are aware that causation is a scientifically controversial component of the plaintiff's case in breast implant litigation. The Mahlums, however, did not need to wait until the scientific community developed a consensus that breast implants caused her diseases. If she had, it might have been too late to recover, in light of the doctrine of laches and statutes of limitation and repose. The Mahlums' I complaint was not tried in the court of scientific opinion, but before a jury of her peers who considered the evidence and concluded that Dow Corning silicone gel breast implants caused her injuries. The jury in this case was properly instructed to consider the proof by a preponderance of the evidence. There is no evidence that the jury did otherwise. Science may properly require a higher standard of proof before declaring the truth, but that standard did not guide the jury, nor do we use that standard to evaluate the judgment on appeal. For the foregoing reasons, we therefore conclude that the Mahlums provided substantial evidence on the issue of causation.[259]

In *Mahlum*, the Nevada Supreme Court explicitly declined to adopt *Daubert*, stating that:

> [w]e have considered Dow Chemical's argument that this court should adopt the decision of the United States Supreme Court in *Daubert v. Merrell Dow Pharmaceuticals*, Inc., 509 U.S. 579, 113 S.Ct. 2786, 125 L.Ed.2d 469 (1993), regarding the admissibility of scientific evidence. The interpretation of a federal counterpart to a Nevada rule of evidence may be

persuasive, but is not controlling. We believe that the *Daubert* doctrine is a work in progress, and that we should observe the doctrine's further development in the federal courts before concluding that *Daubert* should be adopted as the law of this state. Above all, we do not presently perceive a need to adopt *Daubert*, based on our perception of developments in Nevada law, and we therefore decline to do so.[260]

New Hampshire

In 2002 New Hampshire adopted *Daubert* in *Baker Valley Lumber v. Ingersoll-Rand*.[261] In *Baker Valley*, the New Hampshire Supreme Court ruled that a witness's extensive background in the profession of fire investigation was sufficient to qualify him to testify about the plaintiff's causation theory despite his lack of experience with the specific type of fire causation alleged in the case.[262] That court observed that New Hampshire Rule of Evidence 702 is identical to the Federal Rule.[263] *Baker Valley* remanded the case back to the trial court:

> In this case, Dr. Paul's hypothesis about the origin of the fire was based largely upon his elimination of other possible causes. We agree with the plaintiff that this sort of methodology may be described as a "differential etiology." Although courts have found differential etiology reliable in medical diagnoses, the record contains no evidence of whether Dr. Paul's methodology was reliable in the fire investigation involved in this case.[264]

Baker Valley held that a party was not entitled to a *Daubert* hearing as of right; rather, that decision rests with the trial court's sound discretion.[265]

Interestingly, in a 2003 murder/rape case, the New Hampshire Supreme Court observed that:

> the defendant argues that the trial court erred in admitting the results of PCR-based STR DNA testing at trial. Although we have adopted the test set forth [in] *Daubert v. Merrell Dow Pharmaceuticals, Inc.*, 509 U.S. 579, 113 S.Ct. 2786, 125 L.Ed.2d 469 (1993), for determining the admissibility of scientific evidence, both parties stipulated that, for the purposes

of this case, the proper standard for determining the scientific admissibility of PCR-based STR DNA testing is that set forth in *Frye v. United States*.[266]

The Court went on to analyze the evidence pursuant to the *Frye* test before finding the evidence admissible.

A defendant is not entitled to a *Daubert* hearing as of right:

> We emphasize that our adoption of *Daubert* does not require a trial court to conduct a pre-trial hearing in every case involving disputed expert testimony. The decision to hold such an evidentiary hearing rests within the trial court's sound discretion. In cases where the testimony's reliability is properly taken for granted, or where the information before the court is sufficient to reach a reliability determination, the trial court need not and should not conduct an evidentiary hearing. Pre-trial hearings, thus, should be limited to the less usual or more complex cases where cause for questioning the expert's reliability arises.[267]

In *State v. Cochrane*, the court determined that testimony from a police officer about horizontal gaze nystagmus testing was not expert testimony, so long as:

> a trained police officer's testimony is limited to: (1) his or her training and experience in administering and scoring the HGN test based upon the NHTSA standards and guidelines; (2) the administration of the HGN test in a particular case; and (3) the results of the HGN test as established by the NHTSA standards and guidelines, we hold that it constitutes lay testimony not subject to pretrial disclosure requirements applicable to expert testimony. In reaching this conclusion, we are particularly persuaded by our previous determination establishing the reliability of the underlying theory, our ruling limiting the admissibility of evidence based upon this theory to circumstantial evidence of intoxication, and our requirements for laying a proper foundation.[268]

The standard for review is that appellate courts:

> will reverse a trial court's determination on expert qualification only when it results from an unsustainable exercise of

discretion. "While the trial court may rule that a certain subject of inquiry requires that a member of a given profession...be called, usually a specialist in a particular branch within a profession will not be required."[269]

The New Hampshire Supreme Court specifically defined the "unsustainable exercise of discretion" standard:

> We review a trial judge's sentencing decision under an "abuse of discretion" standard. Unfortunately, appellate review based upon an "abuse of discretion" standard may be misunderstood by those not familiar with the concept of judicial discretion as misconduct by the trial judge. When we determine whether a ruling made by a judge is a proper exercise of judicial discretion, we are really deciding whether the record establishes an objective basis sufficient to sustain the discretionary judgment made.
>
> Because the "abuse of discretion" standard may carry an inaccurate connotation, we will hereafter refer to it as the "unsustainable exercise of discretion" standard. To show that the trial court's decision is not sustainable, "the defendant must demonstrate that the court's ruling was clearly untenable or unreasonable to the prejudice of his case."[270]

New Hampshire has formulated standards for the admissibility of testimony recovered after so-called "repressed memory syndrome." Testimony recovered under those circumstances must undergo a pretrial reliability determination.

> [D]etermining the reliability of a recovered memory,—that is, whether the recovered memory is reasonably likely to be as accurate as ordinary memory—the trial court should consider the following factors: (1) the level of peer review and publication on the phenomenon of repression and recovery of memories; (2) whether the phenomenon has been generally accepted in the psychological community; (3) whether the phenomenon may be and has been empirically tested; (4) the potential or known rate of recovered memories that are false; (5) the age of the witness at the time the event or events occurred; (6) the length of time between the event and the recovery of the

memory; (7) the presence or absence of objective, verifiable corroborative evidence of the event; and (8) the circumstances attendant to the witness's recovery of the memory, i.e., whether the witness was engaged in therapy or some other process seeking to recover memories or likely to result in recovered memories...

If the witness was engaged in formal psychological therapy or some other process aimed at, or likely to facilitate, the recovery of memories, then further inquiry into that process is required. See Call for Limitations, supra at 511–12 (describing influence of traditional psychotherapy on memory). In the case of recovery attendant to therapy, this inquiry includes an examination of the therapist's qualifications, the type of therapeutic approach used, whether complaints of false accusations have been filed against the therapist, whether the therapist ordinarily seeks hidden memories or believes that many psychological problems stem from sexual abuse, and whether the therapist remains detached during the process or "validates" allegations of abuse that arise.[271]

The *Hungerford* Court viewed the issue as a mixed one involving the reliability of expert testimony and also of the competence of the witness to testify, given the unusual circumstances of the event.

New Jersey
New Jersey is a *Frye* state, and it applies a *de novo* standard of review of *Frye* rulings.[272] In August 2006 in *State v. Moore*, New Jersey reversed its position on hypnotically-induced testimony, holding that:

[w]e are no longer of the view that the *Hurd* guidelines can serve as an effective control for the harmful effects of hypnosis on the truth-seeking function that lies at the heart of our system of justice. Most important, we are not convinced that it is possible to know whether post-hypnotic testimony can ever be as reliable as testimony that is based on ordinary recall, even recognizing the myriad of problems associated with ordinary recall. We therefore conclude that the hypnotically refreshed testimony of a witness in a criminal trial is generally inadmissible and that *Hurd* should no longer be followed in New Jersey.[273]

Analyzing such evidence under the *Frye* test, the *Moore* court held that:

> [p]rior to *Daubert*, New Jersey had adopted a similar standard for the admission of scientific evidence in cases involving environmental torts. *Rubanick v. Witco Chem. Corp.*, 125 N.J. 421 (1991). In *Rubanick*, this Court held that a scientific theory may be found reliable "if it is based on a sound, adequately-founded scientific methodology involving data and information of the type reasonably relied on by experts in the scientific field." *Id.* at 449; *see Kemp v. State*, 174 N.J. 412 (2002) (following *Rubanick* standard in medical malpractice case). In general, to prove the reliability of scientific evidence, we have allowed a proponent of that evidence to offer "'(1) the testimony of knowledgeable experts; (2) authoritative scientific literature; [and] (3) persuasive judicial decisions which acknowledge such general acceptance of expert testimony...'"
>
> In New Jersey, then, hypnotically refreshed testimony must meet the "general acceptance" standard if it is to be admissible in a criminal trial.[274]

The court considered the available scientific data and the courts of other jurisdictions[275] to conclude that hypnotically refreshed testimony could never be reliable.[276] Compounding the problem, such testimony has enhanced credibility among members of the general public, giving such testimony tremendous weight:

> In this vein, we add only that the general public believes that "hypnosis [is] a powerful tool to recover accurate memories." Eighty-eight percent of respondents in a 1999 survey agreed at some level that "hypnosis enables people to accurately remember things they could not otherwise remember." That confidence in the power of hypnosis to produce accurate recall affects individuals undergoing hypnosis who are convinced—wrongly— that they will remember precisely what happened to them after they are hypnotized, and affects jurors, who are likely to reach a favorable verdict when a witness has been hypnotized.[277]

Despite the evident weaknesses of such testimony, the *Moore* Court held in *dicta* that a defendant may testify at his own trial after having been hypnotized, but the right of a defendant to testify at his own trial is protected by the U.S. Constitution as well as New Jersey's constitution.[278]

New Mexico

New Mexico has its own standard for the admissibility of expert testimony. In *State v. Alberico*, New Mexico rejected *Frye*:[279]

> Rules 702, 703, 704, and 705 govern the admissibility of expert opinion testimony... . It is the duty of our courts, therefore, to determine initially whether expert testimony is competent under Rule 702... .[280]

Furthermore, "there 'must be some threshold of independent support for the validity of the witness's methods before testimony based on the methods is admissible.' We find that threshold of validity within Rule 702."[281]

In *Alberico*, the Court ruled that:

> [w]e discern three prerequisites in Rule 702[282] for the admission of expert opinion testimony. *The first requirement is that the expert be qualified.* As noted earlier, the qualifications of the experts in these cases were not contested, and thus it is not an issue on appeal.
>
> *The second consideration for the admissibility of scientific evidence in the form of expert testimony is whether it will assist the trier of fact.*
>
> The third requirement in Rule 702, which is closely related to assisting the trier of fact, *is that an expert may testify only as to "scientific, technical or other specialized knowledge."* Scientific knowledge is what distinguishes Rule 702 expert opinion testimony from Rule 701 lay opinion testimony, which requires personal observation. Otherwise, an expert's testimony would be nothing more than lay opinion testimony, which is generally not allowed except in limited circumstances involving value, voice and handwriting identification, sanity, or speed... .[283]

The *Alberico* Court also observed that the questioned evidence must be admissible under Rule 401 (relevance standard) and Rule 403 (probative value must outweigh prejudicial effect, etc.).[284]

Alberico ultimately held that testimony about PTSD is admissible in a rape case, but the expert cannot testify as to the ultimate issue that the complainant was, in fact, raped. Rather, the expert can testify that the victim's symptoms were consistent with those of a person suffering from PTSD.[285] However, the expert may not testify that the PTSD was caused by rape, or identify the victim's alleged assailant. Moreover, testimony about rape trauma syndrome is inadmissible because the probative value is outweighed by the prejudicial effect.[286]

In *State v. Anderson*, the New Mexico Supreme Court referred to the test in *Alberico* as the "*Alberico/Daubert*" test.[287]

> Post-*Alberico* cases have adopted specific factors that are considered in determining the validity of certain scientific tests. See, *e.g., Torres*, 1999-NMSC-010, (Horizontal Gaze Nystagmus (HGN) test); *State v. Stills*, 1998-NMSC-009, 125 N.M. 66, 957 P.2d 51 (DNA test); *State v. Morales*, 2002-NMCA-052, ¶ 8, 132 N.M. 146, 45 P.3d 406 (field test used to determine if a substance was heroin); *State v. Lasworth*, 2002-NMCA-029, ¶ 12, 131 N.M. 739, 42 P.3d 844 (HGN test); *State v. Anderson*, 118 N.M. 284, 881 P.2d 29 (1994) (DNA test). Other cases have held that the *Alberico* standard does not apply when the legislature by statute has made other provisions for determining the validity of the equipment or testimony at issue. See *State v. Onsurez*, 2002-NMCA-082, ¶ 10, 132 N.M. 485, 51 P.3d 528 (holding that the state is not required to show that a Breathalyzer machine meets the *Alberico* standard because the legislature has provided by statute other ways to insure the accuracy of the machine); *Banks v. IMC Kalium Carlsbad Potash Co.*, 2003-NMCA-016, ¶ 2, 133 N.M. 199, 62 P.3d 290 (holding that testimony of treating physician in workers' compensation case is not required to meet the *Alberico/Daubert* standard because the legislature has provided different standards for who may testify in compensation matters), *cert. granted*, 133 N.M. 7, 57 P.3d 861, [*affirmed, Banks v. IMC Kalium Carlsbad Potash Co.* (N.M., 2003) at ¶ 390].[288]

In *State v. Fry*, the New Mexico Supreme Court applied the *Alberico* test and ruled that expert testimony about blood spatter analysis was admissible; furthermore, the Supreme Court concluded that the trial court's observation that the state's blood spatter expert had been qualified as an expert in 25 states and had testified as an expert in 300 cases, and that 26 states admitted blood spatter analysis testimony, did not violate *Alberico*'s admonition that "[i]t is improper to look for scientific acceptance only from reported case law" because the trial court had conducted a full *Daubert/Alberico* hearing and had put the bases for its findings under *Alberico* and *Torres* on the record.[289]

In *State v. Lente*, the New Mexico Court of Appeals observed that New Mexico has not yet adopted *Kumho Tire*.[290]

New York

New York is a *Frye* state.[291] But in *People v. Wesley*, the New York Supreme Court distinguished between a technique's reliability under *Frye* and the establishment of an adequate foundation for a technique's admissibility in a particular case:

> The DNA evidence was presented as novel scientific evidence requiring a determination as to its...reliability (see, *People v. Magri*, 3 N.Y.2d 562, 565-566, 170 N.Y.S.2d 335, 147 N.E.2d 728 [approving the use of radar in speed detection]; *People v. Middleton*, 54 N.Y.2d 42, 49-50, 444 N.Y.S.2d 581, 429 N.E.2d 100 [holding that identification through bite marks is accepted by the scientific community]. While foundation concerns itself with the adequacy of the specific procedures used to generate the particular evidence to be admitted, the test pursuant to *Frye v. United States*, 293 F. 1013 poses the more elemental question of whether the accepted techniques, when properly performed, generate results accepted as reliable within the scientific community generally. Only that *Frye* question is before us. The issues of a proper foundation and of the adequacy of laboratory procedures here are not before us, *though some of the arguments made by the parties appear not to make this distinction*.[292]

The *Wesley* Court noted that "the particular procedure need not be 'unanimously indorsed' [*sic*] by the scientific community but must be "generally acceptable as reliable."[293] In its holding that DNA evidence was admissible under the *Frye* test, the *Wesley* Court cautioned that:

> [w]e hold that since DNA evidence was found to be generally accepted as reliable by the relevant scientific community and since a proper foundation was made at trial, DNA profiling evidence was properly admitted at trial. It was admitted under customary foundation principles. The foundation included testimony that the appropriate steps were taken in analyzing the DNA evidence and an analysis and explanation of the assumptions underlying the probability calculations. The foundation did not and should not include a determination of the court that such evidence is true. That function should be left to the jury.[294]

The *Wesley* Court said in *dicta* that "the modern trend in the law of evidence has been away from imposing a special test on scientific evidence and toward using the 'traditional standards of relevancy and the need for expertise.'"[295]

> After the *Frye* inquiry, the issue then shifts to a second phase, admissibility of the specific evidence—i.e., the trial foundation—and elements such as how the sample was acquired, whether the chain of custody was preserved and how the tests were made. This distinct voir dire foundation is presented at the trial and is the same as that applied to all evidence, not just to scientific evidence. This was not part of the *Frye* hearing or ruling and was not addressed by the trial court here. Indeed, Lifecodes had not completed all the testing here at the time of the *Frye* hearing. Once *Frye* has been satisfied, the question is "whether the accepted techniques were employed by the experts in this case." The focus moves from the general reliability concerns of *Frye* to the specific reliability of the procedures followed to generate the evidence proffered and whether they establish a foundation for the reception of the evidence at trial. The trial court determines, as a preliminary matter of law, whether an adequate foundation for the admissibility of this particular evidence has been established.[296]

New York has a procedure for a posttrial *Frye* hearing if the trial judge fails to conduct a necessary *Frye* hearing pretrial:

Where, as here, the trial court admits expert testimony without conducting a preliminary inquiry into the reliability of the procedures utilized by the experts, the proper course is to hold the appeal in abeyance while the matter is remanded for a post-trial *Frye* hearing. At such a hearing, plaintiffs' experts would need to establish, inter alia, the general acceptance of their combination of the tests discussed *supra*, and substantiate how the precise measurements of angle, weight, height, time, and other components were taken. Plaintiffs' experts would be limited to discussing the experiment they presented at trial, and would be precluded from offering any new or supplemental tests.[297]

New York rejected the admissibility of the so-called "neonaticide syndrome:"[298]

Before an expert may testify about the existence of a mental disease or syndrome, the party seeking the introduction of such testimony must establish that the disease or syndrome is generally accepted in the field of psychiatry or psychology and that it would assist the jury in rendering a verdict. The general acceptance of novel scientific evidence such as a psychological syndrome may be established through texts and scholarly articles on the subject, expert testimony, or court opinions finding the evidence generally accepted in the relevant scientific community.

The defense in this case failed to establish that the neonaticide syndrome is generally accepted in the fields of psychiatry and psychology.[299]

In a leading *Frye* case, the Court ruled that bite mark comparisons did not fall within the ambit of *Frye* because they were not novel science:

Identification through configuration of and marks upon teeth has long been permitted in New York. Bite mark evidence, however, requires comparison of impressions made upon a victim's body with a suspect's dentition as a means of identifying him as the perpetrator of a crime. Defendant argues that the procedure, while it may be a valid means of excluding suspects from consideration, has not been sufficiently accepted by the scientific community to permit its use as a

272   Malingering, Lies, and Junk Science in the Courtroom

means of identifying a perpetrator. But the test is not whether a particular procedure is unanimously indorsed by the scientific community, but whether it is generally acceptable as reliable. The techniques employed (photography, freezing of tissue specimens, the taking of dental molds, visual observation) are accepted and approved by the majority of the experts in the field. The reliability of the procedures has, moreover, been accepted by all of the appellate courts that have addressed the issue. It was not error, therefore, for the Trial Judge, without a hearing concerning the scientific principles involved, to hold the evidence generally reliable.

The only remaining question, then, is whether the accepted techniques were employed by the experts in this case in reaching the conclusion that the bite marks on the decedent's back were made by defendant's teeth.[300]

North Carolina

North Carolina relies upon a standard set out in *State v. Goode*:[301]

Thus, under our Rules of Evidence, when a trial court is faced with a proffer of expert testimony, it must determine whether the expert is proposing to testify to scientific, technical, or other specialized knowledge that will assist the trier of fact to determine a fact in issue. As recognized by the United States Supreme Court in its most recent opinion addressing the admissibility of expert scientific testimony, this requires a preliminary assessment of whether the reasoning or methodology underlying the testimony is sufficiently valid and whether that reasoning or methodology can be properly applied to the facts in issue. *See Daubert v. Merrell Dow Pharmaceuticals, Inc.*, 509 U.S. 579, 113 S.Ct. 2786, 125 L.Ed.2d 469 (1993).

State v. Bullard, 312 N.C. 129, 322 S.E.2d 370 (1984), this Court, addressing the reliability of footprint identification, gave a comprehensive review of the law concerning the determination of whether a proffered method is sufficiently reliable. Speaking for the Court, Justice Frye restated the following rule, which is applicable in assessing the reliability issue:

"In general, when no specific precedent exists, scientifically accepted reliability justifies admission of the testimony of qualified witnesses, and such reliability may be found either by judicial notice or from the testimony of scientists who are expert in the subject matter, or by a combination of the two."

The *Goode* Court identified two issues for the trial court in making the reliability analysis: first, the reliability of the underlying procedure or technique, and second the reliability of the expert with regard to that underlying procedure or technique.

> Once the trial court has determined that the method of proof is sufficiently reliable as an area for expert testimony, the next level of inquiry is whether the witness testifying at trial is qualified as an expert to apply this method to the specific facts of the case. N.C.G.S. § 8C-1, Rule 702. "It is not necessary that an expert be experienced with the identical subject matter at issue or be a specialist, licensed, or even engaged in a specific profession."[302]

In *Howerton v. Arai Helmet,* the Court stepped back from *Daubert*:

> The Court additionally suggested that under the *Daubert* analysis it is permissible for a federal trial court to exclude expert testimony that, even though methodologically sound, nonetheless reaches questionable conclusions: [C]onclusions and methodology are not entirely distinct from one another. Trained experts commonly extrapolate from existing data. But nothing in either *Daubert* or the Federal Rules of Evidence requires a district court to admit opinion evidence that is connected to existing data only by the *ipse dixit* of the expert. A court may conclude that there is simply too great an analytical gap between the data and the opinion proffered.[303]

And then, citing *Arai Helmet,* the court in *State v. Anderson* stated flatly that *Daubert* was not the standard in North Carolina.[304]

That 2006 case, ratifying the admissibility of ballistics evidence, set out its own standard for the admissibility of expert testimony in North Carolina.

> As our Supreme Court confirmed *State v. Morgan,* 359 N.C. 131, 159, 604 S.E.2d 886, 903 (2004) (citing *Howerton v. Arai*

Helmet, Ltd., 358 N.C. 440, 469, 597 S.E.2d 674, 693 (2004)), "North Carolina is not a *Daubert* state."

Instead of evaluating expert witnesses under the standard set out in *Daubert,* courts in this State must conduct a three-step inquiry when considering whether to admit expert testimony pursuant to Rule 702 of the Rules of Evidence:

(1)   whether the expert's proffered method of proof is reliable,
(2)   whether the witness presenting the evidence qualifies as an expert in that area, and
(3)   whether the evidence is relevant." When making determinations about the admissibility of expert testimony, the trial court is given wide latitude and "rulings under Rule 702 will not be reversed on appeal absent an abuse of discretion.[305]

The *Anderson* Court held that a court may take judicial notice of the reliability of a technique.

In order to assess reliability, a trial court may look to expert testimony regarding reliability, may take judicial notice, or may use a combination of the two approaches. The Supreme Court has indicated that the trial court should first review precedent "for guidance in determining whether the theoretical or technical methodology underlying an expert's opinion is reliable." "[W]hen specific precedent justifies recognition of an established scientific theory or technique advanced by an expert, the trial court should favor its admissibility, provided the other requirements of admissibility are likewise satisfied."

If no precedent exists, such as when an expert is proposing "novel scientific theories, unestablished techniques, or compelling new perspectives on otherwise settled theories or techniques," the trial court is required to focus on "indices of reliability" to determine reliability, including the expert's use of established techniques, the expert's professional background in the field, the use of visual aids before the jury, and independent research conducted by the expert. These indices are not, however, exclusive.[306]

Once a trial court makes the determination as to the reliability of the technique and the qualifications of the expert, lingering "questions or controversy" regarding the expert's conclusions go to weight, not admissibility.[307]

North Dakota

North Dakota adheres to its own standard for the admissibility of expert testimony:

> If scientific, technical, or other specialized knowledge will assist the trier of fact to understand the evidence or to determine a fact in issue, a witness qualified as an expert by knowledge, skill, experience, training, or education, may testify thereto in the form of an opinion or otherwise.

> Under Rule 702, expert testimony is admissible whenever specialized knowledge will assist the trier of fact. Rule 702 envisions generous allowance of the use of expert testimony if the witness is shown to have some degree of expertise in the field in which she is to testify. Whether a witness is qualified as an expert and whether the witness's testimony will assist the trier of fact are decisions within the sound discretion of the trial court which will not be overturned on appeal absent an abuse of discretion.

> Dolund challenges Dr. Griffin's qualifications to testify about Gonzalez's loss of consciousness and brain injury because he was not a fire safety expert and did not specialize in neurology.

> ...an expert need not be a specialist in a highly particularized field if his knowledge, training, education, and experience will assist the trier of fact. The rule does not require an expert to have a formal title or to be licensed in any particular field, but recognizes it is the witness's actual qualifications that count by providing that an expert can be qualified by knowledge, skill, experience, training, or education.

> We have previously held a trial court does not abuse its discretion by admitting expert testimony whenever specialized knowledge will assist the trier of fact, even if the expert does not possess a particular expertise or specific certification.[308]

Once a court deems testimony admissible, any deficiencies in methodology are a matter of credibility, not admissibility: "The trial court decides the qualifications of the witness to express an opinion on a given topic, but it is the trier of fact whose job it is to decide the expert witness's credibility and the weight to be given to the testimony."[309]

The *Gonzalez* Court rejected *Daubert* in a footnote, observing that:

> It is unnecessary to decide whether we should adopt the standards for admitting expert or scientific evidence under Fed. R. Evid. 702 articulated in *Daubert v. Merrell Dow Pharm., Inc.*, 509 U.S. 579 (1993) and *Kumho Tire Co. v. Carmichael*, 526 U.S. 137 (1999), because the result in this case would be the same under those standards and under our traditional standards governing admission of evidence under N.D.R.Ev. 702.[310]

In North Dakota, an expert may testify to otherwise-inadmissible evidence if such forms the basis of his opinion, but

> an expert's testimony may not be used merely as a conduit to place otherwise inadmissible evidence before a jury, because an expert who simply relates inadmissible hearsay to the factfinder is not acting in the capacity of an expert and is not being of any assistance to the factfinder... .[311]

In such a case, the trial court must ascertain whether the probative value of the disputed testimony outweighs the prejudicial effect.[312] "There is often a fine line between an expert merely relating inadmissible hearsay and an expert giving testimony about inadmissible facts or data upon which the expert's opinion is based."[313]

North Dakota employs an abuse of discretion standard for the admissibility of expert testimony:

> A trial court has broad discretion on evidentiary matters, and we will not overturn its admission or exclusion of evidence on appeal unless that discretion has been abused. A trial court abuses its discretion when it acts arbitrarily, unconscionably, or unreasonably, or when its decision is not the product of a rational mental process. Even if the trial court commits an error on an evidentiary matter, N.D.R.Civ. P. 61 provides that "[n]o error in either the admission or the exclusion

of evidence...is ground for granting a new trial or for setting aside a verdict or for vacating, modifying or otherwise disturbing a judgment or order, unless refusal to take such action appears to the court inconsistent with substantial justice." We apply this deferential standard of review to provide trial courts with greater control over the admissibility of evidence.[314]

In North Dakota, experts may testify as to the ultimate issue in a case.

Rule 704, N.D.R.Ev., specifically provides: "Testimony in the form of an opinion or inference otherwise admissible is not objectionable because it embraces an ultimate issue to be decided by the trier of fact." Thus, an expert is authorized to give his opinion even though it embraces an ultimate issue of fact to be decided by the trier of fact. Rule 702, N.D.R.Ev., envisions "generous allowance" of the use of expert witness testimony where a witness is shown to have some degree of expertise in the field of which the expert testifies.[315]

Ohio

Ohio is a *Daubert* state.[316] In *Miller v. Bike Athletic Co.*, Ohio outlined the standard of admissibility of expert testimony in Ohio:

In deciding whether [the expert's] testimony was proper, we begin our analysis with a consideration of Evid.R. 702, which governs the admissibility of expert testimony. It provides:

"A witness may testify as an expert if all of the following apply:

(A) The witness' testimony either relates to matters beyond the knowledge or experience possessed by lay persons or dispels a misconception common among lay persons;

(B) The witness is qualified as an expert by specialized knowledge, skill, experience, training, or education regarding the subject matter of the testimony;

(C) The witness' testimony is based on reliable scientific, technical, or other specialized information. To the extent that the testimony reports the result of a procedure, test, or experiment, the testimony is reliable only if all of the following apply:

(1) The theory upon which the procedure, test, or experiment is based is objectively verifiable or is validly derived from widely accepted knowledge, facts, or principles;

(2) The design of the procedure, test, or experiment reliably implements the theory;

(3) The particular procedure, test, or experiment was conducted in a way that will yield an accurate result."

There is no question that [the witness] is a qualified expert who testified about a subject beyond the knowledge of lay persons. Evid.R. 702(A) and (B). Thus, at issue in this case is whether [the witness's] testimony complied with the requirements of Evid.R. 702(C), i.e., whether his opinion was reliable. In making this determination, our inquiry focuses on whether the principles and methods [the witness] employed to reach his opinion are reliable, not whether his conclusions are correct.[317]

Ohio reviews trial court decisions with regard to admissibility of evidence under the "abuse of discretion" standard, which it defines as " 'perversity of will, passion, prejudice, partiality, or moral delinquency.' When applying the abuse of discretion standard, this Court may not substitute its judgment for that of the trial court."[318]

In Ohio, a party is not entitled to a *Daubert* hearing as of right:

This Court itself has recently held that the *Daubert* analysis only applies if there has been a proper objection or proffer of evidence, and that a failure to object to the admission of expert evidence constitutes a waiver of any evidentiary errors pursuant to Evid.R. 103(A) (1). This Court held that:

"[T]he 1994 Staff Note to Evid.R. 702 states that the issues can typically be resolved by objection and decision during trial but that sometimes the issues may need to be heard in pretrial hearing where they were raised in a proffer. In either case, the Staff Note does not contemplate a strict duty on the part of the trial court to ensure that the state meticulously explains the methodology of the scientist. Rather, it contemplates objection during trial or presentation in a proffer before trial."

Because Appellant did not properly object at trial, his alleged error is subject only to the plain error rule. See Evid.R. 103(A) (1). Crim.R. 52(B) provides that plain errors affecting substantial rights may be noticed although they were not brought to the attention of the court. Plain error only exists when the outcome of the trial clearly would have been different but for the error.

The decision to correct plain error must be made with utmost caution under exceptional circumstances and only to prevent a manifest miscarriage of justice. *Id.* Crim.R. 52 allows a reviewing court to take corrective action, but it does not require such action. Based on the record before us, the exceptional circumstances contemplated by Crim.R. 52 do not exist in this case.[319]

There is no "no requirement that an expert utter any 'magic language;' i.e., that his opinion was within the reasonable degree of certainty or reasonable degree of certainty within the particular knowledge of his professional experience."[320]

Oklahoma

"Expert testimony is admitted at trial pursuant to the Oklahoma Rules of Evidence, 12 O.S.1991, §§ 2702-2703."[321]

Oklahoma adopted *Daubert* in *Taylor v. State.*[322] The Oklahoma Courts use a *de novo* standard of review in analyzing trial court decisions about admissibility of expert testimony:

Accordingly, in recognition of the fact that the formulation of the law of this jurisdiction is a quintessentially appellate function, we engage in a broad review of the trial judge's determination whether the forensic use of DNA technology has gained general acceptance. In doing so, we may consider not only expert evidence of record, but also judicial opinions in other jurisdictions, as well as pertinent legal and scientific commentaries.[323]

The *Taylor* Court held that because it determined that RFLP DNA evidence, and DNA statistics calculated through standard population genetics formulas, was admissible, future *Daubert* hearings were unnecessary as to that identical issue.[324]

Oklahoma has also adopted *Kumho Tire*.[325]

In *Dunkle v. State*, the Court emphasized that computer-generated or live video crime scene reconstructions are not inadmissible *per se*, and they do not implicate *Daubert*. In:

> order for a video or computer crime scene reenactment to be seen by a jury, as an aid to illustrate an expert witness' testimony, the court should require (1) that it be authenticated—the trial court should determine that it is a correct representation of the object portrayed, or that it is a fair and accurate representation of the evidence to which it relates, (2) that it is relevant, and (3) that its probative value is not "substantially outweighed by the danger of unfair prejudice, confusion of the issues, misleading the jury, undue delay, needless presentation of cumulative evidence, or unfair and harmful surprise."[326]

Oregon

Oregon relies on its rules of evidence, and standards set out in *State v. Brown*,[327] for the admissibility of expert testimony:

> In *Brown*, this court abandoned special tests for the admissibility of scientific evidence in favor of resolving the problem by relying on traditional evidence law as codified in the Oregon Evidence Code (OEC), specifically OEC 401 (relevance), OEC 702 (opinions of experts), and OEC 403 (exclusion of relevant evidence on ground of prejudice, confusion or undue delay).

> "In applying OEC 401, 702 and 403, the court must identify and evaluate the probative value of the evidence, consider how it might impair rather than help the factfinder, and decide whether truthfinding is better served by exclusion or admission."[328]

In a case holding that horizontal gaze nystagmus testimony was admissible to prove that the defendant was under the influence of alcohol, but not that he had a BAC of 0.08 or greater, the Oregon Supreme Court in *State v. O'Key* interpreted *Brown* in light of *Daubert*:

> "[T]raditional admissibility standards for expert testimony as set forth in the Oregon Evidence Code" govern the admissibility of proffered scientific evidence. Addressing the admissibility

of polygraph evidence, this court held that OEC 401, 702, and 403 are to be applied to determine the admissibility of proffered scientific evidence. Under OEC 401, "'[r]elevant evidence' means evidence having any tendency to make the existence of any fact that is of consequence to the determination of the action more probable or less probable than it would be without the evidence." "[P]roffered evidence, [although relevant, nonetheless] may be subject to exclusion under one of the exceptions to the admissibility of relevant evidence in OEC 402 (e.g., decisional law)."

OEC 702, which defines the permissible sphere of expert testimony, provides:

"If scientific, technical or other specialized knowledge will assist the trier of fact to understand the evidence or to determine a fact in issue, a witness qualified as an expert by knowledge, skill, experience, training or education may testify thereto in the form of an opinion or otherwise."

The requirement in OEC 702 that the evidence or testimony "assist the trier of fact to understand the evidence or to determine a fact in issue" is intended to serve multiple functions, such as:

"(1) supplying general propositions which will permit inferences from data which the trier of fact would otherwise be forced to find meaningless; (2) applying general propositions to data so as to generate inferences where the complexity of the body of propositions applied, the difficulty of the application, or other factors make the expert's conclusion probably more accurate or precise than that of the trier of fact; (3) modifying, qualifying, and refining general propositions which the trier of fact may reasonably be expected to use; and (4) adding specialized confirmation and, thus, confidence to general propositions otherwise likely to be assumed more tentatively by the trier."

Once the testimony is determined to be relevant under OEC 401, helpful under OEC 702, and not barred by OEC 402, it will be excluded only if its probative value is substantially outweighed by one or more of the countervailing factors set forth in OEC 403, which provides:

"Although relevant, evidence may be excluded if its probative value is substantially outweighed by the danger of unfair prejudice, confusion of the issues, or misleading the jury, or by considerations of undue delay or needless presentation of cumulative evidence."

In evaluating the incremental probative value of the proffered evidence, the court must assume that the evidence will be believed by the trier of fact. When the incremental probative value of the proffered scientific evidence is relatively slight, and when the jury is likely to overvalue or be misled into giving the evidence undue weight, the likelihood of exclusion under OEC 403 is enhanced.

In applying OEC 401, 702, and 403, the court must identify and evaluate the probative value of the proffered scientific evidence, consider how that evidence might impair rather than help the trier of fact, and decide whether truthfinding is better served by admission or exclusion. In *Brown*, this court identified a number of factors that could affect a trial court's decision on admissibility of proffered scientific evidence:

"(1) The technique's general acceptance in the field;

(2) The expert's qualifications and stature;

(3) The use which has been made of the technique;

(4) The potential rate of error;

(5) The existence of specialized literature;

(6) The novelty of the invention; and

(7) The extent to which the technique relies on the subjective interpretation of the expert."

Those factors were not intended to be exclusive, nor were they intended to be taken as a mechanical checklist of foundational requirements. "What is important is not lockstep affirmative findings as to each factor, but analysis of each factor by the court in reaching its decision on the probative value of the [proffered scientific] evidence under OEC 401 and OEC 702."[329]

Oregon holds that *Daubert* is helpful but not mandatory:

We decide this case under the Oregon Evidence Code. When we cite a decision of the Supreme Court of the United States in interpreting a provision of the Oregon Evidence Code, we do so because we find the views there expressed persuasive, not because we consider this court bound to do so by our understanding of federal doctrines. *Daubert* rests on an interpretation of the Federal Rules of Evidence, a federal statute. As a statutory case, rather than a constitutional case, *Daubert* is not binding on the states. That is true even though the Oregon Evidence Code is modeled on the Federal Rules of Evidence.[330]

Oregon generally requires expert testimony with regard to causation evidence:

Oregon cases discussing the sufficiency of expert opinion testimony about a "reasonable medical probability" of causation have primarily focused on (1) whether such expert testimony is required, *see Chouinard*, 179 Or.App. at 513, 39 P.3d 951 (whether a brain tumor caused the plaintiff's headaches was a sufficiently complex medical question to require expert testimony); (2) whether the expert is qualified in a field that is recognized as scientifically valid, *see State v. O'Key*, 321 Or. 285, 899 P.2d 663 (1995) (laying out multifactor analysis to determine scientific validity); or (3) whether the expert testified that causation was probable or merely possible, *Joshi v. Providence Health System*, 198 Or.App. 534, 545, 108 P.3d 1195 (2005) (testimony that there was a 30 percent chance that defendant's alleged negligence caused injury was insufficient to allow issue to go to the jury).[331]

With regard to the contents of an expert's opinion, "[t]he expert's failure to explain how he arrived at his opinion could result in the jury giving the opinion less weight than it otherwise might, but that omission is not grounds for a directed verdict."[332]

There are exceptions when the issue of causation is so simple that there are no alternative explanations and the effect of the injury would be within the ken of the average juror:

Nevertheless, with respect, it is precisely that sort of intuitive resort to lay logic that the requirements of competent expert opinion on causation in complex medical cases is imposed to forestall. *See Baughman*, 200 Or.App. at 18, 113 P.3d 459; *accord Chouinard*, 179 Or.App. at 513, 39 P.3d 951 ("Although plaintiff argues that tumors and their effects on the body are a matter of common knowledge, we agree with the trial court that the issue of causation was a complex medical question that required expert testimony."). Consequently, exceptions to that rule of proof appear to have been limited to cases of simple injuries, generally without a substantial possibility of alternative causation. *Compare Wheeler v. LaViolette*, 129 Or.App. 57, 877 P.2d 665 (1994) (no expert medical testimony regarding causation of knee injury was required where the plaintiff stepped into space left by a missing plank in a dock and promptly sought medical attention for knee pain, and where contemporaneous emergency room report noted a "superficial abrasion" just above the knee), with *Myers v. Dunscombe*, 64 Or.App. 722, 669 P.2d 388, *rev. den.*, 296 Or. 236, 675 P.2d 490 (1983) (affirming directed verdict where the plaintiff offered no expert opinion that negligently administered dental injection had caused her nerve damage and there was at least one alternative explanation for causation of the plaintiff's injury).[333]

The Court of Appeals recently held that "[t]he primary criterion of whether certain evidence constitutes 'scientific evidence' is therefore whether the evidence 'possesses significantly increased potential to influence jurors as a scientific assertion.'"[334] That court held that:

[w]e conclude that the disputed evidence here is not "scientific evidence" that requires a foundation based on the *Brown* factors. As discussed, this is not the type of evidence that can be presented and explained only by an expert. Lay factfinders can reasonably be expected to understand and weigh the credibility and strength of evidence about who performed a blood draw by syringe and how the person did so. The evidence proffered about the blood collection is simply not the type of evidence that possesses significantly increased potential to influence jurors as a scientific assertion.[335]

Pennsylvania
Pennsylvania is a *Frye* state, and held in *Commonwealth v. Dengler* that actuarial risk assessment of sex offenders is not subject to the *Frye* test because it does not involve "novel scientific evidence."[336]

In *Dengler*, the Pennsylvania Supreme Court observed that "the *Frye* test, which was adopted in Pennsylvania *Commonwealth v. Topa*, 471 Pa. 223, 369 A.2d 1277 (1977), is part of Rule [Pa.R.E.] 702."[337] The *Dengler* Court gave a history of *Frye's* application in Pennsylvania:

> The requirement of general acceptance in the scientific community assures that those most qualified to assess the general validity of a scientific method will have the determinative voice. Additionally, the *Frye* test protects prosecution and defense alike by assuring that a minimal reserve of experts exists who can critically examine the validity of a scientific determination in a particular case. Since scientific proof may in some instances assume a posture of mystic infallibility in the eyes of a jury of laymen, the ability to produce rebuttal experts, equally conversant with the mechanics and methods of a particular technique, may prove to be essential.

> ...This Court has consistently followed this manner of approach when confronted with novel scientific evidence in the three decades since our adoption of *Frye*. *Commonwealth v. Nazarovitch*, 496 Pa. 97, 436 A.2d 170 (1981) (process of refreshing recollection by hypnosis not yet accepted); *Commonwealth v. Dunkle,* 529 Pa. 168, 602 A.2d 830 (1992) ("Sexually Abused Child Syndrome" evidence not admissible); *Commonwealth v. Zook*, 532 Pa. 79, 615 A.2d 1 (1992) (electrophoresis test of dried blood stains deemed admissible); *Commonwealth v. Crews*, 536 Pa. 508, 640 A.2d 395 (1994) (certain DNA evidence deemed inadmissible); *Dalrymple v. Brown*, 549 Pa. 217, 701 A.2d 164 (1997) (repressed memory theory deemed inadmissible); *Commonwealth v. Crawford*, 553 Pa. 195, 718 A.2d 768 (1998) (revived repressed memory testimony rejected); *Blum ex rel. Blum v. Merrell Dow Pharmaceuticals, Inc.*, 564 Pa. 3, 764 A.2d 1 (2000) (expert testimony regarding causal link between mother's ingestion of drug and child's birth defect deemed too unreliable to be admitted where it involved recalculation of data used in other studies); *Grady, supra* (expert witness's conclusion concerning safety of food product inadmissible because expert's methodology lacked general acceptance in relevant scientific community for purposes of reaching such conclusion). In addition, in *Grady*,

this Court recently made clear that *Frye* would remain the governing Pennsylvania standard, and not the newer federal standard represented by *Daubert v. Merrell Dow Pharmaceuticals, Inc.*, 509 U.S. 579, 113 S.Ct. 2786, 125 L.Ed.2d 469 (1993). *Grady*, 839 A.2d at 1044–45.[338]

A party is not entitled to a *Frye* hearing as of right. Instead,

[t]his Court has made it clear that *Frye* is not implicated every time science comes into the courtroom; rather, it applies only to proffered expert testimony involving novel science. *Commonwealth v. Delbridge*, 580 Pa. 68, 859 A.2d 1254, 1260 (2004) (plurality opinion) (citing Pa.R.E. 702 and *Grady*, 839 A.2d at 1044). What constitutes novel scientific evidence has historically been decided on a case-by-case basis, and there is some fluidity in the analysis; indeed, science deemed novel at the outset may lose its novelty and become generally accepted in the scientific community at a later date, or the strength of the proponent's proffer may affect the *Frye* determination.[339]

Rhode Island

Rhode Island adopted *Daubert* in 1996:

We can only determine at this time that when such testimony is offered, particularly expert testimony relating to the basis for such repression of recollection and for the diagnosis of PTSD, which provides the rationale for such repression and flashbacks, the trial justice should exercise a gatekeeping function and hold a preliminary evidentiary hearing outside the presence of the jury in order to determine whether such evidence is reliable and whether the situation is one on which expert testimony is appropriate. *State v. Wheeler*, 496 A.2d 1382, 1386–88 (R.I.1985) (involving the admission of voice identification evidence produced by spectrographic analysis). Subsequent to that case, the Supreme Court of the United States in the landmark case of *Daubert v. Merrell Dow Pharmaceuticals, Inc.*, 509 U.S. 579, 113 S.Ct. 2786, 125 L.Ed.2d 469 (1993), also determined in construing Rule 702 of the Federal Rules of Evidence (which is identical to Rule 702 of the Rhode Island Rules of Evidence) that guidelines should be provided for a trial judge to follow in determining the admissibility of scientific evidence: (1) whether the proffered knowledge can be or has been tested, (2) whether the theory or technique has been subjected to peer review and publication, (3) the known or the potential error rate, and (4) whether the theory or technique has gained general acceptance in the relevant scientific discipline. 509 U.S. at 593–94, 113 S.Ct. at 2796–97, 125 L.Ed.2d at 482–83.[340]

A defendant is not entitled to a *Daubert* hearing as of right:

> Likewise, we reject defendants' contention that they were entitled to a *Daubert* hearing to determine the scientific validity of Mr. Dalbec's loss revenue calculations. A party makes a proper motion for such an evidentiary hearing only when he or she sufficiently alerts the trial justice of the scientific issue at stake by presenting an affidavit or offer of proof to substantiate his or her claim that the opposing party's proposed expert testimony is scientifically invalid. The defendants in the present case offered virtually no explanation of why a *Daubert* hearing was necessary. We therefore are satisfied that the trial justice did not err in failing to hold a *Daubert* hearing concerning Mr. Dalbec's testimony.[341]

However, if a party makes a proper objection pursuant to the relevant rule, the party is entitled to a *Daubert* hearing:

> We are persuaded that in Rhode Island a trial justice in a criminal as well as in a civil case must exercise this gatekeeping function and shall conduct a preliminary examination prior to allowing scientific evidence that supports repressed recollections or flashbacks to be submitted to the jury, if such evidence is challenged by an appropriate objection or motion to suppress. The trial justice in this case, perhaps for lack of adequate guidance from our prior opinions, did not hold such a preliminary hearing. Our decision today, we hope, will provide such guidance in the future. This holding is, of course, applicable to the case at bar. We agree with the dissent that our prior opinions and the language of Rule 104(c) of the Rhode Island Rules of Evidence do not give adequate guidance to a trial justice when confronted with the proffer of a novel and controversial body of scientific

evidence. It is intended that this opinion should clarify the obligation in accordance with the standards set forth above.[342]

Rhode Island has also adopted *Kuhmo Tire*:

> In *Daubert*, 509 U.S. at 589, 113 S.Ct. at 2795, 125 L. Ed. 2d at 480, the United States Supreme Court announced that all scientific evidence must be relevant as well as reliable pursuant to the Federal Rules of Evidence. Specifically, the trial justice must regulate the admission of scientific evidence to ensure that the proposed scientific testimony "rests on a reliable foundation and is relevant to the task at hand." In carrying out this regulatory duty, the trial justice "exercises a gatekeeping function." 'Those gatekeeping duties apply "not only to testimony based on 'scientific knowledge,' but also to testimony based on 'technical' and 'other specialized' knowledge." We have recognized the applicability of *Daubert* and *Kumho Tire* to situations in which scientific evidence is offered pursuant to the Rhode Island Rules of Evidence.[343]

The application of these standards is not uniform, however. In a 2006 case involving the admissibility of DNA, the trial judge applied an alternative state standard:

> After considering the state's evidence regarding the reliability of PCR testing and its acceptance in the scientific community, the trial justice found that the defendant had failed to raise a sufficient challenge to this evidence. The trial justice went on to apply the three-prong analysis set out in *State v. Wheeler*, 496 A.2d 1382, 1388 (R.I.1985), and applied *State v. Morel*, 676 A.2d 1347, 1354–55 (R.I.1996), for analyzing the admissibility of expert testimony based upon novel scientific evidence The trial justice found (1) that the DNA evidence was relevant, (2) that the subject matter was one for which expert testimony was appropriate and that the experts who would testify in this case were qualified to render an opinion, and (3) that the DNA evidence would be helpful to the trier of fact. Accordingly, defendant's motion *in limine* was denied.[344]

The appellate court observed dryly that:

> [in] the present case...the trial justice admitted the DNA evidence in this case only after a lengthy pretrial hearing, at which she considered extensive testimony concerning the reliability of the PCR DNA analysis conducted by Bode and its acceptance in the scientific community. *While it is not necessary for us to pass upon the continued necessity of such a pretrial hearing to determine the admissibility of DNA evidence in cases such as this*, it is clear that, following such a comprehensive hearing, the trial justice certainly did not err in ruling that the state's DNA evidence was admissible at trial.[345]

South Carolina

South Carolina has its own standard for the admissibility of expert testimony, as set out in *State v. Douglas* (clarifying existing state standards and when such standards may or may not need to be applied):

> The test for qualification of an expert is a relative one that is dependent on the particular witness's reference to the subject. (Rule 702, SCRE, articulates guidelines for the admissibility of expert testimony. Rule 702 provides: "If scientific, technical, or other specialized knowledge will assist the trier of fact to understand the evidence or to determine a fact in issue, a witness qualified as an expert by knowledge, skill, experience, training, or education, may testify thereto in the form of an opinion or otherwise." There is no abuse of discretion as long as the witness has acquired by study or practical experience such knowledge of the subject matter of his testimony as would enable him to give guidance and assistance to the jury in resolving a factual issue which is beyond the scope of the jury's good judgment and common knowledge. For a court to find a witness competent to testify as an expert, the witness must be better qualified than the fact finder to form an opinion on the particular subject of the testimony. An expert is not limited to any class of persons acting professionally. There is no exact requirement concerning how knowledge or skill must be acquired.

The party offering the expert has the burden of showing the witness possesses the necessary learning, skill, or practical experience to enable the witness to give opinion testimony. Generally, however, defects in the amount and quality of the expert's education or experience go to the weight to be accorded the expert's testimony and not to its admissibility.

The admissibility of scientific evidence is dependent on whether the expert relied on scientifically and professionally established techniques. This standard is designed to prevent the fact finders from being misled by the aura of infallibility surrounding unproven scientific methods. However, not all expert testimony is subject to a *Jones* challenge. "If the expert's opinion does not fall within *Jones*, questions about the reliability of an expert's methods go only to the weight, but not admissibility, of the testimony." For instance, this includes the testimony of behavioral science experts. In finding that expert testimony on eyewitness reliability was found admissible, the supreme court in *Whaley* rejected the necessity of a *Jones* analysis for that type of evidence to show that the field was a recognized area of expertise:

The admissibility of *scientific* evidence depends upon "the degree to which the trier of fact must accept, on faith, scientific hypotheses not capable of proof or disproof in court and not even generally accepted outside the courtroom." Dr. Cole's testimony, however, is distinguishable from "scientific"evidence, such as DNA test results, blood spatter interpretation, and bite mark comparisons. An eyewitness identification witness gives expert opinion evidence similar to the type given by doctors or psychiatrists. Where the witness is a qualified psychologist who simply explains how certain aspects of every day experience shown by the record can affect human perception and memory, and through them, the accuracy of eyewitness identification, we see no reason to require a greater foundation. Consequently, we are not persuaded that this type of testimony is required to meet the *Jones* test.[346]

The *Douglas* Court listed areas in which expert testimony is required:

South Carolina recognizes a veritable plethora of areas in which an expert "has acquired by study or practical experience such knowledge of the subject matter of his testimony as would enable him to give guidance and assistance to the jury in resolving a factual issue which is beyond the scope of the jury's good judgment and common knowledge." *State v. Henry*, 329 S.C. 266, 273, 495 S.E.2d 463, 466 (Ct.App.1997); *see, e.g., Fields v. Regional Med. Ctr. Orangeburg*, 363 S.C. 19, 609 S.E.2d 506 (2005) (upholding the South Carolina Court of Appeals' decision that a physician's lack of board certification in a specialized area goes to his weight and credibility, and not his qualification as an expert); *Ellis v. Davidson*, 358 S.C. 509, 595 S.E.2d 817 (Ct.App.2004) (reversing the decision of the trial court disallowing the expert affidavit of a law school professor that defendant law firm had an attorney-client relationship with plaintiff); *Burroughs v. Worsham*, 352 S.C. 382, 574 S.E.2d 215 (Ct.App.2002) (affirming the admission of the expert opinion of a medical doctor that if defendant had diagnosed decedent's cancer earlier, cancer would have been more curable); *Means v. Gates*, 348 S.C. 161, 558 S.E.2d 921 (Ct. App. 2001) (finding a neuropsychologist qualified to offer his opinion of the cause and extent of plaintiff's injuries despite his not being a medical doctor); *Small v. Pioneer Mach., Inc.*, 329 S.C. 448, 494 S.E.2d 835 (Ct.App. 1997) (holding a licensed professional engineer may offer his opinion that a log skidder was defectively designed because it allowed debris into the throttle chamber, which caused the throttle to stick).

South Carolina appellate courts recognize the significance of expert testimony to assist or guide the trier of fact in criminal cases. *See, e.g., State v. Ellis*, 345 S.C. 175, 547 S.E.2d 490 (2001) (clarifying that while police officer may testify as expert in crime scene processing and fingerprint identification, he may not testify to ultimate issue as to whether defendant acted in self-defense); *State v. Von Dohlen*, 322 S.C. 234, 471 S.E.2d 689 (1996) (upholding trial court's decision to allow forensic pathologist to testify, during sentencing, about the amount of pain victim suffered); *State v. Whaley*, 305 S.C. 138, 406 S.E.2d 369 (1991) (finding eyewitness identification expert qualified); *State v. Myers*, 301 S.C. 251, 391 S.E.2d 551 (1990) (allowing expert in blood spatter interpretation to testify); *State v. Childs*, 299 S.C. 471, 385 S.E.2d 839 (1989) (qualifying a bloodhound handler as an expert witness).

More specifically, South Carolina courts allow the testimony of experts evaluating victims in sexual abuse cases. In *State v.*

Schumpert, the Supreme Court of South Carolina held the trial court did not abuse its discretion in qualifying a mental health counselor to testify about rape trauma syndrome. *Schumpert*, 312 S.C. 502, 435 S.E.2d 859 (1993). The Court of Appeals, in *State v. Weaverling*, determined the trial court properly qualified a social worker as an expert in the field of victims of sexual abuse. *Weaverling*, 337 S.C. 460, 523 S.E.2d 787 (Ct.App. 1999). Similarly, this court allowed the testimony of a mental health counselor in the field of evaluation and treatment of sexually abused children and posttraumatic stress. *See State v. Morgan*, 326 S.C. 503, 485 S.E.2d 112 (Ct.App.1997).[347]

In *Douglas*, the Court found that expert testimony of a forensic interviewer was admissible to describe the conditions under which complainant made her abuse allegations:

> [T]he testimony was not presented to bolster the victim's credibility, but as a measure to prevent a defense or argument that the victim's testimony was the result of police suggestiveness. The RATAC method [of forensic interviewing] was developed in response to concerns about child victims' testimony being tainted by police suggestiveness, as exemplified by *State v. Michaels*, 136 N.J. 299, 642 A.2d 1372 (1994).[348]

South Carolina interpreted a South Carolina licensing statute so as to hold that an expert engineer licensed in California could testify in South Carolina even though he was not licensed to practice engineering there.[349]

An expert witness was not permitted to testify that, because of Asperger syndrome, a defendant lacked the capacity to form the intent to commit murder because he perceived himself at risk when he should not have:

> On appeal, Santiago argues the trial court erred in refusing to allow the testimony of Schwartz-Watts because the evidence was relevant to Santiago's mental state, both at the time he made the statement to police and at the time of the shooting. At trial, defense counsel offered Schwartz-Watts as an expert witness to testify that Santiago's asperger's [*sic*] disorder

caused him to fear for his life, and accordingly, Santiago did not have the requisite mental state to commit murder. Essentially, defense counsel argued that Santiago was culpable of a lesser offense because of his diminished capacity. However, the diminished capacity defense is not recognized in South Carolina. In *Gill*, defense counsel wanted a forensic psychiatrist to testify that because Gill had a low IQ, he did not have the requisite mental state to commit murder. The Supreme Court held the trial judge properly excluded this testimony because South Carolina does not recognize the diminished capacity defense. Thus, the trial judge did not commit an abuse of discretion when she refused to allow Schwartz-Watts to testify regarding Santiago's diminished capacity.[350]

Furthermore, the South Carolina Supreme Court ruled that a police officer could not offer testimony about gangs because it was all derived from inadmissible hearsay (informants).[351]

South Dakota
South Dakota adopted *Daubert* in 1994 in *State v. Hofer*.[352]

A defendant is not entitled to a *Daubert* hearing as of right. In *Moeller v. Weber*, the Court held that expert testimony identifying soil samples as "gahnite"[353] was not novel, and therefore any quarrels with regard to the methodology used by the expert went to weight and not to admissibility.[354]

> Expert testimony need only be based on a "reliable foundation." There is no requirement that the foundation be one that is absolutely accepted throughout the scientific community. Moeller rests his entire argument on the premise that the State's expert failed to meet the rigorous validation processes of the DNA community. He devotes no ink to explaining where the State's expert failed to meet our admissibility requirements... .

> In furtherance of our belief that the trial court did not err in admitting the disputed DNA evidence, we note that the *habeas* court effectively conducted what might be referred to as a "post-conviction"*Daubert* hearing. During the habeas hearing, Moeller's DNA expert was allowed to testify at length on problems she perceived in the APO-B testing. However,

even at this stage, Moeller's expert was unable to convince the *habeas* court that the evidence based on the APO-B marker failed to meet our admission standards. All the *habeas* court found was that there is disagreement in the DNA community on whether APO-B is a valid marker. Again, perfect agreement is not a prerequisite to admission of scientific evidence.[355]

But the South Dakota Supreme Court held that experts are limited to offering opinions within their area of expertise and not outside of it:

Frankenfeld, a forensic economist, specializes in projecting earning loss over time, not in assessing vocational disabilities. He conceded as much in the pretrial hearing: "[a] vocational expert has competence that I do not have to take physical limitations and translate those into vocational limitations. That's not an area that I get into, but it is possible."According to his chiropractor, Garland suffers a seven percent physical impairment rating; however, a physical impairment does not directly translate into any vocational disability. Frankenfeld's opinion did not hinge on a physical impairment rating. Instead, he relied solely on Garland's assertion that he must take a thirty minute break every four hours. Thus, Frankenfeld, who admits that he has no competence as a vocational expert, converted one hour of claimed nonproductivity a day into a ten percent disability. Frankenfeld also acknowledged that in most instances where he testifies concerning economic loss, he does so based on the analysis of a vocational expert. We conclude that his opinion cannot be considered reliable.[356]

Interestingly, a circuit court judge reduced the fees to a court-appointed attorney by more than a third because the 14-hour *Daubert* hearing on the issue was unnecessary—and because she drove up the expert's fees by having him sit in the courtroom even though his testimony was unrelated to his viewing the testimony of the child witness in the case and because, under *Daubert*, the issue she covered went to weight, not admissibility.[357] The Supreme Court remanded only to have the Court take into consideration the issue of whether the effort was reasonable in light of the exposure of the defendant since he was facing a life sentence.

South Dakota has also adopted *Kumho Tire*, citing it in an opinion that required that an expert have more than anecdotal evidence in support of his conclusions:

> To abide by *Daubert-Kumho,* the proponent offering expert testimony must show that the expert's theory or method qualifies as scientific, technical, or specialized knowledge. One method of meeting this burden is by establishing that there has been adequate empirical proof of the validity of the theory or method. As the Supreme Court stated, "[t]he focus...must be solely on principles and methodology, not on the conclusions they generate."
>
> Lorenzen's opinion was unreliable because it could not be substantiated by showing what the electrical fault was that caused the claimant's electrical shock. Without knowing this, we cannot know if a GFCI would have prevented the claimant's injury. Lorenzen's proof was purely anecdotal: he performed the same job using the portable GFCI and did not experience a shock. His opinion on causation was not admissible as expert testimony. SDCL 19-15-2.[358]

Meanwhile, South Dakota has formulated standards for whether defendants are entitled to postconviction relief based on a desire for further testing of evidence:

> After careful consideration, we have formulated the following guidelines for when post-conviction scientific analysis may be authorized: First, the evidence and test results must meet the *Daubert* standard for scientific reliability. A showing must be made that if the matter were presently tried the defendant would be entitled to the testing and the results would be admissible. Second, because convicted defendants may not obtain reconsideration of their cases whenever some new technology promises to reveal another angle on the evidence against them, it must be shown that a favorable result using the latest scientific procedures would most likely produce an acquittal in a new trial. Third, testing should not be allowed if it imposes an unreasonable burden on the State. An exorbitant cost may be grounds for denial, for example, especially if anticipated test

results promise to be less than definite. If testing is allowed, the court should impose reasonable safeguards to ensure the preservation and integrity of the evidence. With biological evidence, courts have generally found post-conviction testing most suitable when (a) identity of a single perpetrator is at issue; (b) evidence against the defendant is so weak as to suggest real doubt of guilt; (c) the scientific evidence, if any, used to obtain the conviction has been impugned; and, (d) the nature of the biological evidence makes testing results on the issue of identity virtually dispositive.[359]

Finally, South Dakota does not allow expert testimony as to the credibility of a witness:

> A trial court has broad discretion concerning the qualifications of an expert and the admissibility of expert testimony, and it will not be reversed on appeal without a clear showing that it abused its discretion. It is also true that as a general rule, expert testimony regarding credibility is inadmissible. The fundamental test for admission of expert testimony, however, is whether it will assist the jury in resolving the factual issues before it.
>
> The trial court correctly limited [defendant's psychologist's] testimony to the reliability of Corey's statements. *Id.* Corey argues that [his psychologist] should have been allowed to also testify to Corey's frame of mind during the police interviews and explain why Corey resorted to role-playing games as a way to protect himself. Corey set out no scientific basis for the proposed testimony. In fact, Corey could not point to any psychological tests that would make [the psychologist's] testimony credible or reliable for these extended purposes. The limit placed on [the psychologist's] testimony by the trial court was within its discretion. The additional testimony may have added confusion rather than making things clearer for the jury. As such, the trial court did not err by limiting [the psychologist's] testimony.[360]

Tennessee

After observing that the trial judge had listed several different standards for the admissibility of expert testimony in Tennessee,[361] the

Tennessee Supreme Court fixed the standard for the admissibility of expert testimony in *McDaniel v. CSX Transp., Inc*:

> We...conclude that Tennessee Rules of Evidence 702 and 703 impose a duty upon trial courts to determine whether scientific evidence will substantially aid the trier of fact and whether the underlying facts and data relied on by the expert witness indicate a lack of trustworthiness. The trial court must further determine whether the reasoning or methodology underlying the scientific evidence is sufficiently valid and reliable, and whether it can properly be applied to the facts at issue.
>
> In making this determination, the trial court should focus on the principles and methodology underlying the science, and not on the conclusions of experts. The trial court is not required to determine that the principles and methodology employed are generally accepted by the scientific community. The court needs only to determine that the principles and methodology are scientifically valid and reliable.[362]

After comparing the admissibility of the disputed testimony under *Frye* and *Daubert* in two jurisdictions, the Tennessee Supreme Court announced its standard:

> After examining the basic legal principles governing the admissibility of scientific evidence and the change in direction by the federal courts, we turn to Tennessee to clarify our standard of admissibility.
>
> In general, questions regarding the admissibility, qualifications, relevancy and competency of expert testimony are left to the discretion of the trial court. The trial court's ruling in this regard may only be overturned if the discretion is arbitrarily exercised or abused. The specific rules of evidence that govern the issue of admissibility of scientific proof in Tennessee are Tenn. R. Evid. 702 and 703. The former provides:
>
> If scientific, technical, or other specialized knowledge will substantially assist the trier of fact to understand the evidence or to determine a fact in issue, a witness qualified as an expert by knowledge, skill, experience, training, or education may testify in the form of an opinion or otherwise.

And Tenn. R. Evid. 703 states:

The facts or data in the particular case upon which an expert bases an opinion or inference may be those perceived by or made known to the expert at or before the hearing. If of a type reasonably relied upon by experts in the particular field in forming opinions or inferences upon the subject, the facts or data need not be admissible in evidence. The court shall disallow testimony in the form of an opinion or inference if the underlying facts or data indicate lack of trustworthiness... .

Although the advisory comments to Rule 702 indicate that Tennessee has followed the *Frye* test in analyzing the admissibility of scientific evidence, one commentator, recognizing the similarity between Tennessee Rule 702 and Federal Rule Evid. 702, has raised the question of whether the *Frye* test of "general acceptance" should be abolished in Tennessee. Indeed, as the trial court in this case noted, there is some evidence of a departure from the strict adherence to the *Frye* test by courts in this State.

In our view, determining the standard for the admissibility of scientific evidence requires an analysis of the unique language found in Rules 702 and 703 of the Tennessee Rules of Evidence. For instance, Tenn. R. Evid. 702 requires that the scientific evidence "*substantially* assist the trier of fact," while its federal counterpart requires only that the evidence "assist the trier of fact." Fed.R.Evid. 702. This distinction indicates that the probative force of the testimony must be stronger before it is admitted in Tennessee.

Similarly, Tenn. R. Evid. 703 states that "[t]he court shall disallow testimony in the form of an opinion or inference if the underlying facts or data indicate lack of trustworthiness."

There is no similar restriction in the federal rule. Fed.R.Evid. 703. Thus, as one writer has observed, "the additional language ...[in the Tennessee rule] is obviously designed to encourage trial courts to take a more active role in evaluating the reasonableness of the expert's reliance upon the particular basis for his or her testimony." In sum, even though the facts and data need not be admissible, they must be reviewed and found to be trustworthy by the trial court.

Based on the foregoing analysis, we conclude that Tennessee's adoption of Rules 702 and 703 in 1991 as part of the Rules of Evidence supersede the general acceptance test of *Frye*. In Tennessee, under the recent rules, a trial court must determine whether the evidence will substantially assist the trier of fact to determine a fact in issue and whether the facts and data under-lying the evidence indicate a lack of trustworthiness. The rules together necessarily require a determination as to the scientific validity or reliability of the evidence. Simply put, unless the scientific evidence is valid, it will not substantially assist the trier of fact, nor will its underlying facts and data appear to be trustworthy, but there is no requirement in the rule that it be generally accepted.

Although we do not expressly adopt *Daubert*, the non-exclusive list of factors to determine reliability are useful in applying our Rules 702 and 703. A Tennessee trial court may consider in determining reliability: (1) whether scientific evidence has been tested and the methodology with which it has been tested; (2) whether the evidence has been subjected to peer review or publication; (3) whether a potential rate of error is known; (4) whether, as formerly required by *Frye*, the evidence is generally accepted in the scientific community; and (5) whether the expert's research in the field has been con-ducted independent of litigation.

Although the trial court must analyze the science and not merely the qualifications, demeanor or conclusions of experts, the court need not weigh or choose between two legitimate but conflict-ing scientific views. The court instead must assure itself that the opinions are based on relevant scientific methods, processes, and data, and not upon an expert's mere speculation. The trial court should keep in mind that the preliminary question under Tenn. R. Evid. 104 is one of admissibility of the evidence. Once the evidence is admitted, it will thereafter be tested with the cru-cible of vigorous cross-examination and countervailing proof. After that occurs, a defendant may, of course, challenge the suf-ficiency of the evidence by moving for a directed verdict at the appropriate times. See Tenn. R. Civ. P. 50. Yet it is important to emphasize that the weight to be given to stated scientific theo-ries, and the resolution of legitimate but competing scientific views, are matters appropriately entrusted to the trier of fact.[363]

In affirming that the relevant witness's testimony was correctly held to be admissible, the Court made a point of observing that "the research in this area, including that of several of the plaintiffs' experts, was conducted independently of this litigation."[364]

In *State v. Stephens*, the Court held that the *McDaniel* analysis applies to nonscientific expert testimony as well.[365] The Court ruled that:

> when the expert's reliability is challenged, the court may consider the following nondefinitive factors: (1) the *McDaniel* factors, when they are reasonable measures of the reliability of expert testimony; (2) the expert's qualifications for testifying on the subject at issue; and (3) the straightforward connection between the expert's knowledge and the basis for the opinion such that no "analytical gap" exists between the data and the opinion offered. Subject to the trial court's discretion, once the evidence is admitted, "it will thereafter be tested with the crucible of vigorous cross-examination and countervailing proof."*McDaniel*, 955 S.W.2d at 265.[366]

Clarifying the standard, the Tennessee Supreme Court noted that:

> In addition to the *McDaniel* factors, we have identified other nondefinitive factors that a trial court may consider in assessing the reliability of an expert's methodology. One such factor is the expert's qualifications for testifying on the subject at issue. This factor is applicable particularly where the expert's personal experience is essential to the methodology or analysis underlying his or her opinion. We, however, caution that using this factor as the sole basis of reliability would result in a reconsideration of the Rule 702 requirement that the expert witness be qualified by knowledge, skill, experience, training, or education to express an opinion within the limits of the expert's expertise. As a result, the expert testimony would become "perilously close to being admissible based upon the ipse dixit of the expert." Furthermore, the trial court should distinguish between "'the marginally-qualified full-time expert witness who is testifying about a methodology that she has not employed in real life' and 'the highly credentialed expert who has devoted her life's work to the actual exercise of the methodology upon which her testimony is based.'"[367]

The Court went on to note that "[a]nother factor that we have identified is the connection between the expert's knowledge and the basis for the expert's opinion.... . The purpose of this factor is to ensure that an "analytical gap" does not exist between the data relied upon and the opinion offered."[368]

In medical malpractice cases, the requirements for the qualifications of experts are fixed by statute.[369]

Texas

Texas has not adopted a pure *Daubert* standard. In *E.I. du Pont de Nemours v. Robinson*, Texas adds additional requirements to the factors listed in *Daubert*, citing *Kelly v. State* with approval:

> The Court of Criminal Appeals approved, holding that evidence is reliable if the underlying theory and the technique applying it are valid, and if the technique was properly applied on the occasion in question. *Kelly*, 824 S.W.2d at 573. Under *Kelly*, factors affecting the trial court's determination of reliability include: (1) general acceptance of the theory and technique by the relevant scientific community; (2) the expert's qualifications; (3) the existence of literature supporting or rejecting the theory; (4) the technique's potential rate of error; (5) the availability of other experts to test and evaluate the technique; (6) the clarity with which the theory or technique can be explained to the trial court; and (7) the experience and skill of the person who applied the technique on the occasion in question.[370]

The *Robinson* Court gave a grocery list of reliability factors:

> These factors include, but are not limited to:
>
> (1) the extent to which the theory has been or can be tested;
>
> (2) the extent to which the technique relies upon the subjective interpretation of the expert;
>
> (3) whether the theory has been subjected to peer review and/or publication;
>
> (4) the technique's potential rate of error;

(5) whether the underlying theory or technique has been generally accepted as valid by the relevant scientific community; and

(6) the non-judicial uses which have been made of the theory or technique.[371]

In *Gammill v. Jack Williams Chevrolet*, the Court held that the *Daubert-Robinson* standards applied to nonscientific expert testimony, observing that:

> [i]f one wanted to explain to a jury how a bumblebee is able to fly, an aeronautical engineer might be a helpful witness. Since flight principles have some universality, the expert could apply general principles to the case of the bumblebee. Conceivably, even if he had never seen a bumblebee, he still would be qualified to testify, as long as he was familiar with its component parts.

> On the other hand, if one wanted to prove that bumblebees always take off into the wind, a beekeeper with no scientific training at all would be an acceptable expert witness if a proper foundation were laid for his conclusions. The foundation would not relate to his formal training, but to his firsthand observations. In other words, the beekeeper does not know any more about flight principles than the jurors, but he has seen a lot more bumblebees than they have.

> The court concluded that plaintiff's expert was more like the beekeeper than the aeronautical engineer, but that the reliability of the expert's testimony must nevertheless be evaluated.[372]

The Court in *Gammill* approved evaluating the evidence in light of *Joiner*:

> The Robinson factors for assessing the reliability of scientific evidence cannot be applied to the testimony offered by the Gammills' experts, even though mechanical engineering, the expertise claimed by the witnesses, is scientific in nature. But Rule 702's general requirement of reliability must still be satisfied, and the district court concluded that Huston's testimony was unreliable. In essence, the district court applied the test

stated in *Joiner*: whether "there is simply too great an analytical gap between the data and the opinion proffered."[373]

The Court applied *Gammill* in a parental termination case in which a burn expert testified that the burns on the child were inconsistent with the two (mutually exclusive) explanations provided by the appellant:

> Appellant argues that Dr. Hunt's theory that D.S. had been forcibly immersed in hot water was unreliable because it could not be evaluated under the *Daubert/Robinson* factors. Although the State concedes that Dr. Hunt's testimony does not conform to the *Daubert/Robinson* factors, it argues that those factors are not exclusive and that reliability can be achieved based upon the expertise and skill of a testifying expert. We agree that Dr. Hunt's expert testimony is not the type of testimony that can be easily evaluated under the *Daubert/Robinson* factors. Courts are often confronted with both scientific and non-scientific evidence in determining the admissibility of expert testimony. The difference between these two types of evidence is that the former is based on the application of scientific principles which can be readily tested by those factors, while the latter is based on skill or on experience based on observation. Dr. Hunt testified that his theory was not subject to human testing in medical laboratories because it would be immoral to intentionally submerge children in hot liquids in order to study the effects of the burns. Dr. Hunt also testified that there is not any statistical data showing the potential rate of error due to the fact that no one conducts this type of experiment. Dr. Hunt did specify, however, that there are objective criteria that people who have experience treating pediatric burns identify to determine the cause and nature of the burn. Because Dr. Hunt's opinion concerning the cause of D.S.'s burns is not the type of evidence that can be readily evaluated under the *Daubert/Robinson* factors, we will apply the more general reliability test espoused in *Gammill*.

To resolve the controversy when faced with non-scientific evidence like Dr. Hunt's testimony, courts must analyze the underlying data forming the basis for the expert's opinion. The critical inquiry is whether there is an "analytical gap" between the opinion and the basis on which it is founded. Dr. Hunt testified that he was a general surgeon on staff at the Southwestern Medical School in Dallas and co-director of the Parkland Burn Unit (Burn Unit). He has over twenty-five years' experience in treating both adult and pediatric burn victims. Dr. Hunt observed and treated D.S. after her arrival at the Burn Unit on May 6. He explained the principles and methods used to determine whether or not abuse was involved in causing the victim's burns. Dr. Hunt stated that it is crucial to study the distribution of the victim's burns and to compare it with the explanation given based on the body's normal response when contacted with a hot liquid. For instance, a person typically will try to withdraw from the hot liquid; therefore, accidental burns are characterized by splash marks and uneven distributions of burned skin. On the other hand, where abuse is involved, the burn's distribution is fixed and appears as a straight line. Dr. Hunt testified that D.S.'s burns were evenly distributed and that there were no splash marks on her. Based on this testimony, the trial court could have found that Dr. Hunt's testimony regarding the cause of D.S.'s burns was reliable.[374]

In Texas, an expert must be an expert in the specific field under discussion:

> In deciding whether an expert is qualified, the trial court "must ensure that those who purport to be experts truly have expertise concerning the actual subject about which they are offering an opinion." General experience in a specialized field is insufficient to qualify a witness as an expert. "What is required is that the offering party establish that the expert has 'knowledge, skill, experience, training, or education' regarding the specific issue before the court which would qualify the expert to give an opinion on that particular subject."[375]

Utah

Utah has a rule of evidence governing expert testimony that mirrors FRE 702.[376] But Utah uses an alternative common-law state standard for the admissibility of expert testimony—*State v. Rimmasch*.[377] That case ruled upon the admissibility of expert witness testimony as to whether or not a victim's behavior was consistent with sexual abuse: "We join these courts and hold that rule 608(a) (1) bars admission of an expert's testimony as to the truthfulness of a witness on a particular occasion."[378]

In *Rimmasch*, the Court held that there were two ways to determine the reliability of expert testimony: "a request that the trial court take judicial notice of the 'inherent reliability' of the testimony's foundational principles or techniques or, alternatively, a request that the trial court determine that these principles or techniques are inherently reliable after an evidentiary hearing... ."[379]

Once the court determines whether a hearing is required, *Rimmasch* requires that a trial court determine "whether the testimony was founded upon scientific principles or arrived at through scientific techniques that satisfy the requirement of inherent reliability; if so, then we proceed to balance the probativeness of the evidence against its potential for unfair prejudice."[380] Furthermore, in a footnote, the *Rimmasch* Court notes that the "trial court must still make a separate determination...that the scientific principles or techniques have been properly applied to the facts of the particular case by qualified persons and that the testimony is founded on that work."[381]

In sum, "the trial court should carefully explore each logical link in the chain that leads to expert testimony given in court and determine its reliability."[382]

The Utah Supreme Court rejected *Daubert* in *State v. Crosby*.[383]

In 2005, the Court responded to *Kumho Tire* by holding that "the Utah Supreme Court has reiterated that the *Rimmasch* test:

> applies only to novel scientific methods and techniques." A careful review of the Utah decisions, however, indicates that "scientific" evidence is not narrowly defined to include only evidence developed using principles or techniques found in what are traditionally thought of as the "hard sciences."[384]

However, if *Rimmasch* does not apply, this does not end the inquiry:

The trial court is required to apply the inherent reliability test of *Rimmasch* only when there is a "plausible claim," that the expert testimony sought to be admitted is based on "novel scientific principles or techniques."

When expert testimony does not require evaluation under the inherent reliability test announced in *Rimmasch*, we evaluate the testimony according to the standard set forth *State v. Clayton*, 646 P.2d 723 (Utah 1982):

[O]nce the expert is qualified by the court, the witness may base his opinion on reports, writings[,] or observations not in evidence which were made or compiled by others, so long as they are of a type reasonably relied upon by experts in that particular field. The opposing party may challenge the suitability or reliability of such materials on cross-examination, but such challenge goes to the weight to be given the testimony, not to its admissibility.

[S]ee also Utah R. Evid. 703 ("The facts or data in the particular case upon which an expert bases an opinion or inference may be those perceived by or made known to the expert at or before the hearing.").[385]

Vermont

Vermont held that its rules of evidence were identical to the FRE, and adopted *Daubert*, in *State v. Streich*.[386] Vermont also follows *Kumho Tire*:

In Vermont, we adopted the *Daubert* analysis, concluding that because our rules of evidence are "essentially identical to the federal ones on admissibility of scientific evidence" it makes sense to adopt admissibility principles similar to those used in the federal courts. This decision was typical of the at least thirty states that have done the same, based on similar reasoning. Following the Brooks decision, in *Streich*, we reiterated our decision to follow *Daubert* and reject *Frye*. In 2000, although not explicitly, we followed *Kumho Tire*, when we applied the *Daubert* standard *State v. Kinney*, 171 Vt. 239, 248–49, 762 A.2d 833, 841–42 (2000), where an expert testified about rape trauma syndrome. Recently, we made our adoption of *Kumho*

Tire explicit by amending V.R.E. 702 to include its holding. See 2004 Amendment to V.R.E. 702 (effective July 1, 2004) (making V.R.E. 702 identical to Fed. R. Evid. 702, note 4, *supra*).[387]

That court adopted the "abuse of discretion standard" for evaluating trial court decisions at the appellate level.[388] Moreover, in a bench trial, a court may conduct a *Daubert* inquiry in "a somewhat more relaxed manner."[389]

In a murder case, the Court ruled that the substance of the testimony of an expert witness could easily be inferred by his findings on an autopsy report, and so additional notice was unnecessary:

> While there is no question that defendant was entitled to pretrial notice of the substance of Dr. Morrow's testimony, such notice was not lacking here. ...Dr. Morrow's testimony as to Jessica Bishop's paralysis was an "obvious inference" from the autopsy report's description of the path of the bullet, which included a lengthy description of the damage to Jessica Bishop's spinal cord. Moreover, defense counsel could have received more detailed notice of this testimony had he not chosen to waive deposition of Dr. Morrow during discovery. At a pretrial status conference, the State informed defense counsel that Dr. Morrow would testify not only as to the cause of each victim's death, but also as to the range at which the shots were fired, the path of the bullets, and the "physical manifestations." Defense counsel commented that this testimony "might go beyond the scope of what's in the autopsy report" and expressed interest in discussing that possibility with Dr. Morrow, but evidently chose not to pursue the matter further. If defendant wanted more explicit information in advance of Dr. Morrow's testimony, he had ample opportunity to gather it.[390]

Virginia

Virginia has rejected *Frye* and *Daubert*.[391] The test for admissibility of expert testimony is contained within *Spencer v. Commonwealth*:

> *Spencer v. Commonwealth*, 240 Va. 78, 97, 393 S.E.2d 609, 621, *cert. denied*, 498 U.S. 908, 111 S.Ct. 281, 112 L.Ed.2d

235 (1990) [and] *O'Dell v. Commonwealth*, 234 Va. 672, 696, 364 S.E.2d 491, 504, *cert. denied*, 488 U.S. 871, 109 S.Ct. 186, 102 L.Ed.2d 154 (1988), [t]he Supreme Court has set forth explicitly the standard for determining the competence of scientific evidence.

When scientific evidence is offered, the court must make a threshold finding of fact with respect to the reliability of the scientific method offered, unless it is of a kind so familiar and accepted as to require no foundation to establish the fundamental reliability of the system, such as fingerprint analysis; or unless it is so unreliable that the considerations requiring its exclusion have ripened into rules of law, such as "lie-detector" tests; or unless its admission is regulated by statute, such as blood-alcohol test results.

In making the threshold finding of fact, the court must usually rely on expert testimony. If there is a conflict, and the trial court's finding is supported by credible evidence, it will not be disturbed on appeal. Even where the issue of scientific reliability is disputed, if the court determines that there is a sufficient foundation to warrant admission of the evidence, the court may, in its discretion, admit the evidence with appropriate instructions to the jury to consider the disputed reliability of the evidence in determining its credibility and weight.[392]

The Court must also analyze whether the prejudicial effect of the contested testimony exceeds its probative value:

"Expert testimony is appropriate to assist triers of fact in those areas where a person of normal intelligence and experience cannot make a competent decision." The expert testimony must be relevant, and the trial judge must determine whether the subject matter of the testimony is beyond a lay person's common knowledge and whether it will assist the trier of fact in understanding the evidence or in determining a fact in issue. "The admission of expert testimony is committed to the sound discretion of the trial judge, and we will reverse a trial court's decision only where that court has abused its discretion."[393]

In civil cases, the standard is different, but *Frye* and *Daubert* also do not apply:

> In civil cases, expert testimony generally is admissible if it will assist the trier of fact in understanding the evidence. See Code 8.01-401.1 and -401.3; However, the admission of expert testimony is subject to certain basic requirements, including the requirement that the evidence be based on an adequate foundation. The decision whether to admit such testimony is a matter committed to the trial judge's sound discretion, and we will reverse a trial court's determination in this regard only when the court has abused its discretion.
>
> Expert testimony is inadmissible if it is speculative or founded on assumptions that have an insufficient factual basis. Such testimony is also inadmissible when an expert has failed to consider all variables bearing on the inferences to be drawn from the facts observed.
>
> In reviewing a trial court's ruling on the admissibility of expert testimony, we are limited to an examination of the record before us. Thus, in deciding this appeal, we decline John's request that we consider several articles concerning QEEG testing that she failed to submit to the trial court.[394]

In Virginia, expert testimony is inadmissible as to the ultimate issue in a criminal case.[395] Consistent with this prohibition, Virginia prohibits expert testimony about eyewitness identification.[396]

Experts can, however, testify that an injury suffered by the victim in a case would be *inconsistent* with consensual sexual intercourse, and that certain indicia in a drug case render the amount of controlled substances *inconsistent* with personal use.[397]

Expert testimony is not required in an insanity case, but a defendant must establish that he had a "disease of the mind."

> ...both the irresistible impulse test and the M'Naghten test require a showing of a disease of the mind, a defendant must present more than a scintilla of evidence of a mental disease in order to receive a jury instruction. Although lay testimony may support a plea of insanity, "it is generally recognized that it is advisable

to adduce expert testimony to better resolve such a complex
problem." Two doctors examined appellant after the attack was
committed, but appellant did not introduce testimony or reports
from the doctors. Appellant presented the testimony of Selvog,
but Selvog did not testify that appellant suffered from a disease
of the mind. Selvog acknowledged treating appellant, but only
testified that he found appellant "disjointed" and that appellant
raced from one topic to another during their conversation. The
record contains no expert testimony from which the jury could
infer that appellant suffered from a mental disease.[398]

Washington

Washington is a *Frye* state, and it applies a *de novo* standard of review
of *Frye* rulings.[399]

The admissibility of expert testimony in Washington is governed by ER 702, which provides as follows:

If scientific, technical, or other specialized knowledge will
assist the trier of fact to understand the evidence or to determine a fact in issue, a witness qualified as an expert by knowledge, skill, experience, training, or education, may testify
thereto in the form of an opinion or otherwise.

As reflected in recent Washington cases, the rule involves a
two-step inquiry—whether the witness qualifies as an expert
and whether the expert testimony would be helpful to the trier
of fact. *State v. Russell*, 125 Wash.2d 24, 69, 882 P.2d 747
(1994), *cert. denied*, --- U.S. ----, 115 S.Ct. 2004, 131 L.Ed.2d
1005 (1995); *State v. Kalakosky*, 121 Wash.2d 525, 541, 852
P.2d 1064 (1993); *State v. Cauthron*, 120 Wash.2d 879, 890,
846 P.2d 502 (1993), [*overruled in part, State v. Buckner*, 941
P.2d 667, 133 Wn.2d 63 (Wash., 1997)]... . The bases of an
expert's opinion are set forth in ER 703:

The facts or data in the particular case upon which an expert
bases an opinion or inference may be those perceived by or
made known to the expert at or before the hearing. If of a type
reasonably relied upon by experts in the particular field in
forming opinions or inferences upon the subject, the facts or
data need not be admissible in evidence.

When the admissibility of novel scientific evidence is at issue, Washington courts initially turn to the general acceptance test derived from Frye. The general acceptance standard serves as a shorthand method for judges in deciding whether novel scientific evidence, or evidence which is in the "twilight zone" between the "experimental and demonstrable stages," has a valid scientific basis. See Cauthron, 120 Wash.2d at 887, 846 P.2d 502 (citing *Frye*, 293 F. at 1014). Once novel scientific evidence has been deemed admissible under Frye, the trial court must analyze whether that testimony is proper expert testimony under ER 702. Cauthron, 120 Wash.2d at 889–90, 846 P.2d 502.[400]

The *Frye* test only applies to novel evidence:

[E]xpert opinion regarding application of an accepted theory or methodology to a particular medical condition does not implicate Frye. *State v. Ortiz*, 119 Wash.2d 294, 831 P.2d 1060 (1992) (Frye inapplicable where testimony based not on novel scientific procedures but on practical experience and acquired knowledge). Admissibility of a causation opinion under these circumstances is weighed under the general reliability standards of ER 702 and ER 703. While we acknowledge the invitation to adopt the federal test for reliability under Fed. R.Evid. 702 as outlined in Daubert, we decline to do so in this case... .[401]

If evidence is admissible under *Frye*, the court analyzes whether it is helpful to the trier of fact under Washington's Rule 702.[402] "Judges do not have the expertise required to decide whether a challenged scientific theory is correct... . If there is a significant dispute between qualified experts as to the validity of scientific evidence, that evidence may not be admitted."[403]

Washington has a *de novo* standard of review. "A reviewing court will undertake a searching review that is not confined to the record and may involve consideration of scientific literature."[404]

West Virginia
West Virginia adopted *Daubert* in *Wilt v. Buracker*:

> [W]e believe that *Daubert* is directed at situations *where the scientific or technical basis for the expert testimony cannot be judicially noticed* and a hearing must be held to determine its reliability. We conclude that *Daubert's* analysis of Federal Rule 702 should be followed in analyzing the admissibility of expert testimony under Rule 702 of the West Virginia Rules of Evidence.[405]

In *Gentry v. Mangum*, the Court held that the trial court determines whether a *Daubert/Wilt* hearing is necessary pursuant to West Virginia Rule of Evidence 104(a) (similar to FRE 104(a)), and West Virginia employs a *de novo* standard of review.[406] But once a court determines that *Daubert/Wilt* does not apply, expert testimony may still be rejected under Rule 403 (probative value outweighed by prejudicial effect, etc.) or Rule 703 (foundation issues); such rulings are reviewed under the abuse of discretion standard.[407] The *Gentry* Court observed that:

> [a]ctually, most scientific validity issues will be resolved under judicial notice pursuant to Rule 201. Indeed, most of the cases in which expert testimony is offered involve only qualified experts disagreeing about the interpretation of data that was obtained through standard methodologies. *Daubert/ Wilt* is unlikely to impact upon those cases.[408]

As the *Gentry* Court cogently observed,

> [t]he problem is not to decide whether the proffered evidence is right, but whether the science is valid enough to be reliable. When scientific evidence is proffered, the circuit court in its "gatekeeper" role must engage in a two-part analysis in regard to the expert testimony. First, the circuit court must determine whether the expert's testimony reflects "scientific knowledge," whether the findings are derived by "scientific method," and whether the work product amounts to "good science." Second, the circuit court must ensure that the scientific testimony is "relevant to the task at hand."[409]

The *Gentry* Court meticulously describes the correspondence that is required between the expert and the proffered testimony. Furthermore, the court emphasizes that degrees are not required of an expert if practical experience exists instead:

> Our cases indicate that in determining who is an expert, a trial court should conduct a two-step inquiry. First, a circuit judge must determine whether the proposed expert (a) meets the minimal educational or experiential qualifications (b) in a field that is relevant to the subject under investigation (c) which will assist the trier of fact. Second, the circuit court must determine that the expert's area of expertise covers the particular opinion as to which the expert seeks to testify. There must be a match ... . What must be remembered, however, is that there is no "best expert" rule. Because of the "liberal thrust" of the rules pertaining to experts, circuit courts should err on the side of admissibility... .[410]

These cases were applied in *State v. McCracken*, in which a fire-fighter and investigator with 40 years' experience testified that a lit cigarette could not ignite gasoline and demonstrated the same to a jury by throwing a lit cigarette into a container with gasoline and water.[411]

West Virginia has not adopted *Kumho Tire*:

> Based upon the foregoing, we hold that unless an engineer's opinion is derived from the methods and procedures of science, his or her testimony is generally considered technical in nature, and not scientific. Therefore, a court considering the admissibility of such evidence should not apply the gatekeeper analysis set forth by this Court in *Wilt v. Buracker*, 191 W. Va. 39, 443 S.E.2d 196 (1993), and *Gentry v. Mangum*, 195 W. Va. 512, 466 S.E.2d 171 (1995). Applying the foregoing holding, we conclude that the circuit court was clearly wrong in applying a *Wilt/Gentry* gatekeeper analysis to the testimony of Mr. Sevart. Rather, the proper analysis of the admissibility of Mr. Sevart's testimony is conducted pursuant to Rule 702 of the West Virginia Rules of Evidence.[412]

Wisconsin

Wisconsin has its own state standard for the admissibility of expert testimony:

In Wisconsin,...our Supreme Court expressly rejected the *Frye* test in favor of the relevancy test. Because Wisconsin rejected the *Frye* test and adopted a test unrelated to that used by the federal courts and many state courts, our standard for the admission of scientific evidence was unaffected by *Daubert*. Thus, the rule remains in Wisconsin that the admissibility of scientific evidence is not conditioned upon its reliability. Rather, scientific evidence is admissible if: (1) it is relevant, § 904.01, STATS.; (2) the witness is qualified as an expert, § 907.02, STATS.; and (3) the evidence will assist the trier of fact in determining an issue of fact, § 907.02. If these requirements are satisfied, the evidence will be admitted.

Moreover, scientific evidence is admissible under the relevancy test regardless of the scientific principle that underlies the evidence. As our Supreme Court noted in *Walstad*:

The fundamental determination of admissibility comes at the time the witness is "qualified" as an expert. In a state such as Wisconsin, where substantially unlimited cross-examination is permitted, the underlying theory or principle on which admissibility is based can be attacked by cross-examination or by other types of impeachment. Whether a scientific witness whose testimony is relevant is believed is a question of credibility for the finder of fact, but it clearly is admissible.[413]

Judges in Wisconsin also enter into an analysis that considers all the factors encompassed by FRE 403.[414]

Courts in Wisconsin take the position that "[r]eliability is not part of the trial court's function. Rather, '[r]eliability is an issue for the trier of fact, not the trial judge as a predicate for admissibility.'"[415]

Wyoming

Wyoming adopted *Daubert* in 1993.[416]

In Wyoming we find the interesting case in which a party claims that an expert is unqualified after unsuccessfully attempting to retain that expert:

On appeal, the husband contends, for the first time, the wife's expert, Lawrence McGovern, was not qualified to provide an expert opinion regarding the value of the business. It is interesting to note the husband actually tried to retain Mr. McGovern as his expert prior to trial. Further, the husband made no objection to this witness' qualifications or expertise prior to or during trial.[417]

Wyoming has adopted *Kumho Tire*.[418]

Wyoming permits testimony about posttraumatic stress disorder and child abuse accommodation syndrome, but only in rebuttal, to explain behavior of the victim that would otherwise seem inconsistent with having been raped or sexually abused:[419]

> An explanation of the victim's behavior was necessary at Chapman's trial due to the course the testimony took. During cross examination of the victim, Chapman sought to establish that the victim had created the story about Chapman's abuse, during an argument with her mother, in order to divert the mother's attention from the victim's boyfriend, a young man of whom the mother apparently disapproved. After both mother and daughter testified, the State called its expert, who explained that it was normal for victims of sexual abuse to delay in reporting, thus refuting, at least in part, Chapman's theory that the story had been created to divert attention from the issue of the [boyfriend]. In addition, the expert explained why the victim would continue to venture to the Chapman's home even after the sexual abuse. Therefore, because the expert's testimony was used to explain the victim's behavior, we reject Chapman's contention that the testimony was used to prove the claim of abuse.[420]

Furthermore, Wyoming applies a *de novo* standard of review as to whether the trial court applied the proper legal standard in admitting or excluding expert testimony, and an "abuse of discretion" standard for other evidentiary rulings.[421]

CROSS-EXAMINATION OF THE EXPERT WITNESS

Good cross-examination of the expert begins with identification of that expert. Sources of information about the expert include published articles, his own curriculum vitae (CV), a weblog (if he has one), and Google. Has the expert lent his name to any organizations? If so, what are their agendas? Has he published anything that he has not listed on his CV? Has he had any complaints filed with his relevant licensing board? Does he have an office? Does he have appointment hours, or does he just testify? How many cases has he testified in and for whom? Has he given newspaper interviews or written letters to the editor of any professional journals? What journals does he subscribe to?

Occasionally, a witness does misstate his credentials.[422] More commonly available avenues for cross-examination, however, would include articles published by the witness that contradict the assertions in his testimony, evidence of bias, evidence that the area of expertise claimed for the witness by counsel is inconsistent with his actual credentials (such as a chemist who has never examined a fire scene being certified as an orgin-and-cause expert), evidence that the witness has not practiced in his chosen field but earns his living exclusively by testifying as a witness, and the like.

In the case of medical or mental health practitioner experts, what tests did they perform? Did they attempt to verify the subjects' statements from collateral sources? Can they produce the raw test forms completed by the defendant (preferably in time for examination by your own expert, if time, and local rules of discovery, permit)?[423] In making their conclusions about the defendant, did they consult school records, speak to treatment providers or jail personnel, listen to 911 tapes, or view reports from arresting officers? Did they have occasion to view the defendant outside an evaluative context (such as in the recreation yard)? Witnesses may testify without having made necessary examinations or may have examined a defendant in an insanity case months, or even years, after the fact and may not have any safeguards against subjects who malinger.

It may also be helpful to view the ethical guidelines of the expert's profession, particularly in a context in which a treating therapist is testifying as a witness for one party or the other.[424] Additionally, some university departments monitor the content and compensation of faculty members who testify as expert witnesses.[425]

At an admissibility hearing challenging an eyewitness identification expert, sample cross-examination questions can be gleaned from Preussel (2006).[426] But the following list, first published in *The Prosecutor*, includes the following questions:

- Is it true that most of the research upon which your testimony is based uses crime simulations rather than actual crimes?
- Is it true that identifications in crime simulations have no real consequences for criminal suspects and that most of the time the mock witnesses are aware that there are no such consequences?
- Is it true that most of the research uses college students as subjects?
- Is it true that extreme stress has never been simulated in an eyewitness testimony experiment?
- Is it true that eyewitness researchers have expressed concerns about whether the research is reliable enough to discuss in court?[427]

CONCLUSION

Laws governing the admissibility of expert testimony are always evolving. At first glance it seems that the states are relatively uniform on some issues—such as the admissibility of polygraph evidence. On some others, they are not in ways that could ultimately affect the admissibility of the disputed evidence regardless of whether the methodology is considered reliable—such as when they speak to the ultimate issue in the case. It is important to keep in mind the relevant laws of relevant jurisdiction when evaluating the potential admissibility of expert testimony and the uses to which it could be put.

ENDNOTES

1. Daubert v. Merrell Dow Pharmaceuticals, Inc., 509 U.S. 579, 113 S.Ct. 2786, 125 L.Ed.2d 469 (1993), *on remand*, 43 F.3d 1311 (9th Cir.1995), *cert. denied*, 516 U.S. 869, 116 S.Ct. 189, 133 L.Ed.2d 126 (1995).
2. Goodstein, D. (2000). How science works. In J. Cecil & D. Miletich (Eds.), *Reference manual on scientific evidence* (2nd ed., pp. 67–82, 76). Federal Judicial Center. Retrieved August 29, 2006, from http://air.fjc.gov/public/pdf.nsf/lookup/sciman00.pdf/$file/sciman00.pdf
3. See, e.g., Meadow, W., & Lantos, J. (1998). A proactive, data-based determination of the standard of care in pediatrics. *PEDIATRICS, 101*(4), e6-e11. Retrieved September 2, 2006, from http://pediatrics.aappublications.org/cgi/reprint/101/4/e6; Berlin, L. (2003). The miasmatic expert witness. *American Journal of Roentgenology, 181*(1), 29–35, 30.
4. State v. Coon, 974 P.2d 386, 396 (Alaska, 1999), citing *State v. Carter*, 246 Neb. 953, 524 N.W.2d 763, 777–778 (1994).
5. Ibid. at 397
6. Halsey v. A.B. Chance Company, 695 S.O.2d 607, 613 (Ala. 1997).
7. Syndrome evidence will be explored in more depth in this book by other authors.
8. Werner v. State, 711 S.W.2d 639, 649 (Tex. Crim. App., 1986), *dissent.* citations omitted.
9. Bryant v. State, 881 A.2d 669, 678–680, 163 Md. App. 451 (Md. 2005). [italics added]
10. Schafersman v. Agland Coop, 262 Neb. 215 (NE, 2001), ¶ 43–47.
11. Easter v. Aventis Pasteur, Inc., 358 F.Supp.2d 574 (E. D. Tex., 2005) (testimony disallowed because plaintiffs, who concede that they cannot prove that Thimerosal causes autism, sought to prove that Thimerosal caused the co-morbid conditions of ADHD and reduced cognitive capacity, with no evidence to support same, and with no ability to separate cause of autism from cause of co-morbid conditions); *Doe v. Bayer Corp.*, 367 F.Supp.2d 904, 909–910 (M.D.N.C., 2005) (Over the past few years, the Vaccine Court has seen several thousand petitions alleging a causal connection between certain vaccinations, Thimerosal, and "autism spectrum disorder" ("autism"). *In re:* Claims for Vaccine Injuries Resulting in Autism Spectrum Disorder or a Similar

Neurodevelopmental Disorder v. Secretary Health & Human Servs., 2004 WL 1660351, *1 (Fed.Cl. July 16, 2004) (Ruling Mot. Disc. Merck Re: MMR Vaccine) [hereinafter, "Autism Discovery Ruling # 1"]. *Because scientific data on the causal connection are still developing and posing problems of proof and discovery,* the Vaccine Court adopted a procedure to conduct a single discovery proceeding (the "Omnibus Autism Proceeding"). *In re:* Claims for Vaccine Injuries Resulting in Autism Spectrums Disorder or a Similar Neurodevelopmental Disorder v. Secretary Health & Human Servs., 2002 WL 31696785, *3 (Fed.Cl. July 3, 2002) (Autism Gen. Order # 1) [hereinafter, "Autism General Order # 1"]. This proceeding will create the "Autism Master File" as an evidentiary record for these cases. Ibid. To opt into the Omnibus Autism Proceeding and make use of the Autism Master File, petitioners (often referred to as "vaccinees") must file a Short-Form Autism Petition for Vaccinee Compensation ("Short-Form Petition"), which alleges that a measles-mumps-rubella (MMR) or Thimerosal-containing vaccination (or some combination of the two) caused the vaccinee's autistic disorder, and that the vaccinee's claim meets certain other criteria. Ibid. Exs. A-B. Among these other criteria, vaccinees allege they have a vaccine-related injury, they have not filed any civil action for their injury, and they are filing the petition "within three years after the first symptom of the disorder, or within three years after the first symptom of a vaccine-caused significant aggravation of the disorder" Ibid. [italics added]

12. Muska, D. D. (1999). Lemon tort; Nevada's supreme court upholds junk science. *Nevada Journal, 7*(5), Retrieved September 24, 2006, from http://nj.npri.org/nj99/04/feature.htm

13. Janowsky, E. C., Kupper, L. L., & Hulka, B. S. (2000.) Meta-analyses of the relation between silicone breast implants and the risk of connective-tissue diseases. *New England Journal of Medicine, 342*(11), 781–790.

14. Bar-Meir, E., Eherenfeld, M., & Shoenfeld, Y. (2003). Silicone gel breast implants and connective tissue disease—A comprehensive review. *Autoimmunity, 36*(4), 193–197.

15. The Federal Judicial Center is the education and research agency for the federal courts. Congress created the FJC in 1967 to promote improvements in judicial administration in the courts of the United States. This site contains the results of Center research on federal court operations and procedures and court history, as well as selected educational materials produced for judges and court employees. See, http://www.fjc.gov/, official Web site of The Federal Judicial Center, accessed September 1, 2006.

16. Johnson, M. T., Krafka, C., & Cecil, J. (2000.) Expert testimony in federal civil trials; a preliminary analysis. *Federal Judicial Center*, 3. Retrieved August 30, 2006, from http://www.fjc.gov/public/pdf.nsf/lookup/ExpTesti.pdf/$file/ExpTesti.pdf. *Table, infra.*

Table 7.1. Expertise of witnesses offering expert testimony in 297 federal civil trials in 1998.

Speciality	Count	% of Total
Medical/Mental Health	**520**	**43.2**
Physician (unspecified)	66	5.5
Physician (treating)	46	3.8
Surgeon	46	3.8
Psychiatrist	46	3.8
Neurologist/Neurosurgeon	43	3.6
Psychologist (clinical)	39	3.2
Family/general practitioner	30	2.5
Obstetrician/gynecologist	24	2.0
Other medical/mental health[a]	180	15.0
Engineering/Process/Safety	**290**	**24.1**
Mechanical/industrial engineer	58	4.8
Other engineering experts	33	2.7
Accident reconstruction expert	31	2.6
Police procedure expert	31	2.6
Products engineer	28	2.3
Other engineering/process/safety[b]	109	9.1
Business/Law/Financial	**266**	**22.1**
Economist	131	10.9
Accountant	37	3.1
Patent/trademark expert	18	1.5
Other business/law/financial experts[c]	80	6.7
Scientific Specialties	**88**	**7.3**
Chemist	19	1.6
Toxicologist	10	0.8
Statistician	7	0.6
Metallurgist	7	0.6
Other scientific specialties[d]	45	3.7
Other Speciality	**39**	**3.2**

continued

Table 7.1. *(continued)* Expertise of witnesses offering expert
testimony in 297 federal civil trials in 1998.

[a]Category includes the following; Radiologist; Vocational Rehabilitation
Specialist; Pathologist/ Medical Examiner; Orthopedist; Internist; Rehabilitation Specialist; Cardiopulmonary physican; Nurse; Pediatrician; Oncologist; Social worker/counselor; Dentist; Anesthesiologist; Physical therapist;
Chiropractor; Opthalmologist/optometrist; Osteopath; Pharmacist; Other. No
single contribution accounted for more than 1.7% of the total.

[b]Category includes the following: Safety expert (non-engineer); Fire/arson
investigator; Ballistics experts; Electircal engineer; Biomedical engineer;
Sea captain; Human factors expert; Mechanics; Surveyor; General Contrac-
tor; Envirnomental engineer; Chemical engineer; Safety engineer; Security
expert; Land use/urban planner; Architect; Aerospace engineer, No single
contribution accounted for more than 1.3% of the total.

[c]Category includes the following: Appraiser (not real estate); Attorney (as expert
on law); Expert in business practices; Appraiser (real estate); Insurance experts;
Securities/Banking/Pension; Attorney (as expert on proffesional standards); Other.
No single contribution accounted for more than 1.4% of the total.

[d]Category includes the following: Meterologist; Social/behaviour scientist;
Epidemiologist; Geologist; Physicist; Agricultural scientist; Moloecular
biologist/Geneticist; Computer scientist; Other specialties represented by
a lone testifying expert. No single contribution accounted for more than
0.58% of the total.

17. Johnson, M. T., Krafka, C., & Cecil, J. Ibid. at 4.
18. For example, in Commonwealth v. Harper (accessible at http://
    208.210.219.132/vadistrict/select.jsp) (General District Court,
    Loudoun County, Virginia, GC96001021-1035, Oct. 9, 1996) the
    defendant was prosecuted after she hoarded 117 cats in her modest
    home, and was charged with multiple counts of animal cruelty. Dur-
    ing the trial, which received heavy media coverage, the attorney for
    the defendant forced the Commonwealth (the author) to qualify her
    animal control officer as an expert in cat feces. After the expert was
    so qualified, she was able to testify that the floors of the home were
    covered with it. Of course, the Commonwealth also introduced more
    conventional expert testimony from the veterinarian that examined
    and treated the cats after they were seized. But see, Gates v. State,
    224 Ga. App.216, 480 S.E.2d 263, 264 (1997) (layman can tes-
    tify that a cup of solids thrown at him was human feces); Fulcher

322   MALINGERING, LIES, AND JUNK SCIENCE IN THE COURTROOM

v. Commonwealth, 149 S.W.3d 363, 372 (Ky. 2004) (layman can testify as to odor of ether or ammonia).

19. See, e.g., http://www.hgexperts.com/hg/consultants_expert_witnesses. asp, retrieved September 1, 2006; http://www.daubertontheweb.com/ fields.htm, retrieved September 2, 2006.

20. Retrieved September 1, 2006 from http://www.law.cornell.edu/rules/ fre/ACRule702.htm.

21. For cases discussing "negative evidence," See, e.g., Ford v. State, 534 A.2d 992, 994, 73 Md.App. 391, (Md. App., 1988). The Courts have long recognized the concept of negative evidence. In *Eley v. State*, 288 Md. 548, 419 A.2d 384 (1980), the Court of Appeals ruled that a defendant is entitled to comment on the fact that the State's evidence contains an "unexplained silence concerning a routine and reliable method of identification especially in a case where the identification testimony is at least subject to some question... "*Eley*, 288 Md. at 555, 419 A.2d 384. It is important to note that the Court in *Eley* limited the use of a negative evidence argument to those situations where the absent evidence (1) could have been obtained by routine and reliable means; and (2) the State's failure to offer it was unexplained. Thus, a negative evidence argument is appropriate only where it would be normal to expect that the State would present such evidence; U.S. v. Banks et al., 10 F.3d 1044, 1055 (C.A.4 (Va.), 1992) (conspiracy defendant identified in only one telephone call); Charles Clifton, Claimant Plaintiff in Error v. the United States, 45 U.S. 242, 247-8, How. 242, 11 L.Ed. 957, (1846):

It is well observed...that if the weaker and less satisfactory evidence is given and relied on in support of a fact, when it is apparent to the court and jury that proof of a more direct and explicit character was within the power of the party, the same caution which rejects the secondary evidence will awaken distrust and suspicion of the weaker and less satisfactory; and that it may well be presumed, if the more perfect exposition had been given it would have laid open deficiencies and objections which the more obscure and uncertain testimony was intended to conceal.

We will only add, that practical illustrations of this application of the rule are witnessed daily in the administration of justice in criminal cases, and are too familiar to every lawyer to require a more particular reference. [citations omitted]

But the concept of "negative evidence" has gone beyond the absence of evidence one must expect to see—or raise suspicion with regard to the existence of the relevant material fact—and now extends to evidence that might well be competent to prove the same point the proponent proves with perfectly competent alternative evidence... but, as in the case of the DNA and the skeleton or the fingerprint evidence in the marital home, that "missing evidence" may be irrelevant, nonexistent, impossible to obtain, or cumulative.

22. For a more in-depth examination of this phenomenon, see Cather, K. (2004). The CSI effect: Fake TV and its impact on jurors in criminal cases. *The Prosecutor, 38*(2), 9–15. See also, Maricopa County Attorney's Office. (2005). CSI: Maricopa County; The CSI effect and its real-life impact on jurors. Retrieved September 1, 2006, from http://www.maricopacountyattorney.org/Press/PDF/CSIReport.pdf#search=%22CSI%20Effect%20Maricopa%20County%22; see also Russell McGuire, Esq., Assistant Attorney General, Transcript of Commonwealth v. Jaynes et al., Indictment No. 15885, Loudoun County Circuit Court (Va.), 10/25/2004, 47–48:

It's not beyond a shadow of a doubt, as you may have seen on TV and Hollywood; it's beyond a reasonable doubt. More than the civil, but it's not beyond a shadow of a doubt. That's because all cases have circumstances that you'll have to make the decision. Does anybody think that in a criminal case the standard should be more likely than not, that it's a 50.001 the person should be guilty?

Does anybody think it should be beyond a shadow of a doubt, that the Commonwealth has to come here and show the person that saw the person shoot somebody on day one? Or could you find it through other evidence without an eyewitness? Does anybody have a problem with that? The reason I bring that up is because I take it some of you watch those TV shows, Law and Order, CSI. I think there's a different show like that on every night of the week now. I refer to this as "Hollywood evidence." What is "Hollywood evidence"? You promise not to come hold us to the burden that you see on TV, right? Because I think everyone will tell you that's not the way it happens. You're not going to sit here in the middle of this trial and have a witness in the back row say, I did it. That just doesn't happen. That's on TV; that's Matlock, for those of you who remember that old show Matlock. That stuff happens in Matlock. Also, it's Hollywood evidence if you see these CSI people, these forensic examiners, you have a charge of drunk in public and you're coming up there and they're wiping the scene looking for fingerprints. That doesn't happen in reality. So the standard is beyond a reasonable doubt and that's the standard that you're going to take the oath to follow. We ask that you talk about it.

23. Because, presumably, the home might contain fingerprints of husband, wife, children, various tradesmen, friends of the family...or not, depending the surfaces available and the cleaning habits of the family. Similarly, defense counsel might make much of the fact that no fingerprints were retrieved from the gun, but unless the victim lived in a handgun factory, someone might still be required to point out to the jury that the gun did not float there.

24. Discovery-related issues—for example, establishing a foundation for the inclusion or exclusion of expert testimony based on adherence to (or violation of) various rules of discovery, the particulars of what must be included in reports prepared by experts, the implications in discovery for revealing too much or too little of one's case to an expert in preparation for trial—are fertile grounds for exploration by trial lawyers, but are beyond the scope of this chapter, which focuses solely on the evidentiary bases for the inclusion or exclusion of expert testimony.

   Prosecutors must undertake an additional admissibility evaluation of expert testimony in light of *Crawford v. Washington*, 541 U.S. 36 (2004). *Crawford* is a confrontation clause/hearsay case that applies to evidence already deemed admissible as an exception to the hearsay rule but which is (1) testimonial and (2) offered for the truth of the matter asserted. A *Crawford* analysis is not an analysis of evidentiary reliability but of whether the manner of introduction of evidence that would otherwise be reliable under *Frye*, *Daubert*, or other analogous precedent nevertheless violates the confrontation clause by denying the accused the opportunity to cross-examine. *Crawford* and its progeny are implicated generally, for example, in issues of whether the autopsy report or lab report might be inadmissible solely because the state must bring the medical examiner or chemist—and jurisdictions are splitting on whether the reports can come in by themselves or whether the prosecutor must bring the expert. The *Crawford* analysis is therefore beyond the scope of this chapter because it is unrelated to the issue of scientific reliability.

25. Berger, M. A. (2000). The Supreme Court's trilogy on the admissibility of expert testimony. In J. Cecil & D. Miletich (Eds.), *Reference manual on scientific evidence* (2nd ed., pp. 10–38, 26). Federal Judicial Center. Retrieved September 1, 2006, from http://air.fjc.gov/public/pdf.nsf/lookup/sciman00.pdf/$file/sciman00.pdf

26. "Relevant evidence" means evidence having any tendency to make the existence of any fact that is of consequence to the determination of the action more probable or less probable than it would be without the evidence. Federal Rule of Evidence (FRE) 401.

27. Although relevant, evidence may be excluded if its probative value is substantially outweighed by the danger of unfair prejudice, confusion of the issues, or misleading the jury, or by considerations of undue delay, waste of time, or needless presentation of cumulative evidence. FRE 403.

28. See FRE 704, *infra*.

29. For those readers who are unfamiliar with the legal system, a brief comment on jurisdiction is essential here. Federal criminal and civil trials are heard in federal district courts. Those districts are divided into circuits (see http://www.uscourts.gov/courtlinks/; retrieved September 4, 2006). Appeals from federal district court are heard in Courts of Appeals for the respective circuits in which the district courts are located. Appeals from federal courts of appeals are to the United States Supreme Court. The United States Supreme Court (SCOTUS) is the highest court in the United States, but its rulings with regard to the admissibility of expert testimony apply to the states only in limited circumstances that are beyond the scope of this chapter. However, SCOTUS decisions are binding on all other federal courts. Decisions of federal courts of appeals are binding only in their own circuits. So a decision in the 4th Circuit does not create precedential authority in, say, the 10th circuit, although courts may cite case law in other jurisdiction in their opinions— especially if the issue before them is new (and referred to as a *case of first impression*) or when they are resolving a split between the lower courts in their jurisdiction. States have their own trial courts, appellate courts, and supreme courts. Opinions in the state supreme court are binding on all other courts in the state, but all 50 states have different laws with regard to evidence—although some states' rulings are more similar than others. What is more, federal statutory and case law in a given state will differ from state laws and cases. Because of these jurisdictional differences, there is a whole legal discipline—and statutory and common law—devoted to choice of law.

It is also essential to understand that some jurisdictions have completely codified their rules of evidence. However, there will be case law explaining these rules. If there are no statutory rules of evidence in a jurisdiction, the rules of evidence will take the form of case law. Case law is referred to as the *common law*. In Virginia, for example, robbery is a *common-law crime*; the Virginia State Code for robbery

(Va. Code §18.2–58, 1950, as amended, retrieved September 4, 2006, from   http://leg1.state.va.us/cgi-bin/legp504.exe?000+cod+18.2–58) contains only the punishment for robbery, not the essential elements, which are set out in case law.

30. Retrieved September 1, 2006, from http://www.law.cornell.edu/rules/fre/rules.htm#Rule701

31. Retrieved September 1, 2006, from http://www.law.cornell.edu/rules/fre/ACRule701.htm

32. *Frye v. United States*, 54 App.D.C. 46, 47, 293 F. 1013, 1014 (1923), retrieved September 2, 2006, from http://www.daubertontheweb.com/frye_opinion.htm. *Frye* was a D.C. Circuit case, but it was the leading opinion on the subject, and it was adopted as the standard in almost every state—if not nationwide.

33. See, e.g., Logerquist v. McVey, 196 Ariz. 470 (AZ, 2000).

34. "*Daubert* is a two-sided coin. On the one side, it is expansive, rejecting the exclusivity of the "general acceptance" requirement; on the other side, it is restrictive, with a focus on the Trial Judge's responsibility as a gatekeeper on reliability."Minner v. American Mortg. & Guar. Co., 791 A.2d 826, 841 (Del. Super., 2000); Johnson, M. T., Krafka, C., & Cecil, J. (2000.), *supra*; Dixon, L., & Gill, B. (2001). Changes in the standards for admitting expert evidence in federal civil cases since the *Daubert* decision. Santa Monica, CA: RAND. Retrieved August 30, 2006, from http://www.rand.org/pubs/monograph_reports/MR1439/MR1439.pdf. This study is a good starting point for such analysis.

35. Daubert v. Merrell Dow Pharmaceuticals, 509 U.S. 579, 113 S.Ct. 2786, 125 L.Ed.2d 469 (1993). Retrieved September 2, 2006, from http://www.law.cornell.edu/supct/html/92-102.ZO.html

36. Daubert, Ibid.

37. Daubert, Ibid. [citations omitted]

38. Daubert, Ibid. [citations omitted]

39. Rule 403. Exclusion of Relevant Evidence on Grounds of Prejudice, Confusion, or Waste of Time.

    Although relevant, evidence may be excluded if its probative value is substantially outweighed by the danger of unfair prejudice, confusion of the issues, or misleading the jury, or by considerations of undue delay, waste of time, or needless presentation of cumulative evidence.

    Retrieved September 2, 2006, from http://www.law.cornell.edu/rules/fre/rules.htm#Rule403

40. General Electric Co. v. Joiner, 522 U.S. 136, 118 S.Ct. 512, 139 L.Ed.2d 508 (1997).

41. U.S. v. Scheffer, 523 U.S. 303, 118 S.Ct. 1261, 140 L.Ed.2d 413 (1998).
42. Kumho Tire v. Carmichael, 526 U.S. 137, 119 S.Ct. 1167, 143 L.Ed.2d 238 (1999).
43. A *directed verdict* is a verdict "ordered by the judge as a matter of law when he rules that the party with the burden of proof has failed to make out a prima facie case. The judge under these circumstances orders the jury to return a verdict for the other party." Black, H. C. (1983). *Black's law dictionary: Definitions of terms and phrases of American and English jurisprudence, ancient and modern* (5th ed.). St. Paul, MN: West Publishing Co.
44. Weisgram v. Marley Co., 528 U.S. 440, 120 S.Ct. 1011,145 L.Ed.2d 958 (2000).
45. United States v. Yousef et al., 327 F.3d. 56, 148–9 (2nd. Cir 2003), *cert. denied,* 540 U.S. (2003). See also, U.S. v. Triplett, 195 F.3d 990, 998 (8th Cir., 1999).
46. *Cf.* Caubarreaux v. E.I. du Pont de Nemours, 714 So.2d. 67, 71 (3rd Cir 1998) (defendant entitled to a *Daubert* hearing as of right); Clay v. Ford Motor Company, 215 F.3d 663, 667 (6th Cir., 1999) (trial court not obligated to hold *Daubert* hearing, but subject to review as to whether court made findings with reference to reliability and relevance); U.S. v. Bahena, 223 F.3d 797 (8th Cir., 2000) (*Daubert* applies to civil and criminal cases, and to defendants as well as to the government); and U.S. v. Evans, 272 F.3d 1069, 1094 (8th Cir., 2001) (a court's decision not to hold a *Daubert* hearing will be reviewed under the abuse of discretion standard), U.S. v. Nichols, 169 F.3d 1255, 1262–3 (C.A.10 (Colo.), 1999) (Denial of *Daubert* hearing reviewed by appellate courts under abuse of discretion standard); *but see United States v. Velarde*, 214 F.3d 1204, 1209–10 (10th Cir., 2000) (courts must make some kind of finding of reliability on the record; evidence of expert witness unreliable and Court should have held a *Daubert* hearing); Cook ex rel. Tessier v. Sheriff of Monroe County, 402 F.3d 1092, 1111 (11th Cir., 2005) (*Daubert* hearing not required in order to exclude testimony of expert where proffered testimony concerned matters within the understanding of the average lay person). Of course, if expert testimony is inadmissible under another FRE, a court is not required to hold a *Daubert* hearing to assess its reliability before excluding it. See, e.g., United States v. Campos, 217 F.3d 707, 712 (9th Cir., 2000) ("If evidence is inadmissible by application of one evidentiary rule, there is no need for a court to determine whether it satisfies predicate evidentiary standards pertaining to another rule. By

328   MALINGERING, LIES, AND JUNK SCIENCE IN THE COURTROOM

properly determining that the evidence was not admissible under Rule 704(b), the court obviated the need to conduct an evidentiary analysis under Rule 702 or Rule 403.").

47. Elcock v. Kmart Corp., 233 F.3d. 734, 750–1 (3rd. Cir, 2000).

48. To the extent that a given state has codified its rules of evidence, those rules are generally referenced in the case law. Also, many states have adopted rules of evidence that have reproduced the FRE nearly verbatim, leading the uninitiated to believe that that state essentially follows the Federal Rules; however, that state could nevertheless interpret its rules through case law so as to have a totally different effect. Or, for example, the state could follow *Daubert* but reject *Kumho Tire*— leading to a different application of the rule.

49. Phillips v. Industrial Machine, 597 N.W.2d 377 (NE, 1999) ¶ 80, citing State v. Coon 974 P.2d 386 (Alaska 1999); Jones v. State, 314 Ark. 289, 862 S.W.2d 242 (1993); State v. Porter, 241 Conn. 57, 698 A.2d 739 (1997), *cert. denied*, U.S. 118 S. Ct. 1384, 140 L. Ed. 2d 645 (1998); Nelson v. State, 628 A.2d 69 (Del. 1993); State v. Fukusaku, 85 Haw. 462, 946 P.2d 32 (1997); McGrew v. State, 682 N.E.2d 1289 (Ind. 1997); Leaf v. Goodyear Tire & Rubber Co., 590 N.W.2d 525 (Iowa 1999); Mitchell v. Com., 908 S.W.2d 100 (Ky. 1995), *overruled on other grounds*, Fugate v. Com., No. 98-SC-313-MR, 1999 WL 401667 (Ky. Aug. 24, 1995); State v. Foret, 628 So. 2d 1116 (La. 1993); State v. MacDonald, 1998 Me. 212, 718 A.2d 195 (1998); Commonwealth v. Lanigan, 419 Mass. 15, 641 N.E.2d 1342 (1994); State v. Moore, 268 Mont. 20, 885 P.2d 457 (1994), *abrogated on other grounds*, State v. Gollehan, 274 Mont. 116, 906 P.2d 697 (1995), and City of Billings v. Bruce, 290 Mont. 148, 965 P.2d 866 (1998); State v. Hungerford, 142 N.H. 110, 697 A.2d 916 (1997); State v. Alberico, 116 N.M. 156, 861 P.2d 192 (1993); State v. Goode, 341 N.C. 513, 461 S.E.2d 631 (1995); Breding v. State, 1998 N.D. 170, 584 N.W.2d 493 (1998) (Meschke, J., Concurring specially); Miller v. Bike Athletic Co., 80 Ohio St. 3d 607, 687 N.E.2d 735 (1998); Taylor v. State, 889 P.2d 319 (Okla. Crim. App. 1995); State v. O'Key, 321 Or. 285, 899 P.2d 663 (1995); State v. Morel, 676 A.2d 1347 (R.I. 1996); State v. Hofer, 512 N.W.2d 482 (S.D. 1994); McDaniel v. CSX Transp., Inc., 955 S.W.2d 257 (Tenn. 1997), *cert. denied* U.S. 118 S. Ct. 2296, 141 L. Ed. 2d 157 (1998); E.I. du Pont de Nemours & Co. v. Robinson, 923 S.W.2d 549 (Tex. 1995); State v. Crosby, 927 P.2d 638 (Utah 1996); State v. Brooks, 162 Vt. 26, 643 A.2d 226 (1993); Wilt v. Buracker, 191 W. Va. 39, 443 S.E.2d 196 (1993), *cert. denied* 511 U.S. 1129, 114 S. Ct. 2137, 128 L. Ed. 2d 867 (1994); Springfield v. State, 860 P.2d 435 (Wyo. 1993).

50. Schafersman v. Agland Coop, 262 Neb. 215 (NE, 2001).
51. Barber v. State, [Ms. CR-03-0737, May 27, 2005] So.2d (Ala. Crim. App. 2005), citing §36-18-30, Ala. Code 1975; Bagley v. Mazda Motor Corp., 864 So. 2d 301 (Ala. 2003) Southern Energy Homes, Inc. v. Washington, 774 So. 2d 505, 516 n.5 (Ala. 2000); Turner v. State, 746 So. 2d 355 (Ala. 1998); Minor v. State, [Ms. CR-00-1300, August 27, 2004] So. 2d (Ala. Crim. App. 2004); Hoosier v. State, 612 So. 2d 1352 (Ala. Crim. App. 1992); Rivers v. Black, 259 Ala. 528, 68 So. 2d 2 (1953). Turner, 746 So. 2d at 361 n.7. See also Minor, *supra*; Parker v. State, 777 So. 2d 937 (Ala. Crim. App. 2000). See Minor, *supra*; Simmons v. State, 797 So. 2d 1134 (Ala. Crim. App. 1999). See also Vesta Fire Ins. v. Milam & Co. Constr., 901 So.2d 84, 106 (AL, 2004): "This Court has not yet explicitly adopted the *Daubert* test." General Motors Corp. v. Jernigan, 883 So.2d 646 (Ala.2003), Slay v. Keller Indus., Inc., 823 So.2d 623 (Ala.2001), and Courtaulds Fibers, Inc. v. Long, 779 So.2d 198 (Ala.2000); Martin v. Dyas, 896 So. 2d 436 (Ala. 2004). (Goes through a *Daubert* analysis but calls adopting *Daubert* an "extreme result"); Holcomb v. Carraway, No. 1041471 (AL 4/21/2006) (AL, 2006), citing Dyas.
52. See Ex parte Dolvin, 391 So.2d 677, 679 (Ala.1980) (identification of skeletal remains by a forensic odontologist through his comparison of the remains with photographs of the victim in life); Handley v. State, 515 So.2d 121, 131 (Ala.Cr.App., 1987) (comparison of bite marks in the victim with known impressions of the defendant by forensic odontologist); Stewart v. State, 601 So.2d 491, 499 (Ala. Cr.App., 1992) (luma-lite test of victim's clothing to detect biological fluids).
53. Bird v. State, 594 So.2d 644, 647-8 (Ala.Cr.App., 1990), citing Young v. State, 68 Ala. 569, 574–75 (1881).
54. Preussel, R. (2006). The experts aren't reliable either: Why expert testimony on the reliability of eyewitness testimony is unwarranted in Alabama state courts. *Yale Law School Student Scholarship Series* 28, 1–40.
55. State v. Coon, 974 P.2d 386, 395 (Alaska, 1999). ("We are not convinced that 'junk science' is more likely to be admitted under *Daubert* than under *Frye*. Post-*Daubert* reported decisions suggest that courts are acting with restraint, and are giving rigorous consideration to the reliability of scientific evidence. Furthermore, Frye also potentially permits admission of unreliable scientific evidence, because a methodology that has been generally accepted might nonetheless have been discredited during a *Daubert* inquiry." Ibid. at 397).

56. Marsingill v. O'Malley, 128 P.3d 151, 160 (Alaska, 2006) (Expert physician's testimony based on experience with night-time telephone calls from patients what a "reasonable patient would want to know" not covered by *Coon-Daubert* standard).

57. Marsingill v. O'Malley, 128 P.3d 151 (Alaska, 2006) f.n. 43 citing Marron v. Stromstad, 123 P.3d 992 (Alaska, 2005).

58. Logerquist v. McVey, 196 Ariz. 470, ¶ 103, 1 P.3d 113, (2000).

59. Ibid. at ¶ 48.

60. To earn their right to a *Frye* hearing on previously accepted scientific evidence, the party opposing its admissibility must preliminarily demonstrate that the method 'is no longer accorded general scientific acceptance.'" State v. Esser, 205 Ariz. 320, 324, 70 P.3d 449, 453 (App. 2003).

61. State v. Speers, 1 CA-CR 02-0578 (AZ 9/28/2004) (AZ, 2004), citing Logerquist, *supra,* 196 Ariz. at 480, 1 P.3d at 123; State v. Varela, 178 Ariz. 319, 325–26, 873 P.2d 657, 663–64 (App. 1993).

62. State v. Lucero, 207 Ariz. 301, 85 P.3d 1059 (App.2004).

63. State v. Superior Court in and for Cochise County, 718 P.2d 171, 149 Ariz. 269 (Ariz., 1986). That Court gives an exhaustive overview of HGN and the scientific literature supporting its use.

64. State ex rel Romley v. Fields, 2001 AZ 191 (AZCA, 2001).

65. State v. Lehr, 38 P.3d 1172, (AZ, 2002), citing State v. Bible, 175 Ariz. 549, 580, 858 P.2d 1152, 1183 (1993); State v. Tankersley, 191 Ariz. 359, 364–65, 956 P.2d 468, 491–92, ¶ 14 (1998).

66. State v. Tankersley, 956 P.2d 486, 492, 191 Ariz. 359, (Ariz., 1998).

67. Clark v. Arizona, No. 05-5966 (U.S. 6/29/2006) (2006); Retrieved September 2, 2006, from http://www.law.cornell.edu/supct/html/05-5966.ZO.html

68. Farm Bureau Mutual Insurance v. Foote, 341 Ark. 105,14 S.W.3d 512 (Ark., 2000).

69. Coca-Cola Bottling Company of Memphis, Tennessee v. Gill, 352 Ark. 240, 100 S.W.3d 715 (2003).

70. Jackson v. State, CR 03-800 (Ark. 11/4/2004) (Ark., 2004).

71. Arrow Intern., Inc. v. Sparks, 98 S.W.3d 48, 53 (Ark. App., 2003), citing Collins v. Hinton, 327 Ark. 159, 937 S.W.2d 164 (1997).

72. Sparks, Ibid. at 55. (We recognize that a *Daubert* inquiry *may*, in some instances, help to evaluate the reliability of experience-based testimony.)

73. Turbyfill v. State, CR 04-958, 92 Ark. App. 145, S.W.3d (2005).

74. Turbyfill, Ibid. [italics added]

75. Turbyfill v. State, Ibid.

76. Turbyfill, Ibid.
77. Noel v. State, CR 99-738 S.W.3d (2000):

> The trial court agreed, finding that the question of allowing an expert witness to testify regarding possible unreliability of eyewitness testimony had been addressed by this court and determined to be an invasion of the province of the jury... .

> [T]he question whether these witnesses were mistaken in their identification, whether from fright or other cause, was one which the jury, and not an expert witness, should answer. This was a question upon which one man as well as another might form an opinion, and the function of passing upon the credibility and weight of testimony could not be taken from the jury.

> Ibid. at 409–10, 36 S.W.2d at 401–02 [citations omitted] *Parker v. State*, 333 Ark. 137, 968 S.W.2d 592 (1998); *Jones v. State*, 314 Ark. 289, 862 S.W.2d 242 (1993); *Perry v. State*, 277 Ark. 357, 642 S.W.2d 865 (1982); *Caldwell v. State*, 267 Ark. 1053, 594 S.W.2d 24 (Ark. App. 1980).

78. People v. Kelly, 17 Cal.3d 24, 30, 130 Cal.Rptr. 144, 549 P.2d 1240 (1976).
79. *Leahy* also held as follows:

(a) Our Kelly doctrine survived Daubert and continues to represent the standard by which new scientific techniques should be measured before evidence derived therefrom may be admitted in court.

(b) HGN testing is a new scientific technique requiring compliance with Kelly.

(c) Kelly contemplates appropriate expert testimony and evidence showing that HGN testing is generally accepted by a typical cross-section of the relevant scientific community. Until compliance with Kelly is demonstrated, testimony of police officers who merely administer HGN tests is, by itself, inadequate for this purpose.

(d) "General acceptance" under Kelly means a consensus drawn from a typical cross-section of the relevant, qualified scientific community. *People v. Leahy*, 8 Cal.4th 587, 612-3, 34 Cal.Rptr.2d 663, 679, 882 P.2d 321, 337 (Cal. 1994).

80. People v. Leahy, Ibid.
81. People v. Kelly, 17 Cal.3d 24, 30, 130 Cal.Rptr. 144, 549 P.2d 1240, (1976).

82. People v. Mitchell, 110 Cal.App.4th 772 (2003). [citations omitted]
83. Roberti v. Andy's Termite & Pest Control, Inc., 113 Cal.App.4th 893 (2003).
84. People v. Wilkinson, S111028 (CA 7/29/2004) (CA, 2004) (Defendant cannot persuasively contend that between the time of the *Scheffer* decision and defendant's trial, a span of two and one-half years, the deep division in the scientific and legal communities regarding the reliability of polygraph evidence, as recognized by *Scheffer*, had given way to a general acceptance that would render the categorical exclusion of polygraph evidence "so arbitrary or disproportionate that it is unconstitutional."), citing *In re* Aontae D., *supra*, 25 Cal.App.4th at 177.
85. People v. Therrian, 113 Cal. App. 4th 609, 614–16, 6 Cal. Rptr. 3d 415, 419–20 (2003).
86. [italics added] Colorado Rule 403 parallels the federal rule.
87. People v. Martinez, 74 P.3d 316 (Colo., 2003). (Witness need not describe the minimum force necessary to cause subdural hematomas in shaken-impact syndrome for testimony regarding accident scenarios to be admissible for the purpose of proving Martinez's *mens rea*. Standard of admissibility for CRE 702 is reliability and relevance, not certainty. Admissibility of accident scenario evidence evaluated under CRE 702 and CRE 403 and in the context for which it is offered. Although this evidence is not relevant to prove *mens rea*, it is admissible because it educates the jury about subdural hematomas: Prosecution's expert testimony concerning situations in which infants suffered brain injury inflicted by extreme amounts of force consistent with *People v. Shreck*, 22 P.3d 69 (Colo. 2001) and the Colorado Rules of Evidence.)
88. People v. Wilkerson, 114 P.3d 874, 876–77. (CO, 2005) (Testimony by ergonomics expert on chances that defendant's handgun fired accidentally inadmissible under *Shreck*; furthermore, ergonomics expert's conclusion that the handgun fired accidentally an impermissible comment on the defendant's *mens rea*.)
89. Meier v. McCoy, 119 P.3d 519, 521 (CO, 2005).
90. Masters v. People, 2002 CO 292 (CO, 2002). Although the witness was permitted to discuss the concept of sexual homicide and identify the characteristics of the murder that were consistent therewith, he was not allowed to give opinions on ultimate issues of fact—such as the likelihood that the defendant committed the crimes.
91. People v. Jenkins, 83 P.3d 1122 (Colo. App., 2003), 10–11.
92. People v. Prieto, Court of Appeals No. 02CA2093 (CO, 2005), 14.
93. State v. Porter, 241 Conn. 57, 698 A.2d 739, 746 (Conn., 1997).

94. Maher v. Quest Diagnostics, Inc., 269 Conn. 154, 170–172 (2004) (concept of doubling time in cancer not one of those principles).

95. State v. Reid, 757 A.2d 482 (Conn., 2000) (microscopic hair analysis does not fall within the ambit of *Porter*).

96. Ibid.

97. State v. Griffin, 273 Conn. 266, 280–281 (CT, 2005). A "bench trial" is a trial before a judge, without a jury.

98. State v. McClendon, 730 A.2d 1107 (Conn., 1999), citing State v. Kemp, 199 Conn. 473, 507 A.2d 1387, 1389–1390 (Conn., 1986).

99. State v. Sorabella, 277 Conn. 155, 891 A.2d 897, 918–919 (Conn., 2006).

100. Nelson v. State, 628 A.2d 69, 73–74 (Del. Supr., 1993).

101. Nelson, Ibid. at 74, citing State v. Pennell, Del.Super., 584 A.2d 513, 515 (1989).

102. M.G. Bancorporation Inc. v. Beau, 737 A.2d 513 (DE, 1999).

103. Minner v. American Mortg. & Guar. Co., 791 A.2d 826, 834 (Del. Super., 2000).

104. According to Judge Quillin, in the 18th century, courts responded to the need for expert testimony by convening "special juries" consisting of individuals from the relevant discipline:

> *Special* juries were originally introduced in trials at bar, when the caufes were of too great nicety for the difcuffion of ordinary freeholders; or where the fheriff was fufpected of partiality, though not upon fuch apparent caufe, as to warrant an exception to him...either party is intitled upon motion to have a fpecial jury ftruck upon the trial of any iffue, as well as the affifes as at bar; he paying the extraordinarily expenfe, unless the judge will certify...that the caufe required fuch fpecial jury. [The original Blackstone quote had "f" in place of "s"; Judge Quillen rendered his opinion as such. For clarity, this quote is reformatted for the reader as follows: *Special* juries were originally introduced in trials at bar, when the causes were of too great nicety for the discussion of ordinary freeholders; or where the sheriff was suspected of partiality, though not upon such apparent cause, as to warrant an exception to him...either party is entitled upon motion to have a special jury struck upon the trial of any issue, as well as the assizes as at bar; he paying the extraordinarily expense, unless the judge will certify...that the cause required such special jury.] (William Blackstone, *Commentaries,* pp. 357–358)

105. Minner, Ibid. at 834.

106. Minner, Ibid. at 845.
107. Minner, Ibid. at 859.
108. Flanagan v. State, 625 So.2d 827 (Fla., 1993), f.n. 2: "We are mindful that the United States Supreme Court recently construed Rule 702 of the Federal Rules of Evidence as superseding the *Frye* test., *Daubert v. Merrell Dow Pharmaceuticals Inc.*, U.S. 113 S.Ct. 2786, 125 L.Ed.2d 469 (1993). However, Florida continues to adhere to the *Frye* test for the admissibility of scientific opinions. *Stokes v. State*, 548 So.2d 188 (Fla.1989)."
109. Zack v. State, 911 So.2d 1190, 1198 (Fl, 2005) (Capital murder case; RFLP DNA evidence not new or novel; PCR evidence irrelevant since defense to rape was consent).
110. Ramirez v. State, 651 So.2d 1164, 1167 (Fla., 1995).
111. Ramirez, Ibid. at 1167.
112. "[E]xpert opinion testimony 'which is based on an "expert's personal experience and training" is not subject to *Frye* testing. Therefore, a diagnosis based on an expert's opinion and experience, versus a specific scientific test, would not be subject to a *Frye* hearing (...expert 'testimony concerning the causation of a medical condition will be considered pure opinion testimony—and thus not subject to *Frye* analysis').

     Here, Appellant argues that testimony relating to the diagnosis that the victim suffered from Shaken Baby Syndrome should have been subjected to a *Frye* hearing. However, such testimony is based on an expert's opinion and, as such, is not evidence which would be subject to the *Frye* analysis."

     Herlihy v. State, 927 So.2d 146, 147-148 (Fla. App., 2006). [citations omitted]
113. Hadden v. State, 690 So.2d 573, 577 (Fla., 1997).

     We likewise agree with Judge Ervin's conclusions that syndrome testimony in child abuse prosecutions must be subjected to a *Frye* test and that such evidence has not to date been found to be generally accepted in the relevant scientific community. Therefore, we hold that expert testimony offered to prove the alleged victim of sexual abuse exhibits symptoms consistent with one who has been sexually abused should not be admitted. We recognize that this decision comes after our decision *Glendening v. State*, 536 So.2d 212 (Fla.1988), *cert. denied*, 492 U.S. 907, 109 S.Ct. 3219, 106 L.Ed.2d 569 (1989), and *State v. Townsend*, 635 So.2d 949 (Fla.1994). However, those decisions did not deal with syndrome evidence confronted with a *Frye* objection. The *Frye* challenge now having been made to syndrome testimony, we recede from the parts of those decisions which hold that syndrome evidence is admissible in child sexual abuse prosecutions.

114. Marsh v. Valyou, 917 So.2d 313, 320 (Fl, 2005).
115. Ibid.
116. Castillo v. E.I. Du Pont De Nemours & Co., 854 So. 2d 1264, 1268 (Fla. 2003).
117. Marsh, Ibid. at 327.
118. Retrieved September 8, 2006, from the Georgia General Assembly official Web site at http://www.legis.state.ga.us/legis/2005_06/fulltext/sb3.htm. See also http://www.legis.state.ga.us/cgi-bin/gl_codes_detail.pl?code=24-9-67.1 and http://www.legis.state.ga.us/cgi-bin/gl_codes_detail.pl?code=24-9-67. Both retrieved September 8, 2006.
119. [italics added]
120. Senate Bill 3. Ibid. Section 1.
121. Minner, Ibid. at 837.
122. Unannotated Georgia Code §24-1-1. Retrieved September 8, 2006, from http://www.legis.state.ga.us/cgi-bin/gl_codes_detail.pl?code=24-1-1
123. Harper v. State, 249 Ga. 519, 292 S.E.2d 389, 396 (Ga., 1982) (rejecting testimony about defendant's statements under the influence of sodium amytal, so-called "truth serum").
124. Harper, 292 S.E.2d at 395–396.
125. Carlson v. State, 634 S.E.2d 410, 414 (2006).
126. Barlow v. State, 270 Ga. 54, 507 S.E.2d 416, 418–19 (Ga., 1998). ("Of course, an expert witness for the defense cannot give an opinion that the victim made false allegations of molestation, because such testimony directly addresses the credibility of the victim...However, the fact that limited expert testimony regarding proper interview techniques indirectly involves the child's credibility does not render it inadmissible. See also State v. Gersin, *supra* at 488 (distinguishing a case similar to *Campbell* because the ultimate issue of the particular child's veracity is still left to the jury); State v. Malarney, 617 So.2d 739, 740–741 (Fla.App. 4 Dist.1993); State v. Michaels, 136 N.J. 299, 642 A.2d 1372, 1383 (N.J.1994).").
127. State v. Kim, 64 Haw. 598, 605-6, 645 P.2d 1330, 1336-7 (1982), *overruled on other grounds*, State v. Batangan, 71 Haw. 552, 799 P.2d 48 (1990).
128. State v. Montalbo, 73 Haw. 130, 138-40, 828 P.2d 1274, 1280-1281 (Hawaii, 1992).
129. State v. Vliet, 95 Hawaii 94, 19 P.3d 42 (HI, 2001).

130. State v. Escobedo-Ortiz, 126 P.3d 402, 410–413 (Hawaii.App, 2005).

131. HRE 703 differs from FRE 703 by the addition in the HRE of one significant sentence: "The court may, however, disallow testimony in the form of an opinion or inference if the underlying facts or data indicate lack of trustworthiness."

132. State v. Keaweehu, 129 P.3d 1157, 1164 (Haw. App., 2006) citing State v. Vliet, 95 Hawaii 94, 19 P.3d 42 (2001), "[v]igorous cross-examination, presentation of contrary evidence, and careful instruction on the burden of proof are the traditional and appropriate means of attacking shaky but admissible evidence." Ibid. at 108, 19 P.3d at 56 (quoting Daubert v. Merrell Dow Pharmaceuticals, Inc., 509 U.S. 579, 596, 113 S.Ct. 2786, 125 L.Ed.2d 469 (1993)).

133. State v. Vliet, 19 P.3d 42 (HI, 2001). [citations omitted]

134. State v. Parkinson, 128 Idaho 29, 909 P.2d 647, 652 (Idaho App., 1996).

135. Mains v. Cach, 141 P.3d 1090, 1093-4 (Idaho, 2006).

136. State v. Burrow, 127 P.3d 231, 234 (ID, 2005).

137. State v. Konechny, 134 Idaho 410, ¶ 40-41 (IDCA, 2000). In its analysis of reliability, the court in this case took into account the extent to which the role of forensic investigator and treating therapist should be distinct from each other, for various ethical reasons that the court described in the opinion.

138. People v. Caballes, Docket No. 91547 (IL, 2006), f.n. 1.

139. Donaldson v. Central Il. Public Serv. Co., 767 N.E.2d 314, 199 Ill.2d 63 (Ill., 2002). See also Ferebee, 736 F.2d at 1535-36 ("[A] cause-effect relationship need not be clearly established by animal or epidemiological studies before a doctor can testify that, in his opinion, such a relationship exists. As long as the basic methodology employed to reach such a conclusion is sound, *** products liability law does not preclude recovery until a 'statistically significant' number of people have been injured or until science has had the time and resources to complete sophisticated laboratory studies of the chemical"). [citations omitted]

140. Donaldson v. Central Il. Public Serv. Co., Ibid. [citations omitted]

141. Becht v. Palac, 740 N.E.2d 1131, 1138 (Ill. App. 1 Dist., 2000). [citations omitted]

142. In re Commitment of Simons, 213 Ill.2d 523, 535, 290 Ill.Dec. 610, 821 N.E.2d 1184, (2004).

143. Steward v. State, 652 N.E.2d 490 (Ind., 1995).

144. McGrew v. State, 682 N.E.2d 1289, 1290 (Ind., 1997).

145. Steward, Ibid. at 498.

146. Steward, Ibid.
147. Steward, Ibid. at 499.
148. Steward, Ibid. at 499.
149. McGrew, Ibid. at 1292.
150. Malinski v. State, 794 N.E.2d 1071, 1084 (Ind., 2003).
151. Leaf v. Goodyear Tire & Rubber Co., 590 N.W.2d 525, 532 (Iowa, 1999), *accord, In re* Detention of Rafferty, 2002 IA 1007 (IACA, 2002) ¶ 34.
152. Leaf, Ibid. at 532.
153. Leaf, Ibid. at 534.
154. Leaf, Ibid. at 531.
155. Leaf, Ibid. at 534.
156. Schlader v. Interstate Power Co., 591 N.W.2d 10, 14 (Iowa, 1999) citing Salem v. United States Lines Co., 370 U.S. 31, 35, 82 S.Ct. 1119, 1122, 8 L.Ed.2d 313, 317 (1962) (in suit by seaman expert testimony regarding naval architecture and safety devices not necessary). [citations omitted]
157. Davis v. Montgomery County Memorial Hospital, No. 6-086/05-0865 (Iowa App., 2006).
158. Kuhn v. Sandoz Pharaceuticals Corp, 14 P.3d 1170 (Kan., 2000) (expert testimony admissible that Parlodel caused the plaintiff's decedent's postpartum enclampsia because there was 20 years of research supporting plaintiff's expert's testimony).
159. State v. Patton, 120 P.3d 760, 783 (KS, 2005); citing Kuhn v. Sandoz Pharmaceuticals Corp., 270 Kan. 443, 454, 14 P.3d 1170, (2000). [citations omitted]
160. Patton, Ibid. at 785. [citations omitted]
161. State v. Heath, 264 Kan. 557, 957 P.2d 449, 463 (Kan., 1998). [citations omitted]
162. Heath, Ibid. at 465.
163. State v. Oliver, 124 P.3d 493, 508 (KS, 2005).
164. Oliver, 124 P.3d at 504.
165. City of Owensboro v. Adams, No. 2003-SC-0097-WC (KY, 2004), 6.
166. Mitchell v. Com., 908 S.W.2d 100, 101–2 (Ky., 1995).
167. Goodyear Tire and Rubber Co. v. Thompson, 11 S.W.3d 575, 579 (Ky., 2000).
168. Kaplan v. Puckett, No. 2004-CA-001750-MR (KY, 2005).
169. Louisiana v. Foret, 628 So.2d 1116, 1122–3 (La. 1993).
170. Foret, Ibid. at 1130.
171. Cook v. State, Dept. of Public Safety, 928 So.2d 589, 592 (La. App., 2006).

aaaa

172. Franklin v. Franklin, 928 So.2d 90, 94 (La. App., 2005), citing Evans v. DeRidder Municipal Fire, 815 So.2d 61, 67, 71, (2003), *cert. denied*, 537 U.S. 1108, 123 S.Ct. 884, 154 L.Ed.2d 779 (2003).
173. Corkern v. Valve, 2004 CA 2293 (LA, 2006).
174. Doe v. Archdiocese of New Orleans, 823 So.2d 360, 365 (La. App., 2002) (expert testimony that plaintiff suffered from repressed memory of sexual assault by priest admissible).
175. Franklin v. Franklin, 928 So.2d 90, 95 (La. App., 2005).
176. Independent Fire Insurance Co. v. Sunbeam Corp., 755 So.2d 226 (LA, 2000) ¶ 52.
177. Dinett v. Lakeside Hosp., 811 So.2d 116, 120 (La. App., 2002) citing Independent Fire Insurance Co. v. Sunbeam Corp., 755 So.2d 226, 235–236 (2000). [citations omitted]
178. Green v. Cessna Aircraft Co., 673 A.2d 216, 218 (Me., 1996).
179. *In re* Sarah C, 2004 ME 152 (ME, 2004) ¶ 10–11. [citations omitted]
180. Ibid. Searles v. Fleetwood Homes of Pennsylvania, 878 A.2d 509, 2005 Me 94 (ME, 2005) f.n. 2:

> Fleetwood contends that we should adopt the *Daubert* standard, *Daubert v. Merrell Dow Pharmaceuticals, Inc.*, 509 U.S. 579, 589-95, 113 S.Ct. 2786, 125 L.Ed.2d 469 (1993), based on its contention that we effectively eliminated consideration of "general acceptance" as an element to be considered when determining whether scientific evidence is admissible *State v. Williams*, 388 A.2d 500 (Me.1978). Contrary to Fleetwood's argument, however, the *Williams* standard does not preclude the court from considering the question of general acceptance in undertaking its evaluation of challenged testimony. Ibid. at 504. Moreover, Fleetwood concedes that the result in this case would be the same whether we apply *Daubert* or *Williams*. Accordingly, we decline Fleetwood's invitation to adopt the *Daubert* standard in the present case.

181. Searles v. Fleetwood Homes of Pennsylvania, 878 A.2d 509, 515–516, 2005 Me 94, (ME, 2005). [citations omitted]
182. State v. Irving, 2003 ME 31, 818 A.2d 204 (Me., 2003).
183. Irving, 818 A.2d. at 211, f.n. 2 (The parties framed their arguments on the issue of expert evidence on the basis of *Daubert v. Merrell Dow Pharmaceuticals, Inc.*, 509 U.S. 579, 113 S.Ct. 2786, 125 L.Ed.2d 469 (1993)...We need not address whether to adopt the *Daubert* standards because the interpretation of M.R. Evid. 702 in *Williams* is sufficient to guide our analysis.)
184. Wilson v. State, 370 Md. 191, 201 n.5, 803 A.2d 1034, 1040 n.5 (2002).

185. Clemons v. State, 896 A.2d 1059, 1073–4, 392 Md. 339, (Md. App., 2006), citing Reed v. State, 283 Md. 374, 391 A.2d 364 (1978). [numbered paragraphing added]

186. Clemons, 896 A.2d at 1079, f.n. 7.

187. Armstead v. State, 673 A.2d 221, 228-9, 342 Md. 38, 54 (Md., 1993). [Citations omitted]

188. Ragland v. State, Case No. CR 97541, 385 Md. 706, 725, 870 A.2d 609, (Md.App. 2005).

189. Fullbright v. State, 895 A.2d 1088, 1095, 168 Md. App. 168 (Md. App., 2006) (In *Ragland*, the State introduced the officers' opinions that the events they observed constituted a drug transaction in order to prove that those events were *in fact* a drug transaction. By contrast, in the instant case, the State did not elicit Officer Bechtel's opinion to prove that it was *in fact* hard to get good fingerprints off of wet objects. Rather, the State sought his opinion for the sole purpose of explaining to the jury why Officer Bechtel, as the investigating officer, did not submit the bloody knife for fingerprint analysis. In short, the jury was not called upon to determine the truth or falsity of Officer Bechtel's opinion.).

190. CSX Transportation, Inc. v. Miller, 159 Md.App. 123, 858 A.2d 1025 (2004), 72–73, *cert. denied*, 875 A.2d 702, 387 Md. 351 (Md, 2005). [italics in original]

191. Bryant v. State, 881 A.2d 669, 686–687, 163 Md. App. 451 (Md, 2005), *aff'd*, 393 Md. 196, 900 A.2d 227 (Md. App., 2006).

192. Giant Food, Inc. v. Booker, 152 Md.App. 166, 831 A.2d 481, *cert. denied*, 378 Md. 614, 837 A.2d 926 (2003), citing S.B. Thomas, Inc. v. Thompson, 114 Md. App. 357, 382 (1997).

193. Todd v. State, No. 2160, (Md.App. 2005).

194. Commonwealth v. Lanigan, 641 N.E.2d 1342, 1350, 419 Mass. 15, (Mass., 1994) (expert testimony on DNA relying on "ceiling principle" to calculate probabilities admissible under new test).

195. Commonwealth v. Delisle, 17 Mass. L. Rptr. No. 23, 527, 528 (MA, 2004), citing Barefoot v. Estelle, 463 U.S. 880, 896–97 (1983) (approving the use of expert psychiatric testimony on the issue of an offender's future dangerousness. "The suggestion that no psychiatrist's testimony may be presented with respect to a defendant's future dangerousness is somewhat like asking us to disinvent the wheel"). [citations omitted]

196. Smith v. Bell Atlantic, 63 Mass. App. Ct. 702, 829 N.E.2d 228, 243 (MA, 2005).

197. Tarpey v. Crescent Ridge Dairy, Inc., 713 N.E.2d 975, 979–980, 47 Mass. App.Ct. 380, (Mass. App. Ct., 1999), citing Department of Youth Servs. v. A Juvenile, 398 Mass. 516, 531–532, 499 N.E.2d 812, (1986).
198. Palandjian v. Foster, 842 N.E.2d 916, 922, 446 Mass. 100, (Mass., 2006), citing Canavan's Case, 432 Mass. 304, 313–316, 733 N.E.2d 1042, (Mass., 2000).
199. Palandjian, Ibid. at 923. [citations omitted]
200. Palandjian, Ibid. at 926, f.n. 12.
201. Canavan's Case, 432 Mass at 314 n. 6.
202. Commonwealth v. Patterson, 840 N.E.2d 12, 32–33, 445 Mass. 626, (MA, 2005).
203. People v. Beckley, 434 Mich. 691, 711, 456 N.W.2d 391, 399 (Mich., 1990).
204. Craig v. Oakwood Hospital, 471 Mich 67, 77; 684 N.W.2d 296, (2004).
205. People v. Davis, 343 Mich. 348, 72 N.W.2d 269, 281 (Mich., 1955).
206. Anton and Anton v. State Farm Mutual Automobile Ins. Co., 607 N.W.2d 123, 127–128 (Mich. App., 2000) (In this instance, both testifying experts and the foremost expert, Dr. Volpe, concurred that there is a causal relationship between stress and Graves' disease. The onset of Mr. Anton's symptoms following the accident certainly provides objective manifestation of this relationship. The fact that there was no peer-reviewed research on the subject was irrelevant.).
207. Clerc v. Chippewa War Mem. Hosp., 705 N.W.2d 703, 707 (MI, 2005) (remanded for Davis-Frye hearing as to whether an oncologist could testify that plaintiff's decedent's lung cancer would have been at stage I when the defendant had the opportunity to view the X-rays), citing People v. Beckley, 434 Mich. 691, 456 N.W.2d 391, 399 (Mich., 1990) (Admissibility under [MRE 702] requires that the evidence comply with a three-part test. First, the expert himself must be qualified. Second, the evidence must serve to give the trier of fact a better understanding of the evidence or assist in determining a fact in issue. Finally, the evidence must be from a recognized discipline. The determination of whether a witness is qualified to render an expert opinion rests within the discretion of the trial court. Such a determination will not be reversed absent an abuse of discretion.).
208. People v. Davis, 503 N.W.2d 457, 462, 199 Mich.App. 502, (Mich. App., 1993), citing Jones v. State, 716 S.W.2d 142, 152, 154 (Tex. App., 1986). Coppolino v. State, 223 So.2d 68, 69–71 (Fla.App., 1969)

(expert testimony that the victim was killed by an injection of succinylcholine (SCH) proper where based upon the familiar technique of gas chromatography/mass spectrometry, even if technique used in relatively novel fashion to detect SCH in the tissues of an exhumed murder victim). [This is not the *People v. Davis* that gives rise to the *Davis-Frye* test; that case is *People v. Davis, supra,* 343 Mich. 348, 72 N.W.2d 269 (Mich., 1955)].

209. State v. Mack, 292 N.W.2d 764, 765 (Minn., 1980).
210. Mack, Ibid. at 768–769. [italics added]
211. Mack, Ibid. at 769.
212. Goeb v Tharaldson, Dow Chem. & Silberman, 615 N.W.2d 800 (Minn., 2000).
213. Goeb, Ibid.
214. Goeb, Ibid. [citations omitted]
215. Goeb, Ibid. [citations omitted]
216. Goeb, Ibid.
217. State v. MacLennan, 702 N.W.2d 219 (MN, 2005).
218. See State v. MacLennan, 702 N.W.2d 219, 236 (MN, 2005), f.n. 1:

> Dr. C. Henry Kempe first described the concept of "battered child syndrome" in 1962. *State v. Smullen,* 380 Md. 233, 844 A.2d 429, 445 (2004) (citing C. Henry Kempe *et al., The Battered Child Syndrome,* [181 *Journal of the American Medical Association* 105 (1962)]). Dr. Kempe described battered child syndrome as "a clinical condition in young children who have received serious physical abuse, generally from a parent or foster parent." *Smullen,* 844 A.2d at 445–46.

219. MacLennan, Ibid. at 233.
220. MacLennan, Ibid. at 234 (MacLennan's offer of proof demonstrated a tense relationship between him and his father, but there was little demonstrable evidence of the type of relationship described by MacLennan's own expert that would give rise to battered child syndrome.).
221. Miss. Transp. Comm'n v. McLemore, 863 So.2d 31, 34 (Miss. 2003).
222. McLemore, Ibid. [citations omitted]
223. McLemore, Ibid. at ¶ 27 and ¶ 28. [citations omitted]
224. Jones v. State, 918 So.2d 1220, 1228 (Miss., 2005).
225. Jones, Ibid. at 1233.
226. State Bd. of Reg. Healing Arts v. McDonough, Case Number: WD60501, 123 S.W.3d 146, 153, 2003 MO 425, (Mo.banc 2003).
227. McDonaugh, 123 S.W.3d 146, (Mo.banc 2003). [citations omitted]

228. 490.065 RSMo (2000). Retrieved September 23, 2006, from http://www.moga.mo.gov/statutes/c400-499/4900000065.htm [italics added]

229. McDonaugh, Ibid. at f.n. 9:

> See, e.g., *McReynolds v. Mindrup*, 108 S.W.3d 662, 665–66 & n.2 (Mo. App. W.D. 2002) ("whether [section] 490.065 supersedes the *Frye* doctrine...has not yet been decided by our Supreme Court" and "no Missouri case has yet decided what, if any, impact adoption of [section] 490.065 has on the application of the *Frye* 'general acceptance' rule, much less whether it compels application of the *Daubert* standard," citing section 490.065 for the admissibility of expert testimony, and stating that *Frye* is the proper standard for analyzing the admissibility of expert testimony related to scientific techniques); Keyser v. Keyser, 81 S.W.3d 164, 169 (Mo. App. W.D. 2002) (citing section 490.065.3 as the standard for the admissibility of expert testimony without reference to either *Frye* or *Daubert*); Long v. Mo. Delta Med. Ctr., 33 S.W.3d 629, 642-43 (Mo. App. S.D. 2000) (noting that section 490.065's "adoption may create the question if Missouri courts should continue to apply the *Frye* standard to the admissibility of expert testimony, or if *Daubert* would be more appropriate,"then applying *Frye* to the admissibility of expert testimony regarding scientific techniques, and holding that section 490.065 applies to the admissibility of expert testimony regarding non-scientific evidence); M.C. v. Yeargin, 11 S.W.3d 604, 619 (Mo. App. E.D. 1999) (noting that "[t]he Missouri Supreme Court continues to apply the *Frye* test to the admissibility of expert testimony in criminal cases and in civil cases,"and finding that "the trial court abused its discretion in admitting [the expert's] testimony because the court did not find that he based it on scientific principles generally accepted in the relevant scientific community or within the boundaries of Section 490.065"); Whitman's Candies, Inc. v. Pet, Inc., 974 S.W.2d 519, 528 (Mo. App. W.D. 1998) ("[b]ecause the expert testimony at issue in the case at bar satisfies the requirements of both *Frye* and *Daubert*, this court need not determine whether [section] 490.065 supersedes the *Frye* test in Missouri [italics in original]").

230. McDonaugh, Ibid. at ¶ 31.

231. Ibid. at ¶ 34 (Expert testimony admissible on behalf of an osteopath using chelation therapy in ways not approved by the FDA despite evidence on behalf of the licensing board that chelation therapy with EDTA was not indicated for anything but heavy metal toxicity,

hypercalcemia or digitalis toxicity, and a position statement by the American Medical Association that:

> There is no scientific documentation that the use of chelation is effective in the treatment of cardiovascular disease, atherosclerosis, rheumatoid arthritis, and cancer. If chelation is to be considered a useful medical treatment for anything other than heavy metal poisoning, hypercalcemia or digitalis toxicity, it is the responsibility of its proponents to conduct properly controlled scientific studies to adhere to FDA guidelines for drug investigation and to disseminate study results in the usually accepted channels. The AMA believes that chelation for atherosclerosis is an experimental process without proof in efficacy.) Ibid. at ¶ 19.

232. In Matter of Care and Treatment of Goddard v. State, 144 S.W.3d 848, (Mo.App. 2004). It is interesting to note that the *McDonaugh* Court had the opportunity to explicitly endorse *Daubert* but declined to do so.
233. Goddard, Ibid., citing Wulfing v. Kansas City Southern Indus., Inc., 842 S.W.2d 133, 152 (Mo.App. 1992).
234. Goddard, Ibid. at 854.
235. Goddard, Ibid.
236. McReynolds v. Mindrup, 2002 MO 1197, ¶ 25,108 S.W.3d 662, 665 (Mo. App., 2002).
237. State v. Daniels, 179 S.W.3d 273, 281 (Mo, 2005) (Defendant was entitled to a *Frye* hearing on the issue of whether luminol is generally accepted to be a conclusive test for the presence of blood, and not merely a presumptive test.) [citations omitted]
238. State v. Keightley, 147 S.W.3d 179, (Mo.App. S.D.2004), citing State v. Salmon, 89 S.W.3d 540, 544 (Mo.App. W.D. 2002). (PCR-STR DNA testing technology is generally accepted in the scientific community, and that the request for a *Frye* hearing was overruled as it related to PCR-STR DNA testing, Profiler and Cofiler test kits, and interpretive statistics.).
239. State v. Damon, 2005 MT 218, 119 P.3d 1194, 1197–1198, 328 Mont. 276, (MT, 2005).
240. State v. Moore, 885 P.2d 457, 472, 268 Mont. 20 (Mont., 1994), *overruled on other grounds by* State v. Gollehon, 274 Mont. 116, 121, 906 P.2d 697, 701 (1995).
241. See State v. Cline, 275 Mont. 46, 55, 909 P.2d 1171, 1177 (1996) (determining the age of defendant's fingerprint); Hulse v. State, 1998

MT 108 ¶¶ 55-69, 289 Mont. 1 ¶¶55-69, 961 P.2d 75, 91, ¶¶55-56 (1997). (The HGN test is not novel scientific evidence. Therefore, to determine the admissibility of HGN test results, a district court need not employ the *Daubert* standard. However, the relationship between alcohol consumption and nystagmus, the underlying scientific principle of the HGN test, is still beyond the range of ordinary training or intelligence. Therefore, a district court must still conduct a conventional Rule 702, M.R.Evid., analysis to determine the admissibility of HGN test results while adhering to the principle of *Barmeyer*.); State v. Southern, 1999 MT 94, ¶ 59, 294 Mont. 225, ¶ 59, 980 P.2d 3, ¶ 59 (1999) (expert testimony about microscopic hair comparisons admissible); State v. Hocevar, 2000 MT 157, ¶ 56, 300 Mont. 167, ¶ 56, 7 P.3d 329, ¶ 56 (expert testimony regarding Munchausen Syndrome by Proxy neither novel nor scientific and therefore not subject to a *Daubert* analysis); State v. Ayers, 2003 MT 114, ¶ 37, 315 Mont. 395, ¶ 37, 68 P.3d 768, ¶ 37.

242. Hunt v. K-Mart Corp., 981 P.2d 275, 279 (Mont., 1999).

243. State v. Clifford, 121 P.3d 489, 495, 2005 MT 219, 328 Mont. 300, (MT, 2005) (During his deposition, Blanco made some comparisons for the benefit of the attorneys. He compared Cheryl's known writings to the unknown writings for similarities. He showed them how he compared Cheryl's voluntary statement to the Helena Police Department with the "LYkES" letter. For example, the writings both had distinctive k's. Further, Blanco provided almost 20 documents on which he had made notations next to specific characters. The notations indicated that those characters had similarities with characters from other documents.).

244. Clifford, 121 P.3d at 496.

245. Clifford, 121 P.3d at 497.

246. Hulse, Ibid. 961 P.2d at 69.

247. Schafersman v. Agland Coop, 262 Neb. 215, 631 N.W.2d 862 (NE, 2001) (error to admit testimony that multiple mineral toxicity caused the death of plaintiff's cows due to oats sold by defendant that admittedly were contaminated with "Envirolean 2.5L Swine Concentrate").

248. Schafersman, Ibid. at ¶ 62–63.

249. Schafersman, Ibid. at ¶ 46.

250. Schafersman v. Agland Coop, 262 Neb. 215 ¶ 54 (NE, 2001).

251. Schafersman, Ibid. at ¶ 64. [Citations omitted]

252. Schafersman, Ibid. at ¶ 64–66. [Citations omitted]

253. State v. Davlin, 272 Neb. 139, 272 Neb. 139 (Neb., 2006).

254. State v. Mason, 709 N.W.2d 638, 655–656, 271 Neb. 16 (Neb., 2006), citing Zimmerman v. Powell, 268 Neb. 422, 684 N.W.2d 1 (2004), (in jury trial, the trial court failed to explain its reasoning for its ruling with regard to expert testimony about automobile speeds in a personal injury case, the court had abdicated its gatekeeping duty under *Daubert/Schafersman.*) and State v. Fernando-Granados, 268 Neb. 290, 682 N.W.2d 266 (2004) (extensive findings in nonjury case demonstrated gatekeeping duty performed).

255. Banks v. Sunrise Hospital, 120 Nev. Adv. Op. No. 89, 120 Nev. 822, 102 P.3d 52, 60-61, (2004). See also Yamaha Motor Co., U.S.A. v. Arnoult, 955 P.2d 661, 667, 114 Nev. 233, (Nev., 1998) (Based upon his specialized knowledge as an experienced safety engineer, witness concluded that the owner's manual failed to adequately warn of the dangers which caused plaintiff's injuries.).

256. Banks, Ibid. [citations omitted]

257. Morsicato v. Sav-On Drug Stores, Inc., 121 Nev. Adv. Op. No. 18, 121 Nev. 111 P.3d 1112, (2005).

258. Morsicato, Ibid.

259. Dow Chemical Co. v. Mahlum, 114 Nev. 1468, 970 P.2d 98, 109 (Nev., 1998), *disapproved on other grounds*, GES, Inc. v. Corbitt, 117 Nev. 265, 21 P.3d 11 (2001).

260. Mahlum, 970 P.2d at 142, f.n. 3. [citations omitted]

261. Baker Valley Lumber v. Ingersoll-Rand, 148 N.H. 609, 614, 813 A.2d 409, (2002).

262. Baker Valley, 813 A.2d at 414 (Overruling trial court's disallowing testimony by fire origin and cause expert with 50 years of experience.).

263. Baker Valley, Ibid. at 415.

264. Baker Valley, Ibid. at 416–417. [citations omitted]

265. Baker Valley, Ibid. at 417, citing Kuhmo Tire (Pretrial hearings, thus, should be limited to the "less usual or more complex cases where cause for questioning the expert's reliability arises.").

266. State v. Whittey, 149 N.H. 463, 821 A.2d 1086, 1092 (N.H., 2003). [citations omitted]

267. State v. Pelletier, 818 A.2d 292, 300 (N.H., 2003).

268. State v. Cochrane, 897 A.2d 952, 956 (N.H., 2006) (board-certified family physician with extensive experience with child sexual abuse victims could testify that hymens can heal like any other tissue, despite the fact that the physician was not an obstetrician/ gynecologist, because her background gave her the requisite expertise).

269. McLaughlin v. Fisher Engineering, No. 2002-770, 150 N.H. 195, (2003). slip op. (The plaintiffs' argument that the trial court "erred in allowing defendant's accident reconstruction expert to testify concerning bio-mechanical issues including alternate causes of death which were not properly disclosed" is without merit). [citations omitted]

270. State v. Lambert, 787 A.2d 175, 177 (N.H., 2001). [citations omitted]

271. State v. Hungerford, 697 A.2d 916, 925, 142 N.H. 110, (N.H., 1997).

272. State v. Harvey, 151 N.J. 117, 167, 699 A.2d 596, 619 (1997).

273. State v. Moore, A-38 September Term 2003 (N.J., 2006) at 2.

274. Moore, Ibid. at 35–36.

275. State v. Moore, Ibid. at 40 (Twenty-six states limit the admissibility of posthypnotic testimony).

276. State v. Moore, Ibid. at 37.

277. State v. Moore, Ibid. at 39. [citations omitted]

278. State v. Moore, Ibid. at 43. However, such an act would provide fertile ground for cross-examination.

279. State v. Alberico, 116 N.M. 156, 861 P.2d 192, 203 (N.M., 1993). Several factors could be considered by a trial court in assessing the validity of a particular technique to determine if it is "scientific knowledge" under Rule 702. See Daubert, U.S. at 113 S.Ct. at 2790 (addressing criteria for the admissibility of scientific evidence under Federal Rule 702); Downing, 753 F.2d at 1238–39 (same). First and foremost is the technique's relationship with established scientific analysis. For example, a technique that is grounded in traditional psychiatric or psychological principles, whether or not it is generally accepted, might be found to be admissible whereas we would be inclined to hold inadmissible a technique based upon astrology, even though it might be generally accepted by astrologers. The availability of specialized literature addressing the validity of the technique and whether the technique is generally accepted are two more factors to consider because they "bear on the likelihood that the scientific basis of the new technique has been exposed to critical scientific scrutiny." Downing, 753 F.2d at 1238–39. We will not attempt to etch into stone a list of criteria as the *sine qua non* for the admissibility of scientific evidence, but these criteria will serve as guidelines for our lower courts and allow for further development in this area of our case law.

280. Alberico, 861 P.2d at 199–201.

281. Ibid. at 200–201. The opinion alternates between a substantive description of the state of the law with regard to the admissibility of expert

testimony in New Mexico, the rejection of *Frye* and the adoption of a
new standard described in the case, the application of the new standard to the facts before it, and a scathing and even sarcastic commentary on the intermediate appellate court ruling.
282. New Mexico's Rule 702 reads:

> If scientific, technical or other specialized knowledge will assist
> the trier of fact to understand the evidence or to determine a fact in
> issue, a witness qualified as an expert by knowledge, skill, experience,
> training or education may testify thereto in the form of an opinion or
> otherwise. SCRA 1986, 11-702. *Alberico*, 861 P.2d at 202.

283. Alberico, 861 P.2d at 202, citing Daubert. [italics added; citations
     omitted]
284. Alberico, 861 P.2d at 204.
285. Alberico, Ibid. at 210–211.
286. Alberico, Ibid. at 212.
287. State v. Anderson, 881 P.2d 29, 41, 118 N.M. 284, 296 (N.M., 1994).
288. State v. Tollardo (N.M., 2003) at ¶ 18.
289. State v. Fry, 126 P.3d 516, 541–542, 2006 NMSC 1, (NM, 2005).
290. State v. Lente, 119 P.3d 737, 740, 2005 NMCA 111, (NM, 2005).
291. People v. Wesley, 83 N.Y.2d 417, 611 N.Y.S.2d 97, 100 (N.Y., 1994);
     see also In the Matter of R.B., 2006 NY Slip Op 50122(U) (NY, 2006)
     at 4–5.
292. Wesley, Ibid., 611 NYS at 100. [italics added]
293. Wesley, Ibid.
294. Wesley, 611 N.Y.S.2d at 101.
295. 611 N.Y.S.2d at 102.
296. People v. Wesley, 611 N.Y.S.2d at 103–104 (N.Y., 1994).
297. Styles v. General Motors Corp., M-2353 (NY, 2005), 2–3. [citations
     omitted]
298. People v. Wernick, 632 N.Y.S.2d 839, 841, 215 A.D.2d 50 (N.Y.A.D.
     2 Dept., 1995), *aff'd*, People v. Wernick, 89 N.Y.2d 111, 651 N.Y.S.2d
     392 (N.Y., 1996).
299. People v. Wernick, 632 N.Y.S.2d at 840–841. [citations omitted]
300. People v. Middleton, 54 N.Y.2d 42, 444 N.Y.S.2d 581, 584–5 (N.Y.,
     1981). [citations from scientific publications and cases omitted]
301. State v. Goode, 341 N.C. 513, 461 S.E.2d 631, 639–640 (N.C., 1995)
     (bloodstain pattern interpretation testimony admissible).
302. Goode, 461 S.E.2d at 640.
303. Howerton v. Arai Helmet, Ltd., 358 N.C. 440, 597 S.E.2d 674 (2004).

304. State v. Anderson, 624 S.E.2d 393, 396 (NC, 2006).
305. Anderson, 624 S.E.2d at 397. [numbered headings not set apart in original; citations omitted]
306. Anderson, 624 S.E.2d at 397–398. [citations omitted]
307. Anderson, 624 S.E.2d at 398.
308. Gonzalez v. Tounjian, 2003 ND 121, ¶ 24–¶ 26, 665 N.W.2d 705 (N.D., 2003) [citations omitted] (Dr. Griffin was an experienced emergency room physician who had treated 40 to 50 patients with major burn injuries. In addition to his medical training and experience, Dr. Griffin had served as a firefighter in the National Guard for four years. He had specialized firefighting training, including fire spread principles and carbon monoxide poisoning. Under these circumstances, we conclude the trial court did not abuse its discretion in concluding Dr. Griffin was qualified as an expert to testify about Gonzalez's loss of consciousness and brain injury.). See also State v. Hernandez, 2005 ND 214, 707 N.W.2d 449, 453 (ND, 2005) (expert testimony about handwriting testimony admissible to show that defendant wrote disputed incriminating letter); Forster v. West Dakota Veterinary Clinic, Inc., 2004 ND 207, ¶¶ 50-51 (ND, 2004) (Appellant's expert, a certified public accountant, could offer economic calculations of plaintiff's past and future economic loss. This expert had been providing financial analysis and calculations for 30 years. Appellees argued that the certified public accountant had no education, training, or experience as a vocational expert or in the veterinary business and was therefore not qualified to render an expert opinion on plaintiff's past and future earning potential, but this objection goes to the weight of the testimony rather than to its admissibility.).
309. Gonzalez v. Tounjian, 2003 ND 121, ¶ 27, 665 N.W.2d 705 (N.D., 2003).
310. Gonzales, Ibid., f.n. 1. See also State v. Hernandez, 2005 ND 214, 707 N.W.2d 449, 453 ¶ 6 (ND, 2005):

> This Court has never explicitly adopted Daubert and *Kumho Tire*. See *Howe v. Microsoft Corp.*, 2003 ND 12, ¶ 27 n. 1, 656 N.W.2d 285. Contrary to Hernandez's assertion, this Court is not required to follow *Daubert* and *Kumho Tire*, which involved admissibility of expert testimony in federal courts under the federal rules of evidence. This Court has a formal process for adopting procedural rules after appropriate study and recommendation by the Joint Procedure Committee, and we decline Hernandez's invitation to adopt *Daubert* by judicial decision. *See State v. Osier*, 1997 ND 170, ¶ 5 n. 1, 569 N.W.2d 441 (refusing to adopt procedural rule by opinion in litigated appeal).

311. Davis v. Killu, 710 N.W.2d 118, 122, 2006 ND 32, (N.D., 2006).
312. Ibid. at 122.
313. Ibid. at 123.
314. Davis v. Killu, 710 N.W.2d 118 at 120. [citations omitted]
315. State v. Schmidkunz, 2006 ND 192 ¶ 14 (N.D., 2006) [citations omitted] (State was able to introduce expert testimony to rebut the defendant's contention that he shot the victim because the defendant "was in a state of mind of an 'automaton' that was induced by extreme physiologic excitement fueled by a reaction to a medication withdrawal that created an extreme worsening of his psychiatric symptoms and a sudden onset of novel rage resulting in a prolonged episode of extreme emotional disturbance;" the court did note that the state's expert testified in the rebuttal portion of the state's case).
316. Miller v. Bike Athletic Co., 687 N.E.2d 735, 80 Ohio St.3d 607, 611 (Ohio, 1998).
317. Miller, 80 Ohio St.3d at 610–611.
318. Armbruster v. Hampton, 2006 Ohio 4530 ¶ 69 (Ohio App., 2006).
319. State v. Goins, 2005 Ohio 1439, ¶ 71–73 (OH, 2005). [citations omitted]
320. Ochletree v. Trumbull Mem. Hosp., 2006 Ohio 1006 ¶ 43 (OH, 2006).
321. Harris v. State, 2000 OK CR 20 ¶ 16, 13 P.3d 489 (OKCR, 2000).
322. Taylor v. State, 889 P.2d 319, 328 (Okla. Crim. App., 1995).
323. 889 P.2d at 332.
324. 889 P.2d at 338.
325. Harris v. State, 2000 OK CR 20 ¶ 17, 13 P.3d 489, (OKCR, 2000).
326. Dunkle v. State, 2006 OK CR 29 ¶ 53 (Okla. Crim. App., 2006), citing Harris v. State, 2000 OK CR 20, 13 P.3d 489.
327. State v. Brown, 297 Or. 404, 687 P.2d 751, 776–777 (Or., 1984) ("After analyzing the admissibility of polygraph evidence under the Oregon Evidence Code and existing caselaw, we conclude that *upon proper objection* polygraph evidence shall not be admissible in any civil or criminal trial in this state or any other legal proceeding subject to the rules of evidence under our Oregon Evidence Code."). [italics added]
328. State v. Lyons, 924 P.2d 802, 811, 324 Or. 256, 269 (Or., 1996). [citations omitted]
329. State v. O'Key, 899 P.2d 663, 675–677, 321 Or. 285, (Or., 1995). [citations and pagination omitted]
330. State v. O'Key, 899 P.2d at 689, f.n. 7.
331. Baughman v. Pina, 113 P.3d 459, 461, 200 Or. App. 15 (Or., 2005).
332. Baughman v. Pina, 113 P.3d at 462.
333. Hudjohn v. S&G Machinery Co., 114 P.3d 1141, 1149, 200 Or. App. 340, (Or., 2005)

334. State v. Owens, 0111-53181; A124156 (Or. App., 2006); *aff'd without opinion*, State v. Owens, 129 P.3d 281, 203 Or. App. 639 (Or. App., 2006)
335. Owens, Ibid.
336. Commonwealth v. Dengler, 843 A.2d 1241, 1245 (Pa.Super.Ct.2004). (The testimony of a credentialed psychologist or psychiatrist conducting an SVP assessment which follows the statutory formula for an assessment cannot be deemed "novel science" and therefore no *Frye* hearing is necessary.)
337. Com. v. Dengler, 890 A.2d 372, 380 (Pa., 2005). [internal quotations omitted]
338. Dengler, 890 A.2d at 381.
339. Dengler, Ibid. at 382.
340. State v. Quattrocchi, 681 A.2d 879, 884–885 (R.I., 1996).
341. Narragansett Elec. Co. v. Carbone, 898 A.2d 87, 96 (R.I., 2006). [citations omitted]
342. Quattrocchi, 681 A.2d 879 at 884. See also DiPetrillo v. Dow Chemical Co., 729 A.2d 677, 684 (R.I., 1999).
343. Mills v. State Sales, Inc., 824 A.2d 461, (R.I., 2003). [citations omitted]
344. State v. Motyka, 893 A.2d 267, 280 (R.I., 2006).
345. State v. Motyka, 893 A.2d 267, 283 (R.I., 2006). [italics added]
346. State v. Douglas, 626 S.E.2d 59, 65 (S.C. App., 2006) [citations omitted] (We hold that forensic interviewing is a recognized field of expertise. We rule that Herod is qualified as an expert in forensic interviewing by virtue of her knowledge, skill, experience, training, and education. The judge did not err in allowing Herod to testify as an expert witness in the area of forensic interviewing. Herod's testimony satisfied Rule 702, SCRE. The judge properly concluded Herod's testimony would explain to the jury Herod's role in the process and Herod's decision to recommend a medical examination.).
347. Douglas, 626 S.E.2d at 65–66.
348. Douglas, 626 S.E.2d at 72.
349. Baggerly v. CSX Transportation, Inc., Opinion No. 26208 (S.C., 2006).
350. State v. Santiago, Opinion No. 4127 (S.C. App., 2006). [citations omitted]
351. State v. Price, 629 S.E.2d 363, 366 (S.C., 2006).
352. State v. Hofer, 512 N.W.2d 482 (1994) (The trial court did not err in allowing testimony concerning the intoxilyzer and did not err in allowing admission of the intoxilyzer test results.)
353. Moeller, Ibid. at f.n. 1. Gahnite is a rare mineral. According to Perry Rahn, Moeller's soil expert in his second trial, gahnite is less common

than gold. At trial, Dr. Wehrenberg testified that he found gahnite in both the wheel well of Moeller's pickup and at the crime scene.
354. Moeller v. Weber, 2004 SD 110 ¶ 11–13 (SD, 2004).
355. Moeller, Ibid. at ¶ 40–41. [citations omitted]
356. Garland v. Rossknecht, 624 N.W.2d 700, ¶ 12 (SD, 2001). [citations omitted]
357. Atchison v. Circuit Court for the Seventh Judicial Circuit, 2004 SD 20, 676 N.W.2d 814 (S.D., 2004).
358. Wells v. Howe Heating & Plumbing, Inc., 2004 SD 37 ¶ 16-17, 677 N.W.2d 586, 590, (S.D., 2004). [citations omitted]
359. Jenner v. Dooley, 1999 SD 20, ¶ 20, 590 N.W.2d 463, (S.D., 1999) [citations omitted] (Testing of hairs found clutched in 3-year-old victim's hand and on her arms found not to pass the *Jenner* test because the defendant confessed to the slaying, she admitted her long hair was down when she stabbed her daughter over 70 times, and her detailed confession was corroborated by the physical evidence at the scene).
360. State v. Corey, 624 N.W.2d 841, ¶ 15–16 (SD, 2001). [citations omitted]
362. McDaniel v. CSX Transp., Inc., 955 S.W.2d 257, 258 (Tenn., 1997).
363. McDaniel v. CSX Transp., Inc., 955 S.W.2d at 263–265. [italics added; citations omitted]
364. McDaniel, 955 S.W.2d at 266.
365. State v. Stevens, 78 S.W.3d 817, 832–833 (Tenn., 2002).
366. State v. Stevens, 78 S.W.3d 817, 834–835 (Tenn., 2002) (behavioral science expert prohibited from testifying on behalf of defendant that offense was committed by "disorganized sexual offender" because courts decline to make rulings about guilt or innocence based on the *ipse dixit* of the expert.)
367. Brown v. Crown Equipment Corp., 181 S.W.3d 268, 274 (TN, 2005). [citations omitted]
368. Brown, 181 S.W.3d at 275.
369. Pullum v. Robinette, 174 S.W.3d 124, 128–130 (TN, 2004).
370. E.I. du Pont de Nemours and Co., Inc. v. Robinson, 923 S.W.2d 549, 556 (Tex., 1996).
371. E.I. du Pont de Nemours & Co. v. Robinson, 923 S.W.2d at 557.
372. Gammill v. Jack Williams Chevrolet, Inc., 972 S.W.2d 713, 724-5 (Tex., 1998).
373. Gammill, 972 S.W.2d at 727.
374. Interest of D.S, 19 S.W.3d 525, 529–530 (Tex. App.-Fort Worth, 2000). [citations omitted]
375. General Motors Corporation v. Burry, No. 2-05-216-CV (Tex. App., 2006). [citations omitted]

376. State v. Rimmasch, 775 P.2d 388, 396 (Utah, 1989).

377. State v. Rimmasch, 775 P.2d 388 (Utah, 1989).

378. Rimmasch, 775 P.2d at 392.

379. Rimmasch, 775 P.2d at 398.

380. Rimmasch, Ibid. at 406.

381. Rimmasch, Ibid. at 412, f.n. 7.

382. Rimmasch, Ibid. at 403.

383. State v. Crosby, 927 P.2d 638, 642 (Utah, 1996).

384. Haupt v. Heaps, 2005 UT App 436, 131 P.3d 252, 259 (Utah App., 2005), *cert. denied*, 132 P.3d 683 (Utah 2006).

385. Balderas v. Starks, 2006 UT App 218 ¶ 28–29 (Utah App., 2006) [citations omitted]. See also Alder v. Bayer Corp., 2002 UT 115, ¶ ¶ 62, 66, 61 P.3d 1068 (holding that *Rimmasch* was not implicated by expert testimony based on differential diagnosis, which is "one of the oldest and most widely used and recognized of all the methods").

386. State v. Streich, 163 Vt. 331, 658 A.2d 38, 46 (Vt., 1995).

387. USGen New England, Inc. v. Town of Rockingham, 2004 VT 90, ¶ 18, 176 Vt. 104, 838 A.2d 927, (Vt, 2004). [citations omitted]

388. USGen, Ibid. at ¶ 23.

389. USGen, Ibid. at ¶ 26.

390. State v. Provost, 2005 VT 134, 896 A.2d 55, 63 (Vt., 2005).

391. Billips v. Commonwealth, 630 S.E.2d 340, 356, f.n. 3, 48 Va. App. 278, (Va. App., 2006). (In Virginia, our Supreme Court specifically refused to adopt the *Frye* standard in *O'Dell v. Commonwealth*, 234 Va. 672, 696, 364 S.E.2d 491, 504 (1988), and acknowledged *John v. Im*, 263 Va. 315, 322, 559 S.E.2d 694, 698 (2002), that it had not "considered the question whether the *Daubert* analysis employed by the federal courts should be applied in our trial courts to determine the scientific reliability of expert testimony." Thus, as the Supreme Court noted in *John*, the *Spencer* evidentiary standard still governs the admission of scientific evidence in Virginia. Ibid. at 322 n. 3, 559 S.E.2d at 698 n. 3.)

392. Cotton v. Com., 451 S.E.2d 673, 675–676, 19 Va.App. 306, 310–311 (Va. App., 1994), *aff'd on other grounds*, 20 Va.App. 596, 459 S.E.2d 527 (1995) (en banc). See also Muhammad v. Com., 619 S.E.2d 16 (Va, 2005).

393. Utz v. Com., 505 S.E.2d 380, 386, 28 Va.App. 411, (Va. App., 1998) [citations and pagination omitted] (Expert testimony about gangs admissible to prove motive if the probative value of the evidence does not exceed the prejudicial effect; here such evidence was properly admitted).

394. John v. Im, 263 Va. 315 (Va., 2002). [citations omitted]

395. Brown v. Corbin, 423 S.E.2d 176, 179, 244 Va. 528, (Va., 1992) (accident reconstruction expert testimony is rarely admissible in Virginia because it invades the province of the jury); see also Pritchett v. Commonwealth, 263 Va. 182 (Va., 2002) (expert cannot testify as to ultimate issue of defendant's state of mind); Nobrega v. Com., 628 S.E.2d 922 (Va., 2006).
396. Rodriguez v. Com., 455 S.E.2d 724, 726–727, 20 Va.App. 122, (Va. App., 1995).
397. Hussen v. Com., 511 S.E.2d 106, 109, 257 Va. 93, (Va., 1999) citing Davis v. Commonwealth, 12 Va.App. 728, 731–32, 406 S.E.2d 922, 923–24 (1991) (detective's testimony that a certain quantity of drugs was not consistent with personal use did not constitute an opinion that the defendant intended to distribute marijuana and, thus, did not invade the province of the jury).
398. Herbin v. Com., 503 S.E.2d 226, 231, 28 Va.App. 173, (Va. App., 1998). This case was prosecuted by the author, and the defendant did not present any evidence that he suffered from a disease of the mind; in fact, no evidence that he had consulted with a mental health professional was put before the jury, although the trial court erroneously permitted him to proffer that he was under the influence of narcotics, was having a sexual relationship with the victim's mother, and had generally had a bad day. Virginia does not permit the diminished capacity defense, and voluntary intoxication is irrelevant in all but a first degree or capital murder case.
399. State v. Gore, 143 Wash. 2d 288, 304, 21 P.3d 262, 271 (2001). See also Grant v. Boccia, No. 24320-6-III (WA, 2006).
400. Reese v. Stroh, 128 Wn.2d 300, 305–306, 907 P.2d 282, (Wash., 1995).
401. Reese, 128 Wn.2d at 307–308.
402. State v. Wilbur-Bobb, No. 55872-2-I (Wash. App., 2006).
403. Wilbur-Bobb, Ibid.
404. Grant v. Boccia, No. 24320-6-III (WA, 2006), citing State v. Copeland, 130 Wn.2d 244, 261, 922 P.2d 1304 (1996).
405. Wilt v. Buracker, 443 S.E.2d 196, 203, 191 W.Va. 39, 46 (W.Va., 1994), *cert. denied*, 511 U.S. 1129, 114 S.Ct. 2137, 128 L.Ed.2d 867 (1994) (testimony hedonic damages admissible in general). [italics added]
406. Gentry v. Mangum, 466 S.E.2d 171, 177, 195 W.Va. 512, 518 (W.Va., 1995).
407. Gentry v. Mangum, 466 S.E.2d 171, 179, 195 W.Va. 512, 520 (W.Va., 1995).

408. Gentry v. Mangum, 466 S.E.2d at 181.

409. Gentry, Ibid. at 183.

410. Ibid. at 184.

411. State v. McCracken, 624 S.E.2d 537, 541 (WV, 2005).

412. Watson v. Inco Alloys International, Inc., 2001 WV 18 ¶ 41, 209 W. Va. 234, 545 S.E.2d 294 (WV, 2001). See also State v. Leep, 212 W.Va. 57, 66, 569 S.E.2d, 133, 141 (2002).

413. State v. Peters, 534 N.W.2d 867, 192 Wis.2d 674 (Wis. App., 1995). [citations omitted]

414. State v. Peters, 534 N.W.2d 867, 873, 192 Wis.2d 674, (Wis. App., 1995).

415. Ricco v. Riva, Appeal No. 02-2621 ¶ 21, 2003 WI App 182, 266 Wis. 2d 696, 669 N.W.2d 193, (Wis. App., 2003).

416. Springfield v. State, 860 P.2d 435, 443 (Wyo., 1993); see also Bunting v. Jamieson, 984 P.2d 467 ¶ 41 (WY, 1999).

417. Root v. Root, No. 01-137, ¶ 9 2003 WY 36, 65 P.3d 41, (WY, 2003).

418. Easum v. Miller, 2004 WY 73, ¶ 19 (WY, 2003).

419. Chapman v. State, 18 P.3d 1164, ¶ 18 (WY, 2001), citing Frenzel v. State, 849 P.2d 741 (Wyo., 1993).

420. Chapman, Ibid.

421. Easum, Ibid. at ¶ 21.

422. See, e.g., Bonar v. Dean Witter Reynolds, Inc., 835 F.2d 1378 (C.A.11 (Fla.), 1988); White, J. (2001.) Fake burn expert gets probation for lying in court; perjury case could lead to prosecution elsewhere. *The Washington Post.* Retrieved September 27, 2006, from http://www. corpusdelicti.com/stocco_011301.html; Chein v. Shumsky, 373 F.3d 978, 981–982 (9th Cir., 2004); Norwood, C. (2005.) Man who gives 'expert' medical testimony charged with perjury. *Daily Home Online.* Retrieved September 27, 2006, from http://www.dailyhome. com/news/2005/dh-talladega-0224-cnorwood-5b23v2024.htm

423. An excellent article about malingering in a medicolegal context is Rubenzer, S. (2004). Malingering of psychiatric disorders and cognitive impairment in criminal court settings. *The Prosecutor, 38*(5), 40–47.

424. See, e.g., American Academy of Pediatrics, Committee on Medical Liability. (2002, May). Guidelines for expert witness testimony in medical malpractice litigation. *PEDIATRICS, 109*(5), 974–979. Retrieved September 2, 2006, from http://aappolicy.aappublications.org/cgi/ content/full/pediatrics;109/5/974. American Academy of Psychiatry and the Law. (2005). *Ethical guidelines for the practice of forensic psychiatry.* Retrieved September 2, 2006, from http://www.aapl.org/ pdf/ETHICSGDLNS.pdf. (Psychiatrists who take on a forensic role

for patients they are treating may adversely affect the therapeutic relationship with them. Forensic evaluations usually require interviewing corroborative sources, exposing information to public scrutiny, or subjecting evaluees and the treatment itself to potentially damaging cross-examination. The forensic evaluation and the credibility of the practitioner may also be undermined by conflicts inherent in the differing clinical and forensic roles. Treating psychiatrists should therefore generally avoid acting as an expert witness for their patients or performing evaluations of their patients for legal purposes. When requirements of geography or related constraints dictate the conduct of a forensic evaluation by the treating psychiatrist, the dual role may also be unavoidable; otherwise, referral to another evaluator is preferable.); American Psychological Association. (2002). *Ethical principles of psychologists and code of conduct.* Retrieved September 2, 2006, from http://www.apa.org/ethics/code2002.html#3_05; Smith, D. (2003). 10 ways practitioners can avoid frequent ethical pitfalls. *APA Monitor Online, 34*(1). Retrieved September 2, 2006, from http://www.apa.org/monitor/jan03/10ways.html (Pertains to situations where it's not clear whether the psychologist is serving as an expert witness or advocate for one side. Court-appointed evaluators should express well-balanced, objective opinions, says Ethics Committee member Linda F. Campbell, PhD, while advocates are often therapists for one party who have had little direct contact with the other. Because they cannot provide an objective evaluation, psychologists who are therapists for one of the parties shouldn't serve as expert witnesses.); American Medical Association Council on Ethical and Judicial Affairs. 2006). *Code of medical ethics, 2006–2007: Of the American Medical Association: current opinions with annotations.*

425. See, e.g., Brent, R. L. (1988). Improving the quality of expert witness testimony. *PEDIATRICS, 82*(3), 511–513, Retrieved September 2, 2006, from http://pediatrics.aappublications.org/cgi/reprint/82/3/511

426. Preussel, R. (2006). The experts aren't reliable either: Why expert testimony on the reliability of eyewitness testimony is unwarranted in Alabama state courts. *Yale Law School Student Scholarship Series, 28*, 1–40.

427. Cutler, B. L. (2003). Strategies for mitigating the impact of eyewitness experts. *The Prosecutor, 37*(1), 14, 20.

CHAPTER EIGHT

THE COST
OF REASONABLE DOUBT

Sandra R. Sylvester, JD

When confronted with expert witnesses, it may seem to most prosecutors that reasonable doubt is for sale. Certainly, in complex criminal cases, it is disturbing to find the number of "experts" who are willing to say anything for a price. This occurs with great frequency in child abuse prosecutions. Cases involving shaken baby syndrome could involve a number of medical specialties, including neurology, pathology, ophthalmology, radiology, and hematology.[1] Child sexual abuse cases can attract experts who will testify about the "suggestibility" of children or "parental alienation syndrome."[2] Defendants who raise psychological defenses will rely on psychologists to testify to a host of syndromes.

One can only wonder about the motivations of people who hold themselves out as experts. Is it greed? On the other hand, is it narcissism? Do people seek to profit by denying justice to victims of horrible crimes? All too often, prosecutors face frauds, snake oil salesmen, and charlatans who will say anything for a price. In states that limit discovery, prosecutors are forced to combat trial by ambush. In those jurisdictions, prosecutors may encounter these witnesses for the first time during a trial.[3] The "experts for hire" are very prevalent in cases using psychological defenses. In her book, *Whores of the Court*, Dr. Margaret A. Hagen provides chilling examples of suspect psychiatric testimony.[4] Dr. Hagen offers an interesting analysis of the psychological defenses raised in felony trials. For example, she notes that in one third of all cases where the defense presented a "battered woman syndrome" defense, the defendant was acquitted.[5] In 100% of the cases where the court excluded this defense, Hagen notes that the women were convicted. Since the publication of Hagen's book, psychological defenses such as battered woman syndrome have come under greater scrutiny. One legal article stated, "The paucity of research establishing BWS [battered woman syndrome] as a bona fide reliable condition egregiously undercuts the claim that the condition exists as a distinct diagnostic entity."[6] Questionable expert testimony and suspect psychological or medical findings strike at the core of the criminal justice system, and prosecutors must protect the integrity of that system. Prosecutors need to be aggressive in their efforts to preclude unreliable expert testimony.

Whereas some experts are legitimate and may just be "true believers" in their cause or agenda, there are some experts who are complete frauds and seek to profit from their involvement in the criminal justice system. A good example of the profiteering of experts occurred in Prince William County, Virginia, in March 1999. In July 1998, 2-year-old Sada Hatfield was immersed in a tub of scalding hot water. She received third- and fourth-degree burns over 40% of her body. Sada's caretakers left her unattended, and she did not receive medical attention for 1½ days, before finally succumbing to her injuries. Her caretakers, Billy Leon Smalls and Jennifer Nicole Talley, were charged with a number of criminal offenses, including murder and child abuse.[7]

During the months preceding the trial, prosecutors interviewed a number of burn and child abuse medical experts. All the medical experts agreed that the injuries to Sada Hatfield were classic "immersion burn" injuries, consistent with the child being held down in a tub of hot water. These medical professionals unanimously concluded that there were no other explanations for the child's injuries.

The week before the Smalls and Talley murder trials, the defense made a motion for the court to provide funds for them to hire an expert witness. The prosecution was immediately suspicious of the credentials of any expert who would disagree with an overwhelming consensus of medical experts who concluded that Sada's burns were intentionally inflicted.[8]

Prior to the hearing on this motion, the prosecutors began a massive search to try to identify the mystery defense expert.[9] The first step was to determine if the expert was a Virginia practitioner. After contacting known child abuse and burn experts throughout the state to determine if they were hired by the defense, these experts contacted other colleagues throughout the Commonwealth of Virginia to try to ascertain the identity of the defense expert. Once all of Virginia's experts denied involvement, the prosecution team expanded the search nationwide.

The prosecutors contacted child abuse physicians and academicians in Philadelphia, Pennsylvania, San Antonio, Texas, and Columbia, South Carolina. They indicated that there was only one possible source of expert testimony that would support an accident theory. They were able to provide Prince William County prosecutors with a lead directing the prosecutors to the state of New Jersey.[10] With the search narrowed to New Jersey, prosecutors began calling burn hospitals and prosecutors' offices in attempt to identify the defense expert. This effort led to the National Burn Victim Foundation (NBVF) in Basking Ridge, New Jersey.

The prosecutors learned that New Jersey State officials used the NBVF in their immersion burn cases. Harry Gaynor was the founder of NBVF. He referred to himself as Dr. Gaynor or Professor Gaynor.[11] In reality, Harry Gaynor had no academic degrees. He had received an honorary doctorate degree from China for his efforts to produce a burn treatment. A prosecutor in New Jersey had uncovered

Dr. Gaynor's lack of formal education during cross-examination of him.[12]

Prosecutors from attorneys' offices in a number of states were very helpful and provided curricula vitae, transcripts of prior testimony, and training manuals from the NBVF.[13] On reviewing the documentation, it became clear that some of the conclusions and assumptions made in NBVF training were suspect and of questionable merit. The manuals contained broad statements without supporting documentation and covered a variety of disciplines. Some of the training materials were inconsistent with accepted medical practice.

The next step was to determine which employee of the NBVF was preparing to testify in the Hatfield case.[14] Detective Samson Newsome of the Prince William County Police Department placed a call to NBVF. He pretended to be interested in employment and proceeded to ask a number of questions about the NBVF. He was able to determine that Gary Stocco, Executive Director of NBVF, was planning to testify in the Hatfield case. Having identified Stocco, the focus was on obtaining information about him. Although prosecutors had accumulated a significant amount of information about the founder of NBVF, Harry Gaynor, they knew little of his protégé, Gary Stocco. The prosecutors obtained the curriculum vitae (CV) of Stocco. This became a vital piece of evidence when preparing for cross-examination.

During the hearing on the defense motion for state funds for the expert, the prosecution questioned the credentials and training of the proposed defense expert. The defense refused to identify their expert in the hearing. On the prosecution's proffer to the court about their suspicions regarding the witness being an employee of NBVF and the perceived lack of credentials of this employee, the court ordered the defense to produce their expert for voir dire.[15]

As anticipated by the prosecution, the defense called Gary S. Stocco as their expert witness in the voir dire hearing. This hearing was conducted prior to the murder trial to determine whether the defense witness had the appropriate credentials and a scientific basis for his conclusions. Cross-examination produced the evidence that, in fact, Stocco had no academic degrees. Stocco claimed that he was obtaining a baccalaureate and master's degree combination from Columbia State University in Louisiana.[16] The following exchange occurred regarding Stocco's formal education during a hearing in *Commonwealth v. Billy Leon Smalls* and *Commonwealth v. Jennifer Nicole Talley*:

> Page 47, line 5, Q: You have no formal education, yet; isn't that correct? You have no degrees?
>
> line 7, A: Well, there's questions. I have formal education. I do not have a degree of yet.

A later exchange revealed the following:

> Page 78, line 1, Q: Mr. Stocco, where did you do the course work that prepared you for the BA/MA degree you anticipate receiving?
>
> line 4, A: That's at Columbia State University.
> line 6, Q: Where is that, sir?
> line 7, A: That is in Louisiana.

An investigation into Columbia State University discovered that it was not an academic institution, but rather a diploma mill. The Louisiana attorney general had obtained evidence that it was a mail drop in Orange County, California, and filed injunctions against Columbia State University 1 month prior to Stocco making an application. He, therefore, could not have engaged in any course work.

Another point of contention was the lack of credentials of Harry Gaynor. During cross-examination, Stocco claimed that he did not know of Gaynor's lack of education, but he had altered his own CV by removing any reference to Gaynor.[17]

That exchange went as follows:

> Page 43, line 12, Q: Have you updated your CV, sir?
> line 13, A: Yes, ma'am.
>
> line 14, Q: As a matter of fact, you updated it to the point of taking Dr. Gaynor's name off of your abstract publications: isn't that correct?
>
> line 17, A: I am not aware of that, ma'am.

The fact that Stocco had altered his CV to remove any reference to Harry Gaynor was viewed by the prosecution team as evidence that he was aware of the NBVF founder's lack of credentials. These disclosures later became critical elements in building a case of fraud.

At the conclusion of the hearing, the Honorable William D. Hamblen of the 31st Judicial District determined that Stocco did not have the credentials to render an expert opinion in the criminal trial of Smalls and Talley. The court stated,

> There is a danger in expert testimony, the courts have recognized that. There is a danger to the trier of fact in the presentation of expert testimony. And there is, if you will, a downside risk to the presentation of expert testimony to the trier of fact. Because it is portrayed to them as "expert testimony," it has the potential, if wrongly presented or wrongly utilized, to thwart the fact finding process in ways that aren't necessary... . As I listened to his testimony today and counsels' argument, that opinion, in and of itself, is a product of a number of component findings, evaluations, or opinions that Mr. Stucco [*sic*] would reach in this case which require analysis by him and evaluation of the nerve damage, hot water heaters, how they are regulated, etc., how long water retains its temperature and the like. I am not satisfied that he's demonstrated sufficient expertise in all those areas, the scope of which I find breathtaking... . There has to be, in my view, a showing greater than the showing made today of formal, recognized, acknowledged training, training which is subject to peer review and evaluation.[18]

After a trial that lasted 8 days, Jennifer Talley and Billy Smalls were convicted of the murder of Sada Hatfield. The defense did not produce any expert testimony to support a theory of accidental injury.[19]

THE TRIAL OF GARY STOCCO

Following the trials of Billy Smalls and Jennifer Talley, the prosecution was committed to stopping Gary Stocco from ever testifying again. In the months following his Prince William County appearance, Stocco appeared as a defense expert in Middlesex County, New Jersey. The prosecutors from New Jersey, who had helped Prince William County identify Stocco, contacted Prince William County prosecutors and informed them that Stocco was to testify for the defense in an immersion burn case in Middlesex County, New Jersey. Prince William County prosecutors provided copies of Stocco's previous testimony to the Middlesex County prosecutors. The Middlesex County prosecutors attempted a preemptive strike by filing a motion to preclude Stocco from testifying as an expert. When called to testify in New Jersey, Stocco changed his credentials and claimed to have received a master's degree in public health administration from the University of San Moritz in Leeds, England.[20] An investigation into the University of San Moritz revealed that it, too, was a diploma mill and did not actually exist. Degrees could be purchased from this institution, along with distinctive academic honors and letters of recommendations for an additional fee.

Armed with Stocco's Virginia testimony, Middlesex County prosecutors caught him in a number of fabrications and were successful in precluding his testimony. Because of the joint efforts of both prosecution offices, Prince William County prosecutors were able to identify a number of jurisdictions where Stocco had qualified as an expert in the past. He had previously been qualified as a burn expert in Massachusetts, Indiana, Ohio, and throughout New Jersey, and Prince William County prosecutors ordered court transcripts from every jurisdiction. The efforts resulted in a Prince William County grand jury indicting Gary S. Stocco on two counts of perjury and one count of obtaining money under false pretenses.[21]

Preparation for the trial of Gary Stocco was intensive and expensive. It required a coordinated effort with all the other jurisdictions where Stocco had been qualified as a burn expert. One of the perjury counts required proof that on two occasions, while under oath, Stocco had made conflicting statements of a material fact. Prosecutors from New Jersey, Ohio, and Indiana, along with a Louisiana deputy attorney general and a California postal inspector, were subpoenaed. The Commonwealth had to prove that Columbia State University was, in fact, a diploma mill and that Stocco knew it at the time he testified in Prince William County. It was fortuitous that the California postal inspector had a copy of Stocco's application to Columbia State University as evidence. The application was received after the Louisiana attorney general began the investigation of Columbia State University as a fraudulent institution and following a raid conducted by the California postal inspector on the mail drop location for Columbia State University in Orange County, California.

The conflicting testimony regarding his other credentials was also essential to prove the second perjury count. This testimony included his actual "police experience," which was limited to patrolling parking lots at mental health facilities. He used to be a police officer for the State Department of Human Resources. Despite having testified that he had investigated burn cases when he was employed as a state police officer, the prosecution had evidence that he had investigated only one burn case—that of a mental health patient who suffered a cigarette burn.

Faced with the overwhelming evidence gathered by the prosecution and the prospect of facing charges in multiple jurisdictions, Gary S. Stocco subsequently entered pleas of guilty to perjury and obtaining money under false pretenses. He received a suspended prison sentence and 10 years of probation. A condition of his suspended sentence was the prohibition against testifying as an expert witness again.[22]

INVESTIGATING THE EXPERT WITNESS

Identifying the Expert

The efforts to discover the identity of the defense witness in Sada Hatfield's case illustrate the time-consuming and complicated nature of this process. Prosecutors may consider several strategies that might be effective in uncovering the identity of defense experts. A quick trial date might make it difficult for the defense to retain professional witnesses. Such a strategy may force the defense to move for a continuance. When that happens, a prosecutor can try to force the issue of disclosure. Because such continuances only benefit the defense, a judge may be willing to require the defense to provide information about the expert who they need more time to retain.

The next step would be to try to get concessions from the defense. Consider an agreement between the parties to mutually disclose the information on the record and require the parties to be committed to that selection. Any changes, additions, and so on should be made on the record. A Praecipe or Agreed Order with a full accounting of experts affords both sides the opportunity to investigate the witnesses and their credentials.

A prosecutor may file a simple "Motion to Disclose Experts." This motion should indicate the prosecution's willingness to disclose its experts if the defense agrees. Prosecutors may wish to cite reported cases of fraudulent testimony. The motion should also indicate that, if denied, the prosecutor should be entitled to a brief recess to investigate the credentials of any proposed defense expert.

Defense attorneys may not want to divulge the names of their witnesses. Prosecutors should be suspicious in these circumstances. In such an event, suspect a witness of questionable expertise. Consulting with other experts who specialize in the area of the disputed evidence may yield information regarding identity. Often, experts subscribe to an Internet list service, and it is possible that your case was the subject of one such communication.

Also, keep in mind that defense attorneys will use the same witnesses. Review their older cases and consider the possibility that they have established a relationship with a particular expert.[23] In any event, talk to professionals in the judicial system and the discipline that is the subject of the contest.

Background Investigation of the Expert

Having ascertained the expert's identity, the next step is to verify the credentials. Every professional who is required to be licensed must be regulated by the state. For example, in Virginia, the Board of Medicine maintains licensing and educational information accessible via the Internet. Allied health professionals are regulated in a similar fashion. The Internet provides an immediate and rapid response to inquiries made about these professionals. As a first step in verifying background information, these Web sites may provide education, license status, and employment. Virginia, for example, provides information about the license status and the jurisdiction of professionals.

Prior to the advent of the Internet, one had to investigate credentials the old-fashioned way. Most professions maintain professional directories, such as the Martindale-Hubbell directory for lawyers. Prior to the computer age, information regarding medical experts was obtained by searching the medical directories maintained in a medical library. Now, information about education, specialties, and employment is readily available. Most professional organizations maintain information regarding complaints made against an individual. Be sure to follow up on any complaints, civil law suits, judgments, and so forth.

The National District Attorney Association (NDAA) uses an Internet list service to communicate with prosecutors nationwide. It can assist in making inquiries regarding experts. Other statewide prosecutor associations may maintain an expert witness databank.[24] Such services alleviate much of the painstaking legwork needed to check credentials. Networking among prosecutors also allows for exchange of information.

There are a number of Web sites dedicated to providing information to defense attorneys about experts. Although most of these Web sites require some form of proof that one is a defense attorney, many of them have general information that can be helpful. For example, the "Shaken Baby Defense" Web site provides a significant amount of information about defense theories and defense experts.[25] "Mothers Against Munchausen's Syndrome by Proxy" is another example of a defense-oriented Web site.[26] These Web sites can alert the prosecutor to any potential areas that are subject to debate. Prosecutors need to be familiar with the current defenses raised and who is raising those defenses.

CVs or resumes also contain a host of information. As demonstrated by the Stocco case, one should not assume that the educational institution is legitimate. There are a number of resources available about diploma mills. John Bear maintains a Web site and has coauthored with Allen Ezell, *Degree Mills: The Billion-Dollar Industry That Has*

Sold Over a Million Fake Diplomas.[27] Diploma mills may be hard to detect. As Bear points out, in the past the diploma mill may have had names similar to existing accredited institutions. Bear cautions that as more people are becoming aware of the existence of diploma mills, the current trend is to produce bogus degrees from actual accredited institutions.

Prosecutors should not assume that an expert's credentials are legitimate if they are from an accredited institution. Prosecutors must go one step further and verify not only that the expert is or was at that institution, but also graduated from that institution as well. There have been a number of instances where experts have testified about fraudulent academic degrees from legitimate academic institutions. In *State v. Elder*, 199 Kan. 607; 433 P. 2d 462 (Kansas, 1967), Lyle Elder was prosecuted on two counts of perjury for his prior testimony in a criminal case that he had received a bachelor of science degree in chemistry and bacteriology from Wichita State University. He also testified that he had attended medical school for 2 years at the University of Kansas. No record was found of his enrollment or attendance at either institution.

Once the information about the expert's education has been verified, examine the CV for any mistakes. For example, membership in a professional organization may have lapsed. Make an effort to verify each line of the CV. If it is determined that there are errors in the CV, this provides ammunition for cross-examination.

Be wary of the CV in which salient facts are missing. In the case of Gary Stocco, the CV did not list any academic degrees. He bolstered his CV by listing the courses he had attended and the lectures he had conducted. The fact that he excluded any reference to academic degrees was an obvious omission. Examine any gaping holes in the CV. Also, ascertain if a license to practice was suspended at any time.

Many experts are faculty members of academic institutions. If they are research faculty, investigate fully what their research involves. Teaching faculty leave a paper trail, including a syllabus that includes the text used during the academic year. One may find information in the text to contradict their opinion and bolster your position.

Most professional societies have standards of professional conduct. For example, the American Academy of Pediatrics has "Guidelines for Expert Witness Testimony."[28] Review the professional society guidelines applicable to your case and ensure that your experts and the defense experts meet the minimal standards as set forth by these organizations.

Of course, testimonial transcripts are worth their weight in gold. Obtain transcripts in as many cases as possible. This can be an expensive proposition. Organizations such as the National Center for the Prosecution of Child Abuse maintain a transcript database and will provide copies of transcripts of known experts.[29] Be sure that the credentials are consistent because changes in credentials should raise a red flag.[30] Also, verify the information presented in the testimony. If the expert witness reports that he or she has treated or seen a certain number of cases, investigate that claim if possible.[31]

It is important to verify all employment references. Gary Stocco reported experience as a state police officer. This could mean that he was a sworn officer with the New Jersey State Police. Investigation revealed that this was, in fact, an attempt to mislead. Stocco was a police officer for the "State" Department of Human Services, in which capacity he patrolled parking lots. He had no experience investigating major child abuse cases involving burn injuries.[32]

Prosecutors should investigate the credentials of any expert with the same vigor with which they investigate all aspects of the criminal case. Police agencies can assist the prosecutor with background information by using a number of computer programs, such as Accurint. These computer programs provide background information regarding property holdings and known associates. Armed with this information, prosecutors can contact other professionals within the same geographic area as the witness and interview them regarding the witness's professional reputation.

Preparing for the Expert
Impeachment of the legitimate expert should involve a thorough review of the accepted medical literature in the field. This can be a daunting

prospect for the average lawyer. Preparation for complicated cases involving expert witnesses should begin long before a case is even presented in the prosecutor's office. A prosecutor assigned to handle any serious felony caseload, such as child abuse cases, homicide cases, or domestic violence cases, should be familiar with the common defenses and should collect enough information to fill a library.

There are several resources now available via the Internet that could help the young prosecutor become familiar with the preparation of a complex case. It is imperative that a prosecutor not wait until the "case of the century" falls into his or her lap. A rather unusual, but very helpful, suggestion is to establish a library of "true crime" stories. A young attorney can go through the trials and tribulations of others detailed in this genre of material.

Other references for the prosecutor's library should include treatises and journal articles on the subject. The latest edition of the *Diagnostic and Statistical Manual of Mental Disorders* (*DSM*) is required text for anyone dealing with psychological defenses. The prosecutor should read the introduction and the chapter titled "Uses of this Manual." Too often, prosecutors are too busy to pay attention to these subtle details. The limitations of the *DSM* are contained in this section of the manual. For example, in the introduction section, the caution regarding the "significant risks that diagnostic information will be misused or misunderstood" in the forensic setting provides excellent cross-examination material to gain concessions from the expert witness.[33] Additional resources to consider when dealing with psychological defenses are the texts on malingering.[34]

There are a number of excellent resources on child abuse that would complement one's library. Dr. Robert Reece has edited several texts on this topic published by the Johns Hopkins University Press.[35] Prosecutors should be familiar with the facets of criminal investigation pertaining to their area of interest. For example, the publishing company CRC Press publishes a number of books detailing topics such as bloodstain evidence, homicide investigations, rape investigations, forensic pathology, and so forth.

In addition to the texts, a number of federal agencies provide manuals that can be helpful if funding is limited. The Federal Bureau of Investigation and the Department of Justice have excellent manuals on investigation techniques. Some private agencies also provide free publications on a variety of topics. The National Center for Missing and Exploited Children has a wealth of information on child exploitation issues. The American Prosecutors Research Institute has a number of programs in areas such as child abuse, domestic violence, drugs, and gangs. Many of these programs offer training opportunities as well as technical support. The National Center on Shaken Baby Syndrome in Park City, Utah, has a number of learned treatises on this topic and has visual aids that would be helpful to explain the medical testimony to a jury. Prosecutors should avail themselves of these resources long before they have to prepare for a complex case.

In his chapter, "Prosecuting the Shaken Infant Case," in *The Shaken Baby Syndrome: A Multidisciplinary Approach*, Brian K. Holmgren notes that it is up to prosecutors to distinguish between charlatans and Nobel Prize winners.[36] Holmgren suggests that prosecutors consider Rule 803 (13) of the Federal Rules of Evidence, as well as the now famed expert cases of *Daubert* and *Frye*.[37] Not every state recognizes these authorities, but the logic and reasoning are sound and can be persuasive.

Holmgren also suggests that prosecutors file pretrial motions to compel the defense to make an offer of proof regarding the proposed expert testimony and disclose authority that supports the expert's opinion, and to request that the expert's testimony be heard without the presence of the jury so that the court can rule on admissibility and scope.[38]

Prosecutors need to evaluate the quality of any expert opinion. Physicians may speak in terms of absolutes in the emergency room but become equivocal in the courtroom. Prosecutors should interview their own experts in the presence of the police investigator and verify their conclusions and assertions. During the interview of the defense expert, police should also be present to witness the interview and document the conversation. This effort will prevent the prosecutor from becoming a witness in the event there have been inconsistencies.

In states that allow *one-party consent* for tape-recording, the interviews should be recorded and transcribed. One-party consent simply means that one party needs to consent to the making of a tape-recording of the conversation. Prosecutors should comply with their state's law on tape-recording. Following the interview of all the experts, prosecutors should follow up with a letter memorializing the conversation and ask the expert to contact them immediately if there are any changes regarding their findings.

Typically, the defense expert will rely on the defense to provide the information needed to form an opinion. In the case of the psychological defense, the expert's opinion is usually based on the self-report of the defendant. The prosecutor will be able to gain significant concessions on cross-examination by undermining the basis for the expert's conclusions. Pointing out that an expert never contacted the police or prosecution to verify the information shows bias and undermines the credibility of the expert.

Experts who criticize the findings of other professionals can be questioned about the steps they took to discuss the issues with the prosecution's experts. Cross-examination can focus on whether they contacted the other professionals to discuss concerns. During the cross-examination of a noted pediatric neuroradiologist, the witness was asked about the medical findings of another radiologist that contradicted his own conclusions. The neuroradiologist asserted adamantly, "He's wrong."[39] The prosecutor began questioning him about whether he had contacted the other radiologist to discuss his findings. Like most defense experts, he had not done so. This provided the basis for questioning the defense expert's objectivity and commitment to the fact-finding process. Such a cross-examination provides wonderful concessions. The prosecutor will have already ascertained from the prosecution's own expert that the defense witness had never sought to discuss or investigate the medical findings.

Be diligent to hold the expert to his or her area of expertise only. Experts will often attempt to comment on an area outside their stated areas of expertise. Shaken baby cases encompass so many medical disciplines that experts may try to comment outside their area of expertise to support their own conclusions. A radiologist does not usually consider the clinical picture but may try to comment on the symptoms and treatment of the patient. When the defense is attempting to qualify the expert, make the attorney specify in which areas this expert may venture an opinion. For example, a pediatric emergency room physician who sees hundreds of child abuse cases may be qualified in emergency medicine, pediatrics, child abuse, and neglect.

THE LEGITIMATE EXPERT IN MEDICAL CASES

The fraudulent expert is not someone most prosecutors will encounter in their careers. It is far more common to have to prepare a cross-examination of a legitimate expert. This is also a far more daunting task. For example, the typical child abuse case involving a shaking injury can require the assistance of a number of medical experts. If the child survives for any length of time, the prosecutor may consult with neurologists, pediatric intensive care physicians, pediatric neuroradiologists, and ophthalmologists, to name a few. If the child dies, a medical examiner and a neuropathologist will be involved. The complexity of the average shaken baby case can be overwhelming. When beginning a complex case with medical testimony, the prosecutor must become as conversant with the subject as the experts. Medical experts working with the prosecution should be able to anticipate and help prepare the prosecutor for any problems with the case. The prosecutor should share any medical literature that contradicts the findings in the prosecution's case and ask the medical expert to explain and clarify the medical findings.

Educating oneself is the first step in preparing to work with expert witnesses. Often, medicine is not an exact science. For example, there is dispute in the medical community about the very diagnosis of shaken baby syndrome or abusive head injury or traumatic brain injury. It becomes critical for the prosecutor to be as familiar with the changes, medical discoveries, and controversies in this area. The *Quarterly*

Child Abuse Medical Update aids professionals in achieving a more comprehensive understanding of the issues and research in child abuse and neglect. *Quarterly Update* provides peer reviews of the latest medical research and analyzes its validity. It is an exceptional reference for any prosecutor's office.[40]

On October 9, 1992, 8-week-old Ryan Sanders was brutally shaken by his day care worker, Eleanor Hinegardner. Ryan suffered severe brain damage because of the assault. In the felony trial of Eleanor Kay Hinegardner, the prosecution in Prince William County, Virginia, had a number of legitimate defense experts to prepare to cross-examine.[41]

The defense called Dr. Robert Zimmerman, a pediatric neuroradiologist from the Children's Hospital of Philadelphia. Dr. Zimmerman had an impressive CV that was over 150 pages long, detailing his many publications. Although Dr. Zimmerman was a legitimate expert, the defense attempted to bolster his testimony by trying to establish his lack of bias. The direct examination centered on his assisting the prosecution's efforts:

> Page 10, line 19–20, Q: Have you ever testified as an expert witness in a shaken baby case?
> line 21, A: Yes
> line 22–23, Q: Have you ever been asked by a defendant to testify on their behalf?
> Page 11, line 1, A: Yes
> line 2, Q: Have you ever agreed before this case?
> line 3, A: No.
> line 4, Q: Why not?
> lines 5–11, A: Because basically the findings on the studies would not help the defendant in any way, shape or form. My policy is to give you what the straight story is based on the radiographic evidence. And I think in the couple of cases where I was asked to look at a case for the defense, it would have ended up convicting the defendant.
> lines 12–13, Q: Have you ever helped police authorities or prosecutors on cases of shaken baby or other child abuse?
> line 14, A: Every week

Cross examination of Dr. Zimmerman revealed the following:

> Page 33, line 9, Q: How many times? [Referring to the
> number of times the witness has testified in court.]
> lines 10–11, A: I would guess if you testify in court something
> like ten, eleven times totally.
> lines 16–17, Q: How many times for the prosecution in a
> criminal shaken baby case?
> line 18, A: I would say twice.
> lines 19–20, Q: So you have only testified for the prosecution
> two more times than you have for the defense?
> line 21, A: If you are talking about malpractice cases ...
> line 22, Q: No, I am talking about criminal cases, Doctor.
> line 23, A: Okay, I've only testified twice in criminal cases. ...

The attempt to bolster the doctor's credibility backfired when
confronted with the evidence that he was not choosing to testify
in this case solely because of some perceived injustice. The truth
was that this doctor had very limited experience testifying in any
criminal case. Preparation is essential in cross-examining the expert.
A complete review of the expert's prior court appearances allowed
the prosecutor to point out obvious exaggerations.

As previously mentioned, cross-examination regarding the actions
taken by the defense witness to discuss conflicting medical opinions
with the prosecution's witnesses is very effective. The prosecution
grilled Dr. Zimmerman about the efforts he had made to discuss the
medical conclusions of the prosecution's witnesses that he concluded
were plainly wrong. The fact that he had made no effort to discuss
his concerns with the other treating physicians undermined his
credibility.

Of concern to any lawyer is the notion of cross-examining the
true expert on his or her area of expertise. The seasoned expert
witness poses the greatest amount of difficulty for any attorney.
An excellent example of one prosecutor's ability to grasp intri-
cate medical concepts is that of Assistant District Attorney Martha
Coakley during the trial of Louise Woodward in *Commonwealth v.*

Woodward.[42] The prosecution faced many medical issues, including the dispute over CAT scan interpretations, evidence recovered during neurosurgery, and histological evidence recovered by the neuropathologist. The number of expert witnesses called by the defense was staggering. The defense team, led by Barry Scheck, called a nationally known pathologist, a neuropathologist, a neurosurgeon, and an expert in biomechanics. Despite the contradictory medical evidence, the prosecution presented a case in a manner that was understandable and logical, and it resulted in a verdict of guilt by the jury.

The prosecution's work in the Woodward case exemplifies the effort needed to succeed in cross-examining the defense expert.[43] Because of Coakley's work, the Woodward case provides an excellent primer for the medical controversies of shaken baby syndrome. The transcripts from that case would be helpful to any prosecutor who might face one of the defense experts who testified in that case.[44]

Finally, it is incumbent on the prosecutor to conduct a critical analysis of his or her case. Perhaps the case will have issues that will give rise to legitimate disagreements between medical experts. The prosecutor's experts should be able to point out these problems and suggest ways to deal with the controversies. The prosecutor should look critically at the literature that his or her own expert relies on. Understanding how to evaluate medical literature is essential to this process.

The pitfalls of irresponsible expert testimony cannot be overstated. One court noted, "There is hardly anything not palpably absurd on its face that cannot be proved by the so-called expert."[45] It is the prosecutor's duty to prevent this injustice by being prepared, aggressive, and diligent.

ACKNOWLEDGMENT

I gratefully acknowledge the assistance of Dr. Lyman Hunter, Susan Miles, and D. Bradley Marshall.

ENDNOTES

1. The term *shaken baby syndrome* has fallen out of favor with the medical community. It is now commonly referred to as *traumatic brain injury* or *abusive head trauma*.
2. Gardner, R. A. (1987). *The parental alienation syndrome and the differentiation between fabricated and genuine child sex abuse.* Creative Therapeutics.
3. Some jurisdictions have broad discovery rules that allow for disclosure of witness identity, and other states have very limited rules of discovery that do not require disclosure of the identity of potential witnesses.
4. Hagen, M. A. (1997). *Whores of the court: The fraud of psychiatric testimony and the rape of American justice.* Regan Books.
5. Ibid. at 101.
6. Dixon, J. W., & Dixon, K. E. (2003, summer). Gender-specific clinical syndromes and their admissibility under the federal rules of evidence. *American Journal of Trial Advocacy, 27,* 25. This article explores many of the syndromes raised in defense cases. Now, BWS is not raised as often, but defense experts will characterize the BWS defense as posttraumatic stress disorder.
7. *Commonwealth of Virginia v. Billy Leon Smalls,* CR44275, 44292, 44293 (1999) and *Commonwealth of Virginia v. Jennifer Nicole Talley,* CR 44276, 44294 (1999).
8. Immersion burns are characterized by a number of medical findings, including an area of sparing to the buttocks, a clear line of demarcation surrounding the burn and unburned flesh, and the lack of splash marks. See Reece, R. M. (2000). *Treatment of child abuse, common ground for mental health, medical and legal practitioners* (p. 124). Johns Hopkins University Press.
9. The Commonwealth of Virginia has very limited discovery rules. Rule 3A:11 of the Rules of the Supreme Court govern the discovery process. The identity of witnesses is not subject to the discovery process by either side.
10. Although the child abuse and burn experts all pinpointed an organization from New Jersey, none of them could remember the name of the organization.

11. Harry Gaynor was a member of The American Academy of Experts in Traumatic Stress (AAETS). He was the author of "The Root of Child Abuse: Anger" and referred to himself as Professor Harry J. Gaynor, PhD. As recently as July 26, 2006, the Web site for AAETS still maintained this article.

12. Testimony in the case *State of New Jersey v. Evelyn Orsini*, Cumberland County, New Jersey, Indictment Number 95-04-00354, cross-examination by Assistant State's Attorney Theresa Berresford:

    Page 40, line 8, Q: Do you have a degree?
    line 9, A: No, I do not.

13. Theresa Berresford, Assistant State's Attorney, Cumberland County, New Jersey, overnight expressed delivery of the transcript at her own expense to assist Prince William County, Virginia, prosecutors. Anthony Scarpelli, Assistant State's Attorney, Middlesex County, New Jersey, and Denise Schafer, Deputy Prosecuting Attorney, Jacksonville, Indiana, used the transcript from Prince William County to successfully impeach Gary Stocco when he appeared in their jurisdictions and later provided copies of their transcript for Stocco's subsequent criminal case. Assistant County Prosecutor Ava Rotell, Mansfield, Ohio, also provided transcripts and documents about Stocco.

14. At the time this case was being tried, Harry Gaynor was an octogenarian. It was assumed that he would not be the one to travel to Virginia to testify.

15. Voir dire is the process used to question the venire for jury selection as well as to question witnesses on limited topics, such as evidentiary foundations.

16. Gary S. Stocco was also a member of AAETS. He was the coauthor of "Trauma Dreams in a Pre-Schooler Scaled (sic) as a Toddler: A Clinical Illustration." This article was downloaded as recently as July 26, 2006. Stocco claimed that he has a master's degree in public health.

17. Prosecutors had an older CV of Stocco's. In this CV, Stocco mentioned Gaynor's name throughout the document. When the defense produced Stocco's latest CV, any reference to Gaynor had been removed.

18. Court's ruling during the voir dire hearing of Gary S. Stocco in Prince William County, Virginia, February 26, 1999, pp. 93–94.

19. It should be noted that very early on, the prosecution tried to strike a "gentleman's agreement." They offered to disclose the names of their experts if the defense would do the same. They further offered that the names would be disclosed on the record and that both sides would be

bound to use the experts they named or to update the other side on the record of any changes to the expert witness list. The defense declined the offer and was unprepared to cross-examine the Commonwealth's expert, claiming surprise!

20. An exhaustive investigation into Stocco's credentials revealed that Columbia State University was, in fact, a diploma mill. The Louisiana attorney general and the United States postal inspector had closed down the "mail drop diploma mill" prior to Stocco even completing the purchase of his degree. The University of San Moritz was also considered a diploma mill. A Boston, Massachusetts, news station had previously done an exposé on the University of San Moritz and purchased a doctorate degree for the news producer's dog.

21. The defendant was indicted on one count of perjury pursuant to 18.2-434 of the Code of Virginia, 1950, as amended; one count of perjury pursuant to 18.2-435 of the Code of Virginia, 1950, as amended; and one count of obtaining money by false pretenses pursuant to 18.2-178 of the Code of Virginia, 1950, as amended. The two perjury indictments were obtained because the Commonwealth had two distinct theories. The first perjury charge was based on the defendant's false swearing that he was actively pursuing his degree from Columbia State University. The "school" had been closed down by the Louisiana Office of the Attorney General several months prior to his testifying in Prince William County. The second perjury charge was based on the conflicting testimonies in New Jersey, Virginia, Ohio, and Indiana.

22. *Commonwealth v. Gary S. Stocco*, Criminal Docket Numbers 48156, 48157, 48586.

23. This occurred in a recent shaken baby case. The expert routinely consulted with the attorneys. Talking to prosecutors in the same jurisdiction as the defense experts and defense attorneys produced invaluable information regarding this relationship.

24. In Virginia, the Commonwealth's Attorneys Services Council stores information provided by prosecutors and maintains a closed forum for an exchange of information about experts. The American Prosecutors Research Institute in Alexandria, Virginia, is also very helpful. This is the nonprofit educational arm of the NDAA.

25. www.shakenbabydefense.com

26. www.msbp.com

27. Ezell, A., & Bear, J. (2005). *Degree mills: The billion-dollar industry that has sold over a million fake diplomas.* Prometheus Books. The Web site is www.degree.net. This site provides a vast amount of information detailing how to evaluate secondary education institutions.

28. American Academy of Pediatrics, Committee on Medical Liability. (1989). Guidelines for expert witness testimony. *Pediatrics, 83,* 312–313. See also American Academy of Pediatrics, Committee on Medical Liability. (1994). Guidelines for expert testimony in medical liability cases. *Pediatrics, 94,* 755–756.

29. The National Center for Prosecution of Child Abuse is a division of the American Prosecutors Research Institute and is located at 99 Canal Center Plaza, Suite 510, Alexandria, VA 22314.

30. In the case of Gary Stocco, his testimony dramatically changed in 2000, when he testified in *State of New Jersey v. Sedgewick Paige,* Middlesex County Indictment Number 98-04-00565-I:

> Page 112, line 18, Q: Okay. Now, your college degree that you've obtained, you have a bachelor's degree and a master's degree. Is that correct?
> line 21, A: Yes
> line 22, Q: And where did you obtain that degree from?
> line 23, A: From the University of San Moritz.
> Page 115, line 14, Q: What about Columbia State University, do you remember ever attending there?
> line 16, A: No.

31. In another shaken baby case, a former medical examiner claimed to have performed autopsies on one to two dozen babies who had been shaken. Once the records from the Office of the Medical Examiner had been subpoenaed, it was shocking to learn that he had never reported a case of shaken baby syndrome and had only performed four autopsies on babies under one year with head trauma.

32. Referring to the transcript cited in Reece (2000) (see endnote 8), the cross-examination on this issue was as follows:

> Page 50, line 10, Q: Your CV indicates that you were a state police officer, and you were a New Jersey State police officer?
> line 12, A: No, ma'am.
> line 13, Q: What is a state police officer?
> line 14, A: My title was state police officer, Department of Human Services.
> line 16, Q: So you were not affiliated with the New Jersey State Police?
> line 18, A: No, ma'am.
> line 19, Q: Have you ever told anyone you were?
> line 20, A: No.

By the time he testified in *State of Indiana vs. Guadalupe Morales*, Cause Number 10D01-9902-CF-010, Stocco had changed his title:

Page 6, line 24, Q: What other types of experience have you had, other types of employment.
Page 7, line 2, A: I was a police officer for the State of New Jersey, in the Department of Human Resources which is a specialized police department in New Jersey.

33. American Psychiatric Association (APA). (1994). Issues in the use of *DSM IV* (p. xxiii). In *Diagnostic and statistical manual of mental disorders* (4th ed.). The current edition is the *DSM-IV-TR* (text revised). The *DSM-V* is expected in 2011. One must be sure to have the latest edition of the manual. One must also be sure to check for material changes in the manual from one text to another and investigate these changes for cross-examination purposes.
34. An example is Rogers, R. (1997). *Clinical assessment of malingering and deception* (2nd ed.). The Guilford Press.
35. An example is Reece (2000) (see endnote 8). This text also provides an excellent starting point for gathering medical literature on many topics.
36. Holmgren, B. K. (2001). Prosecuting the shaken infant case (pp. 275–331). In S. Lazoritz & V. J. Palusci (Eds.), *The shaken baby syndrome: A multidisciplinary approach*. Hawthorne Maltreatment and Trauma Press.
37. *Daubert v. Merrill Dow Pharmaceuticals Inc.*, 509 U.S. 579, 113 S. Ct. 2786, 125 L.Ed.2d 469 (1993); *Frye v. United States*, 54 App. D.C. 46, 293 F. 1013(1923).
38. Holmgren, Ibid. at 293.
39. *Commonwealth v. Eleanor Kay Hinegardner*, Criminal Docket Number 32453, May 24, 1993. Transcript from May 26, 1993, pages 40–41.
40. *The Quarterly Update* is supported, in part, by the Massachusetts Society for the Prevention of Cruelty to Children. Their Web site is www.quarterlyupdate.org.
41. *Commonwealth v. Eleanor Kay Hinegardner*, Criminal Docket Number 32453, May 24, 1993. The defendant was indicted on one charge of felony child abuse pursuant to 18.2–371.1 of the Code of Virginia, 1950, as amended.
42. *Commonwealth v. Woodward* (1998) Supreme Judicial Court for Suffolk County, Middlesex Superior Court. Case number 97–433.

43. It is often overlooked that the prosecution was successful in the case against Louise Woodward as the jury convicted her of second-degree murder. The judge reduced the charge to manslaughter and sentenced Woodward to time served.
44. The defense experts included Dr. Jan Leetsma, Dr. Michael Baden, Dr. Alisa Gean, Dr. Lawrence Thibault, Dr. Ayub Ommaya, and Dr. Ronald Uscinski.
45. Holmgren, Ibid. at 313, citing *Chaulk v. Volkswagen of America Inc.*, 808 F. 2d 639, 644 (7th Circuit, 1986).

CHAPTER NINE

MADNESS IN THE SUPREME COURT: NULLIFYING ITS OWN RULES OF SCIENTIFIC EVIDENCE

The Phenomenon of Lack of Insight as a Corrective to Judicial Nullification in Civil Commitment Proceedings

Paul F. Stavis, JD

INTRODUCTION

The Enlightenment essentially planted the seeds of science into the fertile soil of American law and culture. Newtonian science revealed the relationship between "cause and effect," using mathematics and established that the laws of nature were knowable, quantifiable and verifiable through empirical processes. One medical manifestation of this new epistemological energy and optimism was the early 19th-century belief that mental illness was a curable as a disease of the brain and not, as previously believed a divine scarlet letter or a punishment for the unholy.

Yet, despite early psychiatry's gross over-optimism of the complexity of the brain in the 19th century—indeed, a profound under-appreciation that, in fact, persisted until the last 20 years—was the hope and confidence that science would eventually not only understand but also conquer the most enigmatic state of the human condition. This became a goal of medicine and public policy in the early 19th century; that goal continues today.

The optimism of the Enlightenment era was most heartily adopted by the New World's first constitutional democracy. Notably, this was the world's first written constitution that placed the authority and responsibility on government to promote the general welfare by treating the mentally ill in hospitals. This matter of both medical science and public policy were jewels in the crown of the American Revolution. The mentally ill, in theory and in an evolving practice among the states, would no longer be subject to punitive incarceration as exiles but would be treated with public sympathy, and funds would be allotted and a strong effort made to understand and cure mental illness. A scientific point of view was taken by medical professionals, politicians, and the public at large to treat mental illness as a disease.

While science has long been an integral part of American jurisprudence, the courts have only gingerly or superficially probed the scientific method. The so-called *Frye* test has ruled for most of the 20th century, demanding little more than that admissible scientific evidence be "generally accepted" by the relevant scientific community. However, a jurisprudential contradiction was created when the United States Supreme Court developed a new rule in the trilogy of cases known as *Daubert, Joiner,* and *Kumho.*[1] In essence, these cases reiterate that scientific methodology should be the preferred predicate of the Federal Rules of Evidence, in particular Rule 702 (FRE 702). The Court made it very clear that scientific methodology was a fundamental requirement to ensure the reliability and veracity of evidence and to permit its admissibility in a court of law. In its simplest formulation, there is a preference for empirical scientific evidence that is verifiable ("falsifiable") and repeatable, over mere opinionated scientific testimony.

The thesis of this chapter is that the Supreme Court has ignored its own mandate for empirical science when it comes to mental illness issues, particularly those where compulsory treatment is sought by the state. Moreover, this anomaly has led to an unconscious judicial nullification of both the role of science in law as well as the traditional *parens patriae* powers of the states. Every lawyer knows that judges at every level can nullify law;[2] the most well-known example is declaring a statute unconstitutional. However, the type of nullification produced under the Court's mental illness jurisprudence is different in many ways, as will be discussed here, but most of all, it has not been identified in either scholarly literature or in any judicial decision.

There are three types of judicial nullification of mental hygiene law. One occurs at the trial level, the second affects the role of science as a foundation of the rules of evidence, and the third nullifies the traditional authority and responsibility of the government *parens patriae* regarding the treatment of persons with mental illness. Yet all three forms of judicial nullification discussed here have a common genesis in the adoption of the so-called dangerous test for compulsory treatments for mental illness.

The emergence by judicial fiat, in the latter part of the 20th century, that clear and convincing proof of "dangerousness," whether already occurred or predicted, has ironically turned persons with mental illness disabilities from victims into the perpetrators of the dangers they encounter rather than create. Under this new concept, a mentally ill person who cannot avoid committing a dangerous act is labeled "dangerous" in a manner identical to a person who willfully or otherwise is the source of the dangerous acts against him or herself or others. In effect, the conceptual confusion has diminished government benevolence, and its sole function has become one of protecting or policing society and individuals. Even worse, under the guise of civil rights sensitivity, current law masks the inertia of mental health bureaucracies in dealing with mental illness under civil law, making criminal law and the criminal justice system the default for treating mental illness.

Finally, this chapter recommends a return to empirical or "evidence-based" mental hygiene jurisprudence by judicial recognition of the condition known as "anosognosia." There is a growing body of scientific and medical knowledge, well over 100 multifaceted empirical studies that verify the phenomenon of "lack of insight"[3] as an organic product and symptom of most serious cases of mental illness. This criterion of serious mental illness was recently incorporated into the *Diagnostic and Statistical Manual*, version IV-TR (*DSM-IV-TR*).[4] It is argued that this diagnosis has been shown to be scientifically sound, empirically testable, and the closest clinical finding to what approximates the legal notion of competence to make medical and psychiatric decisions.

JUDICIAL NULLIFICATION

"Nullification" simply means "without legal effect or status."[5] It is most well known in the context of jury nullification[6] and more rarely discussed when judges do it—perhaps because we view judges as professionals who are universally sworn to uphold and faithfully follow the laws. The judicial form of nullification, however, produces the most concern for a society based on the rule of law. The founding fathers were quite concerned and deliberated about the idea of judicial nullification—especially of traditional constitutional principles and the use of the Constitution to nullify statutes, the will of the majority, and the role of the legislature.[7]

The three forms of judicial nullification discussed here are, therefore, unusual in that they are clearly based solely on judicial behaviors. They exist by virtue of the neologism "danger to self," and they find no previous expression in judicial opinion or scholarly literature.

De Facto Judicial Nullification by Trial Courts

"De facto" nullification at the trial court level frequently occurs in compulsory treatment cases where judges strongly believe that the person with mental illness needs treatment, and the "dangerousness" standard is weak or inapplicable. Given the ambiguity and malleability of the *dangerous* concept, a trial judge can easily spin the circumstances for almost any homeless, mentally ill person to conjure up a variety of "danger to self" scenarios, such as an inability to dress adequately for severely cold weather—finding in almost every case something that is potentially, actually, or prospectively *dangerous*.

The motivation for this form of nullification is usually far from venal. To the contrary, it becomes a convenience of legal interpretation that allows trial judges, perhaps even unconsciously, to use a commonsense approach based on a traditional *parens patriae* analysis. The constrictions of contemporary mental health law are more than offset by the ambiguities of danger to self, so that the judge can bypass the strictures and address the practical question of whether the patient genuinely needs and would benefit from psychiatric care, despite protestations of incompetence. This type of judicial nullification is beneficent, traditional *parens patriae*.

Evidentiary Judicial Nullification
Parens patriae commitments, formerly based on a clinical determination that a person is sick, in need of care, and unable to competently consent or to refuse, have given way to a homogenous jurisprudence based on an ambiguous notion of *dangerousness*. It is a traditional aspect of government's power and purpose to distinguish and deal with a person who is actually dangerous to society, in contrast with others who a susceptible to dangers. Government, therefore, needs to distinguish who should be detained as a preventive measure from a person who is simply very sick and not able to address his illness due to lack of awareness or inability to consent. These two very different instances of state-imposed treatment call for different approaches, but contemporary jurisprudence has homogenized the two under a univocal legal requirement to show that the patient is dangerous. For the simply sick person, this is inconsistent with contemporary scientific knowledge and good clinical practice. There exists neither a reliable scientific methodology that can assess the likelihood of future dangerousness

nor any expert, particularly in psychiatry, who can predict prospective dangerous behavior with a greater-than-chance level of accuracy.

The Supreme Court has properly acknowledged that predictions of prospective dangerousness, whether highly reliable or not, are necessary and appropriate for many applications of law, such as capital punishment, parole, probation, child custody, protective orders, or pretrial detention. However, for *parens patriae* civil commitments, the *dangerousness* criterion is neither necessary nor desirable. It is not representative of the best science, the best evidence, or the best clinical practice. Although the Court has reaffirmed the existence of the *parens patriae* power of the states, its own decisions have cast doubt on its continuing existence, or at least its traditional meaning, in civil commitment proceedings. To the extent that reliance is exclusively placed on predicting prospective dangerousness, it fails to comport with the Daubert-Joiner-Kumho principles by nullifying their holdings.

Parens Patriae Judicial Nullification
The most pernicious form of judicial nullification has been the conceptual homogenization of the governmental police power and *parens patriae* power. The erosion of the latter was accomplished through largely judicially constructed, nontraditional concepts of liberty and freedom. These decisions have not strictly maintained the distinction between the ancient *authority* of the state to intervene to protect society and the more historically recent *responsibility* of government to assist an individual who is incompetent.

The results of confusing the state's role as policeman with its role as parent are significant inhibitions to assisting seriously and persistently mentally ill citizens who, in fact, are in need of help but are not dangerous in any true sense of the word. In such cases, the state is compelled to use the more stringent justifications of the police power and the difficult and cumbersome process of the criminal law, rather than more conducive and benevolent welfare powers that may often be justified by less than preponderant standard of evidence, for example, by "rational relationship," often meaning application of broad professional standards. Our nation has, perhaps inadvertently, reverted from a compassionate approach to helping persons with serious mental illness, to the approach of a bygone time when the disease was criminalized and the persons suffering from it were persecuted. Our mental health law and policy is once again in a dark age.[8]

It is clinically counterproductive for the courts to use litigation as a substitute for a full range of medical options, including aggressive care where appropriate.[9]

PART ONE: PANDORA'S DANGEROUS BOX

> *"[D]angerousness" is a many splendored thing. Unless muzzled by discriminating analysis, it is likely to weigh against nominally competing considerations the way a wolf weighs against a sheep in the same scales: even if the sheep is heavier when weighed separately, somehow the wolf always prevails when the two are weighed together. Keeping dangerousness on a taut leash is especially difficult where there is danger of murder, since the danger is admittedly grave and since its improbability, which theoretically discounts its gravity, is exceedingly difficult to quantify.[10]*

The two most important judicial decisions to require "dangerousness" for exercise of compulsory treatment were *Lessard v. Schmidt* and *O'Connor v. Donaldson*.[11] In the years following these decisions, almost all state legislatures inserted some notion of "dangerousness" into civil commitment statutes, even to justify the exercise of otherwise *parens patriae* civil commitment power. However, there is good reason to believe that the *Lessard* Court promoted this new meaning of "dangerousness" based on a misunderstood and misrepresented historical role of treatment rendered to the seriously mentally ill in 19th-century psychiatric hospitals.

For more than 150 years preceding these decisions, the law permitted civil commitment on two distinctive bases: The law recognized both the right to restrain persons who were dangerous to others or to social order and the obligation to help those who had a "need for treatment" but incompetently refused or could not to consent to it.[12]

Of course, there were some civil commitments based on governmental police power and the need to protect society and its citizens from those behaviors of persons with mental illness that caused or threatened harm. Where possible, families cared for their mentally ill members unless their condition became unmanageable, such as where a person was dangerous to the safety of other family members. In such cases, hospitalization was sought primarily to deter the patient from causing harm, and secondarily to treat the patient. Such commitments might be based on civil law, such as a commitment to a civil hospital, or pursuant to criminal law by incarceration in a prison or forensic hospital. The latter is a form of preventive detention to protect society from criminal behavior or threats of harm, or could be due to the inability of the person to be held legally responsible due to incompetence caused by mental illness.

The contrast between treating a person for his or her own good and detaining a person primarily for the good of society is essential and fundamental. It reflects the difference between ensuring individual civil rights, as accorded to a competent person, that defines adulthood and rights of citizenship, in contrast to the necessity for state intervention in curtailment of an individual's civil rights for the benefit of society, whether that individual is competent or not. The intervention of the state for benevolent purposes is the polar opposite of state intervention for punitive purposes. In the former case, the patient is a beneficiary, whereas in the latter the patient is a detainee and society is the beneficiary. The *parens patriae* is a much more recent and enlightened understanding by society and a historically novel responsibility of government.

Of course, altruism and the importance of the individual have deep roots in ancient Greek and Roman law and culture.[13] Yet it was English law that allowed the king to take responsibility for the fundamental welfare of individuals who were unable to manage their own affairs, such as children, idiots, and lunatics who had no other direct caregivers or surrogates, such as family, friends, or guardians.[14] The significance of this development in political philosophy and governmental law cannot be overstated. It became a defining element of American law and culture, reflected, among other places, in the Preamble to the Constitution that talks of "providing for the common defense" (police power) and "promoting the general welfare" (*parens patriae* power).

Sir Henry Sumner Maine connects the events and individuals of our Constitution with these Enlightenment ideas:

> The American lawyers of the time [of the American Revolution], and particularly in Virginia, appear to have possessed a stock of knowledge which differed chiefly from that of their English contemporaries including much which could only have been derived from the legal literature of continental Europe. A very few glances at the writings of Jefferson will show how strongly his mind was affected by the semi-juridical, semi-popular opinion which were fashionable in France, and we cannot doubt that it was sympathy with the peculiar ideas of the French jurists which led him and the other colonial lawyers who guided the course of events in America to join the specially French assumption that "all men are born equal" with the assumption, more familiar to Englishmen, that "all men are born free," in the very first lines of their Declaration of Independence.[15]

These rights applied in common to individuals who were incapable of rational behavior in their own self-interests or who engaged in disordered behavior beyond what society or the culture would tolerate.[16] Thus, children, lunatics, and idiots were not considered wholly free like other citizens, but were subject to the guidance of their parents, guardians, or the king. It was assumed by most 17th- to 19th-century European thinkers, such as Hegel, Kant, Rousseau, Locke, and Mill, that the concept of liberty by definition involves a rational or intelligent choice based on enlightened self-interest to also act responsibly. Legal rights that could not be exercised rationally, within acceptable norms of adult competence, did not have meaning and, therefore, were not available to persons who were mentally impaired. Even today, except for the growing "mature minor doctrine,"[17] a minor-aged child is still per se incompetent and, therefore, denied the right to exercise many freedoms accorded to adults. The exercise of liberty is meaningless absent rational decision making.[18]

Dr. Darold Treffert is noted for his article, "Dying With Their Rights On."[19] He has argued that equating liberty and freedom to the absence of physical restraint is simplistic and anti-therapeutic in many cases.

> What kind of "freedom" is it to be wandering the streets severely mentally ill, deteriorating, and getting warmth from a steel grate or food from a garbage can? That's not freedom; that's abandonment. And what kind of "liberty" is it to be jailed for disorderly conduct, crazed and delusional, because that is all the law will allow, instead of being hospitalized, treated and released? That's not liberty, that's imprisonment for the crime of being sick.[20]

Despite the court repeating the mantra that civil commitment is always "massive deprivation of liberty, when it can be fundamental in the restoration of a person's ability to exercise autonomous decision making and to control the debilitations of mental illness, then it is an enhancement of freedom as defined in Enlightenment philosophy.[21] Supreme Court Justice Stephen Field aptly noted a distinction between the misconception of liberty as being free to wander and the essence of liberty as truly free to fulfill one's own destiny and seek the happiness that comes with a rationally sentient existence and to live with the blessing of a social order:

> By the term "liberty," as used in the provision [Fourteenth Amendment], something more is meant than mere freedom from physical restraint or the bounds of a prison. It means freedom to go where one may choose, and to act in such a manner, not inconsistent with the equal rights of others, as his judgment may dictate for the promotion of his happiness, that is, to pursue such callings and avocations as may be most suitable develop his capacities, and give to them their highest enjoyment[22]

Civil commitment by judicial process was largely created in the latter part of the 19th century. The legal justification of civil commitments then was the clinical need for treatment and the disability of a person to realize or obtain it.[23] Naturally enough, persons who were violent due to mental illness, alcoholism, and suicide attempts, or who had strange behaviors with hallucinations, depression, and extraordinary or inappropriate excitement, could be and were committed on the basis of the danger they posed to others and to society generally. Commitments based on such dangerousness could be civil or criminal in nature at the discretion of government authorities, the hospital, or prosecutors in the community. Families, often due to an inability to care for their relatives and the need for more intensive professional attention than available at home, hospitalized the majority of civilly committed patients.[24]

Accordingly, civil commitment was not viewed as a legal matter but as a human need. It was not considered a violation of human rights but a restoration of civil rights, including the possibility of and hope for restoration to the family, community, and society. Although laws became more procedurally involved toward the end of the 19th century, they never posed a serious obstacle to civil commitment when there were clinical grounds indicating a need for treatment. As noted by Professor Paul S. Appelbaum, if *dangerousness* were employed more prominently for purposes of hospitalization, it was only because families cared for and retained their mentally ill member until disordered behavior became more than they could handle and not because dangerousness was in any sense legally required by common or statutory law.[25] Thus, commitment for dangerous behavior did not reflect a legal necessity or common law principle; rather, it reflected the familial reality that when a mentally ill member became violent or dangerous around younger children, older relatives, or other vulnerable persons, they could no longer be cared for in the household or without continuous professional attention.

The other conceptual fallacy that is seen constantly in these cases is the term *free will*. Even for patients who clearly have no capacity for understanding, the courts will refer to their refusals as decisions of their free will.[26] Legal tradition has long held that "where there is no discernment, there is no choice; and where there is no choice, there can be no act of the will... ."[27]

Civil commitment itself was neither automatic nor universal for those presented to the hospitals by families. The hospitals performed triage to allocate limited hospital resources within the prevailing cultural standard that looked to the family to be primarily responsible for their mentally ill members, unless such care became impossibly difficult or treatment required professional intervention. Thus, although the initiation of civil commitment typically came from the family, there was a requirement for clinical ratification by physicians. The oversight by the judicial process simply addressed whether a proper clinical evaluation was made by an appropriate professional but did not address the quality or sufficiency of treatment for which a court was not competent to inquire.[28]

To commit an individual was seemingly a complex process. In 1892, 5 states empowered justices of the peace to commit mentally ill persons to hospitals; 18 granted this authority to judges; 5 required a lay jury trial; and 3 others stipulated that at least one member of the jury had to be a physician. Three states used a court-appointed commission and two an asylum board; nine others required just a medical certificate. Where the power to commit rested with a court, a physician whose findings were binding usually made provision for a medical examination, and the court simply recorded the decision. Despite the complexity of the system, the overwhelming majority of families did not find commitment a difficult undertaking or one that involved lawyers and protracted conflict. Where a prominent person was involved, a particular episode might receive national publicity. But such cases were relatively infrequent. On a different level, the legal and psychiatric professions fought bitterly over commitment procedures. This struggle usually involved varying theoretical assumptions about the nature of individual responsibility, human behavior, and mental illness. Although laws tended to become more specific toward the end of the century, they posed no serious obstacle to commitment. Given an individual with severe behavioral symptoms but without a family, legal procedures were administered in a loose and informal manner. The problem of commitment was for the most part perceived in human rather than strictly legal terms.[29]

If a mentally ill person was considered truly dangerous, the most likely place of his or her incarceration was the jail, not a hospital.[30] The prevalent standard for civil commitment was thus a breakdown of the parenting function of care and guidance whether provided by the immediate family, a guardian for that person, or intervention by the state. If hospitalization was called for, it did not involve steep procedural barriers. This was a true *parens patriae* scenario where the state literally became an extension of the family as a parent of last resort. When mental illness caused violence or a threat of harm, the threatening person was subject to criminal prosecution or commitment based on that dangerous behavior. In the latter case, the commitment under police power is not primarily for the sake of the individual's well being, but rather for the sake of society. The difference between acting in a genuine parental role and imposing punishment is clearly enormous. Only when the family cannot supply the joint parental powers of paternal protection (ordering and supervision) and maternal care (nurturing and healing) would the state be justified in stepping in, since culturally the state defers to the family. The *parens patriae* power was not as much a conceptual justification for intervention by the state, as a discretionary responsibility taken at the request, absence, or inability of the primary family.

The demise of the centuries old doctrine of *parens patriae* and its replacement by a dangerousness prerequisite came with many other judicial mandates during the activist years of the 1960s and 1970s.[31] Roughly, it began with statutory reform in California, most significantly the enactment of the Laterman-Petris-Short Act that required a finding of dangerousness to civilly commit a person with mental illness.[32] Other legislative actions did the same. The District of Columbia reformed its law by adopting a dangerousness standard in place of the *parens patriae* standard.[33] In a comprehensive 1961 study by the American Bar Foundation, only 5 jurisdictions used dangerousness as the singular criterion for civil commitment for inpatient hospital care and 12 other states used it as an alternate justification for commitment. Twenty-four years later, it was a necessary predicate in civil commitment cases in 45 states or jurisdictions.[34] Today, all state statutes, and most courts in their written decisions, utilize either "danger to others" or "danger to self" or a conjunction of the two as a basis of civil commitment.[35]

The *Lessard* decision is considered the "high-water mark in 'dangerousness' law."[36] It held that under the Constitution a patient cannot be civilly committed on the basis of being "in need of treatment." This effectively caused a metamorphosis, converting civil proceedings into crypto-criminal ones by mandating the use of most criminal procedures, for example, requiring "proof beyond a reasonable doubt" as a burden upon the government or proponent of civil commitment,[37] right to counsel,[38] privilege against self-incrimination,[39] exclusion of hearsay testimony,[40] and most significantly the requirement that not only must "dangerousness" be proved, but it must also be "imminent" in nature.[41]

Lessard's fundamental concepts have remained, even though no subsequent decision has gone quite as far in reproducing the complete panoply of criminal law upon a civil commitment.[42]

Ms. Alberta Lessard—the patient-respondent in the case— had schizophrenia, but there was no evidence that she was ever dangerous to anyone. Nevertheless the court, making many analogies to criminal law, equated the fundamental interests of a patient facing civil commitment with a criminal defendant facing jail:

> The power of the state to deprive a person of the fundamental liberty to go unimpeded about his or her affairs must rest on a consideration that society has a compelling interest in such deprivation. In criminal cases, this authority is derived from the police power... . [I]n civil commitment proceedings the same fundamental liberties are at stake.[43]

> The boy is charged with misconduct. The boy is committed to an institution where he may be restrained of liberty for years. It is of no constitutional consequence—and of limited practical meaning—the institution to which he is committed is called an Industrial School. "The fact of the matter is that, however euphemistic the title, a 'receiving home' or an 'industrial

school' for juveniles is an institution of confinement in which the child is incarcerated for a greater or lesser time...for anything from waywardness to rape and homicide."[44]

The facts are that Gerald Francis Gault was charged under a criminal statute and he received a determinate sentence. Thus, the length of the sentence was not directly tied to amelioration as in a civil commitment.[45] In addition, the conviction carried a determination of "immoral" behavior and the institutional incarceration was jail-like in every respect. The Court held that such a proceeding "must be regarded as 'criminal'...[and] [t]o hold otherwise would be to disregard substance because of the feeble enticement of the 'civil' label-of-convenience which has been attached to juvenile proceedings."[46]

Thus, despite strong collateral purposes to rehabilitate the juvenile, avoid stigmatization, raise the quality of moral culpability, and preserve the future of a youth, the *Gault* case unquestionably involved state police power. Nevertheless, the juvenile delinquent is incarcerated primarily to protect public safety even if rehabilitation is also a strong secondary consideration. However, obviously, with a conviction, the youth would not be incarcerated merely for his treatment needs.

Lessard's application of *Gault* could not be more stark. The former involved a woman who was endangered by her ordinary surroundings and activities and needed to be restrained temporarily for psychiatric treatment which would ultimately enhance her quality of life; the latter involved a youth who needed to be restrained for the public's safety, not primarily for his own benefit. *Lessard* characterized its own decision accurately: "We fail to see any distinction between the juvenile delinquency hearing and the civil commitment hearing...the seriousness of the deprivation of liberty and the consequences which follow an adjudication of mental illness...[are] proceedings in which an individual's liberty is in jeopardy."[47] This new unified dangerousness standard, however, failed to distinguish between the label *dangerous* as applied to individuals who were violent, suicidal, and self-destructive as against those who were merely sick, mentally incompetent, and unable to live without being harmed or victimized by dangers outside their control, not emanating from their behavior.[48] Being unable to avoid victimization might be called "jeopardy to self," but surely it is not being any "danger to self" because there is no self-infliction of harm. The significantly heavier burdens of a criminal-type trial made the task and probability of the government intervening to help someone, as opposed to protecting the public, much more difficult and unlikely. The *Lessard* decision was the landmark that reformulated civil commitment proceedings as crypto-criminal.

In Wisconsin, after *Lessard* was decided, it is not surprising that in 2 years the number of criminal commitments related to mental illness institutions showed an increase.[49] With these institutions, the "new" jurisprudence that homogenized the police and *parens patriae* powers also had the volatile effect of mixing patients who were truly dangerous and had aggressive tendencies with those who were merely sick and easy prey.

DANGEROUS ITERATIONS

Dangerousness is not a diagnosis, it is a behavioral consequence; clearly, it is neither a medical condition, nor an illness.[50] Where one person perpetrates or causes harm to another or is the active cause of harm to oneself, the danger is not hard to define or to identify. What internally motivates such behavior is much harder to know, whether it is mental illness, psychopathy, pecuniary gain, negligence, or sheer adventurism. The term that *Lessard* resurrected from earlier cases, *danger to self*,[51] is a befuddling term that has corrupted the law. This is because that term is being used to substitute for a *parens patriae* type of intervention.

The irony of that phrase is that it was intended to enhance the dignity and rights of persons with mental illness, but rather, it has inaccurately ascribed harm-causing tendencies to those who are normally victims.[52] This approach backfires because persons with mental illness are unnecessarily stigmatized as "dangerous" and, due to the complicated nature of due process making intervention much less likely, they also get less treatment and less protection from the state in the way of funds or other social services.[53] In short, *danger to self* tends to discriminate and harm as opposed to protect. *Mentally ill* and *dangerous* describe two different characteristics of the individual neither of which by itself justifies compulsory treatment.[54] "As a consequence, the 'mentally ill and dangerous' classification as a predicate for otherwise impermissible prolonged, preemptive confinement raises a substantial question of discrimination against the mentally ill."[55]

The standard dictionary definition does not define *dangerous to oneself* because the word *dangerous* describes an actor who causes or the object who suffers harm through aggression, destructive behaviors, or potential for inflicting harms.[56] This distinguishes between someone who is harmed from passivity from one who harms by activity upon others. In nature, uninfluenced by a mental illness, self-preservation, self interest, and[57] pain-avoidance are universal behaviors, with few exceptions.[58]

Professor Alexander D. Brooks, a leading authority on mental illness law, has written about the *O'Connor* decision's replacement of traditional *parens patriae* with "danger to self" capping the "trend toward the inclusion of disablement with the concept of dangerous."[59] He says it was:

> [a]n unfortunate development, since the stronger term "dangerousness" does tend to stigmatize. It is inappropriate to refer to a gravely disabled person as a "dangerous" person, with the potential for misunderstanding that may be involved. Yet, by suggesting dangerousness as a constitutional requirement for involuntary civil commitment, the Supreme Court may have boxed itself into a unrealistic label.[60]

The Supreme Court made this momentous change without comment, merely on a footnote concerning the charge to the jury by the trial court judge.[61] More curiously, there was no context or meaning for this phrase supported by any facts of the case. There was no explanation of how the word *dangerous* could accurately be applied to Kenneth Donaldson. For example, Donaldson was not committed due to dangerous behavior, he was never known to be dangerous during his decade and a half in the psychiatric hospital, and he was not dangerous after his release.[62] Any critical reader of this decision must wonder why the concept of dangerous was even mentioned in the decision by either the trial court or the Supreme Court except antithetically to the actual facts of the case.

In the absence of evidence of dangerousness,[63] the Court notes that the grounds for commitment were immaterial to its decision. The case only involved continuing incarceration and, again, there was no evidence of dangerousness nor of a need for care. Indeed, the Court reiterated numerous times that the case was not about which commitment standards are constitutional or legitimate.[64] Yet certainly the case has been interpreted as establishing new standards for civil commitment.

It is difficult to understand how the vast majority of the legal establishment, including virtually every legislature as well as most state and federal courts, have come to understand *O'Connor* as mandating a dangerousness requirement to justify civil commitment for any person who is not the source or threat of harm but more likely the victim of it.[65] The only holding that can unquestionably be distilled from the key, but open-ended, language used by the Court is obvious and does not even need articulation.[66] The Court was saying that mental illness, be it mild, moderate, or severe, alone does not provide a justification to involuntarily hospitalize a person for their own good, for amelioration, or for any other reason.[67] It would be absurd to say otherwise, given that tens of millions of people in the United States will suffer from a mental disorder during their lifetime.[68] Certainly, it is general knowledge that states cannot, for financial reasons alone, hospitalize everyone with any form of mental illness. Rather, the power and justification to compel treatment has two straightforward rationales: a person with mental illness must either (1) be incompetent to make decisions in their own best interests[69] or (2) have a substantially diminished ability to be legally responsible so that they pose a threat to society or civil order—in other words, are dangerous to others.[70]

With a flavor of Alice in Wonderland, the Court misperceived the role of compulsory treatment for mental illness, calling it a "massive curtailment of liberty."[71] This often repeated universal rubric connotes that all persons involved in compulsory care—judges, state officials, physicians, nurses, therapy aides, or family—consort to "deprive" the patient of freedom, as if it were a penal rather than a therapeutic activity.

The Court properly assumed that "[mental illness] can be given a reasonably precise content and...identified with reasonable accuracy"[72] and declared that "[a] finding of 'mental illness' alone cannot justify a State's locking a person up...[and] [a State cannot] confine the mentally ill merely to ensure them a [superior] living standard."[73] The Court was correct in assuming that "mental illness" could be given a reasonably precise clinical definition.[74] Mental illnesses are defined and categorized by many internationally authoritative scientific groups, such as the American Psychiatric Association and the World Health Organization. Their definitions are found in the DSM[75] or in the International Classification of Diseases.[76] Certainly, the etiology of mental illness is still not known, and the definitions, as with many other types of illness, are changed from time to time; but the Court wisely did not reject the concept of "mental health" simply because it is "not easy to define."[77] It is a disease that, like many other formerly mysterious diseases, is being understood with the help of new technologies. The treatments for mental illness are evolving and improving at a pace akin to those more commonly known miracle drugs so often in the news.[78]

Court's enigmatic observation "In short, a State cannot constitutionally confine without more a nondangerous individual who is capable of surviving safely in freedom by himself or with the help of willing and responsible family members or friends,"[79] raises the obvious question "without more WHAT?"[80] What the Court meant by a "nondangerous individual" and "dangerous to self," is determined by reference to the jury charge administered by the trial court:[81]

> The judge's instructions used the phrase "dangerous to himself." Of course, even if there is no foreseeable risk of self-injury or suicide, a person is literally "dangerous to himself" if for physical or other reasons he is helpless to avoid the hazards of freedom either through his own efforts or with the aid of willing family members or friends.... . Where "treatment" is the sole asserted ground for depriving a person of liberty, it is

plainly unacceptable to suggest that the courts are powerless
to determine whether the asserted ground is present.[82]

The Supreme Court and the judiciary generally make little or no
mention of the considerable delays and enormous increase in expense
of such procedures,[83] or of the overwhelming resolution of such cases
in favor of the party petitioning for involuntary treatment—either for
cases of inpatient hospitalization[84] or compulsory administration of
medications.[85] The Court mandates the highest standard of civil proof
for all cases of civil commitment.[86] While this standard has been said
to "allocate the risk of error between litigants"..."[c]andor suggests
that...the particular standard-of-proof catchwords do not always make
a great difference in a particular case."[87] The Court concedes that it
deals with a theory that may have no practical consequence, yet it
fails to draw a distinction between the "dangerous" and "in need of
treatment" civil commitment standards.

In contrast, the higher standard of proof is inappropriate for a
person whose health and personal autonomy will remain untreated for
serious illnesses that present significant threats in terms of death by
suicide or other physical vulnerabilities.[88] In such circumstances, that
court deprives both the individual of the state's benevolent obligation
to ameliorate health that otherwise could be harmful.[89]

Given that juries cannot be expected to fully appreciate these
technical standards of evidence, the comment made by the chief
justice that requiring proof beyond a reasonable doubt "would make
civil commitment well-nigh impossible, thereby doing away with
involuntary commitment altogether"[90] is a dire observation that
such differences will be virtually imperceptible or insignificant to a
jury.[91] Clinicians are also not very accurate at predicting or defining
dangerousness because essentially it is a "low base rate, highly
context-dependent behavior [that is not] simplistically depicted and/
or easily routinized."[92] Protection from such "massive deprivation of
freedom" for a seriously mentally ill person would be purchased at
a high price even according to the Court's own rationale.[93] It might
well be worse to be hospitalized and treated with medication than to

merely be incarcerated in a jail (this does not, of course, factor in the stigma of being labeled a criminal).[94]

In his famous ballad, "Like a Rollin Stone," Bob Dylan sings: "when you ain't got nothin' you got nothin' to lose."[95] In this sense, it is not a massive deprivation of freedom to involuntarily commit someone who does not have the mental health to exercise or enjoy freedom.[96]

The *parens patriae* power of the king was derived from an ultimate decision-making authority.[97] Not only would the law not question the broad discretion of a parent to compel his or her child to undergo various medical procedures (injections) or to impose physical limitations (e.g., preventing children from riding a bicycle or driving a car below a certain age) due to the child's immaturity of judgment, the law would generally support any such decision that is questionable so long as it is within professionally acceptable standards.[98] Further, when the issue is one of health and protection, the exercise of the *parens patriae* power should be given broad leeway and presumptive correctness, so long as prophylactic or ameliorative action is taken. Children simply lack the insight and mental capacity to make proper decisions at certain ages. When children are too young to appreciate the dangers of crossing a busy street, they are not dangerous to themselves. Rather, they are "endangered" by traffic because they are unable to avoid that danger. They are passive to those dangers, that is, endangered by those circumstances. Yet it is the responsibility of parents to nurture, gradually allowing their children to learn and mature through age and experience. As the child matures he or she becomes better equipped to solve or handle the various difficulties of life. To label a person with mental illness that causes a lack of awareness of it as *dangerous* is not only inaccurate, it is heavily stigmatizing.[99] Rather, like the inexperienced child, the mentally ill need to be nurtured and taught to make decisions on their own so that they may cease to be endangered by circumstances that they do not understand. Persons who are potential victims but labeled dangerous are not generally welcome in either civil hospitals or community programs.[100] The label makes no sense and is a gross disservice, except perhaps for the colloquial convenience that the term *dangerous to self* has acquired in the last 3 decades. It is often impossible or futile to learn of a person's true background once they are labeled *dangerous* for whatever reason.

The *ratio decidendi* of *O'Connor* is simply that the state cannot civilly commit a person solely because that person suffers from mental illness.[101] Trying to make more of this holding than is justified, commentators have speculated that the holding was a prohibition on civil commitment "in the absence of dangerousness when no treatment is provided."[102] Yet former Chief Justice Burger argues for less judicial scrutiny and more appreciation of the historical development of the public mental health system. He notes that for many institutionalized people mental disease cannot be treated, and yet these people still need a roof over their heads, food in their stomachs, and someone to tend to their medical needs. However, the difficulties of dealing with dangerousness as legal proof have caused hospitals to turn away persons with serious mental illness.[103] A "lack of insight" is a fundamental component of legal incompetence and a primary rationale for exercising the *parens patriae* power.[104]

Chief Justice Burger in his concurring opinion in *O'Connor* and later writing for the majority in *Addington v. Texas* made it clear that the *parens patriae* authority of the state did not die in the *O'Connor* decision:

> [t]he state has a legitimate interest under *parens patriae* powers in providing care to its citizens who are unable because of emotional disorders to care for themselves; the state also has authority under its police power to protect the community from the dangerous tendencies of some who are mentally ill.[105]

> Even worse, we have been making assessments of potential danger on the basis of nothing as precise as the psychometric test hypothesized. Were we to ignore the fact that no definition of dangerous acts has been agreed upon, our standards of prediction have still been horribly imprecise. On the armchair assumption that paranoids are dangerous, we have tended to play safe and incarcerate them all. Assume that the incidence of killing among paranoids is five times as great as among the normal population. If we use paranoia as a basis for incarceration we would commit 199 non-killers in order to protect ourselves from one killer. It is simply impossible to

justify any commitment scheme so premised. And the fact that assessments of dangerousness are often made clinically by a psychiatrist, rather than psychometrically and statistically, adds little if anything to their accuracy.

We do not mean to suggest that dangerousness is not a proper matter of legal concern. We do suggest, however, that limiting its application to the mentally ill is both factually and philosophically unjustifiable. As we have tried to demonstrate, the presence of mental illness is of limited use in determining potentially dangerous individuals. Even when it is of evidentiary value, it serves to isolate too many harmless people. What is of greatest concern, however, is that the tools of prediction are used with only an isolated class of people. We have alluded before to the fact that it is possible to identify, on the basis of sociological data, groups of people wherein it is possible to predict that fifty to eighty percent will engage in criminal or delinquent conduct. And, it is probable that more such classes could be identified if we were willing to subject the whole population to the various tests and clinical examinations that we now impose only on those asserted to be mentally ill. Since it is perfectly obvious that society would not consent to a wholesale invasion of privacy of this sort and would not act on the data if they were available, we can conceive of no satisfactory justification for this treatment of the mentally ill.... It is sufficient now to observe that there is no reason to believe that the mentally well, but statistically dangerous, individual is any less amenable to treatment, though that treatment would undoubtedly take a different form.[106]

Another problem with the vagueness of danger to self is that experts, typically psychiatrists or psychologists who usually testify to establish this element of proof, are wrong two thirds of the time on such behavioral prognostications.[107] A layman using sheer chance can predict dangerousness as well as a professional.[108]

Clinician accuracy was found to be remarkably high, however, when asked to diagnose what characteristics of mental illness were related to past or present dangerousness (i.e., traditional dangerousness meaning causing harm to others or to oneself, not by omission or neglect) or behavioral states (not predictions of future dangerous behavior) using standard clinical factors.[109] Utilizing dangerousness evidence to prove mental illness is technically questionable and surely inferior to clinical symptoms and standard professional diagnosis. The relative use of dangerousness versus clinical standards will be discussed as a form of judicial nullification under the *Daubert-Joiner-Kumho* principles.[110] Dangerousness is purely a behavioral matter that should be treated as such, even if it is related to or caused by a mental illness.

The history of government treatment of the mentally ill is rife with abuse, neglect, and suffering.[111] Despite the early and substantial government support for persons with mental illness in the United States, there were problems of overoptimism in developing treatment and cures for mental illness and an overcrowding and deterioration of hospitals.[112] They became largely custodial institutions as time passed, particularly near and after the turn of the 19th century.[113] There was also a lack of independent oversight to detect and prevent untoward events in the institutional hospitals or to ensure funds and quality of care being maintained at high levels. The confluence of periodic and horrific scandals, combined with the age of judicial activism beginning with the *Warren* Court, and the public funding of the so-called "public interest lawyers," and the changing economics of our times have influenced courts and legislatures to reform public care by abandoning hospitals.[114] In doing so, however, many patients have obviously been abandoned and banished from public assistance.

DANGEROUS LIBERTY

The misapplications of the philosophical definitions of "liberty" claimed in their rationales of *Lessard*, is shown by court citing only part of John Stuart Mill's seminal work, "*On Liberty*" to argue that freedom is bounded only by the rights of others.[115] Yet as many other legal commentators have done, the court omitted Mill's important qualification that liberty applies only to those of sound mind.[116] Rather, Mill believed that persons afflicted with serious mental illness, which impaired the brain's ability to think rationally and to act in their own best interests, are not able to exercise freedom:

His own good, either physical or moral, is not a sufficient warrant. He cannot rightfully be compelled to do or forbear because it will be better for him to do so, because it will make him happier, because, in the opinions of others, to do so would be wise, or even right. These are good reasons for remonstrating with him, or reasoning with him, or persuading him, or entreating him, but not for compelling him, or visiting him with any evil in case he do otherwise. To justify that, the conduct from which it is desired to deter him must be calculated to produce evil to someone else. The only part of the conduct of anyone, for which he is amenable to society, is that which concerns others. In the part, which merely concerns him, his independence is, of right, absolute. Over himself, over his own body and mind, the individual is sovereign.[117]

The authors of the Constitution subscribed to the philosophies of Mill and Locke believing that rights to liberty depended on having a rational mind.[118] When Mill talked about personal freedom he was referring to a person with a sound mind.[119] He said: "It is perhaps hardly necessary to say that this doctrine is meant to apply only to human beings in the maturity of their faculties."[120] Despite the fact that in today's era of political correctness the term "paternalism"[121]is considered pejorative, giving the government the authority to act *parens patriae* was actually one of the major advances in the law of mankind.[122]

In asserting that both the state's and the individual's interest coincide in the decision to confine, the *Addington* Court assumed a *parens patriae* justification for civil commitment. The Court failed to consider whether police-power-based commitments require a higher burden of proof. Let there be no doubt about the difference between *parens patriae*-based commitments and police-power-based commitments. Society does not civilly commit dangerous mentally disordered persons to bestow a treatment benefit upon them. It commits them to protect itself from the harm that they may commit. Thirty years ago, Judge Bazelon, expressing his unwillingness to sugarcoat this reality, correctly observed:

"Non-criminal" commitments of so-called dangerous persons have long served as preventive detention, but this function has been either excused or obscured by the promise that, while detained, the potential offender will be rehabilitated by treatment. Notoriously, this promise of treatment has served only to bring an illusion of benevolence to what is essentially a warehousing operation for social misfits.[123]

Indeed, Judge Bazelon, who has unassailable credentials as an advocate for the mentally ill and was a strong civil libertarian, questioned the extreme view of civil rights of persons with mental illness who are not a threat to anyone but are in need of supervision, care, or treatment.[124] Shortly after the decision in *O'Connor v. Donaldson*, Judge Bazelon recognized the limitations and dangers of misdefining freedom as the absence of treatment when it can just as easily be the foundation for the exercise of freedom:

The "promise of freedom" may be just as chimerical as the "promise of treatment.". . . How real is the promise of individual autonomy for a confused person set adrift in a hostile world? The benevolent purpose of institutionalization may be perverted into excessive state intervention, but there is no guarantee that the benevolent purpose of deinstitutionalization will not itself be perverted into a justification for excessive neglect. Are back alleys any better than back wards?[125]

Reasoning that mental illness was too vague a diagnosis for due process purposes, the court also tried to objectify the civil commitment issues by defining an illness in terms of a behavior rather than by internationally accepted clinical symptoms[126] and complicated it more by requiring the prospective dangerousness to be "imminent."[127] The elevations in the standards, burdens, and costs of proof in civil commitment hearings and associated costs of care through litigation have been large factors in the retreat of state government, especially the mental health bureaucracy, from helping the most serious cases of mental illness.[128] To avoid the expenses of treatment for individuals who are not dangerous but rather are unable to think rationally, control their lives, or avoid the hazards of freedom and challenges of survival in society, the state mental health bureaucracy is deterred by high-hurdled litigation and the improbabilities of proving *danger-ousness*.[129] Retreat of the mental health bureaucracy has been partly responsible for the large increase in the number of persons with mental illness in the jails and prisons of the United States.[130]

Judge Bazelon suggested that jurisprudential judgments be separated from ensuring that clinical diagnosis and treatment met established standards:

> Of course, courts cannot make psychiatric judgments, just as they cannot make many judgments, which are entrusted to expert administrative agencies. What they can do is ensure that such judgments are in fact made, and made rationally on an individualized basis and recorded for future reference and scrutiny.[131]

Current psychiatric practice tends to be more a trial and error process in terms of both multiple attempts at finding a medication that works and the long "half-lives" of psychotropic drugs, which require weeks to determine their effectiveness for a given patient. The methods of the common law are unsuited to what may broadly be called "managerial" tasks. One cannot, through the adjudicative forms of the common law, accomplish, without a damaging distortion, such tasks as directing the operation of an airline, managing a hospital, or allocating railway facilities within a nation.[132]

In a complex case, a court can (at most) echo what experts tell it, if it is able to choose among diametrically opposed testimonies. This is inexact and unscientific and gives in to a jurisprudential sophistry to obtain needed treatment through distortion and re-characterization of otherwise sound medical advice. These court orders are negotiated, necessarily static, and usually less-than-clear to the nonlawyer clinicians and others who must implement them. Thus, whereas treatment of a marginally competent, mentally ill person is a matter of high complexity, or involving fluidity, close interpersonal observation, medical education from physician to patient ("informed consent"), and negotiation in the therapeutic relationship, it is treated more like a criminal sentencing, probation, rehabilitation of delinquency, supervisory jurisdiction over corporations and state institutions (such as integration, school busing, etc.), and like matters.

Contemporary state governments are certainly not awash in health care resources. Civil commitment entails considerable costs and is, therefore, a great disincentive to its use as a treatment modality for serious mental illness. It is not surprising that state mental health bureaucracies have been reducing its use due to the dollar costs of litigation.[133] Disincentives to civil commitment also include the following: the costs of inpatient hospitalization and incidental litigation costs, such as necessitating substantial staff time to transport or accompany a patient to a hearing; requirements to produce psychiatrists, who are in short supply, and others for the heavy burden of proof; preparation time for the litigation; and, in most states, the bureaucratic need for interagency coordination between the hospital, a central or regional office of the mental health department, and the attorney general, county attorney, or lawyer who will carry the petitioner's burden of going forward and burden of proof It is no wonder that government has little enthusiasm for civil commitment as a mode of treatment.

Unjust, pretextual civil commitment proceedings have certainly occurred and often disproportionately against the poor and indigent immigrants.[134] The abuse of civil commitment has been notorious in totalitarian nations, such as Nazi Germany,[135] the former Soviet Union, and China, to quell political dissent.[136] It is noteworthy, and not surprising, that Chinese law utilizes an overbroad "dangerousness" legal standard to rationalize political oppression.[137]

The understanding of dangerousness as a medico-legal category varies considerably in legal systems around the world, but the question of a mentally ill person's potential for doing physical harm to oneself or others is of central and primary concern in most jurisdictions. Secondary considerations may include psychological harm, danger to property, or damage to the environment. China, however, is today the only country known specifically to include "political harm to society" within the scope of what medico-legal authorities officially regard as being dangerous mentally ill behavior.[138]

Political persecution is not the danger in American society. The opposition to compulsory care is primarily ideological and economic.[139] Parsimonious, cost-conscious state and federal mental health bureaucracies enervated from the struggles of operating large complex hospitals, want the problem cases to be dealt with either by the community or more likely, by jails and prisons.[140]

> In no field of law is the divisive, dualistic character of America's legal system more apparent than in the field known as mental disability law. There, legislatures, courts, and scholarly tradition have combined to produce an unwieldy amalgam of general principles and particularized provisions so riddled with internal conflict as to justify a diagnosis of florid legal schizophrenia. In this field of law, the state's *parens patriae* power competes with its police power; the patient's right to treatment coexists (all so uneasily) with the right to refuse it; the therapist's obligation to preserve client confidentiality militates against the duty to warn others; the psychiatrist's wish to treat is undercut by legal compulsion to deinstitutionalize or to refrain from institutionalization altogether; while the pressure on the provider/administrator toward early release increases the risk of legal liability; and the doctrine to deliver least restrictive treatment threatens the disabled with the reality of being subjected to a regimen that retains most of the coercion and restraints of the institutional setting, but without the treatment, or worse, of being left with the unfettered freedom to deteriorate and die in the streets.[141]

This is particularly true in cases of severe mental illness where the disease is still not fully understood by scientists and is unlikely to be appropriately handled by clinicians in an adversarial courtroom.[142] The patient may appear as competent to the trial court; but he or she, in fact, may not be in reality or only be doing so temporarily and owing to being treated at the time.

Then Mayor Koch began a program called project HELP that was authorized to bring homeless mentally ill persons who met statutory criteria for civil commitment to a city hospital for inpatient treatment. The City of New York's program was challenged in the case of Billie

Boggs, a homeless woman with mental illness, who was claimed to be a "danger to herself." The American Civil Liberties Union challenged Ms. Boggs' commitment arguing that she was not dangerous as evidenced by her physical health, mental acuity, general articulateness, and testimony of psychiatric experts.

By the time of the trial, Ms. Boggs had received treatment that reduced her violent and aggressive tendencies and permitted her to articulate her political and other views cogently to the court. At trial, six psychiatrists testified for the City that Ms. Boggs was dangerous to herself and in need of treatment while three psychiatrists testified for Ms. Boggs that she was competent to refuse and did not need treatment.[143] The trial judge engaged in direct conversation with Ms. Boggs over what appeared to be her bizarre behaviors, for which Ms. Boggs gave plausible political justifications.

During the trial proceedings neither the petitioner nor respondent apparently raised the possibility that the dramatic changes to Ms. Boggs' demeanor and abilities could have been affected by the medications given in her pretrial hospitalization, or the court failed to take note of it. The expert testimony between the psychiatrists for the petitioner and respondent was directly opposite in both observations and conclusion.[144] Oddly, the trial court did not consider in its opinion that Ms. Boggs' amelioration might have been a consequence of the prehearing mental health treatment.

For example, before the involuntary hospitalization, Ms. Boggs was living on the street, sleeping on heating grates, running into traffic, toileting herself on the sidewalk or street gutter, attacking men, refusing money, food, and help, and behaving violently toward certain individuals, including those from the city's social work agency.[145] She talked to herself and was clearly delusional. Yet during the hearing the trial judge had extensive talks with Ms. Boggs who was able to present a cognizant rationale for all of these behaviors, for example, denying she ran into traffic, asserting that she had no home to go to, and living in the city shelters was worse than living on the street.[146]

She said that no local business would let her use its rest room. She asserted that men often solicited her for sex; this was offensive and her actions were self-defensive. Her situation was typical of the modern phenomena of the homeless mentally ill.[147] Owing to the treatment, or at least coincidental with it, after being released Ms. Boggs lectured at Harvard University on her life and "street" experiences and appeared on the very popular "Phil Donahue" television talk show. Schizophrenia produces delusional thoughts and behaviors that fascinate the talk show audience.[148]

Why did the parties, especially the petitioner, the City of New York, not point out that what the judge was seeing in Ms. Boggs was a posttreatment situation that worked![149] Nevertheless, the trial judge, based in part on his own interview with Ms. Boggs, failed to understand the significance of or to comment on Ms. Boggs' treatment before the hearing, refused to continue the order of commitment, and did not attempt to realistically explain the vast disparity between the experts' testimony of her mental illness.[150] Rather, he criticized the City of New York and society in general for failing to provide housing and other assistance to individuals like Ms. Boggs.[151] This was reversed on appeal, for, among other reasons, the judge should not have assessed her mental illness himself but rather based his decision on the expert testimony offered.[152]

Dangerousness is not a diagnosis: At best it is a prediction. This is a very poor basis for assessing the need for treatment, but it is effective at stigmatizing a patient who is not dangerous but merely incompetent to make decisions necessary to live a normal life. The misuse of the term, therefore, often results in "a haphazard system of preventive detention for some and non-therapeutic neglect for others."[153] Often, patients who express incompetent objections to hospitalization and commitment are more sick, will present larger problems relating to treatment and behavior in the hospital, and will cost significantly more to treat.[154] Granting rights, particularly ones that tend to be antitherapeutic as well as often ultimately ungratified after judicial hearings, come at a cost to the patient who might well be "rotting with his rights on."[155] Attorneys and courts are thus self-satisfied that legal rights have been accorded even at the cost of a deteriorating state of mental health, or worse, when various harms might befall them such as frequent rape for mentally ill women.[156]

As Professor Bruce Winick has written about civil commitment hearings:

> In practice, commitment hearings tend to be brief and non-adversarial episodes in which judges appear to "rubber stamp" the recommendations of clinical expert witnesses. Indeed, studies show judicial agreement with expert witnesses in this area ranges from seventy-nine to one hundred percent, and most frequently exceeds ninety-five percent. Civil commitment proceedings are often extremely informal, sometimes occurring in courtrooms set up at the hospital in which patients appear in hospital garb rather than street clothes. Judges frequently fail to advise patients of their rights or permit them to speak. Judges often discourage attorneys from taking an active part in the hearing or themselves take over the role of questioning witnesses. These brief, informal hearings at which the judge defers to the expert witness and seems unconcerned with what the patient or the patient's lawyer may have to say give many patients the impression that the hearing is an empty ritual rather than a serious attempt to achieve accuracy and fairness.

> In *Parham v. J. R.*, former Chief Justice Burger questioned whether the supposed protections of the adversary civil commitment hearing were "more illusory than real," citing studies showing the inadequate job that counsel usually plays at commitment hearings, which last a mean time of from 3.8 to 9.2 minutes. These studies are consistent with others showing that civil commitment hearings are extraordinarily brief, often lasting only minutes. Such hearings can only be perfunctory rituals that either presume the existence of mental illness and the need for hospitalization or only superficially inquire into these issues.[157]

Professor Wexler has also made this point:

> The literal meaning of dangerousness is admittedly ignored in favor of the best interests of the patient, i.e., where he will benefit from treatment. Although it is recognized that such a determination is probably illegal, the psychiatrists feel it more humanitarian to require treatment than to be thwarted statutorily in their attempt to prescribe it.[158]

DANGEROUS PERSONS

A sociological and psychiatric analysis of the dangerousness criterion was conducted by Michel Foucault, one of the most influential writers on asylums and mental illness.[159] Foucault argues that at the turn of the 19th century, psychiatry became an autonomous medical discipline conceived as a reaction to the dangers and negative conditions growing and inhering in the developing social body: overpopulation, over-crowding of the cities, communicable diseases, alcoholism, social deviancy, and so forth.[160] This produced a new concept of crime and social deviance only discernible to psychiatry: irrational dangerousness, crime without apparent purpose or normal economic incentive. These were crimes without reason, and the working of these human minds behind them was hidden from normal view and ordinary understanding.

In other words, psychiatry asked "What makes a criminal?" Reasons, motives, free will, design, tendencies, and instincts are all elements. But in the absence of these, it becomes impossible to understand, control, catch, reform, or effectively punish the criminal. One needs to know the nature of guilt before deciding on imprisonment; one needs to understand the human economics and the personal equation to give legitimacy to attempted reform and punishment. Foucault writes:

> [T]he monstrous crime, both anti-natural and irrational, is the meeting point of the medical demonstration that insanity is ultimately always dangerous, and of the court's inability to determine the punishment of a crime without having determined the motives for the crime.... Increasingly, nineteenth-century psychiatry will also tend to seek out pathological stigmata which may mark dangerous individuals: moral insanity, instinctive insanity, and degeneration. This theme of the dangerous individual will give rise on the one hand to the anthropology of criminal man as in the Italian school, and on the other to the theory of social defense first represented by the Belgian school.... One can see the series of shifts required by the anthropological school: from the crime to the criminal; from the act as it was actually committed to the danger potentially inherent in the individual; from the modulated punishment of the guilty party to the absolute protection of others.... Neither

the "criminality" of an individual, nor the index of his dangerousness, nor his potential or future behavior, nor the protection of society at large from these possible perils, none of these are, nor can they be, juridical notions in the classical sense of the term. They can be made to function in a rational way only within a technical knowledge-system, a knowledge-system capable of characterizing a criminal individual in himself and in a sense beneath his acts; a knowledge-system able to measure the index of danger present in an individual; a knowledge-system which might establish the protection necessary in the face of such a danger. Hence the idea that crime ought to be the responsibility not of judges but of experts in psychiatry, criminology, psychology, etc. Actually, that extreme conclusion was not often formulated in such an explicit and radical way, no doubt through practical prudence. But it followed implicitly from all the theses of Criminal Anthropology. And at the second meeting of this Association (1889), Pugliese expressed it straightforwardly. We must, he said, turn around the old adage: the judge is the expert of experts: it is rather up to the expert to be the judge of judges. "The commission of medical experts to whom the judgment ought to be referred should not limit itself to expressing its wishes; on the contrary it should render a real decision."[161]

Foucault uses insurance principles as the economic rationale for this change in view of mental illness. He argues that the civil law revolved around the concept of accidents and legal responsibility, rather than penal liability. Individual wage earners could not generally cover the possible financial exposure of their work, which required using corporate resources that were potentially lethal to others or capable of causing substantial damage. Accordingly, third-party liability, for example, *respondeat superior*, had to be created for two reasons. First, such vicarious liability would bind the major beneficiary of the worker's product, that is, the corporation or business. Second, it would establish a "no fault" criminality under the aegis of the civil law of compensation and nonculpability. This transference of liability provided for the creation of the civil "criminal," a person who simply harmed others without producing economic benefit for society. The civil criminal is distinguished from the real criminal, the one who harmed society. This conceptual approach thus linked the criminal act to the psyche of the person, that is, that person is "dangerous" to society.

> [H]e is not at fault, since he has not of his own free will chosen evil rather than good.... . The general idea of the *Social Defense* as it was put forward by Prinz at the beginning of the twentieth century was developed by transferring to criminal justice formulations proper to the new civil law.... . [A]ll of these seem indeed to indicate that at that moment the required "shunting switch" has just been found. This "switch" is the key notion of *risk* which the law assimilates through the idea of a no-fault liability, and which anthropology, or psychology, or psychiatry can assimilate through the idea of imputabilty without freedom. The term, henceforth central, of "dangerous being," was probably introduced by Prinz at the September 1905 session of the International Union of Penal Law.... . In the course of the past century, penal law did not evolve from an ethic of freedom to a science of psychic determinism; rather, it enlarged, organized, and codified the suspicion and the locating of dangerous individuals, from the rare and monstrous figure of the monomaniac to the common everyday figure of the degenerate, or the pervert, of the constitutionally unbalanced, of the immature, etc.... . But by bringing increasingly to the fore not only the criminal as author of the act, but also the dangerous individual as potential source of acts, does one not give society rights over the individual based on what he is?.... . A form of justice which tends to be applied to what one is, this is what is so outrageous when one thinks of the penal law of which the eighteenth-century reformers had dreamed, and which was intended to sanction, in a completely egalitarian way, offenses explicitly defined beforehand by the law.... . When a man comes before his judges with nothing but his crimes, when he has nothing to say but 'this is what I have done,' when he has nothing to say about himself, when he does not do the tribunal the favor of confiding to them something like the secret of his own being, then the judicial machine ceases to function.[162]

Thus, for the courts, rationality of the person to be judged is essential to making a judgment and rendering justice. Of necessity, there must be some form of rational dialog between the court and accused. However, "dangerousness," when it is used as a qualifier for irrational behavior, effectively nullifies the judicial process in this regard as well. It avoids dealing with the reasons that make a person human and identifying the mental illness that might be preventing that person from behaving humanly.

PART TWO: A TRILOGY
OF JUDICIAL NULLIFICATION

> *The fathers of the French revolution, such as Le Chaplier and Robespierre, were convinced that written law alone must dominate and that "the judge-made law was the most detestable of institutions, and should be destroyed." Indeed, Robespierre went so far as ordering that the word "jurisprudence" ("case-law" in English)—the heart of the common law system—be banished from the French language.*[163]

A. JUDICIAL NULLIFICATION BY TRIAL COURTS:
A QUESTION OF FACT

No matter what their particular philosophy or training, judges are expected to apply the law faithfully: all "agree that it is the prime duty for a judge to obey the law."[164] However, as H. L. A. Hart has written, a judge ought to think "what he does is the right thing."[165]

Thus, no matter how many choices a rule leaves open, a judge applying the law will be guided in his deliberations by what might be called the *ethos* of his office, by a certain ideal of judicial craftsmanship, and by the habits that a devotion to this ideal and long experience in attempting to achieve it tend to instill.[166]

Judicial nullification is a refusal, either overt or tacit, to enforce an otherwise governing statute or principle of law. The subject of judicial nullification is not widely discussed in the literature. It is most well-known as the exercise of "statutory nullification,"[167] primarily by appellate courts. An example of statutory nullification is the exercise of the power claimed by the Supreme Court and the subordinate federal courts to declare statutes unconstitutional.[168]

> [T]he delegates to the Philadelphia Convention in 1787 still regarded judicial nullification of legislation with a sense of awe and wonder, impressed, as Elbridge Gerry was, that "in some States, the Judges had actually set aside laws as being against the Constitution." This is also why many others in the Convention, including James Madison and George Mason, wanted to join the judges with the executive in a council of revision and thus give the judiciary a double negative over the laws. They considered that the power of the judges alone to declare unconstitutional laws void was too extreme and too fearful an act to be invoked regularly.[169]

When implementing the law, courts often justify their decisions using some combination of the following rationales: (1) the decision is based on expectations of the parties pursuant to an actual agreement; (2) the decision conforms with certain moral or ethical values related to "fairness"; or (3) the decision defers to public policy.[170] However, these rationales also apply to judicial decisions that exist outside of statutory guidance, such as in common law.[171] Thus, courts may find that their own logical conclusion, guided by these concerns, may conflict with controlling statutes[172] and thus courts may use these very same rationales to justify judicial nullification. *Jury nullification* is another form of judicial nullification, and its foundations are analogous. Juries may refuse to convict law-breakers (1) when the jury elects not to apply the law to a particular defendant, (2) when the jury disagrees with the law itself, or (3) in response to social conditions, or it could be due to a combination of these elements.[173]

Despite the obligation to follow the law, legal rules and principles allow judges to realize the results they want or they feel are justified.[174] As every trial lawyer has seen—and of which even the television-viewing general public is aware—every judge has the *de facto* power to exclude evidence or nullify a law. The great justice Oliver Wendell

Holmes claimed that he could "admit any general proposition you like and decide the case either way."[175] The jurisprudence of equity has traditionally been recognized as giving a judge ample means to trump statutory law and render a decision he deems "fair." However, the same result is easily and more subtly accomplished by making findings of fact that allow the judge to apply different, and more favorable, law. The latter method is much safer because factual findings are rarely disturbed on appeal, since appellate courts do not have occasion to hear witnesses and judge their demeanor and the truth of their testimony.[176] If the term dangerous is no longer used to mean causing harm to another then it can mean almost anything.[177]

> The concept of "dangerousness" has been used and misused during the past century in America to achieve a variety of ill-defined and sometimes illegal objectives. Because the concept of "dangerousness" is not clearly defined in behavioral terms, it can be used to describe nearly any socially undesirable behavior. Behavior has been legally labeled as "dangerousness" when: (1) physical harm has been inflicted upon others; (2) physical harm has been inflicted upon oneself; (3) a victim has suffered psychic trauma or mental distress; and (4) a patient has recklessly spent the savings of a family... . The abuses which flow from an ill-defined concept of dangerousness are not difficult to find and have been well-documented.[178]

Not listed among these ambiguities is the spectrum of harms that befall someone through neglect or ignorance. Failing to eat properly, to exercise, to maintain physical hygiene, and to dress consistent with the weather conditions are all potential sources of "dangerousness" as that term is now being used.

> The lawyer's main problem with dangerousness, then, is that dangerousness is a *very* existential term. Like the Queen in *Alice in Wonderland*, people who use the term, people who live by it and build their careers upon it, will tell you that dangerousness simply means what they say it means, what they need it to mean in order to get the job done. It is simply a button that must be pushed at the right time, in proper sequence, to accomplish an outcome determined in advance

to be appropriate. Little wonder, then, that to an extent clearly unparalleled in the history of disciplines that ride on the reputation of science, predictions by so-called experts fail to withstand the simplest scrutiny.[179]

There is strong evidence that trial judges facing the issue of civil commitment of a person who is not really dangerous in any true sense of the word will nevertheless follow their common sense instincts when treatment is clearly needed, but the patient is incompetent to consent, articulates an incompetent refusal, or cannot otherwise seek or authorize treatment for himself or herself. The widespread adoption of the contemporary and inchoate "dangerousness" standard in statute and case law and the lack of either a univocal or conceptual meaning for the terms have given trial court both sufficient reason and a justifiable cause to swing the pendulum back to a *parens patriae* standard.

However, the quieter and more fundamental departure from the abrogation of *parens patriae* consideration by the "dangerousness" standards is found at the trial court level, which is the frontline of civil commitment. The evidence for this is both empirical and anecdotal. In three studies done by Harold Bursztajn et al.,[180] the evidence is clear and consistent that:

> As in previous studies, the *parens patriae* model more closely described the individual judge's decision process than the "police powers" model... . judges described earlier, used *parens patriae* considerations, such as a patient's inability to care for self and potential to commit suicide, in deciding whether to commit psychiatric patients. In this representative set of commitment hearings, both methods for characterizing the judge's decision policy, the impact rating method and the statistical analysis of the relations between the patient factors and the judge's decision, indicated that the *parens patriae* considerations received greater weight than the police power considerations of preventing violence to others.
>
> *Our study, using these methods, also showed that the judge considered factors that are not directly specified in the statement*

of the law. Among the specific factors this judge used in considering whether the law's general principles applied in each case were the patient's competence, predictability, and reliability as an outpatient, as well as whether family and friends favor commitment. Each of these factors can, in specific cases, inform the clinical decision as to the likelihood that the threshold has been crossed for the criteria specified by law for committability. Moreover, the additional factors considered can be also be [*sic*] understood as parameters for translating mental illness narratives into a form in which they can be compared with the statutory principles.

Our findings give further support to the proponents of *parens patriae* as a descriptive model of how both clinicians and judges make decisions regarding commitment. Certainly someone's ability to take care of self, as well as suicidal potential, is a reflection of the degree to which he or she has a social support system... . We recognize that experienced judges know the applicable law, and their task is to apply the general statement of the law to each particular case. The method for applying the law can not be specified in the letter of the law. However, it is a process that can benefit from self-reflection and peer discussion. Judges can be helped to articulate their intuitive decision-making processes by extending their training from the black letter of the law to the clinical factors that they consider to be important in the decision to commit. If judges, like clinicians, intuitively use a variety of *parens patriae*-like factors in their decision-making process, being able to both recognize and articulate these factors is vital [italics added].[181]

This model is an application of common sense or in some cases a capitulation to the demands of day-to-day judicial overload and the inherent inability to second guess professionals, who themselves have learned how to manipulate these nonclinical, or perhaps even mystical, standards of evidence such as *dangerousness*.[182] Other studies made similar findings in the State of California[183] and Arizona.[184]

One of the problems with the dangerousness standard is that the evidence of dangerousness, even when danger to self is included, is often not clear. As Professors Goldstein and Katz have observed, the element of dangerousness to others has, at least in practice, been similarly illusive because "such a test at a minimum calls for a determination not only of what acts are dangerous, but also the probably that such acts will occur."[185]

A study of civil commitment in Wisconsin determined that a significant proportion of detainees evidenced behaviors leading to emergency detention, but their actions caused no actual harm. Significantly, the degree of dangerousness and mental illness had no relationship to the length of their respective hospital stays.[186] Darold A. Treffert kept a catalog of such cases. These cases show the dilemma facing a trial judge when he knows treatment is necessary and likely beneficial to the mentally ill person, but evidence of dangerousness is not clear at the time:

> This is one example from my tragic catalog of over 200 cases of persons who, what I call, "died with their rights on." I have hundreds of such cases previously reported in different articles. Civil libertarians and other critics refer to these cases as Treffert's "anecdotes." They dislike them. The cases are jarring. They are "out-liers," not common, and do not represent the mainstream circumstance, these critics say. They interfere with philosophical musings. But the instances are real. They do exist. These persons, with such tragic outcomes, are not "anecdotes" to their families and loved ones, or to innocent persons or bystanders sometimes harmed by them. So I continue to track and report them... . Many of these "dying with your rights on" cases demonstrate graphically, and tragically, that freedom can be a hazard—or another form of imprisonment—for persons who are obviously ill and in need of treatment; who are not yet dangerous but well on their way to being so, and who, because of that obvious and permeating illness, are unable to care for themselves. The Group for the Advancement of Psychiatry (GAP) report, which the MacArthur Studies cite in the introduction to their work, concluded that "sometimes involuntary psychiatric treatment is necessary, can be effective, and can lead to freedom from the constraints of illness. Conversely, tight restrictions against coercive treatment can have disastrous consequences.[187]

To wait until a person becomes "clearly and convincingly" dangerous is often too late, and judges on the trial level realize the absurdity of mating speculation with uncertainty when life and limb might well rest on the mix. This is a Hobbes's Choice. There is a small risk of erroneous determination and a large one of substantial and usually needless harm to the individual absent treatment. Where the risk of harm can be effectively prevented or ameliorated with low-risk treatment, why is the burden of proof biased against intervention? For those patients who are incompetent to make a rational decision, the treatment also puts them in a position to genuinely refuse the offer once their competency has been restored. It also allows them to execute a psychiatric advance directive to handle the recurrence of this situation.[188]

Once a patient is labeled dangerous, whether that might mean the patient is potentially homicidal or, through lack of insight, wanders delusional and naked in fierce snow storms, the "dangerous" label influences hospitals, community treatment centers, clinicians, therapy aides, and the hospital staff to shy away from them due to that label.[189] Such patients in need of compulsory care are thus often denied the benefits of outpatient commitment and right to remain in their own homes and communities.[190]

There are three reasons for judicial determinations in civil commitment cases ultimately using a *parens patriae* approach. First, a sense that as a trial judge, he or she is on the front line and is the gatekeeper who will authorize treatment that might involve life or death, or in most cases, the ability to live a decent life in freedom within a community. Second, in general, judges and juries lack basic sophistication about mental illness and treatment, and given the often diametric testimony of experts, tend to err on the side of helping the patient through temporary treatment with periodic judicial review. Lastly, judges, being on the front line of criminal and civil law involvement with the mentally ill, must often must fill in the gaps left by the current confusion in mental health law, and the dearth of services. In the view of many, especially family or friends of the patient, the judge is the gatekeeper for treatment or incarceration.[191] It is also worthy of note that sometimes juries might also nullify certain applications of law in other areas that involve application of law to persons with mental illness.[192]

Lon Fuller said that "law might usefully be understood as the purposeful enterprise of applying reason in directing human affairs."[193] In his landmark work, *Anatomy of the Law*, Fuller describes the judgment function under the Anglo-American law as "exercised by human beings for human beings. It cannot be built into a computer."[194] This essential lack of strict adherence to legislation or appellate decisions at the trial court level makes the Anglo-American common law approach superior to the European civil law system.

> The sociologist Max Weber was convinced that in the Anglo-American system of common law "the degree of legal rationality is essentially lower than, and of a type different from, that of continental Europe." Perhaps part of what Weber had in mind was that laws are made most rationally when men lay down rules in advance of actual disputes, while their minds are free from the pull of circumstances and person. On the other hand, in complex human affairs it can be argued that to legislate wisely one must acquire some firsthand feeling for the situations about which one is legislating, and that for this reason the common law is likely to be more intelligently responsive to the needs of society than abstract codification. As is often the case, these divergent opinions reflect different aspects of a complex reality and there is truth in both of them.... In the common law it is not too much to say that the judges are always ready to look behind the words of a precedent to what the previous court was trying to say, or to what it would have said if it could have foreseen the nature of the cases that were later to arise, or if its perception of the relevant factors in the case before it had been more acute. There is, then, a real sense in which the written words of the reported decisions are merely the gateway to something lying behind them that may be called, without any excess of poetic license, "unwritten law".... [Weber] spoke indeed of the judicial process in the Anglo-American countries as taking on a "charismatic quality" and as resting on "the very personal authority" of the "individual judge." Yet in most fields of intellectual activity it would be taken for granted that in difficult

or doubtful matters one man's opinion carries more weight than that of others; no quality of "irrationality" or superstitious awe of the person would be seen in the simple conclusion that "on this matter A is a better guide than B," or "A is better at explaining these things than B."[195]

Professor Bruce Winick has harshly criticized the performance of courts in civil commitment hearings as nullifying the adversarial process. Saying that commitment hearings are supposed to be adversarial, yet "a large gulf exists between law on the books and the law in action."[196] He finds fault with all participants in the process, sparing neither the judge nor the patient's own attorney. Professor Winick believes that attorneys relax their advocacy, or temper their zealous representation based on a notion that the person with mental illness needs care more than rigorous due process. This attitude he labels "paternalistic," "a farce and a mockery," and "a basic dishonesty...shared by judges, lawyers, and clinicians."[197] Studies show that civil commitment hearings last only several minutes on the average because the respondent's attorney usually "rolls over" by failing to challenge whether the patient is mentally ill, deferring to expert witnesses and failing to explore alternatives to hospitalization. He summarizes his viewpoint of civil commitment hearings saying that: "[i]n light of these inadequacies of counsel and the way judges frequently conduct the hearing, from the patient's perspective, the hearing may resemble the one presided over by the Queen of Hearts in Alice in Wonderland, 'Sentence first—verdict afterward'."[198] He concludes that civil commitment processes could be more "therapeutic" to reduce the patient's feeling of being coerced into treatment.[199]

Professor Brooks agrees that trial judges give little time to hearings and much deference to professional judgment:

> In this enterprise, the psychiatrist finds that many judges are eager to defer to them. Self-protectiveness reflects the understandable desire of the psychiatrist not to run unnecessary risks by testifying to the non-dangerousness of a mentally ill person who may later comit [sic] suicide, assault others, or engage in other undesirable acts... . If judges actually wished

a more careful explicitation [*sic*] of the alleged dangerousness of the mentally ill person, they could insist on it. However, trial judges have routinely accepted the conclusory opinions of psychiatrists in hearings that are strikingly superficial and brief. A 1966 study of civil commitment hearings in Texas reported that patients were committed at a rate of 40 within 75 minutes, or at a rate of less than 2 minutes per commitment hearing. Contemporary studies indicate that the situation in many States remains substantially unchanged. Wexler has reported that in 1971 the average duration of a commitment hearing in one Arizona county was 4.7 minutes. Zander has reported that in 1974 the average duration of commitment proceedings in Milwaukee, Wisconsin, under the *Lessard* decision was 13 minutes. In such a short period of time, there is frequently little opportunity for an adequate inquiry into dangerousness. Testimony tends to be conclusory.[200]

At what price comes heightened due process? Is this type of due process traditional for a court? Professor Arthur B. LaFrance wrote an article about his experience as a circuit judge *pro tempore* in civil commitment cases. It is a memoir of the cases where he often saw himself "as stranger in a strange land indeed" because a judge is neither trained nor familiar with the world of mental illness treatment and social services.

Apart from the obvious observation that the process provided for civil commitments creates a high likelihood of error, it also demeans the institution of justice, isolates them from the other players in the system, and provides no chance for control. The law and system are stacked so that burden of error falls on the patient, assuming some need for treatment, when treatment is not permitted. It imposes a high standard of evidence ("clear and convincing") against providing treatment where a reasonable patient would want treatment to be rendered by standards substantially less than even a preponderance of evidence, for example, any reasonably likelihood of a minimal therapeutic success or even just relief of symptoms.[201] What cancer, cardiac, or AIDS patient would want treatment denied unless it was warranted by the highest standard of proof under civil law and only after a full adversarial trial?

LaFrance explains that the reason for this is the distinction between treating the respondent as a quasi-criminal defendant with presumptions against treatment until the highest (civil) burdens of proof are satisfied, rather than as a person in need of medical treatment and other forms of aid and public intervention. It is thus not hard to see why judges, a bit uncomfortable with the arcane medical diagnosis and other circumstances of such cases take the human response and "err" on the side of intervention because it does less harm to treat a person who needs it, albeit erroneously determined incompetent, than to fail to treat someone who could be restored his or her mental health or ability to survive.[202]

In mental commitment proceedings, there is a collision between two very different ways of looking at law. One may be characterized as the due process, which treats hearings as adversarial proceedings between equals. The outcome is truth, and the party bearing the burden of going forward may lose simply by failing to bear the burden of proof. The other view is that the state has an obligation beyond procedural truth, to ensure care, treatment, and rehabilitation. Since these can only be considered good, the need for procedural niceties and burdens of proof may be masked or ignored. If errors of inclusion are made, they will in any event be thought helpful to the person who is in need of treatment.[203] How is a judge to resolve the lack of the traditional distinction of our law and culture between persons who cause harm and persons who simply need care?

> If mental illness and dangerousness had to be proven in court beyond a reasonable doubt, and if patients were provided with aggressive attorneys who demanded that the state satisfy its burden of proof, how could psychiatry beset by inherent uncertainties of human nature, ever meet that standard? Did reason not lead inexorably to the conclusion that the entire commitment system would shrink, perhaps even wither, as a result of the reforms? But these appeals were not enough. Even when they were embraced in principle, they often were abandoned in practice. Confronted with psychotic persons who might well benefit from treatment, and who would certainly suffer without it, mental health professionals and judges alike

were reluctant to comply with the law and release them. They simply could not give credence to a calculus that placed rights above suffering. Attorneys trained to fight for the exculpation of felons whom they knew or suspected to be guilty could not bring themselves to do the same for mentally ill people, whose freedom seemed of dubious value compared with treatment and a place to sleep. The new laws did not alter the behavior of these key actors in the system, because they did not want to change.[204]

What is the meaning of *zealous advocacy*? Do attorneys have a heart and use common sense when their clients are seriously ill and unquestionably in need of care? Attorneys are not hard-wired for litigation; they are dedicated to the best interests of their clients by solving legal problems. This is why the vast portion of both criminal and civil litigation is settled by negotiation, not by verdicts.

The failure of patients' attorneys to assume an adversarial posture has been widely reported as well.... . In nearly 43 percent of the cases, patients' attorneys advocated a more restrictive disposition than the patients desired—either in-patient or out-patient commitment—rather than outright release. When interviewed, they endorsed a role in which they sought patients' best interests, as they understood them, rather than advocating patients' expressed wishes. The pervasiveness of such views among attorneys has been confirmed in other studies.... . Discussions with the attorneys after the training revealed the expected finding: they simply did not see their role as being opposed to commitment of people who were "really sick" and who, in their judgment, clearly needed to be in a hospital.[205]

A person who lacks insight is not necessarily dangerous, and both judges and lawyers recognize this fact to the point of justifying a nullification—under the guise of re-characterization—that the person is dangerous. The ethics of the judge can bend the rules for a decision that is made in the manner of a parent, *parens patriae*, when it is called for.[206] A judge can combine the facts of the individual's need for and lack of insight to pursue treatment to construct a plausible legal rationale sufficient to authorize treatment under the dangerousness standard when common sense dictates that result.[207] Moreover, it is unlikely that a decision of a trial judge, as they are so heavily based on the unique facts of each case, will be successfully challenged on appeal. It is also appropriate that the perceptions and participation of others who genuinely care about the patient are involved, such as a supportive family or social welfare agency, as well as the public demands for social order.[208]

B. NULLIFICATION OF SCIENCE-BASED EVIDENCE

i. Mental Illness: Science and Evidence

The Enlightenment rooted our law in science, as it has in our culture.[209] The meaning of this law is best expressed in the well-known beginning of Oliver Wendell Holmes' classic work, *The Common Law*, in which he stated, "the life of the law is not logic but experience"; by "experience" he meant the ordinary practice of law with the evolving culture; "the felt necessities of our times."[210] His commentary *Science in Law—Law in Science* is also instructive for judicial consideration of scientific and medical issues. Holmes thought that the true science of law does not consist of theological working out of dogma, as a logical development analogous to mathematics, or of a study of anthropology.[211]

Holmes insisted that the application of justice depended on applying the facts to the laws. This emphasis on facts certainly, and perhaps ultimately, would most heavily rely on scientific facts. Holmes notably scoffed at the pseudo-science of law that developed at the Harvard Law School[212] led by its Dean, Christopher Columbus Langdell. "Legal science" recommended a rigorous Spinozistic process of deductive logic by taking axioms derived from legal principles and woodenly applying them to the facts in judicial decisions. Holmes believed this approach was the cart driving the horse. In the following, the three iterations of judicial nullification suffer from this flaw. All take a behavioral condition or act and treat it as a talismanic, pseudo-scientific measure to define mental illness.

If the law is the experience of culture and science, and science has been the jewel in the crown of American culture, then science rests at the foundation of contemporary law. The nation was born on the tidal currents created by the golden age of science in the 18th and 19th centuries. This period marks the birth of modern, mathematically and empirically based science as the primary influence in Western culture, sparking new political thought by the philosophers of the Enlightenment as well as other philosophers and thinkers of that time.[213] Newtonian physics established that there were laws of nature reducible to equations and concepts that led most impressively to accurate predictions of the future. This ushered in an age of determinism. Given enough information about the causes of a phenomenon, the effects could be reliably predicted.[214]

A second scientific revolution occurred at the beginning of the 20th century with Albert Einstein's theory of relativity, Planck's theory of quantum mechanics, and especially Heisenberg's uncertainty principle, which has been called the second revolution in Physics.[215] This undermined determinism by demonstrating that scientific truths were not absolute, but rather, they were more or less true, having a degree of probability and ranges of error varying plus or minus from exactitude.

The law has long accepted the idea that ultimate truth is elusive and probabilities must suffice for its practical operation and application. From at least the time of the Constitution, American law has utilized "reasonable cause," "beyond a reasonable doubt," "preponderance of evidence," and other less-than-certain bases for final judgment. As Justice Blackman noted in his majority opinion in *Daubert v. Merrell Dow Pharmaceuticals*:

> [T]here are important differences between the quest for truth in the courtroom and the quest for truth in the laboratory. Scientific conclusions are subject to perpetual revision. Law, on the other hand, must resolve disputes finally and quickly... Conjectures that are probably wrong are of little use, however, in the project of reaching a quick, final, and binding legal judgment—often of great consequence—about a particular set of events in the past.[216]

Indeed, easily the most ubiquitous legal criterion in law is the test of "reasonableness." This is a less-than-certain legal standard under which both the law and human behavior in general must proceed to survive.

General practitioners in mental illness in the pre-Civil War era agreed that insanity was a disease of the brain and that the examination of tissues in an autopsy would reveal organic lesions, clear evidence of physical damage, in every insane person. Isaac Ray, one of the leading medical superintendents of that period, when presenting the consensus of his discipline to the legal profession, confidently declared:

> No pathological fact is better established…than that deviations from the healthy structure are generally present in the brains of insane subjects… . The progress of pathological anatomy during the present century has established this fact beyond the reach of a reasonable doubt.[217]

According to Rothman:

> Institutionalization was not a last resort of a frightened community; it was quite the reverse. Psychiatrists and their lay supporters insisted that insanity was curable, more curable than most other ailments. Spokesmen explained that their understanding of the causes of insanity equipped them to combat it, and the asylum was a first resort, the most important and effective weapon in their arsenal. The program's proponents confidently and aggressively asserted that properly organized institutions could cure almost every incidence of the disease. They spread their claims without restraint, allowing the sole qualifications that the cases had to be recent… . And professionals and laymen alike desperately wanted to credit calculations that would glorify American science and republican humanitarianism. A cure for insanity was the kind of discovery that would honor the new nation.[218]

The scientific tradition of both law and mental illness that previously characterized our culture has recently suffered serious erosion by decisions that have equated mental illness with dangerous behavior. This misconception abandons the disease theory of the 19th century that has now been scientifically confirmed. Ironically, the result of this has been to revert to the pre-19th century practice of incarcerating the mentally ill in jails and prisons, rather than treating them in hospitals and homes.

Accordingly, judicial and government decisions are inadvertently abandoning another innovative tradition, namely implementing, on a large scale, a *parens patriae* policy of public hospital construction and government assistance to persons with serious mental illness. Fundamental to this process was a policy that utilized the civil law for treatment, to avoid criminal incarceration and inferior treatment in jails and prisons.

ii. Science in the Courtroom

In his book, *Galileo's Revenge: Junk Science in the Courtroom*, Peter Huber[219] coined the pejorative term "junk science" to criticize what he saw as the use of the Federal Rules of Evidence to admit unscientific or questionably scientific evidence, that is, unreliable expert testimony that was couched in scientific jargon.[220] It has been observed that despite the court's attempts to keep so-called junk science out of the courtroom, too many courts today accept outmoded-unscientific testimony on how the brain works. It is unreliable, nonempirical, and itself borders on a junk science[221] approach to dealing with mental illness. This problem has grown as science plays a larger role in the courtroom, especially in criminal cases. Most recently, DNA profiling is prominent in the news, particularly in its use both in exonerating persons wrongfully accused of crime and in building a case where none was possible without DNA technology. Crime laboratories now routinely use electron microscopy, electrophorectic blood testing, voice prints, bite marks, trace metal detection, sophisticated analysis of hair and fabric samples, and many other such advanced technological methods of gathering and assessing physical evidence. Of course, every new scientific discovery is at first viewed skeptically, until later, with verification and familiarity, it becomes routinely accepted.

Although fingerprint analysis is standard and well accepted as highly probative evidence, when it was first used it had its skeptics as well. Recently, the scientific validity of fingerprint evidence has again been questioned by a court.[222]

In the well-known trilogy[223] of cases under FRE 702 that governs the admissibility of expert testimony, the United States Supreme Court held that "there is a special obligation on a trial judge 'to ensure that any and all scientific testimony…is not only relevant, but reliable.'"[224] For proving the existence of serious mental illness as the primary justification for state intervention and compulsory treatment, however, the Court's precedents are palpably inconsistent with its own assertion that the best science makes the best evidence. The Supreme Court trilogy announced a major revision of the previous *Frye* standard for evidence admissible in a federal court of law.

Frye established that evidence would be admissible if it was "generally accepted" in the particular field of inquiry. Now, under *Daubert, Joiner*, and *Kumho*, the Court went beyond the rather simple notion in *Frye* that scientific evidence only had to be accepted in the scientific community. The "general acceptance" test was moved to the last of four criteria: (1) scientific conclusions are testable under a valid methodology; this distinguishes science from other fields of inquiry; (2) science is generally subjected to peer review and publication; (3) science usually has a known or potential rate of error; and (4) not required, but permitted, is general acceptance in the relevant scientific community.[225]

The Court's intent was to educate courts and professionals about the importance of and preference for real science in the courtroom.[226] The lesson of these cases can be summed up in one word: "reliability."[227] Any expert can swear that his opinion would be "generally acceptable" in the field and satisfy the former *Frye* standard. The Court was simply saying that "talk is cheap; show me the science." It is much more important that experts' opinions and conclusions be based on empirical science that is reliable, that is, where the experiment is repeatable and the hypothesis testable.[228] It has been said that:

The key to understanding Rule 702 is not unfathoming the meaning of the word "scientific;" it is unfathoming [the] meaning of the word "knowledge." The *Daubert* Court was correct in asserting that assessing the validity of knowledge rests on assessing the validity of the method by which the knowledge was obtained.[229]

The last of the trilogy, *Kumho*, answered a question left open in *Daubert*: that is, does it apply to all experts, especially those of the so-called "soft" sciences, such as psychology and psychiatry? The Court's unanimous answer was "yes."[230] As for the spectrum of expert opinions, which vary from hard sciences on one end to soft science in the middle, and medical arts on the other, the Court opined that the trial judge would be the gatekeeper charged with applying the relevant considerations as they might apply.[231]

iii. Legal Schismata: Judicial Divorce of Mental Illness From Science

The problem that courts have encountered is that the science of the brain is both an emerging and a complex field. Within the brain's relatively small size lies an electrical system that can easily rival the most complex computers now in existence. People are beginning to understand the human brain, but it remains a complex entity with "non-linear, probabilistic" parameters of operation.[232] The lack of empirical evidence of physical causes for mental illness obviously reduces the availability of hard data in favor of opinion evidence.

Barefoot v. Estelle[233] is a stark example of whether evidence based on psychiatric opinion alone is sufficient in important cases of determining *dangerousness*. In that case, a defendant, Thomas Barefoot, was convicted of capital murder. Under Texas law, the decision on whether to impose the death penalty was made before the same jury in a separate hearing that would decide two issues: (1) whether the death was deliberately caused, and (2) whether there was a probability that the defendant would commit criminal acts of violence that would constitute a continuing threat to society. Thus, the execution of Thomas Barefoot turned primarily on the testimony of two psychiatrists who, in response to a hypothetical question, testified that in their opinion, the defendant would probably commit violent acts and be a threat to society in the future.[234] The jury answered both statutory questions in the affirmative and the death penalty was imposed.

The substantive issue in this case was whether the prediction of future violence was valid enough to be admitted into evidence. Under *Daubert*, what scientific methodology could produce this "knowledge," that is, would be able to predict that the defendant was likely to behave dangerously or violently in the future? This is a particularly curious question since neither psychiatrist ever examined Thomas Barefoot,[235] and "[t]here is no doubt that the psychiatric testimony increased the likelihood that petitioner would be sentenced to death."[236] Despite the American Psychiatric Association (APA) taking the position in its amicus brief that psychiatrists cannot reliably predict future dangerous behavior, the majority brushes aside this assertion by maintaining that reliability can be minimal but still be admissible as evidence:

> We are no more convinced now that the view of the APA should be converted into a constitutional rule barring an entire category of expert testimony. We are not persuaded that such testimony *is almost entirely unreliable*... .[n]either petitioner nor the Association suggests that psychiatrists *are always wrong with respect to future dangerousness, only most of the time* [italics added].[237]

This minimalist standard of reliability has been criticized on many grounds. One commentator considers the "not always wrong" standard to be so unreliable as an evidentiary standard that it "shocks the conscience" when applied to a death penalty case, and added:

> One suspects that the Justices would not choose a neurosurgeon on such a basis, nor even a podiatrist. Thomas Barefoot was executed on October 24, 1984. As Huber notes, one could favor the death penalty and "yet still recoil at the thought that a junk science fringe of psychiatry...could decide who will be sent to the gallows."

Some commentators believe that testimony concerning future dangerousness is so lacking in reliability that it is unethical. Indeed, the APA reprimanded Dr. Grigson [one of the two psychiatric experts who testified against Thomas Barefoot] for claiming 100% accuracy in capital cases in which he did not examine the defendant. Nevertheless, Dr. Grigson continued to testify. By May 1990, juries had returned death penalties in 118 of the 127 cases in which he had testified. It is essentially the same testimony in every case.[238]

Justice Blackmun, joined by Justices Marshall and Brennan, dissented and dissected Dr. Grigson's testimony under a judicial microscope. For example, Dr. Grigson characterized his own prediction of future violence as "within reasonable psychiatric certainty" and rated Barefoot off a "1 to 10 scale" for sociopathy. Grigson asserted he was "one hundred percent and absolute[ly]" certain that Barefoot would be violent again. The dissent noted the undisputed evidence that psychiatric predictions were accurate no more than one out of three times, even for mentally ill individuals with a history of violence.[239] In addition, they noted that "[p]sychiatrists have no special insights to add to this actuarial fact, and a single violent crime cannot provide a basis for a reliable prediction of future violence."[240] The dissent focused its attack on the concept of "reliability" of psychiatric evidence:

> [i]t is impossible to square admission of this purportedly scientific but actually baseless testimony with the Constitution's paramount concern for reliability in capital sentencing... . [t]he admission of unreliable psychiatric predictions of future violence, offered with unabashed claims of "reasonable medical certainty" or "absolute" professional reliability, creates an intolerable danger that death sentences will be imposed erroneously... . Psychiatric predictions of future dangerousness *are not accurate*; wrong two times out of three, their probative value, and therefore any possible contribution they might make to the ascertainment of truth, is virtually nonexistent... . Indeed, given a psychiatrist's prediction that an individual will be dangerous, it is more likely than not that the defendant will *not* commit further violence.[241]

The dissent concluded by saying:

> Our constitutional duty is to ensure that the State proves future dangerousness, if at all, in a reliable manner...not...loading the fact finding process against the defendant through the presentation of what is, at bottom, false testimony.[242]

On the one hand, there is obviously a need to distinguish the pertinent differences between the *Daubert*, *Joiner*, and *Kumho* cases that require the most available and reliable scientific evidence for admissibility and *Barefoot v. Estelle* that allowed concededly unreliable psychiatric testimony about future dangerousness to justify a death sentence. When the State seeks to treat a person for mental illness due to the danger he poses to himself or others, the State is asserting its police power and should be subjected to the same burdens of proof as in *Barefoot*. The state must prove that a future dangerous behavior will manifest by applying the highest standard of the civil law, "clear and convincing evidence."[243] In constitutional terms, when both capital punishment and civil commitment are primarily to protect society, they are "takings" of liberty and should receive the highest forms of protection from erroneous state action.

As the *Barefoot* Court argued, given that the determination must be made and must be legitimate, though inexact, psychiatrists can be helpful to the court. As the Court bluntly put it: "The suggestion that no psychiatrist's testimony may be presented with respect to a defendant's future dangerousness is somewhat like asking us to disinvent the wheel."[244]

In *Barefoot* the only alternative method of determining the statutory issue suggested in the dissent was using lay testimony and statistics.[245] Statistics often do not predict what a particular individual might do, and lay witnesses do not have the benefit of having studied the relationship between mental illness and violence.[246] Yet when practical necessity or moral authority absolutely mandates, we make a decision because a low level of reliability might be better than none at all.

Psychiatric testimony about future dangerousness might not pass the tests of the *Daubert*, *Joiner*, and *Kumho* but for the Court's rationale of legal necessity and legitimacy. Even for the broader *Frye* test, since the American Psychiatric Association has disclaimed any ability of psychiatry to foretell future dangerousness, predicting dangerousness would not appear to meet a standard of general acceptance within the profession. Thus, *a fortiori*, such predictions would not satisfy *Daubert*'s four-pronged test of reliability/testability, or *Kumho*'s refusal to exempt soft science from hard science testimony.

The *Barefoot* decision aptly demonstrates the problems and questions surrounding the role of science as a basis for decisions in the most important issue of the life or death of an individual. There can be justification for the *Barefoot v. Estelle* approach as the Court points out. The majority did not say that under Texas law a court inappropriately relied on psychiatric testimony to aid the jury in its determination of future dangerousness. Use of psychiatric testimony is more complex and subtle than merely making an ultimate prediction, since under FRE 702, the touchstone for utility is "helpfulness." A psychiatrist not only has experience with dangerous individuals but also has studied the possible relationship between mental illness, personality, and violence.

Expert witnesses in psychiatry and psychology may not be able to claim great accuracy or reliability for their prospective evaluations of human behavior. They can, however, offer their experience with certain similarly ill individuals, a collective knowledge of symptomology, and the state of that particular science. The epistemology of such experts is different and certainly more studied than that of nonscientific experts.[247] Surely, testimony such as in *Barefoot* cannot clear the hurdle of other scientific disciplines, yet whatever the factual basis of the expert testimony, it will be subjected to cross-examination that can expose its uncertainties and other shortcomings.[248] Ultimately, one must look to the purpose for which the evidence is being introduced and whether this purpose, inaccurate though it may potentially be, is "helpful" in assisting the court to make the determinations that the law legitimately requires.

iv. Making Liars of Us All: Expert Psychiatric Testimony Under *Frye*, and *Daubert, Joiner*, and *Kumho*

Under *Frye* one could even imagine the admissibility of Freudian analysis based on the extant number of psychiatrists and psychologists still practicing that form of therapy.[249] *"Frye* is too forgiving. *Frye* allows the admission of generally accepted but unreliable testimony."[250] The *dangerousness* test would not satisfy Frye, unless it was necessitated by a valid statute under the rationale approved in the *Barefoot* case: "[a]cceptance of petitioner's position that expert testimony about future dangerousness is far too unreliable to be admissible would immediately call into question those other contexts in which predictions of future behavior are constantly made."[251]

In 1993 the U.S. Supreme Court handed down its landmark decision regarding the admissibility of scientific testimony in *Daubert v. Merrill-Dow Pharmaceuticals*.[252] In *Daubert* the Supreme Court rejected *Frye*, relying instead on FRE 702 as providing the rubric for the admissibility of expert testimony. The Court started with the consideration of Federal Rules of Evidence's provision that the subject of expert testimony must be "scientific ... knowledge."[253] The Court defined "scientific" as "grounding in the methods and procedures of science," and "knowledge" as a body of facts "accepted as truths on good grounds."[254]

Daubert held that, prior to accepting expert scientific testimony, a court must conduct "a preliminary assessment of whether the reasoning or methodology underlying the testimony is scientifically valid and...whether that reasoning or methodology properly can be applied to the facts at issue."[255]

> [FRE 702's] overarching subject is the scientific validity—and thus the evidentiary relevance and reliability—of the principles that underlie a proposed submission. The focus, of course, must be solely on principles and methodology, not on the conclusions that they generate.[256]

An issue left unanswered by *Daubert* was the scope of its application. Was the holding confined solely to "scientific" testimony or did it apply to all expert testimony under FRE 702? Importantly for the purposes of this chapter, one may also question whether psychiatric and psychological testimony would ever constitute "scientific" testimony under *Daubert*.[257]

Application of the *Daubert* criteria to behavioral and social science evidence, particularly psychological syndromes, is problematical for two reasons: (1) judges' level of understanding of scientific principles and methodology may ill prepare them to evaluate science...and (2) the nature of certain social and behavioral science theories may be inherently inconsistent with *Daubert* criteria such as "falsifiability" and "error rates."[258]

Most federal circuit courts of appeal did apply *Daubert* to psychiatric and psychological testimony. In *U.S. v. Shay*,[259] the First Circuit reversed a district court's decision to exclude testimony on a mental disorder. In *Geir v. Educational Service Unit No. 16*,[260] the Eighth Circuit upheld the exclusion of expert psychiatric testimony under Daubert. The Seventh Circuit required application of the Daubert standard to a psychologist tendered as expert witness in *U.S. v. Hall*.[261]

Because the fields of psychology and psychiatry deal with human behavior and mental disorders, it may be more difficult at times to distinguish between testimony that reflects genuine expertise—a reliable body of genuine...knowledge—and something that is nothing more than fancy phrases for common sense. It is nevertheless true that disorders exist, and the very fact that a layperson will not always be aware of the disorder, its symptoms, or its consequences, means that expert testimony may be particularly important when the facts suggest [that] a person is suffering from a psychological disorder.[262]

In The Ninth Circuit, however, *Daubert* was held inapplicable to nonscientific (psychiatric) expert testimony.[263]

The Supreme Court clarified this part of the rule in *Kumho Tire Company, Ltd. v. Carmichael*,[264] holding that *Daubert* applies to all expert witness testimony. While *Kumho* answers the question posed by Chief Justice Rehnquist's dissent in *Daubert*, it does nothing to address the fundamental problem of admitting inherently unreliable testimony of future dangerousness, especially in cases where there is acceptable empirical science that would adequately address these issues if contemporary mental health jurisprudence permitted it.[265] As Justice Scalia said in concurrence in *Kumho*: "[t]hough...the

Daubert factors are not holy writ, in a particular case the failure to apply one or another of them may be unreasonable, and hence an abuse of discretion."[266]

C. Nullification *Parens Patriae*: Supreme Court

Through advances in technology it became possible for the first time to study the brains of individuals who were still alive. Computer tomography (CT) scans were followed by magnetic resonance imaging (MRI) and an array of other techniques, enabling researchers to measure brain structure and function. What has emerged from the past 20 years of research is overwhelming evidence that schizophrenia and manic-depressive illness are diseases of the brain, in the same way that Parkinson's disease and Alzheimer's disease are diseases of the brain. There are measurable structural and functional differences in the brains of individuals affected by each disease. And in each disease, we know that something has changed the brain structure and function, but we do not yet know precisely what it is. The etiology of the disease is still a mystery, but one that will be solved at the rate of current advancement. Evidence that schizophrenia and manic-depressive illness are diseases of the brain includes the following:

1. Individuals with schizophrenia and manic-depressive disorder, including those who have never been treated, have enlarged ventricles in the brain, as demonstrated in over 100 studies to date.[267]
2. Individuals with schizophrenia, including those who have never been treated, have a reduced volume of gray matter in the brain, especially in the temporal and frontal lobes.[268]
3. Individuals with manic-depressive disorder have an enlarged amygdala and increased numbers of white matter hyperintensities.[269]
4. Individuals with schizophrenia and manic-depressive disorder, including those who have never been treated, have more neurological abnormalities, as shown in over 25 studies.[270]
5. Individuals with schizophrenia and manic-depressive disorder, including those who have never been treated, have more

neuropsychological abnormalities that impair their cognitive function, including such things as information processing and verbal memory.[271]

6. Individuals with schizophrenia, including those who have never been treated, show decreased function of the prefrontal area, an area of the brain that we use for planning and thinking about ourselves.[272]

7. Approximately 50% of individuals with schizophrenia and manic-depressive disorder, including those who have never been treated, have impaired awareness of their own illness. This has been shown in at least 50 different studies. Such individuals do not realize that they are sick, and they will therefore usually not accept treatment voluntarily. Studies suggest that this impaired awareness is probably related to the decreased function of the prefrontal area. These individuals are thus similar to some patients who have had a stroke and, because of brain damage, are unaware of their disability and deny it. The lack of awareness of illness in individuals with schizophrenia and manic-depressive disorder is the most common reason that they do not take their medication.[273]

In Israel, for example, all 16- and 17-year-olds must undergo a pre-induction assessment to determine their intellectual, medical, and psychiatric eligibility for military service. Using these records, Davidson et al. were able to correctly predict 72% of the males who later developed schizophrenia on the basis of deficits in social, intellectual, and organizational functioning.[274] Predicting violence on the basis of the markers available is problematic, because it casts too broad a net. It is now established that a history of violence and concurrent substance abuse are the most important predictors of violence.[275] Untreated severe mental illness would appear to be an additional major predictor. Despite such major predictors, there are many severely mentally ill individuals who have a history of violence and concurrent substance abuse who are untreated; only a small number of them will commit a major act of violence within any defined period of time.

Psychiatry has not gotten much better at predicting prospective violent behavior related to mental illness, but actuarial studies have.[276] However, there are serious issues whether actuarial correlations are useable in civil commitment proceedings. Obviously, these actuarial correlations are accurate for *groups* having certain characteristics, such as age, gender, race, severity of mental illness, personality, substance abuse, history of violence, pathological family environment, etc. However, a civil commitment proceeding necessarily focuses on the civil liberties of a specific individual who might or might not reflect the particular characteristics of one or more groups. Perhaps more questionable is that some of these actuarial criteria might be inadmissible in a court of law for equitable and other constitutional reasons, for example, a court might refuse to consider race, gender, childhood background, substance abuse (for Fifth Amendment reasons), and so forth, as grounds to negatively affect a person's liberty.

The use of dangerousness is not a valid scientific or proper clinical litmus test for whether a person needs care and treatment for mental illness. The legal consequence is that it distorts and erodes the legitimate authority of the state to act as a parent. Just as a parent would be considered irresponsible to use such distant behavioral tests to determine whether treatment is needed for their children, the courts are mandating an irresponsible standard for the state. Again, this analysis does not apply to police power cases where behavior to others is the relevant commitment concern, whereas the clinical diagnosis is important for treatment purposes.

PART THREE: LACK OF INSIGHT
AS A CORRECTIVE

The most prolific source of the prevalent impression on this subject is, unquestionably, the stories of the insane themselves.

Generally, insane people do not regard themselves as insane and, consequently, can see no reason for their confinement other than the malevolent designs of those who have deprived them of their liberty. And they are all the more inclined to this conclusion by feelings of hostility already engendered toward their friends and all others who have exercised any control over their movements. Many of them are discharged, much improved perhaps, but before they have fully come to themselves and regained the power of seeing their relations with others in the true light.[277]

—Dr. Isaac Ray (1869)

A. NULLIFICATION DE FACTO

Dr. Isaac Ray was one of the most influential founders of American psychiatry and one of the first to clinically recognize the phenomenon of "lack of insight" as a prevalent condition of serious mental illness, along with the other father of American psychiatry, Dr. Benjamin Rush.[278] It is clear, however, that this condition did not require medical expertise to witness. It was commonly observed that severe mental illness often blinded self-perception as to both the manifestations of the disorder and the need for treatment. This phenomenon has formed the basis of most *parens patriae* civil commitment laws for the past 150 years.[279]

The inability of a person to perceive himself, the condition of his judgmental disabilities or to a lack of reasonably correct perception of fundamental necessities of survival due to a mental deficiency, has for centuries been the criteria of social and legal competence to enjoy and exercise the full rights and accept the responsibilities of adulthood.[280] Under Western law, it has also been the basis for countervailing considerations to protect the mentally disabled, such as the "excusing" and "absolving" conditions of the civil and criminal laws; these include the insanity defense and nullification of contract and marriage.[281]

The phenomenon of lack of insight is essentially an inability to perceive, understand, or think rationally or a failure to be aware of one's own mental illness and a refusal to accept needed treatment. If a person with severe mental illness genuinely, even if erroneously, believes that he is mentally healthy, then is there need for treatment?[282] The phenomenon of lack of insight is the absence of an essential component of rational thinking as well as an incapacity for self-preservation or self-interest. The exercise of autonomous decision-making and other rights make no sense if there is neither understanding nor moral responsibility due to this form of incompetence.

The most recent edition of the *DSM-IV-TR*[283] states in its section "Schizophrenia and other psychotic disorders: Associated descriptive features and mental disorders":

> A majority of individuals with schizophrenia have poor insight regarding the fact that they have a psychotic illness. Evidence suggests that poor insight is a manifestation of the illness itself rather than a coping strategy. It may be comparable to the lack of awareness of neurological deficits seen in stroke, termed *anosognosia*. This symptom predisposes the individual to noncompliance with treatment and has been found to be predictive of higher relapse rates, increased number of involuntary hospital admissions, poorer psychosocial functioning, and a poorer course of illness.[284]

It is an ironic reversal that lack of insight was, in 1869, clinically and legally established as the primary symptom of serious mental illness; but 100 years later, it has been replaced with a more primitive behavioral standard unrelated to medicine or science. It is more remarkable that the impetus for the movement away from scientific criteria was led by the federal courts in stark contrast to the scientific process and empirical fact upon which admissible evidence is based.[285] Few illnesses have their diagnoses or treatments confined to physical manifestations of violent or dangerous behaviors when there are more fundamental and causative clinical explanations. It is particularly inapposite with mental illness because it ignores what is known about the brain's function and its tenuous connection to violence and causative dangerousness. In almost all cases, especially the so-called danger to self type of mental illness, the danger does not emanate from the mental illness. Rather, it exists by virtue of a loss of perception that produces an inability to perceive or to avoid dangers.[286]

In other words, the mental illness produces a lack of insight that in turn cripples the person's danger-avoidance abilities. Mental illness, however, does not necessarily produce dangers, and except for suicide and self-injury, it does not create external causes of danger to the person. For example, the inability to cross a street safely, to maintain a medication regime, or eat are not caused by a mental illness: They are created by the lack of judgment inherent in the illness. Such conditions are not "dangers"; they are endangerments that have nothing specific to do with the brain malfunction. In contrast, lack of insight is a common phenomenon in over half the cases of serious mental illness and that debility might manifest itself in an infinite number of ways.

The legal standard for competency that is used in contemporary law has direct lineage in Greek rationalistic philosophy. Aristotle postulated the definition of justice based on three factors: (1) the actor's rational thinking,[287] (2) knowledge of the nature of the act or of the instrument used, and (3) the existence of voluntariness or "free will."[288] These three elements of consent inform modern legal concepts of legal competence for medical decision making. The formulation used by most courts is whether the patient has "sufficient mind to reasonably understand his condition, the nature and effect of the proposed treatment, attendant risks in pursuing the treatment, and not pursuing the treatment."[289]

The first aspect that a trial judge usually considers is determining legal competence to make a rational decision. That is, whether a person is self-aware of the immediate situation and its long-term benefits, harms, and dangers, and how a person appears to comprehend and plan to cope with this situation.[290] Consent principles and informed consent laws have consistently utilized the Aristotelian formula to define competency. The U.S. Supreme Court has generally and consistently used three elements to define informed consent: knowledge (information), intelligence (rationality), and voluntariness (lack of coercion).[291] With slight variations, this same formulation has been adopted by the most prestigious national consensus of authorities on medical ethics: the President's Commission for the Study of Ethical Problems in Medicine, Biomedical and Behavioral Research,[292] as well as the largest and most comprehensive empirical study of competence ever done.[293]

Dr. Paul S. Appelbaum has written of a similar phenomenon that should be contrasted to avoid confusion with "lack of insight." Dr. Appelbaum argues that the denial of a physical illness ("maladaptive denial of physical illness—MDPI") is neither a diagnosis nor necessarily indicative of legal incompetence to refuse treatment or to be subjected to compulsory treatment.[294] He is correct that merely denying an illness, whether it is a truthful assertion or not, does not prove the existence of a mental illness or supply any basis to civilly commit a person for care and treatment. There can be rational reasons for denial. For example, one might deny signs of a physical illness, such as a heart attack or disability, or ignore the likelihood of harm in a dangerous activity, such as tobacco smoking, illicit drug use, excess alcohol consumption, driving at excessive speed, and so forth. The purpose could be erecting a psychological defense mechanism for self-protection, privacy, preserving ego, avoiding stigma, or other such reasons.

Denial of an illness or refusal of treatment does not necessarily constitute "lack of insight," in the sense that Dr. Appelbaum describes, such as deniers refusing to admit certain facts or the import of those facts to avoid stigma or for other nonclinical reasons. Thus, their denials are often largely conclusory misinterpretations of facts, whether intentional or subconscious, but not a failure to perceive them. In contrast, a person who lacks insight is unable to perceive the reality of their mental illness and the accompanying symptoms such as radical changes in their personality or behavior. Merely denying an illness might well be nothing more than a psychological syndrome or a ploy to protect privacy or ego. Such a situation, without additional objective evidence of a mental illness, would, therefore, form no basis for treatment.

Dr. Appelbaum talks of such things as a failure to admit or perceive that an activity might be harmful or life threatening, such as smoking tobacco. But millions of people either do that or consciously ignore the danger. This does not supply any basis to compel treatment. Society not only tolerates, it often encourages risk-taking behaviors as a matter of lifestyle and sometimes, as in war, as a matter of law.[295] Dr. Xavier Amador often uses the comparison of lack of insight to the phenomenon of anosognosia. Taken from the Greek ("ano" and "gnosia," meaning not to know or recognize, especially connoting at the head or upper body), he describes that some stroke patients having a paralysis of an arm, for example, will deny their inability to move that arm. It is more than a misperception; it is an inability of the brain to perceive that disability—a blind spot on the brain.[296] So, while denial of a physical illness might not be a diagnosis, it can be a symptom or a reasonable suspicion of an underlying problem and consequently provides evidence of a co-occurring mental disease.

The rationality or acceptability of some behaviors is a cultural matter. *Lack of insight* is, however, more than that: It is a medically verifiable symptom that is increasingly being verified as having an organic etiology and physical effect on the brain. Dr. Appelbaum was appropriate to criticize inaccurate statements such as:

> Those who deny their illness cannot rationally evaluate the usefulness of a hospital or of antipsychotic medication, and on that basis they are incompetent to make both decisions.[297]

The first part of this statement is true: that someone who denies an illness or who refuses treatment will likely not be cured or helped because they see no reason for such care. The second part, however, is not true; that is, that they are necessarily incompetent because of that denial. In presenting moral theorists with a map of human abilities and capabilities, neuroscience may also help to identify new classes of people who may not have the adequate capacities to meet the requirements of a moral theory. For instance, theories of responsibility usually require that agents demonstrate a minimum level of rationality. As stated earlier, however, competing theorists have for the most part defined rationality in terms of either cognitive abilities or both cognitive and emotional abilities.

Antonio Damasio's research on frontal lobe patients, for example, uncovered a group of patients who displayed irrational behavior despite having cognitive functions that remained intact. Once the neuroscientist uncovers a potentially new class of individuals who exhibit irrational behavior as the result of neurological or physiological impairment, moral theorists still need to determine whether they ought to excuse or exempt those people from responsibility ascriptions. Conceivably, neuroscientific tests tracing an individual's irrational behavior to permanently impaired neurological systems would be compelling evidence for an argument urging reconsideration of the tenets supporting a given moral theory. Laura Reider discusses this research:

> In his landmark work, the neuroscientist Antonio Damasio discovered that the disruption of emotional and feeling capacities as well as biological regulatory systems impairs personal and social judgments. Having suffered damage in the prefrontal lobe area of the brain, patients who had previously been good decision makers experienced a dearth of emotions and feelings and became poor decision makers. Although they continued to exhibit a full range of intellectual and cognitive abilities, they failed to demonstrate coherent decision-making and judgmental abilities. Curious as to whether cognitive functions alone explained an agent's rationality, Damasio performed research on these patients. He determined that even though the frontal lobe damage resulted in an impaired ability to experience emotions, his patients scored remarkably high on standard intelligence tests and personality profiles.
>
> In addition to their lack of emotional and feeling capacities, Damasio's patients experienced a breakdown in biological regulation. The specific biological mechanisms pertinent in the decision-making process are "drives and instincts [that] operate either by generating a particular behavior directly or by inducing physiological states that lead individuals to behave in a particular way, mindlessly or not." These underlying biological systems not only aid in an individual's

overall plan of survival but also help to sort events into "good" or "bad" classifications, depending upon their possible effect on future survival. Over time, these systems couple with ongoing experiences to develop a "repertoire of things categorized as good or bad...and [an] ability to detect new good and bad things." Consequently, any disruption or abnormality of these biological drives and instincts leads to an inability to categorize appropriately experiences and events in the world.

Brain damage to the frontal lobe that impairs the ability to classify a situation as either beneficial or detrimental accordingly results in a reduced capacity to respond appropriately to social situations. Somatic markers give an individual the capacity to respond automatically to particular stimuli on a precognitive level. They work to limit the array of possible responses before cognitive and rational capacities come into play.[298]

Trial judges see the manifestations of these brain impairments present in the respondents in their courtrooms. Under these circumstances superficial application of the *O'Connor dangerous* standard is necessary to overcome avoidance of treatment due to a patient's lack of insight. The most profound instances are when there is strong evidence of the success of past treatments, refusals by the patient to recognize the viability of treatment, and the support of family or other persons who have the patient's best interest at heart.[299] Although most judges do not have a sophisticated understanding of the biology of the brain,[300] their wisdom and common sense recognizes a lack of insight when they see it.[301] Thus, where dangerousness is not an obvious[302] and easy basis for ordering treatment under current jurisprudence, the trial court can and usually does rationalize nullification of the dangerousness requirement to justify a *parens patriae* civil commitment and the treatment the patient obviously needs.[303] There is a trend to changingback a "lack of insight" standard by incorporating contemporary science to support a full cognitive standard along with a "dangerousness" standard, for example, in states such as Washington, North Carolina and Texas.[304]

Since more patients receive necessary treatment under this pattern of nullification, recharacterizing lack of insight in terms of the dangerousness standard is more a matter of beneficent hypocrisy than dysfunctional dereliction of judicial duty. While this might be beneficent, it is certainly not building respect for law or applying the new scientific standards of evidence in the courtroom.

B. NULLIFICATION OF THE FEDERAL RULES OF EVIDENCE: LACK OF INSIGHT AS SCIENCE

Many studies have described the strong evidence locating the frontal lobes as the site of the neurological impairments that include lack of insight.[305] Technology has allowed scientists to study the brain, the most complex and inaccessible part of the body. Judges and psychiatrists generally want to avoid making what are nonmedical conclusions where a professionally acceptable medical judgment is called for. Predicting dangerousness is simply outside the expertise or experience of psychiatrists,[306] who would, as physicians and scientists, rather use a testable criteria of lack of insight as the first consideration of the need to treat a person with mental illness.[307]

Judicial decisions have become increasingly bizarre as judges make diagnoses, order and reject treatments, and discharge patients. The courts often manifest gross ignorance of the issues about which they create laws, relying on lawyers and doctors who pose as experts but are actually persuaders, advocates, and propagandists with economic or other agendas. In addition, the jury system is not conducive to an accurate evaluation of care.[308]

Unlike an error-prone opinion, even if it is based on some professional expertise, about dangerousness (i.e., where an unambiguous violent or harmful act has not occurred and even the nonexpert could evaluate it), the characterization of dangerous does not rise to the level of scientific probability or really say anything definitive about an individual. In contrast, the phenomenon of lack of insight is testable, verifiable, and individualized. The ability to test lack of insight and growing evidence of the organic relationship of mental illness to specific areas of the brain, illustrates how unacceptable dangerousness, which is not amenable to scientific testing, measurement,[309] or prediction, is as an essential characteristic of mental illness.[310]

Use of the lack of insight phenomenon permits greater adherence to the *Daubert-Joiner-Kumho* rule. It brings real science into the courtroom that can be subject to cross-examination and verification. It also provides a crucial opportunity for a jury to understand for itself the connections between mental illness and the need for treatment, rather than having to accept or reject conclusory statements by psychiatrists and other experts.[311]

> The phenomenon of poor insight is defined as a general lack of awareness of having a mental disorder or needing treatment, for example, psychotropic medications. Contemporary definitions of insight regard this phenomenon as occurring on a continuum which can be assessed by skilled clinicians. Thus, insight can be reliably measured using ratings on standardized instruments. Using standardized scales, researchers have found that ratings of poor insight in schizophrenia are associated with lack of compliance in taking medications, refusal of treatment regimens, poorer over-all recovery after treatment, an increased risk of psychological decompensation, a greater number of rehospitalizations, poorer long-term outcome, and worse over-all treatment outcome.[312]

If professional psychiatrists, with essentially the same training and using similar techniques cannot generally agree on such predictions, then obviously the technique is either flawed or the diagnosis is invalidly descriptive of the disease.[313] Predicting dangerousness is not scientific; it is a legal construct that is sometimes necessary to administer law and policies.[314] At best, the relationship between dangerousness and mental illness is associational rather than clinical. *Daubert* requires the legal system to rely upon quantitative statistical analysis when offered in contrast to subjective and anecdotal opinion.[315]

Justice Blackmun's opinion in *Daubert* has been characterized as epistemological in emphasis[316] and Newtonian in its use of natural science theory.[317] Justice Blackmun makes an important distinction between the ontology of science and the business of a court.[318] The former seeks to find the truth of the universe by verifying theory, where over time those theories will be refined, changed, contradicted, or reinforced. In contrast, a court's business is to settle controversies and render a verdict for a party who has petitioned the court for certain relief. The processes of good science, while a proper basis for evidence, are thus not necessarily the same as due process of law.

The term "epistemic paternalism" means the responsibility of the trial judge to be gatekeeper and guarantor of the integrity of the court's processes and verdict. Simply put, the judge must ensure that the science is reliable as well as understandable to the jury.[319] Judges and juries do not deal with issues of science *per se*; they decide cases and controversies. Nor do similar cases have to come to the same conclusion due to slight variations in the rules of evidence, competence of presentations by lawyers, demeanor, clarity and persuasiveness of witnesses, and many other factors. The judge's responsibility is to control the evidence and presentations in the case in order to give the jury the best chance of coming to a truthful and fair verdict.

On questions of mental illness and the proper exercise of state authority to use civil commitment as a treatment modality, as opposed to a preventive measure for public safety, lack of insight as an empirical phenomenon is within acceptable scientific limits. Dangerousness is largely a guessing game without methodology or testability.

> Now that we view the brain as non-linear, probabilistic, at the transition between equilibrium and non-equilibrium, how are we to view mental disease? Mental disorder is just that—disorder, or brain activity beyond the normal range of probabilities. Normally, we have a wide range of options from which we choose the more or less optimal path. Critical judgment can be said to be the capacity to narrow down the probabilities to a manageable number. Saddled with a mental disease, the range of probabilities increases. There are too many options, too many possible directions in which to go, and far too many of these options appear "logical." In the absence

of critical judgment, it becomes easier to take a "flyer," or to follow a red herring of logic to its illogical—and in some cases criminal—fate.... In order to understand mental disorder, we need to know about normal mental states.... Mental disease has a physical basis, even though we do not yet know exactly how it works. Diagnosis of mental disease, like that of physical disease, is the basis of specialized knowledge, and that is the province of experts.... Even more egregious than permitting lay witnesses to testify about disease is the Supreme Court's position on admissibility of future dangerousness testimony. No one (including psychiatrists) can predict with any degree of reliability that an individual will commit other crimes in the future. Moreover, the psychiatrists in question had never examined the defendant personally.[320]

C. Nullification of the Traditional *Parens Patriae* Authority

What kind of "freedom" is it to be wandering the streets severely mentally ill, deteriorating, and getting warmth from a steel grate or food from a garbage can? That's not freedom; that's abandonment.

And what kind of "liberty" is it to be jailed for disorderly conduct, crazed and delusional, because that is all the law will allow, instead of being hospitalized, treated and released? That's not liberty; that's imprisonment for the crime of being sick.... And what kind of twisted "right" is it to stab or shoot to death yourself or some innocent bystander while in a psychotic frenzy, directed by terrifying voices from a disordered and disabled mind?...

Enough of the helpless have been made homeless, enough of the bystanders have died, enough family members have been exhausted in a fruitless effort to help, and enough patients have "died with their rights on."[321]

There is no better statement of the *parens patriae* power than that made by John Locke, whose political thought dominated American political philosophy:[322]

> The Power, then, that parents have over their children, arises from that Duty which is incumbent on them—to take care of their offspring—during the imperfect state of childhood. To inform the Mind, and govern the Actions of their yet ignorant Nonage, till Reason shall take its place, and ease them of that Trouble, is what the Children want, and the Parents are bound to. For God having given Man an Understanding to direct his actions, has allowed him a freedom of Will, and liberty of Acting, as properly belonging thereunto, within the bounds of that Law he is under.... And so Lunatics and Ideots are never set free from the Government of their Parents; Children, who are not as yet come unto those years whereat they may have; and Innocents which are excluded by a natural defect from ever having; Thirdly, Madmen, which for the present cannot possibly have the use of right Reason to guide themselves, have for their Guide, the Reason that guideth other Men which are Tutors over them, to seek and procure their good for them, says Hooker, Eccl. Pol. Lib. 1, Sect. 7. All which seems no more than that Duty, which God and Nature has laid on Man as well as other Creatures; to preserve their Off-Spring, till they can be able to shift for themselves, and will scarce amount to an instance or proof of Parents Regal Authority.[323]

Parents are not constrained to provide guidance and treatment only when their children are dangerous. Parents must also nurture and inculcate right reason in their children. Government performs the same tasks in maintaining a public educational system, public health and safety, a welfare safety net, and so forth, all enforceable under either criminal or civil laws, but all primarily to help, not punish, an individual.

At the current time, there are approximately 24 states that have "lack of insight" language in their statutes.[324] The lack of insight used in these statutes is consistent with the Aristotelian concept of lack of rationality, reason, or understanding. This is also consistent with the more recent "gravely disabled" standard that generally means a lack of functionality such as a physical inability or lack of capacity to function as an adult.[325] The "lack of insight" is essentially based on the traditional notion of lack of rationality.[326] It incorporates a lack of rationality with a lack of perception.[327]

Conclusion

> *Individualism in the law, as in matters of faith, produces the substitution of private morality for public law and duty. This is precisely what [Thomas] More thought [Martin] Luther was encouraging in his own day, and it is even more prominent in ours. That may be seen in the growth of legal nullification, the refusal to be bound by external rules, that is not only widespread among the American people but, more ominously, in the basic institutions of the law. More applied his injunction as much to the judge on the bench as to rioters in the streets. We all recognize that the judge who ignores law or who creates constitutional law out of his own conscience is equally civilly disobedient.*[328]
>
> —Judge Robert H. Bork (1999)

Judicial nullification is the moral equivalent of civil disobedience, having the destabilizing effect of rioters in the streets. Nowhere is nullification more evident than in the way the judiciary has undermined *parens patriae* civil commitment and compulsory treatment of the severely mentally ill. Since the courts have insinuated themselves as the gatekeepers for the exercise of state authority for civil commitment and undertaken to hamper the clinical judgments of professionals, they can be assigned their share of responsibility for the consequences of this trilogy of nullifications.

For a substantial minority, however, deinstitutionalization has been a denial of sufficient psychiatric care. Many mentally ill wander the streets or are incarcerated, with all of their dignity as well as integrity of body, mind, and spirit dumped on a fiction of self-determination. The Potemkin "choices" offered to them are soup kitchens, back alleys, jail, and social contempt. And for many homeless mentally ill individuals, the so-called "least restrictive setting" is often a lonely card-board box set up on the streets or back alleys that is filled only with a plague of real and imaginary enemies endured with the lack of any meaningful interaction with either society or other individuals.

Equally shameful is the needless criminalization of individuals who should be civil hospital patients. Such large-scale imprisonment for sickness is a 2-century regression to darker ages when the mentally ill, lepers, and other undesirables were believed to be cursed and to deserve punishment rather than treatment. The three largest "treatment" facilities for the seriously mentally ill are the three largest urban jails in the United States—Rikers Island in New York City, Cook County Jail in Chicago, and Los Angeles County Jail in Los Angeles. This nation's jails are "brim-full" of the mentally ill, who are often there for minor crimes, and many are in local jails without charges at all.[329] What is the purpose of imprisonment for someone so schizophrenic that they are not even aware of their own illness or able to control their own behavior?

> People with schizophrenia, for example, are ill-served by incarceration. Imprisoning them may keep them off the streets, but it will not reform them, because they cannot understand that the prison experience is intended to deter repeat offenses. Too confused to defend themselves or read the intentions of others, they are easy prey; victimization only reinforces their perception of threat. Schizophrenia…is not an act, a state of mind, or a fanciful eccentricity. It is a chronic, incapacitating brain disorder that abolishes rational thinking and turns emotional reactions upside down. They cannot and typically will not ask for help, because unlike the depressed, the anxious, or the traumatized, they don't recognize that anything is wrong… . Punishing behavior driven by delusions is equally irrational—and it's expensive, cruel, and ineffective as well… . The mentally ill, who were supposed to be freed, have been abandoned, at the mercy of threatening delusions that prompt tragic attempts at self-defense.[330]

One hundred and eight years ago, Dr. Stephen Smith, a prominent physician and official of New York State's mental health system wrote:

> The lunacy laws of the states of the United States are, for the most part, an incongruous mass of legal verbiage, incapable of explanation or judicial construction. They are in the main an elaboration of the laws of a century ago with scarcely a recognition of the great advances that have been made

in our knowledge of insanity. Notwithstanding the many improvements that have been made in providing for the physical comfort for the insane, there is apparent running through our lunacy laws the dominant idea of the criminality of insanity. Commitment and detention, and even care and treatment are still subordinated to this ancient prejudice of our legislators. We are still governed by the common law of England, which declares that "it is only a person of unsound mind and dangerous to himself and other that may be restrained of his liberty by another." States are making better and better provisions for security and well being of the insane while in custody, but they are doing absolutely nothing directly to restore the insane to health. Every improvement in asylum care is chiefly made for the purpose of safe detention and not for cure. As a result the insane in custody are constantly increasing, while the number of cures among them is at its minimum.... . As a logical necessity it follows that if the insane are simply sick people they should come completely under the jurisdiction and management of the medical profession.... . As we have shown, this relic of ancient jurisprudence has been and still is seriously obstructive of all efforts to elevate the care of the insane and place it on the same basis as that so judiciously and advantageously applied to persons suffering from other diseases. But in an enlightened period and in this republic, so little governed by precedents and by obligations to the civil jurisprudence of the past, we ought to recast our laws in light of modern ideas, the deductions of scientific inquiry, and the demand of a more enlightened philanthropy. Influenced by these considerations the insane should be placed on the same footing before the law as are persons suffering from other diseases requiring isolation in the interests of both the public and the patients themselves.[331]

The fundamental issue is one of discrimination against the mentally ill under a guise of special treatment and based on distorted and nontraditional concepts of their civil rights. This is not the case in Japan,[332] England, and many other countries, which do not emphasize legal process over clinical treatment.[333] Public policy elsewhere largely treats mental illness the way it treats any other sickness and accords the same availability of public hospitals and funding for it. It is the hypocrisy of this era of mental health jurisprudence that care and treatment has become increasingly ineffectual inversely to the intensifying legal processes. The economics of publicly funded health care, and especially mental hygiene care, have dramatically changed and outpatient commitment is an essential element of the community treatment modality that is being supported nationwide because it enhances both individual treatment and the effectiveness of treatment.[333] The law must become more therapeutically oriented and the courts must endeavor to understand both the etiology of the disease of mental illness as well as the mechanics and economics of the public treatment system. I have made this point for many years and it has recently been noted in a law school textbook on mental illness:

> Stavis states that '[c]ourt attitudes [that are] based on an archaic view of civil commitment as a life long imprisonment...ignore[ ] the current reality that government no longer is motivated to hospitalize patients, if al all, for any longer than is absolutely necessary. Indeed, the contemporary problem is obtaining treatment, not refusing its imposition.'[333]

APPENDIX

State	Statutory Language
Alabama	Code of Ala. § 22-52-10.2, § 22-52-10.4 (1999) For outpatient and inpatient: "and (iii) the respondent is unable to make a rational and informed decision as to whether or not treatment for mental illness would be desirable." Note: Per the annotation, the relevant statutory language was enacted in 1991.
Alaska	
Arizona	A.R.S. § 36-540 (1998) "that the proposed patient is, as a result of mental disorder, a danger to himself, is a danger to others, is persistently or acutely disabled or is gravely disabled and in need of treatment, and is either unwilling or unable to accept voluntary treatment..." Note: Per the annotation, the relevant statutory language was enacted in 1979.
Arkansas	
California	Cal Wel & Inst Code § 5250(a) (1999) "the person is, as a result of mental disorder or impairment by chronic alcoholism, a danger to others, or to himself or herself, or gravely disabled...(c) The person has been advised of the need for, but has not been willing or able to accept, treatment on a voluntary basis." Note: The relevant statutory language was enacted prior to 1989 Amendments.
Colorado	C.R.S. 27-10-102(5)(a)(II) (1998) "Gravely disabled" means a condition in which a person, as a result of mental illness:... (II) Lack judgment in the management of his resources and it the conduct of his social

relations to the extent that his health or safety is significantly endangered and lacks the capacity to understand that this is so.

Note: Per the session laws, the relevant statutory language was enacted in 1977.

C.R.S. 27-10-109(4) (1998)
"When a petition contains a request that a specific legal disability be imposed or that a specific legal right be deprived, the court may order the disability imposed or the right deprived if it or a jury has determined that the respondent is mentally ill or gravely disabled and that, by reason thereof, the person is unable to competently exercise said right or perform the function as to which the disability is sought to be imposed."

Connecticut

Conn. Gen. Stat. § 17a-495(a) (1997)
"gravely disabled" means that a person, as a result of mental or emotional impairment, is in danger of serious harm as a result of an inability or failure to provide for his or her own basic human needs such as essential food, clothing, shelter or safety and that hospital treatment is necessary and available and that such person is mentally incapable of determining whether or not to accept such treatment because his judgment is impaired by his psychiatric disabilities.

Note: Per the session laws, the relevant statutory language was enacted in 1994, 1995.

Delaware

16 Del. C. § 5001(1) (1998)
"Mentally ill person" means a person suffering from a mental disease or condition which requires such person to be observed and treated at a mental hospital for the person's own welfare and which both (i) renders such person unable to make responsible decisions with respect to the person's hospitalization, and..."

Note: Per legislative staff, the relevant statutory language was enacted in 1975.

D.C.

Florida

Fla. Stat. § 394.467(1)(a)(1) (1998)
"...a. He or she has refused voluntary placement for treatment after sufficient and conscientious explanation and disclosure of the purpose of placement for treatment; or b. He or she is unable to determine for himself or herself whether placement is necessary; AND..."

Georgia

O.C.G.A. § 37-3-1(12.1)(B) (1999)
For outpatient: "Who because of the person's current mental status, mental history, or nature of the person's mental illness is unable voluntarily to seek or comply with outpatient treatment; and..."
Note: This element applies only to outpatient treatment, not inpatient. Per the annotation, OPC was enacted in 1986 with the relevant statutory language.

Hawaii

HRS § 334-1 (1999)
"Gravely disabled" means a condition in which a person, as a result of a mental disorder, (1) is unable to provide for that individual's basic personal needs for food, clothing, or shelter; (2) is unable to make or communicate rational or responsible decisions concerning the individual's personal welfare; and (3) lacks the capacity to understand that this is so..."
Note: Per the session laws, the relevant statutory language was enacted post 1986.
"Obviously ill" means a condition in which a person's current behavior and previous history of mental illness, if known, indicate a disabling mental illness, and the person is incapable of understanding that there are serious and highly probable risks to health and safety involved in

refusing treatment, the advantages of accepting treatment, or of understanding the advantages of accepting treatment and the alternatives to the particular treatment offered, after the advantages, risks, and alternatives have been explained to the person.
Note: per the session laws, the relevant statutory language was enacted in 1986 (Ch. 335, Sec. 1).

HRS § 334-121 (1999)
For outpatient: (5) The person's current mental status or the nature of the person's disorder limits or negates the person's ability to make an informed decision to voluntarily seek or comply with recommended treatment; and
Note: the relevant statutory language was enacted in 1967.

Idaho

Idaho Code § 66-317(h) (1998)
"Lacks capacity to make informed decisions about treatment" shall mean the inability, by reason of mental illness, to achieve a rudimentary understanding after conscientious efforts at explanation of the purpose, nature, and possible significant risks and benefits of treatment."
Note: per the session laws, the relevant statutory language was enacted pre 1991.

Illinois

405 ILCS 5/2-107.1(4) (1999)
"Authorized involuntary treatment shall not be administered to the recipient unless it has been determined by clear and convincing evidence that all of the following factors are present:
(E) That the recipient lacks the capacity to make a reasoned decision about the treatment."

Indiana

Iowa

Iowa Code § 229.1(15) (1997)
"Seriously mentally impaired" or "serious mental impairment" describes the condition

of a person with mental illness and because
of that illness lacks sufficient judgment to
make responsible decisions with respect to
the person's hospitalization or treatment, and
who because of that illness meets any of the
following criteria..."

Kansas

K.S.A. § 59-2946 (1997)
(f)(1) "Mentally ill person subject to involuntary commitment for care and treatment"
means a mentally ill person, as defined in subsection (e), who also lacks capacity to make
an informed decision concerning treatment,
is likely to cause harm to self or others, and
whose diagnosis is not solely one of the following mental disorders: Alcohol or chemical
substance abuse; antisocial personality disorder; mental retardation; organic personality
syndrome; or an organic mental disorder.
(f)(2) "Lacks capacity to make an informed
decision concerning treatment" means that the
person, by reason of the person's mental disorder, is unable, despite conscientious efforts at
explanation, to understand basically the nature
and effects of hospitalization or treatment or is
unable to engage in a rational decision-making
process regarding hospitalization or treatment,
as evidenced by an inability to weigh the possible risks and benefits.
Note: per the session laws, the relevant statutory language was enacted in 1996 or before.

Kentucky

Louisiana

La. R.S. 28:2(10) (1998)
"Gravely disabled" means the condition of a
person who is unable to provide for his own
basic physical needs, such as essential food,
clothing, medical care, and shelter, as a result
of serious mental illness or substance abuse

and is unable to survive safely in freedom or protect himself from serious harm; the term also includes incapacitation by alcohol, which means the condition of a person who, as a result of the use of alcohol, is unconscious or whose judgment is otherwise so impaired that he is incapable of realizing and making a rational decision with respect to his need for treatment.

Note: the lack of insight language appears to apply only to incapacitation by alcohol, not mental illness. Per the session laws, the relevant statutory language was enacted post 1987.

Maine

Maryland

Md. HEALTH-GENERAL Code Ann. § 10-617(4) (1998)
"The individual is unable or unwilling to be admitted voluntarily; and..."

Massachusetts

Michigan

MCL § 330.1401(1) (1998)
"As used in this chapter, "person requiring treatment" means...(c) An individual who has mental illness, whose judgment is so impaired that he or she is unable to understand his or her need for treatment and whose continued behavior as the result of this mental illness can reasonably be expected, on the basis of competent clinical opinion, to result in significant physical harm to himself or herself or others."
Note: this criteria may only be used for emergency treatment, not for long-term commitment.

Minnesota

Minn. Stat. § 253B.065.Subd.5(b)(3)(i) (1998)
"The court shall order early intervention treatment if the court finds all of the elements of the following factors by clear and convincing evidence: (1) the proposed patient is mentally

ill; (2) the proposed patient refuses to accept appropriate mental health treatment; and (3) the proposed patient's mental illness is manifested by instances of grossly disturbed behavior or faulty perceptions and either: (i) the grossly disturbed behavior or faulty perceptions significantly interfere with the proposed patient's ability to care for self and the proposed patient, when competent, would have chosen substantially similar treatment under the same circumstances; or..."

Minn. Stat. § 253B.092.Subd.5(b) (1998) "For medication: (b) In determining a person's capacity to make decisions regarding the administration of neuroleptic medication, the court shall consider:
(1) whether the person demonstrates an awareness of the nature of the person's situation, including the reasons for hospitalization, and the possible consequences of refusing treatment with neuroleptic medications;
(2) whether the person demonstrates an understanding of treatment with neuroleptic medications and the risks, benefits, and alternatives; and
(3) whether the person communicates verbally or nonverbally a clear choice regarding treatment with neuroleptic medications that is a reasoned one not based on delusion, even though it may not be in the person's best interests. Disagreement with the physician's recommendation is not evidence of an unreasonable decision.
Note: the first criteria applies only to early intervention and the last criteria applies only to the use of neuroleptic medications.

Mississippi

Miss. Code Ann. § 41-21-61(e)(ii)(B) (1998) "Mentally ill person" includes a person who, based on treatment history and other applicable psychiatric indicia, is in need of treatment in order to prevent further disability or deterioration which would predictably result in dangerousness to himself or others when his current mental illness limits or negates his ability to make an informed decision to seek or comply with recommended treatment. Note: Per the annotation, the relevant statutory language was enacted in 1994.

Missouri

§ 632.005(9)(b) R.S.Mo. (1999)
"A substantial risk that serious physical harm to a person will result or is occurring because of an impairment in his capacity to make decisions with respect to his hospitalization and need for treatment as evidenced by his current mental disorder or mental illness which results in an inability to provide for his own basic necessities of food, clothing, shelter, safety or medical care or his inability to provide for his own mental health care which may result in a substantial risk of serious physical harm." Note: per the session laws, the relevant statutory language was enacted in 1980 or before.

Montana

Nebraska

Nevada

New Hampshire

New Jersey

New Mexico

New York

NY CLS Men Hyg § 9.01 (1999)
"in need of involuntary care and treatment" means that a person has a mental illness for which care and treatment as a patient in a hospital is essential to such person's welfare and whose judgment is so impaired that he is unable to understand the need for such care and treatment.

North Carolina

N.C. Gen. Stat. § 122C-3(11)(a)(1)(II) (1999) "A showing of behavior that is grossly irrational, of actions that the individual is unable to control, of behavior that is grossly inappropriate to the situation, or of other evidence of severely impaired insight and judgment shall create a prima facie inference that the individual is unable to care for himself; or..."
Note: Per the session laws and further research, the relevant statutory language was enacted in 1985 (Ch. 589, S.B. 58)

N.C. Gen. Stat. § 122C-263(d)(1)(d) (1999) For outpatient: "The respondent's current mental status or the nature of the respondent's illness limits or negates the respondent's ability to make an informed decision to seek voluntarily or comply with recommended treatment."
Note: Per the session laws and further research, the relevant statutory language was enacted in 1983 (H.B. 124).

North Dakota

Ohio

Oklahoma

Oregon

Pennsylvania

Rhode Island

South Carolina

S.C. Code Ann. § 44-17-580 (1998)
"If, upon completion of the hearing and consideration of the record, the court finds upon clear and convincing evidence that the person is mentally ill, needs treatment and because of his condition: (1) lacks sufficient insight or capacity to make responsible decisions with respect to his treatment; or..."
Note: Per the session laws, the relevant statutory language was enacted in 1974.

South Dakota

Note: As of a 1986 law review article, SD included lack of insight in the definition of mentally ill (See S.D. Codified Laws, Sec. 27A-1-1, -9-18 (1984)). Today the statute does not include it.

Tennessee

Texas

Tex. Health & Safety Code § 574.034(a)(2)(c) (1999)
For temporary inpatient: "is: (i) suffering severe and abnormal mental, emotional, or physical distress; (ii) experiencing substantial mental or physical deterioration of the proposed patient's ability to function independently, which is exhibited by the proposed patient's inability, except for reasons of indigence, to provide for the proposed patient's basic needs, including food, clothing, health, or safety; and (iii) unable to make a rational and informed decision as to whether or not to submit to treatment."

Tex. Health & Safety Code § 574.034(b)(2)(D) (1999)
For temporary outpatient: "and...the proposed patient has an inability to participate in outpatient treatment services effectively and voluntarily, demonstrated by: (i) any of the proposed patient's actions occurring within the two-year period which immediately precedes the hearing; or (ii) specific characteristics of the proposed patient's clinical condition that make impossible a rational and informed decision whether to submit to voluntary outpatient treatment."

Tex. Health & Safety Code § 574.035(a)(2)(C) (1999)
For extended inpatient: "or...is: (i) suffering severe and abnormal mental, emotional, or physical distress; (ii) experiencing substantial mental or physical deterioration of the proposed

patient's ability to function independently, which is exhibited by the proposed patient's inability, except for reasons of indigence, to provide for the proposed patient's basic needs, including food, clothing, health, or safety; and (iii) unable to make a rational and informed decision as to whether or not to submit to treatment;

Tex. Health & Safety Code § 574.035(b)(2)(D)(ii) (1999)
For extended outpatient: "or...specific characteristics of the proposed patient's clinical condition that make impossible a rational and informed decision whether to submit to voluntary outpatient treatment..."

Utah
Utah Code Ann. § 62A-12-234(10)(c) (1998) "the patient lacks the ability to engage in a rational decision-making process regarding the acceptance of mental treatment as demonstrated by evidence of inability to weigh the possible costs and benefits of treatment..."

Vermont

Virginia

Washington

West Virginia

Wisconsin

Wyoming

Note. Bold indicates no statutory language.

ENDNOTES

1. Kumho Tire Co. v. Carmichael, 526 U.S. 137 (1999); Gen. Elec. Co. v. Joiner, 522 U.S. 136, 142 (1997); Daubert v. Merrell Dow Pharm., Inc. 509 U.S. 579, 589–95 (1993). A trial judge must determine whether proposed expert scientific testimony is scientific knowledge, which "entails a preliminary assessment of whether the reasoning or methodology underlying the testimony is scientifically valid." *Daubert*, 590 U.S. at 592–93. The new amendments to Federal Rule of Evidence 702 confirm the centrality of the scientific method in the judicial assessment of expert testimony. See Communication from the Chief Justice, the Supreme Court of the United States, Transmitting Amendments to the Federal Rules of Evidence That Have Been Adopted By the Court, May 2, 2000 [106th Cong. 2d Sess. House Doc. 106.225], at 41–53.
2. Smith, M. B. E. (1999). May judges ever nullify the law? *Notre Dame Law Review, 74*, 1657, 1660.
3. Lack of insight can also be termed "anosognosia," a related Greek term used in medical diagnosis that means "no self-knowledge." See Amador, X. F., & Shiva, A. A. (2000). Insight into schizophrenia: Anosognosia, competency, and civil liberties. *George Mason University Civil Rights Law Journal, 11*, 25, 28.
4. American Psychiatric Association (APA). (2000). *Diagnostic and statistical manual of mental disorders* (4th ed., text rev.). [hereinafter *DSM-IV-TR*]
5. *Black's law dictionary* (7th ed., p. 1095). (1999).
6. See Saks, M. J. (1993). Judicial nullification. *Indiana Law Journal, 68*, 1281 (1993).
7. Smith, *supra* note 2, at 1660; Smith, S. D. (1988). Why should courts obey the law? *George Mason University Civil Rights Law Journal, 77*, 113, 139–46.
8. See generally Stavis, P. F. (2000). Why prisons are brim-full of the mentally ill: Is their incarceration a solution or a sign of failure? *George Mason University Civil Rights Law Journal, 11*, 157.
9. Rubenstein, L. S. (1984). Treatment of the mentally ill: Legal advocacy enters the second generation. *American Journal of Psychiatry, 143*, 1264, 1268.
10. Covington v. Harris, 419 F.2d 617, 627 (D.C. 1969).
11. Lessard v. Schmidt, 349 F. Supp. 1078 (1972); O'Connor v. Donaldson, 422 U.S. 563 (1975).

12. Sydeman, S. J. et al. (1997). Procedural justice in the context of civil commitment: A critique of Tyler's analysis. *Psychology, Public Policy, and Law, 3*, 201; Appelbaum, P. S. (1984). Is the need for treatment constitutionally acceptable as a basis for civil commitment? *Law, Medicine, & Health Care, 12*, 144.

13. Stavis, P. F. (1999). The Nexum: A modest proposal for self-guardianship by contract. *Journal of Contemporary Health Law and Policy, 16*, 1, 4–8; Brakel, S. J. et al. (1985). *The mentally disabled and the law* (pp. 9–10); Stavis, P. F. (1989, August–September). Involuntary hospitalization in the modern era: Is "dangerousness" ambiguous or obsolete? *Quality of Care, 41*, 2, 3. (August–September 1989). The origin of what is now called the "parens patriae" power goes much farther back into history. Roman law recognized the power of the state to act as the head of a family, pater familia. And before that, Greek custom established the state in similar terms known as potestas. This significant development was in part motivated by the role of the state as a parent in caring for and protecting the safety of children, idiots, and lunatics.

14. Brakel et al., Ibid. Perhaps the most significant legal development of Western law, the enforceable contract was not developed to facilitate the bartering of objects but rather as part of the patriarchal power over children. See Sir Henry Sumner Maine, Ancient Law 319 (1907).

15. *Sir Henry Sumner Maine*, Ancient Law 98–99.

16. See generally Moynihan, D. P. (1993). Defining deviancy down. *American Scholar, 61*, 17.

17. See generally Kun, J.-M. (1996). Rejecting the adage "children should be seen and not heard": The mature minor doctrine. *Pace Law Review, 16*, 423.

18. As Chief Justice Burger expressed, "[o]ne who is suffering from a debilitating mental illness and in need of treatment is neither wholly at liberty nor free of stigma." *Addington v. Texas*, 441 U.S. 418, 428–29 (1979).

19. Treffert, D. (1974, February). Dying with their rights on. *American Journal of Psychiatry, 130*, 1041.

20. Treffert, D. (1987, March 5). Don't let rights block needed protection. *USA Today*.

21. Burtt, E. A. (1967). *The English philosophers from Bacon to Mill* (pp. 959, 961).

22. Munn v. Illinois, 94 U.S. 113, 142 (1876).

23. See generally Developments in the law—Civil commitment of the mentally ill. (1974). *Harvard Law Review, 87*, 1190, 1207–1222. This widely cited article also notes that commitment based on

"dangerousness" was premised on the police powers of the state and used largely in criminal commitments, where the therapeutic rationale was secondary. Ibid. at 1222.

24. Wexler, D. B. (1980). Some research and policy implications of "dialectics in the discourse of law and psychiatry." *International Journal of Law and Psychology, 3*, 343, 347. ("[I]n the great bulk of cases, family members rather than the police were responsible for instituting commitment. ...'family member' commitment petitioners may really mask the fact that some such commitments were of dangerous persons... ."); see also Armat, V. C., & Peele, R. *The need-for-treatment standard in involuntary civil commitment in treating the homeless mentally ill: A report of the task force on the homeless mentally ill* (pp. 183–194).

25. Appelbaum, Ibid. at 144, 147.

26. A good example of this is the Russell Weston, Jr. case. See *infra* note 166 and accompanying text.

27. Bitz, D. M., & Bitz, J. S. (1999). Incompetence in the brain injured individual. *St. Thomas Law Review, 12*, 205, 208 (quoting William Blackstone, *Commentaries on the Laws of England, 4*, 32).

28. Rothman, D. J. (1971). *The discovery of the asylum: Social order and disorder in the new republic* (p. 43). Little Brown & Co.

    Patterned after the family, yet considered a place of last resort, the almshouse was typical of all eighteenth-century service institutions. The insane were usually supported at home, their illness making them one of the poor; only when they were uncontrollable, threatening the safety of relatives and neighbors, did towns seek alternatives. Ibid.

29. *Supra* note 94, Grob, G. N. (1983). *Mental illness and American society, 1875–1940* (pp. 10–11). Princeton University Press.

30. Rock, R. S. (1968). *Hospitalization and discharge of the mentally ill* (p. 12).

31. See generally Isaac, R. J., & Armat, V. C. (1990). *Madness in the streets* (pp. 109–160).

32. See Petris, N. C. (2005). The Lanterman-Petris-Short Act with a focus upon dangerousness in dangerous behavior: A problem. In *Law and mental health: A case-based approach* (pp. 102–104).

33. Isaac, R. J., & Brakel, S. J. (1992). Subverting good intentions: A brief history of mental health law "reform." *Cornell Journal of Law and Public Policy, 2*, 89, 99; Hinds, J. T. (1990). Involuntary outpatient commitment for the chronically mentally ill. Nebraska *Law Review, 69*, 346, 402–403; Petris, *supra* note 36 at 104.

34. See Charts *infra* p. 102–108; see also Morris, G. H. (1999). Symposium: Rethinking mental disability law: Resolving old issues in a new millennium defining dangerousness: Risking a dangerous definition. *Contemporary Legal Issues, 10*, 61, 65–66.
35. For a catalog of state statutes and their characteristics, see http://www.bazelon.org/ioccharintro.html; http://www.psychlaws.org
36. See Brooks, A. D. (1978). Notes on defining the dangerousness of the mentally ill. In C. J. Frederick (Ed.), *Dangerous behavior: A problem in law and mental health* (p. 49).
37. Lessard v. Schmidt, 349 F. Supp. 1078, 1093–97 (1972).
38. Ibid. at 1097–1100.
39. Ibid. at 1100–1102.
40. Ibid. at 1102–1103.
41. Ibid. at 1094.
42. Brooks at 49.
43. Lessard, 349 F.Supp. at 1084.
44. Ibid. at 27. [internal citations omitted]
45. The infirmity in *Gault* was it was a punitive sentence without a need for treatment. Ironically, in *Lessard*, the court used that rationale for just the opposite—ignoring a need for treatment and making the proceeding punitive by refusing the state permission to treat.
46. Ibid. at 49–50 (noting the equivalence of exposure to commitment as a juvenile delinquent and exposure to imprisonment as an adult offender).
47. Lessard v. Schmidt, 349 F. Supp. 1078, 1103 (1972).
48. See Dixon v. Pennsylvania, 325 F. Supp. 966, 974 (M.D. Pa. 1971) (stating that the "[t]he standard for commitment...shall be as follows:...the subject of the hearing requires commitment because of manifest indications that the subject poses a present threat of serious physical harm to other persons or to himself.")
49. Treffert, D. A. (1999). The MacArthur coercion studies: A Wisconsin perspective. *Marquette Law Review, 82*, 759, 766.
50. Rachlin, S. (1979). Civil commitment, parens patriae and the right to refuse treatment. *American Journal of Forensic Psychiatry, 1*, 174, 177. ("[T]he weight of our concern in preventing predictable injury should not turn on whether the source of danger is mentally ill or "normal." Ibid. at 718). See generally Giovannoni, J. M., & Gurel, L. (1967). Socially disruptive behavior of ex-mental patients. *Archives of General Psychiatry, 17*, 146; Rappeport, J. R., & Lassen, G. (1965). Dangerousness-arrest rate comparisons of discharged patients and the general population. *American Journal of Psychiatry, 121*, 776; Keveles, H. S. (1972). The

community adjustment and criminal activity of the Baxstrom patients: 1966–1970. *American Journal of Psychiatry, 129*, 304.

51. Lessard, 349 F. Supp. at 1084–86.

52. See, e.g., *In re* Boggs, 522 N.Y.2d 407, 411 (1987), rev'd *sub nom.* Boggs v. New York City Health & Hosp. Corp., 132 A.D.2d 340, 523 N.Y.S.2d 71 (1987), appeal dismissed as moot, 70 N.Y.2d 972, 520 N.E.2d 515, 525 N.Y.S.2d 796 (1988). She had "dangerous tendencies" of, among other things, running into traffic.

53. See Colb, S. F. (1999). Insane fear: The discriminatory category of "mentally ill and dangerous." *New England Journal on Criminal and Civil Confinement, 25*, 341 [internal citations omitted]. Prof. Colb argues that the label "dangerous" doesn't answer the question: "Danger of what?" Furthermore, "being confined as 'mentally ill and dangerous' does not preserve the aura of 'innocence' that criminal incarceration would otherwise strip away... it may be no better—from the patient's perspective—to confine a mentally ill, violent person in a hospital than to incarcerate him in a penitentiary." Ibid. at 360.

54. See Colb, S. F. (1998). The three faces of evil [review of Saks, E. R., & Behnke, S. H., (1997) *Jekyll on trial: Multiple personality disorder & criminal law*]. *Georgia Law Review, 86*, 677, 701–703.

55. Ibid. at 722.

56. *Webster's third new international dictionary* (Unabridged, p. 573) (1993).

57. Lessard, 349 F. Supp. at 1084–86.

58. See, e.g., In the Matter of Torsney, 47 N.Y.2d 667, 672 (1979) (a jury determined 'not guilty' by reason of the mental defect of 'psychomotor' epilepsy—an previously unknown mental illness).

59. Brooks, A. D. (1978). Notes on defining the dangerousness of the mentally ill. In C. J. Frederick (Ed.), *Dangerous behaviour: A problem in law and mental health* (p. 49).

60. Ibid. at 50.

61. O'Connor v. Donaldson , 422 U.S. 563, 574 n.9 (1975) (writing that, "[t]he judge's instructions used the phrase 'dangerous to himself.' Of course, even if there is no foreseeable risk of self-injury or suicide, a person is literally 'dangerous to himself' if for physical or other reasons he is helpless to avoid the hazards of freedom either through his own efforts or with the aid of willing family members or friends. While it might be argued that the judge's instructions could have been more detailed on this point, O'Connor raised no objection to them, presumably because the evidence clearly showed that Donaldson was not 'dangerous to himself' however broadly that phrase might be defined."

62. Ibid. at 574–76. The Court said: "The jury found that Donaldson was neither dangerous to himself nor dangerous to others, and also found that, if mentally ill, Donaldson had not received treatment. That verdict, based on abundant evidence, makes the issue before the Court a narrow one. We need not decide whether, when, or by what procedures, a mentally ill person may be confined by the State on any of the grounds which, under contemporary statutes, are generally advanced to justify involuntary confinement of such a person—to prevent injury to the public, to ensure for the jury found that none of the above grounds for continued confinement was present in Donaldson's case. Given the jury's findings, what was left as justification for keeping Donaldson in continued confinement?" Ibid. at 573–574.

63. Ibid. (stating that "[t]he testimony at the trial demonstrated, without contradiction, that Donaldson had posed no danger to others during his long confinement, or indeed at any point in his life").

64. Ibid. at 575.

65. Hinds, J. T. (1990). Involuntary outpatient commitment for the chronically mentally ill. *Nebraska Law Review, 69*, 346, 402; Appelbaum, Ibid., 144, 146–147.

66. O'Connor v. Donaldson, 422 U.S. 563, 576 (1975) (a finding of mental illness "without more" cannot justify civil commitment Ibid. at 575); see also Tancredi, L. R., & Weisstub, D. N. (1986). Law, psychiatry, and morality: Unpacking the muddled prolegomenon. *International Journal of Law and Psychology, 9*, 1, 12. ("[*Donaldson*] was essentially misshaped through its various stages of evolution until, in its final form, it really only stood for a narrow proposition of law, namely, the question of when a mental patient must be released.... cases are read and, more appropriately, misread for discretionary reasons that reflect political choices which can put judges in close alliance with social reformers.... *Donaldson...has become a [conduit] to the condition in whch we find ourselves today,...experiencing serious shortcomings in the delivery of psychiatric services*."). [italics added]

67. Linburn, G. E. (1998). Donaldson revisited: Is dangerousness a constitutional requirement for civil commitment? *Journal of American Academic Psychiatry & Law, 26*, 343, 345.

68. U.S. Department of Health and Human Services. (1999). *Mental health: A report of the surgeon general on mental illness in the United States* (p. xvii) [Executive summary]. Retrieved March 15, 2004, from http://www.surgeongeneral.gov/library/mentalhealth/summary. html [hereinafter *Mental Health Report Summary*] (noting that one in five Americans suffers from a mental disorder in any one year);

Special report: Health care reform for American with severe mental illnesses: Report of the National Advisory Mental Health Council. (1993). *American Journal of Psychiatry, 150,* 1447. "About 5 million Americans (2.8% of the adult population) experience severe mental disorders in a 1-year period. *Treating* these disorders now costs the nation an estimated $20 billion a year (with an additional $7 billion a year in nursing home costs). These costs represent 4% of total U.S. direct health care costs. When the social costs are also included, severe mental disorders exact an annual financial toll of $74 billion."

69. See Winters v. Miller, 446 F.2d 65, 68 (2d Cir. 1971).

70. See Kansas v. Hendricks, 521 U.S. 346, 371 (1997) (stating that a finding of dangerousness alone is not a sufficient basis for indefinite involuntary commitment); *cf. Kansas v. Crane,* 534 U.S. 407, 413 (2002). "In addition, our cases suggest that civil commitment of dangerous sexual offenders will normally involve individuals who find it particularly difficult to control their behavior"—in an emotional as opposed to purely volitional sense. In neither *Jones v. United States* nor *Addington v. Texas* did the Court craft a distinction between the two impairments." *Crane,* 534 U.S. at 414, 415.

71. See Humphrey v. Cady, 405 U.S. 504, 509 (1972).

72. O'Connor v. Donaldson, 422 U.S. 563, 575 (1975).

73. Ibid.

74. See U.S. Department of Health and Human Services. (1999). *Mental health: A report of the surgeon general on mental illness in the United States* (p. 5, n. 18). Retrieved March 15, 2004, from http://www.surgeongeneral.gov/library/mentalhealth/pdfs/C1.pdf [hereinafter *Mental Health Report Chapter 1*] (explaining that "*Mental illness* is the term that refers collectively to all diagnosable mental disorders. Mental disorders are health condition s that are characterized by alterations in thinking, mood, or behavior (or some combination thereof) associated with distress and/or impaired functioning").

75. [Mental illness is a medically diagnosed disorder that includes clinically significant behavioral or psychological syndrome or patterns that...occurs] in an individual and that is associated with present distress (e.g., painful symptom) or disability (i.e., impairment in one or more areas of functioning) or with a significantly increased risk of suffering death, pain, disability, or an important loss of freedom." American Psychiatric Association (APA). (2000). *Diagnostic and statistical manual of mental disorders (DSM-IV-TR)* (4th ed., p. xxxi).

76. World Health Organization. (1992). *International classification of diseases and related health problems.* (1989 rev. ed.). [hereinafter: *ICD-10*]

77. See U.S. Department of Health and Human Services, Mental Health. (1999). *A report of the surgeon general* (pp. 4–5). Retrieved from http://www.surgeongeneral.gov/library/mentalhealth/home.html

78. Aripiprazole emerging as next great hope for schizophrenia. (2002). *Psychopharmacology Update, 13*, 1, 4–5. Retrieved March 15, 2004, from http://www.medscape.com/viewarticle/422878

79. O'Connor v. Donaldson, 422 U.S. 563, 576 (1975).

80. There has been speculation about the meaning of the phrase "without more." One theory is that more means a "right to treatment." See Shuman, D. (1980). Warren Burger and the civil commitment tetralogy. *International Journal of Law and Psychiatry, 3*, 155–156. ([T]he Court left for another day the existence of a right to treatment; that is the "more" required to confine the non-dangerous mentally ill... .). The late Chief Judge David L. Bazelon also believed that the case was about a right to treatment. As a justification for civil commitment, he wrote, "Donaldson's case is easy...since there was evidence that he... had not received treatment." Bazelon, D. L. (1975). Institutionalization, deinstitutionalization and the adversary process. *Columbia Law Review, 75*, 897, 904. Yet, this is doubtful for two strong reasons:

> (1) The majority specifically says the case does not involve a right to treatment:Specifically, there is no reason now to decide whether mentally ill persons dangerous to themselves or to others have a right to treatment on compulsory confinement by the State, or whether the State may compulsorily confine a nondangerous, mentally ill individual for the purpose of treatment... . There is, accordingly, no occasion in this case to decide whether the provision of treatment, standing alone, can ever constitutionally justify involuntary confinement or, if it can, how much or what kind of treatment would suffice for that purpose. In its present posture, this case involves not involuntary treatment but simply involuntary custodial confinement. O'Connor v. Donaldson, 422 U.S. at 573, n.10; and

> (2) Chief Justice Burger took great pains, in his strongly worded concurring opinion, to refute the possibility and feasibility of recognizing a legal right to treatment, as well as to note a lack of historical roots to support such a position. Donaldson, 422 U.S. at 578, 582-83, 588-89 (Burger, J., concurring). In my view, "without more" could more readily be the *parens patriae* power where a person with mental illness (a) lacks sound judgment and (b) needs and is suitable for some form of treatment, even if that "treatment" is custodial or palliative.

See Paul F. Stavis, *Involuntary hospitalization in the modern era: Is "dangerousness" ambiguous or obsolete?* Quality of Care 41 at 3 (August–September, 1989) (explaining that N.Y. Mental Hygiene Law, with such a relaxed standard, better fits the *parens patriae* doctrine purpose, rather than forcing the incompetent to be seen as a danger to others, they are merely in need of supervision and guidance).

81. In Kansas v. Hendricks, a case involving the post-prison incarceration of a "mentally abnormal" sexual predator, the Court said that dangerousness must be accompanied by "volitional impairment rendering them dangerous beyond their control." 521 U.S. 346, 358 (1997).

82. Donaldson, 422 U.S. at n.9, 10.

83. Morris, G. H. (1999). Defining dangerousness: Risking a dangerous definition. *Journal of Contemporary Legal Issues, 10*, 61, n. 81 (advocating a more rigorous inquiry into the circumstances surrounding commitment, but remaining silent with respect to the cost burden), but see Washington v. Harper, 494 U.S. 210, 232 (1990) (requiring administration of antipsychotic medication involuntarily). ("Nor can we ignore the fact that requiring judicial hearings will divert scarce prison resources, both money and the staff's time, from the care and treatment of mentally ill inmates.")

84. Ibid. at 91, n. 90 (noting that use of certain "factors" to predict dangerousness is not very accurate and very difficult to refute for the alleged incompetent).

85. Washington v. Harper, 494 U.S. at 230 (noting that the inmate's interest in avoiding the medication is not insubstantial, but rather there was a more compelling argument to be made for the State, since "the patient is mentally disturbed, his own intentions will be difficult to assess and will be changeable in any event"); see also Addington v. Texas, 441 U.S. 418, 432–433 (1979) (noting that the standard of proof has been lowered to make it easier for the state to prove); Appelbaum, Ibid., 144, 146 (discussing the evolution of case law toward a "dangerous to self or others" standard, and now a retreat back to the "need for treatment" guideline, previously disfavored by the courts but easier to fit by the state).

86. Addington v. Texas, 441 U.S. at 432–33; see generally, Morris, *supra* note 84 at 72–76 (noting that most state laws crafted a distinction between patients who are "dangerous" but mentally competent, from those who are not "dangerous" but "endangered" due to incompetence and inability to avoid dangers).

87. Addington v. Texas, 441 U.S. at 424, 425.
88. See generally, E. Fuller Torrey, Out of the Shadows 1-4, 13-15 (1997) (describing tragic examples of mentally ill persons who slipped through the cracks of the system because they were not perceived as a danger to themselves or others).
89. See Addington v. Texas, 441 U.S. at 431–33.
90. See Addington v. Texas, 441 U.S. at 429.
91. Chief Justice Burger wrote for the majority that: "If a trained psychiatrist has difficulty with the categorical "beyond a reasonable doubt" standard, the untrained lay juror—or indeed even a trained judge—who is required to rely on expert opinion could be forced by the criminal law standard of proof to reject commitment for many patients desperately in need of institutionalized psychiatric care." Addington, 441 U.S. at 430.
92. Lidz, C. W., Mulvey, E. P., Apperson, L. J., Evanczuk, K., & Shea, S. (1992). Sources of disagreement among clinicians' assessments of dangerousness in a psychiatric emergency room. *International Journal of Law and Psychiatry, 15*, 237 ("This consensus, however, has not stopped both judicial and legislative authorities from concluding that assessments of dangerousness are still the responsibility of mental health professionals in a wide variety of clinical and forensic situations").
93. Chief Justice Burger wrote for the majority that: "If a trained psychiatrist has difficulty with the categorical "beyond a reasonable doubt" standard, the untrained lay juror—or indeed even a trained judge—who is required to rely upon expert opinion could be forced by the criminal law standard of proof to reject commitment for many patients desperately in need of institutionalized psychiatric care." Addington v. Texas, 441 U.S. 418, 429 (1979).
94. An absolutist definition of freedom can negate other humanitarian and ethical principles. It is entirely possible to honor the absolute right to liberty of persons in an advanced state of senility by not hospitalizing them. But at the same time does this not deny them their right to care from society when they are helpless, and allow them to die from exposure, starvation, or neglect? Grob, Ibid. at 319.
95. Dylan, B. (1967). Like a rolling stone. On *Bob Dylan's greatest hits*. Columbia. See also http://bobdylan.com/songs/rolling.html.
96. Metaphorically, compared with the limitations on a court of law, former Chief Judge Sol Wachtler notes that certain limitations are, in fact, freedoms that permit a power to act with legitimacy:

In other words, properly understood and applied, justiciability principles serve as a foundation for legitimate judicial lawmaking, beyond which there is no structure to support the practice. These doctrines, therefore, are a source of power, and it is a perversion to view them as judicial abdication. Perceiving them as 'limitations' in any sense is like believing that a man's legs 'inhibit' his movement because they are not wings. Wachtler, S. (1990). Judicial lawmaking. *New York University Law Review, 65*, 1, 3.

97. Samuel J. Brakel & Ronald S. Rock, The Mentally Disabled and the Law 9–10 (1985).
98. Mtr. of Hofbauer, 47 N.Y. 2d 648 (1979).
99. Colb, S. F. (1999). Insane fear: The discriminatory category of "mentally ill and dangerous." *New England Journal on Criminal and Civil Confinement, 25*, 348–349. Colb states: "[s]ubstantively, the 'dangerousness' requirement thus fails to impose serious limitations on the breadth of permissible civil confinement. This open-endedness effectively leaves to 'mental illness' the job of narrowing the class of individuals subject to preventive detention."

100. The community mental health systems in fact are quite resistant to dealing with patients once they have been processed through the criminal system, particularly, if they have been found not guilty by reason of mental disease or defect. In fact, many of the defendants sent to our forensic hospitals under competency statutes are troublemakers in the jails, and there is tremendous resistance on the part of many sheriffs to bringing them back to the jail, even for their competency hearings. The situation is reversed in the case of civilly committed patients. Rather than resistance (either overt or covert) to the hospital discharging patients, there is immediate and persistent pressure from the community mental health boards (who are footing the bills) to get their patients out of the hospital. Miller, R. D. (1992). Economic factors leading to diversion of the mentally disordered from the civil to the criminal commitment systems. *International Journal of Law and Psychiatry, 15*, 1, 11.

101. "A finding of 'mental illness' alone cannot justify a State's locking a person up against his will and keeping him indefinitely in simple custodial confinement." O'Connor, 422 U.S. at 575.
102. Appelbaum, Ibid. at 144, 146–147. [italics omitted]
103. Stone, A. (1987). Broadening the statutory criteria for civil commitment: A reply to Durham and LaFond. *Yale Law and Policy Review, 5*, 412, 425. Dr. Stone argues that that dangerousness should be eliminated

from civil commitment and that only "persons who suffer, who are incompetent to make treatment decisions, and who could be treated" would be subject to civil confinement. Dangerous persons should be purely a matter for the criminal justice system. Ibid. at 422.

104. The lack of insight or lack of awareness is a very common debility of serious mental illness. See generally Amador, X. F., & Shiva, A. A. (2000). Insight into schizophrenia: Anosognosia, competency and civil liberties. *George Mason University Civil Rights Law Journal, 11*, 25. Additionally, the States are vested with the historic parens patriae power, including the duty to protect 'persons under legal disabilities to act for themselves.' Hawaii v. Standard Oil Co., 405 U.S. 251, 257, 92 S.Ct. 885, 888 (1972). See also Mormon Church v. United States, 136 U.S. 1, 56-58 (1890); see generally, Griffith, D. B. (1991). The best interests standard: A comparison of the state's parens patriae authority and judicial oversight in best interests determinations for children and incompetent patients. *Issues in Law and Medicine, 7*, 283, 287-291. The classic example of this role is when a State undertakes to act as "the general guardian of all infants, idiots, and lunatics." Hawaii v. Standard Oil Co., *supra*, 405 U.S., at 257, 92 S.Ct., at 888, quoting 3 W. Blackstone, Commentaries *47. O'Connor v. Donaldson, 422 U.S. at 583. (Burger, C.J., concurring); This state of immaturity of judgment and the obligations of the king or the state under natural law to care for "children of nonage," lunatics or idiots, was prominently discussed by key philosophers and political thinkers who influenced the Founding Fathers. See Stavis, P. F. (1999). The NEXUM: A modest proposal for self-guardianship by contract. *Journal of Contemporary Health and Policy, 1*, 4–23.

105. Addington v. Texas, 441 U.S. 418, 426 (1979).

106. Livermore, J. P., Malmquist, C. P., & Meehl, P. E. On the justifications for civil commitment. *University of Pennsylvania Law Review, 117*, 75, 85–86.

107. See generally Ennis, B. J., & Litwak, T. R. (1974). Psychiatry and the presumption of expertise: Flipping coins in the courtroom. *California Law Review, 62*, 693; Cocozza, J. J., & Steadman, H. J. (1976). The failure of psychiatric predictions of dangerousness: Clear and convincing evidence. *Rutgers Law Review, 29*, 1084.

108. Thompson, J. S., & Ager, J. W. (1988). An experimental analysis of the civil commitment recommendations of psychologists and psychiatrists. *Behavioral Sciences & the Law, 6*, 119–120.

109. Segal, S. P., Watson, M. A., Goldfinger, S. M., & Averbuck, D. S. (1988). Civil commitment in the psychiatric emergency room: The assessment of dangerousness by emergency room clinicians. *Archives of General Psychiatry, 45*, 748, 751. Accuracy confirms two prior

484 MALINGERING, LIES, AND JUNK SCIENCE IN THE COURTROOM

studies of between 72%–86%. ("[I]ndicating that clinicians are in overwhelming agreement as to the applicability of specific criteria to specific cases.")

110. Slobogin, C. (2000). Doubts about Daubert psychiatric anecdata as a case study. *Washington and Lee Law Review, 57*, 919–923.

111. See generally Foucault, M. (1965). *Madness and civilization: A history of insanity in an age of reason.* Vintage Books.

112. See generally Rothman, D. J. (1980). *Conscience and convenience.* Little Brown Co.; Grob, Ibid.; Deutsch, A. (1937). *The mentally ill in America.* Doubleday, Doran & Company, Inc.; and Rothman, D. J. (1990). *The discovery of the asylum.*

113. See Isaac, R. J., & Armat, V. C. (1990). *Madness in the streets* (pp. 109-160). The Free Press. See also Isaac, R. J., & Brakel, S. J. (1992). Subverting good intentions: A brief history of mental health law "reform." *Cornell Journal of Law and Public Policy, 2*, 116-117, n. 93; Chodoff, P. (1984). Involuntary hospitalization of the mentally ill as a moral issue. *American Journal of Psychiatry, 141*, 384.

114. See Isaac & Armat, Ibid. at 109–160; see also Isaac & Brakel, Ibid. at 89, 116–117, n. 93; Chodoff, Ibid.

115. "The only freedom which deserves the name is that of pursuing our own good in our own way, so long as we do not attempt to deprive others of theirs, or impede their efforts to obtain it. Each is the proper guardian of his own health, whether bodily, *or* mental and spiritual. Mankind is greater gainers by suffering each other to live as seems good to themselves, than by compelling each to live as seems good to the rest." Mill, J. S. (1962). *On liberty* (Gateway ed., p. 18). Lessard v. Schmidt, 349 Fed. Supp. 1078, 1085 n.3 (E.D. Wisc. 1972).

116. See , e.g ., Dresser, R. S. (1982). Ulysses and the psychiatrists: A legal and policy analysis of the voluntary commitment contract. *Harvard Civil Rights-Civil Liberties Law Review, 16*, 777, 787; Perling, L. J. (1993). Health care advance directives: Implications for Florida mental health patients [Comment]. *University of Miami Law Review, 48*, 193, n. 1 (supporting advance directives for psychiatric care); Winick, B. J. (1992). On autonomy: Legal and psychological perspectives. *Villanova Law Review, 37*, 1705, 1707–1715.

117. See Burtt, E. A. (1967). *The English philosophers from Bacon to Mill* (p. 961).

118. See Waithe, M. E. (1983). Why Mill was for paternalism. *International Journal of Law and Psychology, 6*, 101, 108–111.

119. Wertheimer, A. (1993). A philosophical examination of coercion for mental health issues. *Behavioral Sciences & the Law, 11*, 239–258;

Rush, B. (1979). *Diseases of the mind* (pp. 268–269). The Classics of Medicine Library. (Original work published 1812). Dr. Rush, as a psychiatrist and political thinker of the early 19th century and a signer of the Declaration of Independence, stated, "Let it not be said, that confining such (mentally ill) persons in a hospital would be an infringement upon personal liberty, incompatible with the freedom of our governments." Ibid. at 267. Dr. Rush also believed in due process of law; adding, "To prevent injustice or oppression, no person should be sent to the contemplated hospital, or Sober House, without being examined and committed by a court." Ibid. at 268.

120. Mill, J. S. (1962). *On liberty* (Gateway ed., p. 18).
121. "Paternalism" is defined as governing "in the manner of a father dealing with his children." *The Random House dictionary of the English language* (Unabridged, p. 1056) (1966). One could not imagine a stronger or more fiduciary obligation, nor one that is the essence of the *parens patriae* concept. As William Safire of the *New York Times* wrote of paternalism,

> [As fathers] We want our intrinsic authority back [from] children who want us to be their friends and by those children's mothers who insist on shared paternalism. [They]…have stolen the essential prerogative of fatherhood from us. Motherpower is rooted in love, fatherpower in authority…. *New York Times*, June 16, 1994, p. 27.

122. See generally Sunstein, C. R., & Thaler, R. H. (2003). Liberal paternalism is not an oxymoron. *University of Chicago Law Review, 70*, 1159, 1175; Zamir, E. (1998). The efficiency of paternalism. *Virginia Law Review, 84*, 229.
123. Bazelon, Ibid. at 897, 907–908.
124. Thirty years ago, Judge Bazelon, expressing his unwillingness to sugar-coat this reality, correctly observed: "Non-criminal' commitments of so-called dangerous persons have long served as preventive detention, but this function has been either excused or obscured by the promise that, while detained, the potential offender will be rehabilitated by treatment. Notoriously, this promise of treatment has served only to bring an illusion of benevolence to what is essentially a warehousing operation for social misfits." Society may disclaim a punishment agenda, but to the incarcerated person, the confinement is punishment. Ibid.
125. Bazelon, Ibid.
126. Lessard v. Schmidt, 349 Fed. Supp. 1078, 1094 (E.D. Wisc. 1972).

127. If, as Professor Slobogin states,

> [L]egislatures define "dangerousness" as a likelihood rather than a certainty of violence in the future.... [a]ssuming that the state cannot ever prove beyond a reasonable doubt, or even by clear and convincing evidence, that a person *will* act violently, showing by the requisite degree of certainty that a person is "more likely than not" to do so present a far less problematic task." Slobogin, C. (1984). Dangerousness and expertise. *University of Pennsylvania Law Review, 133*, 97, 104.

However, if the concept of compulsory treatment involves a "likelihood" of violence, how does the "more likely" modifier relate to the burden of evidence? Must there also be a showing of either "beyond a reasonable doubt" or "clear and convincing." That is, does the state the have a burden of proving a "likelihood" "beyond a reasonable doubt" or alternatively a "likelihood" by "clear and convincing evidence?" Such compounding of evidentiary probabilities, that is, using two simultaneously applicable standards of proof, either requires too much or, under an alternative interpretation, possibly too little. A "more likely than not" standard appears to be equivalent to a preponderance of evidence standard but clearly less than the "clear and convincing" standard, which the Supreme Court has mandated. Thus, the standard of proof also becomes problematic as a value judgment. Either the individual is per se violent, or if actuarial data can be developed, then for that individual as an identifiable member of a group, a probability can be assigned with some generalized precision, for example, 90% chance of being violent based on multiple hospitalization, diagnosis, etc. This multiple then creates further compounding equations, where factoring one actuarial category or characteristic by another might result in a very complex and questionable mode of proof having little connect to the actual clinical conditions or the individual's own condition and circumstances.

128. See Rhoden, N. K. (1982). The limits of liberty: Deinstitutionalization, homelessness, and libertarian theory. *Emory Law Journal, 31*, 375, 392–395.

129. Appelbaum, P. S. (1994). *Almost a revolution: Mental health law and the limits of change* (p. 36). Oxford University Press. See also Stavis, P. S. (2000). Why prisons are brim-full of the mentally ill: Is their incarceration a solution or a sign of failure? *George Mason University Civil Rights Law Journal, 11*, 157, 195–198.

130. See Stavis, *supra* note 129 at 195–198.

131. Bazelon, Ibid. at 897, 904.

132. See Fuller, L. L. (1968). *Anatomy of the law* (p. 110). Greenwood Press. See also Carnahan, W. A. (2001). *Lessons from the Japanese: Collective choice in public policy decisions to care for and treat the mentally ill in Japan* (p. 20). George Mason University Law and Psychiatry Center.
133. "Court hearings required an average of 31 days to resolve at the private hospital and 68 days to resolve at the public hospital. The legal expense to the private hospital is over $2000 per hearing. Two clinicians and an ethicist, who reviewed patient charts at the public hospital, found no patients who benefited from the hearing requirement." Morris, G. H. (1995). Judging judgment: Assessing the competence of mental patients to refuse treatment. *San Diego Law Review, 32*, 343, 361, n.80: "Judicial review significantly delayed the beginning of treatment for patients found incompetent—an average of 80 additional days. The financial impact of holding patients for 80 days without treatment is enormous."...Costs of hearings include delays in treatment and staff time required for hearings. The willingness of courts to accept telephone testimony eliminated staff travel time and time waiting in court for the case to be called... . In fiscal year 1985, the legislature appropriated $364,000 and in fiscal year 1986, the legislature appropriated an additional $824,000 to fund the personnel costs of conducting hearings. Non-economic costs include damage to the therapeutic relationship and the suffering of patients when treatment is delayed. Delays of 8 to 10 weeks were common." See also Ciccone, J. R., Tokoli, J. F., Gift, T. E., & Clements, C. D. (1993). Medication refusal and judicial activism: A reexamination of the effects of the Rivers decision. *Hospital & Community Psychiatry, 44*, 555, 560. "Excluding the court costs, the price of the patient's refusals in extra institutional care and legal fees was $13,000 for the first and $19,000 for the second patient. None of this, of course, takes into account the 'hidden' costs of managing a deteriorating patient and the attendant effects on the safety and quality of care within the institution generally." Brakel, S. J., & Davis, J. M. (1991). Taking harms seriously: Involuntary mental patients and the right to refuse treatment. *Indiana Law Review, 25*, 429, 460.
134. Rothman, D. J. (1980). *Conscience and convenience* (pp. 27–36).
135. See Frese, F. J. III (2000). Mental illness, treatment & recovery: My experience and insight as a consumer. *George Mason University Civil Rights Law Journal, 11*, 83, 88–90.
136. See Washington v. Harper, 494 U.S. 210, 238 n.2 (1990).

137. "Contortions of Psychiatry in China." (2001, March 25). Editorial, *New York Times*, p. 14 (arguing "Chinese law includes 'political harm to society' as legally dangerous mentally ill behavior").

138. Munro, R. (2000). Judicial psychiatry in China and its political abuses. *Columbia Journal of Asian Law, 14*, 1, 83.

139. Miller, R. D. (1992). Economic factor leading to diversion of the mentally disordered from the civil to the criminal commitment systems. *International Journal of Law and Psychiatry, 15*, 1, 10,

> Economic pressure thus emerges as, if not the sole cause, at least a major contributor to the increase in forensic hospitalizations, which assumed significance not only in terms of statistics, but (more importantly) in terms of utilization of resources... . I believe that the data on relative lengths of stay do permit such differentiation [i.e., between economic and political/ideological causes for the observed increase in forensic admissions], however. The initial decision as to whether to hospitalize a patient in system is most probably multi-factorial, with strict civil commitment criteria and ideological biases playing as great a part as economic factors. The police, who are responsible for initiating a great majority of civil commitments in Wisconsin, are likely to consider effective dispositions rather than economics in deciding what to do with mentally disordered persons they are called to see, as their budgets are not directly affected by the choices they make. Ibid.

140. Two excellent reports have been done on Andrew Goldstein who was convicted of murder for pushing Kendra Webdale off a subway platform into an oncoming train. Both note that he was given numerous instances of treatment for the year prior to his crime and this treatment cost $97,000 in public funds. Yet, the treatment seemed to be inappropriate and ineffective for his condition. He sought a form of inpatient treatment, but the system typically gave him medications and sent him away without the supervision that he needed. See Michael Winerip, Andrew Goldstein, *New York Times*; see also Michael Winerip, Andrew Goldstein, *New York Times*; see also Report of the NYS Commission on Quality Care for the Mentally Disabled and the Mental Hygiene Medical Review Board: "In the Matter of David Dix." (November, 1999) (http://www.cqcapd.state.ny.us/publications/dix.htm).

141. Brakel, S. J. (1987). Legal schizophrenia and the mental health lawyer: Recent trends in civil commitment litigation. *Behavioral Science and Law, 6*, 3, 4.

142. Chief Justice Burger expressed this view: "Common human experience and scholarly opinions suggest that the supposed protections of an

adversary proceeding to determine the appropriateness of medical decisions for the commitment and treatment of mental and emotional illness may well be more illusory than real." Parham v. J.R., 442 U.S. 584, 607–609 (1979); and, "The judicial model for fact-finding for all constitutionally protected interests, regardless of their nature, can turn rational decision-making into an unmanageable enterprise." Ibid. at 608 n.16; see also Lake v. Cameron, 364 F.2d 657, 663 (D.C. Cir. 1966) (Burger, J., dissenting) ("[A] United States court in our legal system is not set up to initiate inquiries and direct studies of social welfare agencies or other social problems. The Court exists to decide questions put before it by parties to litigation on the basis of issues raised by them in pleadings and facts adduced by those parties.").

143. *In re* Boggs, 136 Misc. 2d 1082, 1089, 522 N.Y.2d 407, 411 (Sup. Ct.) rev'd *sub nom.* Boggs v. New York City Health & Hosp. Corp., 132 A.D.2d 340, 523 N.Y.S.2d 71 (1987), appeal dismissed as moot, 70 N.Y.2d 972, 520 N.E.2d 515, 525 N.Y.S.2d 796 (1988).

144. Apparently, oblivious to what happened in the time between Ms. Boggs' admission to the hospital and her court appearance, the trial judge wrote that "[p]erhaps the disparity [in the diagnoses of the psychiatrists] results from the lapse of time between examinations by the two groups." *In re* Boggs, 136 Misc. 2d 1082, 1088, 522 N.Y.S.2d 407, 411 (Sup. Ct. 1987) rev'd *sub nom.* Boggs v. New York City Heath & Hosps. Corp., 132 A.D.2d 340, 523 N.Y.S.2d 71 (1987), appeal dismissed as moot, 70 N.Y.2d 972, 520 N.E.2d 515, 525 N.Y.S.2d 796 (1988); see generally Sattar, S. P., Pinals, D. A., Din, A. U., & Appelbaum, P. S. (2006). To commit or not to commit: The psychiatric resident as a variable in involuntary commitment decisions. *Academic Psychiatry, 30,* 191.

145. See generally Watson, S. D. (2000). Discharges to the streets: Hospitals and homelessness. *St. Louis University Public Law Review, 19,* 357, 363–372.

146. Klein, D. W. (2003). Involuntary treatment of the mentally ill: Autonomy is asking the wrong question. *Vermont Law Review, 27,* 649–650.

147. Watson, Ibid. at 357, 363–372.

148. Torrey, E. F. (2001). Surviving schizophrenia: A manual for families, consumers, and providers (4th ed., pp. 210–254) (discussing classes of drugs used to treat schizophrenia, their effectiveness and side effects).

149. Ms. Boggs was given haloperidol ("haldol"), I.M. (intramuscularly), a very potent psychotropic medication of the "Butyophernone" class that suppresses violent and delusional propensities in a matter of hours or

less: "Parenteral therapy may hasten the onset of sedative, if not antipsychotic, activity; for example, haloperidol's effect becomes apparent about 3 hours after oral administration and 20 to 30 minutes after intramuscular administration. Such rapidity of action may be important in agitated combative patients. American Medical Association. (1986). Antipsychotic drugs. In *Drug evaluations* (6th ed., pp. 111–150). Notably, in a scholarly commentary, one judge did comment on the issue of Ms. Boggs' pretrial treatment with medication but failed to mention the omission by the three courts that passed on the *Bogg's* case. See Ludwig, E. V. (1991). The mentally ill homeless: Evolving involuntary commitment issues. *Villanova Law Review, 36*, 1085, 1107.

150. Cournos, F. (1989). Involuntary medication and the case of Joyce Brown. *Hospital and Community Psychology, 40*, 736, 739–740; see also, *supra*, note 144.

151. Cournos, Ibid.

152. Boggs v. New York City Heath & Hosps. Corp., 132 A.D.2d 340, 523 N.Y.S.2d 71 (1987).

153. Stone, A. (1987). Broadening the statutory criteria for civil commitment: A reply to Durham and LaFond. *Yale Law and Policy Review, 5*, 412, 426.

154. Levin, S., Brekke, J. S., & Thomas, P. (1991). A controlled comparison of involuntary hospitalized medication refusers and acceptors. *Bulletin of the American Academy of Psychiatry & the Law, 19*, 161, 169–170.

155. Appelbaum, P. S., & Gutheil, T. G. (1979). "Rotting with their rights on": Constitutional theory and clinical reality in drug refusal by psychiatric patients. *Bulletin of the American Academy of Psychiatry & the Law, 7*, 306; see also Appelbaum, P. S., & Gutheil, T. G. (1980). The Boston State Hospital case: "Involuntary mind control," the Constitution, and the "right to rot." *American Journal of Psychiatry, 137*, 720; Gutheil, T. G. (1980). In search of true freedom: Drug refusal, involuntary medication, and "rotting with your rights on." *American Journal of Psychiatry, 137*, 327 (editorial).

156. Torrey, E. F. (1997). *Out of the shadows*. New York: John Wiley & Sons, Inc.

157. Winick, B. J. (1999). Symposium rethinking mental disability law: Resolving old issues in a new millennium: Therapeutic jurisprudence and the civil commitment hearing. *Journal of Contemporary Legal Issues, 10*, 37, 42. Given this prevalent lack of clinical understanding and press of judicial time and resources judges simply follow the

recommendations of experts in the vast majority of cases: "studies show judicial agreement with expert witnesses in this area ranges from seventy-nine to one hundred percent, and most frequently exceeds ninety-five percent." Ibid. at 42.

158. Wexler, D. B., Scoville, S. E., et al. (1971). *The administration of psychiatric justice: Theory and practice in Arizona. Arizona Law Review, 13*, 1, 100–101 (This study also reports that attorneys saw their role as merely to prevent commitment for those who did not need it. Ibid. at 52–55).

159. Rothman, D. J. (1971). *The discovery of the asylum: Social order and disorder in the new republic.* London: Little Brown & Co.

160. Foucault, M. (1978). About the concept of the "dangerous individual" in 19th-century legal psychiatry (A. Baudot & J. Couchman, Trans.). *International Journal of Law and P sychiatry, 18*, 1, 6–7.

161. Ibid. at 10, 13–14.

162. Ibid. at 16–18.

163. Wachtler, Ibid. at 1, 4.

164. Gavison, R. (1988). The implications of jurisprudential theories for judicial election, selection, and accountability. *Southern California Law Review, 61*, 1617, 1640.

165. See Hart, H. L. A. (1994). *The concept of law* (2nd ed., p. 115) (noting that 'obedience' under the law means different things for the individual citizen, who may obey a law "for his part only," and for whatever reason he chooses, and for the judge, who must obey laws by regarding them as standards of behavior to be obeyed by all).

166. See Kronman, A. T. (1993). *The lost lawyer: Failing ideals of the legal profession* (pp. 318–319) (noting that since judges, unlike lawyers in private practice, are not subject to ordinary commercial pressures, they are able to act as statesman of the law.)

167. See Estreicher, S. (1982). Judicial nullification: Guido Calabresi's uncomon common law for a statutory age. *New York University Law Review, 57*, 1126–1127 (detailing Professor Calabresi's argument that the proliferation of statutory law, some of which is contradictory and inconsistent, empowers the courts to preempt a statute "that no longer commands majority support and is out of phase with the prevailing legal framework... .")

168. The doctrine is attributed to the Marbury v. Madison, 5 U.S. (1 Cranch) 137, 178 (1803), yet there is some question as to whether this was really its holding. See Wood, G. S. (1999). The origins of judicial review revisited, or how the marshall court made more out of less.

Washington & Lee Law Review, 56, 787, 788–89 (pointing out that the Supreme Court did not cite *Marbury* as precedent for judicial review until the late 19th century, and the term 'judicial review' was not coined until 1910, over 100 years after the *Marbury* decision).

169. Ibid. at 796–97.
170. See Smith, S. D. (1988). Why should courts obey the law? *Georgia Law Review, 77*, 113, 135–137.
171. See Ibid. at 137–138.
172. See Ibid. at 138 (observing that courts may render verdicts they feel are consistent with the best logical reasons, "even if those reasons do not happen to be derived from pertinent statutes").
173. See Marder, N. S. (1999). The myth of the nullifying jury. *Northwestern University Law Review, 93*, 877, 888, 892, 899, 902. However, even though judicial or jury nullification at the trial level has been the subject of some literature, it has never been identified as based on the erroneous concept of dangerousness and "danger to self" applied to civil commitment and compulsory treatment cases and has not been reported or discussed anywhere else in either the literature of evidence or mental illness.
174. Tushnet, M. (1983). Following the rules laid down: A critique of interpretivism and neutral principles. *Harvard Law Review, 96*, 781, 821–822.
175. Letter from Mr. Justice Holmes to Harold J. Laski (February 19, 1920). (1953). In M. DeWolfe Howe (Ed.), *1 Holmes—Laski letters: The correspondence of Mr. Justice Holmes and Harold J. Laski 1916–1935* (p. 243).
176. See Caudill, D. S. (2001). Law and science: An essay on links and socio-natural hybrids. *Syracuse Law Review, 51*, 841, 849–850 (noting that even "contradictory findings can both be declared 'right' in the absence of clear error."). See also Smith, M. B. E. (1999). May judges ever nullify the law? *Notre Dame Law Review, 74*, 1657 ("Hence, the law may effectively be nullified by a judge who knowingly plugs fictive facts into correct doctrine in order to obtain a particular result. Patent nullification of legal doctrine is more risky for a trial judge because it is more easily shown on appeal—and judges dislike being reversed. Nonetheless, patent nullification of law may not be worth appealing as appeals are expensive and rarely succeed. Perhaps in part this is because appellate courts often ratify trial court nullification or else nullify the law themselves. Appellate courts do not like to reverse rulings made below even when they think them in error; and

they will not reverse them if they think they can see some reasonable alternative." Ibid. at 1660)

177. To the extent that appelate [*sic*] courts were called upon, occasionally to consider what the word "dangerousness" meant, they originally defined the term with such sweeping broadness that it was stripped of any significant meaning. To illustrate: In 1960, a three-judge panel of the District of Columbia Circuit Court, in dealing with the release from hospital of an offender acquitted by reason of insanity, defined the term "dangerousness," as used in the District of Columbia involuntary civil commitment statute, as including any criminal act, whatsoever, such as passing a bad check.

See Brooks, A. D. (1978). Notes on defining the "dangerousness" of the mentally ill. In C. J. Frederick (Ed.), *Dangerous behaviour: A problem in law and mental health.* Bethesda, MD: National Institute of Mental Health. (p. 41).

178. Schwitzgebel, R. K. (1978). Legal and social aspects of the concept of dangerousness. In C. J. Frederick (Ed.), *Dangerous behaviour: A problem in law and mental health.* Bethesda, MD: National Institute of Mental Health. (p. 83).

179. Silverberg, H. M. (1978). Dangerousness and the discipline of psychology—The stream of thought of a patient's lawyer. In C. J. Frederick (Ed.), *Dangerous behaviour: A problem in law and mental health**** (pp. 96–97).

180. Bursztajn, H. J., Hamm, R. M., & Gutheil, T. G. (1997). Beyond the black letter of the law: An empirical study of an individual judge's decision process for civil commitment hearing. *Journal of the American Academy of Psychiatry and Law, 25,* 79; Bursztajn, H. J., Gutheil, T. G., Hamm, R. M., Brodsky, A., & Mills, M. J. (1988). Parens patriae considerations in the commitment process. *Psychology Quarterly, 59,* 165; Bursztajn, H. J., Gutheil, T. G., Mills, M. J., Hamm, R. M., & Brodsky, A. (1986). Process analysis of judges' commitment decisions: A preliminary study. *American Journal of Psychology, 143,* 170.

181. Bursztajn, H. J., Hamm, R. M., & Gutheil, T. G. (1997). Beyond the black letter of the law: An empirical study of an individual judge's decision process for civil commitment hearing. *Journal of the American Academy of Psychiatry and Law, 25,* 79, 88–89.

182. Brooks, A. D. (1978). Notes on defining the "dangerousness" of the mentally ill. In C. J. Frederick (Ed.), *Dangerous behaviour: A problem in law and mental health.* Bethesda, MD: National Institute of Mental Health. (pp. 40–41).

183. Warren, C. A. B. (1977). Involuntary commitment for mental disorder: The application of California's Lanterman-Petris Short Act. *Law and Society Review, 11*, 629.
184. Wexler, D. B., & Scoville, S. E. (1974). The administration of psychiatric justice: Theory and practice in Arizona. *Arizona Law Review, 13*, 1, 100–101.
185. Goldstein, J., & Katz, J. (1960). Dangerousness and mental illness: Some observations on the decision to release persons acquitted by reason of insanity. *Yale Law Journal, 70*, 225, 235. See also Livermore, J. M., Malmquist, C. P., Meehl, P. E. (1968). On the justifications for civil commitment. *University of Pennsylvania Law Review, 117*, 75, 81.
186. Leiber, M. J., & Anderson, S. (1993). A comparison of pre-reform and post-reform civil commitment decision-making in Dane County, Wisconsin. *New England Journal on Crime & Civil Confinement, 20*, 1, 19–20.
187. Treffert, D. A. (1999). The MacArthur coercion studies: A Wisconsin perspective. *Marquette Law Review, 82*, 759, 775–778.
188. Stavis, P. F. (1999). The Nexum: A modest proposal for self-guardianship by contract. *Contemporary Health Law & Policy, 16*, 1, 4–23.
189. Treffert, *supra* note 234, at 775–778.
190. Appelbaum, P. S. (2001). *Thinking carefully about outpatient commitment. Psychiatric Services, 52*, 347, 349.
191. See United States v. Thomas, 116 F.3d 606 (2d Cir. 1997).
192. Marder, N. S. (1999). The myth of the nullifying jury. *Northwestern University Law Review, 93*, 877, 910.
193. Smith, S. D. (1988). Why should courts obey the law? *Georgia Law Journal, 77*, 113, 132.
194. Fuller, L. L. (1968). *Anatomy of the law.* Westport, CN: Greenwood Press. (p. 40).
195. Ibid. at 89–92.
196. Winick, Ibid. at 37, 40. See also Perlin, M. L. (1998). "There's no success like failure/and failure's no success at all": Exposing the pretextuality of *Kansas v. Hendricks. Northwestern Law Review, 92*, 1247, 1253.
197. Winick, Ibid. at 37, 41–42.
198. Ibid. at 42–43.
199. The meaning of "therapy" here is ambiguous in apparently applying to both amelioration of the disease and a "feel good" emotional state of the patient, which would necessarily come, one assumes, with

curation or amelioration. Civil commitment proceedings are meant to be inherently coercive, since the patient hasn't volunteered for treatment. The most clear form of "non-involuntary" therapy is when the court finds that treatment is necessary and that the patient, due to the disease, would not have sought or would not have consented to if offered, thus coercion is appropriate under the circumstances. Other antitherapeutic consequences, assuming the clinical propriety of treatment, are simply collateral and unavoidable depending on the attempts of the process to be sensitive and the subjective or psychological state of the patient. However, the function of the court, the state, or family is ultimately to act in the best interests of the patient. If a child resists a polio injection, or would feel better without it, if this emotional feeling cannot otherwise be mollified by the process, then rational health policy as well as the interests of the states, dictate that the parents wishes should surely be implemented and the child's wishes ignored.

200. Brooks, *supra* note 228, at 44–45.
201. See LaFrance, A. B. (1995). Mental commitments: The judicial function—A case perspective. *Journal of Psychiatry and Law*, 1, 35 (both judges and lawyers say they need and would want more education on mental illness issues); see Mossman, D., & Kapp, M. B. (1997). Attorneys' and judges' needs for continuing legal education on mental disability law: Findings from a survey. *Journal of Psychiatry and Law*, 327.
202. Mossman & Kapp, *supra* note 201 at 329.
203. LaFrance, *supra* note 201 at 26.
204. Stone, A. (1975). *Mental health and law: A system in transition* (pp. 40–42). For purposes of stacking the proof against treatment, it is sheer quibbling to argue that there are any meaningful distinctions between "beyond a reasonable doubt" and "clear and convincing evidence." Under either standard, all other things being equal, there is significantly more difficulty in proving a case and a greater likelihood of failure to achieve an order for treatment. Also, it has been noted by the Supreme Court itself that there is questionable appreciation by juries of the real meaning of these technical standards of proof. See Addington v. Texas, 441 U.S. 418, 423–433 (1979).
205. Stone, Ibid. at 44 (Rockville Md., Nimh 1975).
206. See generally Shapiro, M. H. (1997). Lawyers, judges and bioethics. *Southern California Interdisciplinary Law Journal, 5*, 113.
207. Frolik, L. A. (1999). Science, common sense, and the determination of mental capacity. *Psychology, Public Policy, and Law, 5*, 41.

208. Bazelon, D. L. (1975). Institutionalization, deinstitutionalization and the adversary process. *C olumbia Law Review, 75*, 897, 909 ("Courts and other social agencies review and fashion criteria for solving each case as it comes... . Consequently, the judgments are never fixed or frozen—they can be altered in response to new information, new understanding, or new public demands."); see also, Powell v. Texas, 392 U.S. 514, 532 (1968), reh'g denied 393 U.S. 898, (1968). ("[Texas] has imposed upon appellant a criminal sanction for public behavior which may create substantial health and safety hazards, both for appellant and for members of the general public, and which offends the moral and esthetic sensibilities of a large segment of the community. This seems a far cry from convicting one for being an addict, being a chronic alcoholic, being 'mentally ill' or a leper.")

209. See Beecher-Monas, E. (2003). The epistemology of the prediction: Future dangerousness testimony and intellectual due process. *Washington & Lee Law Review, 60*, 353–354 ("One description of reality is emphatically not just as good as another. That is why courts look to science in the first place: science has primacy in describing the world. It works. Reality bites. Descriptive claims need to correspond to the natural world... . [E]mpirical information about how people actually reach decision is important in evaluating the truth-seeking and rationality functions of the law.").

210. Holmes, O. W. Jr. (1983). *The common law 1*. Mark de Wolfe.

211. Grey, T. C. (2000). *Holmes on the logic of the law* (Reprinted from *The path of the law and its influence: The legacy of Oliver Wendell Holmes, Jr.*, pp. 137–138, by Steven J. Burton, Ed.); Dean Langdell said "[I]f law be not a science a university will best consult its own dignity in declining to teach it." Sohlag, P. (1997). Law and Phrenology. *Harvard Law Review, 110*, 877, 897 (quoting C. C. Langdell, *A record of the commemorative , November Fifth to Eight, 1886, on the Two Hundred and Fiftieth Anniversary of the Founding of Harvard College*, p. 85 [1887]).

212. Holmes taught at the Harvard Law School for less than a semester when he abruptly departed to join the Supreme Judicial Court of Massachusetts. See generally, White, G. E. (1993). *Justice Oliver Wendell Holmes: Law and the inner self*. Oxford University Press.

213. Gay, P. (1970). *The enlightenment: An interpretation* (Vol. II: The age of science, pp. 126–127).

214. See Beecher-Monas, E., & Garcia-Rill, E. (1999). The law and the brain: Judging scientific evidence of intent. *The Journal of Appellate Practice and Process, 1*, 243, 252–253.

215. Brennan, R. P. (1997). *Heisenberg probably slept here: The lives, times, and ideas of the great physicists of the 20th century.* New York: Wiley & Co.
216. Daubert v. Merrell Dow Pharmaceuticals, Inc., 509 U.S. 579 at 596–97.
217. Rothman, D. J. (1971). *The discovery of the asylum: Social order and disorder in the new republic* (p. 110). Little Brown & Co.
218. Ibid. at 130–132.
219. See Huber, P. W. (1991). Galileo's revenge: Junk science in the courtroom. See also Huber, P. (1991). Medical experts and the ghost of Galileo. *Law and Contemporary Problems, 54,* 119 ("Modern science is not a solitary undertaking. Litigation is. And that fundamental difference—the difference between the relentless collegiality of science and the hermetic isolation of a trial—is what make it so very difficult to maintain good science in court... . Good science is open, collegial, and cumulative; the courtroom setting is discrete, insular, and closed—a one shot decision. It is not merely possible that bad science will emerge in this kind of environment, it is likely. Unless rules of evidence are carefully maintained, courtroom scientists will soon drift away from the science they purport to represent." Ibid. at 165).
220. Giannelli, P. C. (1993). "Junk science": The criminal cases. *Criminal Law and Criminology, 84,* 105, 107.
221. Beecher-Monas, E., & Garcia-Rill, E. (1999). The law and the brain: Judging scientific evidence of intent. *The Journal of Appellate Practice and Process, 1,* 243.
222. See United States v. Llera Plaza, 179 F. Supp. 2d 492 (2002).
223. Daubert v. Merrell Dow Pharmaceuticals, Inc., 509 U.S. at 589 (1993); Kumho v. Carmichael, 526 U.S. at 141 (1999); Gen. Elec. Co. v. Joiner, 522 U.S. at 142 (1997).
224. Kumho, *supra,* note 223 at 147.
225. Another analysis has distilled six criteria from *Daubert:*
    1. Is the proposed theory, on which the testimony is to be based, testable (falsified)?
    2. Has the proposed theory been tested using valid and reliable procedures and with positive results?
    3. Has the theory been subjected to peer review?
    4. What is the known or potential error rate of the scientific theory or technique?
    5. What standards, controlling the technique's operation, maximize its validity?

6. Has the theory been generally accepted as valid in the relevant scientific community?

Grove, W. M., & Barden, R. C. (1999). Protecting the integrity of the legal system: The admissibility of testimony from mental health experts under Daubert/Kumho analyses. *Psychology, Public Policy, and Law, 5*, 224–226 (1999). For an influential pre-*Daubert* article suggesting eleven criteria, see [Judge] McCormick, M. (1982). Scientific evidence: Defining a new approach to admissibility. *Iowa Law Review, 67*, 879.

226. See generally Scherr, A. (2003). Daubert & danger: The "fit" of expert predictions in civil commitment. *Hastings Law Journal, 55*, 1.

227. Indeed, the emphasis on scientific reliability preceded the revision of the Federal Rules of Evidence by 5 to 7 years, beginning with Judge Weinstein's and Professor Berer's work specifying eleven such factors of reliability, as well as the Second Circuit's opinion in *United States v. Williams*, 583 F. 2d 1194 (2d Cir. 1978) admitting voiceprints into evidence. "Thus, there is an element of magic in the Court's 'discovery' of this analysis in Rule 702's phrase 'scientific knowledge'." Giannelli, P. C. (1994). Daubert: Interpreting the federal rules of evidence. *Cardozo Law Review, 15*, 1999, 2015 (contending, *inter alia*, that Rule 702 was never intended to deal with the *Frye* rule at all).

228. "Prior to *Kumho*, unscientific experts could testify if they showed the 'same level of intellectual rigor that characterizes the practice of an expert in the relevant field.' This loophole was noted by Justice Breyer, writing for the Court: [A]s we pointed out in *Joiner*, 'nothing in either *Daubert* or the Federal Rules of Evidence requires a district court to admit opinion evidence that is connected to existing data only by the *ipse dixit* of the expert'" Kumho v. Carmichael, 526 U.S. at 152, 157; see also Grove & Barden, *supra* note 223 at 225. It is noteworthy that on September 15, 2000, the Judicial Conference of the United States approved changes to FRE 702 that would add three conditions to clarify and reinforce the *Daubert/Joiner/Kumho* insistence on science as the basis of admissible evidence: "1) the testimony is based upon sufficient facts or data; 2) the testimony is the product of reliable principles and methods; and, 3) the witness has applied the principles and methods reliably to the fact of the case." Fed. R. Evid. 702.

229. Ghosh, S. (1999). Fragmenting knowledge, misconstruing rule 702: How lower courts have resolved the problem of technical and other specialized knowledge in Daubert v. Merrell Dow Pharmaceuticals, Inc. *Journal of Intellectual Property Law, 1*, 60.

230. Kumho v. Carmichael, 526 U.S. at 147.
231. Ibid. at 149, 152. For considerations on how *Daubert's* four criteria might apply to the social sciences, see Renaker, T. S. (1996). Evidentiary legerdemain: Deciding when Daubert should apply to social science evidence. *California Law Review, 84*, 1657, 1660.
232. Beecher Beecher-Monas, E., & Garcia-Rill, E. (1999). The law and the brain: Judging scientific evidence of intent. *The Journal of Appellate Practice and Process, 1*, 243, 264.
233. Barefoot v. Estelle, 463 U.S. 880 (1983).
234. Ibid. Despite the availability of state payment for defense experts, no contradiction of these two psychiatrists was offered. Ibid. at 899 n.5.
235. Barefoot v. Estelle, 463 U.S. at 896. Indeed, the dissent noted that the American Psychiatric Association declared "it is unethical for a psychiatrist to offer a professional opinion" without conducting an examination. Ibid., 463 U.S. at 924 n. 6; for a thoughtful criticism of the Supreme Court's *Barefoot* majority decision as being unscientifically based, see Beecher-Monas, E. (2003). The epistemology of the prediction: Future dangerousness testimony and intellectual due process. *Washington & Lee Law Review, 60*, 353.
236. Barefoot v. Estelle, 463 U.S. at 905.
237. Ibid. at 899–901
238. Giannelli, *supra* note 220 at 114–15.
239. Barefoot v. Estelle, 463 U.S. at 920.
240. Ibid. at 922–23 n. 5.
241. Ibid. at 923–24 and 928.
242. Ibid. at 938.
243. Addington v. Texas, 441 U.S. 418, 419-20, 431–33(1979).
244. Barefoot v Estelle, 463 U.S. at 896.
245. Ibid. at 922 and 938. See also Heilbrun, K., & Witte, G. (1999). The MacArthur risk assessment study: Implications for practice, research, and policy. *Marquette Law Review, 82*, 733–737, 754–757 (detailing an alternative method for making such a determination).
246. Barefoot, 463 U.S. at 927, 932. See, e.g., Grimes, A. L., McCullough, L. B., Kunik, M. E., Molinari, V., & Workman, R. H. Jr. (2000). Informed consent and neuroanatomic correlates of intentionality and voluntariness among psychiatric patients. *Psychiatric Services, 51*, 1561.
247. Renaker, T. S. (1996). Evidentiary legerdemain: Deciding when Daubert should apply to social science evidence. *California Law Review, 84*, 1657, 1673, 1682.

248. [T]he rules of evidence generally extant at the federal and state levels anticipate that relevant, unprivileged evidence should be admitted and its weight left to the fact finder, who would have the benefit of cross examination and contrary evidence by the opposing party. Psychiatric testimony predicting dangerousness may be countered not only as erroneous in a particular case *but also as generally so unreliable that it should be ignored* [italics added]. Barefoot, 463 U.S. at 898.

249. See, e.g., People v. Sanchez, 208 Cal. App.3d 721, (1989) ("[H]ysteria... was studied by Freud."). Some commentators even questioned the objective reality of mental illness. See, e.g., Albers, D. A., Pasewark, R. A., & Meyer, P. A. (1976). Involuntary hospitalization and psychiatric testimony: The fallibility of the doctrine of immaculate perception. *Capital University Law Review, 6*, 11, 33 ("we have attempted to suggest that 'mental illness' is not a disease process or a medical process but merely a label ascribed to a set of behaviors deemed deviant by a particular society.")

250. Bernstein, D. E. (1988). The science of forensic psychiatry and psychology. *Psychiatry, Psychology, and the Law, 2*, 75, 78 (1995), citing Black, B. (1988). A unified theory of scientific evidence. *Fordham Law Review, 56*, 595.

251. Black, B., *supra* note 250 at 595, citing Barefoot v. Estelle, 103 S.Ct. 3383, 3397 (1983) (Prediction of future dangerousness are necessary in life and in many legal determination); *In re* Harris, 654 P.2d 109, 111 (1982). ("Petitioner's argument would eviscerate the entire law of involuntary commitment as well as render dubious the numerous other areas where psychiatry and the law intersect. There is no question the prediction of dangerousness has its attendant problems... .")

252. Daubert v. Merrell Dow Pharmaceuticals, Inc., 509 U.S. 579 (1993).

253. Ibid. at 589–90.

254. Ibid. at 590.

255. Ibid. at 592–93.

256. Ibid. at 594–95.

257. Ibid. at 598 (Rehnquist, C.J., dissenting).

258. Richardson, J. T., Ginsburg, G. P., Gatowski, S., & Dobbin, S. (July–August 1995). The problems of applying Daubert to psychological syndrome evidence. *Judicature, 79*, 10, 10–11.

259. 57 F.3d 126, 133–34 (1st Cir. 1995).

260. 66 F.3d 940, 944 (8th Cir. 1995).

261. 93 F.3d 1337, 1339 (7th Cir. 1996).

262. Ibid. at 1343.

263. See, e.g., U.S. v. Bighead, 128 F.3d 1329, 1330 (9th Cir. 1997).
264. Kumho v. Carmichael, 526 U.S. 137 (1999).
265. There is no question that the likelihood of future dangerousness should remain a component of involuntary commitment law; and it is not the purpose of this chapter to argue otherwise. Numerous and sensational examples exist of individuals whose propensity for future dangerousness is so obvious that no reasonable mental health care provider or trier of fact would disagree as to the need for involuntary commitment to protect both society and the respective individuals. It is those individuals in whom there is no clearly reliable indication of future dangerousness, but who nonetheless are in need of care and treatment, have no awareness of their need of care and treatment and who would benefit from such care and treatment, to which these observations are addressed.
266. Kumho v. Carmichael, 526 U.S. at 157–58
267. Van Horn, J. D., & McManus, I. C. (1992). Ventricular enlargement in schizophrenia. A meta-analysis of studies of the ventricle: Brain ratio (VBR). *British Journal of Psychiatry, 160,* 687; Soares, J. C., & Mann, J. J. (1997). The anatomy of mood disorders: Review of structural neuroimaging studies. *Biological Psychiatry, 41,* 86; Elkis, H., Friedman, L., Wise, A., & Meltzer, H. Y. (1995). Meta-analyses of studies of ventricular enlargement and cortical sulcal prominence in mood disorders: Comparisons with controls or patients with schizophrenia. *Archives of General Psychiatry, 52,* 735.
268. Lawrie, S. M., & Abukmeil, S. S. (1998). Brain abnormality in schizophrenia: A systematic and quantitative review of volumetric magnetic resonance imaging studies. *British Journal of Psychiatry, 172,* 110.
269. Strakowski, S. M., DelBello, M. P., Sax, K. W., Zimmerman, M. E., Shear, P. K., Hawkins, J. M., et al. (1999). Brain magnetic resonance imaging of structural abnormalities in bipolar disorder. *A rchives of General Psychiatry, 56,* 254.
270. Young, D. A., Zakzanis, K. K., Bailey, C., DaVila, R., Griese, J., Sartory, G., et al. (1998). Further parameters of insight and neuropsychological deficit in schizophrenia and other chronic mental disease. *Journal of Nervous and Mental Disorders, 186,* 44–50.
271. Goldberg, T. E., & Gold, J. M. (1995). Neurocognitive functioning in patients with schizophrenia: An overview. In F. E. Bloom & D. J. Kupfer (Eds.), *Psychopharmacology: The fourth generation of progress* (p. 1245).

272. Berman, K. F., & Weinberger, D. R. (1991). Functional localization in the brain in schizophrenia. *Review of Psychiatry, 10*, 24.

273. McEvoy, J. P. (1998). The relationship between insight in psychosis and compliance with medications. In X. F. Amador & A. S. David (Eds.), *Insight and psychosis* (p. 289); Nassir, S. (1997). Insight and psychiatric disorders: A review of the literature, with a focus on its clinical relevance for bipolar disorder. *Psychiatric Annals, 27*, 782; Peralta, V., & Cuesta, M. J. (1998). Lack of insight in mood disorders. *Journal of Affective Disorders, 49*, 55.

274. See Davidson, M., Reichenberg, A., Rabinowitz, J., Weiser, M., Kaplan, Z., & Mark, M. (1999). Behavioral and intellectual markers for schizophrenia in apparently health male adolescents. *American Journal of Psychiatry, 156*, 1328, 1328–1335.

275. See generally, Krongard, M. L. (2002). A population at risk: Civil commitment of substance abusers after Kansas v. Hencricks. *California Law Review, 90*, 111.

276. Monahan, J. (2006). A jurisprudence of risk assessment: forecasting harm among prisoners, predators, and patients. *Virginia Law Review, 92*, 391 (a thorough review and explanation of the superior accuracy of actuarial techniques of predicting dangerousness in comparison to expert opinion testimony or predictions of a particular individual's prospective dangerous behavior).

277. See Ray, I. (1869). Confinement of the insane. *American Law Review, 3*, 193, 215.

278. Rush, B. (1979). *Diseases of the mind.* The Classics of Medicine Library. (Originally published in 1812) ("Derangement in the understanding has been...the first object of a physician's inquiry on entering the sick room, it shall be the first subject of our consideration in the present inquiry." Ibid. at 13)

279. See Slovenko, R. (2000). Civil commitment laws: An analysis and critique. *T.M. Cooley Law Review, 17*, 25, 35.

280. See Pound, R. (1954). The role of the will in law. *Harvard Law Review, 68*, 1, 2–3; Posner, R. (1998). The problematics of moral and legal theory. *Harvard Law Review, 111*, 1637, 1639–1641 ("1997 Oliver Wendell Holmes Lecture")

281. See Hart, H. L. A. (1958). Legal responsibility and excuses. In S. Hook (Ed.), *Determinism and freedom in the age of modern science* (pp. 81–104). These categories of "absolving" and "excusing" conditions are a heuristic created by the author. They are not discussed as such in this two-volume work, but rather are distilled from the theoretical framework of legal rights of the mentally disabled presented in it. See

also Carnahan, W. A. (Ed.). (1978). *A report to Gov. Hugh L. Carey on the insanity defense in New York*. Although guardianship is a long recognized authority of the state that can be imposed on children of minor age or the mentally disabled, it is neither an absolving nor an excusing condition of law. Guardianship is a fiduciary relationship meant to preserve autonomy or the enjoyment of legal rights and privileges notwithstanding the decision-making impairment due to age or illness. It should also be noted that the government's authority for civil commitment can be considered a form of guardianship by the state pursuant to its *parens patriae* authority. Foucha v. Louisiana, 504 U.S. 71, 103 (1992). Thomas, J., dissenting, uses this concept, saying: "Insanity, in other words is an affirmative defense that does not negate the State's proof, but merely 'exempt[s the defendant] from criminal responsibility.'"

282. Taking his own case history as evidence, Beers skillfully describes how the behavior of the insane followed an internal logic. Seemingly bizarre or unpredictable responses were part of a system, delusional to be sure, but nevertheless consistent. Beers recalled, for instance, that he would not swallow a medicated sugar tablet because "that innocuous sugar disc to me seemed saturated with the blood of loved ones." The asylum staff, however, rather than understanding his fears, interpreted the refusal "as deliberate disobedience," deserving punishment. The ward staff was the obvious villains in Beers' story. He would often hear "the dull thud of blows: on an inmate," "the cries for mercy until there was no breath left the man with which he could beg even for his life." Rothman, D. J. (1980). *Conscience and convenience* (p. 299); see also Link, B. G., & Stueve, A. (1999). Psychotic symptoms and the violent/illegal behavior of mental patients compared to community controls. In J. Monahan & H. J. Steadman (Eds.), *Violence and mental disorder: Developments in risk assessment* (p. 143). Chicago Press.

283. *DSM-IV-TR.*

284. *DSM-IV-TR* at 304.

285. See Slovenko, R. (2000). Civil commitment laws: An analysis and critique. *T.M. Cooley Law Review, 17*, 25, 35. For example, *The Act and Laws, of His Majesties Colony of Connecticut in New England* (1702) provided:

[W]hen so often as it shall happen, any person to be naturally wanting of understanding, so as uncapable, and become for him, or her self; or by the Providence of God, shall fall into Distraction, and become Non Compos mentis, and no Relations appear, that will undertake the care of providing for them; or that stand so near in degree, as that by law they may be compelled thereto; in every such case the Select men, or overseers of the poor of the Town or Peculia, where such person was born, or is by Law an Inhabitant, be and hereby are Empowered and required, to take effectual care, and make necessary Provision, for the relief, support, or safety, of such impotent or distracted persons... . Ibid. at 36.

286. See generally Bitz, D. M., & Bitz, J. S. (1999). Incompetence in the brain injured individual. *St. Thomas Law Review, 12*, 205.
287. Thus, the existence of a rationale mind distinguished mankind from other animals, thus defining mankind as the "rational" animal. Aristotle. (1963). *Nicomachean ethics of Aristotle* (pp. 12–13) (D. Ross, Trans.).
288. "Acts just and unjust being as we have described them, a man acts unjustly or justly whenever he does such acts voluntarily; when involuntary, he Acts neither unjustly or justly except in an incidental way; for he does things which happen to be just or unjust. Whether an act is or is not one of injustice (or of justice) is determined by its voluntariness or involuntariness; for when it is voluntary it is blamed, and at the same time is then an act of injustice; so that there will be things that are unjust but not yet acts of injustice, if voluntariness be not present as well. By the voluntary I mean, as has been said before, any of the things in a man's own power which he does with knowledge, i.e., not in ignorance either of the person acted on or of the instrument used or of the end that will be attained." Aristotle. (1966). Nicomachean ethics. In McKeon, R. (Ed.), *The basic works of Aristotle* (p. 1015).
289. Saks, E. R. (1991). Competency to refuse treatment. *North Carolina Law Review, 69*, 945, 978–979.
290. Morris, G. H. (1995). Judging judgment: Assessing the competence of mental patients to refuse treatment. *San Diego Law Review, 32*, 343, 368.
291. See Johnson v. Zerbst, 304 U.S. 458, 464–68 (1938); Godinez v. Moran, 509 U.S. 389 (1993).
292. See *President's commission for the study of ethical problems in medicine, biomedical and behavioral research* (pp. 20–21). (1998). (hereinafter *President's Commission*); see Johnson v. Zerbst, 304 U.S. 458, 464 (1938).
293. Grisso, T., & Appelbaum, P. S. (1995). The MacArthur treatment competence study III. *Journal of Law and Human Behavior, 19*, 149, 169–173.

294. Appelbaum, P. S. (1998). Why denial of physical illness is not a diagnosis. *International Journal of Psychiatry in Medicine, 28,* 479, 481.

295. See Saks, E. R. (1991). Competency to refuse treatment. *North Carolina Law Review, 69,* 945, 978–979; Appelbaum, P. S. (1998). Why denial of physical illness is not a diagnosis. *International Journal of Psychiatry in Medicine, 28,* 479 ("To avoid infringement on individual liberty, we tolerate a panoply of self-injurious behaviors, from cigarette smoking to erratic compliance with medication for hypertension, to (in many states) riding motorcycles without helmets. All of these behaviors are based to some degree on denial of the possible consequences." Ibid. at 281).

296. Amador, X. F., & Shiva, A. A. (2000). Insight into schizophrenia: Anosognosia, competency, and civil liberties. *George Mason University Civil Rights Law Journal,* 11, 25.

297. Beck, J. C., & Parry, J. W. (1992). Incompetence, treatment refusal, and hospitalization. *Bulletin of the American Academy of Psychiatry & the Law, 20,* 261, 263–264.

298. Reider, L. (1998). Toward a new test for the insanity defense: Incorporating the discoveries of neuroscience into moral and legal theories. *UCLA Law Review, 46,* 289, 313–319.

299. See Schwartz, R. C. (1998). Symptomatology and insight in schizophrenia. *Psychology Report, 82,* 227 (noting that "[t]he phenomenon of poor insight is defined as a general lack of awareness of having a mental disorder or needing treatment, for example, psychotropic medications"); see also Amador, X. F., & Seckinger, R. A. (1997). The assessment of insight: A methodological review. *Psychiatric Annals, 27,* 798, 804 (stating that: "[t]he correlation between psychopathology and insight is consistent across several subscales concerning insight into previous episodes of the illness... . As we have reported before, insight into having an illness or into particular symptoms may be less important than an awareness of the previous efficacy of pharmacotherapy").

300. Beecher-Monas, E., & Garcia-Rill, E. (1999). The law and the brain: Judging scientific evidence of intent. *The Journal of Appellate Practice and Process, 1,* 243.

301. See Morris, G. H. (1995). Judging judgment: Assessing the competence of mental patients to refuse treatment. *San Diego Law Review, 32,* 343, 369.

302. Miller, R. D. (1992). Need-for-treatment criteria for involuntary civil commitment: Impact in practice. *American Journal of Psychiatry, 149,* 1380, 1381, 1383 (noting that two research groups estimated that

a need-for-treatment standard might result in twice as many commitments as a "dangerous to self or others" standard).

303. The awkwardness of this hybrid standard has been aptly, if sarcastically, described by columnist Charles Krauthammer as "not just unfeeling, it is uncivilized. The standard should not be dangerousness but helplessness. Society has an obligation to save people from degradation, not just death." Krauthammer, C. (1988, December 23). the homeless who don't want help. *Washington Post*, at A19., as quoted in Torrey, E. F. (1997). *Out of the shadows: Confronting America's mental illness crisis* (pp. 157–158).

304. Appelbaum, P. S. (1984). Is the need for treatment constitutionally acceptable as a basis for civil commitment? *Law, Medicine, & Health Care, 12*, 144, 147; see Miller, *supra* note 358, at 1383 (commenting on the fact that Alaska and Colorado also have enacted "need for care" criteria); see, e.g., *In re* the Detention of Labelle, 728 P.2d 138, 145 (Wash. 1986) (quoting Washington's involuntary commitment statute, which identifies the requirements for defining a person as gravely disabled as "manifests severe deterioration in routine functioning evidenced by repeated and escalating loss of cognitive or volitional control, but also that he or she is not receiving care as is essential for his or her health or safety... .").

305. Amador, X. F., & Shiva, A. A. (2000). Insight into schizophrenia: Anosognosia, competency, and civil liberties. *George Mason University Civil Rights Law Journal, 11*, 25, 29; Young et al. (1998). Further parameters of insight and neuropsychological deficit in schizophrenia and other chronic mental disease. *Journal of Nervous and Mental Disorders, 186*, 44, 48–49.

These results suggest that in chronic schizophrenia, frontal-executive neuropsychological deficit and lack of awareness of illness are consistently associated. This finding supports the hypothesis that frontal cerebral dysfunction makes a substantial contribution to such unawareness... . This suggests that illness awareness is more attributable to neurological factors, probably involving frontal lobe dysfunction, than to a general deficit state engendered by the illness... .

...Our findings support the hypothesis that illness unawareness is more prevalent in schizophrenics than in other major mental disorders... .

...The finding that, among chronic schizophrenics lack of selfawareness in other domains is significantly associated with the lack of insight into illness suggests that such deficits may be a relatively global phenomenon... .

...neurologically based factors rather than psychological motivation play a more central role in illness unawareness among schizophrenics.

Young, *supra* note 270 at 48–49; see also Fenni, S. et al. (1996). Insight in first-admission psychotic patients. *Schizophrenia Research, 22*, 257, 261–262: "Amador, et al. (1991) & David, et al. (1992) suggest that in some cases, lack of insight might be a form of neuropsychological deficit.... the present study suggests that the association is rather robust. Another finding that indirectly connects lack of insight and frontal lobe impairment concerns the deficit symptoms. Amador, et al. (1994) commented that the insight scale was significantly associated with the deficit syndrome in a chronic schizophrenic sample.... (Amador, et al. 1993). Our findings in a sample at a relatively earlier stage of their illness further support their subsequent observations on the deficit syndrome." Kemp, R. A., & Lambert, T. J. R. (1995). Insight in schizophrenia and its relationship to psychopathology. *Schizophrenia Research, 18*, 21–28; and, this particular dimension into effective past treatment is likely the most important to have.

306. Appelbaum, P. S. (1998, March 13). The medicalization of "judicial decision-making" (Keynote address at the Judicial Training Conference on Mental Health Testimony in the Courtroom, sponsored by Mental Health Legal Advisors Committee and Flaschner Judicial Institute) (p. 2); see Brief Amicus Curiae for the American Psychiatric Association at 8–9, Barefoot v. Estelle, 463 U.S. 880 (No. 82-6080) (noting that many studies have confirmed that psychiatrists do not have the ability to predict dangerousness in the long-term to any reasonable degree of certainty).

307. Thompson, J. S., & Ager, J. W. (1988). An experimental analysis of the civil commitment recommendations of psychologists and psychiatrists. *Behavioral Sciences and Law, 6*, 119, 127.

308. Perr, I. N. (1990, November). Commentary in forensic psychiatry. *The Psychiatric Times—Medicine & Behavior*, p. 31; see also Owens, H. et. al. (1985). The judge's view of competency evaluations. *Bulletin of the American Academy of Psychiatry & the Law, 13*, 389, 390.

309. Insight is classified in gradations from severe to moderate. See Amador & Shiva, *supra* note 3 at 27 (noting that insight can be modality specific).

310. Lack of insight correlates with other behaviors, outcomes and other characteristics of mental illness such as lack of compliance with treatment, refusal of treatment, poorer recovery, poorer socialization, increase in the likelihood and number of relapses, more hospitalizations for mental illness treatment, worse overall outcome, poor IQ, delusional thinking, anomie, etc. See, e.g., Young, *supra* note 270 at

48; Schwartz, *supra* note 299, at 23; Kemp, R. A., & Davis, A. S. (1995). Insight and adherence to treatment in psychotic disorders. *British Journal of Hospital Medicine, 54,* 222; McEvoy, J. P., Freter, S., Everett, G., Geller, J. L., Appelbaum, P., & Roth, L. (1989). Insight and the clinical outcome of schizophrenic patients. *Journal of Nervous and Mental Disease, 177,* 48, 50 (1989); Peralta, V., & Cuesta, M. J. (1994). Lack of insight: Its status with schizophrenic psychopathology. *Journal of Biological Psychiatry, 36,* 559–560; McEvoy, J. P., Appelbaum, P. S., Apperson, L. J., Geller, J. L., & Freter, S. (1989). Why must some schizophrenic patients be involuntarily committed? The role of insight. *Comprehensive Psychiatry, 30,* 13, 17 (1989); Davis, J. M., & Andriukaitis, S. (1986). The natural course of schizophrenia and effective maintenance drug treatment. *Journal of Clinical Psychopharmacology, 6,* 28.

311. See generally DeVyver, K. I. (1999). Opening the door but keeping the lights off: Kumho Tire Co. v. Carmichael and the applicability of the Daubert test to nonscientific evidence [Comment]. *Case Western Reserve Law Review, 50,* 177.

312. Schwartz, *supra* note 299 at 227–28 and 231.

> Most notable [implication] is the diagnostic utility of insight. This study may lend further support for the necessity of using thorough assessments of insight during evaluations at intake. For example, if poor insight is related to more severe positive symptoms, increasing insight for these symptoms may lead to better self-control over or a reduction in symptomatology. Ibid. at 231.

313. Bernstein, D. E. (1995). The science of forensic psychiatry and psychology. *Psychiatry, Psychology and Law, 2,* 75, 78.

314. Playing the psychiatric odds: Can we protect the public by predicting dangerous? [Symposium]. (2000). *Pace Law Review, 20,* 315.

315. Meadow, W., & Sunstein, C. R. (2000, November 20). *Statistics, not experts* (John M. Olin Law & Economics Working Paper No. 109, 2d Series) (It can be downloaded without charge at: The Chicago Working Paper Series Index: http://www.law.uchicago.edu/paper.taf?abstract_id=252824).

316. Golanski, A. (2001). Why legal scholars get Daubert wrong: A contextualist explanation of law's epistemology. *Whitter Law Review, 22,* 653, 699.

> [It has been argued] that Daubert's rule represents a "revised empiricist" philosophy of science, entailing a social, naturalized epistemology... .

[T]his philosophy of science revises logical empiricism, which sees testability as "the sole distinguishing feature of science." Because revised empiricism emulates actual scientific practice. Daubert stresses not only testability, but also such factors as peer review, publication, and general acceptance as guidelines for identifying good science. Ibid. at 699.

Compare Brewer, S. (1998). Scientific expert testimony and intellectual due process. *Yale Law Journal, 107*, 1535, 1542 "The Court does take quite seriously the phrase 'scientific knowledge,' but it is clear on reflection that this cannot quite be the same concept that has concerned traditional epistemology—at least not those epistemological theories for which *truth* is a necessary condition of knowledge." Ibid. at 1598.

317. Smoger, G. H. (2001, February). *From rule 702 to Daubert to Joiner to Kunho tire: A review of the supreme court's analysis of the admissibility of expert testimony, ATLA Winter Convention reference materials hot topics: Daubert/Evidence Association of Trial Lawyers of America* (pp. 2185, 2194); Beecher-Monas, E., & Garcia-Rill, E. (1999). The law and the brain: Judging scientific evidence of intent. *The Journal of Appellate Practice and Process, 1*, 243, 267; DeVyver, *supra* note 369, at 183–84.

318. Daubert v. Merrell Dow Pharm., 509 U.S. 579, 596–597 (1993).

319. Leiter, B. (1997). The epistemology of admissibility: Why even good philosophy of science would not make for good philosophy of evidence. *BYU Law Review*, 803, 814–815.

320. Beecher-Monas, E., & Garcia-Rill, E. (1999). The law and the brain: Judging scientific evidence of intent. *The Journal of Appellate Practice and Process, 1*, 243, 264, 270.

321. Treffert, D. (1987, March 5). Don't let 'rights' block needed protection. *USA Today*, as quoted in Isaac, R. J., & Armat, V. C. (1990). *Madness in the streets* (p. 283). The Free Press (Dr. Treffert's seminal article, "Dying With Their Rights On," was published in *Prism*, February 1974).

322. Locke was the great practical success; the new English and American regimes founded themselves according to his instructions... . The notion that man possesses inalienable natural rights, that they belong to him as an individual prior, both in time and in sanctity to any civil society, and that civil societies exist for and acquire their legitimacy from ensuring those rights, is an invention of modern philosophy....Hobbes initiated the notion of rights, and it was given its greatest respectability by Locke... . [T]he whole world is divided into two parts, one of which

traces its intellectual lineage back to Locke and the other to Marx, and the latter is much readier to acknowledge its parent than is the former. Bloom, A. (1987). *The closing of the American mind* (pp. 162, 165, 217). Simon & Schuster.

Historian Louis Hartz holds that: "Locke dominates American political thought, as no thinker anywhere dominates the political thought of a nation." Hartz, L. (1955). *The liberal tradition in America* (p. 140). Harcourt, Brace, & World, Inc.

323. Locke, J. (1965). *Two treatises of government* (pp. 348–352) [Peter Laslett, Ed.] (written approximately in 1690, although there is some dispute within a 3-year period).
324. See "Appendix: Statutory Language of Lack of Insight Examples by Selected States"; see also http://www.psychlaws.org/LegalResources/statechart.htm
325. See Geller, J., & Stanley, J. A. (2005). Settling the doubts about the constitutionality of outpatient commitment. *Criminal and Civil Confinement, 31*, 127, 130.
326. Colyar v. Third Judicial Dist. Ct. for Salt Lake County, 469 F. Supp. 424, 432–33 (D. Utah 1979).
327. *In re* Melas, 371 N.W. 2d 653, 654–55 (Minn. App. 1985).
328. Bork, R. H. (1999, June/July). Thomas More for our season. *First Things*, 17, 20. (Judge Bork discusses the morality of Senate nullification in terms of the impeachment and acquittal of President William Jefferson Clinton.)
329. See generally, Stavis, P. F. (2000). Why prisons are brim-full of the mentally ill: Is their incarceration a solution or a sign of failure? *George Mason University Civil Rights Law Journal, 11*, 157, 189.
330. Niehoff, D. (1999). *The biology of aggression* (pp. 285–286). New York: Oxford University Press.
331. Smith, S. (1894). Proposed change of the legal status of the insane, in accordance with our present knowledge of the nature of insanity, for the purpose of securing for them more rational and efficient treatment, commitment, detention, care and treatment of the insane. In G. A. Blumer & A. B. Richardson (Eds.), *The Fourth Section of the International Congress of Charities, Correction and Philanthropy, Chicago, June, 1893* (pp. 105, 110–111).
332. See generally Carnahan, W. A. (2001). *Lessons from the Japanese: Collective choice in public policy decisions to care for and treat the mentally ill in Japan.* George Mason University Law and Psychiatry

Center; Appelbaum, P. S. (1997). Almost a revolution: An international perspective on the law of involuntary commitment. *Journal of American Academic Psychiatry & Law*, 135.

333. Zanni, G., & Stavis, P. F. (in press). The effectiveness and ethical justification of psychiatric outpatient commitment. *American Journal of Bioethics*.

334. Reisner, R., Slobogin, C., & Rai, A. (2004). *Law and the mental health system: Civil and criminal aspects* (4th ed., American casebook series, p. 728). Thomson-West, quoting, Stavis, P. (2000). Foreword: First Annual Symposium on Mental Illness and the Law. *George Mason University of Civil Rights Law Journal, 11*, 1, 7.

CHAPTER TEN

POSTTRAUMATIC STRESS DISORDER IN LITIGATION

Susan B. Trachman, MD

The diagnosis of posttraumatic stress disorder (PTSD) has been the subject of both skepticism and controversy ever since its inclusion in the *Diagnostic and Statistical Manual of Mental Disorders* (*DSM*) in the early 1980s (American Psychiatric Association [APA], 1968). One of the criticisms of (PTSD) is that it was constructed out of a group of social and political ideas rather than based on empirical study. In spite of a growing body of research supporting this diagnosis as a separate entity, there has been some concern that it has spurned a "growth industry" in civil litigation cases. It is the only psychiatric diagnosis for which compensation may be sought, and as such it has the potential to give rise to the intentional production or exaggeration of psychiatric disability (Mezey & Robbins, 2001).

Literature and history are filled with descriptions of people who appear to suffer from a constellation of symptoms that are remarkably similar to what we today would recognize as posttraumatic stress. Homer's *Iliad* contains powerful descriptions of symptoms that were experienced by soldiers as a result of war trauma and stress. He describes accounts of "disappointment, withdrawal, grief, and feelings of guilt toward fallen comrades" (Lamprecht & Sack, 2002). Daly, who wrote of the Great Fire in London in 1666, said:

> How strange that to this very day I cannot sleep at night without great fear of being overcome by fire. And last night I lay awake until almost 2 o'clock in the morning because I could not stop thinking about the fire. (p. 222)

The English surgeon Erichson appears to have written one of the first articles in the medical literature on this subject. He attributed "conspicuous psychological abnormalities following railway accidents to microtraumas of the spinal cord." This was later termed "railroad spine syndrome" (Lamprecht & Sack, 2002, p. 222).

Interestingly, these types of claims increased in frequency following the development of public transportation systems. At the same time that the railways were replacing horse-drawn carriages, personal liability and accident insurance were introduced. Rail accidents were among the first accidents for which a person could sue for damages. After the introduction of the personal liability law in Germany, the number of invalids from rail accidents had increased ninefold in the period between 1871 and 1876. Numerous accounts of combat reactions during World War II and after the Korean War led to the *DSM-I* (first edition of *DSM*) diagnosis of "gross stress reaction" (McNally, 2003). The current diagnosis is in many ways the legacy of the war in Vietnam. PTSD was introduced in the third edition of the *DSM* in 1980, primarily as a result of the requirement that U.S. psychiatry manage the needs of Vietnam veterans. Military psychiatrists have long recognized that horrific events could trigger acute stress symptoms in previously well-adjusted individuals. Most of them believed that these reactions abated after the soldier left the battlefield. Others, however, such as Robert Lifton, argued that some veterans continued to suffer severe stress symptoms long after having returned home. Some initially appeared well adjusted but developed the onset of a delayed set of symptoms months or years later. At the time, no diagnosis existed to account for either a chronic or a delayed syndrome, so these psychiatrists lobbied for the inclusion of a "post-Vietnam syndrome" in the forthcoming edition of the *DSM*. Members of the task force were initially hesitant to include a diagnosis that was tied to a historical event. However, they eventually agreed when veterans' advocates persuaded them that the same stress syndrome occurred in survivors of other traumatic events such as rape or natural disaster (McNally, p. 230).

Subsequent editions of the *DSM* led to a more refined approach to diagnosing PTSD. In the DSM-II version, the equivalent diagnosis became known as "transient emotional reaction," which emphasized the temporary nature of a psychological reaction to an overwhelming traumatic experience (APA, 1968). The more modern conception was first introduced in the *DSM-IV-R* and then later in the *DSM-IV*. The earlier edition initially required the presence of symptoms for a period of 6 months or more. The later editions required a period of only 1 month and were based on a conceptual model that separates PTSD from other stressful experiences. In addition, the more modern versions describe the criteria in both temporal and phenomenological terms that are in proportion to the underlying trauma. In the *DSM-IV* version, a change was made to the stressor criterion; no longer did one have to experience the traumatic event themselves, it could be experienced subjectively (APA, 1994). For example, the death of a loved one due to any kind of cause could lead to posttraumatic stress if the death occurred suddenly or unexpectedly. However, in addition to witnessing or hearing about a traumatic event, the current diagnosis requires that symptoms be evident in five different areas. Criterion A requires that a traumatic event be experienced personally or subjectively. Criterion B is a cluster of symptoms that include flashbacks or re-experiencing of the event while awake or as nightmares. Criterion C includes symptoms such as avoidance of activities that remind the victim of the event or a sense of psychological numbing. Criterion D includes symptoms such as a sense of being hypervigilant or irritable. Criterion E requires that the symptoms described be in evidence for at least 1 month. And, finally, Criterion F requires that these symptoms cause significant impairment of the victim's functioning either professionally or personally. Another result of the new definition is the acceptance of the possibility that not just one major trauma but a series of smaller traumas could lead to this disorder. An example of this would be a child being bullied in school or an employee being harassed verbally or physically in the workplace over a period of time.

Given the fact that theoretically there are now more ways to be effectively exposed to potential traumas, how has this affected the incidence of this disorder? Surprisingly, epidemiologic surveys indicate that although a large proportion of the American population has been exposed to traumatic stressors, only a minority develop PTSD. The National Comorbidity Survey revealed that 60.7% of a random sample of American adults had been exposed to traumatic events, but only 8.2% of the men and 20.4% of the women had ever developed the disorder. Among the survivors of the Oklahoma City terrorist bombing, only 34.3% developed PTSD (McNally, 2003, p. 237). How is it then that although a majority of people have experienced what most would consider a significant stressor, only a minority will go on to develop the disorder? The research that has been done in an attempt to answer this question is in the area of risk factors, physiologic response to stress, and individual vulnerabilities.

A major cornerstone for the early conceptions of PTSD was the field of biological studies of stress. These studies described a normal continuum of responses to adversity. The early studies of the biology of PTSD postulated that the physiologic response in this disorder would be similar to those already documented in earlier studies of reactions to stress. One of the pioneers in this area was Hans Selye (Yehuda & McFarlane, 1995). His early findings proved that any adversity could provoke a biologic stress response. This scientific documentation served as a counterargument to those who argued that PTSD was a diagnosis created to serve a social and political agenda.

Another area of research addressing this subject was drawn from the literature on life events. This body of research provided indirect support for the notion of PTSD as a normative response to stress by drawing a temporal relationship between adverse life events and the development of physical and psychiatric symptoms (Yehuda & McFarlane, 1995, p. 1708). The fields of bereavement and crisis intervention supported the idea that transient traumatic events could produce symptoms that were responsive to treatment. These findings were important to the mental health field because they helped in the development of a model of how to treat those who had experienced a traumatic event.

When evaluating the findings on the prevalence of PTSD, it is important to consider that it is likely that some types of trauma are more significant than others, which explains the variability in the rates reported. However, given the fact that some victims of trauma do not develop symptoms, it seems likely that trauma perhaps is not a sufficient determinant of the disorder. In other words, there may be risk factors that account for an individual's vulnerability to developing this disorder (Yehuda & McFarlane, 1995, p. 1710). Some risk factors have been identified among people who already have the disorder. One group for whom this is true is the Vietnam veterans. In general, they report lower levels of social support than do those without the disorder. This is a difficult fact to interpret since it is unclear whether the lack of social support hinders recovery or the mere presence of the disorder alienates victims from those who could help them (McNally, p. 238). Risk factors identified from a cross-sectional analysis have been deemed to be independent of the consequence of the illness. They are lower intelligence, nonspecific behavioral indicators of central nervous system impairment, unstable family history, or a history of a mood or anxiety disorder. Unfortunately, prospective studies designed to identify risk factors of PTSD are scarce.

The nature of acute traumatic reactions may be modified by a range of factors other than the severity of trauma. One such factor is a prior history of trauma. Research studies have shown that women with a prior history of rape were three times more likely to develop PTSD than those who were raped for the first time (Yehuda & McFarlane, 1995, p. 1711). Cortisol is a hormone that is released from the adrenal glands in response to stress. In the individuals studied who had been raped previously, the cortisol levels measured were significantly lower in the hours after they had been raped. Much higher levels were measured in those individuals who did not have a prior rape history. The level of their cortisol response was commensurate with the severity of the assault they had endured. Thus, responses to stress are not uniform but rather depend on variables including not only the trauma itself but also other predisposing factors. Studies such as this one call into question the idea that PTSD is a continuation of a normal stress response. This argues against Selye's earlier theory. The most important conclusion to be drawn from studies such as these is that there is a distinct set of biological alterations that serves to characterize the state of prolonged or persistent symptoms in response to a traumatic event. However, the nature of these disturbances suggests that the biological correlates of long-term psychological responses to trauma are far more complex than was originally believed (Yehuda & McFarlane, p. 1712).

PTSD has been used as a defense in the criminal court as well as a diagnosis in pursuit of damages in the civil court. Given the fact that this diagnosis first came to light in modern times in the Vietnam veteran population, it is not surprising that some of the literature in this area is based on studies of soldiers. Breslau and Davis found that the same individuals who served in intensive combat zones and were at high risk for PTSD might also be at high risk of being charged with criminal offenses. The same study also found that these individuals scored high on a test measuring narcissism, the tendency to see the world solely from one's own perspective and essentially treat others in ways that only serve the affected individual's purpose. Thus, there was a correlation between the potential for violence and a form of personality disorder. This raises the question of whether it is the stress disorder or the personality disorder that predisposes one to potential criminal behavior. In jurisdictions where the insanity defense is based on a cognitive test, a dissociative reaction is the type of traumatic stress reaction that would most likely fulfill the test for "lack of criminal responsibility" (Rosner, 1994, p. 216). A dissociative reaction is one that often occurs in response to stress and is characterized by alterations in memory, state of awareness, or personal identity. A benign form of this reaction and one that may occur during stressful times is the phenomenon of sleepwalking. In this phenomenon, the individual looks and acts as though awake and alert, as described by witnesses, but in reality is in an altered state of consciousness that is not recalled on awakening. In a more severe form of this reaction, one who has developed PTSD may have a symptom called flashbacks or re-experiencing. In these situations, the individual believes that he or she is in the situation in which the trauma occurred despite the fact that he or she may be far removed from the event by time or space. It is this second form of dissociation that is most often used in a criminal defense. Unfortunately, in the absence of witnesses, it is difficult to verify that the alleged criminal behavior was actually caused in the course of a flashback. Criteria for assessing flashback-induced behavior were addressed by Blank in 1985. These include the following: The flashback behavior is unpremeditated and sudden, the flashback behavior is uncharacteristic of the individual, there is a retrievable history of one or more traumatic events enacted in the flashback episode, amnesia for some or all of the episode is reported, the flashback behavior lacks current motivation, the stimuli for the flashback behavior may be current or environmental features that are reminiscent of the traumatic event (combat or otherwise), the patient is mostly unaware of the specific ways in which he or she has enacted war-related or other traumatic experiences, the choice of the victim may be fortuitous or accidental, and the patient has or has had other symptoms of PTSD (Rosner, p. 216).

In the forensic literature on PTSD in criminal cases, it is most often cited with regard to the insanity defense, the mens rea defense, and the area of law related to the defense of justification. A well-known case in which an insanity defense based on PTSD was raised was *State v. Heads* (1981). Charles Heads was a decorated marine veteran who had served as a "point man" on multiple long-range reconnaissance patrols in Vietnam. He had an excellent service record and no prior criminal convictions. He did, however, have a history of at least two dissociative reactions after his return from Vietnam. Mr. Heads was charged with the murder of his brother-in-law after breaking into his house in search of his estranged wife. Mr. Heads shot and killed his brother-in-law and claimed that he had killed him while in the midst of a dissociative episode. He was convicted of murder in 1978. The case was later reversed on appeal after the publication of the *DSM-III*. On appeal, he claimed that he was not criminally responsible for his actions because at the time of the offense he was not able to distinguish right from wrong. He cited the fact that on the day in question he was under great duress because of his wife's departure and that the wooded surroundings of his brother-in-law's home were reminiscent of the woods in Vietnam. These factors together, he claimed, had triggered a dissociative episode. He stated that while in this state, he was acting on "automatic" as if he was on a search and destroy mission and recalled little else. The jury deliberated for 2 weeks before determining that he did not, in fact, know right from wrong at the time of the offense and was therefore not guilty by reason of insanity.

Mens rea, interpreted as guilty intent, has been another area in which PTSD has been used as an unconsciousness defense. In these cases, the defense rests on the assumption that the accused lacked the ability to formulate the intent to commit the crime. If there is no intent, there is no culpability. One example of this defense was in *People v. Tse* (1991). Mr. Tse was a successful Chinese businessman who was at work in his office when a well-known member of a local Chinese gang entered his office, pointed a gun at him, and demanded a large sum of cash. Mr. Tse was able to avert the assailant's gaze momentarily, grabbed his own licensed handgun, and shot and killed him. When the police arrived, Mr. Tse acknowledged shooting the man but stated that he did not recall firing more than one or two shots. On investigation, it was revealed that the dead man had 18 bullets fired into him and that Mr. Tse's gun only had a six-bullet capacity. Therefore, he must have fired and reloaded his gun at least twice. Mr. Tse's handgun was licensed and had been purchased years earlier after an incident in which he was held up at gunpoint. He admitted that he had practiced shooting the gun under the supervision of a former marine who was his trainer. The trainer taught him to fire "combat style," which meant that he was taught to fire 18 shots at a time as quickly as possible and reload the gun twice. At trial, an expert psychiatric witness testified that Mr. Tse had acted while in a dissociative state as if "on automatic pilot," like soldiers in combat. The psychiatrist was able to explain that even complex behaviors can occur while a person is in this altered mental state. As a result, Mr. Tse was acquitted on all charges.

The defense of justification has been used in cases in which the defendant has been victimized, such as battered woman syndrome or rape trauma syndrome. Battered woman syndrome has been used to explain two components of a self-defense claim: the defendant's subjective fear of serious injury or death and the reasonableness of that belief (Rosner, 1994, p. 217). A landmark case in this area is *Ibn-Tamas v. United States* (1979). Mrs. Beverly Ibn-Tamas was convicted of second-degree murder while armed, because she shot her husband, a neurosurgeon, to death. Substantial evidence was presented at the time of trial to indicate that the victim had committed violent acts toward his wife and others. On the morning of the shooting, Mrs. Ibn-Tamas was beaten by her husband and ordered out of the house. The case was overturned on appeal because it was ruled that the trial judge erred by not allowing expert testimony on the subject of battered woman syndrome. The psychologist who was to testify at trial was Dr. Lenore Walker, an expert in the field. Dr. Walker's planned testimony was based on her experience of studying over 100 women who had been battered. The defense claimed that the testimony was relevant because it would help the jury appraise the credibility of Mrs. Ibn-Tamas's contention that she perceived herself in such imminent danger that she shot her husband in self-defense. The Appeals Court's decision concluded that the trial court erred in not permitting this expert testimony because such testimony would aid the trier of fact (the jury) in understanding:

> why the mentality and behavior of such battered women are at variance from the ordinary lay perception of how someone would be likely to react to a spouse who is a batterer; and thus provide a basis from which the jury could understand why Mrs. Ibn-Tamas perceived herself in imminent danger at the time of the shooting.

In cases such as these, the prosecution has argued that the defense is not justified because the woman could have left the abusive situation. In defense, the battered woman syndrome has been used to explain how a woman's state of mind might prevent her from doing so. For example, in *State v. Kelly*, the court ruled that:

> only by understanding these unique pressures that force battered women to remain with their mates, despite their long-standing and reasonable fear of severe bodily harm and the isolation that being a battered woman creates, can a battered woman's state of mind be accurately and fairly understood.

Rape trauma syndrome, generally considered to be a subtype of PTSD, has been used to support an allegation of rape or sexual assault and to explain the behavior of the alleged victim. An example of this is when the victim delays reporting the event or at some point recants her allegations. To be admissible, this syndrome must generally corroborate and not generally bolster the claimant's credibility (Rosner, 1994, p. 218). Testimony that the complainant suffers from symptoms commonly found among rape victims and not that the complainant is truthful is corroborative. Testimony that the complainant is telling the truth that the rape occurred is bolstering. Landmark cases in this area of law have had conflicting outcomes. For example, in *State v. Marks* (1982), the Kansas Supreme Court found that a psychiatrist's testimony that the claimant suffered from rape trauma syndrome was admissible, concluding that:

> an examination of the literature clearly demonstrates that the so-called rape trauma syndrome is generally accepted to be a common reaction to sexual assault and as such qualified expert psychiatric testimony regarding the existence of rape trauma syndrome is relevant and admissible.

In contrast, in *Minnesota v. Saldana* (1982), the Minnesota Supreme Court ruled that testimony from a rape victim's counselor indicating that she believed the victim had been raped rather than having fantasized it was inadmissible, concluding that:

rape trauma syndrome is not a fact finding tool, but a therapeutic tool useful in counseling. Because the jury need be concerned only with determining the facts and applying the law, and because evidence of reactions of other people does not assist the jury in its fact finding function, we find the admission of expert testimony of rape trauma syndrome to be error.

Most forensic cases involving PTSD fall within the realm of civil litigation and are generally filed under the category of psychological injury. This diagnosis has been called "a defense attorney's nightmare" because it is based entirely on self-report. The fact that the finding is incident specific allows the plaintiff to arrive in court with both the cause and the nature of the injury contained within the same diagnosis. From a forensic standpoint, it is critical that a thorough and careful evaluation of the plaintiff and the facts of the case be conducted to prevent unnecessary and, in some cases, exorbitant claims from being handed down. In addition, this is a diagnosis that lends itself to possible malingering, so this must be ruled out as well.

For a claim of psychological damages to be viable, it must meet strict criteria. The first of these is that the defendant must have demonstrated negligence or responsibility for the injury that the plaintiff claims to have suffered. Second, the plaintiff must have some documented mental disorder that poses significant losses to his or her occupational or social functioning. Third, the disorder must have been caused or worsened by the negligent act. The defendant is only responsible for harm that he or she has caused and not for injuries that existed prior to the defendant's alleged act or as a result of a subsequent event unrelated to the defendant. However, the defendant may be liable where the plaintiff has a preexisting vulnerability and the defendant's actions trigger the onset of full symptoms. The relationship between current symptoms and past trauma is complex and not always clear. The challenge in the legal setting is to distinguish between emotional distress resulting from the behavior in question and the emotional distress that existed prior to the behavior or as a result of other events (Shouten, 2002). Fourth, the injury must have resulted in some loss by the plaintiff in either occupational or social functioning and may extend to pain and suffering associated with the injury. Robert Simon, an expert in the area of PTSD litigation, has proposed the following guidelines for the evaluation of PTSD cases:

- The claimant must meet the criteria for the disorder as diagnosed by the *DSM-IV*.
- The traumatic stressor must have been of sufficient severity to produce the disorder.
- The pre-incident psychiatric history of the claimant must be assessed.
- The diagnosis should not be based solely on subjective reporting by the claimant, but it should in addition be supported by objective corroborating data to support the symptoms claimed.
- The claimant's actual level of functional psychiatric impairment must be carefully assessed (Simon, 2003, pp. 32–76).

To satisfy the current *DSM-IV* criteria for PTSD, *each* of the following categories must be met:

A. The person has been exposed to a traumatic event in which both of the following were present:

1. The person experienced, witnessed, or was confronted with an event or events that involved actual or threatened death or serious injury or a threat to the physical integrity of self or others.
2. The person's response involved intense fear, helplessness, or horror. In children, this may be expressed instead by disorganized or agitated behavior.

B. The traumatic event is persistently re-experienced in at least one or more of the following ways:

1. There may be recurrent and intrusive distressing recollections of the event, including images, thoughts, or perceptions. In young children, repetitive play may occur in which themes or aspects of the trauma are expressed.

2.   Recurrent distressing dreams of the event may occur. In children, there may be frightening dreams without recognizable content.
3.   The person may act or feel as if the traumatic event were recurring (this includes a sense of reliving the experience, illusions, hallucinations, and dissociative flashback episodes, including those that occur on awakening or when intoxicated). In children, trauma-specific re-enactment may occur.
4.   There may be intense psychological distress on exposure to internal or external cues that symbolize or resemble an aspect of the traumatic event.
5.   There may be physiological reactivity on exposure to internal or external cues that symbolize or resemble an aspect of the traumatic event.

C. There is persistent avoidance of stimuli associated with the trauma and numbing of general responsiveness (not present before the trauma), as indicated by three or more of the following:

1.   Efforts to avoid thoughts, feelings, or conversations associated with the trauma
2.   Efforts to avoid activities, places, or people that arouse recollections of the trauma
3.   Inability to recall an important aspect of the trauma
4.   Markedly diminished interest or participation in significant activities
5.   Feelings of detachment or estrangement from others
6.   A restricted range of affect (e.g., unable to have loving feelings)
7.   A sense of a foreshortened future (e.g., does not expect to have a career, marriage, children, or a normal life span)

D. There are persistent symptoms of increased arousal (not present before the trauma), as indicated by two or more of the following:

1.   Difficulty falling or staying asleep
2.   Irritability or outbursts of anger
3.   Difficulty concentrating

4.   Hypervigilance
5.   Exaggerated startle response

E. The duration of the disturbance (symptoms in Criteria B, C, and D) is more than 1 month.

F. The disturbance causes clinically significant distress or impairment in social, occupational, or other important areas of functioning (APA, 1994).

Simon (2002) strongly recommends that:

> in evaluating the diagnostic criteria for PTSD, the forensic examiner should be guided by official diagnostic manuals, the professional literature, and current research. Idiosyncratic definitions of PTSD must be avoided. If official diagnostic criteria are not used, the burden of proof should be on the forensic examiner to provide the scientific evidence for his or her diagnosis. (p. 33)

The definition of the traumatic event is of critical importance to making the diagnosis. The stressor is an event of such magnitude that it is outside the realm of usual human experience and would be experienced by most people as markedly distressing. Examples of such stressors would be witnessing a murder, experiencing a rape, or involvement in a natural disaster. This is to be distinguished from events such as chronic illness, divorce, or loss of a job, which are traumatic in and of themselves. However, the magnitude is not of a sufficient degree to meet the diagnosis. An example from the author's forensic practice will serve to illustrate this:

> Several years ago I was asked to serve as a forensic expert in evaluating a family who all claimed that they suffered from PTSD. The family consisted of an elderly mother, a middle aged brother and sister, and a teenage daughter. Each of these family members suffered a loss when a middle aged brother died suddenly and unexpectedly from a pulmonary embolus. The event occurred in the summer in a rather small college town in the south. Unfortunately, the air conditioning in the morgue of the hospital was not working and the ambient temperature rose to over 70 degrees Fahrenheit. This caused the

decedent's body to undergo decay in a rapid fashion so that when the family came to identify his body the results were rather gruesome. Each of the family members claimed that they had symptoms consistent with PTSD. Indeed, they each had experienced flashbacks of the sight of the body, as well as nightmares of being in the morgue. Some of them reported avoiding going past funeral parlors or cemeteries, symbols that reminded them of their loved one's death. Several of them reported feeling "shut down" or distant from others and had difficulty enjoying once pleasurable activities. However, the main reason that this case was not settled in the plaintiff's favor was that none of them met Criterion A. The trauma never rose to the level that was required to meet the diagnosis of PTSD. It is most likely that their experience was very traumatic but was not of sufficient magnitude in the forensic sense to lead to a successful civil suit.

It is critical for the forensic examiner to explore a claimant's prior psychiatric history. No examination is credible without a thorough examination of the plaintiff's past. This is true not just in forensic evaluations but in any complete clinical examination as well. Any past history of PTSD should be documented in detail. Breslau has found that approximately 9% of people who are diagnosed with PTSD have experienced it in the past (Simon, 2003, p. 58). As noted earlier in this chapter, certain risk factors increase a person's vulnerability to developing PTSD once exposure to traumatic events occurs. Particularly pertinent are a history of a major mood disorder, such as depression or bipolar disorder, or a history of anxiety, all of which have been found to coexist with significant frequency with PTSD. Traumatic stressors may exace rbate or reactivate preexisting diagnoses or contribute to the development of a new mental disorder. There is also an association between personality disorders and substance abuse with PTSD (Simon, p. 59). A study by Cottler in 1992 found that cocaine and opiate abusers are over three times as likely as comparison subjects to report a traumatic event and to report more symptoms as well as to meet the diagnostic criteria for PTSD (Simon, p. 61). Given the fact that there is such a high incidence of other psychiatric disorders associated with PTSD, it is imperative that the forensic examiner rule out other possible conditions when a claim of PTSD is made. To do so, a thorough examination of the claimant's psychiatric and medical record must be completed.

One of the inherent problems in performing a forensic examination of a litigant who claims PTSD is the fact that the examiner must rely on the subjective complaints of the examinee. A well-informed claimant who familiarizes himself or herself with the diagnostic criteria can make a convincing case for this disorder, particularly in the event of malingering. Thus, it is imperative to find additional sources for corroboration of the claimed symptoms. Collateral information should include police reports regarding the traumatic event, if available; witness statements; and an interview either by phone or in person of a family member or friend regarding the specifics of the symptoms claimed. For example, the assertion that the claimant dreams of or thinks about the traumatic event should be verified by relatives who have heard him or her talk about it in situations unrelated to the litigation. A detailed history of the traumatic event itself should be ascertained, as well as treatment efforts and changes in living patterns. In addition, any history of prior law suits should be collected. If malingering is being considered, the claimant should be asked if he or she is familiar with the criteria for the diagnosis. Additionally, inquiry should be made into whether the claimant saw the trauma coming. Persons who feel helpless while anticipating a traumatic event are more likely to develop the diagnosis (Simon, 2003, p. 58).

Standardized psychological tests may prove helpful in the collection of objective data. This is particularly true when litigants lack the verbal skills to accurately relate their distress or when they lack credibility. Testing may also be useful in detecting a coexisting illness that may be presenting as PTSD or may be worsening the traumatic symptoms. Testing may also be useful in ruling out the diagnosis of malingering. The Minnesota Multiphasic Personality Inventory (MMPI) is the most validated test to ascertain malingered psychiatric illness. The MMPI profiles of persons with true PTSD resemble those of persons who have organic disease. Malingerers generally exaggerate their symptoms and are more likely to endorse statements on this profile that have little or nothing to do with PTSD (Simon, 2003, p. 68). In assessing functional impairment, it is important to remember that just because a person has traumatic symptoms, it does not mean that he or she is functionally impaired. A case example will serve to illustrate:

> I was asked to review the case of four international business students who were studying in the U.S. and survived a very serious motor vehicle accident while on vacation in the western United States. All of the students were in their twenties and in good physical health. They were driving on a major highway when they were hit on the passenger side of the vehicle by a tractor trailer. Two of the students wore seat belts, two did not. The two who were unbelted were thrown from the vehicle and landed on the side of the highway. Of the four students, only two were awake at the time of impact and of the two, only one saw it coming. Each of the students had some physical injury, fortunately none of them was life threatening. The one who was awake at the time of the incident had a moderately severe back injury which was improving at the time I examined him. Although each of them had some symptoms of PTSD, none of them met the full criteria for the disorder. The student who had the most severe physical injuries met all of the criteria except for functional impairment. He worked as a waiter at an ethnic restaurant, and although sore from his back injury did not have any psychological injury that prevented him from performing the duties of his job. Socially, he was a bit more isolated but not to the degree that it met the full diagnostic criteria. All of students went on to recover fully from their injuries.

In cases in which disability is determined, it should be expressed quantitatively if possible with a numeric or percentage evaluation. In the case that was presented earlier that involved the family who claimed PTSD, the American Medical Association Guides to Evaluation of Permanent Impairment was used for each family member. Other sources that may be helpful are Guidelines for Handling Psychiatric Issues in Workers' Compensation Cases or the Social Security Administration's Functional Impairment Scale. The concept of convenient focus should be considered in every evaluation (Simon, 2003, p. 124). This states that a preexisting disorder is uncovered by stress rather than created by it. In addition, when an individual is not working, certain secondary effects take hold. The various beneficial effects of work are not available. Often, financial and marital difficulties ensue. The examiner must distinguish this as a response to PTSD rather than the secondary consequence of being unemployed. Two researchers, Hirshfield and Behan, developed a paradigm of the injured worker that takes into account his or her personality difficulties and troubled life situation. In several cases, they found that an "accident" provided the occasion to assume a formerly unacceptable disabled role. The claimant's tendency to ascribe all difficulties as stemming from the traumatic event should not be initially accepted as factual (Simon, p. 68). Courts rely on the claimant's actual level of functioning in assessing damages. Thus, a specific diagnosis by itself does not imply a given level of impairment. The ubiquitous nature of potential traumatic life experiences as well as the increasing willingness of the courts to compensate for psychological damages has led to an explosion in civil actions that claim PTSD as the basis of litigation. Prior to the conclusion that a plaintiff suffers from this disorder, it is essential to perform a thorough trauma history and to exclude other diagnostic entities including malingering as the real cause of the symptoms.

PTSD has been called the "chameleon of psychiatry" (Rosenbaum, 2004). Since 1980, when it was first introduced into the official classification of psychiatric disorders, it has undergone many alterations and permutations. However, history has shown that this diagnosis existed long before the development of the *DSM* classification; it was just called something else commensurate with the times. Indeed, as Charles Dickens wrote long ago, after he was involved in a serious train crash that killed numerous other passengers, "I am curiously weak, weak as if recovering from a long illness. I begin to feel it more in my head. I sleep well and eat well; but I write a half a dozen words and turn faint and sick" (Lamprecht & Sack, 2002, p. 222). Imagine what would have happened if the English courts of the time had allowed him to sue for damages based on his decreased occupational functioning!

REFERENCES

American Psychiatric Association (APA). (1968). *Diagnostic and statistical manual of mental disorders* (2nd ed.). Washington, DC: Author.

American Psychiatric Association (APA). (1994). *Diagnostic and statistical manual of mental disorders* (4th ed.). Washington, DC: Author.

Ibn-Tamas v. United States, 407A.2d606 (D.C. Cir., 1979).

Lamprecht, F., & Sack, M. (2002). Posttraumatic stress disorder revisited. *Psychosomatic Medicine, 64,* 222–237.

McNally, R. (2003). Progress and controversy in the study of posttraumatic stress disorder. *Annual Review of Psychology, 54,* 229–252.

Mezey, G., & Robbins, I. (2001). Usefulness and validity of posttraumatic stress disorder as a psychiatric category. *British Journal of Psychiatry, 323,* 561–563.

Minnesota v. Saldana, 234. N.W. 2d227 (Minn.1982).

People v. Tse, Indictment No. 1123-90, Supreme Court, New York County (1991).

Rosenbaum, L. (2004). Post traumatic stress disorder: The chameleon of psychiatry. *N ordic Journal of Psychiatry* (5), 343–348.

Rosner, R. (1994). *Principles and practice of forensic psychiatry.* New York: Chapman & Hall.

Shouten, R. (2002). Compensation for victims of trauma in the United States. *Seishin Shinkeigaku Zasshi, 104*(12), 1186–1197.

Simon, R. (2003). *Post traumatic stress disorder in litigation: Guidelines for forensic assessment* (2nd ed.). Washington, DC: American Psychiatric Press.

State v. Heads, Case No. 106-126, First District Court of Caddo Parish Louisiana (1981).

State v. Kelly, 97 N.J. 178, 478 A.2d 364 (1984).

State v. Marks, 647 P.2d 1292 (Kan.1982).

Yehuda, R., & McFarlane, A. (1995). Conflict between current knowledge about post-traumatic stress disorder and its original conceptual basis. *American Journal of Psychiatry, 152,* 1705–1713.

Chapter Eleven

"Into the Wonderland of Clairvoyance": Faulty Science and the Prediction of Future Dangerousness

*John S. Carbone, MD, JD, MBA**

Prediction is very difficult, especially if it's about the future.
—attributed to Nils Bohr (1885–1962),
Nobel Laureate in physics[1]

I remember clearly the first time I was asked to testify in a civil commitment proceeding involving one of my patients. It was the summer of 1988, and several weeks into the ordeal that was my internship, one of the chronically mentally ill men on the inpatient service wanted to leave the hospital, and a hearing was hastily convened to decide whether to force his continued institutionalization. While I had observed numerous hearings as a student, this was my first time testifying solo, and it suddenly seemed liked uncharted territory.

After giving a synopsis of the patient's hospital course, and in my opinion, his decidedly unwise desire to be discharged at that time, the court-appointed defense counsel asked a perfectly predictable question: "Doctor, is the patient dangerous?"

Starting to re-summarize the clinical information on his chronic mental illness and his long history of treatment noncompliance and absent insight, the attorney interrupted, wanting to know if the patient was dangerous to himself or anyone else at *that specific time.*

I found this question perplexing. Given the patient's long history of hospitalizations, indisputably disordered and delusional thinking, and previous assaults on caretakers in the community and officers who responded to the frantic calls of family members, anyone could see that the patient was dangerous. However, as I looked at the patient sitting at the table—stable on injectable antipsychotic medication for the past several months—it didn't seem so clear cut.

"He has a history of assaulting ..."

"No, I mean is he dangerous right now, on the unit today?"

My hand forced by the attorney's perseverance, with reluctance it seemed necessary to answer, "no, he's not dangerous right at this moment." I then wanted to elaborate, but as soon as the negative word was uttered, the attorney pounced. "Your honor, the doctor has testified that the patient is not dangerous at this time. We move to have the state's petition for commitment dismissed, and the patient discharged to his home in the community, as he wishes, with outpatient follow-up to be arranged." The judge agreed, and the patient was hastily discharged later that day. As a neophyte, I was crestfallen... and worried. Needless to say, the patient assaulted one of his family members within a week of leaving, and was back on the unit before the discharge summary was even completed. Though feeling personally vindicated, I also felt broadsided by the attorney, whom I held to have played word games that were certainly not in the patient's best interest. The attorney had "won" for his client, but had he really done a favor for this mentally ill man, his family, the hospital and the community?

I remember this hearing because it was then that the essence of civil commitment seemed to come into focus. One has to be careful of just how phrases in court are constructed and words are used. "Dangerous" means different things to different people; answering too concretely—"the patient is not dangerous this very second as he sits before the judge with two muscular orderlies standing behind him"—accomplishes nothing. In order to see that patients receive the care that they desperately need, thought I, it is necessary to predict what will happen 5 hours, 5 days, and 5 weeks in the future. That's what the court really wants: no waffling, just the "facts." The proper answer to the sharp but misguided attorney, I mused later, would have been, "yes, the patient *is* dangerous right now. He has a long history of assaultive behaviors and he could become agitated and dangerous at any moment, especially once he predictably stops his medication again. He cannot safely be released to the community because he presents an imminent risk of danger to himself and others the minute that he is not in a structured milieu as we have on this locked ward."

It was then, too, that I fell prey to the quagmire of prognostication that ensnares many clinicians for most of their careers. Courts rarely see things in shades of grey, instead wanting clear-cut answers from those of us—mental health professionals—who are supposedly trained to field just such questions in black and white, and make the job of the finder of fact that much easier.

Were that reality so neatly packaged! As a profession, we have done little to divorce ourselves from the judiciary's expectations. Though my concerns had proven correct in my first time at the plate, could any clinician reliably and consistently bat 1,000 throughout a career?

Volumes have been written on the validity of predictions of future dangerousness, and I do not intend to wade into that controversy with heretofore unpublished data that will somehow turn the tide. I do

536 MALINGERING, LIES, AND JUNK SCIENCE IN THE COURTROOM

not even intend to review everything that has been written on this subject, a Herculean cleansing of the psychiatric Augean stables that is well beyond the scope of this work. Instead, I wish to provide an overview of what we do know about the ability of practitioners to predict future dangerousness, and what scholars, legislators, attorneys, judges and juries have subsequently said about the practice. In doing so, it is my wish that future mental health practitioners who are called to render expert testimony will be better armed with objectivity, and accordingly freed of the vague and dangerous expectations that the legal system has placed upon them.

WHAT DO THE SECONDARY SOURCES SAY?

> *Those who have knowledge don't predict. Those who predict don't have knowledge.*
> —attributed to Lao Tzu (6th century B.C.),
> Chinese philosopher[2]

Imagine that the reader is examining a defendant who has just been convicted of two first degree murders, and assault with the intent to murder, and psychiatric testimony is requested by the court for purposes of sentencing. The defendant had approached a young mother at the time of the crime and propositioned her for sex. The woman refused his advances. Enraged and intoxicated, the defendant proceeded to brutally assault and subsequently murder the woman in the presence of her children, inflicting over forty stab wounds to her with a butcher knife. He then turned his rage on her toddlers. The little girl was also killed, but the little boy miraculously survived, despite having several knife wounds that penetrated his entire torso from front to back. Given the heinous nature of the crimes and the apparent subsequent remorselessness of the defendant, what would most people think? Would they want this individual eventually released into their community after supposed "rehabilitation"? Would they trust this individual to develop a conscience after-the-fact? Even assuming that the individual would never be released from prison, would he ever be deemed nondangerous in any environment? Should he be put to death based on his incorrigibility? Would it be wrong for a mental health professional, empowered by the court to offer opinions as an expert witness, to evaluate this individual and, finding a severe personality disorder, then state a position on his likely future dangerousness given the above?

The United States Supreme Court heard this case in 1991, in *Payne v. Tennessee*. The high court allowed for the admission of expert testimony on future dangerousness despite professional misgivings as to the reliability of such testimony. In justifying the admission of this evidence, the high court stated,

> as we explained in rejecting the contention that expert testimony on future dangerousness should be excluded from capital trials, the rules of evidence generally extant at the federal and state levels anticipate that relevant, unprivileged evidence should be admitted and its weight left to the fact-finder, who would then have the benefit of cross-examination and contrary evidence by the opposing party.[3]

This sounds reasonable, doesn't it? Give the jury all of the information, and then let the jury decide.

Here is another example: A petty criminal killed a state trooper more than a decade ago during a drug arrest, but was acquitted of the resulting murder charge as his attorney successfully argued self-defense. Fifteen years later, the former defendant, now a hospitalized psychiatric patient, began to write death threats in letters to local policemen and judges; found capable of standing trial, he was accordingly convicted of multiple counts of communicating threats. When determining his sentence, the district court judge deviated from the guidelines, which call for a sentence of 30 to 37 months, and instead handed down the maximum statutory sentence of 120 months, saying in part that the defendant's history makes it more likely that he will commit additional violent offenses in the future. As a mental health professional, do you feel that this is a plausible conclusion?

The federal court of appeals for the seventh circuit in Illinois heard this case in 1990, in *United States v. Fonner*. That court eventually vacated and remanded the case based on its determination that the district court judge had not clearly enough articulated his reasons for deviating from sentencing norms. However, the circuit court did not specifically disapprove of the district court judge's analysis of mental state and future dangerousness. A conclusion that the defendant was likely to commit more crimes, perhaps because of mental problems and the known history of homicide, was felt to be an acceptable basis for upward deviation of sentencing, at least if clearly articulated. In other words, the circuit court permitted a determination of future dangerousness grounded on at least some actions for which the defendant had not been held legally culpable, but which were arguably related to his mental instability nevertheless.[4]

This, too, sounds reasonable, doesn't it? Involvement with a killing, for any reason, followed by sending threatening letters to other individuals certainly suggests that the individual in question presents a danger to others he may encounter.

However, what if the information given to the jury in either of the above cases was false? What if the information was predominantly but not entirely false? What if the information was of a degree of veracity that could not be readily determined by the court? What if the information was true but presented in a misleading manner? Would it be correct then to ask a jury to decide a case on the basis of that information? *Should there be standards regarding what the jury is allowed to hear*, regardless of whether it comes from a 'reliable' professional source or not?

There *are* standards, and before reviewing primary and secondary sources on this issue, some background on the admissibility of evidence in the form of expert opinion is requisite. In 1923 from the District of Columbia circuit came *Frye v. United States*. In that case, it was held by the federal district court that expert scientific opinion was admissible only if the principles on which the opinions were based had gained general acceptance in the relevant scientific community. This was an attempt by the *Frye* Court to avoid the testimony of charlatans and quacks. However, for those courts that adopted it—and there were many—the common law *Frye* test also succeeded in preventing the fact-finder from hearing expert opinions from accomplished scientists who were intellectually credible and yet novel or cutting-edge (i.e., they had not yet gained general acceptance within the relevant scientific community). Many felt that the *Frye* test was thus unduly restrictive.[5]

Seven decades later, by the time that the soon-to-be-landmark case of *Daubert v. Merrell Dow* came along in 1993, lower federal courts wanted to know if the *Frye* test had been supplanted by the adoption, 20 years earlier, of 28 U.S.C.A. §702, the Federal Rules of Evidence (FRE).[6] In lieu of the general acceptance stipulation for expert opinion found in *Frye*, the FRE simply provide that,

> if scientific, technical, or other specialized knowledge will assist the [finder] of fact to understand the evidence or to determine a fact in issue, a witness qualified as an expert by knowledge, skill, experience, training, or education, may testify thereto in the form of an opinion or otherwise.[7]

In its holding, the *Daubert* Court did indeed indicate that the FRE had supplanted the common law *Frye* test regarding admissibility of expert scientific testimony. A careful reading of 28 U.S.C.A. §702 demonstrates its three-pronged approach:

- First, there must be "scientific, technical, or other specialized knowledge" involved. *Daubert* described such knowledge as that which "applies to any body of *known facts* or to any body of ideas inferred from such facts or *accepted as truths* on good grounds [italics added]." Expert opinions with such a foundation would possess per se the necessary evidentiary reliability to be admissible. *Daubert* identified four queries that bear on this determination; they ask (1) have the theories been tested on which the expert opinions are based? (2) have the theories been published in professional journals and subjected to peer review? (3) when the scientific theories are applied, is there a known error rate? and as a residual nod to *Frye*, (4) do the theories enjoy acceptance within the relevant scientific community? Later, in *Kumho Tire Company v. Carmichael*, the U.S.

Supreme Court held that the four *Daubert* queries regarding scientific knowledge are neither exhaustive nor necessarily applicable in every case; flexibility within the guidelines, the high court said, is imperative.[9]

- The second prong of 28 U.S.C.A. §702 is thatthe expert scientific opinion must "assist the finder of fact to understand the evidence or to determine a fact in issue." In short, it must be relevant and helpful.
- The final prong of 28 U.S.C.A. §702 holds thatthe expert himself must have superior "knowledge, skill, experience, training, or education." He must be qualified to offer his opinion on the matter at hand.

Of the three prongs for admissibility of expert scientific testimony found in 28 U.S.C.A. §702 and expounded by *Daubert*, the relevance of testimony and the qualifications of the expert are probably the least theoretically controversial, if for no other reason than courts have been determining relevance and qualifications for years prior to the advent of either the FRE or *Daubert*. Thus it is the first prong—that of the quality of scientific knowledge—that may cause the most consternation. Any federal court faced with expert scientific testimony has to determine for itself if 28 U.S.C.A. §702 and *Daubert* have been satisfied.[10]

With the above in mind, a number of secondary sources have commented on the reliability of predictions of future dangerousness and, by extension, whether such predictions fulfill the FRE's requirement of "scientific, technical, or other specialized knowledge." The following encapsulate the tip of the proverbial iceberg of what has been written:

- "Can psychiatrists predict danger with reasonable accuracy? Are there well established clinical symptoms which, if present, can be relied upon to indicate potential danger? Can one be reasonably sure that persons who are not dangerous will not be labeled as such and unnecessarily confined? I believe the answer to all these questions is an emphatic 'no.' There are a number of statistical studies which amply demonstrate that the predictions of dangerousness by psychiatrists are unreliable. ...The findings so consistently demonstrate that psychiatrists over-predict dangerousness by huge amounts that the reports must be taken seriously."[11]

- "Study shows that psychiatric predictions of dangerousness were as likely to produce false positives as to correctly predict future dangerousness."[12]

- "In general, mental health professionals...[w]hen predicting violence, dangerousness, and suicide...are far more likely to be wrong than right."[13]

- "Reliance by the courts on testimony by psychotherapists may be misplaced, since the ability to accurately predict danger-ousness has not been demonstrated."[14]

- "In April 1983 the District of Columbia's Superior Court ruled, *In re Wilson,* that psychiatrists may not testify about the dan-gerousness of individuals subjected to the civil commitment process. In June of that year the United States Supreme Court decided *Jones v. United States,* which strongly implied that psychiatric testimony on dangerousness is admissible in com-mitment proceedings for individuals acquitted by reason of insanity. Shortly thereafter, in *Barefoot v. Estelle,* the Supreme Court explicitly stated that a mental health professional may address the dangerousness of a capital murder defendant at the sentencing proceeding. The chasm between the lower court's decision and the Supreme Court's two opinions could hardly be more pronounced: the District of Columbia court found expert testimony predicting the probability of antisocial behavior too unreliable to support a hospital commitment of six months, while the Supreme Court held the same type of testimony sufficiently trustworthy to support not only prolonged com-mitment to a maximum security mental hospital but also the ultimate penalty of death."[15]

- "One of the most controversial aspects of the...statute is its reli-ance upon prediction of the offender's future dangerousness by a mental health professional. The most persistent objection to the use of such predictions is their lack of accuracy. Opponents of the new statute claim that the prediction accuracy of individual recidivism is so low that it seriously threatens individual freedom and autonomy without adequate justification."[16]

- "A large literature indicates that neither actuarial nor clinical modes of predicting the dangerousness of mental patients released from maximum security have fared very well."[17]

- "Predictions of violence have been the subject of extensive literature that consistently criticizes psychiatrists'ability to gauge individuals'long-term future dangerousness."[18]

- "The courts have increasingly relied upon the psychiatrists'and psychologists'predictions in determining an offender's potential for future dangerousness, even though the psychiatric literature stresses the unreliability of these expert predictions."[19]

- "The American Psychiatric Association disclaims such predictions [of future dangerousness], admitting that they are wrong twice as often as they are right. ...Psychiatrists should not be permitted to offer a prediction concerning the long-term future dangerousness of a defendant in a capital case, at least in those circumstances where the psychiatrist purports to be testifying as a medical expert possessing predictive expertise in this area. Although psychiatric assessments may permit short-term predictions of violent or assaultive behavior, medical knowledge has simply not advanced to the point where long-term predictions—the type of testimony at issue in this case—may be made with even reasonable accuracy. The large body of research in this area indicates that, even under the best of conditions, psychiatric predictions of long-term future dangerousness are wrong in at least two out of every three cases."[20]

- "Psychiatric predictions based on hypothetical situations sometimes bear more resemblance to medieval fortune-telling than to modern scientific techniques."[21]

- "Lay people can predict future dangerousness as well as medical experts. ...Although the testimony of clinicians about future dangerousness offers little more than that of an astrologer, such clinical testimony is pervasive, and courts persist in circumventing any inquiry into the scientific validity of expert future dangerousness predictions. This is an important concern because giving the imprimatur of science to chicanery undermines our justice system."[22]

- "The opinions of experts in prediction should help the courts in this task, but over thirty years of commentary, judicial opinion, and scientific review argue that predictions of danger lack scientific rigor. ...Scientific studies indicate that some predictions do little better than chance or lay speculation, and even the best predictions leave substantial room for error about individual cases. The sharpest critique finds that mental health professionals perform no better than chance at predicting violence, and perhaps perform even worse. ...Given their notorious unreliability and deep division in the professional community, we might predict that no court would admit predictive opinions either under *Daubert* or *Frye*. Yet no appellate court has ever ordered exclusion of expert psychiatric testimony about danger in a civil commitment case, either before or after *Daubert*. Courts have shown an extraordinary receptiveness to such opinions, admitting and relying on them in their commitment decision-making. Moreover, courts have had their eyes open: Judicial opinions regularly refer to, and explicitly accept, the imperfections of predictive testimony. What is going on? How can such unreliable opinions survive *Daubert*'s stress on scientifically valid and reliable expertise?"[23]

- "Juries give great credence to expert testimony, and the scientific literature evaluating the predictive value of clinical judgments about future violence has shown that these expert predictions are no better than lay judgments. If courts applied *Daubert* standards to the kinds of clinical predictions currently offered in our courts, they would not admit the predictions because they do not meet any of the criteria for scientific validity."[24]

- "Predictions of future dangerousness were inaccurate in forecasting serious assaultive behavior in prison 95% of the time."[25]
- "The prediction of dangerousness is arguably the most difficult aspect of the [adjudication] process, largely because of its uncertainty. Research over the past thirty years shows a significant degree of inaccuracy in clinicians' predictions of dangerousness, especially with false positives."[26]
- "The courts reasoned...that predictability in psychiatric matters is notoriously poor."[27]
- "Studies have not been heartening about the ability of psychotherapists to predict dangerousness...finding that only one in three predictions of long-term dangerousness among institutionalized population were correct. Even with relatively sensitive tests for dangerousness, a substantial number of false positives occur because of the low base rate of dangerousness among the patient population."[28]

The above is hardly a resounding endorsement of admissibility under under "scientific, technical, or other specialized knowledge" of 28 U.S.C.A. §702. With experts in courtrooms across the country still predicting dangerousness more than 30 years after the adoption of the FRE, though, one must ask how this mess came about.

TRYING TO MAKE SENSE OF CONFUSION

An unsophisticated forecaster uses statistics as a drunken man uses lamp posts—for support rather than illumination.
—Andrew Lang (1844–1912),
Scottish author[29]

In 1908 Professor Hugo Munsterberg of the psychology department at Harvard University compiled a collection of his earlier articles into a work entitled, *On the Witness Stand.* This tome extolled the virtues of using psychologists as expert witnesses in criminal and civil actions, and advocated a rational and scientific means for probing facts endorsed by (fallible) human witnesses. In criticizing then-current courtroom procedure, Munsterberg wrote, "the lawyer and the judge and the juryman are sure that they do not need the experimental psychologist. They go on thinking that their legal instinct and their common sense [alone] supplies them with all that is needed."[30] Munsterberg hoped to change that policy with his publication.

In the first decade of the 20th century, the foremost expert on evidence in the United States was John Wigmore, then professor emeritus of law at Northwestern University in Chicago. Wigmore wrote a scathing rebuttal of Munsterberg's book which appeared in the *Illinois Law Review* in 1909. Following this public rebuke of the perceived value of psychologists as expert witnesses by such an august authority, few if any articles were written for almost a quarter of a century advocating the discredited Munsterberg's view. Even as recently as the 1950s, there are documented episodes of trial judges dismissing psychologists from court, not because their credentials within the field of psychology were lacking, but rather because they belonged to the discipline itself![31]

The loss of autonomy following civil commitment to a psychiatric facility historically was justified on the basis of either of two compelling societal demands: the state's legitimate interest under *parens patriae* to provide care for citizens who were deemed unable to care for themselves, and the state's authority under its police powers to protect the community from the dangerous tendencies of some unstable individuals. With the rise of consciousness about civil rights and patients' rights in the 1960s, mental health professionals found themselves in demand for a service which was rarely requested in the days of lifelong institutionalization, and especially after Professor Wigmore's lambasting: prediction of future dangerousness in court, as dangerousness increasingly replaced the paternalism of *parens patriae* as the primary grounds for commitment and long-term hospitalization.

The momentum of change picked up markedly in 1974, when Steadman and Cocozza published their work on the *Baxstrom* cohort, a sociological follow-up study of individuals released from maximum security forensic wards. In 1966, the U.S. Supreme Court, in *Baxstrom v. Herold*, had ruled that an inmate, J. K. Baxstrom, had been denied equal protection by being confined on the forensic unit of Dannemora State Hospital beyond the expiration of his prison sentence. The inmate had been held on the locked forensic unit due to purported mental illness, but had not been given the legal safeguards of a contested civil commitment prior to his institutionalization. Because of a successful legal challenge, inmate Baxstrom and 967 other offenders being similarly held were released to nonforensic hospitals throughout New York State. Havoc was expected, but none occurred. The offenders had a very low rate of re-offending in the nonforensic settings. Over a period of almost 5 years, more than half of the cohort members were discharged entirely from their respective hospitals to the community, and fewer than 3% of the total were reincarcerated due to violent crimes.[32]

Still, in the minds of many remained the association between mental illness and violence, even if few in relative terms were responsible; one study claimed that almost half of recorded incidents of violence in a particular group were perpetrated by the most seriously unstable 5% of patients.[33] The American Psychiatric Association's Model State Law on Civil Commitment from 1983 contemplated involuntary hospitalization of those with mental illness only when they were deemed "likely to cause harm to others." As recently as 1999, the U.S. Surgeon General's Report on Mental Health opined that the continued fear and stigmatization of the mentally ill was largely due to the public's fear of violence.[34] Monahan, one of the foremost researchers in the prediction of violence, put it thus: "The presumed link between mental disorder and violence has been the driving force behind mental health law and policy for centuries."[35]

It was generally held, at least initially, that psychiatrists had the requisite expertise to pass judgment on whether a patient had achieved maximum benefit from institutionalization, and perhaps more importantly, if that person presented a danger to himself or others outside of a structured inpatient setting.[36] There seemed to be little doubt expressed about the accuracy of such professional opinions, and certainly there was no dispute as to relevance. Laypeople, and especially attorneys, were felt by the mental health profession to have no role in the determination of such matters.[37]

Sepejak et al. in 1983 said that 39% of those patients rated to be "medium" and "high" risk for future violence in one study committed violent acts in the 2 years following discharge, compared to those classified as "low" risk, who became violent during the follow up period 26% of the time. Lidz et al. in 1993 asked psychiatrists and nurses in psychiatric emergency rooms to predict future dangerousness in patients they examined, the premise being that anyone who has regularly cared for patients has at some point felt strongly that they knew how a patient would react, including the possibility of violence. In the Lidz group's study, 53% of those deemed at risk of violence by the staff eventually did become violent, whereas 36% of those not deemed at risk of violence later became violent.[38] In both example studies, many of those deemed at risk did not become violent during the follow-up period, and many of those not deemed at risk did experience violent outbursts. Just like the wives' tale about emergency rooms and the full moon, though, assumptions regarding the prescience of clinicians convinced many, then as now, that behavior can be predicted. Little to none of this was at first empirically tested on a large scale basis, and no one initially seemed to dispute it.

Inevitably, some doubts slowly began to arise. To cite the Quinsey group, "people often think that they have more information than they actually have, [and they] are therefore willing to make more extreme judgments than are necessary."[39] In a recent legal text is written,

> there are [numerous]…flaws and limitations in human information processing, such as the propensity of human decision makers to be distracted by irrelevant aspects of the alternatives…the tendency of decision makers to be swayed by the form in which the information about risks is packaged and presented…

[the] reliance on faulty categories and stereotypes...and [the] illusion of control.[40]

Such flawed opinions can have wide-reaching effects. Take for example one review from 2005 which revealed,

> a meta-analysis of 82 recidivism studies, [with] 1620 findings from 29,450 sex offenders, identified deviant sexual preferences and antisocial orientation as the major predictors of sexual recidivism for both adult and adolescent sexual offenders. ...Many of the variables commonly addressed in sex offender treatment programs (e.g., psychological distress, denial of sex crime, victim empathy, stated motivation for treatment) had [therefore] little or no relationship with sexual or violent recidivism.[41]

Commenting on the imperfect nature of individual risk assessment calls, "clinicians will weigh the factors, unfortunately, often *due to their personal bias*: Freudian psychologists might consider the [offender's] relationship with the mother as paramount, while a cognitive psychologist might consider the offender's thoughts and perceptions as more important [italics added]" in determining and predicting the risk of future dangerousness.

In time the pro-prediction camp developed more detractors. Repeated studies were performed, and the empirical data on such predictions did not support the conventional wisdom of clinical judgment resulting in good forecasting. Predictions of long term dangerousness were not being made with anything approaching the accuracy needed to meet a standard of proof. An accuracy level that is slightly above chance, possibly not even reaching a difference of statistical significance when compared to that accomplished by laymen, should not suddenly confer upon professionals, it was felt in some quarters, the expertise to testify in court to largely unsubstantiated facts. The courts and the public had conferred upon mental health providers in general, and on psychiatrists in particular, a belief of near-omniscience in predicting such matters. Though a surprising amount has been written on this topic in more recent years that does not support anything near such omniscience, this has not apparently filtered down to all attorneys, courts or laypeople. The American Bar Association's National Benchbook on Psychiatric and Psychological Evidence and Testimony in 1998 admitted as much, stating that, while imperfect, such predictions of future dangerousness are the best information that courts currently have available to them! Thus, "imperfect" apparently became "good enough."

So how *do* clinicians arrive at these faulty opinions? One study delineated six ways along a continuum in which mental health professionals go about making determinations of future dangerousness:

- First, there is that of "unguided clinical judgment," what has been called by some researchers nothing more than a likeability test and a personal morality judgment.[43]
- There is that of "guided clinical judgment," which involves the clinician formulating an opinion based on a checklist of risky characteristics for which to look in old records and during current examinations; this method seems hardly different than the unguided method, and might include elements, personally derived by the clinician, such as irritability, impulsivity, the presence of psychosis, expansiveness and inappropriateness of affect, and evidence of impaired judgment.[44]
- There is that of "clinical judgment based on an anamnestic approach," which involves the clinician examining the subject's history and seeing what, if any, dangerousness characteristics still exist; often this method includes looking for the well known childhood triad of enuresis–vandalism–animal abuse, along with evidence of pyromania, intense jealousy, and feelings of hopelessness, frustration, and rage.[45]
- There is that of "research guided clinical judgment," which involves the clinician employing a more detailed and "scientifically" generated list of dangerousness characteristics, based on actuarial red flags.
- There is that of "clinically adjusted actuarial procedures," which involves employing actuarial instruments which the clinician can then adjust according to his own clinical observations.

- Finally, there is that of "pure actuarial procedure," in which the clinician essentially has no personal input, and only collects the data and crunches the numbers.[46] A few early studies dating back to that of Paul Meehl in 1954 suggested that the purely actuarial method is superior to anything that has in it the clinician's personal input, even taking into account those instances in which the clinician reports a subjectively high degree of certainty in his opinion!

Before commenting further on the assumption that actuarial models succeed over clinical guesswork, though, Monahan's 2001 study on the prediction of future dangerousness, said to have been the largest study of this topic undertaken up to that point, needs to be discussed. Those who wish to review the very detailed statistical data presented by the Monahan group are referred to the work itself; a summary of some of their findings for our purposes will here hopefully suffice.

The Monahan group reviewed at length the MacArthur Violence Risk Assessment Study (MVRAS), research that had been conducted using almost 1,000 patients who were released from inpatient settings and then followed for a year postdischarge. The MacArthur study found in their monitoring of this patient population some interesting facts. Of those diagnosed with schizophrenia, 14.8% were violent at some point during the follow up period. Of those with depression, the number was 28.5%. Of those with bipolar disorder, the number was 22%. Of those with dual-diagnoses including substance abuse, the number jumped to 31%. Overall, 18.7% of the patients followed in the MacArthur study were violent at some point postdischarge.[47]

The MacArthur study went on to state:

> "People discharged from psychiatric hospitals" is not a homogeneous category regarding violence. People with a major mental disorder diagnosis and without a substance abuse diagnosis are involved in significantly less community violence than people with a co-occurring substance abuse diagnosis. The prevalence of violence among people who have been discharged from a hospital and who *do not* have symptoms of

substance abuse is about the same as the prevalence of violence among other people living in their communities who [also lack] symptoms of substance abuse. ...Violence committed by people discharged from a hospital is very similar to violence committed by other people living in their communities in terms of type (i.e., hitting), target (i.e., family members), and location (i.e., at home).[48]

Only 13% of the violent incidences that were documented involved the patient actually seeking out the victim, and whether dually diagnosed or not, substance abuse was involved in fully 75% of the violent episodes. There was also a drop-off in incidences of violence after twenty weeks postdischarge. It was felt that this represented the re-institutionalization or incarceration of those who had failed their placement, removing the unstable individuals from inclusion in the community data post-20 weeks.[49]

The patients who did become violent were further examined, both from a criminologic aspect (age, gender, sociodemographics of the home environment) and from a clinical aspect (symptoms and diagnoses), and some trends were noted. Prior childhood exposure to violence was one of the strongest actuarial predictors for future violent behavior. Not having lived with either biological parent while young, the occurrence of deviant behavior on the part of either parent in the home setting, substance abuse as noted above, antisocial orientation, and past physical abuse were all associated with later tendencies toward violence.[50]

The presence of delusions was not at first noted to contribute to violent tendencies unless the delusions were of threats to self or control by others, in which case there was an increase in subsequent violence by those who were delusional and felt thus threatened.[51] However, when using the MacArthur-Maudsley Delusions Assessment Scale (MMDAS), there was no association noted between delusional thinking and later violence, even when the content of the delusion was accordingly taken into account; it was noted, however, that under the MMDAS, nondelusional suspiciousness *was* related to later violence, probably because those individuals might feel threatened while at the same time not being as functionally impaired—and thus being more capable of executing a violent plan—as those individuals with full blown psychotic delusions.[52] Command hallucinations with a violent theme were also found to increase the risk of future violence, though nonviolent command hallucinations, or hallucinations of a noncommand nature, showed no increase in the likelihood of violent acts.[53] Interestingly, anger was not seen to be a statistically significant risk factor for violence. The researchers felt that this confirmed that not all violence has an anger component, and conversely anger does not always lead to violence.[54]

The influence that environment exerted on violent predisposition was difficult to study, since high crime and poverty stricken neighborhoods were found to have high degrees of transience, injecting unpredictable influences coming and going into the milieu with variable frequency.[55] Notably, when subjects within a study environment were adjusted for income, there were no racial or ethnic differences in violence demonstrated.[56]

In reviewing the MacArthur data, the Monahan group opined that a few variables could be suggestive of a violent predisposition, whereas many other variables, some of which run counter to the so-called conventional wisdom, did not have any predictive value. Even in those cases in which suggestive variables were found, there was a complex relationship between competing variables that was not always readily apparent. As the Monahan group stated, "The complexity of the findings reported here underscores the difficulty of identifying main effect or uni-variate predictors of violence—variables that are across-the-board risk factors for violence *in all populations.* This complexity is no doubt one of the principle reasons why clinicians relying on a fixed set of individual risk factors have had such difficulty making accurate risk assessments [italics added]."[57] While Monahan's group advanced that unaided predictions of future dangerousness in general equal little better than chance, they went on to advocate the use of decision trees which categorize individuals into high and low risk and allow for actuarial study.

This was not the first time that researchers had decided that long-term predictions based on clinical observations are near-worthless, but had attempted to circumvent this worthlessness by developing actuarial instruments to hone and refine clinical observations into hopefully meaningful results. One early protocol, referenced by the Monahan group, was created by Steadman and Cocozza in 1974. Called the Legal Dangerousness Scale, it documented in subjects the presence of juvenile arrest records, the presence of previous violent crimes, the number of past lockups, the abuse of alcohol and drugs, the severity of any current offenses, and the age of the subject, and subsequently postulated a positive association with later acts of violence during the follow up period.[58]

The Quinsey group developed the Violence Risk Appraisal Guide (VRAG) in 1998. The VRAG at first consisted of more than four dozen variables, and after a series of regression models, twelve variables were finally opined to be of predictive value. In addition, the Quinsey group maintained that if a subject scored "high risk" on the Hare Psychopathy Checklist (HPC) and in addition had a documented history of maladjustment in elementary school and a relatively young age at first offense, 55% of those subjects would later offend violently, compared with only 19% of those who rated as 'low risk' on the HPC and who had no early legal infractions nor school maladjustments noted.[59]

Earlier, the Quinsey group had stated that clinicians should be allowed to make 'conservative adjustments' in predicting future dangerousness when using actuarial tools if some facet of the analysis was particularly compelling. As the VRAG was fine-tuned, though, by 1998, the group had changed its outlook, saying, "actuarial methods are too good, and clinical judgment too poor, to risk contaminating the former with the latter."[60] The Quinsey group divided risk factors into those that are fixed (such as prior arrest history, history of abuse as a child, father's criminal and drug abuse history, age of the subject, presence of violence at the time of arrest or hospitalization, and history of head injury with loss of consciousness) and those that are fluid and treatable (presence of anger, ongoing substance abuse, and current violent fantasies).[61] In supporting the use of their actuarial instrument, the Quinsey group added, our data are most consistent with the view that the propensity for violence is the result of the accumulation of risk factors, no one of which is either necessary or sufficient for a person to behave aggressively toward others. People will be violent by virtue of the pressure of *different sets of risk factors* [italics added].[62]

Another research team, Douglas and Webster, in 1999 developed the Historical Clinical Risk-management 20-item checklist (HCR-20) and subsequently suggested that those patients scoring above the median were 6 to 13 times more likely to be violent in the first 2 years following discharge to the community than were those who scored below the median.[63]

Many still search for the magic bullet, that collection of characteristics that, when employed for predictive purposes, will yield accurate and meaningful information for use in a variety of clinical and legal settings. As recently as 2005, Douglas and Skeem wrote an article advocating the development of an analytic instrument using dynamic risk factors, such as impulsiveness, anger, psychosis, antisocial attitudes, substance abuse, unstable interpersonal relationships, and lack of treatment compliance, which they felt could trump predictions based on the so-called static (i.e., unchanging) risk factors, such as age at offense, offense history, and childhood and family background.[64]

Although proponents of actuarial tools may be well meaning and enthusiastic, they often overlook or minimize what I perceive to be serious flaws that greatly curtail the usefulness of such instruments *to the requisite level of accuracy desired by the legal system*. There are a number places in the actuarial chain where unreliability can slip into and pollute the analytic process. For example:

- No one has ever really agreed on the definitions of "violence" and "dangerousness," and thus what is actually being measured. Does it mean attempted bodily harm? Actual bodily harm? If harm does occur, does it have to be serious to be included, or minimal? Does an arrest or official report have to be completed for the act to count, or does self-report by the subject, or the unofficial reports of others, allow for inclusion? Actuarial instruments will be difficult to compare—or even use—unless there is universal agreement as to what is being measured, and in what way. From a 1994 book edited by Monahan: "it is unusual in this field to find two studies that have even defined actuarial predictor variables in the same manner. Given the retrospective nature of much of the research, investigators often have had to rely for predictor variables upon whatever information happened to be in the patient's records...[and additionally] follow up periods vary widely."[65]

- Where are the cut-offs for high risk and low risk? What becomes of the grey zone in the middle? The more tightly defined the parameters of the high- and low-risk groupings, the more likely it appears that some meaningful data can be extracted based on the much smaller and more extreme or homogenous cohorts, but at the same time, the larger becomes the nebulous middle ground. The Monahan group admits that "in practice, the choice of cutoffs for high and low risk must be made on substantive grounds by a decision-maker *legally empowered* to do so [italics added]." Note the use of the word "legally." Just because a person is *legally* empowered to do something—in this case, make a decision on parameters—is no guarantee that the act will be based on anything scientific.[66]

- The MVRAS examined patients from three states (Pennsylvania, Massachusetts, and Kansas) and included only English speaking white, black, and Hispanic males between the ages of 18 and 40. Do the findings of the MacArthur study, or other protocols noted above, such as the VRAG or the HCR-20, easily and accurately extrapolate to other geographic areas and groups, such as women, adolescents, geriatrics, civil patients versus correctional inmates, or inpatients versus outpatients?

- The data collected by researchers and clinicians for inclusion in an actuarial model are only as good, or as useful, as is the collector. I do not mean to impeach the honesty of researchers, but rather to remind the reader that the actuarial camp promotes that, by using actuarial tools, the imperfectness and bias of human examiners can be eliminated. It can't. A summary paragraph at the MacArthur Web site states: "the approach to risk assessment developed in the MVRAS appears to be highly accurate when compared to other approaches to assessing risk among people hospitalized in acute-care psychiatric facilities. But it is also much more computationally complex than other approaches. Five tree-based prediction models need to be constructed, each involving the assessment of many risk factors. It would clearly be impossible for a clinician to commit the multiple models and their scoring to memory, since different risk factors are to be assessed for different patients, and using a paper-and-pencil protocol would be very unwieldy. Fortunately, however, the administration and scoring of multiple tree-based models lends itself to software."[67]

While I agree that the complexity of the model makes its use unwieldy, the employment of software is still dependent on the collection and entry of data. The data do not collect themselves, and as noted above, when definitions and parameters have not been universally defined, the very bias that was supposedly removed is reintroduced. The weak link will always be the imperfect human who is collecting and collating the data, deciding what to include in which category, and what attains significance and what does not.

- Perhaps most practically and realistically, what clinician has the confidence *to go against his gut instincts* in this litigious society and base testimony on future dangerousness on actuarial data with which he doesn't agree, regardless of what the allegedly unbiased numbers show?

In my opinion, damning evidence against the ability to accurately employ actuarial instruments to predict future dangerousness is found on page 117 of the Monahan group's 2001 publication. The study states,

> that different predictions [of future dangerousness] may be obtained for the same individual from risk assessment models that have comparable levels of predictive accuracy is not unique to tree-based models, but rather is a general property of actuarial prediction models.

In other words, even after all of the statistics have been discussed and the data collected and the numbers analyzed, the outcomes can still depend on which elements are included, which questions are asked, what data are even available, and which instruments are used. While the Monahan group purports that employing multiple iterative actuarial tree models is superior to using only one such model—and that certainly may be true—the more complex an available analytic tool becomes, the less likely it will be of any practical use to harried clinicians, and will instead, for whatever it is worth, be restricted to researchers and academicians.

WHAT DO THE COURTS SAY?

> *It is my opinion that such future-telling is admissible under no theory of law and [is] prejudicial beyond belief.*
> —Texas Judge Wendell Odom,
> *State v. Smith,* 1981[68]

Those who look to the courts in order to clarify matters may be sorely disappointed.

Take for example the following two cases:

- From within the first circuit in 2005 is found *United States v. Naparst.* In this case, the federal district court was asked to rule on a motion by a convicted sex offender to terminate his supervised release 4 months earlier than scheduled, a move which was opposed by the U.S. attorney. In granting the motion, the district court acknowledged that the offense in question was serious, but at the same time, the petitioner was noted to have been engaging in therapy on a regular basis, and to have incurred not even minor infractions since his arrest and incarceration. The district court went on to note that the Massachusetts Sex Offender Registration Board rated the convict at the lowest of three levels with respect to the risk of future dangerousness, and his therapist had written to the Board saying, "looking into the future, I can say that [he]... places in the top one percent of individuals...who are at a very low risk of recidivism, and who therefore present very little risk to the community."[69]

- From within the fifth circuit in 2004 is found *Willis v. Cockrell*. In this case, when weighing the validity of predictions by mental health providers on the risk of future dangerousness, the federal district court held that "overall, the theory that scientific reliability underlies predictions of future dangerousness has been uniformly rejected by the scientific community, absent those individuals who routinely testify to, and profit from, predictions of dangerousness."[70]

The *Naparst* Court had no qualms about relying on the predictions of a mental health provider concerning future dangerousness; the *Willis* Court soundly rejected the veracity of such predictions, even calling into question the pecuniary conflicts of interest of those who proffered such opinions.

Confused? Here's a third example: from within the fourth circuit in 2006 is found *United States v. Thomas*. In this case, the federal district court was asked to rule on the supervised pretrial release into the community of an alleged child molester; the expert witnesses were diametrically opposed, with the defense's psychiatrist opining a low risk of harm to children in the community, and the prosecution's law enforcement expert opining a high risk. Though allowing for the release, the court stated that, "it must be acknowledged...that although the law recognizes the relevance and admissibility of psychiatric evaluation and opinion for the purpose of assessing future dangerousness, the use of such evidence has long been criticized as lacking reliability."[71]

Three federal district courts within a 24-month span respectively (1) freely allowed for predictions of future dangerousness, (2) criticized such predictions, and (3) permitted for the admission of such predictions though with a skeptical caveat. Given the volumes that have been written in scholarly journals on this very topic, and especially in light of *Daubert* and the Federal Rules of Evidence, how can there remain such a incongruity of views regarding application?

Looking back, many examples exist of courts in the days before *Daubert* allowing or calling for predictions of future dangerousness:

- In 1961 from within the D.C. circuit, was the case of *Overholser v. O'Beirne*. The petitioner, a psychiatric patient with criminal charges who earlier had been found not guilty by reason of insanity and committed to St. Elizabeth's asylum, sought release on habeas corpus grounds, maintaining that he was by then mentally stable. The federal district court held that the evidence proffered by the petitioner was insufficient to support his release, as it did not prove to the requisite degree of certainty that he would be "free from [his] abnormal mental condition or that his release would not expose him or the public to danger in the reasonably foreseeable future."[72] The court accepted instead the state's expert's testimony and his opinion of the petitioner's future mental instability and dangerousness.
- From the California courts in 1976 came possibly the best-known of the cases involving prediction of future dangerousness, *Tarasoff v. Regents of the University of California*. In 1969 Prosenjit Poddar killed Tatiana Tarasoff, a fellow student whom Poddar perceived as having spurned his romantic overtures; the decedent's parents alleged that 2 months prior to her death, Poddar confided his intention to kill Tarasoff to a psychologist employed at the university. The campus police briefly detained Poddar, but released him as he then appeared rational and voiced no threats to them. No one warned the

Tarasoffs of the possible danger, and it was on this duty to protect theory that the parents sued. The California Superior Court at first sustained the defendants'demurrers. In reversing the Superior Court and deciding for the plaintiffs, the state high court held that "[o]nce a therapist does in fact determine, or under applicable professional standards reasonably should have determined, that a patient poses a serious danger of violence to others, he bears a duty to exercise reasonable care to protect the foreseeable victim of that danger." The state high court went on to say that "professional inaccuracy in predicting violence cannot negate the therapist's duty to protect the threatened victim."[73]

Apparently Poddar never threatened Tarasoff by name, though some of those familiar with the situation maintained that her identity was easily discernible from the context. The *Tarasoff* Court justified this seeming contradiction—a duty to protect despite professional assertions denying an ability to accurately predict—by offering that any uncertainty inherent in the prediction of future dangerousness was outweighed by the public's interest in safety from those who would possibly do harm. This is known in sociological circles as *hindsight bias*, the erroneous belief that once an outcome is known, it was, in fact, predictable all along.[74]

The *Tarasoff* dissent vigorously noted the American Psychiatric Association's amicus brief documenting that, since future dangerousness is not predictable with any accuracy by mental health professionals, there should be no such duty to protect imposed on clinicians. How was a therapist's determination of dangerousness to be judged after-the-fact if the profession itself disclaimed the ability to predict future behavior?[75] Though many courts now feel that, unless there is a specifically named or reasonably foreseeable victim, no duty to warn or protect exists, *Tarasoff* is still regarded in many quarters as putting clinicians between the proverbial rock and hard place.

• In *Barefoot v. Estelle* in 1983, the U.S. Supreme Court explicitly stated that a mental health professional could address the future dangerousness of a capital murder defendant at sentencing. The American Psychiatric Association's amicus brief noted once again that psychiatric predictions of long-term future dangerousness are deemed unreliable by the profession. The APA's best estimate was that two out of three predictions of long-term future violence made by psychiatrists are eventually proven to be wrong, even amongst populations of psychiatrically ill individuals who have committed violence in the past. Justice Blackmun's dissent stated, "neither the court nor the state of Texas has cited a single reputable scientific source contradicting the unanimous conclusion of professionals in this field that psychiatric predictions of long-term future violence are wrong more often than they are right."[76] Yet, in logic that defies reason, the high court majority did not expressly disagree with the APA's assertion, but rather held that since psychiatrists are not incorrect *all* of the time, they are thus correct at least *some* of the time! The high court felt that relevant unprivileged evidence "should be admitted and its weight left to the fact-finder, who would then have the benefit of cross-examination and contrary evidence by the opposing party.")[77]

• In the same train of thought the following year is the majority opinion of the high court in *Schall v. Martin*. Here the U.S. Supreme Court majority held that "[stare decisis] indicate[s]... that from a legal point of view there is nothing inherently unattainable about a prediction of future [dangerous] criminal conduct."[78] However, in opposing the majority, Justice Marshall, citing several scholarly works on mental health and the law, opined that there were no diagnostic tools available which allowed for even the most highly trained professional to predict reliably who would engage in violent crime.[79]

• From within the Arizona court system in 1989 came *Hamman v. County of Maricopa*. The psychiatric patient in question lived with his mother and stepfather. Following release from an inpatient unit and his return home, the patient attacked and killed his stepfather. The mother sued, alleging that a competent psychiatric examination would have revealed that her son was suffering from schizophrenia and was dangerous to others.[80] The state supreme court held that "the rule which we adopt does not impose upon psychiatrists a duty to protect the public from all harm caused by their patients. We do not, however, limit the duty of the psychiatrist to third parties only in those instances in which a specific threat is made against them. We hold that the duty extends to third persons whose circumstances place them within the reasonably foreseeable area of danger where the violent conduct of the patient is a threat."[81] Here we find ourselves again in the shadow of *Tarasoff*, with the expectation of the legal system that mental health professionals are not only able to accurately predict future dangerousness, but also know who victims of the predicted violence will be even when they are not even identified by name!

• In *Peterson v. Murray*, the defendant, convicted and sentenced to death by a jury that had heard expert testimony on his likelihood of future violent acts, argued in 1990 that the imposition of capital punishment based on such an opinion is unconstitutionally arbitrary because dangerousness predictions cannot be made accurately or reliably by anyone. The court of appeals for the federal fourth circuit, in rejecting that argument, compared such predictions to those made in parole board hearings, and held that the jury's task "in answering the [question of future dangerousness] is... basically no different from the task performed countless times each day throughout the American system of criminal justice."[82]

There were, nevertheless, some court opinions in the days before *Daubert* that refuted the science of predicting dangerousness:

- One such case was seen in 1975 in California state court, *People v. Burnick*. The *Burnick* court, asked about expert opinions of future dangerousness, quoted the American Psychiatric Association's amicus brief, and stated, "[n]either psychiatrists, nor [any other mental health or law enforcement professionals], have reliably demonstrated an ability to predict future violence or dangerousness. Neither has any special psychiatric 'expertise' in this area been established."[83]

- In *Lindabury v. Lindabury*, a Florida state court held in 1989 that, "[psychiatry] represents the penultimate grey area...particularly with regard to issues of foreseeability and predictability of future dangerousness."[84]

- In *Fischer v. Metcalf*, another Florida state court issued an even harsher opinion: "unlike other branches of medicine in which diagnoses and treatments evolve from objective, empirical, methodological foundations, psychiatry is at best an inexact science, if, indeed, it is a science [at all]. ..."[85]

- In rejecting *Tarasoff's* logic 15 years after that opinion, the state court in *Boynton v. Burglass* offered, "Florida courts have long been loathe to impose liability based on a defendant's failure to control the conduct of a third party." Continuing by quoting Justice Mosk's partial dissent in *Tarasoff*, the *Boynton* court added, "when the duty sought to be imposed is dependent upon standards of the psychiatric profession, we are asked to embark upon a journey that 'will take us from the world of reality into the wonderland of clairvoyance.'"[86]

- From Minnesota in 1982 came *Johnson v. Noot*. The state supreme court, when faced with a situation calling for a prediction of future dangerousness, held that "many psychiatrists themselves admit that their ability to predict future dangerousness is not reliable; to date, no valid clinical experience or statistical evidence describes psychological or physical signs or symptoms that can be reliably used to discriminate between the harmless and the potentially dangerous individual." Quoting an expert witness from the mental health profession, the court went on to state that "neither psychiatrists nor other behavioral scientists are able to predict the occurrence of violent behavior with sufficient reliability to justify the restriction of freedom of persons on the basis of the label of potential dangerousness. Accordingly, it is recommended that courts no longer ask such experts to give their opinion of the potential dangerousness of any person."[87]

Which brings our overview of the common law to the post-*Daubert* era. Given that expert opinions of future dangerousness should have by then encountered considerable difficulty fulfilling the first facet of the 28 U.S.C.A. §702 three-pronged approach on admissibility of scientific evidence, recent contradictions between courts—especially federal courts—regarding prognostications are all the harder to understand. One might think that *Daubert* had leveled the evidentiary landscape, but this has not uniformly proven so.

There are courts that have started questioning more assertively the veracity and usefulness of expert predictions on behavior. Like an addict needing a fix and shunning rehab, though, many courts continue to rely on flawed science from expert witnesses:

- The ink had barely dried on *Daubert* when, in 1997, the U.S. Supreme Court heard *Kansas v. Hendricks*.[88] Hendricks was convicted of molesting children and, as he was nearing release from prison, the state petitioned to have him civilly committed under the Kansas Sexually Violent Predator Act (SVPA), as it was alleged that he had a 'mental abnormality or personality disorder' that made him likely to engage in predatory acts of sexual violence in the future. Hendricks agreed that he had pedophilic thoughts when under stress. Once committed to the hospital, however, Hendricks appealed, saying that the act of commitment represented for him double jeopardy, as he had already served his penal sentence. The high court disagreed, and, in upholding the constitutionality of the SVPA, noted that, at the trial court level, the state presented predictive testimony from the chief psychologist at Larned State Hospital offering that the defendant was likely to commit sexual offenses against children in the future if not confined.

- In 2002 *Kansas v. Crane* was heard. After his prison term, a sex offender was committed to the state psychiatric hospital, again under Kansas' Sexually Violent Predator Act. The state supreme court reversed the commitment. In reversing the state supreme court and reaffirming the constitutionality of the SVPA, however, the U.S. Supreme Court held that states retain considerable leeway in statutorily defining mental abnormalities and personality disorders, and in accepting the testimony on future dangerousness that render individuals eligible for commitment.[89]

- From within the fifth circuit came the especially egregious *Saldano v. Cockrell* in 2003. After conviction on murder and kidnapping charges in state court, an expert for the prosecution testified in the penalty phase that, based on his use of an assessment instrument that included 24 elements deemed to be predictive of future dangerousness, he believed the defendant likely would again be violent. Two of the 24 elements in the assessment were "race" and "ethnicity" (the defendant was Hispanic). The prosecution expert said that Hispanics were over-represented in the Texas Department of Criminal Justice, and to him, that suggested a predilection toward criminal behavior amongst Texas Hispanics. Under cross-examination, the expert admitted that economics and lack of education could also explain the over-representation of some Hispanics in Texas prisons. Oddly, the defense attorney did not object to the prosecution expert's testimony, though the defense did offer its own expert testimony to refute race and ethnicity as predictive factors.

The *Saldano* prosecution's closing argument stated,

> our expert told you [that there was a probability that the defendant would be dangerous in the future], and you can have *confidence in his opinion beyond a reasonable doubt* because of his *qualifications* and his *background* and his *expertise.*

...[His assessment instrument] is a formula *recognized in the field* as to what would constitute dangerousness in a person [italics added].

After two remands the defendant was finally granted federal habeas relief of his death sentence based on the constitutional error of employing race and ethnicity as predictive of future dangerousness. Still, it is worth noting that not only did the prosecution's expert employ flawed science which was nevertheless admitted into evidence, but the prosecution's closing statement stressed to the jury the veracity of predictions stemming from that flawed science, using words such as "confidence," "qualification," "background," and "expertise," and falsely emphasizing claims of recognition of the predictive instrument within the profession itself![90]

- Yet another recent holding involving predictions of future dangerousness, from 2005, is found in *U.S. v. Rodriquez*. The federal district court, relying on what it called "well established precedent," denied the defendant's motion to exclude testimony on future dangerousness. The *Rodriquez* court said that the U.S. Supreme Court had upheld the use of psychiatric testimony on future dangerousness previously in *Barefoot,* and further offered that the adversarial process can be trusted to sort out reliable from unreliable information, especially when the defendant is able to present his own story to the finder of fact. The *Rodriquez* court failed to mention, however, the amicus brief of the American Psychiatric Association, filed unsuccessfully in *Barefoot* in the pre-*Daubert* days, likely because the theory contained in that brief would have succeeded in excluding much of the state's expert testimony in the case at bar.[91]
- *In re G.R.H.*, dealt in 2006 with a sex offense against a minor. Before the completion of a prison sentence for gross imposition of sexual acts on a child, the state's attorney general filed a petition to involuntarily commit defendant G.R.H. as a sexually dangerous individual under North Dakota state law. The district court found probable cause and transferred G.R.H. to

a state hospital on his prison release date. Three psychologists testified in court that his antisocial personality disorder made him highly likely to engage in similar behavior in the future. G.R.H. argued that committing him thus was unconstitutional, since he was able to control his behavior when so motivated. After an evidentiary hearing, the court upheld the commitment order, finding that a sexually dangerous individual is one who has trouble controlling his behavior, and while G.R.H. was not *entirely* incapable of controlling his behavior, he had a difficult time doing so outside of a structured milieu. G.R.H. appealed, and the North Dakota Supreme Court upheld the lower court ruling, saying that the defendant's diagnosed personality disorder rendered him likely to engage in future acts of sexual predation. The North Dakota high court specifically cited *Hendricks* and *Crane* as justification for their opinion.[92]

WHAT IS THE CLINICIAN TO DO?

> *Say you were standing with one foot in the oven and one foot in an ice bucket. According to the percentage people, you should be perfectly comfortable.*
>
> —Bobby Bragan (1917–),
> erstwhile Brooklyn Dodgers catcher[93]

To argue against the use of expert mental health opinion testimony concerning future dangerousness is difficult, as such a stance is oft-perceived by providers and the public alike as being either foolishly soft on crime, or unconcerned about safety and attempts to sort the seriously disturbed from those who pose no threat. Instead, arguing against the use of such predictions as they are often employed today should be viewed as an attempt to restore vitality, common sense, and evidence-based practices to an aspect of mental health that has long suffered from unchallenged hubris. No one wishes to see dangerous individuals released wholesale into our communities, but at the same time, few accomplished professionals would likely want to knowingly put their names to reports lacking scientific validity, often at the behest of the courts that have baited the profession for so long.

To briefly review what has been previously discussed:

- For at least half a century, mental health professionals have been asked by courts to predict the future dangerousness of subjects who are felt to be at risk of violence and yet often need placement or sentencing.
- While courts may prefer facts in black and white, data does not support that clinical judgment by any mental health professional is reliably accurate regarding predictions of future dangerousness. Numerous briefs, articles, studies, holdings, and statements support this finding of general lack of validity regarding such clinical predictions.
- Actuarial instruments for predicting future dangerousness, while identifying some traits that indicate a predilection for violence, suffer nonetheless from flaws that limit their practical usefulness, either because they are too complex and cumbersome, too narrow in scope, suffer from too many interrelated and poorly understood variables, lack the requisite sensitivity and specificity, or are tainted by subjectivity and lack of uniform definitions and parameters, the assertions of their proponents notwithstanding.
- Case law has been anything but uniform, despite the advent of the Federal Rules of Evidence and *Daubert*, and what would otherwise seem to be clear guidelines for analyzing and rejecting expert testimony of dubious reliability.
- Existing statutory law is largely imperfect, and often suffers from what appears to be a lack of understanding of the limitations inherent regarding mental health evaluation and treatment.

Accordingly, the role of the mental health professional should be to educate the nonclinician, present clinical descriptions and raw data, *avoid personal opinions of future behavior*, and allow the finder of fact or policymaker to draw a conclusion. In doing so, the mental health professional is not only being faithful to high professional ethical standards, but is doing his part to make the system—imperfect as it is—work to the best of its ability.

With italics added, the U.S. Supreme Court, in *Ake v. Oklahoma* in 1985, may have inadvertently come closest to that for which we are, as a profession, searching:

> Psychiatry is not...an exact science, and psychiatrists disagree widely and frequently on what constitutes mental illness, on the appropriate diagnosis to be attached to given behavior and symptoms, on cure and treatment, and on likelihood of future dangerousness. Perhaps *because there often is no single, accurate psychiatric conclusion*...in a given case, juries remain the primary fact-finders on this issue, and they must resolve differences in opinion within the psychiatric profession on the basis of the evidence offered by each party.[94]

ENDNOTES

* The author is a graduate of the College of William and Mary (BA) in Williamsburg, Virginia; the University of Virginia (MD) in Charlottesville; King College Graduate School of Business and Economics (MBA) in Bristol, Tennessee; and North Carolina Central University (JD) in Durham. He is a diplomate of the American Board of Psychiatry and Neurology, and currently serves as chief of psychiatry for the North Carolina Department of Correction in Raleigh. He may be reached at cjs29@doc.state.nc.us. I am deeply appreciative of my family's love and support throughout, and wish to dedicate this work to my parents, Ralph Carbone, MD, USAAF, MC (1911–2002) and Jean Gove Carbone, RN.

1. Available at http://www.met.rdg.ac.uk/cag/forecasting/quotes.html
2. Ibid.
3. 501 U.S. 808, 823.
4. 920 F.2d. 1330.
5. 293 F. 1013.
6. 509 U.S. 579. See also 28 U.S.C.A. §702.
7. 28 U.S.C.A. §702.
8. 509 U.S. at 590.
9. 526 US 137 (1999).
10. Piorkowski, J. (2001). Medical testimony and the expert witness. In A. Bibofsky et al., *Legal medicine* (5th ed., pp. 93–107). Mosby.
11. Diamond, B. (1975). The psychiatric prediction of dangerousness. *University of Pennsylvania Law Review, 123*, 439, 440.
12. Cocozza, J., & Steadman, H. (1976). The failure of psychiatric predictions of dangerousness. *Rutgers Law Review, 29*, 1084, 1096–1099.
13. Morse, S. (1978). Crazy behavior, morals, and science: An analysis of mental health law. *Southern California Law Review, 51*, 527, 600.
14. Hammond, M. (1980). Predictions of dangerousness in Texas. *St. Mary's Law Journal, 15*, 141–142.
15. Slobogin, C. (1984). Dangerousness and expertise. *University of Pennsylvania Law Review, 133*, 97–98.
16. Bochnewich, M. (1992, fall). Prediction of dangerousness and Washington's sexually violent predator statute. *California Western Law Review, 29*, 277, 283.
17. Long, L. (1993, fall). Rethinking selective incapacitation: More at stake than controlling violent crime. *UMKC Law Review, 62*, 107, 110.

18. Mossman, D. (1995). Dangerousness decisions: An essay on the mathematics of clinical violence prediction and involuntary hospitalization. *University of Chicago Law School Roundtable, 2*, 46.

19. Skaggs, C. (1995, spring). Kansas' sexual predator act and the impact of expert predictions: Psyched out by the Daubert test. *Washburn Law Journal, 34*, 320, 327.

20. Regnier, T. (2003). Barefoot in quicksand: The future of 'future dangerousness' predictions in death penalty sentencing in the world of Daubert and Kumho. *Akron Law Review, 37*, 469, 482.

21. Texas Defender Service. (2003, May). Junk science. In A *state of denial: Texas Justice and the death penalty* (p. 45). Retrieved October 21, 2006, from http://www.texasdefender.org

22. Beecher-Monas, E., & Garcia-Rill, E. (2003). Danger at the edge of chaos: Predicting violent behavior in a post-Daubert world. *Cardozo Law Review, 24*, 1845–1855.

23. Scherr, A. (2003). Daubert & danger: The 'fit' of expert predictions in civil commitments. *Hastings Law Journal, 55*, 1, 2–3.

24. Beecher-Monas, E. (2003, spring). The epistemology of prediction: Future dangerousness testimony and intellectual due process. *Washington and Lee Law Review, 60*, 353, 356.

25. Texas Defender Service. (2004). Overwhelmingly inaccurate predictions of future dangerousness. In *Deadly speculation: Misleading Texas capital juries with false predictions of future dangerousness* (p. 22). Retrieved February 5, 2007, from http://www.texasdefender.org

26. Menninger, K. (2005, September). Proof of qualification for commitment as a mentally disordered sex offender. *American Journal of Proof of Facts, 51*, 3d 299.

27. Sarno, G. (2005, September). Mental or emotional disturbance as defense or mitigating factor in attorney disciplinary proceedings. *American Journal of Proof of Facts, 46*, 2d 563.

28. Restatement (Third) of Torts: Liability for Physical Harm, Affirmative Duties, Duty to Third Persons Based on Special Relationship with Person Posing Risk §41 (2005).

29. Retrieved from http://www.whatquote.com/quotes/Andrew-Lang/7286-An-unsophisticated-f.htm

30. Blau, T. (1984). *The psychologist as expert witness* (Vol. 1). Wiley & Sons.

31. Ibid. at 3.

32. Quinsey, V., Harris, G. T., Rice, M. E., & Cormier, C. A. (1998). *Violent offenders: Appraising and managing risk* (p. 31). American Psychological Association Press. See also 383 US 107.

33. Douglas, K., & Skeem, J. (2005). Violence risk assessment: Getting specific about being dynamic. *Psychology, Public Policy, and Law, 11,* 347–348.

34. Monahan, J., Steadman, H., Silver, E., & Appelbaum, P. S. (2001). *The MacArthur study of mental disorder and violence* (p. 2). Oxford University Press.

35. Ibid. at 4.

36. Quinsey et al., *supra*, 6.

37. Ibid. at 8.

38. Monahan et al., *supra*, 6.

39. Quinsey et al., *supra*, 56.

40. Garrison, M., & Schneider, C. (2003). *The law of bioethics: Individual autonomy and social regulation* (p. 121). Thomson-West.

41. Hanson, K., & Morton-Bourgon, K. (2005, December). The characteristics of persistent sexual offenders: A meta-analysis of recidivism studies. *Journal of Consulting and Clinical Psychology, 73,* 1154, 1158.

42. Douglas & Skeem, *supra*, 349.

43. Turney, B. (1996, March). *Dangerousness: Predicting recidivism in violent sex offenders.* Knowledge Solutions Library. Retrieved from http://www.corpus-delicti.com/danger.html

44. Monahan et al., *supra*, 6.

45. Stone, A. (1976). *Mental health and the law: A system in transition* (p. 30). U.S.Govt Printing Office.

46. Doren, D. (2002). *Evaluating sex offenders: A manual for civil commitment and beyond* (p. 43). Sage.

47. Monahan et al., *supra*, 43.

48. Available at http://www.macarthur.virginia.edu/violence.html

49. Monahan et al., *supra*, 44.

50. Ibid.

51. Ibid. at 73.

52. Ibid. at 77.

53. Ibid. at 80.

54. Ibid. at 86.

55. Ibid. at 59.

56. Ibid. at 44.

57. Ibid. at 90.

58. Ibid. at 8.

59. Ibid. at 8.

60. Ibid. at 130.

61. Ibid. at 140.

62. Ibid. at 142.

63. Ibid. at 8.
64. Douglas & Skeem, *supra*.
65. Monahan, J., & Steadman, H. (1994). Toward a rejuvenation of risk assessment research. In J. Monahan & H. Steadman (Eds.), *Violence and mental disorder* (p. 12). University of Chicago Press.
66. Monahan et al., 2001, *supra*, 98.
67. Retrieved from http://www.macarthur.virginia.edu/risk.html
68. 534 S.W.2d. 900, 905 (Tex.Crim.App. 1981).
69. 2005 WL 1868173 at 1.
70. 2004 WL 1812698 at 34.
71. 2006 WL 140558 at 10.
72. 302 F.2d. 852, 863.
73. 17 Cal.3d. 425, 439.
74. Quinsey et al., *supra*, 4.
75. Firestone, M. (2001). Psychiatric patients and forensic psychiatry. In A. Bibofsky et al., *Legal medicine* (5th ed., pp. 479). Mosby.
76. 463 U.S. 880, 921.
77. 463 U.S. at 898.
78. 467 U.S. 253, 278.
79. 467 U.S. at 294. Cocozza, J., & Steadman, H. (1974). The failure of psychiatric predictions of dangerousness. *Rutgers Law Review, 29,* 1084, 1088. See also Ennis, B., & Litwack, T. (1974). Psychiatry and the presumption of expertise: Flipping coins in the courtroom. *California Law Review, 62,* 693, 705.
80. 161 Ariz. 58, 59.
81. 161 Ariz. at 65.
82. 904 F.2d. 882, 885.
83. 14 Cal.3d. 306, 327.
84. 552 So.2d. 1117, 1118.
85. 543 So.2d. 785, 787.
86. 590 So.2d. 466, 470.
87. 323 N.W. 2d. 724, 728.
88. 521 U.S. 346.
89. 534 U.S. 407.
90. 267 F.Supp. 2d 635, 639.
91. 389 F.Supp. 2d. 1135.
92. 711 N.W. 2d. 587.
93. Retrieved from http://www.hickoksports/com/quotes/quoteb01.shtml#braganbob
94. 470 U.S. 68, 81.

CHAPTER TWELVE

ARE SEXUAL OFFENSES THE RESULT OF AN ADDICTIVE PATTERN?

Stanton E. Samenow, PhD

Addiction! We hear about it constantly in one form or another. The word is commonly used to characterize a person's consuming passion for a particular substance or activity. A person who loves chocolate and devours a lot of it is called a chocolate addict or a "chocaholic." A physical fitness enthusiast who is intent on never missing his daily jog is a running addict or a "jogaholic." There is even a term for the incessant reader; she is a "bibliomaniac," addicted to reading. And now there is a book about people who constantly seek to please others, a condition termed "approval addiction."

The word "compulsive" is often used to characterize addictive behavior. The man who gambles away money he cannot afford to part with becomes known as a compulsive gambler, addicted to this past time. The young woman who steals wherever she goes is considered a compulsive thief or kleptomaniac—addicted to stealing. And so it goes with other types of behaviors that are repetitive, persistent, and destructive. They are diagnosed as addictions that are considered diseases.

I do not intend to tackle the wide range of these behaviors but rather to focus on so-called sexual addiction—in particular the person who gets into legal trouble because of it.

Gary appeared to be a successful professional and a responsible husband and father. He had everything going for him until the day he was arrested for attempting to expose his penis to a 13-year-old girl. It happened shortly after three in the afternoon when Gary saw the youngster leaving school. He pulled over and parked his car under a tree. As she drew near, he called to her. The girl approached to see what he wanted, thinking he was lost and needed directions. Nearing the door, she looked in and saw him with his pants down. She fled! Not long after the encounter, Gary was arrested for indecent exposure and solicitation of a minor. I interviewed Gary upon referral by his attorney for a psychological evaluation.

As it turned out, there was an entire dimension to Gary's existence that lay behind the responsible facade. Cheating on his wife, Gary had occasional one-night stands with women, including paid prostitutes. Reluctantly, he admitted involvement in sexual contacts with men. Asked about interest in pornography, Gary first said he occasionally glanced at pictures of scantily clad adult females. Eventually and with considerable embarrassment, he admitted downloading many types of pornography. In what had become a ritual on weekdays before work, he would leave his slumbering wife and stealthily enter the den, switching on the computer in the darkness of early morning (usually around 4 a.m.) and then masturbate while viewing pornography.

Since adolescence, Gary had peered into windows hoping to glimpse females engaging in sexual activity. He had exposed himself in the past both to juveniles and adults. With all this going on, he still managed to maintain good standing at his accounting firm and spend time with his wife and little boy.

Gary said that he was "addicted" to sex. It was constantly on his mind. No matter how many sexual outlets he had, he sought more. He regarded the urgency of his sexual drive as a force over which he had no control.

Tony, a man in his forties, had a top secret security clearance and was on track for promotion to be a high-ranking government official. Married and with two children, he was arrested for exposing himself in a community park. Tony confessed to me he had been exposing himself since the age of 11 but never before was apprehended by authorities. He told me about the careful calculations he made while on business trips. It was easier to remain anonymous in locations where he did not live and would spend only a short time. He would request a hotel room several stories up but not too high, overlooking a pedestrian area or parking lot so he could be seen. He would part the curtains in his room but not open them all the way. He would stand naked with an erection in the window but partially hide his face behind the curtain. As soon as he saw someone look up, he would instantly draw back and then masturbate in private. He also staked out parks and exposed himself there. Women who saw him continued about their business or else did not want to get involved reporting him to authorities.

It is understandable that people like Tony and Gary would be considered to have a disorder because they risked everything they valued by a quest for cheap thrills. People would naturally conclude that such individuals are in the grips of a compulsion or addiction—that they must be sick. During 35 years of specializing in the evaluation and treatment of criminal offenders, I have interviewed many men like Gary and Tony. Some were arrested for their sex offenses. Many who had similar sexual patterns were not arrested for these but for other types of crimes.

An in-depth psychological analysis of these individuals revealed that sex was a vehicle for conquest, excitement, and an ego boost. Their preoccupation with sex had nothing to do with the lack of a responsible sexual outlet. Like Gary and Tony, most had spouses or partners who were available for them. These men were far more conquering individuals than sexual. One told me, "I find 'em, feel 'em, fuck 'em, and forget 'em." Another asserted, "I don't care if she's deaf, dumb, and blind; all I wanted was her body."

Even with a valued job, a spouse, children, and financial security, these men sought excitement by doing the forbidden. Sex with a consenting partner left them restless and dissatisfied. "Take my crime away, and you take my world away," one offender exclaimed. Like Gary and Tony, he meant that life without the excitement of his sexually illicit activities was not worth living.

There is increasing excitement during every phase of a sex offense—fantasizing, the pursuit, the commission of the act, and the aftermath. Some offenders report experiencing pangs of guilt, but these are fleeting and are of little value in deterring future misconduct. These men know the ruinous consequences to themselves of being discovered, but they have a chilling capacity to banish these considerations from their thoughts while they pursue their objectives. Twinges of conscience are similarly brushed aside.

Sex offenders differ in their modus operandi. Some are deceptive, insinuating themselves into others' lives to extract sexual favors. Once they obtain what they want, they are opt to discard their partners like used Kleenex. Others resort to intimidation or force. Regardless of the modus operandi, they share similar thinking patterns as they pursue power and control. The voyeur has a sense of power while secretly intruding into private lives. The "flasher" has a sense of control as he surprises his victim, attracting or, more often, repelling her. Rape is a raw act of exercising power as the perpetrator reduces a woman to a quivering, pleading speck of humanity who submits and does his ultimate bidding. A rapist recalled, "I brandish my penis like a sword."

I interviewed Gary's wife, Alice, and Tony's wife, Diane. Naturally, they were shocked and devastated by their spouses' arrests. Eager to get help for their husbands, each spoke to me candidly. Both Alice and Diane thought their spouses were "sick." It is my experience that in trying to make sense of deviant and shocking behavior, the concept of an addiction is seen as explanatory both by professionals and the public.

Alice informed me that several years ago, she had caught Gary with another woman. She left him but reconciled several months later. Chastened by the experience, Gary resolved to be faithful. The couple went ahead and had a child. One day, as Alice went to check e-mails, she was horrified by what she saw on the computer screen— graphic images of women in sexual acts. When confronted by his wife, Gary acknowledged he had been "curious," but avowed he had no farther interest in pornography. Alice did her best to convince herself that he meant it.

Alice remained frustrated, as she long had been, by her husband's failure to communicate. But she reassured herself that many men are that way. She also observed that her husband constantly complained about being exhausted. Alice attributed this to Gary being so worried about work that he would go to the office early, even on Saturdays. She did not have the faintest idea of his early morning forays into computer pornography. Alice's main concern, however, was that when Gary was home, he seemed distracted, like he was in another world.

Diane told me that Tony was a control freak. She was expected to run the household like clockwork, precisely on the schedule he dictated. She was tired of his constant criticism. She could not fathom how he found time to prowl around parks and other public places as busy as he was at work and home.

Both Gary and Tony disclosed to me how they managed to find the time and opportunity for their sexual adventures. They lived a double life, carefully concealing their behavior from the very people who ostensibly knew them best.

Like scores of other sex offenders whom I have evaluated, Gary and Tony constantly were making choices. Sex offenders plan what they are going to do. If they think the risk is too great, they are not compelled to go ahead with their actions. The person who exposes himself scouts out the area. If he thinks a getaway will be problematic, he will wait for a more propitious opportunity or search out a different spot. Sometimes, a perpetrator becomes complacent or careless and takes an unnecessary risk. He miscalculates and is caught. This becomes more likely if he has been drinking or using drugs. Whatever behavior he engages in, it is freely chosen and not a compulsion or addiction.

Pedophilia—sexual activity with prepubescent youngsters—is *not* characterized as an addiction in the American Psychiatric Association's *Diagnostic and Statistical Manual of Mental Disorders*. Nonetheless, many individuals with pedophilic interests and behaviors describe their experience in terms of having obsessive thoughts, then compulsively engaging in the sexual behavior. The repetitive and urgent nature of pedophilia, as experienced by the pedophile, very much resembles features of addiction.

Edgar immersed himself in child pornography, spending hours on most days searching the Internet. He located an abundance of sites depicting boys engaged in sexual acts. The children shown appeared to be as young as six and ranged in age well into puberty. Edgar also sought out sites with images of adult males engaged in sex with young adolescents. No matter how many sexual images and scenes he saw, it was never enough. His appetite was insatiable when it came to viewing naked boys in countless poses and positions. And so he moved on to downloading brief film clips that graphically depicted sexual activity. The very young boys featured in them did not seem to know what to do but were being coached step by step by an adult whose voice was clearly audible. Some of the film clips showed adult men spanking and anally penetrating prepubescent males. Edgar then started paying for access to Internet pornography, which opened up many more selections. He ordered videos lengthier than the Internet film clips. These he could view at leisure at home. He amassed a huge collection of child pornography, which he locked away in a closet.

Employed as a legal assistant, Edgar knew that possessing child pornography wais illegal. As a precaution, he discovered through search engines programs advertised as having the capacity to delete anything from a computer. He paid for several of these programs, relieved that no trace of his search for child pornography would ever be found.

Edgar lived in an apartment building where young families resided. He watched children playing on a nearby playground and casually began talking to boys who appeared to be approaching puberty. Edgar chatted with these youngsters about all sorts of things—sports, cars, friends, school, their family life. He offered help to kids having difficulties with school work. He invited them up to his apartment and had them bring their school books so he could tutor them.

Boys liked Edgar because he was friendly, funny, easy to talk to, and ready to discuss anything. Youngsters experiencing family problems were especially open, pouring out their hearts. An excellent listener, Edgar provided helpful advice to these needy children. Gradually, he insinuated himself into personal aspects of their lives and became a confidante and advisor. He talked to them about girls, eventually about their own physical development, and provided information about sex. He was affectionate, embracing them with hugs and giving them back rubs. One thing led to another, with Edgar offering assurance that sexual curiosity, experimentation, and play were normal. He intrigued boys by showing them pornography, persuading those who were hesitant that sex between guys of their age was not abnormal, also assuring them that participating signified nothing about being gay. The boys trusted him. They were aroused by the pornography and were open to participating in various sexual activities.

Edgar's life appeared to be taken over by his voracious sexual appetite. His pornography collection grew too large for its storage area. Viewing pornography and masturbating to it did not diminish Edgar's sexual drive. Rather, it fueled his fantasies and provided ideas for varying the form of sexual activity. To an outsider, he might seem to have been in the grips of something similar to an addiction, so pervasive was the collecting of pornography, so frequent the masturbation, then the seeking out of youngsters and engaging in sexual activities with them.

Perpetually on the prowl, Edgar was methodical and careful about the manner in which he selected boys for participation. Patiently, he developed relationships. Gaining a boy's confidence, earning his trust, and becoming privy to his personal secrets had to precede anything overtly sexual. By the time sexual activity began, Edgar had convinced a boy of the necessity of keeping private anything physical that happened between them. This was easy to accomplish! These boys were extremely unlikely to disclose anything for fear of the trouble they knew they might get into. And they did not want to jeopardize Edgar, their friend and confidante.

The inevitable finally occurred. A neighbor from an apartment in Edgar's hallway thought it extremely odd that young boys unaccompanied were frequently entering and leaving his apartment. Unsure of what to do, she spoke to a friend who agreed something was not right and urged her to call the police. Law enforcement officers staked out the apartment and watched young boys come and go. Obtaining a search warrant, they found the pornography and came upon a list of names and phone numbers of the boys.

When I interviewed Edgar, he steadfastly maintained that he had hurt no one, that he loved children and had helped many academically and personally. He had tutored several and helped them raise their grades. And, for nearly all, he had become a refuge from family turmoil. No matter how fond he genuinely was of these boys, Edgar did not stop at that but pursued sexual contact. He asserted that the physical aspect was a natural form of expressing affection in an emotionally close relationship. Moreover, he maintained, the boys had desired sexual activity, and, in some instances, initiated it.

Edgar contended that it was the criminal justice system, not he, that inflicted untold distress, subjecting the boys to humiliating interrogations by social service and law enforcement personnel and causing them untold embarrassment with their families. Edgar explained that he emphasized secrecy to protect the boys from encountering all that when, in fact, they were doing absolutely nothing that was wrong.

Edgar exclaimed that life without boys would be intolerable. One might say Edgar was obsessed about sex with boys. It was true that, day and night, he thought about it. He even used a computer during work hours to view child pornography. He could barely wait to end his work day so he could visit the playground. Considering the extent to which his life was absorbed by pedophilic interests, one might observe that Edgar was engaged in a lifestyle similar to that of an addict who need to have his next "fix."

A careful analysis of Edgar's sexual life, however, reveals that he made deliberate and calculated choices. Many people are not aware that it is illegal to view child pornography in the privacy of their own homes. However, they do know that it is illegal to have sex with young children. As a legal assistant, Edgar knew both. And, as I mentioned, he took pains to conceal his accessing child pornography on the computer both by trying to eradicate it from his hard drive and securing it in a locked closet. He recognized that buying child pornography placed him at risk since suppliers and credit card companies would have records of his purchases. Edgar knew that actual sexual contact with anyone under 18 years of age could result in his arrest and prosecution. When he instructed the boys not to tell anyone, he was warning them to conceal that which he knew was a crime. Even if he thought of the sexual activity as consensual—that is, the boy did not object—he still was breaking the law.

Some boys develop precociously and are willing to be initiated into sexual activity. Some might be eager enough to seek it out. Whatever the case, the pedophile is fully aware of potential consequences to himself even if he is not considering the legal, social, and emotional consequences to the youngsters.

Was Edgar so taken over by his sexual obsession for young boys that he could not help himself? Clearly, this was not what was going on. He selected for sex only boys whom he could befriend and groom for that purpose, youngsters who he was certain would protect the privacy of what they did together.

A discussion of pedophilia brings into focus the question of why some people are sexually attracted to children, sometimes to the exclusion of anyone else. Children are inexperienced, vulnerable, naive, and easy to control. These features render them ready targets for sexual exploitation. Although this is all true, we still know little about the origin and development of sexual orientations—in this instance, why some people are attracted to children. It is unlikely that a person such as Edgar would deliberately choose to be attracted to children versus a less problematic sexual orientation. Although controversy abounds as to the "why" of human sexual preferences, people do make choices regarding the expression of their sexual desires.

Bear in mind that Edgar and others like him refrain from acting on pedophilic urges if they ascertain it is not safe to do so. Edgar selected some boys, not others. He chose the time of day to have them visit in his apartment. He discussed with each youngster what, if anything, to tell his parents about what he was doing. And entire weeks passed when he had no contact with any of the boys.

In the case of the pedophile, we do not know how to change a person's sexual orientation. However, in clinical practice, we can work with a person's thought processes—teaching him to consider foremost the harm he does to the very children whom he claims to love as well as heightening his awareness of the risk to himself of engaging in sex with children. The question as to how best to manage these individuals if they are on probation or parole is another matter. Needless to say, intensely monitoring them is required in many instances.

An offender remarked, "If I didn't have enough excuses for crime, psychiatry gave me more." The concept of addiction as a disease to explain sexual offenses falls into that category. I am *not* suggesting that a person's sexual orientation is freely chosen. I am saying that people make choices in how they conduct themselves sexually, whatever their orientation. Engaging in behavior that victimizes other people is not a disease. It is freely chosen by men and women who seek excitement at the expense of other people. As one fellow said of his so-called addiction, "I like it too much to quit!"

Sex offenders are not suffering from the disease of addiction. They are excitement seekers in pursuit of conquests. They do not have a condition over which they are helpless and lack control. Sex offenders make choices to do what they do. If the consequences of their behavior become unbearable, they are able to make other choices that are more responsible. Some do, in fact, change their thinking and become disgusted with behavior that they formerly found exciting.

Successful treatment entails a cognitive-behavioral approach. The individual is taught to recognize the thinking processes that gave rise to the irresponsible and destructive behavior. He is encouraged to look in the mirror, so to speak, at the harm he has inflicted in order to generate motivation to change. He is taught corrective concepts. Essential to this process is becoming constructively self-critical. Throughout the process, the offender becomes aware of his thoughts, deters the thoughts, thinks of the potential impact of acting on such thoughts, and changes the thinking so he can act in a responsible manner. With prolonged effort, sex offenders can succeed in living a life in which they do not have to look over their shoulders to avoid apprehension. Abandoning criminal patterns of thinking and behavior, they eventually earn the trust of others.

ABOUT THE CONTRIBUTORS

Alan A. Abrams, MD, JD, FCLM, is a psychiatrist and a lawyer whose practice includes providing expert testimony and evaluations in criminal, civil, disability, competency, and worker's compensation cases.

Lee Bewley, PhD, MHA, is a major in the U.S. Army, Medical Service Corps and an assistant professor in the Army-Baylor University Graduate Program in Health & Business Administration.

Robert W. Bigelow, JD, is a managing partner in the law firm of Bigelow & Narra, LLC (NY, NJ). He is an author, educator, and frequent television commentator on legal issues. He is a former senior supervising attorney with the Legal Aid Society-Criminal Defense Division (LAS-CDD) in New York City.

Ariana M. Brooks, MA, is a research assistant with the Berger Institute for Work, Family, and Children at Claremont McKenna College.

John S. Carbone, MD, JD, MBA, serves as chief of psychiatry for the North Carolina Department of Corrections. A lawyer as well as a psychiatrist, he is also a fellow of the American College of Legal Medicine.

Karin Horwatt Cather, JD, is a former assistant commonwealth attorney in Virginia. She is a writer with the National District Attorney's Association and writes articles on technical topics for *The Prosecutor* magazine.

M. Nicholas Coppola, PhD, MHA, FACHE, is program director and associate professor at the U.S. Army-Baylor Graduate Program in Healthcare & Business Administration. He is a lieutenant colonel in the U.S. Army Medical Service Corps.

Diane F. Halpern, PhD, is director of the Berger Institute for Work, Family, and Children, as well as a professor of psychology, at

Claremont McKenna College. She is a past president of the American Psychological Association.

Jeffrey P. Harrison, PhD, MBA, MHA, FACHE, is president of the Harrison Consulting Group, Inc. (HCG, Inc.), a consulting firm specializing in health care organizations including hospitals, health systems, and medical practice groups. Consulting services include strategic planning, market development, health care operations, health care reimbursement, and corporate compliance.

Alan Newman, MD, is a psychiatrist in private practice.

Maheen Patel, MD, is a psychiatrist in private practice.

Richard G. Salamone, PhD, ABPP, is in the private practice of neuropsychology, clinical psychology, and biofeedback. He provides outpatient and inpatient neuropsychological assessments and consultations with neurologic and psychiatric populations, as well as psychological assessment of psychiatric and medical/surgical populations (including pre-surgical psychological evaluations). Dr. Salamone also provides psychotherapy with a broad range of adult patient populations including mood and anxiety disorders, personality disorders, psychotic disorders, and chronic pain. He is on the active medical Staff of the Wellmont-Bristol Regional Medical Center.

Stanton E. Samenow, PhD, is a clinical psychologist in Alexandria, Virginia, specializing in forensic psychology. He has served as an expert witness in criminal and civil matters. Among the books that he has written are *Inside the Criminal Mind*, and *Before It's Too Late: Why Some Kids Get Into Trouble and What Parents Can Do About It*.

Antoinette Collarini Schlossberg, PhD, is an associate professor of Criminal Justice in the School of Professional Studies at St. John's University.

Harvey Schlossberg, PhD, is an associate professor of Criminal Justice in the School of Professional Studies, St. John's University. He is the author of *Psychologist With a Gun*.

Meghan Shapiro, MHA, CHE, is assistant administrator of Stokes Reynolds Memorial Hospital.

Nesibe Soysal, MD, is a psychiatrist in private practice.

Paul F. Stavis, JD, was the founding director of the Law and Psychiatry Center at the George Mason University School of Law. He has been a professor of health, mental health, criminal, and bioethics law at various institutions of higher learning. He is an experienced litigator in large-scale civil rights class actions and in general private practice. He is currently the director of the Bureau of House Counsel for the NYS Department of Health. He has written extensively in many areas of law and psychiatry, including empirical studies of public policy, care, and treatment.

Clayton Stephenson is a graduate student at Claremont Graduate University.

Sandra R. Sylvester, JD, has been an assistant commonwealth's attorney in Prince William County, Virginia, since 1988. She has prosecuted child abuse cases for 17 years and lectures throughout the Commonwealth of Virginia on topics relating to prosecuting and investigating child abuse cases and dealing with expert witnesses. She started the "Expert Witness Database" and maintains information on common defenses and defense experts. Ms. Sylvester was the 2005 recipient of the Von Schuch Distinguished Assistant Commonwealth's Attorney Award for her work in child abuse and her assistance to Virginia's prosecutors.

Susan B. Trachman, MD, is currently in private psychiatric practice in Fairfax, Virginia. She is an associate clinical professor of psychiatry at Georgetown University and George Washington University.

INDEX

Printed in the United States
103673LV00002B/229-237/A